Drug Use and Abuse

SECOND EDITION

Drug Use and Abuse

SECOND EDITION

Stephen A. Maisto
Syracuse University
Syracuse, New York

Mark Galizio
University of North Carolina
at Wilmington

Gerard J. Connors
Research Institute on Addictions
Buffalo, New York

THE HARCOURT PRESS

HARCOURT BRACE COLLEGE PUBLISHERS

Fort Worth Philadelphia San Diego New York Orlando Austin San Antonio
Toronto Montreal London Sydney Tokyo

Publisher • Ted Buchholz
Acquisitions Editor • Tina Oldham
Developmental Editor • Karee Galloway
Project Editor • Laura J. Hanna
Production Manager • Thomas Urquhart IV
Art Director • Burl Sloan
Literary Permissions Editor • Julia C. Stewart
Cover Illustration • Ron Lusk

Address for Editorial Correspondence
   Harcourt Brace College Publishers
   301 Commerce Street, Suite 3700
   Fort Worth, Texas 76102

Address for Orders
   Harcourt Brace & Company
   6277 Sea Harbor Drive
   Orlando, FL 32887
   1-800-782-4479, or 1-800-433-0001 (in Florida)

Printed in the United States of America

Library of Congress Catalog Card Number 94-75452

ISBN 0-15-501007-7

   67890123 066 987654

Preface

The preface to the first edition of this book included a discussion of the grave concern that drugs were to the people of the United States. Although drugs do not seem to be the salient concern they were just three or four years ago, they still are perceived as a serious social problem, especially because of the association of drugs and violence. It is as important now as ever for students to have a textbook that reflects an up-to-date and accurate portrayal of the complexity of human drug use and its consequences.

There were several reasons for writing a second edition of this book. The study of drug use and its consequences is one of the most dynamic fields in science, with seemingly continual new contributions from the biological, behavioral, and social sciences. Many important changes and discoveries have occurred since the first edition was published in 1991. Accordingly, each chapter of the second edition has been updated to represent findings from the latest research and debates on drugs.

There are other changes evident in this edition. Most fundamental of these is the change of the book title from *Drug Use and Misuse* to *Drug Use and Abuse*. This change was made to achieve consistency between concepts presented in the book and the most widely used psychiatric diagnostic system in the United States, the American Psychiatric Association's *Diagnostic and Statistical Manual* (DSM). The most recent version of this system, DSM-IV, revives the importance of the classification "substance abuse," which had a lesser status in the last DSM edition, DSM-III-R.

We have also added a new chapter on psychopharmacology. We hope that the inclusion of separate chapters on pharmacology (Chapter 4) and psychopharmacology (Chapter 5) will help emphasize that the effects of drugs depend not only on the chemical properties of the drug itself and its interaction in the body, but on the individual characteristics of the user (both biological and psychological) and the setting in which the use occurs. This theme is continued throughout the presentation of the individual classes of drugs and the discussions of treatment (Chapter 16) and prevention (Chapter 17).

This edition also includes several new pedagogical features designed to increase student interest and learning. Diagnostic pretests (What Do You Think?) at the beginning of each chapter challenge students to test their knowledge of drugs and key their attention to concepts or facts that are important to learn. Answers and explanations at the end of each chapter provide an important review of the main concepts. In addition, new quotes appearing in the margins throughout the book help abstract concepts come to life by relating personal accounts and other comments about drug use and its ramifications.

Another new feature is the Drugs and Culture boxes, which highlight the importance of differences in drug use associated with factors such as race, gender, ethnicity, and time period. The Drugs and Culture boxes have been added to give these powerful factors more prominence than they had in the first edition.

A number of strengths of the first edition remain. For example, the book is sufficiently comprehensive to cover all the major drugs that humans use from biological, psychological, and social/environmental perspectives. We also have kept full chapters on the prevention and treatment of substance-related disorders, both extremely important to readers. Finally, the popular chapter-by-chapter margin glossary, with a cumulative glossary at the end of the book, remains.

Our goals for this edition were the same as for the first: to provide a textbook that is scholarly yet understandable to the student with little background in the biological or behavioral–social sciences, and to write a textbook that reflects the complexity of human drug use on biological, psychological, and social levels. We feel we have met these goals even more effectively in the second edition than we did in the first, by keeping what was best about the former edition and by updating the book's contents to reflect the field's latest scientific discoveries and directions.

We are pleased that the new edition of *Drug Use and Abuse* was selected for publication under a new imprint, The Harcourt Press, which was recently introduced by Harcourt Brace College Publishers to offer an economically priced alternative to the rising cost of college textbooks. Every book published by The Harcourt Press is a proven success in the classroom; production costs are kept low by using black and white, rather than color photos. This substantial savings has been passed on to students. In keeping with The Harcourt Press' commitment to the instructor as well as the student, this edition is also accompanied by an instructor's manual that includes a revised and expanded test item file.

Completion of a book like this is impossible without help. Most essentially we thank acquisitions editor Christina Oldham and developmental editor Karee Galloway of the Harcourt Brace editorial staff for their endless patience, encouragement, and guidance in getting all the chapters revised to meet high standards of currency and quality. Project editor Laura Hanna skillfully saw the book through production.

We owe special thanks to Chris Newland of Auburn University whose insightful comments and constructive criticism of the first edition helped to launch the second edition. We would also like to thank the following reviewers for their helpful suggestions and expert advice. Their work played a big part in creating the strengths in this book: Lisa E. Baker, Western Michigan University; Bob Banks, Amarillo College; Patricia Baasel, Ohio University; N. Jay Bean, Vassar College; W. William Chen, University of Florida; Eileen Clifford, North Hennipen Community College; Jacqueline L. Daley, Bowling Green State University; Marc Gellman, University of Miami; Charlotte Hales, Lower Columbia College; Richard Hurley, Brigham Young University; Wesley P. Jordan, St. Mary's College of Maryland; Carolyn Mathews, Auburn University; Fathy S. Messiha, University of North Dakota; James V. Noto, San Diego State University; Mitchell J. Picker, University of North Carolina at Chapel Hill; Kerry J. Redican, Virginia Polytechnic Institute and State University; Laurna Rubinson, University of Illinois at Urbana-Champaign; Freddie Thomason, Wallace State College; Ray Tricker, Oregon State University; Larry Waldrop, Wallace

State College; Bill C. Wallace, The University of Tennessee, Knoxville; Roger B. Weller, Illinois State University.

There are other special people each of us wants to thank for helping us to finish the second edition. Stephen Maisto would like to thank Patricia Hutchins and Katherine Mastrocola for their superlative word processing skills and never-failing willingness to type material without delay. Stephen also thanks his wife Mary Jean and son Eddy, who gave unwavering support to completing this book, even in the face of frequent sacrifices of family time together. Mark Galizio thanks his students—who taught him how to teach. Gerard Connors thanks Mark R. Duerr and Teddy Cephas for their tireless patience and assistance in preparing the revised chapters for this edition. Gerard also thanks his wife, Lana Michaels Connors, and daughter Marissa for their constant support and love throughout the process of preparing this second edition.

Brief Contents

Detailed Contents

8 CAFFEINE   173

9 ALCOHOL   191

To my father and the memory of my mother.
SAM

To Rachel and Joey.
MG

To my parents.
GJC

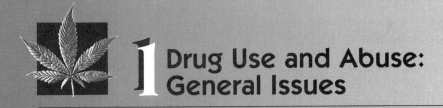

1 Drug Use and Abuse: General Issues

WHAT DO YOU THINK?

True or False?   ____   Because the effects of drugs are both predictable and obvious, it is relatively easy to define drug abuse.

____   A drug's street name often describes the actual effect of that drug.

____   A person's reaction to a drug depends mostly on the biological action of the drug in the body.

____   Because drug use is complicated, it is impossible to estimate patterns of drug use for the population of a whole country.

____   Within the United States similar patterns of alcohol and other drug use are found even among different subgroups of the population.

____   The highest rates of alcohol and other drug use are found among 18- to 25-year-olds.

____   A person's use of more than one drug at a time is of little concern because it happens so infrequently.

____   The total economic cost of alcohol and drug abuse in the United States is about a billion dollars annually.

____   Alcohol and other drug use causes violence and crime.

____   Modern researchers rely on definitions of alcohol and other drug use that are free of social or cultural biases.

____   A diagnosis of drug abuse is made when a person has become either physically or psychologically dependent on a drug.

____   Definitions of addiction center on overwhelming involvement with a drug.

____   The continued use of any drug will eventually lead to tolerance and physical dependence on that drug.

ATHLETIC   MEDICAL
BIOLOGICAL   POLITICAL
ECONOMIC   PSYCHOLOGICAL
EDUCATIONAL   RELIGIOUS
LEGAL   SOCIAL/CULTURAL

Q: *How are these 10 systems alike?*
A: They influence or are influenced by alcohol and other drug use.

You will see in this text that drugs[1] may affect us in many ways, whether or not we use them. You also will see that a person's drug use may be affected by a number of different factors.

What influences drug use and how that use affects us make up the subject of drugs and human behavior and are what this text is about. Because our subject matter is so wide-ranging, this introductory chapter spans a variety of topics. We include formal definitions throughout the chapter, beginning with terms such as "pharmacology," "drug," and "drug abuse."

Introducing a lot of terms in one chapter might be confusing at first, but there is no need to feel that all the terms have to be grasped immediately. Since the terms will be used repeatedly throughout the book, there will be time to learn them. Introducing the terms now will give you the vocabulary to read later chapters more easily, beginning with Chapter 2.

In this chapter we also explain the drug-classification systems used in this book, and then move to a discussion of who uses drugs. The final sections of the chapter cover ways to define harmful drug use. The chapter closes with a brief overview of the rest of the text.

> [The use of cigarettes, alcohol, and drugs is] "destroying families, driving up health-care costs, overwhelming the education, criminal justice, and social systems of this nation and contributing to an unprecedented wave of violence and homelessness."
>
> Joseph A. Califano
> (cited in *The New York Times*, October 24, 1993)

PHARMACOLOGY AND DRUGS

Humans have used drugs for several thousand years, but the scientific study of drugs is more recent. The scientific study of drugs is called **pharmacology,** which is concerned with all information about the effects of chemical substances (drugs) on living systems. Pharmacology is considered a part of biology and is allied with physiology and biochemistry (Blum, 1984). **Psychopharmacology** is an area within the field of pharmacology that focuses on the effects of drugs on behavior. Although psychopharmacology is a joining of the words **psychology** and pharmacology, it is now recognized that understanding how drugs affect human behavior requires knowledge about social and environmental factors as well. This book is about human psychopharmacology.

Drugs are easy enough to talk about, or so it seems from the numbers and variety of people who do so. However, defining "drug" is not so simple. Although they have run into confusion along the way, experts have arrived at a workable definition. According to a World Health Organization (WHO) report published in 1981, **drug** is defined in the broadest sense as "any chemical entity or mixture of entities, other than those required for the maintenance of normal health (like food), the administration of which alters biological function and possibly structure" (p. 227).

These fundamental definitions bring us to the question of what is drug use and what is drug abuse. We will discuss this distinction in more detail later in this chapter, but it is important for you to get an idea at the outset of what is called drug use and drug abuse. Abuse has been referred to in different ways when people write about drugs, and there is no generally accepted

Pharmacology
The scientific study of drugs; concerned with all information about the effects of drugs on living systems.

Psychopharmacology
The subarea of pharmacology that concerns the effects of drugs on behavior.

Psychology
The scientific study of behavior.

Drug
Broadly defined as any chemical entity or mixture of entities, not required for the maintenance of health, that alters biological function or structure when administered.

---

[1]Sometimes in this book we use the term "alcohol and drugs"; at other times we use "drugs" as the inclusive term. Because alcohol is a drug, saying "alcohol and drugs" is redundant. However, we do so on occasion, when it seems useful, to distinguish alcohol from all other drugs.

Drug abuse
Any use of drugs that causes physical, psychological, legal, or social harm to the individual user or to others affected by the drug user's behavior.

definition. In such circumstances, one way to define a term is by a consensus of experts. A study by Rinaldi, Steindler, Wilfrod, and Goodwin (1988) achieved such a consensus definition for a number of terms used in research and clinical work on alcohol and drugs. In the Rinaldi et al. study, the experts defined **drug abuse** as, "any use of drugs that causes physical, psychological, legal, or social harm to the individual or to others affected by the drug user's behavior."

As you can see, the definition of abuse centers on the consequences of the drug user's behavior, both to him or herself and to others in the person's social environment. Our leading paragraph on the 10 systems and drug use comes into sharper relief with this definition of abuse. The definition also illustrates the difficulties in defining abuse. A major problem is that the behavior that causes consequences in one community or culture may not cause them in another, or not to the same degree. Therefore, the goal to have a standard referent for drug abuse has proved elusive. Nevertheless, in writing and other forms of communication about alcohol and other drugs, abuse is a word that is used extremely frequently, and therefore efforts to arrive at a more generally applicable definition should continue. Along these lines, toward the end of this chapter we discuss a new "diagnostic" definition of substance (alcohol or other drugs) abuse that has been developed by the American Psychiatric Association. For now, however, our initial definition of abuse is sufficient for understanding what we say in this chapter up to that point.

With the definition of drug abuse, "use" simply is any drug use that is not abuse. This may sound a little circular, but the level of definition of a number of terms in human psychopharmacology is relative.

Drug Classification

As the WHO panel of experts understood, their definition of drug is very broad. To make the definition useful for research and practical purposes, it is necessary to order the substances that fit the definition of drug into smaller categories. Pharmacologists have done this with their many systems for classifying drugs. These classification systems have been based on the primary properties of drugs, in order to communicate a drug's nature and ways that it can be used. The ways of classifying drugs in this text are as follows (Jacobs & Fehr, 1987, pp. 12–15):

1. By origin—An example within this system is drugs that come from plants, such as the opiates, which are derived from the opium poppy. The "pure" (nonsynthetic) opiates include compounds such as morphine and codeine. Heroin, which is a semisynthetic compound, often is called an opiate drug. As this classification distinguishes only the source of the drug, a given drug class may include many drugs with different chemical actions.

2. By action, according to similarity of **drug effects**—For example, marijuana and atropine both increase heart rate and cause dryness in the mouth. According to this system, therefore, marijuana is called an atropine-like drug.

3. By therapeutic use, or according to similarity in how a drug is used to treat or modify something in the body—For example, with this

Drug effects
The action of a drug on the body. Drug effects are measured in different ways.

system amphetamines are called appetite-suppressant drugs. Note that the reasons some drugs are used can be much different from their therapeutic effects. When amphetamines are used nonmedically it is often because of their stimulant effects. Similarly, morphine may be used medically as a powerful painkiller, but the street user takes morphine for its euphoric effects.

4. By site of drug action, which pertains to where in the body the drug is causing physical changes—For example, alcohol often is called a depressant drug because of its depressant action on the central nervous system (CNS). Conversely, because of its CNS stimulant properties, cocaine often is called a stimulant drug. The utility of this system can be limited when a drug has an effect on several different body sites. One example is the CNS stimulant cocaine, which also has local anesthetic (pain-reducing) effects. Furthermore, drugs that differ widely in chemical structure or mechanisms of action may affect the same body site.

5. By chemical structure—For example, the barbiturates (such as phenobarbital, Amytal, and Seconal) are synthetic compounds derived from the chemical structure of barbituric acid, the synthetic compound forming the chemical base for barbiturate drugs.

6. By mechanism of action, which means how a drug produces its effects—This is a good system in principle, but we still do not know the details about how some drugs produce their effects.

7. By street name, which comes from drug "subcultures" and the street drug market—For example, amphetamines are called "speed," and drugs like the barbiturates or depressants such as methaqualone (Quaalude) are called "downers." As these latter examples show, classification by street names sometimes does reflect actual drug effects.

Of all the types of drugs that are known, we are most interested in what are called **psychoactive** drugs—those that affect moods, thinking, and behavior. Some substances have been designated formally as psychoactive, while others have not. Psychoactive drugs are of most importance in this text because they are the ones that people are most likely to use, often in ways that create serious problems for them. This text mainly concerns the nonmedical use of psychoactive drugs, but we also discuss medical uses.

Psychoactive
Pertaining to effects on mood, thinking, and behavior.

The Drug Experience

Because humans have an affinity for nonmedical drug use, it might be said that people like the experiences they have when they take drugs. This raises an extremely important question: What causes the "drug experience"? The drug's chemical action is part of the answer, but how much? Not too long ago, the chemical actions of drugs were viewed as the primary reason people experienced certain changes when they took different drugs. However, in the past 30 years or so research from different disciplines, such as pharmacology, psychology, and sociology, has shown that the drug experience is a product of more factors than the drug's pharmacological action.

Drug dosage
Measure of the quantity of drug consumed.

Route of drug administration
The way that drugs enter the body.

Psychological set
An individual's knowledge, attitudes, expectations, and other thoughts about an object or event, such as a drug.

Placebo
In pharmacology, refers to a chemically inactive substance.

"I could have easily gotten stoned [before coming to this interview]; it wouldn't have bothered me. It depends on the situation. I wouldn't like to smoke in the middle of the day if I have things to do. Or I wouldn't smoke in the middle of a class. Things like that"
research subject in Zinberg
(1984, p. 140)

Generally, we can look at three sets of pharmacological and nonpharmacological factors to help us understand the drug experience. The first set includes **pharmacological factors,** and three stand out. First are the chemical properties and action on the body of the drug used. Another is **drug dosage** (or dose), which is the measure of how much of the drug is consumed. The third pharmacological factor is the **route of drug administration,** or the way the drug enters the body. This is important because the route affects how much of a dosage reaches its site(s) of action and how quickly it gets there. Chapter 4 discusses major routes of drug administration and their effects on the drug experience in detail.

The second set of factors is nonpharmacological and consists of the **characteristics of the drug user.** Included are such factors as the person's genetic makeup (biologically inherited differences among people govern their bodies' reaction to the ingestion of different drugs), gender, age, drug tolerance, and personality. An important part of personality is the person's **psychological set** about a drug, which refers to knowledge, attitudes, expectations, and thoughts about a drug. For example, sometimes the strong belief that a drug will produce a certain effect will be enough to produce the effect, even though the person has ingested a chemically inactive substance (**placebo**).

The third and last set of factors, also a nonpharmacological one, is the setting in which a drug is used. The factors in this group span a wide range and include laws pertaining to drug use in the community where the drug is taken, the immediate physical environment where the drug is used, and whether other people are present at the time of drug use.

Together these three sets of factors influence what a person experiences when he or she takes a drug. You may have guessed that the path to a drug experience is not always easy to chart. However, many people are trying to do just that—to understand how drugs affect people. The accumulated knowledge from these efforts is the foundation of this book.

ALCOHOL AND DRUG USE IN THE UNITED STATES

The way the popular media tell it, it may seem as if virtually everyone has positive experiences using drugs, since everyone seems to be using them. However, scientists learned long ago that our impressions or feelings about a subject often are inaccurate, and to find out what is really going on it is best to study the subject systematically. This means using the scientific method, which is the major way we have learned as much as we do know about drugs. One of the best ways to answer questions about the uses of alcohol and drugs in a community or larger region is to do a survey study. When we want to learn about a whole country, we do what is called a national survey study.

In the United States, national survey studies of alcohol and drug use have involved interviewing a sample of individuals (in this case, age 12 or older) across the country. Such studies generally ensure that those interviewed are as similar as possible to the U.S. population as a whole, regarding, for example, factors such as gender, age, race, region of the country, and rural-versus-urban living environment. The national survey data give us the

People use drugs in a variety of situations and experience different reactions to them.

Contemporary Issue
U.S. SOCIETY AND DRUG USE

Learning about alcohol and drug use in the United States is important. One reason is the sheer number of people in the United States who use alcohol or other drugs. Another reason is the negative consequences associated with alcohol and drug use, which are discussed later in more detail. A third reason is the amount of controversy that drugs, especially illicit drugs, create. Despite the prevalence of drug use among Americans, as a population the U.S. attitude has been toward eradicating illicit drug use, often ranking such use as the nation's number one problem. Think of some of the major headline events that have occurred and controversies they have generated in the last few years. Some of them touch upon the basic constitutional rights of Americans:

- The right of the federal government and other public and private employers to conduct urine screens (tests for drug taking) of employees as a way to control drug abuse in the workplace
- The use of illegal drugs by professional and other athletes—some prime examples are Len Bias, the star University of Maryland basketball player who died in 1987 from an overdose of cocaine; Ben Johnson, Canadian track star, whose use of anabolic steroids nullified his gold medal in the 1988 Summer Olympics in Seoul, Korea, and resulted in 1993 in his being barred for life from track and field.
- The uproar resulting from the revelation that Douglas H. Ginsberg, a 1987 Supreme Court nominee, smoked marijuana at a party in the 1970s and the ensuing controversy, which revolved around Ginsberg's fitness to be a Supreme Court judge, resulting in the withdrawal of his nomination
- Some proposed legal penalties related to selling or using drugs—requirement of life sentences to drug dealers who are convicted twice of selling drugs to teenagers, and the imposition of the death penalty on dealers when a murder occurs during a drug deal
- President Clinton's decision to elevate the directorship of the Office of National Drug Control Policy to a Cabinet-level post

Many Americans use alcohol or other drugs. But the country's attitudes toward such use, especially regarding illicit drugs, are far from permissive. Society's proposed and actual solutions to drug use in the United States have far-reaching legal, social, and financial implications. Which stand out to you?

best estimate we have of what the findings would be if we studied every person in the population that was sampled for the survey. In this case that means a population of around 200 million people.

The federal government goes to great trouble and expense to support these national surveys of drug use because the knowledge gained from them is extremely valuable in making legal, tax, educational, and health policy decisions. More narrowly, we are interested in the information from national surveys for this text because many people do not know the typical patterns of drug and alcohol use among Americans. For example, in the popular media we are exposed primarily to extreme cases of use and problems associated with it. So, the national survey data on alcohol and drug use give us a more balanced reference for understanding any one person's or group's use. In the same way, our brief review of national survey data in this chapter will help you understand drug-use patterns and related problems that we write about in later chapters of this book.

National Household Survey

To provide you with an overview of current alcohol and drug use, we used a national survey that is conducted every few years by the National Institute on Drug Abuse (NIDA). The "National Household Survey" includes households in the contiguous 48 states. In this section we refer to findings from the 1992 survey (U.S. Department of Health and Human Services [USDHHS], 1993a).

This survey included individuals 12 years of age or older. Personal and self-administered interviews were completed with 28,832 respondents. Since it was a household survey, people living in places like military installations, drug-treatment programs, or jails were excluded from the sample. Although these people constitute only about 2% of the population, the data cannot be viewed as representative of everyone in the contiguous 48 states as a result. Nevertheless, the national household surveys provide the best single description of frequency and quantity of different drug use among a broad age range of people in U.S. society.

In the 1992 NIDA survey a variety of data about drug use in the United States was collected. We first discuss data on overall **prevalence** of use in the last year and last month for different drugs, including alcohol and tobacco cigarettes. In this case, "use" means the person used the drug in question at least one time during the time in question. We also offer counterpart prevalence data from the 1988 and 1990 surveys to allow a comparison with the 1992 data. Table 1-1 presents this first set of percentages. Several findings stand out in Table 1-1. First, alcohol leads the use list, followed by cigarettes in a distant second place. Marijuana and hashish head the list of illicit drug use (drug use not in accord with legal restrictions). These relationships hold up both for use in the past year and in the past month. Notably, with a few exceptions, the trend in legal (alcohol, cigarettes) and illicit drug use seems to be a decline, again both for the last month and the last year. However, a good deal of attention has been given to the exceptions: hallucinogens and heroin in the past year, and hallucinogens in the past month.

Table 1-1 gives you an overall picture of drug use, but as we noted before, drug use differs with characteristics of people. Tables 1-2 and 1-3 give you an initial look at some of the characteristics of the person that are highly associated with drug-use differences. Table 1-2 centers on age differences in drug use in the past year and month, as reported in the 1992 national survey. As you can see in Table 1-2, individuals in the age range 18–34 have the most prevalent substance use. Respondents aged 18–25 stand out in particular for illicit drug use. For example, more than one of every four of such participants in the survey reported at least one occasion of illicit drug use in the past year.

Prevalence
The general occurrence of an event, usually expressed in terms of percentage of some population. Another common statistic in survey studies is incidence, or the number of first-time occurrences of an event during some time period.

Table 1-1   Percentages of Individuals Aged 12 and Older Who Reported Use of Different Drugs for the Past Year and Past Month, 1988, 1990, 1992

Drug	Past Year			Past Month		
	1988	1990	1992	1988	1990	1992
Marijuana & hashish	10.6	10.2	8.5	5.9	5.1	4.4
Cocaine	4.1	3.1	2.4	1.5	.8	.6
Inhalants	1.3	1.2	1.0	.6	.6	.4
Hallucinogens	1.6	1.1	1.2	.4	.3	.3
Heroin	.3	.2	.2	.0	.0	.0
Nonmedical use of any psychotherapeutic	5.7	4.3	3.8	1.7	1.4	1.3
Alcohol	68.1	66.0	64.7	53.4	51.2	47.8
Cigarettes	4.2	32.0	31.2	28.8	26.	26.2

Note: Psychotherapeutic drugs include any prescription-type stimulant, sedative, tranquilizer, or analgesic. Do not include over-the-counter drugs. "Use" means used at least one time.

Source: U.S. Department of Health and Human Services (1993a).

Table 1-2   Percentages of Individuals in Different Age Groups Who Reported Use of Different Drugs for the Past Year and Past Month, 1992

Drug	Past Year				Past Month			
	12–17 yrs.	18–25	26–34	>34	12–17 yrs.	18–25	26–34	>34
Any Illicit Drug	11.7	26.4	18.3	5.1	6.1	13.0	10.1	2.2
Alcohol	32.6	77.7	79.0	62.6	15.7	59.2	61.2	46.5
Cigarettes	18.2	41.1	38.8	28.8	9.6	31.9	33.7	25.3

Note: Any Illicit drug use includes nonmedical use of marijuana or hashish, cocaine, inhalants, hallucinogens, heroin, or psychotherapeutic drugs at least one time.

Source: U.S. Department of Health and Human Services (1993a).

Table 1-3   Percentages of Individuals Aged 12 and Older of Different Ethnic and Gender Groups Who Reported Any Illicit Drug Use or Any Alcohol in the Past Month, 1992

		Any Illicit Drug	Alcohol
Ethnic/Racial Group	White	5.5	49.7
	Black	6.6	39.8
	Hispanic	5.3	45.0
	Other	3.6	38.4
Gender	Male	7.1	55.9
	Female	4.1	40.4

Note: Any Illicit Drug Use includes nonmedical use of marijuana or hashish, cocaine, inhalants, hallucinogens, heroin, or psychotherapeutic drugs at least one time.

Source: U.S. Department of Health and Human Services (1993a).

In Table 1-3 we provide 1992 substance-use data for the past month according to ethnic/racial group and gender. The most striking findings in Table 1-3 are the gender differences. Men were almost twice as likely as women to report any illicit drug use in the past month, and almost 50% more likely than women to report any alcohol use. For ethnic/racial differences, whites and Hispanics did not show large discrepancies in alcohol or illicit drug use.

However, blacks reported more prevalent illicit drug use than either of these two groups, and less prevalent alcohol use.

Summary of Survey Data

The national survey data suggest that people in the United States use a variety of drugs, and that some drugs are far more commonly used than others. For example, alcohol and nicotine use is considerably more prevalent than is use of any illicit drug. (This finding evokes the question of whether the "war on drugs" is fighting only part of the battle.) Furthermore, substance use for the past year and past month seems to have declined since 1988. Two exceptions in the 1992 data, however, were heroin and hallucinogen use for the past year, and hallucinogen use for the past month. Characteristics of the respondents can make a considerable difference in prevalence for substance use, as we showed for age, gender, and ethnic/racial groups in the 1992 data.

Multiple Drug Use

The person who increases the percentage of, say, marijuana users in a survey sample may be the same person who increases the percentage of alcohol users. Such multiple drug use (also called **polydrug use**) is extremely important because of the effects that drug combinations have on the body. We will explore those effects in detail in Chapter 4. For now, it is important to know that polydrug use is a critical health and social problem.

Polydrug use
The same person's regular use of more than one drug.

At this writing the best and most recent information we have on the prevalence of polydrug use is from the 1991 National Survey of Drug Use (US-DHHS, 1993b). Table 1-4 presents 1991 survey data on single and multiple drug use patterns in the last year in different age groups. The table shows, again, how alcohol is far and away the most popular drug in the United States. But the table also shows a considerable rate of multiple drug use,

Table 1-4   Percentages of People of Different Ages Reporting Single and Multiple Drug Use in the Last Year, 1991 National Survey of Drug Use

	Age Group (Years)			
Pattern of Use	12–17	18–25	26–34	>34
Alcohol Only	27.4	54.3	63.2	59.3
Illicit Drugs Only	1.9	.6	.7	.7
Marijuana only	.4	.2	.3	.2
Psychotherapeutics only	.7	.3	.2	.5
Other drugs & drug combinations	.8	.2	.2	*
Alcohol and Illicit Drugs	12.9	28.5	17.7	5.6
Alcohol and marijuana only	5.4	13.0	8.1	2.3
Alcohol & psychotherapeutics only	1.6	2.4	2.5	1.4
Alcohol and other drugs & drug combinations	5.9	13.2	7.2	1.9

Note: Illicit Drugs = marijuana or hashish, cocaine (including crack), inhalants, hallucinogens (including PCP), heroin, or nonmedical use of psychotherapeutics; Psychotherapeutics = prescription-type stimulants, sedatives, tranquilizers, or analgesics. Does not include over-the-counter drugs; Use = consumption at least one time; * = no estimate available because of lack of precision.

Source: USDHHS (1993b, p. 92).

DRUGS AND CULTURE
THE NATIONAL SURVEY AND SUBGROUP DIFFERENCES

You know from our discussion that the national survey data give us a great description of drug use among people living in the contiguous 48 states. At the same time, the national surveys do not tell us as much as they do tell us. The beginnings of understanding this is in some of the differences in use patterns according to characteristics of the user—such as age, sex, and race—and to the user's environment—such as the person's area of residence and local laws and policies regarding alcohol and drug use.

Demographic group differences in drug use reflect differences in complex historical or current factors that are common to some group of people or to some region. Therefore, the differences could reflect biological, psychological or social/environmental factors that distinguish a group from other groups or from the population as a whole. The complexity of the factors is such that certain groups have been designated "special populations." This label represents the idea that in order to understand the respective group's drug use you need to understand its unique history and current circumstances. Groups that today are considered special populations by experts who study drug use include women, native Americans, African Americans, the homeless, and Asians. You will note later that the drug chapters in this text incorporate cultural and regional differences with features such as a historical account of the drug or drug class in question, and with attention to special cultural differences in use of the drug.

Given the importance of subgroup differences within a total survey sample, how might you adjust the sampling in a national survey to get a better, more accurate look at a subgroup that is of particular interest to you?

especially the use of alcohol with illicit drugs. Overall, the prevalence of such a pattern of use in the past year is 11.9% (not shown in Table 1-4). However, age is strongly associated with such use: 28.5% of respondents aged 18–25 used alcohol and illicit drugs, compared to 17.7% of 26- to 34-year-olds, who had the next highest rate. A total of 12.9% of respondents aged 12–17 also reported combined alcohol and illicit drug use in the past year—a substantial prevalence when it is considered that alcohol cannot be purchased legally by people in this age group.

In its extreme, multiple drug use can include taking drugs with different or opposite physical effects in sequence on the same occasion. In such cases, the motive for use seems to be change, positive or otherwise, from one drug experience to another. An instance of extreme polydrug use, excerpted from Goldman (1971) and cited in Mendelson and Mello (1985, pp. 200–201), illustrates how people may use one type of drug after another, without apparent rhyme or reason. The example involves famous comedian Lenny Bruce, who died in 1966 at age 40, and an associate of his:

The night before, they ended a very successful three-week run in Chicago by traveling to the Cloisters (in New York City) and visiting the home of a show-biz druggist—a house so closely associated with drugs that show people call it the 'shooting gallery.' Terry smoked a couple of joints, dropped two blue tabs of mescaline, and skin-popped some Dilaudid; at the airport bar he also downed two double Scotches. Lenny did his usual number: 12, ⅟₁₆-**grain** Dilaudid pills counted out of a big brown bottle, dissolved in a 1-cubic centimeter (cc) ampule of Methedrine, and heated in a blackened old spoon. The resulting soup was drawn into a disposable needle and then whammed into mainline (intravenously) until you feel like you're living inside an igloo.

Grain
As a measure, a unit of weight equal to .0648 of a gram.

Lenny also was into mescaline that evening: Not just Terry's two little old-maidish tabs, but a whole fistful, chewed up in his mouth and then washed down with a chocolate Yoo-Hoo.

Negative Consequences of Alcohol and Drug Use

Describing alcohol and drug use brings up the question of the consequences of such use. As we will discuss in detail in later chapters, people experience positive consequences of their use of drugs. But they also may experience negative effects, which definitions of drug abuse try to capture. One way to look at the negative consequences of alcohol and drug use for society is to conduct a "cost of illness" study. The purpose of these studies is to quantify in dollars what society "pays" for its members incurring specific illnesses. It is important to note that focusing on economic factors does not mean there are no psychological costs associated with illness. However, psychological consequences are not easily quantified and thus are much more difficult to analyze.

Two major "illness" distinctions that have been studied in detail are alcohol abuse and other drug abuse. In such research, "drug abuse" concerns the use of illegal drugs and the nonprescription use of drugs typically used for therapeutic purposes. Nicotine use has not been included. (However, this is not to understate the costs of nicotine use to United States society. The costs are devastating and are reviewed in detail in Chapter 7.)

A study by Rice, Kelman, Miller, and Dunmeyer (1990) included estimates of the economic costs to U.S. society of alcohol abuse and other drug abuse. The study yielded the estimate that in 1985, alcohol abuse cost the United States about $70.3 billion, and drug abuse cost $44.1 billion. The total: over $114 billion. These figures were updated for 1988. The estimates, adjusted for inflation and other factors, grew to $85.8 billion for alcohol abuse and $58.3 billion for drug abuse (Rice et al., 1990). The new total is over $143 billion. And in October 1993 a report published by the Robert Wood Johnson Foundation had the total economic cost in 1990 of alcohol abuse at $99 billion and of drug abuse at $67 billion.

Most people cannot even conceptualize what $1 billion is, never mind hundreds of billions of dollars. To help you understand how much money we are talking about, here is one illustration: A wealthy woman gives her sister $1 million to put in a drawer, telling her she can spend $1,000 a day and to call when the money is spent. Three years later, the sister calls. If the original sum had been $1 billion, the sister would not have called for 3,000 years. In

The sometimes tragic consequences of drug use have drawn national attention and response.

any case, our difficulty in picturing billions of dollars does not make the cost of alcohol and drug abuse any less real.

For both alcohol and drug abuse the costs come from a wide range of sources, although not distributed in the same proportions for the two types of illnesses. The sources include direct treatment costs, the value of reduced or lost productivity, and the value of productivity lost due to premature death. Other costs include those related to crime expenditures, motor vehicle crashes, fires, and the value of lost productivity for victims of crime, incarceration, crime "careers," and caregivers (Rice et al., 1990). Crime-related costs are especially significant for drug abuse.

A Closing Note

Cost-of-illness studies give us a good, well-rounded estimate of what society pays for its members' involvement with alcohol and other drugs. The multi-billion-dollar cost estimates are staggering but ironically understate the impact, perhaps, because most of us have little direct experience with even $1 million. Yet some of the consequences of alcohol and drug use come into stark reality with a little thought of what events make up the cost computations. For example, there are the lifetimes of individuals that will not be lived fully because the individuals were born with fetal alcohol syndrome (Chapter 9). Or, there is the jamming of hospital emergency rooms in 1990 with 80,000 visits related to cocaine use (Chapter 6). Then there is the suffering of a family who lost one of its young members because he was shot and killed in a robbery to obtain drugs. And maybe you have experienced what it is like to lose a friend or family member in one of thousands of fatal alcohol-related traffic accidents that occur every year in the United States. It is important to step down from the statistics to these and other events to help crystallize the real costs of alcohol and drugs to society.

Contemporary Issue
DRUGS, CRIMINAL ACTIVITY, AND AGGRESSION

We noted how costs associated with criminal behavior are especially significant for drug abuse. The association of alcohol, drugs, and crime is one we seemingly see and hear about continually in the popular media. The association also is one that very likely has frightened each of us in one way or another.

The problem of drugs, alcohol, and crime is an old one, and much studied. First, that we are dealing with associations, or correlations, and not causes should be clear. For example, the pharmacological effects of cocaine are not known to cause a person to commit murder. Yet the high positive correlation between drugs and crime remains a fact: as drug use in a community increases so does the occurrence of certain kinds of crimes, depending on the drug.

Much of the research on drugs and crime has concerned heroin. Most of the crimes committed by heroin addicts are either violation of the drug laws or ways to get money to buy more heroin. Therefore, the addict's most commonly committed crimes are burglary, larceny, assault, and other street crimes. These crimes are indeed serious and sometimes result in injury or death to the victims. But the direct intent of the crime is not to harm the victim, but to get his or her money. This same motive probably applies to much of the violence around cocaine, and to conflicts over money among cocaine dealers and their customers.

Surprisingly, the use of some drugs has no relationship with criminal activity, or there is negative association between use of the drug and crime. Use of the hallucinogens, for example, is not associated with crime, and marijuana seems to fall in the same category. The evidence is mixed for barbiturates and tranquilizers: some studies show no relationship, but others suggest that the relationship between use and crime is the same for barbiturates and alcohol.

Alcohol intoxication has a high correlation with criminal activity. Because alcohol is legal and very available, little violence is connected with violating drug laws or stealing to obtain alcohol. Most of the crimes associated with alcohol intoxication are assaultive. That is, they are committed with the intent to harm the victim. Alcohol is correlated with other types of crime as well, such as aggravated assault, homicides, property offenses, sexual offenses, and writing bad checks.

So one point is clear: some types of drug use are associated with criminal activity. But what is the explanation? Pharmacology figures complexly in the answer but seems to be only one of many factors. Others include the person's expectations about the drug's effects, the setting where the drug is being used, and personality characteristics of the user.

The drug-crime problem is a good example of how a society and its individual members are affected by drug use. It also illustrates that drug use and its effects on the user are influenced by many factors working together.

DEFINING HARMFUL DRUG USE

Discussing cost-of-illness research brings our focus back to what might be called harmful drug use, or use that is associated with detrimental consequences to the drug user or to others. Indeed, in order to reflect harmful use, cost-of-illness studies have used terms like "alcohol abuse" and "drug abuse." Yet in the beginning of this chapter we mentioned how widely different are the meanings the users of these terms have ascribed to them. This is a problem most essentially because it hampers communication about drug use. Relatedly, lack of standard definitions tends to slow the advance of knowledge. If there is disagreement about what it is we are trying to gain knowledge about, you can see why scientific advances might be impeded.

In the United States and other countries providers of care for physical and mental illness have handled the problems of definition by developing systems of definitions of illnesses, or diagnostic systems. A diagnosis typically is based on a cluster of symptoms that is given a name (the diagnosis). The advantage is that, say, if two physicians are communicating about pneumonia in a patient, and they are following the same diagnostic system, each knows exactly what the referent of the other is when the term "pneumonia" is used. That is, a specific cluster of symptoms is being referred to. It also is possible to create diagnostic systems of mental illnesses. In the United States the primary organization responsible for doing that has been the American Psychiatric Association (APA). Since the early 1950s the APA has published formal diagnostic systems of different mental illnesses, or disorders. These have appeared under the publication name of *Diagnostic and Statistical Manual* (DSM). The most recent version (systems are revised because of ongoing research that provides new information about different disorders) appeared in May 1994. It is called DSM-IV. The DSM-IV has a section called "substance-related" (alcohol- or other drug-related) disorders, which includes definition of "substance-related dependence" and "substance-related abuse."

Table 1-5 lists the criteria for defining substance-related dependence and abuse according to DSM-IV (American Psychiatric Association, 1994). It is important to make a few comments about the criteria. Most generally, the same criteria are applied in defining dependence and abuse for all drugs and drug classes that people tend to use for nonmedical reasons. That includes all the

"Unlike others, he (a heroin addict) could not find a vocation, a career, a meaningful, sustained activity around which he could wrap his life. Instead he relied on the addiction to provide a vocation around which he could build a reasonably full life and establish an identity"

Psychologist Isidor Chein
(Quoted in Krogh, 1991, p. 133)

Table 1-5   Diagnostic Criteria for Psychoactive Substance Abuse and Dependence, DSM-IV

Substance Dependence

A maladaptive pattern of substance use, leading to clinically significant impairment or distress, as manifested by three or more of the following occurring at any time in the same 12-month period:

1. tolerance, as defined by either of the following:
   (a) need for markedly increased amounts of the substance to achieve intoxication or desired effect.
   (b) markedly diminished effect with continued use of the same amount of the substance.
2. withdrawal, as manifested by either of the following:
   (a) the characteristic withdrawal syndrome for the substance.
   (b) the same (closely related) substance is taken to relieve or avoid withdrawal symptoms.
3. the substance is often taken in larger amounts or over a longer period than was intended.
4. a persistent desire or unsuccessful efforts to cut down or control substance use.
5. a great deal of time is spent in activities necessary to obtain the substance (e.g., visiting multiple doctors or driving long distances), to use the substance (e.g., chain-smoking), or to recover from its effects.
6. important social, occupational, or recreational activities given up or reduced because of substance use.
7. continued substance use despite knowledge of having had a persistent or recurrent physical or psychological problem that is likely to be caused by or exacerbated by the substance (e.g., current cocaine use despite recognition of cocaine-induced depression, or continued drinking despite recognition that an ulcer was made worse by alcohol consumption).

Specify if:

With physiological dependence: Evidence of tolerance or withdrawal (i.e., either items |1| or |2| are present).

Substance Abuse

A maladaptive pattern of substance use leading to clinically significant impairment or distress, as manifested by one or more of the following:

1. recurrent substance use resulting in a failure to fulfill major role obligations at work, school, or home (e.g., repeated absences or poor work performance related to substance use; substance-related absences, suspensions, or expulsions from school; neglect of children or household).
2. recurrent substance use in situations in which it is physically hazardous (e.g., driving an automobile or operating a machine when impaired by substance use).
3. recurrent substance-related legal problems (e.g., arrests for substance-related disorderly conduct).
4. continued substance use despite having persistent or recurrent social or interpersonal problems caused or exacerbated by the effects of the substance (e.g., arguments with spouse about consequences of intoxication, physical fights).

Does not meet the criteria for substance dependence for this substance.

---

drugs we will discuss in this text. Another general point is that dependence and abuse are considered separate diagnoses. A person could not be diagnosed with both dependence and abuse of a given substance, although it is possible to meet criteria for dependence on one substance and for abuse of another.

Regarding dependence, criteria 3-6 focus on what traditionally has been called "compulsive drug use," or drug **addiction.** In essence, the individual's life centers on drug use and its procurement to the point of reduced attention to or outright neglect of other aspects of life. Similarly, drug use persists despite the risk of incurring serious consequences by doing so. There also is an inability to stop or to reduce drug use for any length of time, if that is the intention. This phenomenon has been called "loss of control."

The first two criteria for dependence introduce two terms to you—tolerance and withdrawal. We will have more to say about them later in this chapter and in other chapters in this text. In DSM-IV, a distinction is made between a diagnosis of dependence without meeting criteria for either tolerance or withdrawal, and a dependence diagnosis that does meet either of those two criteria. At least three of the total of seven criteria that are listed for dependence must be met for the diagnosis to be made.

While we are discussing the DSM definition of dependence, we would like to define a term that you probably have heard or read because it is so commonly used: **psychological dependence.** As with many terms that are used in communicating about drugs and their use, psychological dependence has had different meanings. So the Rinaldi et al. (1988) consensus definition is useful again. In the Rinaldi study psychological dependence was defined as "the emotional state of **craving** a drug either for its positive effect or to avoid negative effects associated with its abuse" (p. 557). As you can see, psychological dependence is far more narrowly but less precisely defined than is dependence in DSM-IV and focuses on the strong desire to use a drug in order to alter a psychological state or to escape or avoid some unpleasant experience.

The criteria for substance-related abuse center on consequences in different areas of life (family, social, job) that may reasonably be connected to substance use. Four criteria are listed for abuse, and a person has to meet at least one of them to receive the diagnosis.

We would like to say a few more words about the DSM-IV definitions before concluding our discussion of them. The DSM-IV criteria, which are based on the most current knowledge about substance-use disorders that comes from research and clinical practice, ease problems in communication because they are clearly written descriptive criteria. This does not mean that the criteria are perfect—indeed the expectation is that the criteria will continue to evolve as new knowledge accrues. In this regard, a generally accepted definition of a phenomenon makes it far more likely that we will acquire new knowledge about substance use and eventually have a good understanding of it. Another point you may have noticed is that the DSM offers definitions of dependence on and abuse of drugs, but provides no definition of drug use. In DSM terms, drug use would be any consumption of alcohol or other drugs and related events that does not meet criteria for dependence or abuse.

In summary, although we may never get away entirely from the influence of societal values on definitions of substance-use disorders, the creators of

Addiction
In reference to drugs, overwhelming involvement with use of a drug, getting an adequate supply of it, and a strong tendency to resume use of it after stopping for a period.

Psychological dependence
The emotional state of craving a drug either for its positive effect or to avoid negative effects associated with its abuse.

Craving
A term that has been variously defined in reference to drug use. Typically it refers to a strong or intense desire to use a drug.

DSM-IV have considerably advanced our ability to communicate about harmful drug use. Because of this, DSM is ubiquitous in alcohol and other drug treatment and research settings in the United States. Accordingly, we follow the DSM-IV definitions where relevant in the remaining chapters of this text.

Drug Tolerance and Withdrawal

The DSM-IV criteria for dependence include the term drug **tolerance,** which was defined in criterion 1 of Part B in Table 1-5. Another new term is **withdrawal** symptoms. Withdrawal is a definable illness that occurs with a cessation or decrease in drug use, after the body has adjusted to the presence of a drug to such a degree that it cannot function without it. Not all drugs are associated with an identifiable withdrawal **syndrome** (also called abstinence syndrome). For any drug associated with withdrawal symptoms, the severity of those symptoms may change with the characteristics of the user and his or her history of use of that drug. Furthermore, psychological symptoms, such as anxiety, depression, and craving for drugs, are often part of withdrawal syndromes. These psychological symptoms strongly influence whether the individual can stop using drugs for any length of time.

Tolerance, Withdrawal, and Drug-Taking Behavior

We drew your attention to drug tolerance and withdrawal in this introductory chapter because they are central topics in psychopharmacology. Tolerance and withdrawal are addressed as part of any evaluation or study of a drug. As a result, we will discuss these concepts in far more detail in later chapters. It is critical to mention further in this chapter, however, that tolerance and withdrawal affect drug-use patterns. For example, if tolerance to a drug develops, the individual must consume increasing amounts of it to achieve a desired drug effect. Such a trend in use may affect how much time the person may devote each day to acquiring the drug and to using it. Furthermore, with greater quantities and frequencies of drug use, the person becomes more susceptible to experiencing various physical, social, or legal negative consequences.

Similarly, drug withdrawal makes more likely a person's continued use of a drug or resumption of use after a period of abstaining. Many studies have shown that relief from withdrawal is a powerful motivator of drug use. In this regard, drug withdrawal may begin when the level of drug in the blood drops. If more of the drug is taken at this point, the withdrawal symptoms are relieved. Here the motivating force is the "turning off" of unpleasant withdrawal symptoms, working to perpetuate a powerful cycle of drug use–drug withdrawal–drug use.

We want to emphasize here that the influences of tolerance and withdrawal are at the heart of psychopharmacology—the incentives or motivators that drive human (and other animal) drug use. Chapter 5, on principles and methods of psychopharmacology, addresses this question in detail.

This discussion shows that using a drug for a long period alters the patterns of use for that drug. Long-term use also relates to the DSM-IV criteria. Tolerance and withdrawal may result not only in changes in drug use and preoccupation, but also in the likelihood that the person's life and the lives of

Tolerance
Generally, a diminished drug effect with its continued use.

Withdrawal
A definable illness that occurs with a cessation or decrease in use of a drug.

Syndrome
In medicine, a number of symptoms occurring together and characterizing a specific illness or disease.

those around him or her are affected by the drug in a snowballing effect, with one consequence building upon another. The outcome can reflect some of the criteria included in the DSM-IV definition of substance-use disorder.

OVERVIEW OF THE TEXT

We close this chapter by giving you a brief overview of what is to follow. As was the goal of this chapter, the next four are designed to give you information about the history of drug-taking behavior and basic concepts in psychopharmacology. Accordingly, Chapter 2 places human drug use in a historical context, giving you a better appreciation of today's use patterns and the social and political contexts in which they occur. Chapter 3 is a basic discussion of the nervous system and how drugs affect it. This knowledge is essential to understanding drug effects because, no matter what drug effect or experience you consider, some change in the nervous system is inevitable. Chapter 4 concerns pharmacology, as we review the methods scientists use to study drugs and their effects. Chapter 5 focuses on principles and methods of psychopharmacology, which is the central topic of this text. Chapters 4 and 5 will help you to understand how we have learned much of what we know about drugs.

Over-the-counter drugs
Drugs that can be legally obtained without medical prescription.

Chapters 6–15 concern individual drugs and drug classes, including the major stimulants, nicotine, caffeine, alcohol and other depressant drugs, psychiatric drugs, opiates, marijuana, hallucinogens, and **over-the-counter drugs.** These chapters broadly follow an outline of historical overview and epidemiology; mechanisms of drug action; medical and psychotherapeutic uses; and physiological, psychological, and social/environmental effects. Your study of each of the drug chapters offers good understanding of that drug (or drug class) and its use.

The last two chapters concern topics often discussed in media geared to the general public. Chapter 16 is a review of treatment of the substance-use disorders, and Chapter 17 covers prevention of substance-use disorders before they occur. Prevention is a fitting topic on which to end this book because that is what all the research, politics, and discussion are about—reaching the goal of living in a society free of substance-use disorders.

summary

- Psychopharmacology—the scientific study of the effects of drugs on behavior—is the subject of this text.

- Drugs may be classified in different ways; seven of the major ones are reviewed in this chapter.

- The experience that humans have from taking drugs is influenced by three sets of factors, including pharmacological factors, characteristics of the drug user, and the setting in which the drug is used.

- National survey data show that people in the United States use a variety of drugs. With a few exceptions, the overall trend from 1988 to 1992 is a decline in licit and illicit drug use.

- Alcohol, tobacco cigarettes, and marijuana/ hashish consistently have appeared as the most commonly tried and currently used psychoactive drugs.

- An accurate picture of drug use is possible only if use is looked at by characteristics of the person. For example, the heaviest and most frequent illicit drug use is among young adults (age 18–25). Another example is that men are far more likely than women to report alcohol and drug use in the past month.

- Some individuals use more than one drug regularly and may use different drugs together on the same occasion.

- In 1990 the estimated economic cost of alcohol and illicit drug abuse to the United States totaled over $160 billion.

- The formal way used to define substance-use disorders in the United States is the fourth edition of the American Psychiatric Association's *Diagnostic and Statistical Manual*.

- The DSM-IV definition includes drug tolerance and withdrawal, which may powerfully affect drug-use patterns.

- This book covers basic psychopharmacology concepts, details on major drugs and drug classes and those who use them, and discussions of prevention and treatment toward a better understanding of drugs and human behavior.

ANSWERS TO WHAT DO YOU THINK?

1. Because the effects of drugs are both predictable and obvious, it is relatively easy to define drug abuse.

F *Drugs have a variety of effects on people, and how they are perceived may vary in different cultures and subcultures. As a result, it has proved difficult to create a definition of drug abuse that is generally agreeable.*

2. A drug's street name often describes the actual effects of that drug.

T *Street names, which come from drug subcultures and the street drug market, sometimes do reflect actual drug effects.*

3. A person's reaction to a drug depends mostly on the biological action of the drug in the body.

F *Biology is important, but psychological and social/environmental factors also must be included to explain the effects of psychoactive drugs on humans.*

4. Because drug use is complicated, it is impossible to estimate patterns of drug use for the population of a whole country.

F *Drug use is complicated, but sophisticated sampling methods and computers have made it possible to select large numbers of people and survey them to derive precise estimates of drug use in a given population.*

5. Within the United States similar patterns of alcohol and other drug use are found even among different subgroups of the population.

F *Drug use has been found to vary with characteristics of the person and of the environment.*

6. The highest rates of alcohol and other drug use are found among 18- to 25-year-olds.

T *People in this age group, called "young adults," have the highest rates of alcohol and other drug use in the United States.*

7. A person's use of more than one drug at a time is of little concern because it happens so infrequently.

F *Although multiple drug use is not as frequent as use of a single substance, it is hardly rare, especially among young people. It is of great concern because* *combining drugs sometimes has unpredictable effects that may be life-threatening.*

8. The total economic cost of alcohol and drug abuse in the United States is about a billion dollars annually.

F   *The most recent estimates suggest it is more than 160 times that amount.*

9. Alcohol and other drug use causes violence and crime.

F   *Use of alcohol and other, but not all other, drugs is associated with violence and crime, but does not directly cause such behavior.*

10. Modern researchers rely on definitions of alcohol and other drug use that are free of social or cultural biases.

F   *We are improving our ability to rid our definitions of biases, but due to the influence of social and cultural factors on alcohol and other drug use and the perception of such use, it is unlikely that we ever will arrive at bias-free definitions.*

11. A diagnosis of drug abuse is made when a person has become either physically or psychologically dependent on a drug.

F   *Dependence and abuse are considered separate diagnoses. A person could not be diagnosed with both dependence on and abuse of a single drug.*

12. Definitions of addiction center on overwhelming involvement with a drug.

T   *Addiction is identified when a person has overwhelming involvement with using a drug. His or her life centers on getting an adequate supply of the drug, with priority over most or all other parts of life, such as school, job, family, and friends.*

13. The continued use of any drug will eventually lead to tolerance and physical dependence on that drug.

F   *The continued use of many, but not all, drugs may lead to tolerance to and physical dependence on that drug.*

2 Drug Use: Yesterday and Today

WHAT DO YOU THINK?

True or False?

____ The first recorded use of cannabis occurred in the early 1800s.

____ Grape wine was the first alcoholic beverage to be used.

____ The Opium Wars between China and Great Britain in the mid-1800s occurred in large part because Britain was unwilling to curtail its trade of opium into China.

____ Columbus and his crew were responsible for introducing tobacco to the New World.

____ Many of the drugs that are now illegal in the United States were widely used in the 1800s and early 1900s to treat a broad spectrum of maladies.

____ The first notable drug law in the United States—the 1875 San Francisco Ordinance—banned the smoking of opium.

____ The Pure Food and Drug Act of 1906 had little impact on individuals who were addicted to drugs.

____ The Harrison Narcotic Act of 1914 sharply curtailed the prevalence of heroin use in the United States.

____ The Eighteenth Amendment, which prohibited the production, sale, transportation, and importing of alcohol, failed because it did not have a substantial effect on drinking in the United States.

____ Federal anti-drug legislation between 1940–1970 failed to have a sustained influence on drug use or dependence.

____ The most successful aspect of the Reagan and Bush administrations' war on drugs was the effort to intercept drugs.

____ Urine screening is a reliable method for detecting drug use.

The use of drugs dates back thousands of years. Drugs have been used for a variety of reasons in different cultures, including for religious purposes, for recreation, for altering states of consciousness, and for obtaining relief from pain or distress. In this chapter we have several objectives. One is to provide you with a historical overview of drug use, from prehistory to recent times. This is a general overview only. More detailed histories of specific psychoactive substances appear in their respective chapters. Nevertheless, a general overview is useful for studying the evolution of drug use and as a background for considering the patterns of today's drug use described in Chapter 1. A second goal is to discuss some parallels between developments in medicine and the nonmedical use of drugs. Finally, we review the types of restrictions that have been placed on drug use historically and summarize current drug laws.

HISTORICAL OVERVIEW

Indications of psychoactive substance use date to the beginnings of recorded history and revolve around the use of alcohol and plants with psychoactive properties. Investigations by archeologists suggest that beer and hackleberry wine were used as early as 6400 B.C. (Mellaart, 1967). Alcohol probably was discovered following accidental **fermentation.** (Grape wine, incidentally, did not appear until around 300–400 B.C.) The earliest reference to use of an intoxicant appears to be Noah's drunkenness, cited in the Book of Genesis. Also, various plants were used for the physical and psychological changes they produced, usually within religious or medicinal contexts. As an example, what probably was the **opium poppy** was used in Asia Minor about 5000 B.C. as a "joy plant" (Blum, 1984; O'Brien & Cohen, 1984). The use of **cannabis sativa** (brewed as a tea) dates to around 2700 B.C. in China. It was recommended by Emperor Shen Nung to his citizens for the treatment of gout and absentmindedness, among a host of other ailments. People in the Stone Age are thought to have been familiar with opium, **hashish,** and cocaine, and to have used these drugs to produce altered states of consciousness (typically within a religious context) or to prepare themselves for battle (GPO, 1972). Chewing coca leaves (one procedure for ingesting cocaine) is recorded among Indian burial sites in Central and South America as far back as 2500 B.C. Something to keep in mind is that the use of a drug in one culture does not necessarily mean people in another culture were at the same time exposed to or using that substance. Instead, cultures (now as well as then) are characterized both by diversity and by similarity in their patterns of drug use.

Throughout history contact between distant cultures has often been forced by trade agreements or by wars or other hostilities. For example, the Crusades and the expeditions of Marco Polo exposed Europeans to the drugs, particularly opium and hashish, that were popular in Oriental and Asian cultures. Other contacts were opened later through the travels of European explorers (particularly from England, France, Portugal, and Spain) to the Americas. The predominant psychoactive substances brought to Europe from the Americas were cocaine (from South America), various hallucinogens (from Central America), and tobacco (from North America). And according to O'Brien and Cohen (1984), the exchange was not one-sided. The trees producing the caffeine-containing coffee bean were native to Ethiopia. The coffee beverage derived from this bean was brought to Europe in the 1600s, and European seagoers were responsible for the eventual spread of coffee bean cultivation to the current world-leading supplier of coffee, South America. In addition, Europe introduced distilled alcoholic beverages to the Americas generally and cannabis to Chile in 1545 (O'Brien & Cohen, 1984).

There were few restrictions on drug availability or drug use prior to the beginning of the twentieth century. Occasional efforts were made to decrease or eliminate certain substances, but these efforts tended to be short-lived or ineffective. For example, initial introductions to Europe of tobacco, coffee, and tea were all met with some resistance. Rodrigo de Jerez, a colleague of Columbus and thought to be the first European to have smoked tobacco, was jailed in Spain because the authorities felt the devil had overtaken him

Fermentation
A combustive process in which yeasts interact with the sugars in plants, such as grapes, grains, and fruits to produce an enzyme that converts the sugar into alcohol.

Opium poppy
A plant cultivated for centuries, primarily in Eurasia, for opium—a narcotic that acts as a central nervous system depressant.

Cannabis sativa
The Indian hemp plant popularly known as marijuana; its resin, flowering tops, leaves, and stem contain the plant's psychoactive substances.

Hashish
Produced from the resin that covers the flowers of the cannabis hemp plant. This plant resin generally contains a greater concentration of the drug's psychoactive properties.

(Whitaker, 1987). Also, at different times efforts were made to ban the use of coffee and tea.

Cases are also known in which governments acted not to make drugs unavailable but rather to keep drug trade open and flourishing. The best example of this involved armed conflicts between China and Great Britain in the mid-nineteenth century. These conflicts, because they dealt with British traders bringing opium into China, are known now as the Opium Wars. By the mid-1800s several million Chinese men had become addicted to opium. In fact, China appears to have had the highest national use of opium by that period of time. Most of the opium being used in China was cultivated in India and brought to China by British traders. A variety of laws was passed by Chinese officials to control or eliminate opium imports, but none (including **prohibition**) had the desired effect of reducing opium use or the prevalence of addiction. Further, the British were unwilling to curtail trade of opium into China, in part for financial reasons and in part because they did not witness such a degree of addiction among users in England (where opium was widely used in medicine). Relations came to a crisis point in 1839, when the Chinese government destroyed large shipments of opium being brought into China by several British and American traders. Thus began the first Opium War between China and England. The British won the conflict, and as part of the 1842 Treaty of Nanking received rights to the port of Hong Kong as well as reimbursement for the shippers who lost their opium cargo. The opium trade continued until 1856, when the second Opium War commenced. The war ended in 1858, and the Treaty of Tientsin mandated that China would continue to import opium but could impose heavy taxes. Not until the beginning of the twentieth century was this trade reduced and eventually terminated, dovetailing with a growing international recognition of **narcotic** drug abuse.

Prohibition
The legislative forbidding of the sale of a substance, as in the alcohol Prohibition era in the United States, 1920–1933.

Narcotic
A central nervous system depressant that contains sedative and pain-relieving compounds.

Several million Chinese men were addicted to opium in the mid-to-late 1800s. This woodcut depicts two opium and water pipe smokers around 1880 in China.

In the twentieth century, few differences existed between Europe and the United States in the types of drugs being used. What is of interest is that a large number of new or "rediscovered" drugs were first popularized in the United States, and later became popular in other countries (Brecher, 1972), making the United States something of a trendsetter in drug use.

Drug Use in the United States

The use of psychoactive substances in the United States has a history as old as the country itself. Upon their arrival in the New World, Columbus and his crew were startled and amazed when they saw Indians smoking tobacco. Indeed, they described to their countrymen that these natives ate fire and belched out smoke like a dragon! The Indians inhabiting this land also introduced Columbus and the later explorers and settlers to a wide variety of psychoactive plants, including **peyote.** The Europeans, in turn, introduced to the Americas distilled spirits, a major staple on the long and arduous voyage across the Atlantic. The Pilgrims, for example, brought with them large stores of alcoholic beverages.

One of the most interesting periods of time in this country, in terms of drug use, was the nineteenth century. Into the middle 1800s, few restrictions were placed on drugs. Drugs such as opium, **morphine,** marijuana, heroin (at the end of the century), and cocaine all were easy to obtain without prescription, and often at grocery stores or through mail order. Opium, for example, was on sale legally and at low prices; some opium poppies were grown in the United States (a national outlawing of opium cultivation did not occur until 1942). Morphine was commonly used, especially during and after the Civil War, and both opium and morphine could be obtained in a variety of patent medicines readily available in stores. Examples include Godfrey's Cordial and Mrs. Wilson's Soothing Syrup. Opium was frequently taken in liquid form in mixtures such as laudanum (which contained one grain of opium to 25 drops of alcohol), and one of its more common uses was in calming and quieting crying babies!

Most narcotic use throughout this period was legal—whether through over-the-counter "tonics" or through prescription. Physicians recommended these substances widely, and referred to opium and morphine as "God's own medicine," or "G.O.M." (Morgan, 1981). And, indeed, these were effective calming agents. The list of ailments for which opium was recommended was nearly endless. A short list includes dysentery, pain, swelling, delirium tremens (associated with withdrawal from alcohol), headache, and in certain cases mental illness. Morphine, the active agent in the opium poppy, was isolated in 1806. It was named after Morpheus, the god of sleep and dreams, and was used widely during and after the Civil War, its administration greatly facilitated by the introduction of the hypodermic needle in the late 1840s. In fact, the widespread use of morphine during the Civil War is generally held responsible for large numbers of soldiers developing the "soldier's disease"—morphine addiction. The smoking of opium was introduced in the United States by Chinese laborers and was a widespread practice in the mid-1800s, especially on the West Coast. However, increased recognition by medical experts and others of the addictive aspects of the opium poppy products—opium,

Peyote (Pay-yo-tea)
A cactus plant, the top of which (a button) is dried and ingested for its hallucinogenic properties.

Morphine
A derivative of opium that is best known as a potent pain-relieving medication.

morphine, and heroin—triggered efforts to control their use and availability. We discuss some of these efforts later in this chapter.

Marijuana is another substance with a long history of use. A liquid extract of the cannabis sativa plant was used by physicians in the 1800s as a general all-purpose medication (Nahas, 1973). Its use nonmedically was noted to be much wider in the 1920s, probably in part a result of alcohol prohibition (Brecher, 1972). The use of marijuana was fairly steady in the 1930s through the 1950s but generally limited to urban areas and to the rural areas in which the marijuana was grown and harvested. In the 1960s, its popularity soared, and that popularity has remained strong. Coinciding with this popularity has been an effort to decriminalize or even legitimize marijuana sale and use. The most active organizations in this effort are the National Organization to Reform the Marijuana Laws, or NORML, and the Cannabis Action Network.

A drug that has had a fluctuating popularity among drug users in this country is cocaine. Cocaine was widely used in various "tonics" and patent medicines in the late 1800s and early 1900s. Despite concerns over negative effects associated with extended use, not until 1914 was cocaine brought under strict legal controls and penalties. Its use was apparently fairly limited in the United States until into the 1960s. In the late 1960s and up to now it has been, in various forms, in much wider use. Some experts believe cocaine will be the drug of choice for many drug users in upcoming years, and that it has not yet achieved its peak in popularity.

Other psychoactive substances have had their distinct periods of popularity during this century. **Amphetamines,** for example, were widely used throughout the 1930s to treat depression. In addition, they were given to soldiers during World War II in the belief the drug would enhance alertness (O'Brien & Cohen, 1984). Obtaining amphetamines through medical outlets such as physician prescriptions was not particularly difficult. When concern arose about the dangers inherent in continued use of these drugs, restrictions on their availability became much tighter. At this juncture, the stage was set for a much greater production and distribution of amphetamines through illicit channels. Later, in the 1960s and 1970s, amphetamines went through another period of heavy use, during which there was an overprescribing of amphetamines for weight control. Amphetamines also became widely available on the street during this period. The abuse of amphetamines remains a significant problem today, particularly when these drugs are taken intravenously.

The 1950s were the era for two central substances. During this decade the minor tranquilizers first became popular, a trend that continues today. As we discuss in Chapter 10, minor tranquilizers are the most commonly prescribed psychiatric drugs in this country. The 1950s also are associated with the contemporary appearance of **solvent** inhaling. The first report of such abuse was in 1951 by Clinger and Johnson. They described the intentional inhalation of gasoline by two young boys. However, solvent abuse tended to be more common with other substances, such as model cements, lighter fluids, lacquer thinner, cleaning solvents, and more recently the propellant gases of aerosol products (see Hofmann, 1975). The problem was marked in the early 1960s, with solvent inhaling producing deaths and leading hobby glue producers to remove the two most toxic solvents—benzene and carbon tetrachloride—from their products (Blum, 1984). A more recent example has been the sniffing of correction fluids that contain the solvent trichloroethane. However, manufactur-

Amphetamine
A central nervous system stimulant whose actions are similar to those of the naturally occurring adrenaline.

"The universal, immediate reaction is that the amphetamine high is like nothing else. You fix up a shot. You dissolve it in water. You draw it up into the dropper. You put a belt or a tie around your arm. In the meantime, you're very excited, your heart's beating fast. 'Cause you know you're going to get happy in a couple minutes. Then you give yourself a shot." Drug use description provided by an amphetamine addict

Goode
(1972)

Solvent
A substance, usually a liquid or gas, that contains one or more intoxicating components. Examples include glue, gasoline, and nonstick frying-pan sprays.

DRUGS AND CULTURE
KHAT: INCREASED U.S. EXPOSURE TO A NEW DRUG

We note elsewhere in this chapter that drugs popular in one country or region can gain popularity in another as contacts between the cultures increase. Such a concern emerged in the early 1990s when the United States participated in a massive food-relief program in Somalia, and the source of that concern was a leafy plant called khat (pronounced "kaht"). Some newspaper reports suggested that Somalian gunmen hijacking relief supplies were under the influence of the drug.

Khat is a stimulant that most users ingest by chewing. Two substances secreted by its leaves—cathine and cathinone—are categorized as controlled substances, making khat illegal. Its use is most common in East Africa, including Somalia and Ethiopia. Users report that khat provides energy and a euphoric feeling. An initial period of several hours of euphoria generally is followed by a period of depression. The substance has a bitter taste that for some users in the United States is similar to that of cocaine, although its effects are much less than those experienced when using cocaine. Khat also is known as Abyssinian tea, African tea, and Bushman's tea.

There was some initial concern that servicemen stationed in Somalia would become addicted to khat, and that the drug would gain a foothold in the United States. The fear that servicemen would become addicted to the drug appears to have been unfounded, but the drug has developed at least some temporary popularity. It has been available in a number of larger cities, including New York, Washington, Los Angeles, Boston, Dallas, and Detroit. And while technically an illegal substance, law enforcement officials initially were not placing a high priority on khat. For around $25–$30 the buyer receives a handful of stems and leaves that can be chewed for several hours with gradually accumulating effects. Some experts have stated that the drug is not dangerous. Not having it, according to Dr. Lester Grinspoon of Harvard Medical School, would be analogous to missing a morning cup of coffee. Other experts, such as Dr. Ansley Hamid at John Jay College of Criminal Law, say that heavy khat users often become anxious and irritable, and that they can lapse into depressed states.

While khat in its plant form may not represent a significant social or health problem, synthetic form analogues may. Several Drug Enforcement Administration raids (in Michigan and in Washington state) have been made at sites where a potent synthetic form of the active ingredients of khat was being produced.

---

ers of correction fluid have begun to replace trichloroethane with other solvents or to add unpleasant substances to the fluid, such as mustard oil. As such, solvent inhalant abuse (such as the current "huffing" of propane and spray paint fumes) is still a serious problem, especially among males in their teens.

A historical view of psychoactive substance use might show the 1960s as the era of lysergic acid diethylamide-25, most commonly known as LSD. The drug had been used in various tests during the 1950s (for example, as an adjunct to psychotherapy) but did not reach the zenith of its popularity (in the mid-1960s) until Dr. Timothy Leary, a Harvard psychologist, began to expound on what he found to be its mind-altering advantages. LSD eventually was banned (in 1967), and its use appears to have waned (but not ended) during the years since. A more recent psychedelic substance to appear on the scene is methylenedioxymethamphetamine, better known as MDMA or Ecstasy.

Heroin is another drug with a long history of use in the United States. Heroin was first synthesized in the late 1890s, and it has been available for use since the early 1900s. The extent of use traditionally has been greater among two populations—lower and higher socioeconomic groups (O'Brien & Cohen, 1984). During a certain period in the Vietnam War, the incidence of heroin use among U.S. soldiers in Vietnam was a significant concern, but soldiers who used the drug overseas did not tend to continue its use following return to the States. In recent years heroin has been showing a renewed popularity. The same factors that contributed to the spread of crack—low price and easy availability—appear to be behind this increase in heroin use. But there are some new wrinkles and concerns. First, the level of purity of the currently available heroin is higher than in the past. Second, there are fewer users injecting the drug. Instead, users have been mixing heroin and crack and smoking the combination.

This overview provides only a sample of the major drugs that have been used over the years for their psychoactive properties. Importantly, patterns of drug use and abuse are not static. The drugs more frequently used next year might include a drug used in the past that develops a renewed popularity, or they might include a newly synthesized substance, such as one of the so-called "designer drugs." The only thing that can be said with confidence is that drugs will continue to be used, and that some drug abuse will be associated with any given psychoactive substance.

Medical Science and Drug Use

Before leaving our section on historical perspective, we should note the interesting, long-term parallel between the development and use of psychoactive substances in medicinal forms (discussed in more detail in Chapter 5) and the nonmedicinal use/misuse of these drugs. Many of the drugs described in this text were used for medicinal purposes at one time or another. Medical science only gradually became the well-respected institution that we know today. Even in the twentieth century, folk cures, potions, and so-called "patent medications" were freely available and widely used.

Perhaps the best examples of this are the opiates opium and morphine, which throughout most of the 1800s were used for a variety of complaints, including rheumatism, pain, fever, delirium tremens, and colds. The opiates also were used as an anesthetic for some surgeries and for setting broken bones. As we noted earlier, the opiates were widely used and prescribed by physicians, despite the lack of understanding of how they acted in the body. All that was known was that opium and morphine seemed to help alleviate pain and symptoms that simply were not understood (Morgan, 1981). Unfortunately, such widespread use contributed to a considerable number of persons becoming physically addicted to these substances. Not until the 1870s did a clearer picture of the addictive properties of these drugs emerge.

Numerous other examples can be cited. Chloroform and ether were developed as anesthetics, but each also went through a period in the 1850s when its nonmedical use was quite fashionable. Cocaine went through a period in which it was used to treat complaints, such as depressed mood and pain. In fact, one of its uses was as a treatment for opiate addiction! In the latter half of the nineteenth century physicians recognized an array of uses for cannabis, including treatment of insomnia and nervousness, although its prescribed use was not nearly as extensive as with the opiates. In the twentieth century, we witnessed the development of the synthetic stimulant amphetamines, some of which initially were available without prescription.

We could provide other examples similar to those noted, but the important point is that medicinal uses of psychoactive substances (whether folk medicine or more contemporary medicine), medical science, and nonmedical drug use and abuse will always be closely intertwined. In the past, folk or cultural use of a substance often became incorporated into the practice of medicine. More common today is that a substance developed for the practice of medicine will be incorporated into the array of drugs that can be used in nonmedicinal ways. In any event, keeping these processes separate is impossible.

DEVELOPMENT OF DRUG LAWS

Legislation is the main way society establishes formal guidelines regarding drugs. Further, such legislation essentially reflects society's beliefs about drugs. Laws regarding drugs generally establish restrictions or prohibit the manufacture, importation, sale, and/or possession of the substance under evaluation. Interestingly, actual use under federal law is not a crime, nor is it a crime to be a drug addict or an alcoholic.

Drug laws for the most part have had limited effectiveness in reducing overall illicit drug use. In fact, the more restrictive the laws, the less effective they have tended to be in the long run (Brecher, 1972). The only circumstance in which these laws seem to have a stronger effect is during periods in which drug use or abuse is particularly unpopular (Hofmann, 1975). However, the duration of these periods, as well as the time between them, is quite variable. Nevertheless, legislation remains society's central means for addressing its concerns regarding drugs.

A history of drug laws in this country does not really begin until the turn of the twentieth century. Various efforts were mounted to regulate opiates in the second half of the nineteenth century, but these were largely halfhearted and not effective. That is not to say sanctions regarding drug abuse did not exist, but rather that there were no legal penalties to speak of. However, at different times and in different locations varying degrees of social sanctions existed, such as the ostracism of citizens showing certain forms of drunkenness in Colonial times.

The San Francisco Ordinance

The only notable law regarding drug use in the nineteenth century with any effect was a city ordinance passed in San Francisco in 1875. A number of

Chinese men had entered this country throughout the mid-1800s in response to labor demands in the rapidly expanding West. Most of these immigrants were working on the building of the railways. When this construction was finished, many of the laborers made their way back to San Francisco, where they frequented "opium dens"—places where people could smoke their opium. Although little negative effect of this drug use was substantiated on the San Francisco community *per se*, some thought the practice was sinister. Rumors began to circulate that the houses were evil and that unsuspecting members of the community—frequently young women were used as examples—were at risk for unknowingly heading down dangerous paths toward disrepute and drug addiction. This concern led to the 1875 ordinance. However, only opium dens were banned, not the smoking of opium. Conviction for operating or frequenting an opium den carried a fine of between $50–$500 and/or a jail sentence of 10 days to 6 months. The actual impact of the ordinance was not great; the larger and more obvious opium dens closed, and the number of smaller dens increased. The effect was greater in the sense of setting the stage for drug regulation in other parts of the country, as a number of other cities and states passed similar ordinances in later years. Not until 1909 did Congress pass a law banning the importation of opium for smoking.

Pure Food and Drug Act

The first federal legislative action of note occurred in 1906 with the passage of the Pure Food and Drug Act. This act, which was designed to control opiate addiction, legislated that producers of medicines indicate on the packaging of their products the amount of drug contained therein. The law was particularly

Addicts gathered outside a New York City drug clinic in 1920.

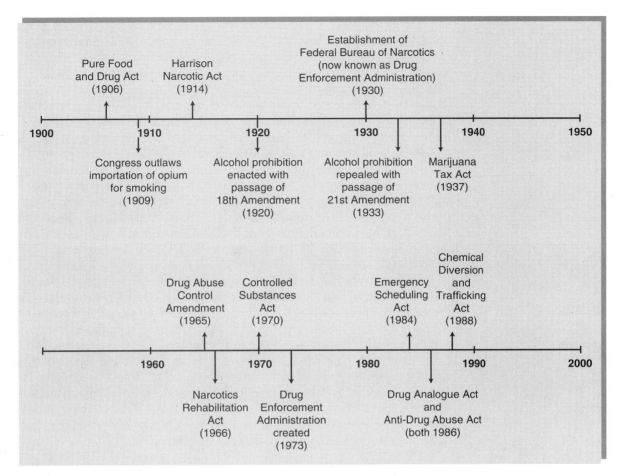

Figure 2-1   Major U.S. Drug Legislation in the Twentieth Century

focused on the opiates opium, morphine, and heroin, but also mandated the accurate labeling of products containing alcohol, marijuana, and cocaine. The overall effect of the act was mixed: it did not ban opiates in patent medicines, and thus had little impact on the addicts at the time, but the legislation may have served to decrease the number of new addicts, given the subsequent political and educational efforts to describe the addictive potential of patent medicines containing opiates (Brecher, 1972).

Harrison Narcotic Act

Another major piece of federal legislation, the Harrison Narcotic Act, was passed in 1914. Curiously, this law was passed not in response to domestic demand, but rather as a consequence of the United States signing the Hague Convention of 1912, an international agreement that directed signing nations to regulate opium traffic within their respective countries (Brecher, 1986). The Harrison Act strictly regulated, but did not prohibit, the legal supply of certain drugs, particularly the opiates. The law stated that the marketing and prescribing of these drugs required licensing. Further, the physician was directed to prescribe narcotics only "in the course of his professional practice." This phrase is certainly general and open to interpretation, and controversy between law enforcement agencies and physicians ensued. The central debate was whether the prescribing of an opiate for an addict was part of a treatment plan or merely serving to maintain the addict's dependence on the drug. Although this confusion on interpretation of the act's intent led to greater restriction on the prescribing and supplying of opiates, the result had little effect on opiate abuse (even when subsequent amendments through the years mandated more severe penalties for possession). In fact, Brecher (1986) argued that the ultimate outcome was actually counterproductive. Brecher maintained that the law, in the years since its passage, actually has served to shift opium and morphine addicts to heroin (which became easier to obtain on the black market) and overall to double the number of addicts in the United States. And this occurred despite more than 50 modifications to the act during the 50 years following its passage, each designed to toughen the law (Brecher, 1972).

Several other facets of the Harrison Narcotic Act should be mentioned. The first is that the act did not restrict patent medicine manufacturers, with the exception that their preparations could "not contain more than two grains of opium, or more than one-fourth of a grain of morphine, or more than one-eighth of a grain of heroin . . . in one **avoirdupois** ounce" (U.S. Pure Food and Drug Act of 1906, cited in Brecher, 1972). A second interesting aspect of this narcotic control act was its inaccurate inclusion of cocaine as a narcotic. Finally, one treatment-related result of the Harrison Act was that treatment centers for addicts began to open in some of the larger cities (Morgan, 1981). Most of these centers, however, were open for only a few years and thus had limited opportunity to help alleviate opiate addiction.

Avoirdupois
Something sold or measured by weight based on the pound of 16 ounces.

Alcohol Prohibition

"Our country has deliberately undertaken a great social and economic experiment, noble in motive and far-reaching in purpose. It must be worked out constructively."
President-elect Herbert Hoover
(1928, on Prohibition)

Alcohol prohibition was enacted several years later, in 1920, when Congress passed the Eighteenth Amendment. The legislation was a victory for the forces that viewed alcohol as evil and destructive, notably the Anti-Saloon League and the Women's Christian Temperance Union. And the legislation was not vague about its intent: it prohibited the production, sale, transportation, and importing of alcohol in any part of the United States. The only exception was that alcoholic beverages kept in the home, such as naturally fermented hard cider, could be consumed but not offered for sale (Lender & Martin, 1982).

As you may be aware, and as discussed further in Chapter 9, Prohibition was an experiment in drug control that did not succeed and was repealed 13 years later by the Twenty-first Amendment. Although Prohibition is commonly cited as a drug-use control measure that failed overall, it nevertheless did have a substantial effect on drinking in the United States. For example, the rate of drinking was reduced markedly (reasonable estimates range from one-third to one-half); other reductions included decreases in the death rates attributable to liver cirrhosis, admission rates to state hospitals for alcoholism, and arrest rates for alcohol-related offenses (Aaron & Musto, 1981). The greatest degree of decrease in alcohol consumption was among the working population, which opened the legislation to widespread criticism that it was a biased law. Unfortunately, a variety of other undesired consequences was

Prohibition was enacted to terminate the production, sale, and distribution of alcohol. These federal agents have just completed a raid on a Washington, DC, speakeasy in 1923.

associated with Prohibition, including more extensive use of marijuana, a shift in drinking habits away from beer to distilled spirits, the advent of the **speakeasy,** and the takeover of alcohol distribution by criminal groups. (Coffee intake, incidentally, according to Brecher, 1972, also soared during this period.) Thus, while Prohibition was successful in achieving some of its intended effects, these outcomes were sharply tempered by other undesired results. Ultimately, however, Prohibition was repealed because it lacked sufficient public sentiment necessary to maintain it.

Speakeasy
A slang expression used to describe a saloon operating without a license. The term was popularly used during Prohibition.

Post-Prohibition Legislation

The 1930s, following repeal of Prohibition, were characterized by stricter guidelines and penalties regarding drug possession and sale, particularly of marijuana. Legislative action taken in 1930 provided independent status for narcotic control agents through the establishment of the Federal Bureau of Narcotics (later to be called the Bureau of Narcotics and Dangerous Drugs and now the Drug Enforcement Administration). One of the major thrusts of the Federal Bureau of Narcotics, spearheaded by Commissioner Harry J. Anslinger, was the eradication of marijuana use. Anslinger's crusade resulted in the Marijuana Tax Act of 1937. As with the Harrison Narcotic Act, this measure did not ban marijuana, but instead required authorized producers, manufacturers, importers, and dispensers of the drug to register themselves and pay a yearly license fee. Outlawed was only the nonmedical possession or sale of marijuana (Brecher, 1972). The recognition of some medical uses for marijuana continued. Legislative actions regarding marijuana gradually grew more restrictive and provided for greater penalties until the decriminalization movement began in the latter part of the 1970s.

Additional federal legislation was passed periodically between 1940–1970. However, as with previous legislation, these actions failed to have a sustained influence on the prevalence of drug use or dependence, despite the increased severity of the penalties for drug law infractions. However, two trends are worth noting. The first is increased attention to nonnarcotic drug

Contemporary Issue
THE WAR ON DRUGS

One of the foremost efforts of the Reagan and Bush administrations was the "war on drugs," implemented throughout the 1980s and into the 1990s. Hallmark features of this "war" were efforts to catch drug smugglers and sellers (in this country and overseas) and the implementing of a "zero-tolerance" approach to drug users, including casual users of drugs. Throughout the early 1990s, the U.S. government was spending approximately $1 billion a year on anti-drug operations overseas alone, most of it used to catch drug smugglers.

Despite all of these efforts, it does not appear that there has been much of an impact on drug use. This is particularly the case regarding efforts to intercept drugs, which most experts conclude has been a failure. Hundreds of millions of dollars have been spent on these efforts, yet the flow of drugs into the United States has not been significantly altered. All of which raises the question of what is the best strategy for combating the drug problem. Some organizations have been pushing for a greater focus on demand reduction, such as prevention efforts and treatment.

The Clinton administration considered these issues while developing its approach to the drug problem. Indications are that there will be more balance between law enforcement activities and demand reduction strategies. Further, efforts have been initiated to streamline the approach to drug problems. For example, the Drug Enforcement Administration now is devoting more of its resources to reducing the supply of cocaine and heroin, and reducing its focus on marijuana, methamphetamines, and other drugs that are viewed as less threatening, at least in a relative sense. In addition, more attention is being placed on disrupting the overall flow of drugs as opposed to focusing specifically on one or two major drug lords. Finally, coordination of all government efforts in this realm is being placed under the head of the White House Office of National Drug Control Policy, better known as the "drug czar."

It remains to be seen whether these changes in drug control policy will have greater success than those experienced during the "war on drugs." But before closing, it is noteworthy that the two drugs most associated with deaths in this country—tobacco and alcohol—are not a focus of attention in any of the above efforts.

use, whereby stimulants, depressants, and hallucinogenic substances became regulated under legislation such as the Drug Abuse Control Amendment of 1965. The second notable change in federal legislation was a shifting of some of its attention to treatment of drug abuse through such measures as the Community Mental Health Centers Act of 1963 and the Narcotic Rehabilitation Act of 1966.

The last major piece of legislative action was the Comprehensive Drug Abuse Prevention and Control Act. This measure, more commonly known as the Controlled Substances Act, was passed in 1970, and forms the basis for drug regulation in the United States today.

CURRENT DRUG LAWS

Drug classifications for law enforcement purposes are rooted in the 1970 Controlled Substances Act. Under this measure, drugs are not classified according to pharmacological action, but according to their medical use, their potential for abuse, and their likelihood for producing dependence. Almost all psychoactive substances have been placed in one of the five categories, or schedules, generated by the act. A description of each of the five schedules is shown in Table 2-1, and Table 2-2 lists examples of the drugs in each classification. Several substances having little or no potential for abuse or dependence are

Table 2-1   Schedules of Controlled Substances

Schedule I: High potential for abuse and dependence. No accepted medicinal use in the U.S. Not available with prescription. Available for research purposes only. Included in this category are narcotics and hallucinogens.

Schedule II: Medicinal drugs with accepted therapeutic use. High potential for abuse and dependence. Requires written prescription. No refills allowed for user without first being seen again by doctor for new prescription. Providers must keep these drugs in secured area. Included in this category are certain narcotic (e.g., opium, morphine, and codeine), stimulant, and depressant drugs.

Schedule III: Medicinal drugs with accepted therapeutic use. Potential for abuse and dependence greater than for Schedule IV and V drugs but less than for drugs in Schedule I or II. Abuse can lead to moderate or low physical dependence or high levels of psychological dependence. Prescription can be written or phoned in by doctor. Prescription must be renewed every six months and can be refilled up to five times. Included in this category are the less abusable sedative-hypnotics and narcotics.

Schedule IV: Medicinal drugs with acceptable therapeutic use. Less potential for abuse and dependence than for Schedule III drugs. Abuse can lead to limited physical or psychological dependence. Same prescription guidelines as for Schedule III drugs. Included in this category are sedative-hypnotics, drugs used for weight reduction, and minor tranquilizers.

Schedule V: Medicinal drugs with accepted therapeutic use. Lowest potential for abuse or dependence. Abuse leads to only limited physical or psychological dependence. Prescription not needed for many of these drugs, which often are sold over the counter. Need to be 18 years of age. Purchaser in some cases needs to sign a dispensing log maintained by the pharmacist. Included in this category are medicines containing small amounts of a narcotic.

Adapted and updated from Blum (1984).

Table 2-2   Examples of Scheduled Drugs

Schedule I	
Heroin	Marijuana
Peyote	Lysergic acid diethylamide (LSD)
Mescaline	Dimethyltryptamine (DMT)
Psilocybin	Quaalude

Schedule II	
Opium	Cocaine
Morphine	Benzedrine
Codeine	Dexedrine
Percodan	Dilaudid
Ritalin	Demerol

Schedule III	
Empirin with codeine	Butisol
Tylenol with codeine	Fiorinal
Paregoric	

Schedule IV	
Luminal	Serax
Darvon	Dalmane
Valium	Tranxene
Librium	Miltown

Schedule V	
Cheracol with codeine	Cosadein
Robitussin A-C	

Adapted and updated from Cohen (1981).

not classified. These include the major tranquilizers, such as chlorpromazine (trade name Thorazine), thioridazine (Mellaril), and haloperidol (Haldol), and the antidepressants, such as imipramine (Tofranil) and amitriptyline (Elavil). (We discuss these drugs in greater detail in Chapter 11.)

The Controlled Substances Act contains provisions for adding drugs to the schedules and for rescheduling drugs. For example, diazepam (Valium) and other benzodiazepines were unscheduled when the act was passed but were classified as Schedule IV drugs in 1975. Similarly, phencyclidine (PCP, "Angel Dust") was initially unscheduled but quickly classified as a Schedule II substance in 1978 when it began to be abused. A variety of Schedule III substances were reclassified into Schedule II during the early 1970s, including amphetamine (Benzedrine), methylphenidate (Ritalin), and secobarbital (Seconal).

Consistent with its intended comprehensive character, the Controlled Substances Act also establishes the penalties for criminal manufacture or distribution of the scheduled drugs. Many of these penalties, particularly those for drug trafficking, were increased during the 1980s through legislation such as the 1986 Anti-Drug Abuse Act. The penalties are greatest for trafficking Schedule I and II drugs (excluding marijuana, hashish, and hashish oil, for which a less severe set of penalties has been established), and the penalties increase with the quantity involved and the number of previous offenses. For example, a first conviction for trafficking 100–999 grams of heroin mixture or

500–4999 milligrams of cocaine mixture carries a sentence of not less than 5 years (up to 40 years) and a fine of up to $2 million. If a death or serious injury is associated with the drug trafficking, the sentence is not less than 20 years' imprisonment. Greater quantities carry greater penalties, as do subsequent offenses. Penalties for trafficking any amounts of Schedule III-V substances are less but still substantial. A first conviction for trafficking a Schedule III substance is up to 5 years and a $250,000 fine. A subsequent conviction can result in up to 10 years' imprisonment and up to a $500,000 fine.

Penalties for possession of lesser amounts of the drug without intent to distribute are less severe, though still substantial. As part of the "no-tolerance"

Contemporary Issue
DRUG TESTING IN THE WORKPLACE

One result of the growing concern over drug use and misuse has been efforts by corporations to have their workers submit to mandatory drug tests. The employers argue the tests are needed to identify those workers who, because of their drug use, may be at risk for subpar or even dangerous work performance. Further, employers often believe random drug tests serve as a deterrent to drug use. About one-third of the largest American corporations currently use drug screens as part of their hiring process. And according to a report in U.S. *News & World Report* (July 28, 1986), anywhere between 8%–35% of these applicants will test positive for recent drug use (a "positive" result means the test revealed indications of drug use).

The argument put forth by employers may appear relatively straightforward: if drugs can impair work performance, then checking for drugs is a legitimate practice. But drug testing remains controversial for several reasons. Consider the three following aspects of the controversy.

First is the issue of the possible infringement on constitutional rights of privacy when tests are administered randomly (that is, without warning and independent of "probable cause"). This has led some to suggest tests should be used only if a demonstrable "reasonable cause" exists to believe a person is under the influence of a drug.

A second issue is the relationship between a positive test result and actual job performance. For example, traces of marijuana can be detected in the system for several weeks and sometimes much longer after it was smoked, even though no associated impairment in the person's functioning can be proven. Is drug use a legitimate reason for termination or other disciplinary action if no obvious effect of that drug use on the worker's job performance can be demonstrated?

A third issue is very basic, yet crucial. Unfortunately, questions abound regarding accuracy of the drug tests themselves. A study by the Centers for Disease Control, a federal agency, found that many urinalysis test results were unreliable. In some cases the poor reliability was a result of primitive technology in testing for the presence of particular drugs. Sometimes the presence of a drug was missed, and in other cases a legitimate drug use (such as a prescribed medication) was identified by the test as an illicit substance. Examples of such false

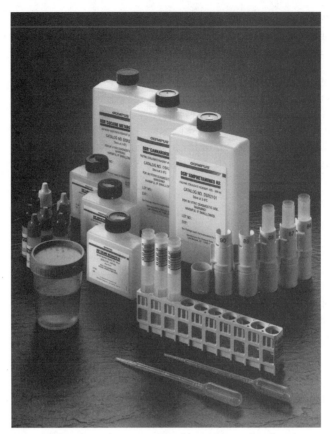

Materials such as these are used in testing urine for the presence of drugs such as cocaine, cannabis, and amphetamines.

positives include ibuprofen being mistakenly identified as marijuana, codeine as opiates, and Valium as PCP. However, the biggest factor contributing to the poor test reliability often has been human error and carelessness on the part of the people doing the urinalysis at the laboratory.

It should be noted that most of the problems with false readings have been associated with use of immunoassay or thin-layer chromatography tests. These urine tests are best viewed as screening tests; they test not for the presence of the drug in the urine but rather for the metabolic products of drugs. Although not always done, positive readings using immunoassay procedures should be followed by mass spectrometer procedures that identify chemical compounds associated with specific drugs.

Before the question of drug testing is resolved, these issues are going to have to be addressed. A balancing of employee rights with the perceived needs of employers, along with improvements in the drug-testing process itself, still seems a distance away. But progress is being made, and one notable new development is the use of radioimmunoassay procedures to test for the presence of particular drugs (such as heroin, cocaine, and marijuana) in strands of hair.

feature of the "war on drugs" implemented in the late 1980s (see nearby Contemporary Issue box on the war on drugs), law enforcement agencies have been seizing assets of persons possessing or selling drugs. For example, individuals caught with drugs in their cars or boats have had their vehicles seized and sold by government agencies, such as Customs or local authorities.

We should make several final comments before closing this section on current drug laws. First, each state has the opportunity to modify many of these guidelines according to its own needs and preferences. Most states have adopted these guidelines but may have changed certain components of them. For example, marijuana is classified as a Schedule I substance, but the penalties for possession in many states are generally less severe than those applied to other Schedule I substances. In fact, at least 11 states at some time or another have passed legislation to decriminalize marijuana possession. Finally, it is important to recognize that new legislation always is on the horizon, whether in response to the latest trends in the arena of drug use and abuse or to emergent political mandates. During the 1980s, law enforcement agencies were having difficulties controlling the production of the so-called "designer drugs"—drugs that were structurally similar but not identical to illegal substances. Each time a slight modification in the chemical structure of the drug was made, enforcement officials were forced to go through a time-consuming process of documenting the drug and having it certified as a controlled substance. In response, Congress in 1986 passed the Controlled Substances Analogue Enforcement Act, which allowed for the immediate classification of a substance as a controlled substance. In this way, drug enforcement officials were in a position to address the arrival of a new drug as soon as it appeared in circulation. Similarly, legislation has been put in place to allow the Drug Enforcement Administration to monitor and regulate the distribution of chemical substances and other equipment needed for the preparation of illegal drugs. Titled the Chemical Diversion and Trafficking Act of 1988, this legislation controls the distribution of particular chemicals, tabulating machines, and encapsulating machines that are used in the manufacturing of illicit substances.

> "Will *we be able to teach the dangers of drugs to later generations who have little or no experience with them?"*
>
> David F. Musto, Yale School of Medicine professor of psychiatry and history, asked to ponder life in the year 2053.
>
> (U.S. *News & World Report,* October 25, 1993)

summary

- Drugs have been used for a variety of reasons in different cultures for thousands of years; earliest drug use involved ingestion of alcohol and of plants with psychoactive properties.

- Prior to the twentieth century, few restrictions were placed on drug availability or drug use.

- During the nineteenth century, drugs such as opium, morphine, marijuana, heroin, and cocaine could be easily obtained without prescription.

- Marijuana was used by physicians during the 1800s as a general all-purpose medication; its nonmedical use increased during the Prohibition era of the 1920s.

- Different drugs have enjoyed periods of relatively greater popularity in the United States. Cocaine was widely used in medicines and tonics during the late 1800s and early 1900s. Cocaine use again became popular in the 1960s and its popularity continues today. Amphetamines were used relatively widely during the 1930s, minor tranquilizers and inhalants during the 1950s, and LSD during the 1960s. Heroin has been showing signs of increased use in recent years.

- A parallel exists between the development and use of psychoactive substances in medicinal forms and the nonmedical use/abuse of these drugs.

- The main mechanism through which society establishes formal guidelines regarding drugs and drug use is legislation. However, a history of drug laws in the United States does not really begin until the turn of the twentieth century.

- The first major federal legislation regarding drugs was the 1906 Pure Food and Drug Act, which mandated a listing of the types and amounts of drugs contained in the medicines.

- Other major legislation of note included the 1914 Harrison Narcotic Act, which regulated the legal supply of certain drugs, and alcohol prohibition, which spanned the years 1920–1933.

- Drug classifications for law enforcement today are rooted in the 1970 Controlled Substances Act, which classifies drugs according to their legitimate medical uses and their potential for abuse and dependence.

ANSWERS TO WHAT DO YOU THINK?

1. The first recorded use of cannabis occurred in the early 1800s.

F *The use of cannabis sativa dates to around 2700 B.C. in China, where it was recommended by Emperor Shen Nung for the treatment of various ailments.*

2. Grape wine was the first alcoholic beverage to be used.

F *Beer and hackleberry wine were used as early as 6400 B.C. Grape wine did not appear until 300–400 B.C.*

3. The Opium Wars between China and Great Britain in the mid-1800s occurred in large part because Britain was unwilling to curtail its trade of opium into China.

T *Most of the opium used in China at the time was cultivated in India and brought to China by British traders. Although opiate addiction was a major problem for China, the British were unwilling to curtail this trade in part because of financial reasons and in part because this degree of addiction was not experienced by users in England.*

4. Columbus and his crew were responsible for introducing tobacco to the New World.

F *The Indians whom Columbus encountered introduced him and later explorers to tobacco and other psychoactive plants. The Europeans, in turn, introduced alcohol to the New World.*

5. Many of the drugs that are now illegal in the United States were widely used in the 1800s and early 1900s to treat a broad spectrum of maladies.

T *The opiates, marijuana, cocaine, and amphetamines were all used at one time or another to treat various ailments. Use of these drugs was restricted when their addictive natures were recognized.*

6. The first notable drug law in the United States—the 1875 San Francisco Ordinance—banned the smoking of opium.

F *The San Francisco Ordinance banned opium dens, but not the actual smoking of opium.*

7. The Pure Food and Drug Act of 1906 had little impact on individuals who were addicted to drugs.

T *This act was designed to control opiate addiction and legislated that producers of medicines indicate on the packaging of their products the amount of drugs contained therein. It had little impact on the addicts at the time, but may have served to decrease the number of new addicts.*

8. The Harrison Narcotic Act of 1914 sharply curtailed the prevalence of heroin use in the United States.

F *This act strictly regulated the legal supply of certain drugs, but actually served to shift opium and mor-*

phine addicts to heroin (which became easier to obtain on the black market).

9. The Eighteenth Amendment, which prohibited the production, sale, transportation, and importing of alcohol, failed because it did not have a substantial effect on drinking in the United States.

F *Prohibition did have an effect on drinking. In fact, the rate of drinking was reduced markedly. In addition, death rates attributable to liver cirrhosis decreased, and there was a decline in both admission rates to state hospitals for alcoholism and in arrest rates for alcohol-related offenses.*

10. Federal anti-drug legislation between 1940–1970 failed to have a sustained influence on drug use or dependence.

T *This is true despite the increased severity of penalties for drug law infractions. However, there was increased*

attention to nonnarcotic drug use and to drug abuse treatment during this period.

11. The most successful aspect of the Reagan and Bush administrations' war on drugs was the effort to intercept drugs.

F *Most experts conclude that this effort has been a failure, despite the fact that hundreds of millions of dollars were spent on it. The flow of drugs into the United States has not been significantly altered.*

12. Urine testing is a reliable method for detecting drug use.

F *A study by the Centers for Disease Control found that many urinalysis tests were unreliable. Factors affecting reliability include primitive technology and human error.*

3 Drugs and the Nervous System

WHAT DO YOU THINK?

True or False? ____ Certain cells found in the nervous system have the unique ability to "talk" with each other.

____ The effects of drugs always involve naturally occurring physiological processes.

____ Some drugs may act by mimicking a neurotransmitter.

____ All drugs have the same basic effect on a cellular level; that is, they all block neural firing.

____ The brain is shielded from many toxic substances by a protective barrier.

____ The two main branches of the nervous system are the peripheral nervous system (PNS) and the autonomic nervous system (ANS).

____ The brain and the spinal cord comprise the peripheral nervous system.

____ The brain is firmly attached to the inside of the skull by a tough membrane known as the meninges.

____ The autonomic nervous system is responsible for regulating food and water intake.

____ Animals will work for the electrical stimulation of certain parts of the brain.

Every feeling or emotion you have—in fact, all psychological experience—is based on brain activity. The fact that this physical entity, the brain, is the basis of conscious experience is the key to understanding how the chemical agents we call drugs alter psychological processes.

One feature all psychoactive drugs have in common is that they produce their effects by acting in some way on nervous system tissue, and this chapter focuses on these physiological actions of drugs. Most of these actions occur at the level of the brain. As recent discoveries in the neurosciences have led to a greater understanding of how the brain works, parallel advances have taken place in our understanding of drug actions. These developments have led to some radically new ways of conceptualizing drug effects and drug problems such as addiction. However, in order to discuss how drugs act on the brain, we first must cover some of the fundamentals on just how the brain works.

THE NEURON

Neuron (NUR-on)
The individual nerve cell that is the basic building block of the nervous system.

The basic building blocks of the nervous system are cells called **neurons.** Neurons are similar to other cells in the human body, such as blood cells or muscle cells, but they have the unique feature of being able to communicate with each other. The unique structural properties of neurons provide us with some clues as to the nature of the neural transmission process.

Notice in Figure 3-1 that the neuron depicted have cell bodies similar to those of any other cell. These cell bodies include a nucleus containing the genetic material for the neuron and other processes that control the metabolic activities of the cell. Extending from the cell body of the neuron are a number of small spine- or branch-like structures called **dendrites** and one long cylindrical structure called the **axon.** These structures are unique to the neuron and responsible for some of its remarkable properties.

Axons vary in length but are usually much longer than shown in the illustration—sometimes as many as thousands of times longer than the diameter of the cell body. The axon depicted in Figure 3-1 is enclosed within a sheath of a white, fatty substance called **myelin** (not all axons are covered by myelin sheaths, and "unmyelinated" axons are gray in color). Myelin provides insulation for the axon, similar to insulation for a wire. That comparison is fitting, for the principal function of the axon is to conduct electrical current. The axon transmits information by conducting an electrical signal from one end of the neuron to the other. The current flow is always initiated in the cell body, which sends its electrical message (called the **action potential**) to the small branches at the end of the axon. The change in potential is small (about 110 millivolts), and is said to be "all or none," in that the axon is either firing— conducting its full current—or is quiescent.

Dendrite (Den-drite)
Spiny branch-like structures that extend from the cell body of a neuron. Dendrites typically contain numerous receptor sites and are thus important in neural transmission.

Axon (AKS-on)
A long cylindrical extension of the cell body of the neuron. The axon conducts an electrical charge from the cell body to the axon terminals.

Myelin (MY-a-lin)
A fatty white substance that covers the axons of some neurons.

Action potential
The electrical impulse along the axon that occurs when a neuron "fires."

NEURAL TRANSMISSION

The branches at the end of the axon shown in Figure 3-1 terminate in small button-like structures known as **axon terminals** or **terminal buttons.** These axon terminals hold the key to an important puzzle: how the electrical message actually gets from one neuron to another. When advances in microscopy made possible the viewing of neurons as they are seen here, a surprising finding was that most axon terminals of one neuron do not come into direct contact with the dendrites of the neighboring neuron as had been supposed; instead they are separated by a space called the **synapse** (shown in Figure 3-2). The question, of course, is how does electrical current flow from one neuron to another without direct contact between them? It is now known that when electrical current reaches the axon terminal, chemical substances stored in the terminal button are released into the synapse and these chemical substances, called **neurotransmitters,** actually trigger activity in the adjacent neuron.

Axon terminal (or terminal button)
Enlarged button-like structures that occur at the end of axon branches.

Synapse (SIN-naps)
The junction between neurons.

Neurotransmitters
Chemical substances stored in the axon terminals that are released into the synapse when the neuron fires. Neurotransmitters then influence activity in postsynaptic neurons.

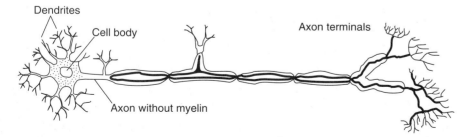

Figure 3-1   Diagram of a neuron.

Thus, neural transmission is an electrochemical event—electrical along the axon, and chemical at the synapse. This is of some importance for our purposes as it suggests that drugs may interact with the nervous system at the synapse, because that is where the chemical transmission takes place. In fact, most of the psychoactive drugs we discuss produce their important effects by action at the synapse. Therefore, more detailed analysis of the chemical processes occurring at the synapse seems justified.

A lock-key analogy is useful for depicting the neural transmission process. Scattered along the dendrites and cell body are special structures known as **receptor sites** or receptors. These structures may be viewed as locks that keep the neuron from firing. In order to fire, the locks must be opened, which is accomplished by the neurotransmitter substances released at the terminal button. The neurotransmitter molecules may be thought of as keys. The point is illustrated in Figure 3-2. Receptor sites are depicted as circular holes in the dendrite and neurotransmitters as circles being released from the axon terminal. The notion is simple: the key must fit the lock in order to trigger an event such as neural firing.

Receptor sites
Specialized structures located on dendrites and cell bodies for neurons that are activated by neurotransmitters.

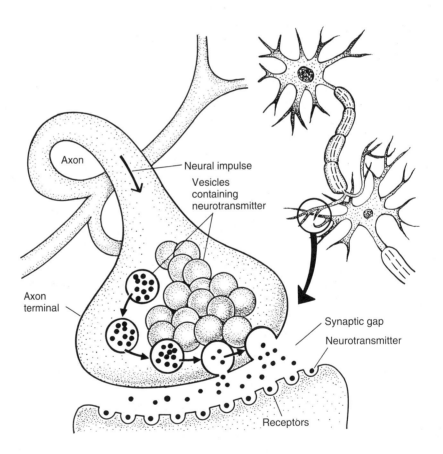

Figure 3-2   Diagram of a synapse showing enlarged axon terminal with vesicles containing neurotransmitter molecules.

In fact, neurotransmitter molecules and receptors have chemical structures that are considerably more complex than is illustrated, and the lock-key analogy doesn't completely explain the process. Because of their electrical charges, transmitters and their receptors are attracted to one another and when a transmitter key occupies a receptor lock they are said to bind to one another. When a neurotransmitter molecule binds to a receptor, changes occur in the neuron that may trigger neural firing. An important point is that there are many different types of neurotransmitter keys and many corresponding receptor site locks. We now understand that the brain is chemically coded with different pathways that respond to different neurotransmitter chemicals.

DRUGS AND NEURAL TRANSMISSION

Several ways that drugs can interfere with synaptic transmission may have already occurred to you. For example, suppose the chemical structure of some drug is quite similar to that of a naturally occurring (or endogenous) neurotransmitter. If the similarity is close enough, the drug molecules might bind to the receptor sites, thus duping the receptor into reacting as if the natural transmitter is present and stimulating the neuron. Just such a process, called mimicry, actually does occur with a number of drugs. For example, drugs such as morphine and heroin are now thought to act by mimicking a recently discovered natural neurotransmitter called endorphin.

Mimicry is an obvious mechanism of drug action, but drugs can influence neural transmission in numerous other ways. A sampling of these mechanisms is listed in Table 3-1. Neurotransmitters must be manufactured from simpler building blocks, or precursor molecules. The manufacture of transmitters usually takes place in a cell body or axon terminal, but if the substance is manufactured in the cell body it must still be transported to the

Table 3-1   Neurochemical Mechanisms of Drug Action

Drug Effects Can Be Produced by Altering the Following Neurochemical Systems:

1. *Neurotransmitter Synthesis.* A drug may increase or decrease the synthesis of neurotransmitters.
2. *Neurotransmitter Transport.* A drug may interfere with transport of neurotransmitter molecules to the axon terminals.
3. *Neurotransmitter Storage.* A drug may interfere with the storage of neurotransmitters in the vesicles of the axon terminal.
4. *Neurotransmitter Release.* A drug may cause the axon terminals to prematurely release neurotransmitter molecules into the synapse.
5. *Neurotransmitter Degradation.* A drug may influence the breakdown of neurotransmitters by enzymes.
6. *Neurotransmitter Reuptake.* A drug may block the reuptake of neurotransmitters into the axon terminals.
7. *Receptor Activation.* A drug may activate a receptor site by mimicking a neurotransmitter.
8. *Receptor Blocking.* A drug may cause a receptor to become inactive by blocking it.

Vesicles (VES-ik-ulls)
Tiny sacs located in axon terminals that store neurotransmitters.

Enzyme breakdown
One process by which neurotransmitters are inactivated. Chemicals called enzymes interact with the transmitter molecule and change its structure so that it no longer is capable of occupying receptor sites.

Reuptake
Another process by which neurotransmitters are inactivated. Neurotransmitter molecules are taken back up into the axon terminal that released them.

Acetylcholine (ass-it-teel-KOLE-een)
A neurotransmitter found both in the brain and in the parasympathetic branch of the autonomic nervous system.

Agonist (AG-o-nist)
A substance that occupies a neural receptor and causes some change in the conductance of the neuron.

Antagonist
A substance that occupies a neural receptor, but blocks normal synaptic transmission.

terminal before it is functional. Some drugs interfere with transmitter production or transport. Neurotransmitter molecules are stored in small packages called **vesicles,** located in the terminal buttons. Some drugs affect the ability of the vesicles to store neurotransmitter substances. For example, the drug reserpine, once used to treat high blood pressure, causes certain vesicles to become leaky and the transmitters involved are not effectively released into the synapse. Alternatively, other drugs can enhance the release of neurotransmitter substances into the synapse and this is one of the ways stimulants such as amphetamines act.

Another important rule of neural transmission is that neurotransmitters, once released, must be deactivated. The neuron can be thought of as a rechargeable battery—once it fires it may be recharged and fired again. But first, we need to get those keys out of the locks so that the recharging process can take place. The deactivation of the neurotransmitter keys is accomplished in two ways: **enzyme breakdown** and **reuptake.** Certain chemicals called enzymes act both to build the complex molecules of neurotransmitters and to break down neurotransmitters to inactive form. These processes are complex and reveal one reason that identifying and isolating the functions of neurotransmitters in the brain is difficult. There are a number of different chemicals in the brain, and they are constantly changing form. Consider the processes involved in the production and destruction of **acetylcholine,** one of the most important neurotransmitters. The precursor molecule choline is acted on by an enzyme (choline acetyltransferase) to make acetylcholine. Acetylcholine itself is broken down by a different enzyme—acetylcholinesterase—to yield two metabolites: choline and acetate. (Enzymes are named by the stem of the chemical that they influence and always take an "-ase" ending.) A drug can alter neural transmission by affecting enzyme activity. For example, some antidepressant drugs alter the deactivation of the neurotransmitters norepinephrine, dopamine, and serotonin by inhibiting the activity of monoamine oxidase, the enzyme that breaks down these compounds.

A second mechanism for removing neurotransmitters from the synapse is called reuptake. Some neurotransmitters are taken back up into the terminal button after they have been released, thus the term reuptake. Reuptake is an economical mechanism of deactivating transmitters, because the neurotransmitter molecule is preserved intact and can be used again without the energy involved in the manufacture of new transmitters. Some drugs (notably cocaine and the amphetamines) exert some of their action by blocking the reuptake process.

A final site of drug action is directly at the receptor. Some drugs directly affect the receptor by mimicking the activity of natural neurotransmitters— similar to a duplicate key that fits into and opens the locks. But other drugs seem to act as if they fit into the lock, but then jam the lock, and prevent the neuron from firing. Such a drug is called a blocking agent. In general, any chemical—natural or otherwise—that fits a receptor lock and activates it is said to be an **agonist** of that receptor. Any compound that occupies a receptor and does not activate it, but rather prevents other compounds from activating the receptor, is said to be an **antagonist.**. For example, naloxone is an antagonist of the receptors on which opiate drugs such as heroin work. If naloxone is administered to a patient who has just taken a normally lethal

Table 3-2   Major Neurotransmitters With Representative Agonists
and Antagonists

Neurotransmitter	Agonist	Antagonist
acetylcholine	nicotine	atropine
dopamine/norepinephrine	cocaine/amphetamines	chlorpromazine
serotonin	LSD	chlorpromazine
endorphins	morphine	naloxone
GABA	barbiturates	bicuculline

dose of heroin, the patient not only does not die, but is rapidly brought to a state in which the patient acts as if the heroin had not even been taken. In fact, all of the effects of heroin and other opiates are blocked completely or reversed by naloxone. Thus, naloxone is called an opiate antagonist.

We have seen a number of ways that drugs can act to influence neural transmission. (See Dykstra, 1992; Johanson, 1992, for more detailed reviews.) However, a point to remember is that although drugs can interact with the brain in many different ways, the effects of the drugs always involve naturally occurring processes. That is, some systems in the brain or body with defined natural functions are made more or less active by the drug. The differences between the effects of various drugs are coming to be understood in terms of which transmitter systems they influence, and exactly how they influence them. Therefore, next we take a brief look at the neurotransmitter systems of the human brain and note some of their known functions.

MAJOR NEUROTRANSMITTER SYSTEMS

Acetylcholine

One of the first neurotransmitters to be discovered was acetylcholine, probably because it is found in the more easily studied neurons located outside the brain. Acetylcholine resides in the axon terminals of neurons that activate the skeletal muscles. At sites where nerves meet muscles there is a space similar to the synapse called the **neuromuscular junction.** When the neurons that synapse with muscle fibers are fired they release acetylcholine into the neuromuscular junction and the muscle contracts. Acetylcholine is also important in the brain, but as with most neurotransmitters, its function in the brain is not thoroughly understood. However, the body of evidence is that acetylcholine is important in the regulation of thirst. (By the way, if a neurotransmitter is to be used in the adjectival form, one simply takes the stem of the name [i.e., choline] and adds the suffix "-ergic." Thus, thirst is said to be a cholinergic function, neurons containing acetylcholine are said to be cholinergic neurons, and drugs that block acetylcholine are said to be anticholinergic drugs.) Acetylcholine is also thought to be important in memory. In fact, substantial evidence is mounting that **Alzheimer's disease,** a progressive loss of memory function that occurs in the elderly, is related to the loss of neural function in some of the brain's cholinergic pathways. Much current research on Alzheimer's disease is attempting to determine just what might be

Neuromuscular junction
Junction between neuron and muscle fibers where release of acetylcholine by neurons causes muscles to contract.

**Alzheimer's disease
(ALLZ-hi-merz)**
One of the most common forms of senility among the elderly, Alzheimer's disease involves a progressive loss of memory and other cognitive functions.

going wrong in these pathways and to develop ways of correcting or preventing the problem. In fact, in 1993 Parke-Davis announced the first drug approved to treat the symptoms of Alzheimer's disease, Cognex (tacrine), which is thought to act by elevating brain levels of acetylcholine. The problem of Alzheimer's disease underscores an important point: when neurotransmitter systems malfunction, disease states are a likely consequence. This point is at the heart of contemporary theories of the biological basis of mental illness, which is considered in the next section.

Monoamines

Norepinephrine (nor-ep-in-EFF-rin)
A neurotransmitter found in the brain and involved in activity of the sympathetic branch of the autonomic nervous system.

Dopamine (DOP-ah-meen)
A neurotransmitter found in the brain.

Serotonin (sair-o-TONE-in)
A neurotransmitter found in the brain.

Monoamine (mon-o-AM-mean)
A class of chemicals characterized by a single amine group. This class includes neurotransmitters: norepinephrine, dopamine, and serotonin.

Parkinson's disease
A disease that primarily afflicts the elderly and involves a progressive deterioration of motor control.

L-dopa (el-DOPE-ah)
A chemical precursor of dopamine used in the treatment of Parkinson's disease.

Blood-brain barrier
A term given to the system that "filters" the blood before it can enter the brain.

Three important neurotransmitters, **norepinephrine (noradrenaline), dopamine,** and **serotonin,** are collectively known as the **monoamines** because the chemical structure for each contains a single amine group. Like acetylcholine, norepinephrine was discovered early on because it is found outside the brain. It serves as a key chemical mediating the physical changes that accompany emotional arousal. Norepinephrine is also found in the brain as a neurotransmitter, where it seems important in the regulation of hunger, alertness, and arousal. Serotonin is found throughout the brain and has been shown to be important in the regulation of sleep. Dopamine is a key neurotransmitter in the pathways that regulate coordinated motor movements. This discovery led to the hypothesis that dopamine insufficiency may be the basis of **Parkinson's disease,** a disorder characterized by progressive loss of fine motor movements, muscle rigidity, and tremor primarily afflicting elderly persons. The dopamine deficiency hypothesis of Parkinson's disease led to new treatment approaches involving the administration of **L-dopa,** a precursor of dopamine. L-dopa was administered to patients in the hopes of correcting the dopamine deficiency and proved to be dramatically effective in relieving the symptoms of this disease. Dopamine itself is not effective because it does not enter the brain from the bloodstream. The brain is protected from toxic compounds that might enter the bloodstream by a **blood-brain barrier** that screens many chemicals, including dopamine. But L-dopa does penetrate the barrier and once it reaches the brain, it is converted to dopamine (Bradford, 1986; Kruk & Pycock, 1979). The use of L-dopa in the treatment of Parkinson's disease is a dramatic example of the value of new knowledge about neurotransmitters in the treatment of disease. Although L-dopa does not cure the disease process (loss of dopaminergic neurons continues to take place and eventually even L-dopa cannot correct the loss), it has brought years of productive living to many whose lives would otherwise have been prematurely ended by Parkinsonism.

In addition to these functions, the monoamine neurotransmitters norepinephrine, dopamine, and serotonin have been closely linked to mood states and emotional disorders. In fact, drugs that influence the monoamine systems have revolutionized modern psychiatry. For example, considerable evidence shows that severe clinical depression may have a biological basis (see Chapter 11). Current theories propose that clinical depression results from a disregulation of monoamines, particularly norepinephrine and serotonin. This monoamine theory of depression originated with the finding that certain drugs that depleted monoamines seemed to produce depression. Reserpine, once used to treat high blood pressure, makes monoaminergic vesicles leaky (as we noted earlier) and the transmitters are then destroyed by enzymes, resulting in a depletion of norepinephrine, serotonin, and dopamine. This process often causes depression in persons whose mood states were normal before treatment (as you may have guessed, it also produces Parkinson's symptoms due to dopamine depletion and this side effect helped lead to the use of L-dopa previously mentioned). The drugs that are useful in the treatment of depression generally influence either norepinephrine or serotonin transmission or both, which further supports this monoamine-disregulation hypothesis (see Bradford, 1986; Cooper, Bloom & Roth, 1991; Kramer, 1993).

Monoamines, particularly dopamine, appear to be important as the biochemical basis of another important mental illness, schizophrenia. Schizophrenia involves a major loss of reality contact characterized by false beliefs or delusions, hallucinations, social withdrawal, and distortions of emotionality. The evidence relating these symptoms to high levels of monoamine activity is strong. First, all of the drugs that are effective in the treatment of schizophrenia block monoamine transmission. In fact, a very close correlation exists between the clinical potency of the various drugs used and their ability to block dopamine receptors (Snyder, Burt, & Creese, 1976). Moreover, compounds that fail to block dopamine receptors generally do not relieve schizophrenic symptoms even though such compounds possess the other neurochemical properties of the more effective drugs (see Carpenter & Buchanon, 1994; Crow & Deakin, 1979). Another interesting piece of evidence is that stimulant drugs such as cocaine and amphetamines increase dopaminergic activity of the brain. Although low or moderate doses of these stimulants enhance mood, overdose levels often lead to paranoid delusions and a loss of reality contact that strongly resembles symptoms of schizophrenia. When the drug wears off and dopamine activity returns to normal, these symptoms dissipate, a finding that provides further support for the link between abnormally high dopamine activity and schizophrenia.

Other Transmitters

The four neurotransmitters previously discussed (acetylcholine, norepinephrine, dopamine, and serotonin) have been relatively well studied, and until recently were thought to be the main chemicals involved in neural transmission. However, the development of more sophisticated research techniques has led to the recognition that many more neurotransmitters await discovery. Thorough discussion of the recent advances in neuropharmacology is beyond the scope of this text, but some of the recent advances have already caused a substantial impact on our understanding of psychoactive drug actions.

During the late 1970s, compounds were discovered in mammalian brain tissue that were functionally similar to opiate drugs such as morphine and heroin. Because these chemicals were similar to naturally occurring morphine, they were named **endorphins**—a contraction of the term endogenous morphine. We now understand that the effects of opiate drugs are mediated through endorphinergic activity. The natural functions of the endorphins

Endorphins (en-DORE-finz)
Neurotransmitters found in the brain that are mimicked by opiate drugs.

GABA
Short for gamma-aminobutyric acid, a neurotransmitter found in the brain.

themselves are still far from clear but they certainly modulate pain relief. The endorphins are explained in more detail in Chapter 12.

Another important neurotransmitter is gamma-aminobutyric acid, commonly referred to as **GABA.** GABA is among the most abundant of the known neurotransmitters in brain tissue, and it acts somewhat differently from the way neurotransmission was previously described. The lock-and-key analogy still holds, but when GABA binds to a receptor it seems to "turn the lock the wrong way." That is, GABA does not cause the neuron to fire; instead it impedes the neural firing. Thus, it is often referred to as an inhibitory transmitter (although the other transmitters can be inhibitory at some synapses). If a neuron has a GABA-ergic receptor site that is activated, a larger quantity of the excitatory transmitter is required in order for the neuron to fire. A number of drugs are now thought to act on the GABA system; as you might guess, they are the classic depressant drugs: barbiturates, tranquilizers such as Valium (diazepam) and Librium (chlordiazepoxide), and alcohol. Another inhibitory neurotransmitter, adenosine, is thought to be blocked by caffeine (see Chapter 8).

THE NERVOUS SYSTEM

We have been focusing on a microscopic view of the nervous system as we considered how drugs might act at the level of the single neuron. We now turn to the larger picture and consider a macroscopic view of the nervous system. The basic structure of the nervous system is outlined in Figure 3-3. The major distinction is between the **central nervous system** or CNS and **peripheral nervous system** or PNS. The CNS includes the brain and spinal cord. All nervous tissue outside (or peripheral to) the CNS is part of the PNS. The PNS includes nerves (nerves are simply bundles of axons) that send input from the senses to the brain (sensory nerves) and nerves that send output from the brain to muscles (motor nerves).

Central nervous system
The brain and the spinal cord comprise the central nervous system or CNS.

Peripheral nervous system
Sensory nerves, motor nerves, and the autonomic nervous system comprise the peripheral nervous system or PNS.

The Autonomic Nervous System

Autonomic nervous system
Part of the PNS, the autonomic nervous system or ANS has two branches: the sympathetic and parasympathetic.

Sympathetic branch
Branch of the ANS that is activated during emotional arousal and is responsible for such physiological changes as increased heart and respiratory rate, increased blood pressure, and pupil dilation.

Sympathomimetic
Term applied to drugs such as cocaine and amphetamines that produce the physiological effects of sympathetic activity.

Additionally, the PNS includes an important regulatory system known as the **autonomic nervous system** (ANS). The ANS regulates various nonconscious or automatic functions and is divided into two parts. The **sympathetic branch** of the autonomic nervous system is activated during emotional arousal by a release of epinephrine and norepinephrine from the adrenal glands. This branch is responsible for the various physiological changes that characterize the "fight or flight" reaction. During sympathetic arousal, heart rate increases, blood pressure increases, respiratory rate increases, sweating increases, pupils dilate, the mouth becomes dry, and changes occur in blood flow, as blood is shunted away from the internal organs and to the brain and large muscle groups. These physiological effects are important to keep in mind because some psychoactive drugs mimic sympathetic arousal. Such drugs are said to be **sympathomimetic;** they include cocaine, amphetamines, and some hallucinogens such as LSD. Another group of drugs blocks a type of norepinephrine receptors in the sympathetic system called "beta" receptors. These

The Brain   55

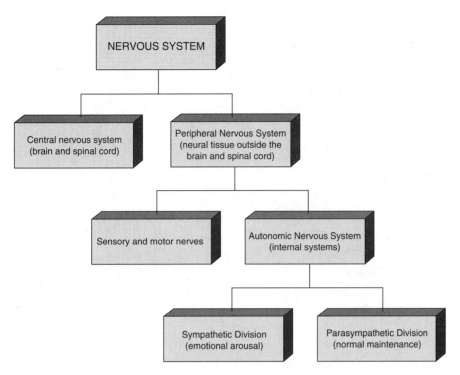

Figure 3-3   Organizational structure of the nervous system.

beta receptors regulate blood pressure and the so-called **beta-blockers** (drugs such as propranolol) are widely used in the treatment of hypertension.

The other branch of the autonomic nervous system is the **parasympathetic branch,** which in general exerts actions opposite those of the sympathetic branch. Parasympathetic activity reduces heart rate, blood pressure, and so on. In contrast to sympathetic neurons, parasympathetic synapses are primarily cholinergic. Drugs that act directly on the parasympathetic system can be highly toxic. For example, nerve gases such as Sarin and Soman act to inhibit acetylcholinesterase, which results in excessive parasympathetic activity. The result can be death through respiratory or cardiovascular failure.

Beta-blockers
Drugs that block beta-adrenergic receptors of the sympathetic system and thus act to relieve high blood pressure.

Parasympathetic branch
The branch of the ANS that is responsible for lowering heart rate, blood pressure, and so on.

THE BRAIN

The key organ of the nervous system is, of course, the brain (see Figure 3-4). Covered with a tough membrane called the meninges, the brain floats within the skull in a liquid known as cerebrospinal fluid. Though just a few pounds in mass, the human brain is an extremely complex structure. We have just examined the various processes involved when a single neuron fires. Now consider that the human brain contains literally billions and billions of neurons. Many of the neurons of the brain synapse with several thousand other neurons because of an elaborate branching of axons. The complexity of billions of neurons and more billions of synapses is absolutely staggering and a bit

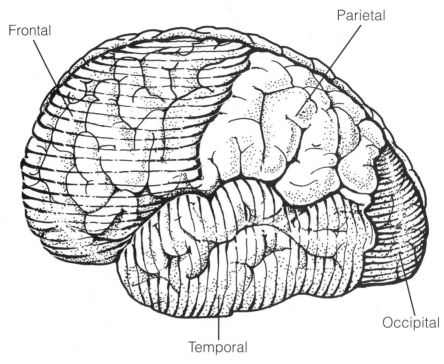

Frontal

Parietal

Occipital

Temporal

Figure 3-4   The four lobes of the human cerebral cortex.

Hindbrain
The lower part of the brain including the medulla, pons, and cerebellum.

Midbrain
Includes the inferior and superior colliculi.

Forebrain
The largest part of the human brain, the forebrain includes the cerebral cortex, thalamus, hypothalamus, and the limbic system.

Medulla oblongata (meh-DULL-ah ah-blong-GOT-ah)
The lowest hindbrain structure of the brain, the medulla is important in the regulation of breathing, heart rate, and other basic life functions.

Cerebellum (sair-ah-BELL-um)
Hindbrain structure important in motor control and coordination.

Pons (pahnz)
Hindbrain structure important in the control of sleep and wakefulness.

beyond comprehension. Despite the sheer enormity of the task, great strides have been made in understanding how this most complex of organs works. One fruitful approach is considering the different parts of the brain separately in an attempt to determine their individual functions.

The major divisions of the human brain are the **hindbrain, midbrain,** and **forebrain.** Figure 3-5 shows the relative locations of these three levels of the brain. If a voyage through the brain began at the spinal cord and moved up, the first part of the brain encountered would be the hindbrain.

The Hindbrain

The hindbrain consists of three main components: the **medulla oblongata,** the **cerebellum,** and the **pons** (see Figure 3-5). The medulla is located just above, and is really a slight enlargement of, the spinal cord. A highly significant structure for the regulation of basic life functions, the medulla controls breathing, heart rate, vomiting, swallowing, blood pressure, and digestive processes. As you can see, normal functioning of the medulla is critical, and when drugs begin to affect the medulla the person is often in danger. When toxic chemicals reach high levels in this area, the vomit center is often triggered to purge the body, which may be why drinking large quantities of alcohol often causes nausea and vomiting. Further up the hindbrain is an enlarged section called the pons. In addition to providing the pathways for input up and output down from the spinal cord, the pons plays a role in the control of sleep and wakefulness. Running along the pons and through the medulla is a

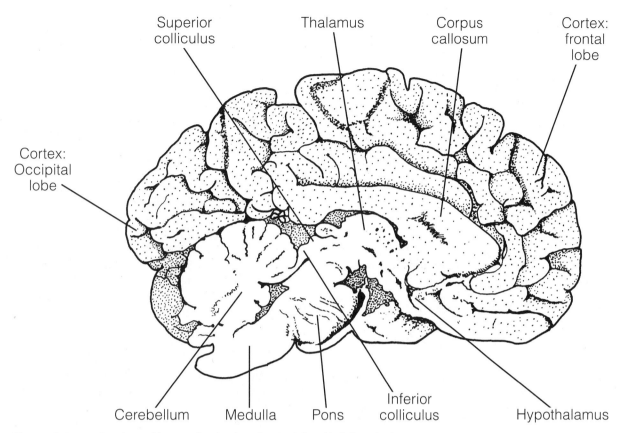

Superior colliculus — Thalamus — Corpus callosum — Cortex: frontal lobe

Cortex: Occipital lobe

Cerebellum — Medulla — Pons — Inferior colliculus — Hypothalamus

Figure 3-5   Section of human brain showing inside of left hemisphere.

pathway (not visible in Figure 3-5) known as the **reticular activating system,** which is critical for alertness and arousal. Drugs that lower arousal and induce sleep (such as barbiturates or tranquilizers) are thought to act in this region of the brain.

The cerebellum, the last major organ of the hindbrain, is a highly complex structure containing several billion neurons itself. The cerebellum is critical for motor control. Activities of the cerebellum are largely unconscious, but do involve balance, coordinated movement of all kinds, speech, and other aspects of movement. The loss of motor control and balance produced by drugs such as alcohol may be caused by their action on the cerebellum.

The Midbrain

The midbrain consists of two small structures: the **inferior colliculi** and the **superior colliculi** (see Figure 3-5). The inferior colliculi are two structures that are part of the auditory system. The superior colliculi function in localization of visual stimuli. These structures are specifically involved with localization of stimuli and mediation of reflexes. The actual recognition and interpretation of visual and auditory stimuli takes place elsewhere in the brain (see the section on cerebral cortex).

Reticular activating system
Pathway running through the medulla and pons that regulates alertness and arousal.

Inferior colliculi (ko-LICK-you-lie)
Midbrain structures that control sound localization.

Superior colliculi
Midbrain structures that control visual localization.

The Forebrain

The Thalamus and Hypothalamus   The most important brain regions from the perspective of interpreting drug actions are in the forebrain, which includes the **thalamus, hypothalamus,** and several other higher structures, particularly the cortex (see Figure 3-5). The thalamus is often referred to as a relay station because it receives incoming sensory stimuli and then "relays" that information to relevant centers throughout the brain. The hypothalamus is a critical structure in the motivation of behavior. The hypothalamus contains areas that appear to be central in the control of eating, drinking, control of body temperature, aggression, and sexual behavior. Worth noting is that information about the particular function of given brain regions has not been easily determined and remains somewhat controversial. The methods for analysis of brain structures involve primarily lesions and stimulation. Lesioning a structure involves performing surgery on an animal subject and causing localized damage to the structure in question. When the animal has recovered from surgery, changes in behavior are then attributed to the damaged structure. For example, lesions in one part of the hypothalamus result in greatly reduced food intake, while if another part is damaged overeating and obesity occur. Thus, the hypothalamus contains at least two sites that appear to be important in the regulation of food intake. One area seems to inhibit eating (because its loss results in overeating) and the other seems to excite hunger (because its loss results in less eating). The effects of electrical stimulation of a brain region generally are the opposite of the effects of lesioning or removing that region.

However, a note of caution accompanies these findings. When cells in the brain are lesioned or stimulated, the effects extend beyond those specific cells, and indeed entire pathways may become damaged or stimulated. Thus, rather than speak of the hunger or satiety *centers,* more appropriate terms are hunger or satiety *pathways.* However, even this may be an oversimplification, as some researchers have noted the role of these pathways may not be as specific to hunger as we first thought. That is, these pathways could affect motor movements, the sensation of taste, or more general motivational variables, and much current research is devoted to these effects. However, there is general agreement that the hypothalamus is an important structure in the regulation of hunger, thirst, and other basic biological motives (Carlson, 1991; Logue, 1991).

The Neural Basis of Reward   Despite the difficulties of such research, electrical stimulation of brain regions was the basis of one of the most significant discoveries in the quest to understand the relationship between brain, behavior, and drugs. During the 1950s, the psychologist James Olds was trying to map the effects of stimulation on the rat brain by implanting electrodes into various regions. In some areas of the brain, the rat seemed to enjoy the electrical stimulation. Here is how Olds describes his serendipitous discovery:

> I applied a brief train of 60-cycle sine wave electrical current whenever the animal entered one corner of the enclosure. The animal did not stay away from the corner, but rather came back quickly after a brief sortie which followed the first stimulation and came back even more quickly

Thalamus (THAL-ah-muss)
Forebrain structure that organizes sensory input.

Hypothalamus (HIGH-poe-THAL-ah-muss)
Forebrain structure that regulates eating, drinking, and other basic biological drives.

Contemporary Issue
DESIGNER DRUGS AND THE BRAIN

Designer drugs are synthetic chemicals produced by making a small chemical change in the structure of previously known psychoactive drugs. If the change does not alter the receptor-activating properties of the compound, the drug will still produce the psychoactive properties desired by the user, but not be specifically controlled by federal law. In other words, a clever chemist could make a slight change in the heroin molecule and produce a new drug with the effects of heroin, but because it would be unknown, the new compound would be completely legal. (The 1986 Drug Analogue Act changed that.) Thus, designer drugs placed the dealer at less risk, but not necessarily the user. Recently in California, an underground chemist began to produce a designer heroin called MPPP, but due to poor laboratory technique some of what hit the streets was a closely related but highly toxic compound called MPTP. The error was discovered when a number of young drugs users were hospitalized with complete paralysis. At first the cause of this epidemic of paralysis was a mystery. The symptoms were similar to those of advanced Parkinson's disease. But because Parkinson's is a disease of the elderly, only an inspired guess from a physician named William Langston solved the puzzle. He tried to use L-dopa with these "frozen" addicts. The L-dopa was successful enough that the paralyzed patients were able to at least talk a little. Eventually they were identified as heroin addicts who had tried the misdesigned heroin, MPTP.

We now know that MPTP selectively attacks the substantia nigra and causes rapid destruction of this organ. Thus, the addicts who became victims of MPTP have sustained permanent damage, although some symptom reduction is possible with L-dopa (Markey, Castagnoli, Trevor, & Kopin, 1986).

A couple of important points: the tremendous hazard associated with designer drugs is obvious. Because these drugs are not tested in animals and screened by the FDA, the risks they pose to the user are great. An additional point is that brain damage can occur without overt symptoms. Many people who were exposed to MPTP only once or twice probably do not show any Parkinson's symptoms at present. Nonetheless, some damage to the substantia nigra has occurred. As more cells are lost during the normal aging process, the 80% threshold may be reached and these individuals may yet pay the price by developing premature Parkinsonism.

---

after a briefer sortie which followed the second stimulation. By the time the third electrical stimulus had been applied the animal seemed indubitably to be "coming back for more" (Olds, cited in Carlson, 1980, pp. 540–541).

Following up this finding, Olds and Milner (1954) discovered that when electrodes are implanted in some brain areas, particularly the **medial forebrain bundle,** rats could actually be trained to press a lever in order to electrically stimulate themselves. The medial forebrain bundle involves a group of neurons

Medial forebrain bundle
Pathway that is rewarding when stimulated.

that travel through the lateral part of the hypothalamus. When rats have been trained to self-stimulate this area they often respond with great vigor (over 1,000 responses per hour), and the potency of the reinforcement related to this center led Olds and others to refer to it as the "pleasure center." The notion is that the region may represent the final common pathway for pleasurable stimulation and reward. While this claim is controversial, clearly this brain region is of significance in understanding the rewarding properties of drugs. One of the major neurotransmitter pathways that is associated with the medial forebrain bundle and surrounding area is a dopamine pathway, and some investigators have suggested that dopamine is a critical chemical in producing the rewarding properties of drugs (see Wise, 1989). In support of this, studies have shown that rats will learn to press a lever that results in the delivery of cocaine through a micropipette implanted in one of the medial forebrain bundle regions that primarily involve dopaminergic neurons (Goeders, Dworkin, & Smith, 1986). As Dackis and Gold (1985) put it, cocaine addicts can be seen as individuals who have "tampered chemically with endogenous systems of reward and lost control of this shortcut to pleasure" (p. 476).

The forebrain also includes three complex systems: the **limbic system,** the **basal ganglia,** and the **cortex.** The aspects of behavior that are most uniquely human such as complex reasoning, memory, logic, speech, and planning, are largely derived from these structures.

The Limbic System   The limbic system includes several structures in the interior of the forebrain. One limbic structure, the amygdala, is important in mediating certain types of aggression. Another important limbic system structure is the **hippocampus,** which appears to be critical in memory storage. Persons with damage to the hippocampus can remember things that occurred in their lives prior to the damage, but are unable to store new memories. In other words, their long-term memories are intact but they cannot form new permanent memories. Heavy use of alcohol, coupled with malnutrition, in "skid row" alcoholics often produces a severe psychotic state known as **Korsakoff's Syndrome.** Korsakoff's patients often show this sort of memory problem that appears due to brain damage to the hippocampus and perhaps other structures as well.

The Basal Ganglia   The basal ganglia include the caudate nucleus, the putamen, and the globus pallidus. These structures are critical for motor movements. The problem of Parkinson's disease involves damage to the basal ganglia. Specifically, Parkinson's develops when a group of nerve cells known as the **substantia nigra** begins to degenerate. The substantia nigra produces dopamine, which is transported to the basal ganglia, and as the substantia nigra deteriorates, less and less dopamine is available for neurotransmission. Interestingly, Parkinson's symptoms do not appear until about 80% of the substantia nigra is destroyed.

Some of the recent controversy about designer drugs involves the substantia nigra (see nearby Contemporary Issue Box).

The Cerebral Cortex   Figure 3-4 shows the lobes of the cerebral cortex. The occipital lobe is at the back of the brain and is often referred to as the visual

Limbic system
Forebrain structures including the amygdala, hippocampus, and others.

Basal ganglia (BAY-sell GANG-lee-ah)
Forebrain structures important for motor control. The basal ganglia include the caudate nucleus, the putamen, and the globus pallidus.

Cortex
The cerebral cortex or cortex is the outermost and largest part of the human brain.

Hippocampus (hip-poe-KAMP-us)
A structure of the limbic system thought to be important in the formation of memories.

Korsakoff's Syndrome
A disorder characterized by memory loss and psychotic behavior and related to heavy use of alcohol and malnutrition.

Substantia nigra (sub-STAN-shah NIE-gruh)
Literally, "black substance" this basal ganglia structure is darkly pigmented. The substantia nigra produces dopamine. Damage to this area produces Parkinson's disease.

projection area. Stimulation of the eye is eventually perceived as a visual stimulus when the signal reaches the occipital cortex. The temporal lobe is similarly specialized for auditory stimulation, and also appears to be important in language. Damage to the left temporal lobe results in severe impairment of

Contemporary Issue
ASSESSMENT OF BRAIN DAMAGE

An important question that comes up whenever chronic effects of drugs are discussed is the issue of drug-induced brain damage. We discuss this problem throughout the text with each drug we consider, but now, after this lengthy discussion of the brain, a few general comments are warranted. First, detecting brain damage caused by drugs is often very difficult. Rarely do psychoactive drugs produce such dramatic destruction as is seen with MPTP, so more often we must rely on specialized methods to determine whether damage has occurred. Various tests are available that can be used to detect impairment in memory, perceptual motor skills, language, or other functions that may be influenced by chronic drug use. More direct analysis of brain tissue may be accomplished through **electroencephalography (EEG).** This technique involves measuring the brain's electrical activity through the scalp. These brain waves change in predictable ways with sleep or various kinds of arousal, and abnormalities in EEG patterns can reveal gross brain damage.

Electroencephalography (EEG)
Technique used to measure electrical activity in the brain.

A more recently developed and more sensitive measure of brain impairment is the technique of **Computerized Axial Tomography,** better known as the CAT scan. The CAT scan involves passing X-rays through the head in a circular pattern, resulting in a three-dimensional image of the brain. The focus can be changed to different depths of the brain so that internal tumors, enlarged spaces or ventricles, or other internal abnormalities can be detected.

Computerized Axial Tomography (CAT)
The CAT scan is a technique for developing a three-dimensional X-ray image of the brain.

CAT scans can provide a picture of the brain but reveal nothing about its functioning. However, a newly developed technique called the PETT scan may greatly increase our ability to detect brain activity. **Positron Emission Transaxial Tomography (PETT)** involves injecting weak radioisotopes into the brain. Radioactive glucose or oxygen or even radioactive neurochemicals are then measured by sensitive detectors that can determine where the isotopes are absorbed, their rate of absorption, and so on. Then changes in activity in various brain regions can be assessed. The PETT scan is just beginning to be widely used but offers promise to greatly increase our ability to detect the forms of subtle brain damage that drugs may induce. On the horizon may be an even more sophisticated and sensitive technique to image the brain called **Magnetic Resonance Imagery (MRI).** With this technique, a strong magnetic field is passed through the person's head. Radio waves are then generated, causing the molecules of the brain to emit energy of different frequencies, depending on their properties. This technique creates a localized and detailed brain image and eventually may greatly improve our ability to detect and understand brain dysfunction (Carlson, 1991).

Positron Emission Transaxial Tomography (PETT or PET)
The PET scan is a technique used to measure activity in selected brain regions.

Magnetic Resonance Imaging (MRI)
This technique creates a high-resolution, three-dimensional image of the brain.

language abilities (at least for most right-handed individuals). Right temporal lobe damage often results in disregulation of emotions. This relationship between right and left temporal lobe mediation of language and emotions is reversed in some cases (e.g., left-handed individuals). The frontal lobe is important in the initiation of motor movement (precentral gyrus) and also is involved with emotionality, intelligence, and personality. Tactile stimuli are registered in the parietal lobe.

summary

- All psychoactive drugs produce their effects by action on the nervous system—primarily by altering normal brain function.

- The brain is composed of specialized cells called neurons. Neurons transmit information by conducting electrical currents along their axons and releasing chemical substances called neurotransmitters into the synapse. Most drugs act by altering this chemical phase of neural transmission.

- Neurotransmitters work through a "lock-and-key" mechanism. The transmitter substance is like a key, and specialized areas on the neuron, called receptor sites, are like locks. Neurotransmitter chemicals must occupy the receptor sites in order for the neuron to fire.

- Drugs alter neural transmission in several ways. For example, a drug may mimic a natural or endogenous neurotransmitter by activating receptor sites. Alternatively a drug may block a receptor site. Drugs can also affect the deactivation or release of neurotransmitters.

- Although dozens of different chemicals have been proposed to act as neurotransmitters in the human brain, six are known to be related

to drug effects. These are acetylcholine, dopamine, endorphins, GABA, norepinephrine, and serotonin.

- The nervous system is divided into two main sections. The central nervous system includes the brain and spinal cord. The peripheral nervous system includes the sensory nerves, motor nerves, and the autonomic nervous system.

- The autonomic nervous system is divided into two branches. The sympathetic branch produces the physiological effects that accompany emotional arousal, and the parasympathetic controls the body when at rest.

- For convenience of description, the brain is divided into three divisions: the hindbrain, the midbrain, and the forebrain.

- The evolutionarily primitive hindbrain includes the medulla, the pons, and the cerebellum.

- The midbrain includes the superior and inferior colliculi.

- The forebrain includes the cerebral cortex, the thalamus, the hypothalamus, the basal ganglia, and the limbic system.

ANSWERS TO WHAT DO YOU THINK?

1. Certain cells found in the nervous system have the unique ability to "talk" with each other.

T   *Neurons are able to communicate with each other through an electrochemical process known as neural transmission.*

2. The effects of drugs always involve naturally occurring physiological processes.

T   *Drugs act by making defined natural functions of the brain or body either more or less active.*

3. Some drugs may act by mimicking a neuro-transmitter.

T *Some drugs bind to receptor sites just as natural transmitters do.*

4. All drugs have the same basic effect on a cellular level; that is, they all block neural firing.

F *While some drugs, called antagonists, do block receptor sites and prevent activation of the receptor, other drugs, called agonists, act by activating the receptor.*

5. The brain is shielded from many toxic substances by a protective barrier.

T *The brain is protected from toxic compounds that might enter the bloodstream by a blood-brain barrier that screens many, but not all, chemicals.*

6. The two main branches of the nervous system are the peripheral nervous system (PNS) and the autonomic nervous system (ANS).

F *The two main branches of the nervous system are the central nervous system (CNS) and the peripheral nervous system (PNS).*

7. The brain and the spinal cord comprise the peripheral nervous system.

F *The brain and spinal cord comprise the central nervous system.*

8. The brain is firmly attached to the inside of the skull by a tough membrane known as the meninges.

F *The brain floats within the skull in a liquid known as cerebrospinal fluid.*

9. The autonomic nervous system is responsible for regulating food and water intake.

F *Food and water intake appear to be regulated by the hypothalamus—a structure found in the brain.*

10. Animals will work for the electrical stimulation of certain parts of the brain.

T *The medial forebrain bundle is sometimes called the pleasure center.*

4 Pharmacology

WHAT DO YOU THINK?

True or False?   ____   A given amount of a drug has similar biological effects on people.

____   Despite the large number of known drugs, there are only three ways that drugs are commonly administered or taken.

____   The safest way to take a drug is orally, but it also is the slowest way of getting the drug into the blood.

____   Taking a drug intravenously is a highly efficient, safe way to get a drug into the blood.

____   Smoking is a relatively slow way of getting a drug into the blood.

____   Some drugs can enter the body through the skin.

____   The body protects the brain from toxic substances.

____   The kidneys play the major part in drug metabolism.

____   Scientific study of the effects of drugs is difficult because there is no way to represent such effects quantitatively.

____   When more than one drug is taken at a time, the effects of one can enhance or diminish the effects of the other(s).

____   Caffeine and alcohol have antagonistic effects.

____   It is important to know about drug interactions because there is an increasing prevalence of using more than one drug at a time among people who present themselves for drug treatment.

Control
In research, control means to be able to account for variables that may affect the results of a study.

Feedback
In this context, in a series of events, what happens in a later event alters those preceding it.

Absorbed
Drugs are absorbed by, or entered into, the bloodstream.

The aim of this chapter is to cover basic principles and methods of pharmacology that apply to the description and evaluation of all drugs. We will achieve this aim by elaborating on an idea we first mentioned in Chapter 1—the drug experience, or a person's perception of the effects of a drug. A series of interrelated factors contributes to a given drug effect. The importance of any one factor, or set of factors, for a given drug-taking occasion depends on the importance of the other factors. This complicated-sounding idea is even more complicated to analyze in practice. To evaluate the importance or contribution of any one factor to a drug effect or experience, the researcher must comprehend or at least somehow **control** the effects that other relevant factors are having.

We will try to walk down the path of the drug experience from beginning to end as if it were always a logical and linear route. However, that analogy is not fully accurate, because not only are the contributory factors of a drug effect interdependent, but also **feedback** relationships may occur among those factors. For example, a large quantity of some drugs may be taken and then **absorbed** into the blood. Then the drug is carried to its site of action (**distributed**). But in some cases a large quantity of a drug may cause the body to slow absorption or quicken **metabolism** of the drug in order to defend itself against a toxic drug effect. In this event, the distribution of the drug is information that the body "feeds back" to its regulators of absorption and metabolism to, in effect, reduce drug quantity.

However, including all the possible feedback loops would strangle this discussion so we review the drug experience and factors influencing it as if everything proceeds linearly. We chart the path as outlined in Table 4-1. For each of the "steps" included in Table 4-1 there may be two or more factors to consider. By the end of this chapter you will begin to understand the great complexity of what humans experience when they take drugs.

To the pharmacologist the ideas of the drug experience mean two branches of that science—**pharmacokinetics** and pharmacodynamics. Pharmacokinetics concerns "the absorption, distribution, biotransformation, and excretion of drugs (Benet, Mitchell, & Sheiner, 1990, p. 1). Drug absorption and distribution are the essentials for determining how much drug reaches its sites of action, and therefore its effects. As such, absorption and distribution make major contributions to the drug experience (step 4 in Table 4-1).

Once in the body drugs do not stay forever. The basics of how the body eliminates drugs, and how that is studied, will also be covered in this chapter. Knowing about drug excretion or elimination is required for learning what effect a drug will have at some time after it enters the body.

Pharmacokinetics might be viewed as the vehicle for **pharmacodynamics,** which is the study of the "biochemical and physiological effects of drugs and their mechanisms of action" (Benet, Mitchell, & Sheiner, 1990, p. 1). The neural mechanisms of drugs already have been discussed in Chapter 3. In this chapter we will further your introduction to some of the language that pharmacologists use in describing drug effects, and some of the ways that have been developed to depict them. In later chapters on individual drugs and drug classes, you also will see some pharmacodynamics in our description of a respective drug's biological mechanism of action. Pharmacodynamics is relevant to the drug experience because this branch of pharmacology concerns drug effects. It will be valuable for you to know what standards are followed in describing and representing these effects.

Distribution
Drugs are distributed, or transported, by the blood to their site(s) of action in the body.

Metabolism
The process by which the body breaks down matter into more simple components and waste.

Pharmacokinetics
The branch of pharmacology that concerns the absorption, distribution, biotransformation, and excretion of drugs.

Pharmacodynamics
The branch of pharmacology that concerns the biochemical and physiological effects of drugs and their mechanisms of action.

Table 4-1   "Steps" to the Drug Experience

1. A drug of specified chemical structure is
2. Measured in a certain quantity. It is then
3. Administered in one of a number of possible ways and
4. Absorbed into the blood and distributed to site(s) of action
5. To achieve some pharmacological effect.
6. But in humans, the drug effect depends not only on the chemical properties of the drug and its physiological consequences,
7. But also on characteristics of the person, such as genetic constitution, gender, age, personality, and drug tolerance.
8. The setting or context of drug use may also affect the drug experience.
9. Steps 1-4 and 6-8 combine to produce the drug experience.

The emphasis of this chapter will be on characteristics of the drug and the part the body plays in producing drug effects. Characteristics of people that distinguish them from each other (step 7 in Table 4-1) and setting factors (step 8 in Table 4-1) that play a part in the drug experience will be the subject of Chapter 5.

PHARMACOKINETICS

We begin our overview of pharmacokinetics by showing how to specify and measure a desired amount of a drug and the ways to get the drug into the body. These essentials form the combination of drug and body chemistry that contributes to the drug experience.

Drug Dose

You know from Chapter 1 that the effect of a drug depends most fundamentally on how much of the drug is taken (steps 1 and 2 in Table 4-1). A science about drugs relies on a standard way to determine drug quantities. Thus the questions: How do pharmacologists compute drug dose? How is that quantity communicated? A drug's dose is computed according to a person's body weight because heavier people have a higher volume of body fluid than lighter people do. Therefore, a given amount of a drug is less concentrated in the body of a heavier person, and similarly at the site of drug action, than it is in the body of a lighter person (e.g., White, 1991). As you will see later in this chapter, generally the greater the drug concentration at a site, the greater the drug effect. Therefore, the amount of drug that is administered has to be adjusted according to body weight to assure that a drug is given in equivalent strength (dose) to people who weigh different amounts.

The first step is to determine the desired dose, expressed in milligrams of the drug per kilogram (mg/kg) of body weight. The next step is to weigh the person and record the weight in kilograms. With these two quantities the amount of drug required for the desired dose is easily determined. For example, if the desired dose is .08 mg/kg and the subject weighs 80kg, the necessary amount is .08 × 80 = 6.4 mg of the drug (Leavitt, 1982).

Routes of Administration

In pharmacology, the "route of drug administration" may refer to the site where a drug is taken, or to how a drug is taken.[1] Drug administration route can strongly influence the effects that a drug has (step 3 in Table 4-1). In this section we will discuss eight administration routes. The five most common of these are oral, by injection (includes three ways—subcutaneous, intramuscular, and intravenous), and inhalation. Three other important routes we will discuss are intranasal (sniffing), sublingual (under the tongue), and transdermal (through the skin).

---

[1]Our discussion of routes of drug administration draws heavily from Benet, Mitchell, and Sheiner (1990, 1990a) and Jacobs and Fehr (1987).

Oral Oral administration, or swallowing, is the route that you probably are most familiar with. Orally taken drugs generally are in the form of pills, capsules, powders, or liquids. Numerous examples include the variety of headache medicines, cough syrups, cold remedies, and so on available at any drugstore. That such accessible medications are virtually always prepared for oral administration is a result of a major feature of this route: It usually is the safest, most convenient, and most economical way to administer a drug.

When drugs are swallowed, they pass through the stomach and are absorbed primarily through the small intestine. This travel course has several consequences for the speed with which a drug can register its effect physically as well as how much effect is registered. A major factor in determining the effect is how much food is in the digestive tract when the drug is taken. The presence of food delays stomach emptying and may dilute the concentration of a drug. The result: delayed absorption and a decrease in the maximum drug level achieved. Perhaps people most commonly notice this result when they compare drinking alcohol after eating a full meal to drinking on an empty stomach. Another point about oral administration is that food may encapsulate the drug so that it is passed out of the body in the feces. Finally, taking a drug orally, even without the complications of food in the stomach, causes the drug to be absorbed into the blood more slowly than with other routes.

So, the pluses of oral administration—relative safety, convenience, and economy—must be balanced against considerations of time to absorption and the maximum drug effect that can be reached with a particular drug dose. With some drugs, such as heroin, the stomach acids used for digestion actually break down the drug to some degree before it is absorbed into the blood. Once in the blood the chemically altered drug is passed through the liver before reaching the brain. Because the liver is the major site of the metabolizing of most drugs, only a fraction of the drug dose actually reaches the brain. The outcome is a diminished drug effect.

Injection Three of the most common routes of drug administration involve injecting drugs into the body using a needle and syringe. When drugs are taken this way they typically are **dissolved** or **suspended** in some solution ("vehicle") before injection. The routes for administration when injecting drugs are: subcutaneous, intramuscular, and intravenous.

Subcutaneous This route involves injecting the drug under the skin. It is the easiest of the injection routes to use, because the target site of the needle is just below the skin surface. Many beginning drug abusers take their drugs subcutaneously. This route may also be preferred medically for drugs that are not irritating to body tissue, because of the route's relatively slow (but faster than oral) and constant absorption rate. In fact, the solution the drug is administered in may be selected to adjust the drug's absorption rate. Two reasons for not taking a drug subcutaneously are when the drug irritates body tissue and when large volumes of solution must be taken in order to introduce enough drug to achieve the desired effect.

Intramuscular The name of this route means within the muscle. Intramuscular injection requires a deeper penetration than the subcutaneous method

Dissolved
A drug is dissolved by converting it from solid to liquid by mixing the drug with a liquid.

Suspended
A drug is suspended in solution if its particles are dispersed in solution but not dissolved in it.

but is associated with a faster absorption rate when the drug is prepared in a water solution and there is a good rate of blood flow at the site of administration. Absorption rates may differ, depending on what muscle group the drug is injected into. Absorption rate can also be modulated by the type of solution that the drug is prepared in for administration.

One disadvantage of intramuscular injection is that it can result in localized (at the site of injection) pain. Furthermore, when drugs are administered intramuscularly by a person who is not formally trained to do so, the risk of infection from irritating drugs and tissue damage is high.

Intravenous   "Intravenous" means into the veins, and because of that most of the problems in absorption are averted. A common street term for the route

Intravenous drug injection is associated with rapid drug effects, making it the preferred route of some drug abusers. Intravenous injection of drugs is considered dangerous because large quantities can reach the site(s) of action so quickly.

is "mainlining." The drug is injected, in solution, directly into the veins. The effects can be immediate. As a result, intravenous administration is valuable for emergency medical situations, and doses can be precisely adjusted according to the person's response. In addition, irritating drugs as well as irritating vehicles can be taken intravenously (as opposed to, say, subcutaneously or intramuscularly) because blood vessel walls are relatively insensitive and the drug is further diluted by blood.

The apparent advantages of intravenous administration raise the question of why this is not the preferred route for prescribed medications. A major reason is that the intravenous route is the one most highly associated with complications, because large quantities of the drug very quickly can reach the site of action. Another point to consider: if a drug is repeatedly administered intravenously, maintenance of a healthy vein is necessary. In general, intravenous injection is associated with such risk that administration must be done slowly and with careful monitoring of a person's response. Obviously, this is much more likely to happen in a controlled medical environment than in other settings where drugs are taken.

Those who regularly take drugs like heroin, cocaine, or heroin and cocaine together (called speedball) intravenously are called "hard-core addicts." These users take drugs intravenously because they want immediate and powerful drug effects. However, the risks of taking a drug intravenously, coupled with the assault that such drug taking has on the body, usually take a toll on a person. Drug-induced deaths, intentional or not, are an ever-present danger among addicts and other nonmedical drug users who take their drugs intravenously.

Another critical point to consider when drugs are taken by injection is that to prevent diseases such as AIDS, hepatitis, or tetanus, drugs must be injected using sterile needles and solutions. When any of the three injecting routes are used, the body's natural protections from microorganisms, such as skin and mucous membranes, are bypassed. Therefore, dirty needles or non-sterile solutions may carry illness-inducing microorganisms that the body cannot "screen out." This is why, for instance, street drug abusers are at high risk for contracting AIDS.

Inhalation   Some drugs may be inhaled and then absorbed through the lung's membranes. For such drugs, inhalation results in a fast (faster than subcutaneous or intramuscular injection) and effective absorption. To inhale a drug it has to be in one of a few states. Drugs that can be changed into gaseous states may be inhaled. For example, the vapors of one class of substances may be inhaled. Some examples of these substances, which typically are ingredients of commercial products and are aptly called inhalants when used for their psychoactive properties, are benzene, toluene, and naphtha. We will have more to say about this important group of substances in Chapter 10. Drugs that can be administered in the form of fine liquid drops also may be inhaled. Furthermore, drugs in small particles of matter that are suspended in a gas (Jacobs & Fehr, 1987, p. 22) may be inhaled. Included here is the smoke from tobacco and from **freebase** cocaine (crack).

As we noted, inhaling a drug results in rapid and effective absorption. A disadvantage of inhalation is that it is possible to absorb only a small amount of a drug in one administration.

Freebase
A substance may be separated, or "freed," from its salt base. The separated form of the substance is thus called "freebase."

Contemporary Issue
NEEDLE SHARING AND AIDS

Intravenous (IV) drug use has become the highest risk factor for AIDS among heterosexuals (Schleifer, Delaney, Tross, & Keller, 1991). The reason that the risk for AIDS is high among IV drug users is that they often share needles while taking drugs. Risk for becoming HIV positive goes up when one or more of the needle sharers is HIV positive and the needle is not sterilized before being passed from person to person.

There are several reasons for needle sharing among IV drug users. For example, it may be a simple matter of syringe availability. If there are few needles around, then sharing becomes more likely. In this regard, the addict's first priority is to get the drug into his or her body. However, a more entrenched and difficult-to-modify reason for needle sharing is that it may be part of local drug-taking social norms. In addition, needle sharing often is part of socialization into the drug-taking subculture and has been viewed as a way that the addict can feel a sense of group belonging and friendship.

Several approaches have been taken to combat the problem of HIV risk and needle sharing. One is education, and in the last 10 years or so it would be difficult not to have heard or read about one or more campaigns directed at addicts and alerting them to avoid needle sharing or, if the practice is followed, to clean the needle before using it. A related approach has been to directly supply addicts with clean syringes. So-called needle exchange programs, in which addicts trade their used syringes for clean ones, seem promising. That is, review of programs in the United States, Canada, and Europe shows that addicts in exchange programs do less needle sharing, and more often clean their syringes with bleach. In addition, needle exchange programs have not increased IV drug use where they have been implemented (Hilts, 1993).

In spite of signs that needle exchange programs can make inroads into the HIV risk-IV drug use problem, such programs are locally restricted in 47 of 50 of the states in the United States. In such localities, there are laws against free exchange of syringes without a physician's prescription, because of fear of aiding and abetting the spread of IV drug use. If you were a local official, what would you consider as the pros and cons of needle exchange programs in your city?

Intranasal   In this route, also called sniffing, a drug in powdered form is taken through the nose. Absorption then occurs through the mucous membranes of the nose and the sinus cavities. Examples of drugs commonly absorbed this way include cocaine, heroin, and powdered tobacco snuff. When a drug is fat-soluble, sniffing is a rapid and effective way to absorb it. However, if a drug is irritating and disrupts blood flow it can cause damage if sniffed. An example that has been cited often is the damage cocaine sniffing causes to the nasal septum and lining of the nose.

Sublingual   With this route a drug tablet is placed under the tongue and dissolves in saliva. It is absorbed through the mouth's mucous membranes. Ni-

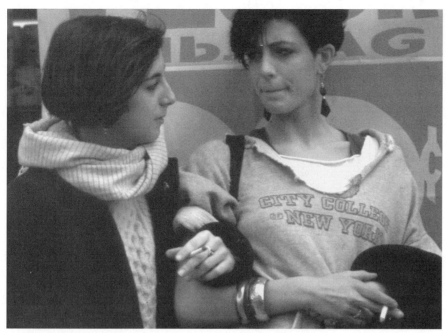

Probably the best known way of ingesting a drug by inhalation is taking nicotine by smoking cigarettes.

troglycerin, which is taken for treatment of angina pectoris (heart pain), usually is taken sublingually. Nicotine may be taken in the form of chewing tobacco or "dipping" snuff by the sublingual route.

The sublingual route results in faster and more efficient drug absorption than oral administration. It also is preferred to oral administration for drugs that irritate the stomach and cause vomiting. Almost any drug with the right chemical properties may be taken in pill form sublingually. However, this route is used less frequently than might be expected because of the unpleasant taste of many of the drugs that may be taken sublingually.

Transdermal   Some drugs may be taken transdermally, or through the skin (Wester & Maibach, 1983). One common medical use of the transdermal route is to provide an alternative to oral administration when a drug may cause unwanted gastrointestinal effects. The transdermal route actually is not an effective one for many drugs, because the skin acts as a barrier to some chemicals and thus is relatively nonpermeable. For those drugs that do more readily penetrate intact skin, absorption is better the wider the area the drug is applied to.

Absorption of drugs that penetrate the skin is enhanced if sites are selected that have a higher rate of cutaneous blood flow. In addition, a drug dose may be modified by mixing it with other substances (for example, an oily preparation) to improve penetration at the site of administration. In this regard, in Chapter 7 we will discuss a patch containing a preparation of nicotine and other substances that is applied to the skin for entry of nicotine into the body. This is one type of pharmacological treatment of nicotine dependence.

Nitroglycerine may be administered by patch, which avoids the problem of metabolizing the drug before it reaches its site of action when it is taken orally (see discussion of the oral route earlier, and discussion of "first pass" effects later in this chapter). Finally, patches may be used to place a drug at a site of the skin that is advantageous for increased blood flow.

To conclude this section, routes of drug administration should be thought of as ways to get drugs into the body, and they can have a considerable influence on the drug experience. No route is inherently better than any other. Rather, determining the preferred route depends on the drug administered, the goals of administration, and the advantages and disadvantages of using a particular route with a particular drug under particular circumstances. Table 4-2 is a summary of general considerations in using the eight routes of drug administration that we discussed, and Table 4-3 is a summary of the routes typically used with a number of drugs taken for medical or nonmedical reasons.

Table 4-2   General Considerations in Using Eight Routes of Drug Administration

Route	Considerations
Oral	—Among the safest, most convenient, and most economical of routes of administration —Presence of food in the stomach retards absorption or may diminish the amount of drug absorbed —Stomach acids may break down some drugs, resulting in reduced drug effect
Subcutaneous	—Easiest of the three injection routes to use —Associated with absorption rates faster than oral administration but slower than intramuscular and intravenous routes —Preferred for medical use of drugs that are not irritating to body tissue, because of its relatively slow but constant absorption rate with sustained drug effects —When a drug irritates body tissue or when large volumes of solution must be used for taking the drug, the subcutaneous route should not be used
Intramuscular	—Requires deeper penetration of injection than subcutaneous but results in a faster absorption rate with proper preparation of solution and an injection site with good blood flow —May be painful at the injection site —Use of this route by medically untrained people is associated with a high risk of injection from irritating drugs and tissue damage
Intravenous	— Considered the fastest absorption rate of all routes —Because the resulting drug effects can be immediate, this route is valuable for emergency medical needs —Doses can be adjusted precisely according to the person's response, because of immediacy of drug effects —Better than subcutaneous or intramuscular routes for taking irritating drugs, because blood vessel walls are relatively insensitive and the blood further dilutes the drug —Danger exists in the potential for a large quantity of a drug to reach its site of action

Table 4-2   (continued)

Route	Considerations
Intravenous (continued)	—Repeated use of this route requires maintenance of a healthy vein
	—A drug dose must be administered gradually and the person's response monitored carefully to prevent serious complications
Inhalation	—When feasible to inhale a drug, the resulting absorption is effective, and more rapid than it would be by the intramuscular or subcutaneous routes
	—Only a small amount of drug can be absorbed in any one administration
Intranasal	—When a drug is fat soluble, this route results in absorption that is rapid and effective
	—A drug can cause damage, if sniffed, when the drug is irritating or disrupts blood flow
Sublingual	—Potentially many drugs could be taken in pill form sublingually
	—Results in faster and more efficient absorption than oral administration
	—Preferable to oral administration for drugs that irritate the stomach and cause vomiting
	—Route not used as often as it might be because of the unpleasant taste of many of the relevant drugs
Transdermal	—An alternative to the oral route when a drug may cause unwanted gastrointestinal effects
	—A number of drugs cannot be taken by this route because the skin is a relatively impenetrable barrier to many chemicals
	—Resulting absorption is enhanced at sites that have greater cutaneous blood flow, and mixing a drug with another substance may improve penetration of the skin

Drug Absorption

Absorption also may be defined as the rate and extent to which a drug leaves its site of administration, and it plays a major part in the drug experience. Absorption and the factors that affect it are extremely important because they influence **bioavailability.** Bioavailability is the portion of the original drug dose that reaches its site of action or that reaches a fluid in the body that gives the drug access to its site of action (Benet et al., 1990a). As such, the bioavailability of a drug tells us about its effects.

We have just explained in detail how the route of administering a drug affects its absorption. Actually, differences among the routes in absorption rate are related to a number of factors that in general influence absorption. We will cite a few major examples here (Benet et al., 1990a; White, 1991). For all routes besides intravenous, the drug must pass through at least one body membrane before it can reach the circulatory system. Since membranes largely consist of lipids (fats), drugs that are more soluble in lipids are much more readily absorbed. The solvents and alcohol are examples of drugs that dissolve in lipids. Another factor is the form in which the drug is administered—drugs taken in aqueous solution are more rapidly absorbed than are drugs taken in suspension, in oily solution, or in solid form, because they are dissolved more readily at the site of absorption. Relatedly, when a drug is

Bioavailability
The portion of the original drug dose that reaches its site of action, or that reaches a fluid in the body that gives it access to its site of action.

Table 4-3   List of Drugs and Drug Classes Used for Medical or Nonmedical Reasons and the Ways They Are Most Often Administered

Drug	Route
Alcohol	Oral
Amphetamines	Oral; intravenous (preferred by the chronic, high-dose abuser); sniffed by occasional or new users
Barbiturates	Oral; rectal (through the mucous membrane of the rectum); subcutaneous; intramuscular; intravenous
Benzodiazepines	Most common is oral; some of these drugs may be administered intravenously or intramuscularly
Caffeine	Most common is oral; medically, occasionally by injection for mild stimulant properties; abusers have injected caffeine intravenously
Cannabis	Almost all routes have been used, but the most common is by smoking (inhalation)
Cocaine	Cocaine hydrochloride is taken through the nasal or other mucous membranes, such as those of the mouth, vagina, and rectum. Also taken intravenously. Cocaine freebase (crack) is volatile and, therefore, is most often vaporized in a freebase pipe and inhaled into the lungs
Heroin	Most commonly dissolved in water and injected subcutaneously, intramuscularly, or intravenously. May be inhaled by smoking or sniffed
Nicotine	Inhaled by smoking (cigarettes), nicotine in cigar or pipe smoke mainly absorbed across membranes of the mouth and upper respiratory tract. Also may be absorbed through membranes of the mouth (chewing tobacco) and nose (snuff), and through the skin
LSD (Lysergic Acid Diethylamide)	Oral; inhalation; the three injection routes; through the skin
PCP (Phencyclidine)	Oral; sniffed; inhalation by smoking (sprinkled on marijuana, parsley, tobacco or other smokable substance); intravenous injection

taken in solid form, as aspirin is, for example, its degree of solubility depends on conditions at the site of absorption. For instance, aspirin is fairly insoluble in the acidic environment of the stomach, and this places a limit on its absorbability. This relates to the importance of the environment in the gastrointestinal system and its influence on absorption for drugs that are taken orally, as we have discussed. Circulation at the site of absorption also influences it, as more blood flow speeds absorption. Finally, size of the absorbing surface makes a difference. Drugs are absorbed more rapidly from larger surface areas.

Since each of these and other factors may singly or in combination affect absorption, you can see why it is so difficult to specify a drug effect for a person under specific conditions at a specific time. This discussion also might have reaffirmed why intravenous injection is the most efficient way to get a drug to its sites of action. Many factors that may retard absorption are bypassed, because the drug is put in direct contact with the blood—the vehicle of drug distribution.

Drug Distribution

The biochemical properties of both the body and the drug have a lot to do with distribution of a drug to its sites of action. Because the blood transports a drug, it follows that regions of the body receiving the most blood get the most drug. Indeed, the heart, brain, kidney, liver, and other systems that receive a lot of blood get major portions of the drug shortly after absorption. Other parts of the body that receive less blood flow, such as muscle, viscera, and fat, may take considerably longer to receive the drug. Besides blood flow, **diffusibility** of membranes and tissues affects distribution: the more diffusible tissues receive the drug more rapidly.

> **Diffusibility**
> A more diffusible substance is more easily entered into, or "receptive" of, another.

Drug properties may influence distribution considerably. A major example is fat **solubility.** Drugs that are more soluble in lipids penetrate body membranes, and therefore reach sites of action more easily than do less soluble drugs.

> **Solubility**
> The ease with which a compound can be dissolved or entered into a solution.

The fat solubility of a drug plays a substantial role in how much of it can reach the brain. This is most important to us, as in this text we concentrate on drugs that affect the CNS. Although the amount of blood flow to the brain would make it a natural repository for drugs (and other chemicals) that enter the body, substances must cross the blood-brain barrier before they can reach the brain. As we noted in Chapter 3, the blood-brain barrier serves as a natural filter of toxins from the blood before they reach the brain. The filtering is accomplished because pores of the capillary walls in the brain are small and close together, which restricts the passage of substances through them. In addition, a thick wall of glial cells encloses the capillaries to form another line of defense. When a drug is highly fat soluble, like the benzodiazepine diazepam (Valium), it easily can pass through the capillary and glial cell membranes. However, passage of less fat soluble drugs is impeded (Johanson, 1992).

Another feature of a drug's chemistry that affects its distribution is whether it selectively binds to elements of the body. For example, some drugs, such as the barbiturates, may bind chemically to certain proteins in the plasma. The more "tightly" bound a drug is, the slower is its distribution to sites of action (Benet et al., 1990a; Leavitt, 1982; White, 1991). Similarly, some drugs have an affinity for fatty tissue in the body. In this case, the drug may be released but it can take a relatively long time. With such longer term unbinding, the drug may register in the blood for some time, yet the drug's release from fat tissues is slow enough that the psychoactive effects are negligible (White, 1991). A notorious example of a drug that has an affinity for fat is marijuana. With such a drug, its distribution is not even throughout the body because of selective binding, and the effects achieved by taking the drug are attenuated. Part of the dose does not immediately reach its sites of action.

In summary, the processes of drug absorption and distribution illustrate that a drug is a chemical that, when entered into the body, disrupts its steady biochemical state and produces system-wide reverberations. Absorption and distribution are the complex fundamentals of bioavailability, or how much drug reaches its sites of action. Bioavailability tells us most about drug effects. To understand the effects of a drug over time, it is essential to track its excretion or elimination from the body.

Drug Elimination

Drugs may be excreted from the body directly or first metabolized into products that are less likely to be reabsorbed. The metabolic by-products then are excreted. Enzymes in the liver play the major part in drug metabolism. Importantly, these enzymes also are present in other organs such as the kidneys and gastrointestinal (GI) tract. As a result, a drug administered orally is subject to a "first-pass effect," which means that enzymes in the GI tract break down a drug to some degree. Therefore, less drug than what was administered is eventually distributed to its sites of action. In Chapter 9 we discuss a study of differences between men and women in first-pass effects with alcohol.

One question that may have occurred to you is whether the drug metabolic by-products themselves have pharmacologic action. If this were true, then it would be difficult to see how a drug state ever would become deactivated. In fact, some drug metabolites are pharmacologically active and are responsible for unwanted **side effects** of different medications, for example. The metabolites of other drugs have desired psychoactive effects. Two examples are the metabolites of diazepam (Valium) and of chlordiazepoxide (Librium). In fact, one of Valium's metabolites is eliminated from the body more slowly than is Valium (Jacobs & Fehr, 1987). When metabolites are active, the action ends with further metabolism of the by-products or by their direct excretion in the urine (Benet et al., 1990a).

The kidney is by far the most important organ for excretion of both drugs and their metabolites, but excretion may occur in other ways. For example, drugs that are taken orally may be excreted directly in the feces. Drug metabolites may be excreted in liver bile. Drugs are excreted in mother's milk, which is not critical so much because of the proportion of drug that leaves the body this way, but because of the dangers posed to the nursing infant. Drugs also may be excreted through the lungs, which is why you can smell alcohol on a person's breath after he or she drinks it. Finally, drugs may be excreted in perspiration.

Pharmacologists have discovered that the rate of elimination of drugs from the body obeys two general laws called zero-order kinetics and first-order kinetics (e.g., Clark, Brater, & Johnson, 1988). Although we will not discuss these laws here, we want to note that knowledge of these laws is a great help to people who do research on drugs and to physicians when they prescribe medications. A term relevant to drug elimination that you may come across often is **half-life,** which is the time that must pass for the amount of drug in the body to be cut by half. Drug half-life actually is a term that has been given more importance than is warranted. In this regard, drug half-life has been discovered to be a result of other statistics that reflect the body's ability to clear a drug. These other statistics are directly linked to the kinetics law that the drug is obeying. In any case, you will see the term half-life again in this source and, likely, in others, so it is useful for you to know it.

Side effects
Effects of a drug other than those of central interest. Used most often in reference to the other-than-therapeutic effects of medications, such as the side effect of drowsiness for antihistamines. Note that what are considered a drug's side effects depends on what specifically the drug is being used for.

Half-life
The amount of time that must pass for the amount of drug in the body to be reduced by half.

Drug Testing   Discussing drug-elimination processes raises the topic of procedures that are used in drug testing. Drug testing is a term applied to various methods of determining drug use by analysis of urine or blood samples. Actually, analysis of urine samples (urinalysis) is more sensitive, because the drug's metabolites may be detected in urine. If the drug is detected in the blood directly, it is an indication of recent use (Miller, 1991).

The validity of drug testing depends on a variety of factors, including the dose of the drug last taken, the testing method used, and the laboratory quality-control procedures that are followed in testing. The detectability of use of a drug essentially depends on its clearance rates from the body and the clearance rates of the drug's metabolites. Table 4-4 is a list of common drugs of abuse, their range of elimination times, and their range of detectability in days by testing. The range of elimination times in Table 4-4 pertains to elimination of the drug itself (shorter time) and to elimination of the drug's metabolites (longer time) from the body. Alcohol has no range because its metabolites are used too efficiently in the body to be measured reliably (Miller, 1991).

The right-hand column of Table 4-4 gives a range of detection times under the best testing conditions. Detection times are enhanced substantially if the drug's metabolites can be measured by the testing method. Along these lines, note that detection time ranges are generally much shorter than elimination ranges of drugs and their metabolites. This is because the testing method is not sensitive enough to pick up the metabolite(s) at some point. Where that point is depends on the metabolite and the testing method. This also implies that a positive drug test does not necessarily give you precise information about when the drug actually was used. The exception, as we noted, is that if the drug is detected in blood, we then know that use was recent. A final point about Table 4-4 is that an acute dose of marijuana can be detected for up to eight days after use. In chronic users, the drug can be detected for well over a month after the last dose was taken.

Summary   Our discussion of drug elimination concludes our review of the first four steps of the drug experience and of pharmacokinetics. Figure 4-2 is a summary of what we have covered in this chapter so far. Given that we have a quantity of a drug (dose), we can administer it by one of several methods

Table 4-4   Common Drugs of Abuse, Range of Elimination Times, and Range of Detection Times

Drug	Range of Elimination Times	Range of Detection Times (Days)
Alcohol	Hours	Up to 1 Day
Cocaine	Hours–Days	.2–4.0
Marijuana	Weeks–Months	2–8 (Acute)
		14–42 (Chronic)
Benzodiazepines	Weeks–Months	7–9
Opiates	Days–Weeks	1–2
Barbiturates	Weeks–Months	3–14

Note: Shorter time in the elimination range refers to the drug itself, and the longer time to the drug's metabolites. (Adapted from information in Miller 1991, p. 299)

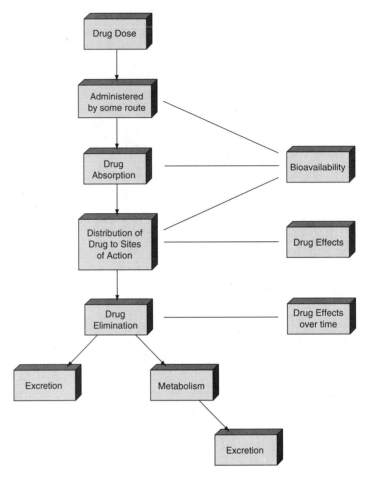

Figure 4-1   A summary of the first four steps of the drug experience and pharmacokinetics.

(route of administration). The drug then leaves its site of administration (absorption) to be distributed to the sites of drug action. The route of administration and biochemical factors influence the speed and amount of drug absorption. Biochemical factors also affect the amount of drug that is distributed. The latter refers to bioavailability, which tells us what portion of our original dose reaches sites of drug action. Bioavailability is the pharmacological basis of the drug experience. Once reaching their sites of action drugs are eliminated from the body, either by direct excretion or by metabolism into by-products that are excreted. The course of elimination of a drug is one influence of a drug effect over time.

It is important to point out that a drug's exit from the body may not be the end of the drug experience. In this regard, you will see in later chapters on specific drugs that elimination of a drug from the body often is associated with physical and psychological changes that are opposite to those that were caused by the drug. For example, the feelings of euphoria and tranquility that heroin causes switch to irritability and intense, extremely unpleasant physiological changes when the drug leaves the addict's body. The euphoria and high energy that typically are induced by cocaine and amphetamines turn to lethargy and depression as the drugs end their course of action. Such opposite (sometimes called "rebound") effects are important to us because of their influence on drug-use patterns. The rebound effect of depression that follows cocaine use is sometimes so unpleasant, for example, that the user feels a strong need to take more cocaine in order to stop the bad feelings. Avoiding the effects of heroin abstinence is a powerful force in the addict's continued use of the drug. When coming down from a dose of alcohol, people often feel sleepy and somewhat depressive, so they may try to recapture the more euphoric mood associated with just starting to drink by starting again.

PHARMACODYNAMICS

Our overview of pharmacokinetics prepares you for the description and explanation of drug effects—the subject of pharmacodynamics. In the remainder of this chapter we will present terms that pharmacologists use to describe drug effects, and the way such effects are represented graphically. This standard language of drug effects is essential to your understanding not only information in this text, but also much other information that is available on drugs and human behavior.

The Dose-Effect Curve

Knowing the size or magnitude of an effect for a range of drug doses is important. Earlier we saw that drug effects differ according to drug doses. Because representing the different effects a drug can have over a number of doses can become complicated quickly, a tool that would represent such information as clearly and efficiently as possible would be quite useful. In pharmacology, this tool is the dose-effect curve (formerly commonly referred to as dose-response curve), a standard way of representing drug effects resulting from taking different drug doses. This curve is a representation of some effect according to a dose of the drug. For example, several groups of people may drink different doses of alcohol and at a given point be asked to report their degree of relaxation. If the average reports of relaxation for each group were then plotted, we would have a dose-effect curve.

Figure 4-2 is a prototypic dose-effect curve. The vertical axis of the graph, which we have labeled "effect size," represents the change we are interested in recording. The kinds of changes that we emphasize in this text are reported in some generally accepted method of measuring mood, behavior, or nervous system function. Examples might include memory task performance, ratings of mood, or some measure of physiological arousal such as heart rate. On the vertical axis of the graph, the size of some effect is represented. Generally, the effect is depicted as going from smaller to larger. On the graph's horizontal axis the range of doses under investigation is represented, from smaller doses to larger ones. (Often the logarithm of the drug dose is represented on the horizontal axis.) Typically a minimum of three doses is studied. Creating the curve then is simply a matter of plotting the

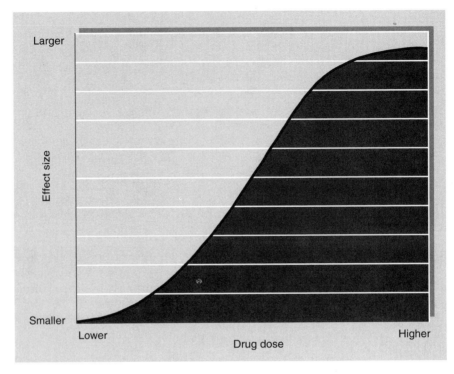

Figure 4-2   A typical dose-effect curve.

As a function of
A term expressing causality. In graphing functional relationships between two variables, changes in one variable (in this case, drug effect) resulting from changes in another (in this case, drug dose) are represented.

effect, however measured, for the individuals who have received a given dose of the drug under evaluation. Usually, different groups of subjects each receive a given dose, or the same subjects receive all the doses studied in an experiment lasting a number of days. In either case the average effect of each dose is plotted. When the effect is plotted for each dose investigated, the resultant graph represents effect **as a function of** drug dose.

Figure 4-2 shows that the effects of this hypothetical substance are not constant across different drug doses. Rather, the S-shape (sigmoid) of the curve reflects that an accurate description of this drug's effects requires specification of a dose. For instance, the hypothetical drug in Figure 4-2 produces greater effects as the dose increases. However, a limit exists; there is a plateau in the graph for the highest doses. This means that increasing the dose beyond a given level does not yield increased effects. One illustration of this is the effect of alcohol on simple reaction time, which is formally measured by timing a person's "yes-no" response to the presence or absence of some stimulus, such as a light. For the "average" drinker (see Chapter 9), having two 12-ounce beers in an hour has little effect on simple reaction time. However, after about four beers, reaction time is significantly increased (the person's response is slower). After five beers, reaction time is slowed even further. If the person had about nine beers in an hour, he or she might find it quite hard to stay awake, so that our ability to measure further deterioration in reaction time with additional drinking would yield little. At that point, if the person is having a hard time maintaining consciousness, then the possibility of—and the utility of—measuring further slowing of reaction time with a higher dose of alcohol would hover around zero. The plateau of the dose-effect curve in this instance would be reached at the alcohol dose equivalent of about nine beers.

The case of alcohol and simple reaction time shows that the question is not what effects does drug "X" have, but rather what is the effect of drug "X" at a specified dose.

Variations of the Dose-Effect Curve   Not all the effects of any drug may look like Figure 4-2 when plotted for a range of doses. One variant is a biphasic drug effect. This means an effect of a drug may go in one direction, say increase, as dose goes up, but then the effect changes direction (decreases) as the dose continues to go up. A biphasic drug effect is represented in Figure 4-3.

As illustrated, the drug effect increases in size as the drug dose increases to the moderate range. However, as the dose continues to increase, the curve changes direction to represent the decrease in drug effect with higher drug doses. In this example, the size of the effect essentially returns to close to the lowest drug doses. Heart rate is an effect that has been reported to be biphasic for both alcohol and marijuana (Blum, 1984).

Any drug may cause many different effects that can be measured. For each of these effects, a dose-effect curve can be plotted. Many of the curves look alike, and they usually are similar to that represented in Figure 4-2. However,

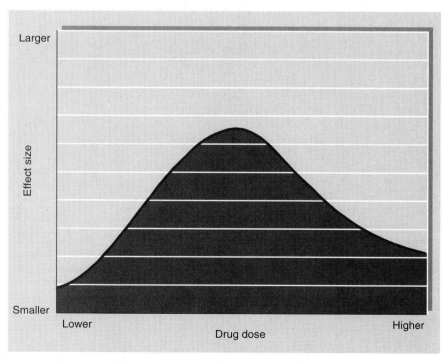

Figure 4-3   Dose-effect curve for a biphasic drug effect.

some of the dose-effect curves for a given drug could look quite different, depending on what effects are being compared. This brings out a major point: The dose-effect curve for a drug depends on the effect being measured. This is illustrated in Figure 4-4, which shows how college women in laboratory studies perceive their sexual arousal (one effect) and a physiological measure (such as vaginal blood flow) of their sexual arousal (a second effect) at lower to moderate doses of alcohol. Figure 4-4 looks a bit different from the other dose-effect curves we have depicted because we have changed how effect is represented (vertical axis) to accommodate a negative drug effect. As the figure shows, the college women perceived that their sexual arousal increased with increasing doses of alcohol, at least up to moderate doses (very high doses have not been studied). However, physiological measures of the women's sexual arousal show decreases as dose increased (Abel, 1985).

Slope, Maximal Effect, and Potency   Pharmacologists have a few terms they use to more specifically describe a drug's action. These are illustrated in Figure 4-5, which shows the dose-effect curves for two hypothetical drugs, A and B. The first feature of the curves is the slope, which refers to steepness. This aspect of the curve reflects the amount of latitude there is in drug dose before a stronger effect is reached. Slope can have very practical implications in prescribing drugs therapeutically or in considering potentially life-endangering

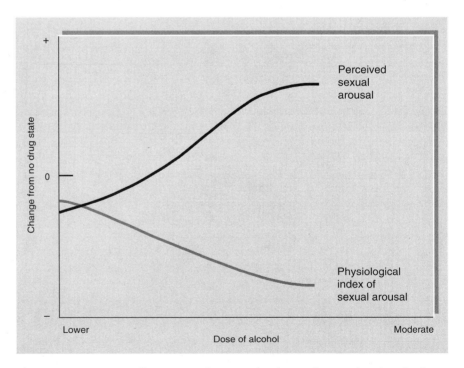

Figure 4-4   Dose-effect curves for perceived sexual arousal and a physiological measure of sexual arousal in college women after drinking low to moderate doses of alcohol.

effects of drugs taken nonmedically. Examples of the latter are the sedating effect of the barbiturates or of the effects that occur when taking a benzodiazepine drug (Chapter 10) and alcohol together. In Figure 4-5 curve A has a steeper slope than curve B, so as the curves rise to a plateau, a given dose of A yields a larger effect.

Two other terms illustrated in Figure 4-5 are a drug's **maximal effect** and **drug potency.** Maximal effect is defined by finding the peak of the dose-effect curve for a given effect. In Figure 4-5 that peak is where the curves reach a plateau. Drugs A and B are drawn to show two drugs with the same maximal effect. The last concept we have included in Figure 4-5 is drug potency—the dose of a drug that yields its maximal effect. On the dose-effect curve a line extending from the point of maximal effect down to the horizontal axis gives the dose called the drug's potency for an effect (Ross & Gilman, 1985).

Maximal effect
The most intense, or peak, level of a drug effect.

Drug potency
The dose of a drug that yields its maximal effect.

Effective and Lethal Doses

The last two terms we define to describe a drug's effect are its effective and lethal doses. Both terms arise from observing the considerable variability in individuals' reactions to a dose of a drug. As a result, testing one person does not accurately show a drug's effect at a given dose. Rather, an effect is viewed

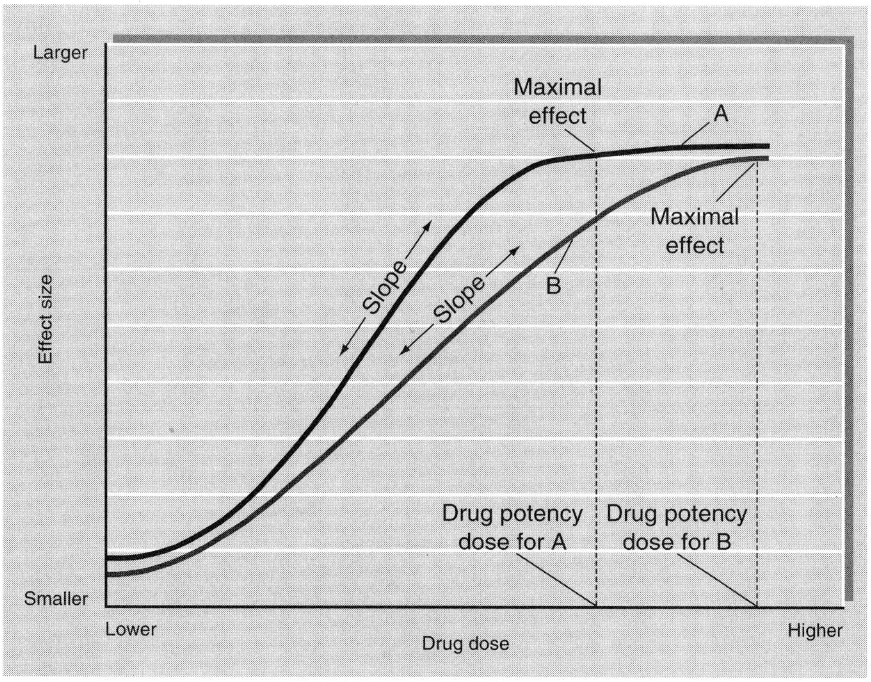

Figure 4-5   The dose-effect curves for two hypothetical drugs, A and B— the terms slope, maximal effect, and potency, which are used to further describe a drug's effects, are illustrated on the curves. (Adapted from information in Ross & Gilman, 1985)

in relative terms, or in the proportions of groups of people showing an effect at a specified dose.

Figure 4-6 shows the dose-effect curves for two effects of a hypothetical drug. One difference in Figure 4-6 from the previous dose-effect curves we have presented is that the percentage of individuals showing an effect rather than the effect size is represented on the vertical axis. This slight change allows for the illustration of effective and lethal doses. With these terms, an effect is specified, and then the drug dose associated with different percentages of people experiencing the effect is found.

The **effective dose** (ED) is the percentage of individuals who show a given effect of a drug at a given dose. Another way of expressing this is the dose at which a given percentage of individuals shows a given effect of a drug. The ED is found on a dose-effect curve by extending a horizontal line from the vertical axis at a given percentage to the relevant effect curve and from there dropping a vertical line to the drug dose axis. That point represents the ED for a given percent. The ED 50 is a standard term pharmacologists use, and the ED 50 for sedation for the hypothetical drug in Figure 4-6 is illustrated there. This means 50% of the people receiving that amount of the drug will experi-

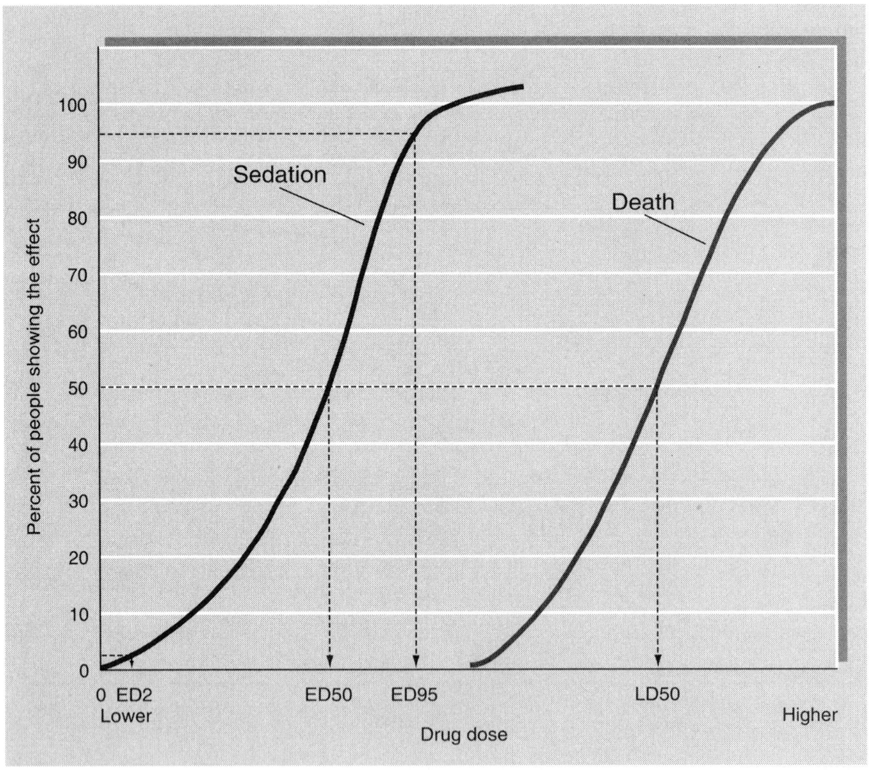

Effective dose
The percentage of individuals who show a given effect of a drug at a given dose.

Figure 4-6   The dose-effect curves for two of a hypothetical drug's effects, sedation and death—the curves are used to compute three effective doses for sedation and the drug's LD 50. (Adapted from information in Ross & Gilman, 1985)

ence sedation. Of course, the ED for any percent can be found in the same way. Two others are shown in Figure 4-6.

The **lethal dose** (LD) of a drug is a special case of effective dose. As the name implies, in lethal dose the effect of interest is death, and the LD is the percentage of nonhumans (human subjects are not used in experiments to determine the lethal doses of drugs) that die at a given dose of a drug within a specified time. A standard referent in pharmacology is a drug's LD 50, which is the dose at which 50 percent of the animals administered a given dose of a drug died within a stated time. Determining the LD 50 of a drug in humans is a matter of extrapolating the findings with animal subjects to humans. The LD 50 of our hypothetical drug is illustrated on the curve on the right in Figure 4-6.

A drug's EDs and LDs are of more than casual interest. Of particular importance for a city's health officials, for example, is the difference between a drug's ED and LD. When the difference is small, much more danger of accidental suicide exists for a person who is using drugs for nonmedical reasons. For some drugs such as caffeine or marijuana, the ED-LD difference is large. However, other drugs pose more of a problem. Accidental deaths due to heart damage from a dose of cocaine are referred to (case of Len Bias) in one Contemporary Issue Box in Chapter 1. Alcohol is another example. A 160-pound man with average tolerance to alcohol typically would report feeling relaxed after drinking about two drinks in an hour on an empty stomach. However, the LD 50 for alcohol would be reached if that same person drank about a fifth (25.3 oz) of whiskey in an hour. Such drinking occurs more often than you might think and has been responsible for the serious injuries or deaths that have occurred in fraternity hazings (initiation rites). Furthermore, when some drugs are combined, such as alcohol and the barbiturates, the resulting ED and LD are pushed even closer and the danger higher. We discuss the effects of combining drugs in the next section of this chapter.

A final point: the ED-LD difference is also important when a drug is administered by physicians for medical reasons. In medicine the goal is to find a drug that can be given in a dose that is therapeutic (that is, effective) for all patients, has no side effects, and that is not lethal. Accordingly, the **therapeutic index** has been derived. It is the ratio (LD 50/ED 50) for a given drug. Here, the ED of interest is the alleviation of the symptoms of some disease or injury. You can see that the larger a drug's therapeutic index, the more useful the drug is in medical treatment. Another point is that steeper dose-effect curves tend to have smaller therapeutic indices. The therapeutic index gives physicians a quick idea of the benefits of prescribing a drug as part of a specific treatment.

Drug Interactions

So far we have simplified our discussion by considering only one drug at a time. However, the study of pharmacodynamics often involves the consideration of the action of two or more drugs. A person could take multiple drugs at the same time, or take one drug before another has totally cleared his or her body. The extremes of this are seen in polydrug abuse, which we illustrated in Chapter 1.

Lethal dose
The percentage of individuals who are killed by a given dose of a drug within a specified time.

Therapeutic index
A measure of a drug's utility in medical care, it is computed as a ratio, (LD 50/ED 50).

The use of more than one drug at a time increases the complexity of the drug experience, because when two or more drugs enter the body they **interact.** An interaction between two drugs occurs if the effect of one modifies or alters the effect of the other. Drug interactions may be analyzed qualitatively or quantitatively; the degree of effect, or quantitative study, is by far the better understood in pharmacology. For quantitative study of drug interactions, there are both enhancing and diminishing effects of combining drugs.

Enhancing Combinations   Drug **synergism** is a term that is confusing because it has been used in different ways. Here we will use it to denote any enhancing drug interaction. Another word that currently is used in the same way as synergism is "potentiation." When two drugs are synergistic, the effects of taking them together are greater than the effects of taking either drug alone. In practice, pharmacologists find it difficult to tell for sure if synergistic effects are a simple result of adding the separate effects of the two drugs together, or if somehow one of the drugs is "multiplying" the effects of the other.

In quantitative studies of combining drugs interactions are represented by changes in the dose-effect curve. Figure 4-7 represents a synergistic relationship between drug A and drug B. You can see that the solid line is the typical dose-effect curve for a drug that we illustrated in Figure 4-2. The effect of

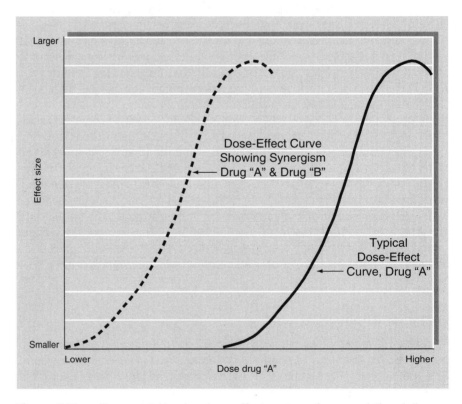

Figure 4-7   Representation by dose-effect curves of a synergistic relationship for drugs A and B.

People often use more than one drug at the same time, which sometimes can pose considerable risks to safety. The woman in the photograph is smoking a marijuana cigarette and drinking a glass of wine.

synergy between two drugs, then, is to "shift" the dose-effect curve for a drug to the left, represented by the broken line function in Figure 4-7. The broken line curve shows that more intense effects of drug A are evident at lower doses of it when drug B is present.

Diminishing Combinations   Drug **antagonism** is a term that refers to the diminished or reduced effect of a drug when another drug is present. As you might guess, drug antagonism is represented by a shift to the right in a drug's dose-effect curve. For example, the amphetamines, which are CNS stimulant drugs, antagonize alcohol's CNS depressant effects. However, the amphetamines do not reduce alcohol's impairment of motor skills, like driving (Blum, 1984).

The Importance of Interactions Between Drugs   An awareness of interactions between drugs is important for several reasons. In medical practice, knowledge of drug interactions is vital, because drugs often may be used in combinations for more effective treatment of an illness. Therefore, drug interactions may be used to improve medical care. On the other hand, interactions could be a problem for a physician. Usually difficulties occur if the physician is not aware of all the drugs a patient may be using at a given time. For example, the effects of one drug could cancel the therapeutic effects of another. Furthermore, prescribed medication could have detrimental or even lethal effects in the presence of other drugs. In this regard, an increasingly common practice is for pharmacies to have computerized profiles of the medications that a patient has been prescribed. Such information allows the pharmacist to inform customers how newly prescribed medications interact with other medications

Antagonism
The diminished or reduced effect of a drug when another drug is present.

they may be taking and what precautions should be followed to avoid harmful combined drug effects. This backup system to physician advice is available to all patients but is probably of most help in treating the elderly, who often take more than one prescribed medication at a time.

Drug interactions also may cause problems when considering different nonprescribed drugs, or combinations of prescribed and nonprescribed drugs. The most common examples are mixing drugs that depress the central nervous system (see Chapters 9 and 10). For example, as we said earlier, alcohol and the barbiturates may be lethal in their enhancement of each one's sedative effects. This drug combination has caused many intentional and accidental deaths.

Drug interactions also are important for their influences on the reasons for and patterns of human drug use. Accordingly, they are of central concern in this text. In this respect, individuals may intentionally combine drugs with the same or similar action to achieve a "super" high or effect. Or, individuals may use drugs that are opposite in effects in a deliberate effort for one drug to modify the other. An example heard commonly in treatment settings is the use of alcohol's depressant effects to modify the sometimes overstimulation induced by a dose of cocaine. Drinkers sometimes consume large amounts of black coffee (containing caffeine) in hopes of antagonizing alcohol's CNS depressant effects. Surprisingly, however, caffeine seems to do little to counter alcohol's effects on the CNS. These two examples refer broadly to the drug user's attempt to modify the intensity (quantitative) of drug effects. However, drugs also may be combined in order to achieve **qualitative** interaction effects that could not be achieved by any of the drugs separately. For example, users might take a depressant drug, such as one of the benzodiazepines, along with LSD to have a tranquil state while they experience the perceptual alterations that result from LSD (Jacobs & Fehr, 1987).

Qualitative
The kind, as opposed to quantity, of effect.

summary

- The basic principles of pharmacology emerge in discussing what contributes to the drug experience.

- To the pharmacologist, principles of pharmacokinetics and pharmacodynamics are most relevant to the drug experience.

- Drug dose is computed according to the recipient's body weight. A standard way of expressing dose is by milligrams of drug per kilogram of body weight.

- Eight routes of drug administration are discussed in detail: oral, subcutaneous, intramuscular, intravenous, inhalation, intranasal, sublingual, and transdermal. A route of administration is selected according to the drug taken and the goals and circumstances of administration.

- The route of drug administration affects the drug experience primarily through the rate of drug absorption and the amount of drug absorbed.

- Once they enter the body, drugs are absorbed into the blood and distributed to their site(s) of action. The body also works to metabolize and excrete drugs that enter it.

- Drug elimination may occur either by direct excretion of the drug from the body or by metabolism of the drugs and excretion of its by-products.

- A term related to drug elimination that is frequently used is drug half-life.

- Drug absorption, distribution, and elimination are affected by different biochemical factors and accentuate the complexity of the drug experience.

- Pharmacodynamics most directly concerns actions of the drug on the body and thus drug effects. This chapter covered fundamental terms that pharmacologists use to describe drug effects and ways to depict them.

- Pharmacologists use the dose-effect curve as a standard way to represent graphically the size of an effect according to the dose of a drug taken. The prototypical dose-effect curve has an "S" shape, but variations depend on the effects studied.

- Three concepts derived from a dose-effect curve offer valuable information about a drug's action: slope of the curve, drug maximal effect, and drug potency.

- Two other important features of a drug's actions are its effective dose and lethal dose. The relationship between these two doses is essential information for medical and nonmedical drug use.

- Pharmacodynamics often involves consideration of more than one drug in the body at the same time. Multiple drugs interact to contribute to the drug experience. Such interactions may be enhancing or diminishing.

- Drugs that enhance the effects of each other are called synergistic. Antagonism between drugs creates diminished drug effects.

- Enhanced and diminished drug effects refer to a quantitative (degree of effect) study of drug interactions. Qualitative study of drug interactions also is possible.

- It is essential to be aware of drug interactions for an understanding of both medical and nonmedical drug use.

ANSWERS TO WHAT DO YOU THINK?

1. A given amount of a drug has similar biological effects on all people.

F *The quantity of drug is adjusted for a person's body weight to yield pharmacologically equal amounts of drug.*

2. Despite the large number of known drugs, there are only three ways that drugs are commonly administered or taken.

F *There are a variety of ways to take drugs; we described eight of them in this chapter.*

3. The safest way to take a drug is orally, but it also is the slowest way of getting the drug into the blood.

T *The most common, and the safest, way to take a drug is orally. However, the speed of absorbing a drug when it is taken orally is slowed by several factors.*

4. Taking a drug intravenously is a highly efficient, safe way to get a drug into the blood.

F *The intravenous route is highly efficient because it bypasses problems of absorption associated with, say, the oral route. However, because the drug is injected directly into veins, the intravenous route is the most risky because of problems due to overdosing. Great caution is required if drugs are administered intravenously.*

5. Smoking is a relatively slow way of getting a drug into the blood.

F *For drugs that can be taken by inhalation, that route results in quicker absorption than does subcutaneous or intramuscular injection.*

6. Some drugs can enter the body through the skin.

F   *Some drugs can be taken through the skin, or trans-dermally. Nicotine is among the best known of such drugs.*

7. The body protects the brain from toxic substances.

T   *The blood-brain barrier prevents many toxic substances from reaching the brain. Drugs that are less fat soluble have a tougher time getting through the blood-brain barrier.*

8. The kidneys play the major part in drug metabolism.

F   *The liver is the organ primarily responsible for drug metabolism.*

9. Scientific study of the effects of drugs is difficult because there is no way to represent such effects quantitatively.

F   *The effects of drugs can generally be measured and can be represented by using dose-effect curves.*

10. When more than one drug is taken at a time the effects of one can enhance or diminish the effects of the other(s).

T   *Drugs modify the effects of each other when taken simultaneously. Sometimes the outcome is difficult to predict.*

11. Caffeine and alcohol have antagonistic effects.

F   *Although it is intuitive that caffeine and alcohol are antagonists, research shows that caffeine does little to alter alcohol's effects on the CNS.*

12. It is important to know about drug interactions because there is an increasing prevalence of using more than one drug at a time among people who present themselves for drug treatment.

F   *Although use of more than one drug is more common among people who present themselves for treatment, knowledge of drug interactions also is important because many people are prescribed more than one medication.*

5 Psychopharmacology and New Drug Development

WHAT DO YOU THINK?

True or False?

____   Gender differences in the effects of drugs are due primarily to body-weight differences.

____   There are individuals who have an "addictive" personality that predisposes them to have alcohol- or drug-use disorders.

____   Expectancies about alcohol's effects may be a more powerful determinant of its effects than is the pharmacological action of alcohol.

____   Theories about the effects of drugs on humans always have taken into account social and environmental factors.

____   Tolerance to a drug develops because of biological changes that occur as a result of using the drug.

____   Tolerance to a drug may be evident within the same occasion of using it.

____   A person who has tolerance to alcohol will also demonstrate tolerance to barbiturates the first time he or she uses the latter drugs.

____   There is no relationship between the drugs that animals show preference for and the drugs humans prefer.

____   The effects of a drug on animals tell us little about how that drug will affect humans.

____   In general, drug researchers are not concerned with placebo effects when studying the actions of a drug.

____   Because of the need for new medications to treat diseases like AIDS, government regulation of the process of drug development and marketing has been greatly simplified.

____   Folk uses of naturally occurring products are important sources of discovering new drugs.

In Table 4-1 we listed eight steps of the drug experience, but only six were discussed in Chapter 4. In this chapter we focus on steps 7 and 8; step 7 concerns biological and psychological characteristics of the drug user that affect the experiences humans have when they use drugs, and step 8 concerns social and environmental factors and their influence on the drug experience. Completing our drug experience steps listed in Table 4-1 raises the question of how that experience relates to human drug use, which opens our discussion of research methods in the field of psychopharmacology. (Another, narrower use of the term "psychopharmacology" is the study of drugs used to treat mental illness.) Psychopharmacology research, as you might guess, centers on the reasons behind drug-use patterns, and on the patterns of use themselves. Information on research basics will prepare you for understanding the process of discovering and developing new drugs, which we review in the last sections of this chapter.

CHARACTERISTICS OF THE USER

Differences among people probably account for most of the differences in how they react to a given dose of a drug. We will present only the major factors in this section, since any more extended discussion would preclude presentation of anything else in this book. Roughly, we can divide the characteristics into two types—biological and psychological.

Biological Characteristics

Inherited Differences in Reactions to Drugs There are genetically based differences in how people react to some drugs (Nurnberger, 1987). For example, differences among people in how their first dose of a drug affects them is called their **initial sensitivity** to a drug. Such differences are thought to be determined genetically. More generally, a lot of money is spent on research to discover the role genetics plays in causing the various substance-use disorders. Alcohol-use disorders in particular have received much attention from scientists. It is believed that inherited differences in how alcohol is experienced (as a result of action in the brain) and metabolized may be of major importance in some individuals' developing alcohol abuse or dependence.

Initial sensitivity
The effect of a drug on a first-time user.

Gender A specified dose of a drug administered to a man and a woman on average will have greater effects on the woman. This is due to the higher percentage of body fat, and therefore, a lower percentage of body water in women than in men. So, based on information you learned in Chapter 4, percentage of body fat may influence drug effects in two ways. If there is less body water because of more body fat, a drug will be more concentrated in the body and thus have greater effect. In addition, some drugs selectively bind to fat molecules in the body, so that the drug is eliminated more slowly with a higher percentage of body fat, and thus remains active in the body for a longer time.

Weight In Chapter 4 you saw that body weight is part of the formula for computing drug dose. This is because the concentration of a drug in the blood depends on how much blood and other body fluids are in the body. These fluids dilute an absorbed drug. Simply, a heavier person has more blood and other fluids, so for a given quantity of drug he or she would have less of a concentration of it than would a lighter person. As we noted above for gender differences, this contributes to a lesser drug effect in the heavier person.

Age Age can influence drug effects if the user is very young or old. Children are more sensitive to drugs because enzyme systems that metabolize drugs may not be fully developed. As a result, the drug stays active longer. In the

People differ in how they react when they use drugs in a given setting as a result of differences in biological and psychological factors.

elderly, these same enzyme systems may be impaired, with the same effect of increased duration of drug action.

Psychological Characteristics

How an individual's psychological characteristics affect the drug experience has often been studied in research on personality and drug use. Not surprisingly, how personality affects the drug experience is not easy to answer. Personality is a term used to represent a cluster of characteristics that describe the ways in which an individual thinks, perceives, feels, and acts. These characteristics are thought to be fairly constant, although variations occur in how a person acts in different situations. Nevertheless, personality characteristics are for the most part viewed as enduring.

One personality characteristic that has received a lot of attention regarding its relationship to drug use is sensation seeking. Zuckerman (1979) defined sensation seeking as "the need for varied, novel, and complex sensations and experiences and the willingness to take physical and social risks for the sake of such experience" (p. 10). Four different aspects of sensation seeking have been discovered: thrill and adventure seeking, experience seeking, disinhibition, and boredom susceptibility.

A number of studies have shown a positive relationship between sensation seeking and frequency of drug and alcohol use and the variety of drugs that are used. Thus, the more sensation seeking a person is, the more he or she tends to use alcohol and drugs, and to use more kinds of drugs. One explanation for these findings is that sensation seeking represents the individual's higher degree of sensitivity to the pleasurable effects of drugs. That is, sensation seeking is a summary term to represent one source of differences among people in how they experience drugs.

Personality factors also have been shown to influence the degree of stress reduction that is achieved from taking alcohol and other drugs. This is particularly important, because stress reduction has long been held to be a major reason why people drink and use drugs, particularly people who develop drug- or alcohol-use disorders. Sher (1987) developed the "stress response dampening" (SRD) model of alcohol and other drug use. Alcohol and other drugs such as the benzodiazepines are seen as having anxiety-reducing effects. People who experience such effects, therefore, are more likely than others to use drugs to cope with unwanted stress. Of particular interest here is that individuals seem to vary in the SRD of alcohol they experience according to their personality characteristics. For example, Sher and Levenson (1982) showed that people characterized as aggressive, impulsive, and extraverted were more sensitive to alcohol's SRD effects. Notably, studies have shown that those individuals who developed alcohol-use disorder tended to be high on these characteristics before they began to experience problems with alcohol.

A general discussion of research on personality and drug use cannot ignore the topic of the **addictive personality.** Essentially, this refers to an idea of a personality structure common to all individuals with substance-use disorder. The notion of addictive personality has generated a lot of research and discussion, and it remains a popular idea among people who practice treatment

Addictive personality
The hypothesis of a personality structure common to all people with substance-use disorder.

Individuals who enjoy bungee jumping probably would score high on a measure of sensation seeking.

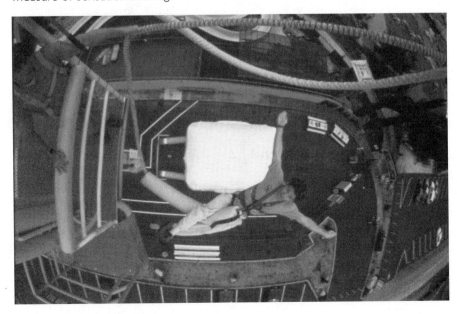

of individuals with the substance-use disorders. The addictive personality idea is important to us here for two reasons. The idea implies that people with a particular personality make-up experience a unique reaction to alcohol and drugs, or that they find alcohol and drugs especially valuable in coping with life's stressors. As a result, people with an addictive personality would be more likely to develop substance-use problems than people who do not have such a personality.

Although the idea may have some appeal, the research yields little evidence for an addictive personality. Instead, it seems that there are considerable personality differences among people identified as having substance-use disorder. In short, people who have problems with drugs and alcohol may have as many personality differences as any group of people does. However, we should note that studies of men and women who have developed substance-use disorders may be distinguished from people who did not develop such problems by personality characteristics predating development of the disorders (Barnes, 1979; Cox, 1986; Goldstein & Sappington, 1977). For example, characteristics of young men who later developed alcohol problems include self-centered, rebellious, impulsive, talkative, gregarious, and in need of personal power. Importantly, these studies do not provide evidence for an addictive personality. But this research does suggest that some personality characteristics may interact with other factors, like stress, the influences of peers, and the quality of family life to make it more likely that a person will develop problems with alcohol and drugs.

Drug Expectancies and Beliefs   A person's history of experience with drugs, his or her beliefs, knowledge, attitudes, and other thoughts about drugs are part of his or her uniqueness and, therefore, personality. These nonpharmacological variables can exert powerful influences on the drug experience. One factor that is prominent in this regard is what a person expects to achieve or happen when using a drug. This anticipation is called a **drug expectancy.**

Drug expectancy
A person's anticipation of or belief about what he or she will experience upon taking a drug.

A person's expectancies are based on previous experiences regarding a given psychoactive substance and its effects. These experiences could have been direct (that is, the person has used the substance) or indirect (that is, the person has been exposed to the substance and its effects through instruction, friends' use, television, advertising, reading, and so on).

Most of the research on expectancy has been conducted on alcohol use, and we review some of that work in Chapter 9. In one early discussion by MacAndrew and Edgerton (1969), it was proposed that what people have learned and believe about alcohol is an important determinant of how they conduct themselves while drinking. Thus, what people expect to happen when they drink can be an important factor in determining their response to the alcohol consumed. In some cases this may be more influential than alcohol's pharmacological action! Researchers have investigated alcohol-related expectancies by conducting studies in which some participants are told they are drinking alcohol but actually receive a nonalcoholic "placebo" beverage. A summary of such research (Hull & Bond, 1986) showed that expectancy effects seem most prominent with behaviors or emotions that society proscribes from free expression. Examples include aggression, sexual arousal, and humor. Therefore, it would be predicted that people who believe alcohol fosters aggression or enhances sexual arousal would experience those effects, but more because they expect that result than because of any specific pharmacological effect of alcohol.

Expectancies appear to have a considerable effect on the way people respond to other drugs as well. The use of marijuana is a good example (Orcutt, 1987). The person who anticipates a relaxed, "mellow" feeling is more likely to experience that result than the person who anxiously anticipates some type of drug-induced "loss of control" over his or her behavior. In part this relates to the ways the various sensations produced by the marijuana are interpreted or understood by the smoker. The same sensation might be interpreted positively by one user but negatively by another, and much of that discrepancy likely will be attributable to what the user expected to occur as a result of smoking.

SOCIAL AND ENVIRONMENTAL FACTORS

Although a relatively recent discovery, it now is generally accepted that the drug effects people experience are strongly influenced by social and environmental (setting) factors (Zinberg, 1984). The "environment" is an extremely broad term, and its study ranges from the level of government laws about alcohol and drug availability (Chapter 2) to the people and places that define the immediate drug-use setting (McCarty, 1985).

Setting factors seem to be particularly important in the effects of alcohol, marijuana, and hallucinogenic drugs. Pliner and Cappell (1974) demonstrated this point with alcohol. In this study, men and women drank moderate amounts of alcohol alone or with others. When subjects drank alone they mostly reported experiencing physical changes, like fuzzy thinking, sleepiness, and dizziness. In contrast, subjects who drank the same amount of alcohol but with others said their mood changed to feeling friendly and more pleasant. Since subjects who drank an alcohol placebo beverage reported no changes whether drinking alone or with others, it seems that the number of people you drink with affects how you interpret the physiological changes that alcohol induces.

Another example of the influence of the setting involves reactions to marijuana. Carlin, Bakker, Halpern, and Post (1972) noted that at lower doses of marijuana, smokers viewed others in the setting as more intoxicated than they actually were. The experimenters were able, again at lower doses of the drug, to enhance or diminish the degree of reported marijuana intoxication by having an accomplice act "up" or "down." Setting was not as influential at higher doses of marijuana. Studies such as these support Becker's (1963) ideas about the "making" of a marijuana user. Becker described this as a sociocultural process in which experienced users essentially "teach" new users what to anticipate, how to interpret the effects, what effects to enjoy, and what effects to ignore. Becker's ideas imply that what a person experiences when taking marijuana is influenced by his or her expectations about the drug's effects and by who is present in the drug-taking setting.

"I wasn't really persuaded to smoke [marijuana], I just watched everybody. I saw nobody going mad or anything; they were all laughing and having a good time. So . . . I smoked and got high. I liked the high and I smoked"

Research participant
(Cited in Zinberg, 1984, p. 85)

TOLERANCE

Repeated administration of a given dose of a drug often results in reduced response to the drug. This phenomenon, known as tolerance, was defined in Chapter 1. Here we will summarize major principles and explanations of tolerance. Our discussion of tolerance follows our overview of biological, psychological, and social/environmental characteristics of the user because, as you will see, tolerance involves all three types of factors.

Types of Tolerance

There is widespread agreement that there are three distinct types of tolerance involving quite different mechanisms. Regular use of a given drug results to some degree in **dispositional tolerance.** This refers to an increase in the rate of the metabolism of a drug, so that the user must consume greater quantities of it in order to maintain a certain level of the drug in his or her body.

Dispositional tolerance
An increase in the rate of metabolizing a drug as a result of its regular use.

Another type of tolerance is **functional tolerance.** Functional or pharmacodynamic tolerance means that the brain and other parts of the central nervous system become less sensitive to a drug's effects. There are two types of functional tolerance—*acute* and *protracted*. **Acute tolerance** (sometimes called tachyphyllaxis) is measured within the course of action of a single dose or first few doses of a drug. In this respect, when a person takes a dose of a drug, the amount of drug in his or her body—measured as the amount of drug in the blood, or blood level—rises to some peak level. For some drugs, at any point when the blood level is rising to peak there may be greater drug effects than there are at that same point when the blood level is falling. For example, people show acute tolerance to alcohol. One effect of alcohol when consumed in moderate amounts is impairment of short-term memory, or memory for events that occurred, say, in the past 30 seconds. Because there is acute tolerance to alcohol, we are more likely to see impairment in short-term memory when the blood level of alcohol is rising than when it is falling.

Functional tolerance
Decreased behavioral effects of a drug as a result of its regular use.

Acute tolerance
A type of functional tolerance that occurs within a course of action of a single drug dose.

A second example of acute tolerance is with regard to stimulant drugs like cocaine. Cocaine is a short-acting drug, and when the highly pleasurable effects of an initial dose begin to wear off, users are prone to taking another dose. However, the second administration—even when the same amount is taken—generally produces much less of a pleasurable high due to rapidly developing acute tolerance.

Protracted tolerance pertains to the effects of a given dose of a drug when it is administered more regularly or chronically. Protracted tolerance requires that the individual consume greater amounts of a drug in order to achieve an effect that was once achieved with a lesser dose. So, in our example of alcohol and short-term memory, a person may show impairment in memory today after drinking six cans of beer, when he or she formerly showed the same degree of impairment after drinking only three beers.

Protracted tolerance
A type of functional tolerance that occurs over the course of two or more drug administrations.

The third mechanism of tolerance involves a behavioral adjustment by the subject and is called **behavioral** or learned **tolerance.** For example, an individual with considerable experience with the effects of alcohol on motor coordination may learn to compensate for his or her intoxication by walking

Behavioral tolerance
Adjustment of behavior through experience using a drug to compensate for its intoxicating effects.

slowly or with a lower center of gravity to keep from falling—even if he or she is quite drunk. Other examples of learned or behavioral tolerance are discussed below.

In addition to the above mechanisms for tolerance, there are other types of tolerance to be introduced. For example, tolerance to one drug may extend to other closely related drugs—a phenomenon called **cross tolerance.** A person who has developed tolerance to one drug also will have tolerance to certain other drugs, even though he or she may never have taken those other drugs. A practical consequence of cross tolerance commonly occurs in surgical treatment. A person who is highly tolerant to drugs that depress the central nervous system, such as alcohol or the barbiturates, creates problems for the anesthesiologist. Anesthetic drugs are useful in surgery because of their depressant effects. As a result, drugs like alcohol or the barbiturates would show cross tolerance to drugs used medically as anesthetics.

Our discussion of types of tolerance suggests how complicated it is. There are further complications. For example, tolerance may develop to some of the effects of a drug but not to others. For instance, the barbiturates present a complex case. Tolerance develops rapidly to the sleep-inducing and pleasantly intoxicating (e.g., euphoria) effects of these drugs. However, tolerance does not develop as readily to their effects of impaired motor coordination and slowed reaction time. And, tolerance to the anticonvulsant effect of the barbiturate phenobarbital does not seem to occur at all (Jacobs & Fehr, 1987). Another example is the amphetamine drugs. Tolerance to their appetite-suppressant and euphoric effects may develop rapidly. However, the **psychosis**-like effects of amphetamines are not subject to tolerance. Similarly, one amphetamine drug, methylphenidate (Ritalin), is used to treat **attention deficit disorder** in children. Fortunately, tolerances do not develop to the **paradoxical** attention-focusing and calming effects that Ritalin has on these children. Finally, **reverse tolerance** to a drug also may occur, which is increased sensitivity to the effects of a drug with its repeated use. Reverse tolerance has been reported, for example, for marijuana and cocaine.

Explanations of Tolerance

Because tolerance is so important in psychopharmacology and is so fascinating, there has been no shortage of effort to explain how tolerance to a drug develops. So far, no one theory has been able to account for all the nuances in tolerance that have been observed, but there are a few themes that can account for portions of what has been discovered about tolerance. These theories reflect current thinking that tolerance is multifaceted and involves both biological and learning processes.

Cell Adaptation Theory   One explanation for tolerance that has been around for over 40 years is called the adaptation-**homeostasis** hypothesis (Cicero, 1980). It is assumed in this theory that a drug's action occurs on specific cells in the central nervous system (CNS). Because of the plasticity of the CNS, the cells become "adapted" to the presence of the drug with repeated exposure to it. The adaptation allows the cells to maintain normal functioning at a given

Cross tolerance
Tolerance to a drug or drugs never taken that results from protracted tolerance to another drug or drugs.

Psychosis
A severe mental disorder whose symptoms include disorganized thinking and bizarre behavior.

Attention deficit disorder
A disorder of childhood with features such as greater-than-normal amount of activity, restlessness, difficulty concentrating or sustaining attention, and impulsivity.

Paradoxical
Contrary to what is expected. A paradoxical drug effect is one that is opposite in direction to what is expected, based on the drug's chemical structure.

Reverse tolerance
Increased sensitivity to a drug with repeated use of it.

Homeostasis
A state of equilibrium or balance. Systems at homeostasis are stable; when homeostasis is disrupted the system operates to restore it.

drug dose. As a result, more drug is required to disrupt cell functioning. This required increase is called tolerance.

The idea of cell adaptation actually is a general one that refers to the notion that some kind of changes occur in the cells of the CNS to account for the changes we call tolerance to drugs. The idea of cell adaptation is important, because it seems that changes in a drug's effects as a result of its repeated use are due only in minor part to dispositional tolerance. Instead, protracted functional tolerance is more important, and the reduced sensitivity to a drug in the CNS seems to be due to cellular changes there. Several hypotheses have been proposed regarding the specific changes that might explain tolerance at the cellular level. For example, chronic exposure to a drug that affects a particular neurotransmitter system results in a reduced synthesis of that transmitter. Because of reduced transmitter levels, it might then require more drug to effect the same overall neurochemical actions. Alternatively, there is evidence that repeated exposure to drugs may reduce the number of receptor sites on neurons that are activated by the drug. This process is called down-regulation and could also explain the phenomenon of cellular tolerance. However, the specifics of those changes have not yet been determined (Koob & Bloom, 1988; Tabakoff & Hoffman, 1988).

Drug Compensatory Reactions and Learning   In the 1970s scientists discovered that tolerance to drugs is in part learned. To illustrate the type of observations that led to this conclusion, imagine that two people who are "theoretically equal in all ways" take a particular dose of a drug on 10 occasions. Person A takes the drug every time under the same conditions, while person B takes the drug under different conditions every time. For example, the room where B takes the drug may vary, the color of the drug tablets may change, and so forth. Then on the 11th occasion, tolerance for some effect of the drug at the specified dose is measured in A and B under the conditions that A took the drug 10 previous times. Who would show a greater degree of tolerance? The cell adaptation hypothesis, for example, would predict equal tolerance for A and B. Yet numerous studies of humans and other animals show that A would show the greater degree of tolerance (Hinson, 1985). Such findings have led to the idea that tolerance may be in part learned.

In order to understand this idea you have to know about compensatory reactions. When an event, like taking a drug, occurs to disrupt the body's homeostasis, then sometimes the body counteracts the disruption with a reflex-like response. In this case the counterreaction would be an effect opposite to the drug effect. So, for example, when you drink two cups of coffee, the caffeine is absorbed and acts to increase your heart rate. Simultaneously, your body begins to work to counteract this effect, that is, a compensatory reduction in heart rate begins. This aspect of compensatory reactions tells you that when you take a drug, there are two major actions that are biologically triggered: one is the drug effect, whatever it might be, and the other is homeostatic counterreaction.

One more part of compensatory reactions is that, with repeated use of a given dose of a drug they are thought to become stronger. You can see that we have the makings of an explanation of tolerance here, and one that was made very prominent about 20 years ago by two psychologists, Richard Solomon and John Corbit, when they published their "opponent process" theory of motivation (Solomon & Corbit, 1974).

Learning enters with the final part of the explanation, which involves the phenomenon of classical conditioning.[1] The cues associated with drug taking, such as where it is taken, who is there, and what colors the pills are, are "conditioned stimuli" that become associated with drug actions and compensatory reactions. Over repeated occasions of pairing drug taking and drug-taking cues, just presenting the drug-taking cues alone may elicit a drug compensatory reaction. For example, presenting drug-taking paraphernalia, such as syringe and tourniquet, may elicit strong urges in IV heroin or cocaine abusers to use their respective drugs. This urge to use is based on elicitation of biological reactions associated with drug deprivation. Therefore, drug compensatory reactions—one hypothesis of what underlies tolerance—seem to build in strength with their repeated pairing with the same environment. They seem to be tied to the specific drug-taking context. As a result, the "sum" of the drug effect and countereffect that is observed when a person takes a drug depends on how often the same drug-taking conditions have occurred in the past. The higher the number of pairings, the larger the compensatory reaction, and the smaller the observed drug effect. In our initial example, that is why person A showed more tolerance than B did—the drug-taking event never changed for A, so that conditioning or learning in that context was stronger than it was in B, who changed contexts every time.

In addition, because these stimuli associated with drugs come to elicit reactions opposite the drug, exposure to these stimuli in the absence of the drug may produce discomfort or craving in the user. For example, people trying to quit cigarette smoking often report that the smell of tobacco produces cravings, and cocaine crack users may react strongly to the sight of a crack pipe. Only when people have been exposed to these stimuli many times without the drug do these effects dissipate—a process called extinction.

Final Notes on Tolerance   Once tolerance to a drug effect has developed, it is not irreversible. In this regard, a period of abstaining from a drug increases the user's sensitivity to drug effects that he or she may have become highly tolerant to in the past. This, for example, has resulted in the deaths by overdose of some heroin abusers who have resumed heroin use after a relatively long time of not using the drug. When use was resumed there was a failure to take into account the loss of tolerance that resulted from the long period of abstinence. In general, acute tolerance reverses in a short time period, while protracted tolerance requires more extended abstinence to reverse. Learned or behavioral tolerance may not reverse at all unless special procedures such as extinction are used.

Another point about tolerance concerns its reacquisition. Often, resumption of use of a drug after a long period of abstinence from it results in

[1]Classical conditioning is a type of learning in which, by repeated pairing, a second stimulus elicits a response similar to that elicited without prior learning by another stimulus. For example, a puff of air, a type of stimulus, blown at the eye elicits an eye blink. If, say, a buzzer, which normally does not elicit an eye blink, repeatedly follows by about a half-second an air puff directed at the eye, at some point presenting the buzzer alone will elicit an eye blink. We then would say that classical conditioning has occurred: the buzzer now elicits a reaction that it did not before the repeated pairing with the puff of air.

Contemporary Issue
TOLERANCE AND DUI LAWS

There have been almost radical changes in the attitudes and behaviors of U.S. politicians and other citizens about the availability of alcohol and its legal and social consequences. For example, the legal drinking age in the United States is now 21 for all alcoholic beverages, compared to less than 10 years ago when many states had legal drinking ages of 18 or 19. Another major area is laws about driving under the influence (DUI) of alcohol (and other drugs). These laws pertain to an established blood alcohol level. At this writing, the point at which the individual is declared legally intoxicated is .10% in 40 states and .08% in the other states. Arrest and conviction for driving at this level of intoxication now bring far harsher penalties than before, especially for repeat offenders. The main reason behind this change is compelling: for years it had been a consistent finding that about 50% of the traffic fatalities in the United States are associated with alcohol.

A blood alcohol level of .10% was chosen for several reasons, but a central one is that the driving skills of the average person are greatly impaired at that level. Now that you know something about tolerance to a drug, and alcohol is one of the drugs that tolerance develops to, what do you think of the "average driver" approach to the DUI law? Do you see any value in the argument that arrest should be based on behavioral (especially driving skills) impairment of the driver at a given blood alcohol level, whether it is above or below .10%? What do you see as the health, social, and political consequences of this stance?

---

the reacquisition of tolerance more quickly than it developed when first acquired (Kalant, LeBlanc, & Gibbins, 1971).

The information so far in this chapter and in Chapter 4 completes our overview of the drug experience and the factors that affect it. We have shown you that in humans the drug experience is complex, as it is influenced by biological, psychological, and social/environmental factors. This knowledge about the drug experience prepares us to address the fundamental topic of this text: the links from the drug experience to the behavior of drug use, or as commonly referred to by scientists, "drug-taking behavior." To begin answering this question we turn to some of the principles and methods of **behavioral pharmacology,** which is the specialty area of psychopharmacology that concentrates on drug use as a learned behavior.

Behavioral pharmacology
The specialty area of psychopharmacology that concentrates on drug use as a learned behavior.

BEHAVIORAL PHARMACOLOGY

The premise of behavioral pharmacology is that drug use is a learned behavior that is governed by the same principles as any other learned behavior. We already saw in this chapter how some aspects of drug use may be influenced by a learning process called classical conditioning, so we will not discuss that further. Instead, we will emphasize in this section drug use as an "operant" or voluntary behavior.

Reinforcement and Punishment

The basic principle of operant learning is that behavior is controlled by its consequences: reinforcement and punishment. A **reinforcer** is a consequence of a behavior that increases the likelihood that it will occur in the future. As some everyday examples, if studying for an exam is followed by getting an "A" on it, then studying is more likely to occur when it is time for the next exam. If a person who has not eaten for 12 hours goes to the refrigerator and finds food, then at the next occasion of food deprivation going to the refrigerator is a more likely event. In these two examples, getting an "A" and food are reinforcers.

When receipt of something, such as an "A" or food, results in an increase in the behavior it followed, it is called positive reinforcement. Another concept is negative reinforcement. A behavior may increase in frequency if it results in avoidance of or escape from something. In this case, the reinforcer is avoidance of or escape from something, in contrast to receipt of something in positive reinforcement. When a behavior increases in likelihood because it results in avoidance of or escape from a stimulus, it is called negative reinforcement. Common examples include turning on the air conditioning to escape the heat of a summer day, slamming on the brake of your car to avoid an accident, or changing the subject of conversation to escape an unpleasant topic.

A **punisher,** on the other hand, is a consequence of a behavior that suppresses or decreases its likelihood. We touch a hot stove only once because of the consequence that was transmitted to our finger tips. If inviting an attractive friend out for a date is followed by insults and rejection, the likelihood of trying again will probably decline.

You may reasonably wonder what getting an "A," changing conversation topics, and burnt fingers have to do with drug use. If, as behavioral pharmacologists believe, drug-taking behaviors are controlled by their consequences, then drug users must derive either positive or negative reinforcement from their behavior, and experience relatively little punishment for it. Thus, the study of drugs as reinforcers has become an important research area. Behavioral pharmacologists often study drug access as consequences for behavior in what are called **self-administration studies.** As the name implies, a drug self-administration study involves testing whether the research participants will "give themselves," or self-administer, a drug. Imagine that an animal, say a rat, has no experience whatsoever in psychopharmacology experiments. The essential question is whether the rat can be trained to perform a simple behavior, like pressing a lever, if the lever press is followed by access to or infusion of some drug. Further, if the rat meets the challenge of learning the lever press, the question becomes whether it will continue to lever press in order to get the drug. Based on about 25 years of research, the answer to both questions is a resounding "yes." And not just rats—the yes applies to monkeys, baboons, dogs, mice, and humans as other examples. An impressive array of drugs has been tested and includes alcohol, cocaine, opioids, PCP, barbiturates, benzodiazepines, amphetamines, and nicotine (Bozarth, 1987; Mello & Griffiths, 1987; Young & Herling, 1986).

What could be said about these strong and consistent findings is that humans and other animals, under given environmental, biological, and

Reinforcer
A consequence of a behavior that increases its likelihood.

Punisher
A consequence of a behavior that suppresses or decreases its likelihood.

"I think maybe it is time we stopped all the . . . nonsense about social milieus and how your daddy fell off a horse . . . and just say . . . what you mean which is 'I get loaded because I love to do it' "
Respondent cited in Le Dain Commission *Interim Report*
(Cited in Brecher, 1972, p. 456)

Self-administration study
A study that involves testing whether research participants will "give themselves" a drug.

psychological conditions, "prefer" the drug experience. They show this preference experimentally by voluntarily working to obtain the drug. As one research group put it: "abused drugs are those that serve as positive reinforcers and thereby maintain drug-seeking behavior" (Henningfield, Lukas, & Bigelow, 1986, p. 75).

In our concern about human drug use, the temptation is strong to "get behind" the preference to find out its basis, to discover why the drug state is a preferred one under some circumstances. This question has been the topic of numerous studies. For example, we did an informal review of survey questionnaire items that have been used among adults (18 years of age or older) in the United States. We came up with almost 50 reasons for using alcohol! Some examples are to expand awareness and understanding, to celebrate something important, to relax, to make sex better, to overcome shyness, to help forget worries, and to increase courage and self-confidence. The same array of mood and behavior changes has been recorded for the "drugs of abuse" other than alcohol (Barrett, 1985).

It is important to insert a note of caution here. There is a high, positive correlation, or association, between pleasant or desired drug effects and their reinforcing effects in humans (Griffiths & Woodson, 1988). However, the correlation is not perfect. Therefore, asking people why they use a drug or what they like about it is only an indirect way of studying a drug's reinforcement value. Technically, the reinforcement efficacy of a drug is measured by its ability to maintain or increase the frequency of a behavior that access to the drug follows.

Self-administration studies also are a powerful source of knowledge about drug use because they show that not all drugs have reinforcement value. Again, it seems that drugs that tend not to be abused by humans, such as the psychiatric drugs (see Chapter 11) chlorpromazine and imipramine, are not self-administered by other animals. Another insight about drug abuse that can be derived from reinforcement principles is that in general reinforcers are most effective when they are presented immediately following a behavior. When a drug like crack is smoked or heroin is injected intravenously, the drug taking is reinforced almost instantly by the "rush" or flash and it is thus not surprising that these methods of delivery lead to addiction more frequently.

Operant Principles and Drug Dependence

Principles of operant learning and drug self-administration may help us understand changes that take place in drug use over time. For example, initial use of most drugs is not determined by drug reinforcement, but rather is typically in response to the instructions or advice of peers, parents or a physician. Only when the individual has actually taken the drug will the user experience the drug effects that may reinforce behavior. Thus, in regard to drugs with powerful reinforcing properties the observation that an "ounce of prevention is worth a pound of cure" may be quite valid.

Although initial drug use may be instigated by social factors, continued use will more likely be determined by the sorts of positive reinforcement effects noted above. However, as drug use continues and increases in frequency, a change in motivation may occur. Consider that with chronic use tolerance develops to the effects of many drugs, and that withdrawal symptoms may occur when the drug wears off. Thus, because of tolerance the effects desired by the user are more difficult to experience, but unless the user takes the drug, withdrawal distress is felt. Taking the drug now relieves the unpleasant withdrawal symptoms and thus produces negative reinforcement. The general principle is that, for some drugs, especially those associated with significant levels of physical dependence, as initial use becomes more chronic incentives for use may come to include negative as well as positive reinforcement contingencies (Crowley, 1981). Negative reinforcement may also be important in early use of some drugs. For example, alcohol is often reported used to escape unpleasant feelings of anxiety or depression. Because drugs such as alcohol can elevate mood rapidly, persons who are prone to negative mood states may be more vulnerable to abuse.

So far we have illustrated that access to a drug as a consequence of behavior can be a powerful force in maintaining it. But we still have not addressed the negative drug effects we reviewed in Chapter 1 that have been extremely serious for some individuals and for society in general. Perhaps the major challenge for people in the addictions field is to explain humans' continued use of drugs in the face of punishing consequences. At least part of the explanation may be that punishment, like reinforcement, is most effective when it is immediate. In general, the impact of a consequence decreases the further removed it is from the target behavior. For example, the decision of whether to eat a piece of luscious chocolate cake is usually more powerfully affected by how the cake will taste if eaten now than by the weight gain or tooth decay later. Similarly, some of the negative consequences of drug use,

Despite the possible consequences of a hangover from overindulgence in alcohol, its consumption remains quite popular.

like social, family, and health problems, do not tend to occur until some time after any given episode of drug use. Even at that such consequences are not certain. This contrasts sharply with the immediate, desirable effects of drugs of abuse. As such, immediate consequences have a lot more control over an individual's drug-use patterns than do the distant, more negative consequences. Note that this idea of delay of reinforcement holds even if the delay is not that long. People have been known to put off considerations of a hangover tomorrow for the pleasures of drinking alcohol tonight, for example.

These behavioral principles have proven to be useful in developing treatment strategies for drug dependence. The idea is to reduce drug use by arranging punishment for drug use and reinforcement for abstinence (see Budney, Higgins, Delaney, Kent & Bickel, 1991; Higgins, Delaney, Budney, Bickel, Hughes, Foerg & Fenwick, 1991 for examples). We will say more about these approaches to treatment in Chapter 16.

The drug self-administration procedure is perhaps the most obvious method in behavioral pharmacology through which research with animals can provide important information about human drug abuse. However there are other important methods, and we will consider two of them: drug discrimination and the anticonflict procedure.

Drug Discrimination

Drug-discrimination study
A research procedure that primarily concerns the differentiation of drug effects.

Another method in behavioral pharmacology is the **drug-discrimination study,** which is important because it provides a way of asking nonhuman subjects about the subjective effects of drugs. It has been shown that multiple species of animals can be trained to make a target response in order to achieve some reinforcer, such as food, based only on a drug state. For example, a rat may first learn to press a lever for food reinforcement. Then over multiple sessions it is injected either with some drug, for example, an amphetamine, or a "placebo" saline solution (a solution containing salt), and placed in an experimental chamber that has two levers for pressing. A press of one of the levers results in food when the animal has been injected with the amphetamine, and a press of the other lever is reinforced when the animal has been given the placebo. Pressing the "wrong" lever for a respective drug state (here, drug or placebo) results in no food. With just the internal drug state as the animal's signals, it can learn what lever to press to receive food. This shows that the animal can learn to discriminate between drug and nondrug states. Naturally, this basic paradigm can be extended to test ability to discriminate among different doses of a drug, and among different drugs. Drug-discrimination studies are important for knowledge about drug use because they can help us to explain the bases of perceived similarities and differences between internal changes produced by different drugs and by different doses of the same drug (part of what we have called the drug experience). Thus, an animal trained to discriminate amphetamine from saline will respond on the amphetamine lever when injected with the related stimulant cocaine, but not when alcohol or other depressants are administered. Similarly, if LSD is the training drug, other hallucinogens will be "recognized." These techniques have allowed behavioral pharmacologists to classify experimental drugs according to their "subjective" effects even before they have been administered to people (Colpaert, 1987).

Conflict Paradigm

The last major method of behavioral pharmacology that we will present is called the **conflict paradigm.** The conflict paradigm is generated by creating a history of some behavior being followed by both reinforcement and punishment. So, to return to our previous example, a rat may be trained to press a lever for food reinforcement. Once this learning occurs, then the lever press is also punished, say by administering electric shock to the animal if the lever is pressed during some programmed time period. You can see why this is called the conflict paradigm: the rat has a learning history of both reinforcement and punishment for the same behavior. This arrangement of consequences typically suppresses the behavior in question.

Conflict paradigm
A research procedure that concerns the effects of a drug on a behavior that has a history of both reinforcement and punishment.

The conflict paradigm is important to us because it has been shown to be sensitive to drugs such as benzodiazepines that are in the family we call "antianxiety drugs." In this regard, when an animal is injected with such drugs the usual disruption in behavior seen by introducing the punishment component of the conflict does not occur when the animal has been given an antianxiety drug. Anticonflict effects in animals have been found for a range of drugs that have been shown in humans to have the effect of reducing the perception of anxiety (see Chapter 10).

These basics of behavioral psychopharmacology have been extremely important in advancing our knowledge about drug use and drug effects. As such, a lot of what we say in the rest of this text about specific drugs or drug classes was discovered using behavioral pharmacology principles and methods. Another way those principles and methods have been extremely important is in the development of new drugs, which we will review in the next section of this chapter. For example, self-administration studies with animal subjects can tell us a lot about the abuse potential of a drug that is being developed for medical reasons, or whether prolonged use of a new drug has toxic consequences.

Therefore, knowledge of principles and methods of behavioral pharmacology in animals is essential to your understanding new drug development. Before we get to that, however, we will address questions of the generality of animal research and of the use of human subjects in drug research.

ANIMAL MODELS AND HUMAN DRUG USE

Much has been learned about drug effects in humans from research on animals other than humans. Yet a question that still is asked frequently is the relevance of findings about drugs based on nonhuman animals. A more technical way to ask this question is, how **generalizable** to humans are findings based on animals? The answer is that generalizability is remarkably good. In our discussion of drug self-administration studies, you saw the similarities between different species of animals, including humans, in the reinforcement

Generalizable
Applicability of a research finding from one setting or group of research participants to others.

value of drugs. Other areas of comparable generalizability include the effects of drug dose, age, the presence of other drugs in the body, and the influence of environmental factors on drug use (Johanson & Uhlenhuth, 1978; Vuchinich & Tucker, 1988).

It is highly fortunate that what we learn about drugs in animal studies can be used to learn more about human drug use and effects. Such research has vastly increased our knowledge about human drug use and effects with-

Contemporary Issue
ANIMAL RIGHTS AND ANIMAL RESEARCH

Research with nonhuman subjects became a highly controversial issue in the last 15 years. Animal rights activists have sought to ban or disrupt research at many different laboratories. Activists charge that animal research has little or no value in human affairs and that researchers are unnecessarily cruel to animals.

Regarding their value in human affairs, animals have contributed greatly to modern medicine, in general, and to our understanding of drugs and behavior in particular. Drugs used to treat or prevent rabies, smallpox, polio, diphtheria, rickets, beriberi, diabetes, tetanus, schizophrenia, anxiety, thyroid disorders, arthritis, and leprosy are some notable examples of treatments developed through animal research. Virtually all the techniques of modern surgery, treatment of disease with antibiotic drugs, and drug treatments for pain owe their developments to animal research. However, some of the studies that led to these developments involved exposing animals to pain or distress, and practically all of these studies involved sacrificing animals' lives to improve human welfare.

Serious ethical issues are raised by the assumption that human welfare is paramount. Those who defend animal rights argue animals have rights equivalent to those of humans. If this position is taken, then most animal research would have to be viewed as unethical, but so would the practices of killing animals for food, or destroying their habitat for human cities. Furthermore, if animal research is discontinued, we would lose important tools in helping to improve our ability to treat and prevent diseases like cancer, heart disease, AIDS, mental disorders, and substance-use disorders.

To ensure that animal welfare is given high priority in animal laboratories, the federal government and professional organizations have placed animal research under tight regulations. For example, all animal research at institutions receiving federal funding must be reviewed by the Institutional Animal Care and Use Committee, or IACUC. Members of the IACUC must include a veterinarian and nonscientists who are not affiliated with the institutions. The research must conform to accepted ethical standards, and all possible steps to minimize animals' discomfort must be taken. The IACUC makes unannounced site visits to laboratories, and if regulations are not followed, can shut down research projects. Thus, measures are being taken to assure that when animals are used in research, they are treated as humanely as possible, and that the research is justifiable.

out unduly risking human health. Furthermore, there are some **causal relationships** between drugs and functioning in parts of the human body, like the brain, that never could have been established with certainty without animal studies.

You should keep in mind that, in science, generalizability is always an "empirical question." That is, we cannot safely assume that what we find in one experimental setting will automatically apply to the next. Rather, we do a second experiment, varying some essential factor about the individual or the setting, to see if what was found in the first experiment applies to the second one, too.

Causal relationship
There is a causal relationship between variables if changes in a second variable are due directly to changes in a first variable.

HUMAN BEHAVIORAL PHARMACOLOGY

Ethical Issues

Just as there are ethical issues involving animal research (see Contemporary Issue Box), when humans become subjects in drug research a number of ethical dilemmas are posed. In many kinds of biomedical research, there is potential for harm to befall subjects. Some of the atrocities committed in the name of biomedical research in Nazi Germany led the post-war scientific community to adopt a set of ethical guidelines called the Nuremberg Code to govern scientific research. The basic principles of the code are that research with humans cannot be conducted without the subjects' responsible, voluntary, informed consent. That is, the subjects must agree to participate in the study and must give consent without coercion after being told all risks or potential problems related to the experiment.

Despite the principle of informed consent, there can still be ethical difficulties in human research. After all, when a new drug is developed, someone has to be the first person to take it. Even though by federal law a drug must be extensively tested in animals before it is tried with people, there is always the possibility that some side effect not detected in the animal studies may occur. Fortunately, serious side effects have been rare and have been more than offset by the value of the drugs developed.

Placebo Controls

A second research issue in human behavioral pharmacology is a methodological one: the need for placebo controls. A **control group** or control condition is a referent that scientists usually build into their experiments in order to tell if the drug they are investigating is really causing an effect. In psychopharmacology an important kind of control condition is the **placebo control.** The idea that such a control is essential to determining the pharmacological part of a drug's effect arose long ago, when placebo effects were discovered. Earlier in this chapter we noted that drug effects can be influenced by subjects' histories with and beliefs and expectancies about drugs. These nonpharmacological effects of drug administration are often called placebo effects, and may be difficult to disentangle from the pharmacological effects of drugs. In many experiments, only by comparing conditions in which people are told

Control group
In an experiment, the control group is the reference or comparison group. The control group does not receive the experimental manipulation or intervention whose effect is being tested.

Placebo control
A type of control originating in drug research. Placebo subjects are of the same makeup and are treated exactly like a group of subjects who receive a drug, except that placebo subjects receive a chemically inactive substance.

that they receive a drug, and then half actually get a chemically active substance and half do not, can the effects of the chemical compound of interest be specified. Sometimes all of the experimental participants are told that they may or may not receive the real drug and then half really get the drug and half do not. In either case, neither the experimenter nor the subjects knows, for any one subject, whether the drug or placebo is being administered. This "double blind" method is used so that biases from the experimenter or subject, according to their respective beliefs and expectancies about the drug or the experimental situation in general, are less likely to affect the results of the study. For example, the person taking the drug may have specific expectancies about what effects it will have. Similarly, the person administering the drug may have expectancies about its effects, and accordingly may react to the person receiving the drug in a certain way. Both the subject's and the experimenter's expectancies may influence the effects of the drug that the subject experiences.

Group design
A type of experimental design in which groups (as compared to individual cases) of subjects are compared to establish experimental findings.

Using a placebo control **group design** can get complicated, as you can imagine. However, many view such a design as essential to learning how drugs affect people. The idea behind a placebo control is that it allows the experimenter to say with confidence what the chemical action of a drug has to do with the way a person reacts upon taking it. In this respect, it is reasoned that, if the measured effect in the people who take the real drug is greater than it is in the people who take the placebo, then the chemical action of the drug must be responsible for the effect.

You now have the foundation for understanding the last section of this chapter, which concerns how a new drug is developed according to guidelines established by the U.S. government. All of what we have discussed in this and Chapter 4 enters into drug development.

You have seen that this text mostly concerns nonmedical drug use. Yet such an emphasis should not be seen as diminishing the importance of drugs developed legally for medical reasons. First of all, many of these drugs are, in fact, used in a way that was not prescribed by a physician. Second, medical drug use is far more prevalent among adults than is nonmedical use. A final point is that legal drug development and distribution make up a major economic force in the United States. For these reasons your knowledge about drugs and human behavior would not be complete without knowing about how legal drugs are developed.

NEW DRUG DEVELOPMENT

The "discovery" of new drugs generally occurs in one of three ways (Baldessarini, 1985): The rediscovery of folk usages of various naturally occurring products; the accidental observation of an unexpected drug effect; or the synthesizing of known or novel compounds. No matter how a drug's potential usefulness is discovered, however, the procedures for testing and marketing it are fairly standard. In the United States, these guidelines are detailed by the Food and Drug Administration (FDA). The typical stages are shown in Table 5-1.

A "new" drug may consist of a novel molecular synthesis, a recombination of known ingredients, or a new use of an existing compound (Walters,

Table 5-1   Stages in the Testing and Marketing of a Drug

1. Belief that a particular compound has clinical value
2. Animal studies
3. Experimental studies with healthy volunteers
4. Experimental studies with clinical patients, rigorously conducted
5. Broader clinical trials
6. Licensing and marketing approval
7. After-marketing evaluation of clinical use, particularly short-term and long-term effects

1992). In all these cases the FDA has guidelines that must be met in order to make a "new drug application," which must be approved before a drug can be marketed. The extensive process of meeting the guidelines is outlined in Table 5-2.

As you can see in Table 5-2, the first step is, where relevant, synthesis and adequate chemical description of the compound and a series of preclinical or animal studies. The animal studies are done to establish the safety of the compound for use by humans. The first step in the process may take one to three years, and the animal research relies heavily on research designs such as drug self-administration and drug discrimination that we described earlier. If the compound at this point is deemed to have therapeutic potential, then the drug developer applies to the FDA for designation of the new product as an Investigational New Drug (IND) which, if approved, allows the drug to be distributed for purposes of completing the three phases of clinical trials or studies in humans, as outlined in Table 5-2.

The three phases of clinical trials are straightforward, if not easily accomplished. Phase 1 involves normal (not ill), human volunteers and is completed to specify human reactions to the drug and to determine that it is safe for human use. In phase 2, the efficacy of the drug in alleviating or curing a

Table 5-2   Steps, According to FDA Guidelines, in Development of a New Drug

Step	Duration
Initial synthesis and preclinical studies	1–3 years
↓	
Phase 1 Clinical Trials, to establish safety, up to 50 normal volunteers	
↓	
Phase 2 Clinical Trials, controlled studies in patients with a target disease, 50–200 patients	2–10 years
↓	
Phase 3 Clinical Trials, controlled and open studies of 1,000 or more patients. These patients are monitored for drug effectiveness and for adverse reactions. Data are used for determining doses and labeling requirements.	

Note: Adapted from information in Walters (1992), especially p. 334.

Contemporary Issue
ADVANCES IN DISCOVERING DRUGS

The great success that has marked efforts to find new drugs in the twentieth century has its roots in the earth. Soil and plants are sources of microbes that produce disease-fighting compounds. For example, penicillin was discovered in mold over 60 years ago, and many painkillers have their sources in plants and soils.

Advances in technology have helped us to tap another of earth's resources—the sea—to find drugs. For example, animal and plant microbes taken from the sea in the Bahamas provide chemicals that seem to inhibit the growth of certain cancer cells. Bacteria taken from jellyfish in Florida produce compounds that kill some cancer cells and fight inflammation and swelling.

There also have been advances in ways to discover drugs that do not have their source in nature, as developments in biochemistry make the synthesis of useful new drugs more promising than ever before. For instance, new knowledge of neurotransmitter and receptor chemistry has made it possible to design drugs by computer that are tailored to bind to specified brain receptors and thus have highly selective biological activity.

Whether their roots are natural or synthesized, large groups of compounds traditionally have been screened to test their potential value as drugs. Advances in biotechnology in the last few years have allowed the definition of "large" to go from about 5,000 a year to billions (Fisher, 1992). The advance is not so much in synthesizing compounds to be screened, but in the ability to generate and screen large numbers of them. The method essentially involves generating millions of peptides, which are chains of amino acids that constitute proteins. Then through successive stages of screening it is discovered which peptides bond best (and thus neutralize) with disease-causing bacteria or viruses. Although these methods have been used only in the last few years, some drugs have been developed that are ready for human clinical trials. Examples are drug treatments for blood clots, high blood pressure, and asthma.

---

target disease is determined through controlled clinical trials in humans who are diagnosed as having the disease. Phase 3 expands phase 2 by increasing the number of patients involved in clinical trials, and also by evaluating the drug's effects in less controlled trials (Spiegel & Aebi, 1983). Throughout the phase 1–3 trial process, the drug developer is required to be in frequent contact with the FDA to monitor the development of the drug. Phases 1–3 may take a total of 2 to 10 years (Tyrer, 1982; Walters, 1992).

If phase 1–3 clinical trials are completed, then the developer files a New Drug Application with the FDA, which contains the data on the drug that have been collected so far. The FDA has up to six months to act on the application; if it is approved, or determined to be safe and effective, then the developer may market the drug within the United States and may export the drug for sale outside the United States. Anything less than approval means more time must be spent to correct deficiencies or solve problems so that a new application for approval may be filed.

Contemporary Issue
AWAITING DRUG APPROVAL

The period of time between preliminary indications of a drug's usefulness and its final approval for prescription use is a long and rigorous process. Before some recent changes in the FDA's regulations, the average time for drug approval was about 10 years (McKercher, 1992). There are valid reasons for the process taking so long; these reasons primarily are to ensure the drug's effectiveness and to study possible side effects. However, the time can seem interminable to the person who now suffers from the fatal disease that in a few years may be treatable with the new drug.

A case in point is the ongoing testing of potential drug treatments for AIDS. This syndrome, first identified in the early 1980s, grew in five years from being an isolated clinical oddity to near epidemic proportions. While researchers quickly were able to identify and trace the actions of the AIDS virus, efforts to develop a vaccine to combat it have not progressed at the same quick pace. This is not to say that AIDS-fighting drugs are not being tested. Indeed, a number of drugs are being looked at singly and in combination in various types of trials, but they are not available for general distribution to physicians treating AIDS patients.

This has produced a major debate between research clinicians and AIDS patients. The majority of those who suffer from AIDS die within three years of their first seeking medical treatment. Given this rapid course and the severity of the symptoms, there has been pressure to use potential anti-AIDS drugs before they have been through the full route of traditional drug approval requirements.

Some scientists argue that the distribution of a drug not fully tested would be short-sighted and potentially dangerous for the person. On the other hand, some patients argue that using a drug with AIDS-fighting potential is preferable to no treatment, and that they should be allowed to take the risk if they so choose. In fact, in 1987 the FDA eased its regulations in order to expedite commercial use of the drug AZT, which then seemed to be a major and singular hope for slowing the advance of AIDS in some patients. That change has become a more general policy that allows less lengthy approval requirements for drugs that may be of help in fighting fatal diseases like AIDS.

This change was a victory for patient advocate groups, but a 1993 study conducted in England, Ireland, and France, called the Concorde study, shows the importance of scientists' concerns about the risks of short-cutting drug-approval requirements. The Concorde study suggests that AZT may show benefits in slowing the progression of AIDS during the first several months, but not in the longer term.

Decisions about drug-approval requirements are extremely complex and are of interests to patients, scientists, clinicians, and drug companies. If you were a top FDA administrator, would you relax drug-approval requirements for quicker distribution of a drug that may help fight a fatal disease? Why?

"Silence = Death"
Campaign banner to lobby for the FDA to release experimental drugs to AIDS patients
(1987)

"Don't stop trials too early. Whatever the pressures are, keep going as long as possible. We must look to the longer term regarding benefit and harm"
Dr. Ian Weller, head of the British Concorde research team
(Cited in *The New York Times*, April 6, 1993, p. C3)

Distribution and Marketing

Once the developer begins distributing and marketing the new drug, monitoring is not over. In this regard, clinical researchers continue to evaluate the effectiveness of the drug and the appearance of any unforeseen side effects associated with its use.

Drugs are designated in different ways once they reach commercial status. First is the **chemical name** of the drug, which is technical and allows chemists to reproduce the drug's structure. The chemical name indicates the drug's structural formula. The manufacturer of the drug also gives it a **brand name** or trademark. This is the name of a drug that most people would know, since it is the commercial name for the drug that the manufacturer uses exclusively until its sole rights to market the drug expire. The brand name says nothing about the drug's chemical structure. Finally, a drug also is given a **generic name,** which is a general name for a drug that is shorter than its chemical name. Like its trade name, a drug's generic name tells nothing about its chemical structure.

To give you one example, we will cite the three names of Valium (brand name). The generic name of this drug is diazepam, and its chemical name is 7-chloro-1, 3-dihydro-1 methyl-5-phenyl-2H-1, 4-benzodiazepine-2-one.

Generic Drugs

No introduction to marketing and distributing new drugs would be complete without mention of generic drugs. Generics have fueled heated debate in the last several years. When a drug is approved, the source of its invention, usually a drug company, is granted sole rights to market the drug for 17 years. After that, generic drug companies can sell their versions of the same compound just as long as they use the generic rather than the brand name. Generic versions are not chemical copies of the respective brand-name drugs, but the FDA officially designates the generics as equivalent in effect to the brand names. Generic drugs usually are sold at a price lower than that charged for the drug of the company that invented it.

Generic drug companies have made a significant impression in the drug market. For example, an article that appeared in the *New York Times* in July, 1987, noted that between 1981 and 1986 generic drug sales tripled, to $5.1 billion. This was 23% of the $21 billion prescription drug market for 1986. This trend has continued. Furthermore, health insurers structure financial incentives in their benefits rules for people to select lower priced medication when a choice is available.

The drug companies that are awarded patents do not appreciate the generic drug onslaught. Their gripe is understandable, considering all the time, money, and energy that are spent in gaining new drug approval, as we just described. And we did not discuss compounds that fail to meet all the criteria for approval. Efforts put into such compound testing are written off as losses. Brand-name drug companies have been trying to fight back by claiming that using generics may be unsafe for some patients, and in some cases generics may not be as potent as brand-name drugs. The brand-name drug companies also have offered incentives to physicians for prescribing brand-name medications. But the generics are probably here to stay. Their use is supported by both consumer groups and the American Medical Association.

Chemical name
The name given to a drug that represents its chemical structure.

Brand name
The commercial name given to a drug by its manufacturer.

Generic name
The general name given to a drug that is shorter (and easier for most people to say) than its chemical name.

summary

- Step 7 of the drug experience concerns characteristics of the user, which broadly may be classified as biological or psychological.

- Personality and drug use has been the subject of considerable research attention. Although some personality characteristics seem to be associated with the drug experience, there is no evidence for an "addictive personality."

- Step 8 of the drug experience concerns environmental factors, which range from the level of government laws about alcohol and drug availability to the immediate drug-use setting.

- Tolerance is extremely important in understanding human drug-use patterns. In this chapter several different types of tolerance are reviewed.

- Both biological and learning factors seem to be involved in the development of tolerance.

- Behavioral pharmacology gives us the link between the drug experience and drug use.

- Drug use has been shown to follow the operant principles of reinforcement and punishment.

- An extremely important way to learn about drug use is self-administration studies.

- The effects of delay of consequences on behavior may be at least part of the explanation of continued drug use by humans in the face of negative consequences.

- Two methods of learning about drug effects are drug discrimination and conflict studies.

- A lot of knowledge that we have today in psychopharmacology is the result of experiments with nonhuman animals. Yet the question of what research on nonhuman animals says about the human drug experience still is debated.

- Ethical questions must also be addressed carefully in the administration of both active and inactive (placebos) drugs to human research participants.

- New drugs become available through a process of drug discovery, development, and marketing and distribution.

- Once a drug is commercially available it is given a chemical name, a brand name, and a generic name.

- The increasing popularity of generic drugs is affecting the profit margins of brand-name drug companies. Generics have caused some controversy in the United States.

ANSWERS TO WHAT DO YOU THINK?

1. Gender differences in the effects of drugs are due primarily to body-weight differences.

F *Although men tend to be heavier than women, the reason that a drug tends to have a greater effect on a woman than a man is that men tend to have less body fat.*

2. There are individuals who have an "addictive" personality that predisposes them to alcohol- or drug-use disorders.

F *The idea of an addictive personality is a popular one in some circles, but there is no scientific evidence for it.*

3. Expectancies about alcohol's effects may be a more powerful determinant of its effects than is the pharmacological action of alcohol.

T *Alcohol expectancies may be powerful determinants, especially at lower doses of alcohol, of behaviors and emotions that normally are socially proscribed.*

4. Theories about the effects of drugs on humans always have taken into account social and environmental factors.

F *The importance of social and environmental factors in understanding the effects of drugs on humans* *has been generally recognized only in the last 20 years.*

5. Tolerance to a drug develops because of biological changes that occur as a result of using the drug.

F *Important biological changes do seem to occur at the cellular level, and this seems to explain tolerance in part. However, learning and environmental variables also seem related to demonstrations of tolerance.*

6. Tolerance to a drug may be evident within the same occasion of using it.

T *For example, impairment in some behavior like driving at a given concentration of alcohol in the blood will be greater when the blood alcohol level is rising than it is at that same concentration when the level is falling.*

7. A person who has tolerance to alcohol will also demonstrate tolerance to barbiturates the first time he or she uses the latter drugs.

T *This person would be demonstrating cross tolerance to the two drugs, which have similar action in the body.*

8. There is no relationship between the drugs that animals show preference for and the drugs that humans prefer.

F *Self-administration studies show that the drugs that animals "take" are similar to the ones subject to human abuse. Conversely, the drugs that animals tend not to self-administer are less prone to abuse by humans.*

9. The effects of a drug on animals tell us little about how that drug will affect humans.

F *There is remarkably good generalizability from how drugs affect animals to how they affect humans. Some examples include the effects of drug dose, age, and the influence of environmental factors on drug use.*

10. In general, drug researchers are not concerned with placebo effects when studying the actions of a drug.

F *As we noted above, subjects' expectancies and beliefs about a drug may affect what effects of a drug are experienced. Therefore, when studying drugs, often a "placebo control" group(s) has to be included in the experiment.*

11. Because of the need for new medications to treat diseases like AIDS, government regulation of the process of drug development and marketing has been greatly simplified.

F *There has been some easing of the regulations, which primarily has resulted in a potentially shorter time from drug discovery to distribution for public use. However, the process still is extensive and still takes a considerable amount of time.*

12. Folk uses of naturally occurring products are important sources of discovering new drugs.

T *Rediscovery of old folk medicines based on, for example, plants growing "wild" is an important source of creating new drugs.*

6 Cocaine and the Amphetamines

WHAT DO YOU THINK?

True or False?

____ Cocaine is a synthetic drug developed during World War II.

____ Cocaine abuse was epidemic in the United States in the 1880s.

____ Stimulant drugs are often used to treat children with attention deficit hyperactivity disorder.

____ Amphetamine effects are highly similar to cocaine effects.

____ Overdoses of cocaine and amphetamine may produce a psychotic state.

____ Amphetamine has been used medically as a sleeping pill.

____ Crack is a smokable form of amphetamine.

____ The most common withdrawal symptom associated with cocaine is depression.

____ Stimulant drugs enhance learning and intellectual performance.

____ Some chronic users of cocaine may develop reverse tolerance, or increased sensitization to the drug's effect.

____ One difference between cocaine and the amphetamines is that cocaine has a longer duration of action.

____ Severe physical withdrawal symptoms occur following heavy cocaine use.

A number of drugs used for recreational as well as medical purposes can induce stimulation of the central nervous system and so are referred to as stimulants. We separate these into two groups according to potency. Cocaine and the amphetamines, the major stimulants, are treated in this chapter, and the minor stimulants such as caffeine and nicotine are dealt with in Chapter 7. We first consider the history of major stimulant use and discuss the effects of cocaine and the amphetamines as we review their history. Then we return to a more detailed treatment of the pharmacology of these stimulants.

THE COCA LEAF

Our story begins high in the Andes Mountains of Peru and Bolivia where grows a low shrub called the coca bush or coca tree (Erythroxylum coca). From the leaves of this plant comes the powerful stimulant, cocaine. The use of this drug is truly ancient. For centuries the native inhabitants of this region of South America, including the Inca peoples and their descendants, have engaged in the practice of chewing the coca leaf. Although no one knows when this practice began, archeological evidence suggests several thousand years ago (Siegel, 1985). The coca leaf had important religious significance to the Inca people but was used for medicinal and work-related purposes as well. When the Spanish *conquistadores* encountered the Incas during the sixteenth century, they were at first disturbed by the religious use of coca, which was, of course, inconsistent with Catholicism. (See Drugs and Culture Box: Cocaine and the Inca.) But after conquering the Inca, the Spanish permitted and actually encouraged the use of coca because they believed it helped the Inca to work harder and longer. The Spanish ultimately came to control Inca access to the coca leaf by using it as a form of payment and levying taxes to be paid in coca leaves. The Spanish considered chewing coca a vice, and neither used coca themselves nor encouraged its use among other Europeans (see Grinspoon & Bakalar, 1976; Kennedy, 1985).

Thus, until the 1800s the coca plant was relatively unknown in Europe. Then European naturalists began to explore Peru, experimented with coca, and soon strange and often-conflicting tales began to circulate about coca. Some, such as the German naturalist Edward Poeppig, viewed coca as deadly: "The practice of chewing the leaf is attendant with the most pernicious consequences, producing an intoxication like that of opium. As indulgence is repeated the appetite for it increases and the power of resistance diminishes until at last death relieves the miserable victim" (quoted by Kennedy, 1985, p. 55). Others, such as the Italian biologist Mantegazza who chewed coca while in Peru, were more positive: "I sneered at poor mortals condemned to live in this valley while I, carried on the wings of two coca leaves, went flying through the spaces of 77,438 worlds, each more splendid than the one before" (quoted by Mortimer, 1901, p. 137).

DRUGS AND CULTURE
COCAINE AND THE INCA

Human use of cocaine dates back to prehistoric times. The Inca people of what are now Peru and Bolivia apparently learned the practice of chewing the coca leaf from the Aymara Indians of Bolivia whose use dates back at least as early as 300 B.C. (Grinspoon & Bakalar, 1976). Coca was a sacred drug to the Incas. "Mama Coca" was viewed as possessing a goddess-like essence. One myth had it that coca had been a beautiful woman who had been executed for adultery. From her remains the divine coca plant grew, to be consumed only by royalty, in her memory (Petersen, 1977). In fact, prior to the Spanish invasion, the use of coca was reserved for the members of the highest classes. Coca played an important part in weddings, funerals, initiations, and other major ceremonies. The Spanish missionaries took a dim view of coca because they saw it as idolatry, and thus a barrier to conversion. However, because of its social importance, the Spanish eventually took over coca production and distribution, and used coca as a tool to control the conquered population (Petersen, 1977).

Neither of these quotes represents a very accurate depiction of the effects of chewing the coca leaf. However, of the two, apparently Mantegazza's was more compelling, because nearly every historical reference attributes the rise of scientific interest in coca to his praise. This scientific interest led to the increased availability of the coca leaf in laboratories and in the 1850s European chemists were able to isolate the far more potent active agent in the leaf, which they called cocaine. The extraction of cocaine from the leaf led to a whole new era in the history of stimulant drug use. This is because of the greater potency of cocaine (a single coca leaf contains only a tiny amount of cocaine), and because cocaine seems to produce different and more intense effects when taken through intravenous injection or intranasal absorption (sniffing or snorting)—methods of administration made possible only by the extraction of cocaine from the leaf. Presumably the more rapid delivery of large amounts of cocaine to the brain is responsible for the relatively more intense actions of cocaine when it is injected (Siegel, 1985).

EARLY USE OF COCAINE

The next chapter in the history of cocaine is fascinating because it involves a young physician working in Vienna who was looking for some medical break-

A South American woman tends coca bushes.

through to make his mark. Though he is now best known for other contributions, Sigmund Freud was first recognized for his writings on cocaine. Freud obtained a sample of cocaine in 1884 and, after taking it a few times, felt he had come across a miracle drug. In his first major publication, "On Coca," he advocated cocaine as a local anesthetic and as a treatment for depression, indigestion, asthma, various neuroses, syphilis, and drug addiction and alcoholism. Freud also thought cocaine was an aphrodisiac (Freud, in Byck, 1974).

Only one of these therapeutic uses has turned out to be valid, and that is the use of cocaine as a local anesthetic. When cocaine makes direct contact with peripheral neurons, it prevents neural firing, which has the effect of "numbing" the area. This action is quite unlike cocaine's effects on the central nervous system. Cocaine was the first of the local anesthetics and revolutionized surgery. Now, of course, related "-caine" drugs such as procaine and xylocaine are more frequently used, but because cocaine also constricts blood vessels, it is still used for surgery on areas such as the face because it reduces bleeding as well as pain.

Freud was mistaken in his early suggestions about cocaine, and he helped launch a major period of cocaine abuse. Ironically, one of the first indications of what was to come was observed in one of Freud's friends, Ernst von-Fleischl. Fleischl suffered from chronic pain and had become a morphine addict. Freud prescribed cocaine and Fleischl began to consume larger and larger doses of it. Although doing quite well at abstaining from morphine, Fleischl eventually was consuming a gram of cocaine daily. Not only had Fleischl become the first European cocaine addict, but he began to show bizarre symptoms that we now recognize as characteristic of cocaine overdose. These symptoms included paranoid delusions, which are often seen in paranoid schizophrenia, and a feeling of itching called the **formication syndrome,** which is described as something like insects or snakes crawling on

"Cocaine produces . . . exhilaration and lasting euphoria . . ."
Freud on cocaine

Formication syndrome
Symptoms of itching and feeling as if insects were crawling on skin caused by cocaine and amphetamine.

Cocaine was a popular ingredient in many remedies and tonics of the late 1800s, as shown in this advertisement for toothache drops.

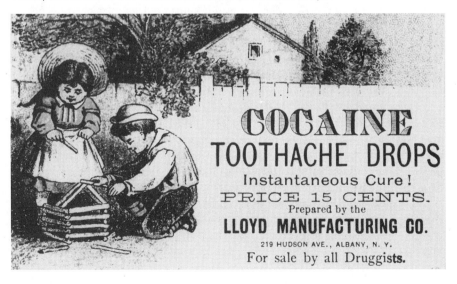

the skin. Today these symptoms are recognized as caused by cocaine overdose, but Fleischl was the first reported of many to experience these effects.

Surprised by the disastrous effects of cocaine on Fleischl, Freud in his later writings on cocaine was not quite so enthusiastic, but the damage had been done. The cocaine epidemic of the '80s was on—the 1880s that is! Not only was cocaine prescribed by physicians, but it also was readily available in patent medicines that could be obtained without prescription, such as Mariani's Coca Wine, a best-seller in Europe, and yes, in Coca-Cola. Coca-Cola's early advertising described its contents as containing the "tonic and nerve stimulant properties of the coca plant"—back when it *was* the real thing! Cocaine was popularized in music and literature as well. The famous fictional detective Sherlock Holmes was depicted by author Arthur Conan Doyle as using cocaine to give him energy and aid his powers of deductive reasoning. Robert Louis Stevenson apparently wrote the Jekyll and Hyde story while taking cocaine treatments for tuberculosis, and others who provided testimonials to the value of cocaine include Thomas Edison, Jules Verne, Emile Zola, Henrik Ibsen, the czar of Russia, and President Ulysses Grant (Grinspoon & Bakalar, 1976).

An advertisement from another coca product, Metcalf's Wine of Coca, again illustrates how cocaine became so popular:

> Public Speakers, Singers, and Actors have found wine of coca to be a valuable tonic to the vocal cords. Athletes, Pedestrians, and Base Ball Players have found by practical experience that a steady course of coca taken both before and after any trial of strength or endurance will impart energy to every movement, and prevent fatigue. Elderly people have found it a reliable aphrodisiac superior to any other drug (Siegel, 1985, p. 206).

It isn't hard to understand how cocaine became popular with this kind of publicity, and with so many people using cocaine, casualties began to emerge. Soon many users of cocaine began to discover firsthand the hazards of cocaine use, and with cocaine psychosis, overdose death, and severe dependence becoming major problems, popular sentiment against cocaine began to rise (Allen, 1987). One of the most influential works that changed ideas about cocaine was an article that described the case of Annie C. Meyers, who had been a successful businesswoman and a "well-balanced Christian woman" before becoming a "cocaine fiend." The depth of addiction to cocaine was well-described by Meyers who, upon finally running out of money for cocaine, recounted: "I deliberately took a pair of shears and pried loose a tooth that was filled with gold. I then extracted the tooth, smashed it up, and the gold went to the nearest pawnshop (the blood streaming down my face and drenching my clothes) where I sold it for 80 cents" (quoted in Kennedy, 1985, p. 93). Thus, beliefs and attitudes about cocaine began to change. In addition to dramatic accounts of addiction to cocaine, reports of violent acts committed under the influence of the drug led to a dramatic swing of public opinion culminating in the control of cocaine under the 1914 Harrison Narcotic Act. Although the Harrison Act was primarily designed to control opiates such as morphine and heroin, cocaine's inclusion as a dangerous drug was no accident.

THE AMPHETAMINES

Use of cocaine in America declined during the years following the Harrison Act, but a new stimulant was soon to enter the scene: the amphetamines. The amphetamines are a class of drugs first synthesized in the late nineteenth century that include amphetamine, dextroamphetamine, and methamphetamine (see Table 6-1). Although amphetamines had been available for research for many years, the first medical applications were developed in the 1920s. Amphetamines were at one time considered to be useful as a treatment for cold and sinus symptoms (the original inhalers contained Benzedrine—amphetamine), obesity, narcolepsy (a disease in which the patient uncontrollably falls asleep), and paradoxically, treatment of **hyperactive children** (see nearby Contemporary Issue Box). Amphetamines are rarely used for any of these purposes today, and a major reason for the decline in medical use is their high abuse potential. These drugs were used for their stimulant properties by soldiers on both sides during World War II. After the war amphetamine abuse reached epidemic proportions in Japan, Sweden, and other parts of Europe, yet was not recognized as a dangerous drug in America until the 1960s. Ironically, amphetamines became a major problem in America when physicians began to prescribe methamphetamine as a treatment for heroin addiction. Like Freud's cocaine treatment of morphine addiction, this treatment backfired, resulting in an explosion of amphetamine abuse, particularly on the West Coast during the early 1960s (Brecher, 1972).

The use of injected amphetamine resulted in a pattern of abuse reminiscent of the cocaine problems seen at the turn of the century and again today. The user experiences a brief but intense "flash" or "rush" immediately after the drug is injected. The strongly pleasurable feeling produced following amphetamine or cocaine injection is often described as orgasmic in nature, but because it lasts only a few minutes, the person is soon craving a return to the heights of pleasure even though the level of the drug in the body remains quite high. A series of injections often follows; the user becomes more and more stimulated but has difficulty obtaining a rush quite as good as the first. Because both cocaine and amphetamines suppress appetite and prevent sleep, persons may go for days without sleep, eating very little, and administering dose after dose. In the 1960s a person who engaged in this pattern of use came to be called a "speed freak." When speed freaks burst on the drug scene, it became clear that amphetamine shares virtually all of the effects of cocaine. For example, when dose levels of amphetamine get large enough, the user develops formication symptoms (called "speed bugs" or "crank bugs" by users) and paranoid delusions. Thus, a psychosis is not produced only by cocaine: amphetamines can cause an almost identical phenomenon. Here is a description of a speed freak from the San Francisco street scene of the late 1960s:

> "He is a very nice person, and extremely generous; however when he gets all jacked up and he is wired (stimulated with speed) . . . then he is in trouble. Because pretty quick he's got a shot gun . . . I've seen him out in front of . . . the freeway entrance herding the hitch-hikers away because he's paranoid of them. At four o'clock in the afternoon with a full length

Hyperactive children
Disorder of childhood involving restlessness, inability to be attentive, and disruptive behavior. Today referred to as "attention deficit hyperactivity disorder."

Contemporary Issue
STIMULANT DRUGS AND HYPERACTIVE CHILDREN

Some children just can't sit still! This can be a problem, especially in the class-room. Historically, when this type of problem became serious and interfered with the child's ability to live at home or perform at school the child was labeled as suffering from "minimal brain damage" (minimal because none was detectable) or "hyperactivity." Today such a child is labeled as suffering from "attention deficit hyperactivity disorder" or ADHD. Typical symptoms include inattention, impulsivity, and hyperactivity in a child of otherwise normal intelligence. In 1937 a physician named Charles Bradley discovered what appeared to be an extraor-dinary paradox: hyperactive children were calmed by a dose of the stimulant drug amphetamine. Since then many millions of ADHD children have been treated with stimulant drugs. In the 1970s when amphetamine abuse led to a stigma associated with these drugs, other stimulants became preferred. Now methylphenidate (Ritalin) and pemoline (Cylert) are the most common pharma-cological treatments for ADHD. However, the effects of these are virtually iden-tical to those of amphetamines. Because of the apparently paradoxical nature of the effects of stimulant drugs on ADHD children, they are often assumed to be biologically different from normal children. But studies have shown that stimu-lants affect both normal and ADHD children in about the same way: they in-crease alertness and attention span. Actually, these drugs have pretty much this effect in adults as well. So the "paradox" may not be real (Rapoport, Buchs-baum, Zahn, Weingartner, Ludlow, & Mikkelsen, 1978).

One thing is certain: stimulant drugs do improve ADHD children's perfor-mance. However, there are costs. Stimulant drugs suppress normal height and weight increases. Often the children will go on a "growth spurt" during the sum-mer if they are taken off the drug (Safer, Allen, & Barr, 1975). Other adverse ef-fects are less well documented, but given the data we have reviewed on stimu-lants, there is some reason for concern. Do the benefits of stimulant treatment for ADHD children outweigh the risks? That remains a controversial issue.

Stimulant psychosis
Paranoid delusions and disorientation resembling the symptoms of paranoid schizophrenia caused by prolonged use or overdose of cocaine and/or an amphetamine.

shot gun, he's screaming 'move on, you can't stand there, move on.' That's just the way he gets." (Brecher, 1972, p. 287)

So the paranoid psychosis produced by cocaine and amphetamine overdose should probably be called **"stimulant psychosis."** By the late 1960s the word was out on the street—"Speed kills!" What was referred to in this slogan was not just death by overdose. Amphetamine overdose deaths did occur, but they were relatively rare. Far more common was the development of a paranoid state that often led to acts of violence. In addition, after a long binge of am-phetamine abuse the user may crash (sleep for an extended period), and then awaken deeply depressed. The depression could last for days and is now rec-ognized as a common withdrawal symptom after heavy use of either amphet-amine or cocaine. The depression often leads the user back to drugs to try to

Table 6-1   Major Stimulants

Generic Names	Brand Names	Slang Terms
Cocaine		Coke, Snow, Freebase, Base Crack
Amphetamine	Benzedrine	Bennies, White Crosses
Dextroamphetamine	Dexedrine, Biphetamine	Black Beauties, Cadillacs, Dexies
Methamphetamine	Methedrine, Desoxyn	Speed, Crank, Ice
Methylphenidate	Ritalin	
Phenmetrazine	Preludin	Bam

get "up" again, and the cycle is repeated. Eventually the user's physical and mental health deteriorates badly unless he or she can break out of the cycle.

As the word spread about the hazards of amphetamine abuse, users tried to obtain other stimulants they thought might be safer. For example, a compound related to the amphetamines called phenmetrazine ("Bam" on the street—see Table 6-1) had a run of popularity in the 1970s, but soon it was recognized that it, too, produced all the adverse effects of the amphetamines. By the middle of that decade a different trend was clear: a "new" stimulant drug was on the scene, an "organic" or "natural" drug—surely there could be nothing wrong with . . . cocaine?

COCAINE EPIDEMIC II

It has been said that those who do not know history are condemned to repeat it, and with cocaine that certainly seems to be true. Why did cocaine reemerge as a stimulant of choice? One reason is that in the early '70s cocaine was fairly difficult to obtain and was quite expensive. It became glamorized as the drug of movie stars and pro athletes (who were among the few who could afford to buy it), and thus acquired a reputation as the "champagne" of the stimulants. Most users during this period experimented with low doses, taken intranasally, and thus rarely encountered the problems associated with intravenous use. Occasional exceptions were encountered: one of the first of many athletes to admit a major cocaine problem was former Dallas Cowboy linebacker Hollywood Henderson who in 1978 acknowledged he had acquired a $1,000-a-day habit. But this type of cocaine casualty was relatively rare. Cocaine was believed to be a fairly innocuous drug. To give you a feeling of the times, Ashley (1975) concluded in a popular-press book that cocaine was "not an addictive, especially dangerous drug" (p. 186) and argued that it should be legalized.

Unquestionably the contemporary view is that cocaine is, in fact, a very dangerous drug. Today Ashley's comments seem hopelessly naive because we have seen too many people die of cocaine overdose and have witnessed the struggles of many famous personalities trying to recover from cocaine dependence. What happened to bring about this change? One factor has been the increased availability of lower cost cocaine. This has led to changing patterns of use, with more people regularly using the drug in high doses. Another

Crack
A freebase cocaine produced by mixing cocaine salt with baking soda and water. The solution is then heated, resulting in brittle sheets of cocaine that are "cracked" into small, smokable chunks or "rocks."

critical factor has been the practice of smoking freebase cocaine, or crack. Although freebasing cocaine has been a problem since at least the late 1970s, **crack** burst upon the national scene in 1986.

However, the more familiar uses of cocaine involve more purified forms. Street cocaine, which takes the form of a white powder, is produced by combining a paste made from coca leaves with a hydrochloric acid solution to form a salt—cocaine hydrochloride. Because it is a salt, street cocaine is water-soluble and can be injected or taken intranasally (sniffed or snorted). Intranasal cocaine can produce quite intense effects, but because cocaine causes constriction of blood vessels in the nose when taken by that route, absorption is slowed. By the way, it is this vasoconstriction that can cause problems with inflammation and tissue damage of the mucous membranes of the nose in chronic intranasal users. Overdose deaths, psychosis, and dependence are all possible as a consequence of intranasal cocaine but are less common than with injected cocaine. Because intranasal cocaine was the major method of administration on the street until the late 1980s, the hazards of cocaine abuse were underestimated.

When cocaine is smoked it is absorbed very rapidly and completely in lung tissue and produces an intensely pleasurable high of very short duration followed by a severe crash. However, cocaine is broken down at the high temperatures necessary to smoke it when it is in the salt form. In order to smoke cocaine the hydrochloride salt must be separated from the cocaine base to create a substance that is called "freebase."

One method of "freeing the base" involves mixing street cocaine with a highly flammable substance—ether. Many people were badly burned by failing to handle the ether properly. The comedian Richard Pryor developed a popular routine in which he spoofs the very severe burns he received in a freebase accident. However, freebase cocaine can be produced more simply and safely by dissolving the cocaine salt in an alkaline solution (for example, baking soda). When the water in the solution is boiled off, what remains is a hard, rock-like substance called "crack" or "rock" cocaine. Crack has a low melting point and thus can be heated and the fumes inhaled while preserving the potency of the cocaine. The name crack comes from the crackling sound made by the baking soda left in the compound when it is heated (Inciardi, Lockwood, & Pottieger, 1993). When crack is smoked it results in rapid and concentrated delivery of cocaine to the brain, and produces an intense "rush" that is so pleasurable, it is actually preferred to comparable doses of injected cocaine by addicts (Foltin & Fischman, 1993). The euphoria is quite short-lived, and within 10–20 minutes users report a "crash," and begin to crave another hit. Perez-Reyes et al. (1982) found that users reported more craving following cocaine smoking than after injection.

Crack is cheaper and less dangerous to produce than other forms of freebase, so dealers became attracted to it. Also it is so potent that it can be sold in small chunks or rocks for $10–$20, and so is relatively affordable. Because it produces such strong cravings and dependence a large market for crack developed almost overnight. While there is evidence of sporadic crack use in the '70s it came to the attention of the media in late 1985, and by early 1986 national media such as *Time*, *Newsweek*, and various television documentaries reported that crack had emerged as a national crisis. By the late 1980s millions of Americans had tried crack. When athletes Len Bias and Don Rodgers died in the same week of cocaine overdose, a new era of cocaine consciousness had begun. Cocaine can kill, especially when smoked. Other cocaine overdose emergencies such as paranoid reactions also rose rapidly during this period. According to NIDA statistics more than 80,000 cocaine-related emergency room visits occurred in 1990, up from 10,000 in 1985, and almost none in the early 1970s (NIDA, 1991). Dependence on cocaine, once viewed as a minor problem, became one of the nation's major health problems with the introduction of crack.

Crack cocaine continues to have a major impact on society today. One aspect of the problem is the enormous amount of criminal activity generated by cocaine. The distribution of cocaine is controlled by large and well-organized criminal groups known as cartels. The largest is the Cali cartel of Colombia, and it supplies most of the cocaine that reaches the United States (*Newsweek*, 1993). As the U.S. and Colombian governments began to crack down on cocaine smuggling, the war on drugs became a shooting war. More than 2,000 murders were reported during the first six months of 1989 in the city of Medellin, Colombia. Hundreds of judges and court employees have been assassinated, and hundreds more have resigned in anticipation of more

Gangs control the sale of crack in many urban areas.

violence. Although Pablo Escobar, former head of the Medellin cartel, was killed in a gunfight with police in 1993, the reach of the cartels has continued to extend to include eastern Europe and Asia and is truly global. A 1993 *Newsweek* story reported that "Organized crime earns annual profits estimated at $1 trillion worldwide, almost as much as the U.S. annual federal budget. The Cali Cartel has tried to lease its own satellite to avoid eavesdropping by the CIA and Drug Enforcement Administration," (p. 18).

Once in the United States, cocaine distribution continues to contribute to crime and violence. Gangs such as the notorious "Bloods" and "Crips" of Los Angeles have infiltrated many other cities and vie with one another and other gangs (some from Jamaica, others from Colombia and other Latin American countries) to gain control of the crack market. These highly organized criminal elements pose a major threat to police and civilians alike. Unlike the traditional notion of the small-time drug dealer, gang members often possess high-tech weapons and sophisticated transportation systems. Many of the incidences of drive-by shootings and other acts of urban violence are crack related.

Crack has also been extremely destructive to users. Because the allure of crack is so great, dependence on the drug leads many people to tragic levels of desperation and self-destruction. The "crack house"—a place where crack is sold and smoked—has become the 1990s den of iniquity, and the media is filled with stories of degradation. When addicts run out of money, sexual activities of various kinds become the medium of exchange, and the transmission of HIV becomes an additional risk factor. Inciardi et al.'s (1993) study of crack house activities chronicles numerous examples of prostitution, murder, rape, child abuse, and other acts of violence that have occurred in the crack house environment. A quote from one user sums it up:

> "I seen things in crack houses that I never seen anywhere else. They're the worst of places. No one cares about anybody, about what they do. I seen everything. I seen a girl get ____ fifty times in a row, 'till she was bloody and couldn't even stand, for a little rock. I saw a guy throw acid in a lady's face, all because she didn't want to go down on him any more. I seen a junkie get his balls blown off with a shotgun because he tried to steal some "white" (crack). They're bad places, man, beyond the extremes . . ." (Inciardi et al., 1993, p. 63).

The publicity about the dangers of crack has been impossible to avoid during the past few years. So why are people still smoking crack?

Consider this seductive and sinister description from a cocaine smoker:

> "Imagine you are on an island and offshore about a dozen yards is this orange-pink haze that is glowing and extremely enticing. So you walk out into that cold, dark water and you swim a ways to get near that glow and you're out on the edge of it and it feels so good and so warm, but it moves away a little. So you swim out into deeper water and this time you get even closer to the center and it is so incredibly seductive. But now it's moving a little faster out into the ocean and you swim harder trying to keep up and you're getting farther and farther away from shore. That's how with the first few tokes you feel pretty good and then with a deep toke you are near the center and it's so exhilarating but you come down and keep

"Every time I gets some money— $2, $10, or $1,000—it all goes for the base. When you have this base habit, that's all you do— base, base, and more base. I base all day . . ."

Crack user
Quoted by Inciardi et al., 1993

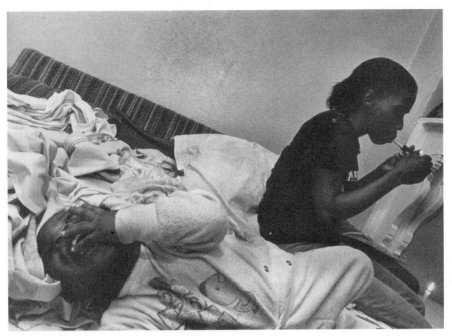

A woman smokes crack while her infant cries.

wanting more. Pretty soon you are way the hell out in the cold black ocean and you're faced with keeping up swimming harder toward that warm, wonderful, glowing haze just out of reach or turning back and swimming miles back to shore in that dark, cold water" (Kirsch, 1986, p. 49).

Contemporary Issue
A NEW ICE AGE?

Considering the widespread awareness of the dangers of cocaine, you might think stimulant drug use would be on the decline. And it might be. But, there is word of a "new" stimulant on the street called "ice," "crystal," "crank," or "speed." But this new drug isn't so new after all. It's methamphetamine or one of the other amphetamine drugs. Will another generation discover the "speed freak" phenomenon? Particularly dangerous is the new smokable form of methamphetamine called ice. Ice is similar in many respects to crack cocaine. It seems to share with crack the capacity to induce rapid addiction, violence, and psychotic behavior. But, unlike the short duration of action associated with crack, the ice high lasts from 4 to 14 hours. Many are concerned that ice could create even more problems than crack has. However, access to ice has been fairly limited except for parts of California and Hawaii. Apparently clashes between rival gangs have restricted ice distribution. The outcome of these battles may determine whether a new "ice age" occurs in the '90s.

More recently, the use of crack and other forms of cocaine has begun to decline among the general population (see Chapter 1). Despite this trend, cocaine use and problems caused by cocaine remain extensive in the United States. In addition, evidence indicates that methamphetamine is returning to popularity among illicit drug users both in an injectable form called "crank," and in a new smokable form referred to as "ice" (see nearby Contemporary Issue Box).

PHARMACOKINETICS OF STIMULANTS

Stimulant drugs may be administered and absorbed in a variety of ways, and the intensity and duration of action vary accordingly. Cocaine, the amphetamines, and amphetamine-like stimulants (methylphenidate, phenmetrazine) are readily absorbed after oral administration, but the onset of drug action is slower and the peak effect somewhat less than with other methods. Both cocaine and the amphetamines are commonly administered intranasally and absorption properties are similar to those associated with oral administration (Jones, 1987). In contrast to oral or intranasal routes, which require 10–15 minutes for drug action to begin, intravenous injection of stimulants results in intense effects within 30 seconds. When cocaine is smoked in the form of crack or freebase, the onset of action is even faster (Jones, 1987).

One important difference between cocaine and the amphetamines is in their duration of action. Cocaine is metabolized quite rapidly with most of its effects dissipating between 20–80 minutes after administration. Cocaine or its metabolites are detectible in human urine for two to three days after administration (Hawks & Chiang, 1986). Amphetamines are much longer acting with effects that persist from 4 to 12 hours, and they or their metabolites are also detectible in urine for two to three days (Goodman, Goodman, & Gilman, 1980; Hawks & Chiang, 1986).

MECHANISM OF STIMULANT ACTION

As noted in Chapter 3, stimulant drugs such as cocaine and the amphetamines are thought to affect the brain primarily through complex actions on monoamine neurotransmitters: dopamine, norepinephrine, and serotonin. For example, both cocaine and the amphetamines block reuptake of norepinephrine and dopamine (Koob & Bloom, 1988). In addition, the amphetamines appear to stimulate the release of norepinephrine and dopamine into the synapse (Ellinwood, 1980). Cocaine also blocks reuptake of serotonin (Jones, 1984). Thus, the initial effect of stimulants is to produce a storm of activity in neural pathways that are sensitive to the monoamine transmitters. However, because of this increased activity, and particularly because reuptake is blocked so that enzymes break down the neurotransmitters, the long-term effects of stimulant use involve depletion of monoamines. If you remember that low levels of monoamines are linked to clinical depression (see Chapter 3), then you have the basis of one theory of why the aftereffects of heavy cocaine use involve depression (Dackis & Gold, 1985). In order to explain this hypothesis, we must turn briefly to data from the animal laboratory.

It has been known for a long time that animals will work to obtain cocaine. Rats and monkeys given a choice between making responses that produce cocaine or other rewards will choose cocaine over other drugs or even over food under some circumstances. (Aigner & Balster, 1978; Bozarth & Wise, 1985). The powerful reinforcing properties of cocaine and amphetamines are thought to stem from their action on dopamine-containing neurons in the neural pathways that make up the medial forebrain bundle (Goeders, Dworkin & Smith, 1986; Wise, 1984). As you may recall from Chapter 3, this brain region is thought to mediate reward, and thus cocaine use has been described as a chemical shortcut to the reward systems of the brain. However, because in the long run a depletion of dopamine (along with other transmitters important in depression) occurs, the cocaine user may then find that his or her ability to experience normal pleasure is diminished. This is consistent with the depression and lack of joy that is so common during cocaine withdrawal it is known as the "cocaine blues." Figure 6-1 illustrates the relationship between mood and cocaine after moderate and heavy use. The peak at the left shows the mood elevation that occurs upon cocaine administration; the valley at right depicts the consequent depression. The depression of mood is greater following heavy use. Note that these general observations seem to hold for amount of use in a single session and for longer term use. However, the depressive abstinence syndrome is thought to be stronger and of greater duration in those who have been abusing the drug for an extended period.

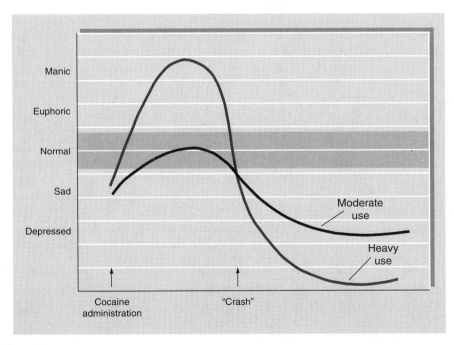

Figure 6-1   Relationship between cocaine dose and mood.

ACUTE EFFECTS AT LOW AND MODERATE DOSES

Stimulant drugs produce a number of physiological effects that are observable outside the brain. We discuss the effects of cocaine and amphetamines together because, for all practical purposes, their measurable effects are identical. Although users often claim to notice subjective differences between stimulants, under controlled laboratory conditions even experienced stimulant users cannot discriminate among the effects of cocaine, amphetamines, and methylphenidate (Fischman, 1984).

Stimulants provide the classic examples of sympathomimetic drugs. That is, they act to stimulate or mimic activity in the sympathetic branch of the autonomic nervous system. Thus, many of their physiological effects are the same as those seen during emotional arousal: heart rate is up, blood pressure is up, respiratory rate is up, and sweating increases; meanwhile, blood flow decreases to the viscera and extremities but increases to the large muscle groups and the brain. Finally, body temperature is elevated and pupils are dilated.

Anorectic effects
Causing one to lose appetite—suppression of eating.

Cocaine and amphetamine also produce appetite-suppressant or **anorectic effects.** People simply do not feel hunger after taking these drugs. It is anorectic effects that were sought when amphetamines and phenmetrazine (Preludin) were prescribed as diet pills. Although patients definitely ate less and lost weight on diet pills, doses had to be escalated to maintain loss, and when patients went off the drugs they typically regained the weight. Thus, the benefits of diet pills were outweighed by the risk of dependence and other side effects, and this approach to the treatment of obesity is considered questionable at best.

Moderate doses of cocaine and amphetamines also produce a sense of elation and mood elevation. Individuals show increased talkativeness and sociability (Higgins & Stitzer, 1988). Alertness and arousal are increased, and marked insomnia often develops. These drugs also enhance performance on a wide variety of tasks involving physical endurance, such as running and swimming, and they increase physical strength. Laties and Weiss (1981) concluded in a review of the literature on amphetamines and sports that amphetamines confer a small but significant edge to the athlete. Consider the effects, shown in Figure 6-2, of methamphetamine on performance on a stationary bicycle machine. Note that a control injection does little to reverse the effects of fatigue on rate of cycling, but that a methamphetamine (Methedrine) injection administered at the three-hour point produces a large improvement that is sustained for several hours. Although the data on cocaine are scantier, it appears to have the same effects but is limited by its short duration of action (Grinspoon & Bakalar, 1976). The expected, and to some extent real, enhancement of performance is probably one reason cocaine abuse has been so prevalent among athletes in recent years. Ironically, when former Maryland basketball coach Lefty Driesell, now coaching at James Madison University, made this very point at a conference on drugs in June 1987, he was sharply criticized. But in fact he was arguing for the need for drug testing in sports—if stimulants provide an edge, even a small one, athletes will be tempted to use them.

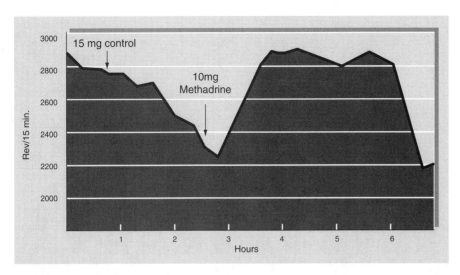

Figure 6-2 Performance on bicycle machine after control and metham-phetamine injections (from Laties and Weiss, 1981).

Because stimulants increase resistance to fatigue and boredom they have often been used to aid studying, resulting in the amphetamine-induced "all-nighter." Several problems occur with this type of stimulant use. One is that information learned under the influence of a drug is best recalled when the individual is in that same drug-induced state. This phenomenon is called **state-dependent learning** and it is true of a number of drugs other than stimulants (Overton, 1985). Now we are *not* suggesting that students should take the test "high" if they study high. Rather, the phenomenon of state-dependent learning suggests there will be problems in learning information when under the influence of a drug because the ability to retrieve the information will not be as good when sober. Furthermore, experimental evidence shows that stimulants actually may impair learning ability (Fischman, 1984). Figure 6-3 shows increased errors produced by cocaine in a learning task. Note that the effects are dose- and time-dependent and that the effects of injections of 32 mg are far greater than even the highest intranasal dose (96 mg). Considerable anecdotal evidence shows that stimulants may impair complex reasoning performance. Consider the case of William Halstead. Halstead became known as the father of modern surgery for his pioneering work at the turn of the century. But later in his career, while studying the anesthetic properties of cocaine, he became probably the first American to become addicted to the drug. At one point during his cocaine dependency he published an article in the *New York Medical Journal* that begins with the following sentence:

> Neither indifferent as to which of how many possibilities may best explain nor yet quite at a loss to comprehend, why surgeons have, and that so many, quite without discredit, could have exhibited scarcely any interest in what, as a local anaesthetic, had been supposed, if not declared, by most so very sure to prove, especially to them, attractive, still

State-dependent learning
Learning under the influence of a drug is best recalled when in the same "state."

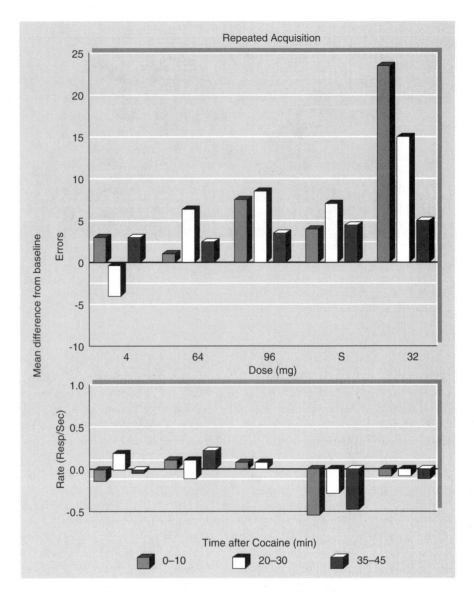

Figure 6-3   Effects of cocaine on learning new behavior patterns. Data collected during each pre-drug, repeated-acquisition task were averaged across subjects; the mean is used as the baseline score. Change from baseline is shown for number of errors and response rate during each of the three 10-minute post-drug tests. Cocaine was inhaled at doses of 4, 64, 96 mg, and 32 mg was injected intravenously. S indicates an intravenous saline injection (from Fischman, 1984).

I do not think that this circumstance, or some sense of obligation to rescue fragmentary reputation for surgeons rather than the belief that an opportunity existed for assisting others to an appreciable extent, induced me, several months ago, to write on the subject in hand the greater part of a somewhat comprehensive paper, which poor health disinclined me to complete (quoted in Grinspoon & Bakalar, 1976, p. 32).

Given the apparent effects of cocaine on Halstead's writing style, it is frightening to imagine how his surgery was going! So the notion that cocaine enhances intellectual performance appears to be a myth.

Another notion about cocaine (and the amphetamines) that appears to be largely mythical is their ability to enhance sexual prowess. Although this has not been well studied, surveys suggest that while some report enhancement of sexual feelings and performance with stimulants, most do not. Many men report impotence with stimulants and women frequently describe a decline in sexual interest, but most report no effects (Abel, 1985).

ACUTE EFFECTS AT HIGH DOSES

As we noted earlier, when high doses of stimulant drugs are taken a characteristic psychotic state emerges. This state can be produced in normal volunteers in a laboratory setting by amphetamines, cocaine, phenmetrazine (Preludin), or methylphenidate (Ritalin) (Davis & Schlemmer, 1980). Such psychotic reactions are currently a serious problem with high-dose use of crack cocaine. Paranoid delusions are the most common symptom of stimulant psychosis, but a second symptom commonly noted is compulsive, stereotyped behavior like rocking, hair-pulling, chain-smoking, or "fiddling with things." Other symptoms may include hallucinations and, as noted earlier, formication. Interestingly, stimulant psychosis can be successfully treated with chlorpromazine (Thorazine) or other drugs used in the treatment of schizophrenia (Davis & Schlemmer, 1980).

Of course, accompanying high doses of cocaine or amphetamines is always the risk of overdose death. Specifying the dose that places the user at risk is difficult. With cocaine in particular, when we speak of low to moderate doses, we refer to 15–60 mgs (a typical "line" contains 10–20 mgs). But cocaine overdose deaths have been reported in cases of individuals who were given as little as 20 mgs as a local anesthetic, apparently because they suffered from a rare deficiency in the enzyme that breaks down cocaine in the blood and liver (Weiss & Mirin, 1987). Such cases would certainly be exceptional, and generally much higher doses are taken before experiencing either stimulant psychosis or death.

A number of cocaine overdose deaths have occurred during the past few years—more than 500 in 1985—but for many people the deaths of athletes Len Bias and Don Rodgers and comedian John Belushi stand out as remarkable illustrations that cocaine can kill. Stimulants can kill in a number of ways:

1. Cocaine can cause convulsions or seizures that may result in respiratory collapse.
2. Cocaine produces a direct action on cardiac nerves, which may cause irregular beating of the heart (arrhythmia). If severe enough this may lead to fibrillation—the heartbeat flutters but does not pump blood through the system.

"I need it. I need it. You couldn't possibly understand."
John Belushi on cocaine
Quoted by Woodward, 1984

Athlete Len Bias and actor River Phoenix were both casualties of cocaine use.

3. Cocaine may produce coronary artery spasm leading to impaired blood flow to the cardiac muscle. This results in myocardial infarction (heart attack) and may cause permanent cardiac damage even if not fatal.
4. Cocaine may cause a cerebral artery to burst because of high blood pressure, which may produce a stroke.

These are the most likely reasons for a cocaine overdose death, but which of these particular factors is responsible is rarely certain (Sorer, 1992). To further complicate matters, users often combine cocaine with other drugs to produce complex and often unpredictable drug interactions (see nearby Contemporary Issue Box).

EFFECTS OF CHRONIC USE

Tolerance

When stimulants are taken regularly over a long period (chronic use), several additional problems and issues arise. One issue involves the development of

Contemporary Issue
COCAINE AND OTHER DRUGS

Cocaine and other stimulant drugs are often taken in combination with other drugs, particularly alcohol and opiates. Recent studies have revealed that when cocaine is combined with alcohol a new compound called cocaethylene is formed in the body. Cocaethylene has pharmacological properties similar to cocaine, but it may be more toxic (Katz, Philip, & Witkin, 1992). Many cases of cocaine overdose may, in fact, involve cocaethylene toxicity caused by combining cocaine and alcohol. The combination of cocaine (or amphetamine) and heroin (or other opiate) is called a "speedball" and is particularly popular among heroin addicts. Combinations of cocaine and heroin have sometimes been blamed for drug overdose deaths (as was the case in the deaths of comedian John Belushi and the actor River Phoenix), but experimental studies of cocaine combined with opiates have not found evidence of additive effects or synergy (Foltin & Fischman, 1992).

tolerance for the drug, and in the case of the stimulants, this turns out to be fairly complex. First, acute tolerance develops for cocaine. That is, the effects obtained from the first administration of the drug are not produced by a second administration shortly after, unless a higher dose is used. This is described by a freebase user as follows:

> "You can do enough freebase to kill you and not realize it because the base numbs your lungs and you can keep sucking it in. After that first hit, you spend the rest of the night trying for that same rush. You keep hoping the next hit will do it, and you add more to the pipe and breathe in deeper, but it's never the same and I mean *never* the same. Nothing compares to that first hit" (quoted by Kirsch, 1986, p. 49).

Acute tolerance to the physiological (heart rate increase) and subjective effects of cocaine also has been demonstrated in humans in laboratory settings (Fischman, Schuster, Javaid, Hatano & Davis, 1985). This acute tolerance dissipates rapidly, too, usually within 24 hours. But studies of the development of long-term, protracted tolerance to cocaine and amphetamines have not yielded consistent findings. Some studies have shown clear development of tolerance to various stimulant effects. For example, tolerance to the hyperthermic (body temperature increasing) effects of amphetamine develops gradually (Caldwell, Croft, & Sever, 1980). However, other studies have shown the development of what might be termed reverse tolerance or sensitization following repeated administration. In these cases, lower doses were sufficient to produce a given effect (Jones, 1984; Post, 1977). This is particularly true for the convulsant effects of cocaine where the ability of the drug to produce seizures appears to be enhanced by repeated use—a phenomenon called **kindling.** Kindling may be of significance when overdose death occurs at relatively low doses of cocaine (Jones, 1984). In any case, the occurrence of reverse or regular tolerance may depend on various complex aspects of the response being studied (Hughes & Branch, 1991).

Kindling
Repeated exposure to a stimulus may lower the brain's threshold for seizures. This effect, which is produced by electrical stimulation or by cocaine, is called kindling.

Dependence

Although the abstinence syndrome associated with cocaine (or amphetamines) does not involve life-threatening physical symptoms, it is real and compelling. The primary symptoms include depression, social withdrawal, craving, tremors, and sleeping disturbances (Jones, 1984). The temptation to resume use of the drug is described by many as overpowering. Gawin (1991) notes three distinct phases of cocaine withdrawal (see Figure 6-7). The "crash" occurs first and involves one to five days of intense craving, exhaustion, and deep depression. Gawin notes that at times during the crash, the addicts may be too tired and exhausted to experience craving, but as they recover their strength the cravings return with great power. The second phase is called withdrawal and for 1 to 10 weeks the addicts continue to feel intense cravings, moderate to severe depression, and an inability to experience normal pleasure (*anhedonia*). Finally, considerable improvement occurs in the third phase, but for many months or even years the addicts may continue to experience intermittent cravings for cocaine. This phase is called the "extinction" phase because the cravings seem to be caused by exposure to particular cues in the environment that were associated with cocaine use in the past and continue to "trigger" craving until eventually, perhaps via classical conditioning, the craving response is extinguished to these cues.

Obviously, not all persons who experiment with cocaine or crack develop a dependence pattern and not all who use the drug regularly even over a period of years experience these severe abstinence symptoms (Siegel, 1984). But for those who do, cocaine dependence can be a living nightmare. In addition to the risk of lethal overdose, stimulant psychosis and severe depression, cocaine smokers often report chest pains related to lung or heart damage, and even intranasal users frequently report insomnia, chronic fa-

Contemporary Issue
COCAINE BABIES: LEGACY OF THE CRACK ERA?

Additional risks occur when drugs are taken during pregnancy. Studies of women who used cocaine during pregnancy have shown higher rates of spontaneous abortion, fetal death, and premature labor and birth. Infants born of cocaine-using mothers had lower birth weights and lengths and were more likely to die during infancy. There has been widespread publicity and concern regarding the possibility that children exposed to cocaine *in utero* would show permanent neurological damage with attendant learning disabilities. However, at the present time long-term consequences of fetal exposure to cocaine are not clear. There are some reports of long-term learning and behavioral problems, but it is not clear that prenatal exposure to cocaine is responsible (Singer, Farkas, & Kliegman, 1992). Remember that "crack babies" are likely to suffer from maternal neglect and an impoverished social and familial environment as well. Finally, although well-intentioned, calling a child a "crack baby" may stigmatize him or her and create a self-fulfilling prophecy of failure.

tigue, severe headaches, nasal and sinus infections, and seizures (Washton, 1987). Many women are unable to quit using cocaine during pregnancy and there are a number of problems associated with fetal exposure to cocaine (see nearby Contemporary Issue Box). Because the unpleasant abstinence symptoms are so long-lasting, many cocaine users relapse back to heavy use even after months of abstinence.

A variety of new approaches are now being tried to help treat the cocaine-dependent individual. In addition to more traditional approaches to drug treatment (see Chapter 16), some therapists are now using antidepressant drugs to help the cocaine user through the abstinence depression, and new drugs that may reduce craving for cocaine, such as amantadine and buprenorphine, are under study (see Gawin, 1991). In addition, special self-help groups have developed for cocaine dependency (for example, Cocaine Anonymous). A national hotline has been established for individuals to get information on cocaine and treatment facilities: 1-800-COCAINE (Washton, 1987). Despite the absence of life-threatening physical withdrawal symptoms, cocaine is as hard an addiction to break as any.

summary

- Cocaine comes from the leaves of the coca bush, and the practice of chewing coca leaves by South American Indians goes back many centuries. Cocaine was introduced to Europe by the Spanish, and when the process necessary to separate cocaine from the leaf was developed in the nineteenth century a major epidemic of cocaine abuse swept the world.

- Amphetamines are synthetic stimulant drugs discovered in the 1920s. They became major drugs of abuse as well, but their popularity waned somewhat in the 1970s and 1980s as cocaine returned to favor.

- Cocaine became one of the most frequently abused drugs in the 1980s with the introduction of an inexpensive smokable form—crack.

- The effects of cocaine and the amphetamines are virtually identical except that cocaine is metabolized very rapidly and thus has a short duration of action (20–80 minutes), while amphetamine effects are more prolonged (4–12 hours).

- Both cocaine and amphetamines act through the monoamine neurotransmitter systems, particularly by enhancing dopaminergic activity. This action in the brain's reward pathways may account for the highly addictive nature of cocaine.

- Both cocaine and amphetamines are sympathomimetic drugs that increase heart rate, blood pressure, respiratory rate, and cause pupil dilation.

- Other effects of stimulants include anorectic effects, increased alertness and arousal, mood elevation, and at low doses, enhanced performance on a variety of tasks.

- High doses of cocaine or amphetamines may produce a paranoid state called stimulant psychosis or death through overdose.

- Dependence may develop after chronic use of cocaine or amphetamines. The abstinence syndrome is characterized primarily by depression and craving with few measurable physiological effects. Thus, a drug that does not cause severe physical withdrawal symptoms can still be highly addictive.

ANSWERS TO WHAT DO YOU THINK?

1. Cocaine is a synthetic drug developed during World War II.

F   *Cocaine is derived from the leaves of the coca bush.*

2. Cocaine abuse was epidemic in the United States in the 1880s.

T   *Cocaine was a legal drug in the United States until the passage of the 1914 Harrison Narcotic Act, and was widely abused around the turn of the century.*

3. Stimulant drugs are often used to treat children with attention deficit hyperactivity disorder.

T   *Ritalin (methylphenidate) and other stimulants are actually effective in the treatment of attention deficit hyperactivity disorder.*

4. Amphetamine effects are highly similar to cocaine effects.

T   *Cocaine and amphetamine are virtually indistinguishable in terms of their major physical and behavioral effects.*

5. Overdoses of cocaine and amphetamine may produce a psychotic state.

T   *The stimulant psychosis resembles paranoid schizophrenia.*

6. Amphetamine has been used medically as a sleeping pill.

F   *Amphetamines cause insomnia. They have been used as diet pills.*

7. Crack is a smokable form of amphetamine.

F   *Crack is smokable cocaine.*

8. The most common withdrawal symptom associated with cocaine is depression.

T   *Depression following cocaine use is referred to as the "cocaine blues."*

9. Stimulant drugs enhance learning and intellectual performance.

F   *Experimental evidence shows that stimulants may impair learning ability and complex reasoning performance.*

10. Some chronic users of cocaine may develop reverse tolerance, or increased sensitization to the drug's effect.

T   *When reverse tolerance develops, lower doses of the drug are sufficient to produce a given effect. This is particularly true for the convulsant effects of cocaine.*

11. One difference between cocaine and the amphetamines is that cocaine has a longer duration of action.

F   *Amphetamine effects last from 6–12 hours, while cocaine is a relatively short-acting drug.*

12. Severe physical withdrawal symptoms occur following heavy cocaine use.

F   *Cocaine produces no major physical withdrawal symptoms.*

7 Nicotine

WHAT DO YOU THINK?

True or False?   ____   Tobacco was once thought to have major medical value.

____   Throughout the age range, men have higher smoking rates than women do.

____   The prevalence of smokeless tobacco use among males is about three times that among females.

____   Nicotine can be considered both a stimulant and a depressant.

____   When using commercial tobacco products, the peak in blood level of nicotine is reached most quickly by using smokeless tobacco.

____   While psychological dependence is common, there have been no identified cases of physical dependence on nicotine.

____   Nicotine's calming effects are a main reason for its use.

____   Nicotine plays a secondary role to learning and social factors in maintaining tobacco use.

____   Health damage from cigarette smoking cost the U.S. economy about $25 billion in 1990.

____   Low-tar, low-nicotine cigarettes are healthier than cigarettes that do not have reduced tar and nicotine content.

____   Despite the media hype, passive smoking actually poses a serious health risk to few Americans every year.

____   A large portion of ex-smokers quit on their own.

In this chapter and in Chapter 8 we review two more stimulant drugs—nicotine and caffeine. We cover these two drugs apart from other stimulant drugs because nicotine and caffeine are so prominent in societies around the world. Other stimulant drugs have a small fraction of the prevalence that nicotine and caffeine do.

This chapter is a review of nicotine and begins with some background information about its source and the ways that nicotine is consumed, followed by a history of tobacco use. We then discuss the prevalence of nicotine use, followed by the mechanisms of pharmacological action. We also review the acute and chronic effects of nicotine. The chapter concludes with a description of professional services available to help individuals stop smoking.

Nicotine occurs naturally from one source: the leafy, green tobacco plant. The plant belongs to the genus Nicotiana and has 60 species. Only two of these can be used for smoking and other human consumption, *Nicotiana rustica* and *Nicotiana tabacum*. The latter species provides all of the tobaccos typically consumed in the United States, including burley, oriental, and cigar tobaccos. Different types of tobacco result mostly from differences in cultivation and processing. In this regard, tobacco leaves are harvested when still green and then undergo curing and fermentation. The tobacco then is converted into the commercial products—cigarettes, cigars, snuff, chewing tobacco, and pipe tobacco (Blum, 1984).

Tobacco has many constituents, but nicotine is singled out as having the broadest and most immediate pharmacological action. Nicotine is extremely toxic, about as toxic as cyanide (Rose, 1991), and only 60 mg are needed to kill humans. When tobacco is burned the smoke has a small portion of nicotine, which the body metabolizes to a non-toxic substance.

The tobacco products meant for smoking—in the form of cigarettes, cigars, or pipes—are generally familiar. Not as familiar are the forms of smokeless tobacco, which include snuff and chewing tobacco (Gritz, Ksir, & McCarthy, 1985). Snuff is powdered tobacco that is mixed with salts, moisture, oils, flavorings, and other additives. It is marketed in two forms—dry and moist. Chewing tobacco is marketed in loose leaf form, pressed as a rectangle called a plug, or in a twist or roll. As with snuff, aroma and flavoring agents are added to chewing tobacco. A quid (piece) of tobacco can either be chewed or held between the cheek and gum. "Dipping" is holding a pinch of moist snuff in the same place. In Europe, snuff is most commonly taken dry and intranasally.

HISTORY OF TOBACCO USE[1]

The West Discovers Tobacco

In the late fifteenth century Columbus and other explorers found Indians in the New World smoking dried tobacco leaves. The pleasant effects of nicotine caught on like fire, and smoking quickly became popular among the Europeans. They brought home seeds of the tobacco plant and spread them to other parts of the world on their ventures. In these early years the Spanish held a monopoly on the world tobacco market because *Nicotiana tabacum* is indigenous to South America. However, the English took a piece of the business when John Rolfe's *Nicotiana tabacum* crop flourished in the colony of Virginia.

At first, only the wealthy could afford tobacco. For example, in England tobacco was worth its weight in silver, and people paid that price. However, by the early seventeenth century tobacco use had become widespread, and even the poor could afford it. In 1614 London had about 7,000 tobacco shops. By the middle of that century tobacco use had spread through central Europe, and signs of the addictive nature of the drug were evident. For example, African natives would trade land, livestock, and slaves for tobacco.

Not everybody regarded tobacco in the highest terms. In the middle 1600s, Popes Urban VIII and Innocent X issued papal bulls against tobacco use, but clergy and laymen alike continued to smoke. In 1633 in Constantinople, the Sultan Murad IV paid surprise visits to his men in combat during war.

---

[1]This section on the history of tobacco use is taken from Brecher (1972), Stewart (1967), and Blum (1984).

These harvested tobacco plants await conversion to commercial products such as cigarettes and chewing tobacco.

If the soldiers were caught smoking, the good sultan punished them by quartering, hanging, beheading, and worse. Yet the soldiers continued to smoke. The Russian czar in 1634 also prohibited smoking. He punished his offending subjects by slitting their nostrils and by imposing other consequences that might impede their smoking. But the Russians did not give up tobacco.

The Japanese were given tobacco by Portuguese seamen in 1542. Like their western counterparts, the Japanese took to smoking quickly—so quickly that by 1603 an edict against smoking already had been issued by the emperor. But the Japanese did not stop. In 1639 smoking had become so established in Japan that a person was offered a smoke with a ceremonial cup of tea. "From these days until today . . . no country that has ever learned to use tobacco has given up the practice" (Brecher, 1972, p. 213). No substance has replaced tobacco in people's hearts, minds, and bodies. When tobacco smokers discovered the pleasures of smoking marijuana or opium, these drugs did not displace tobacco. They merely were smoked in addition to it.

"I cannot but . . . criticize that new . . . fashion . . . which outdoes all passions for indulgence in drink. Dissolute persons have taken to imbibing noisly drinking into their bodies the smoke of a plant they call . . . tobacco, with incredible avidity and inextinguishable zeal."

Palatinate's ambassador to the Netherlands, 1627
(Cited in Schivelbusch, 1992, p. 86)

Tobacco as Panacea

From the time Columbus and his colleagues discovered tobacco use among the Native Americans until about 1860, the tobacco plant was accepted widely as having medical therapeutic value. Probably tobacco reached its peak of recognition as a medicinal herb at the beginning of the seventeenth century, even though at the same time King James I of England published his skepticisms about tobacco's curative powers. The king admonished that using tobacco for pleasure was morally wrong. To give you an idea of how its reputation exceeded its critics' influence, Table 7-1 lists some of the ways to-bacco has been used medically. During the 350 years the table covers, some people believed it was literally possible to breathe life into another, as long as that breath carried tobacco smoke. Tobacco was esteemed at one time as a panacea weed.

From Panacea to Panned

The concept of tobacco as a therapeutic agent took a serious blow in 1828 when two Frenchmen, L. Posselt and F.A. Reimann, isolated nicotine. The chemical was named after a man named Nicot, who was the French ambas-sador to Portugal and who conducted exacting experiments with tobacco as a medicinal herb. He published his purported successes worldwide. The isola-tion of nicotine was damaging to its medical reputation because the toxic and addictive properties of the compound began to be understood.

During the years 1830–1860 the use of tobacco for medicine and plea-sure in the United States was subject to a stream of attacks by clergymen, ed-ucators, and some physicians. This also occurred in Europe. Sometimes the ills attributed to tobacco were not based in medical science. For example, perverted sexuality, impotency, and insanity all were attributed to tobacco. In 1849 Dr. R.T. Trall denounced the medical use of tobacco and illustrated his argument by describing a case of tobacco addiction. By the middle of the nineteenth century tobacco had all but vanished from the United States phar-macopoeia, and the dangers of tobacco as a drug were well-known. As the United States prepared for a civil war in 1860, the use of tobacco as a medical agent had virtually ended. But people continued to use tobacco for pleasure.

PREVALENCE OF TOBACCO USE

History shows that tobacco's popularity can resist even the most severe ob-stacles. In the United States today, cigarette smoking is by far the most com-mon way to use tobacco. Six of every seven pounds of tobacco grown in the United States are used for making cigarettes, and the other pound is used

Table 7-1   Uses for Tobacco as Medical Treatment Agent, 1492–1853

- Application externally in various forms (such as ashes, hot leaves, balm, lotion, mush, oil, many more) for pain due to internal or external disorders and for skin diseases or injuries of any kind
- Introduced into all openings of the head to treat diseases of the ears (such as smoke blown into), eyes (juice to cleanse), mouth (such as small ball chewed) and nose (such as snuff blown up nose of patient by physician)
- Introduced into the mouth to reach other organs, such as the lungs (such as smoke introduced directly by the physician), the stomach (such as through juice, boiled or uncooked), and the teeth (such as use of ashes to clean)
- Introduced into the nostrils to reach lungs (such as inhaled odor of snuff powder)
- Introduced into the intestinal canal (such as smoke or tobacco enema)
- Introduced into the vagina by injection

Note: This table was adapted from Stewart (1967), Appendix 5.

for making pipe and cigar tobaccos and smokeless tobacco products (U.S. Department of Health and Human Services [USDHHS], 1987). Furthermore, cigarette smoking demands the most attention because it is the most toxic way to smoke tobacco, followed in order by cigar and pipe smoking (Blum, 1984). Accordingly we begin this discussion with the prevalence of cigarette smoking.

Smoking in the United States

A number of national surveys of smoking among American adults have been conducted. These studies show that the percentage of men and women who smoke has declined steadily since 1965. Coupled with the decline in smokers is a steady increase in the percentage of adults who identify themselves as former smokers (Hughes, 1993; USDHHS, 1987). That is, increasing numbers of people have said they quit smoking, and most of them did so on their own (Zusy, 1987). Self-quitters are thought to have been "lighter" (fewer than 25 cigarettes a day) smokers. However, there remain many current smokers who say they want to quit but cannot seem to.

It probably is no coincidence that the peak of smoking among Americans was in 1963. In 1964 the U.S. Public Health Service's *Smoking and Health: Report of the Advisory Committee to the Surgeon General* was published. It detailed the health hazards of cigarette smoking in a way then unprecedented in scope and persuasion.

You learned in Chapter 1 that overall prevalence rates of drug use may mask important differences among different subgroups. This also applies to smoking. Table 7-2 summarizes 1992 national survey data for cigarette use in the last 30 days for gender and racial/ethnic subgroups. One point that emerges from Table 7-2 is that age is an important factor, as the highest rates of current cigarette use are among 18–34-year-olds. Note also that rates for men and women are similar throughout the age range. This is because the rates of decline in smoking prevalence since the 1960s have been far steeper for men than for women. However, men started out at a much higher prevalence rate. It is significant that prevalence rates for the youngest ages, 12–17, hover around 10% and are statistically identical for boys and girls.

Table 7-2 Percentages of Individuals in Different Age, Gender, and Racial/Ethnic Groups Who Reported Cigarette Use in the Past Month, 1992

| | Age | | | | |
Sex	12–17	18–25	26–34	>34	Total
Male	9.6	32.8	35.4	27.6	27.9
Female	9.5	31.1	32.1	23.3	24.6
Race/Ethnicity					
White	11.6	35.5	35.5	24.8	26.9
Black	3.2	20.2	33.5	32.5	26.7
Hispanic	7.4	24.1	24.4	23.3	21.5

Source: National Institute of Drug Abuse 1992 National Survey (U.S. Department of Health and Human Services, 1993b).

Racial/ethnic identity also relates to smoking rates. Whites have the highest rates of the three groups in Table 7-2, until we reach the 26–34-year-old group, when the rate among blacks rises to nearly the rate for whites. Among respondents older than 34, the smoking prevalence of whites and blacks essentially is the same.

Two factors not included in Table 7-2 are education and employment status. Although these variables are correlated, it is of interest to look at them separately. Current smoking prevalence for all respondents 18 years or older consistently was highest for individuals who were unemployed. The overall magnitude of difference was about 14 percentage points between the unemployed and those employed full- or part-time. Regarding education among respondents 18 years or older, there was a negative relationship between smoking and education—as years of education went up, prevalence went down. The difference was most marked among 18–34-year-olds (USD-HHS, 1993). Data such as these on education and employment are the bases for arguments that the ills of smoking fall disproportionately on the least-advantaged citizens of U.S. society.

Initiation of Smoking

It is important to know who initiates smoking and the number of people who do so, as people tend to become dependent on nicotine quickly and before they are 20 years old. So, it seems a lot easier to start smoking than it is to stop. An indirect indicator of initiation is smoking among young people. In 1974 national survey data showed that about 23% of respondents aged 12–17 said they smoked cigarettes in the last month. This percentage declined to about 10% in 1988 and has stayed close to that rate through 1992 (USDHHS, 1993 a,b). Given the concern about smoking initiation, the lack of decline since 1988 in past month prevalence among this young age group is noteworthy. Furthermore, the lack of decline in prevalence differs from the trends observed for older respondents. The past month prevalence rates of cigarette smoking for respondents 18–25 years old was about 50% in 1974. That percentage fell to slightly over 40% in 1979 and was about 32% in 1992.

Another good view of smoking among young people can be obtained from the federal government's annual national surveys of drug use among seniors, and now, other high school students. Figure 7-1 shows the trend in high school seniors' reports of cigarette use in the past month since the seniors surveys began in 1975. You can see in Figure 7-1 that reports of cigarette use in the past month have declined since the peak of almost 40% in 1975. The 30% mark was crossed in 1981, with a very gradual further decline to 27.8% in 1992 (Johnston, O'Malley, & Bachman, 1993).

Table 7-2 gave an indication of subgroup differences in young people who smoke. We can further look at such differences among the high school seniors that add to our picture of early smoking. Males (29.2%) reported a prevalence rate slightly higher than females (26.1%) did in 1992. Probably the most important factor was whether the respondents said they planned to attend college. For those who said they had no plans to attend college or to attend fewer than four years of it, the past month smoking prevalence was

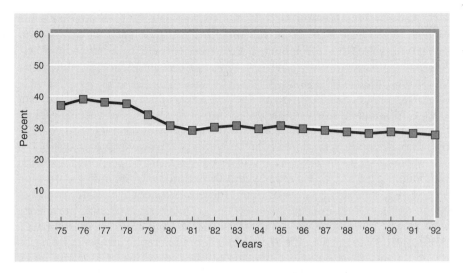

Figure 7-1   Percentage of seniors who report cigarette use in the last 30 days, High School Surveys, 1974–1992. (Source: Johnston, O'Malley, & Bachman, 1993)

38.6%. For seniors who said they planned to complete four years of college, the prevalence was 23.8% (Johnston, O'Malley, & Bachman, 1993).

Per-Capita Cigarette Use and Smoking Prevalence

Consistent with the trends in smoking prevalence, the per-capita annual cigarette consumption among those 18 years and older has declined steadily from its 1963 peak. However, the decline has not been as steady as we saw for current smoking prevalence. There are two reasons for this. Among people who still smoke, a greater proportion of them are heavier smokers than the proportions in previous years. In addition, the cigarette has changed. Currently, more than 90% of smokers in the United States use filtered cigarettes, compared to less than 60% in 1963, and less than 2% in 1952. Tar content has been reduced in today's cigarette by two-thirds, and nicotine content by one-half, compared to the cigarettes of 1954 (Shopland & Brown, 1985). Because of lower nicotine content, smokers today tend to smoke more cigarettes than did smokers in earlier years.

Smokeless Tobacco Use

The use of smokeless tobacco products recently has attracted a lot of attention in the United States. From 1964 to 1986 there appears to have been a steady decline in the use of such products among Americans (pipe and cigar tobacco use declined considerably, too). According to the Centers for Disease Control, the rate of smokeless tobacco use among adult Americans did not change from 1987 to 1991. Among younger people the picture changes, as the use of smokeless tobacco products has increased substantially since the 1970s (USDHHS, 1989).

DRUGS AND CULTURE
MAKING UP FOR LOST PREVALENCE

In Shanghai you can hear a radio program called the American Music Hour that is sponsored by Marlboro cigarettes. In Taiwan you could have attended a fashion show sponsored by Virginia Slims. In 1993 in the Philippines there was a bicycle race called the Marlboro Tour.

All these and more are evidence of the significant inroads American tobacco companies have made into Asian markets. As reported in detail in 1993 by Stan Sesser in the *New Yorker*, the marriage of American cigarette companies and the huge Asian market began in 1985. In that year, the U.S. government, which has gone to great lengths to discourage tobacco use among its own people, put pressure on Japan, Taiwan, South Korea, and Thailand to break their respective governments' monopolies on the sale of tobacco and to permit the sale of American cigarettes. The government of China still has a monopoly over tobacco sales there, but no later than 1995 the Chinese will allow the sale of American cigarettes in China as part of a broader trade agreement with the United States. The huge population numbers in Asia give the potential to greatly rejuvenate the sales of American tobacco companies, which face the steadily declining rates of smoking among many segments of the U.S. population.

The arrival of American tobacco products, essentially cigarettes, has changed patterns of smoking in the affected Asian countries. For example, in Asia smoking among the young and women generally had not been socially acceptable, and the government monopolies did not gear advertisements to those groups. But American advertising promotions such as rock concerts, fashion shows, and bike races have changed all that. For instance, American cigarette products arrived in Taiwan in 1987. In a 1985 survey of 2,000 Taiwanese high school students, 26% of the boys and 1% of the girls said they smoked. In 1991, a comparable survey of 1,100 students showed figures of 48% for the boys and 20% for the girls. Of course, as these trends continue there are profound implications for the health and welfare of the people of Asia. The World Health Organization estimates that in 20 or 30 years smoking-related deaths in "developing" countries will rise from the current one million a year to about seven million. China tops the list of expected death increases.

What would your position be on exporting cigarettes if you were the U.S. Secretary of Agriculture? What are some of the financial, cultural, and ethical questions that you think are important to consider?

Subgroup data on smokeless tobacco use in the past month are available for the 1991 national survey on drug use (USDHHS, 1993a) and are presented in Table 7-3. Smokeless tobacco use varies according to age (most popular among 18–25-year-olds), race/ethnicity (most popular among whites), and region of the United States (most popular in the South). The most striking difference is between men and women—thirteenfold.

"Have you ever experienced the snuff sensation yet? Wow, it's heady stuff. Well here's your chance to delight in the sensual pleasure of snuffing for free."
Promotion of Imperial Tobacco, England
(Cited in Wilkinson, 1986, p. 62)

Table 7-3   Prevalence of Smokeless Tobacco Use by Age, Gender, Race/Ethnicity and Region of the U.S., 1991

Variable Age	Prevalence (%)
12–17	3.0
18–25	5.8
26–34	3.6
>34	2.8
Sex	
Male	6.5
Female	.5
Race/Ethnicity	
White	3.9
Black	2.0
Hispanic	.8
Region	
Northeast	1.2
North Central	3.0
South	5.4
West	2.5
Overall Total	3.4

Source: 1991 National Household Survey on Drug Abuse (USDHHS, 1993a).

The seniors survey of 1992 adds to our view of smokeless tobacco use among young people. A total of 20.8% of the male seniors said they used smokeless tobacco in the last month, compared to 2.0% of the females. The overall rate of use that the seniors reported was 11.4%. As with cigarette use, plans for college made a difference. Among students who said they intended to complete four years of college, 9.4% reported smokeless tobacco use in the last month. The rate for the other respondents was 18.0% (Johnston et al., 1993).

Although all of the subgroup differences in smokeless tobacco use are important, the gender differences are worthy of additional comment. The great disparity between males and females offsets to a degree the steeper decline in smoking among males than females over the years. That is, when considering both smoked and smokeless tobacco, males continue to have a considerably higher exposure to tobacco products than females do.

PHARMACOLOGY OF NICOTINE

Sites of Action

To understand the action of nicotine it is essential to understand the neurotransmitter acetylcholine (ACH), which we reviewed in Chapter 3. Nicotine stimulates the same receptors that are sensitive to ACH and therefore is a cholinergic agonist drug (Julien, 1992). ACH stimulates both the autonomic and central nervous systems. Table 7-4 is a summary of ACH effects on biology and behavior.

The use of smokeless tobacco products among younger
people has increased considerably since the 1970s.

Table 7-4　　Acetylcholine Effects on Biology and Behavior

Increases blood pressure
Increases heart rate
Stimulates release of epinephrine from adrenal glands
Increases tone and activity of the gastrointestinal tract
Involved in CNS functions of arousal, attention, learning, memory storage and
　　retrieval, mood, and rapid eye movement (REM) during sleep

Note: Adapted from information in Julien, pp. 141, 399–400.

In addition, nicotine is called a biphasic drug, because at low doses it
stimulates ACH receptors but at higher doses it retards neural transmission
(Krogh, 1991; Taylor, 1990). This biphasic action partly explains the complex
effects that humans perceive when they ingest nicotine, which we will discuss
shortly.

Pharmacokinetics

Absorption   Nicotine can be absorbed through most of the body's membranes. The drug is rapidly absorbed through the oral, buccal (the cheeks or mouth cavity), and nasal mucosa, the gastrointestinal tract, and the lungs (Russell, 1976). Russell related a story to illustrate how readily nicotine can be absorbed. A florist was using a pesticide spray containing nicotine, and by accident soaked the seat of his pants with it. In only 15 minutes the florist had **nicotine poisoning** and had to be hospitalized for four days. When he recovered and was dressing to return home, the florist put on the same pants, which still had some nicotine on them. He was readmitted to the hospital an hour later with nicotine poisoning.

Nicotine absorption depends on both the site of absorption and how the nicotine is delivered. Nicotine is most readily absorbed from the lungs, which makes inhaling cigarette smoke an efficient way to get a dose of nicotine. Nicotine is not as readily absorbed through the oral, buccal, or nasal mucosa. The nicotine in cigar or pipe smoke, for example, is not as readily absorbed as that in cigarettes because people usually do not inhale cigars or pipes. As a result, the nicotine is absorbed through the mouth. When nicotine is taken by using snuff or by chewing tobacco, it is absorbed through the mucosa of the nose and the mouth, respectively.

How nicotine is delivered also affects absorption for a few reasons. You will recognize some of these differences from reading Chapter 4. One factor is the acidity of the medium (for example, smoke) of delivery. The more alkaline (basic) the medium, the easier the absorption. Cigar and pipe smoke are more basic than cigarette smoke, which compensates to some extent for the difference between the mouth and lungs in ease of absorption. Time of contact of the nicotine-containing substance with the absorption site also is important. The more contact, the greater the amount of nicotine absorbed. For example, the use of snuff and chewing tobacco allows considerable time for nicotine absorption at the nose and mouth (Blum, 1984).

Distribution   After nicotine is absorbed it is distributed by the blood to a number of sites of pharmacological action. For example, when a cigarette is inhaled, nicotine reaches the brain from the lungs within seven seconds. By comparison, it takes 14 seconds for blood to flow from the arm to the brain, which would be the typical route for intravenous injection. Therefore, in delivery of nicotine brain levels rise rapidly and then decline just as quickly as the drug is distributed to other parts of the body. The effects of nicotine can be observed rapidly, as its distribution half-life is only eight minutes. The speed with which absorption and distribution occur is one reason smokers tend to reach for a cigarette so soon after they have finished their last one. The average smoker of a typical cigarette manufactured in the United States absorbs about 1 mg of nicotine for each cigarette that he or she smokes.

Metabolism and Excretion   The major organ responsible for metabolizing nicotine is the liver. The lungs and the kidneys also play a part in the body's chemical breakdown of nicotine. Nicotine is eliminated primarily in the urine, which is the major way nicotine is excreted from the body. About 10% to 20%

Nicotine poisoning
A consequence of nicotine overdose, characterized by palpitations, dizziness, sweating, nausea, or vomiting.

of nicotine also is eliminated unchanged through the urinary tract (Blum, 1984). Less important vehicles of eliminating nicotine and its metabolites are saliva, sweat, and the milk of lactating women (Jones, 1987; Russell, 1976).

One study compared blood nicotine levels over a course of two hours in 10 subjects administered comparable doses of nicotine in cigarettes, oral snuff, and chewing tobacco (Benowitz, Porchet, Sheiner, & Jacob, 1988). The study showed that peak nicotine blood levels reached through the three sources were comparable. However, the rise in nicotine level was sharpest by smoking, with a quick, then a more gradual decline leveling to about one-third the peak level. In contrast, with both snuff and chewing tobacco the rise in blood level was slower, but higher levels of nicotine were maintained considerably longer than were maintained by smoking. These findings follow from the quicker nicotine absorption time through inhalation, but the increased nicotine exposure time gained by using chewing tobacco or snuff.

The course of nicotine blood levels by smoking gives considerable insight into why smokers often smoke many cigarettes a day. This pattern is necessary to maintain a nicotine blood level that is not below a threshold for the beginning of withdrawal symptoms (see below). Figure 7-2 is a graph of the average levels of nicotine in the blood of a cigarette smoker over the course of a full day. The level of nicotine in the blood rises during the course of the 16-hour part of the day when people are awake, with a peak around

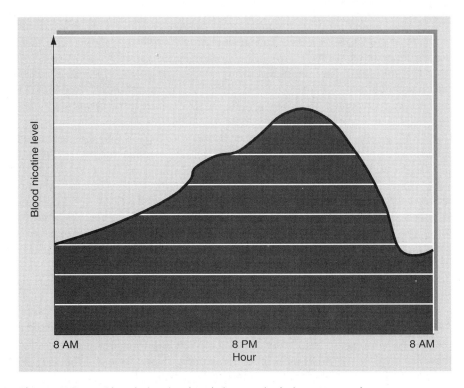

Figure 7-2   Blood nicotine levels in a typical cigarette smoker over a 24-hour period.

midnight. The level then declines during sleeping hours, but there is a positive level upon wakening in the morning.

TOLERANCE AND DEPENDENCE

Tolerance

"Recruits, you'll find that smoking will make you nauseous at first, but you will keep with it, and smoke a little more with each passing month until you level out your consumption, usually at about 20 cigarettes a day, and hold this pattern for years, maybe a lifetime."

Drill sergeant, describing
smoking to new users
of nicotine
(Cited in Krogh, 1991, p. 74)

Tolerance to nicotine develops quickly. For example, first attempts at smoking usually result in palpitations, dizziness, sweating, nausea, or vomiting (Russell, 1976). These are signs of acute nicotine poisoning. However, signs of tolerance to these autonomic effects of nicotine are evident even within the time of smoking the first cigarettes. Similarly, the effects of the nicotine in the initial puffs of the first cigarette of the day are greater than those in the last few puffs of that cigarette (Jones, 1987). The rapid development of tolerance to nicotine also is apparent in the short time it takes some people to reach the status of seasoned smoker. The time from their unpleasant first cigarette to pleasurable smoking of a pack a day or more can be as short as several weeks. Besides tolerance to the effects of nicotine, dispositional tolerance develops. For instance, smokers metabolize the drug more quickly than do nonsmokers (Edwards, 1986).

Physical Dependence

There is no question people can become physically dependent on nicotine. The major criterion for classification of a drug as one that induces physical dependence is what ensues when the drug is taken away for enough time so that the amount of it in the blood drops considerably or is eliminated. When a consistent set of physical symptoms results, it is said that the drug induces physical dependence. The reverse side of this criterion of physical dependence is that readministration of the drug alleviates any withdrawal symptoms that are present. In 1988 the U.S. Surgeon General's Office issued a full report with the conclusion that physical dependence on nicotine develops and that the drug is addicting.

Actually, studies have shown for some time that users of nicotine may become physically dependent on it. For example, Hughes, Grist, and Pechacek (1987) collected smokers' reports of the symptoms they experienced 24 hours after stopping smoking. The most common report (73% of the smokers) was a craving for tobacco, followed in order by irritability, anxiety, difficulty concentrating, restlessness, increased appetite, impatience, somatic complaints, and insomnia. A range of what generally would be considered unpleasant symptoms results when the dependent smoker stops smoking.

Once an individual begins smoking cigarettes there is a high likelihood that he or she will become dependent on nicotine. For example, Blum (1984) noted that among the adolescents who smoke more than 2–3 cigarettes occasionally, about 85% will become dependent on nicotine. In the Hughes study (1987) it was found that of the American adults who smoke, about one-third are dependent on nicotine. Therefore, about one-tenth of adult Americans are nicotine dependent.

ACUTE EFFECTS OF NICOTINE

As we noted, nicotine's effects are pervasive and complex. Table 7-5 is a summary of nicotine's acute pharmacological effects at "normal" doses, or doses that typically would be ingested by everyday smokers, tobacco chewers, or snuff users, for example. Because of nicotine's biphasic effects, its effects at higher doses would tend to be more depressant than are the effects listed in Table 7-5.

A major point to notice in Table 7-5 is that nicotine has ACH-like effects (see Table 7-4), which coincides with its ACH agonist action. Table 7-5 shows that nicotine has major CNS stimulant action, although these effects are not as intense as what is observed with cocaine and amphetamines. Nicotine's enhancing effects on alertness, learning, and memory are of considerable importance to us, because it seems that these effects account for a good part of nicotine's reinforcing effects in humans.

Another point to notice in Table 7-5 is nicotine's autonomic effects, particularly on the cardiovascular system. The stimulation of the heart and its resultant increased demands for oxygen underlie the association of nicotine and heart disease. In this regard, failure to deliver an adequate supply of oxygen to the heart may result in chest pain (angina), or a heart attack (Julien, 1992).

Nicotine is classified as a stimulant drug but people who use it often report a decrease in arousal. That is, the perception is that nicotine has calming effects, and nicotine users find this effect quite reinforcing. The reasons for this perception of lowered arousal are complex and include several factors. One factor may be nicotine's acute effect of relaxing the skeletal muscles (Table 7-5; also see Jones, 1987). Another pharmacological reason is nicotine's biphasic action—at higher doses its effects are more depressant.

However, pharmacology is only part of the explanation of how aroused a person feels when he or she uses nicotine. For example, part of the sedating psychological effects of smoking are due to the smoker's association of successfully coping with stress while smoking (Abrams & Wilson, 1986).

Another factor to consider is the association of nicotine use with pleasant social situations like parties. Many other secondary (associated) effects

Table 7-5   Acute Pharmacological Effects of Nicotine

General CNS Stimulant
- Increases behavioral activity
- May produce tremors
- Stimulates vomiting center in brain stem (tolerance to this effect develops quickly)
- Stimulates release of antidiuretic hormones from hypothalamus, increasing fluid retention
- Reduces muscle tone by reducing activity of afferent nerves from muscles
- Enhances alertness, learning, and memory

Other Actions
- Increases heart rate, blood pressure, contraction of the heart
- Initiates dilation of arteries, if they are *not* atherosclerotic, to meet heart's increased oxygen demand caused by nicotine

Note: Adapted from information in Julien (1992) and Taylor (1990).

of nicotine use exist and can contribute to the user's perception at times that the drug has calming effects.

A final acute effect of nicotine is its relationship to lower body weight. In this regard, nicotine decreases appetite for sweet foods and increases the amount of energy the body uses both while it is resting and while it is exercising (Jaffe, 1990; Russell, 1976; West & Russell, 1985). These features of nicotine help to explain the results of studies that show that smokers tend to weigh less than nonsmokers. Relatedly, it is commonly found that quitting smoking is associated with weight gain. The nicotine-body weight relationship is noteworthy to us, because the perception that smoking controls weight is a powerful motivator for continuing to smoke and for resuming smoking after stopping for a period of time. The motivation seems to be particularly strong among women (Abrams & Wilson, 1986; Klesges, Meyers, Klesges, & La Vasque, 1989). The good news for people who want to stop smoking is that the weight gain associated with quitting may be only temporary (Chen, Horne, & Dosman, 1993).

Nicotine's Dependence Liability

The surgeon general's 1988 conclusion that nicotine is physically addicting stunned many people, although knowledge that physical dependence on nicotine can develop had been around for years. The shock of the surgeon general's report probably lay in the public's failure to view nicotine as a "serious" drug, like cocaine or heroin. Yet, the circumstances are most conducive for developing both psychological and physical dependence on nicotine.

Nicotine's CNS stimulating effects, coupled with the frequent perception that it is sedating, are powerfully reinforcing to humans. Similarly, for some people nicotine's effect on body weight also is a strong motivation for its use. Nicotine remains a highly accessible drug, in spite of the numerous occasions of "sin taxing" that have been levied on its purchase over the years. In addition, although the number of social settings where nicotine use is acceptable has decreased recently, the social environment as a whole is far from hostile toward nicotine use.

The rapid rise and fall of nicotine blood levels, at least by smoking, creates the conditions for many nicotine reinforcements a day. For the smoker, each inhalation results in a drug reinforcement that must be replaced quickly because of a quick fall in blood level of nicotine. For a two-pack-a-day smoker, estimates average 300 nicotine reinforcements a day, which equals more than 15,000 a year.

Reasons such as these make psychological dependence on nicotine so likely once use of the drug starts. We have also noted the many social and environmental associations with nicotine use that strengthen psychological dependence. Additionally, strong incentive to continue using the drug is added when a person becomes physically dependent on it. Use must continue in order to avoid unpleasant withdrawal symptoms, or to escape such symptoms if they begin. Use of nicotine under such conditions is strengthened through negative reinforcement. Therefore, pharmacological, psychological, and social/environmental variables combine to make nicotine a drug with high dependence liability. Indeed, it now is generally agreed that smokers smoke, tobacco chewers chew, and snuffers snuff for the effects of nicotine.

EFFECTS OF CHRONIC TOBACCO USE

Chronic or long-term use of tobacco products is associated with the occurrence of life-threatening diseases. We will begin this section with the effects of chronic cigarette smoking, as it is the dominant way that tobacco is used. In 1990 the U.S. surgeon general estimated that, overall, 390,000 American smokers suffer premature deaths every year. For example, insurance companies have compiled information on differences in survival rates for men smokers aged 35 to 75. These 1980 data show that, by age 55, 10% of the smokers are dead compared to 4% of the nonsmokers. At age 65 the differences widen to 28% and 10%, respectively. And by age 75, the difference is twofold—50% and 25% (USDHHS, 1987). The 1993 Robert Wood Johnson Foundation study we cited in Chapter 1 estimated that the costs to U.S. society in 1990 from its citizens' smoking cigarettes was $72 billion.

Cigarette smoking damages health because of the constituents of tobacco smoke. The three culprits are tar, nicotine, and carbon monoxide, and cigarette smokers face continual exposure to them for years. For example, a two-pack-a-day smoker could be seen 13.4 hours a day with cigarette in hand, mouth, or ash tray, taking about 400 puffs, and inhaling as much as 1,000 mg of tar. Carbon monoxide appears to facilitate many of the disease processes associated with smoking. This is due to carbon monoxide's advantage over oxygen in binding to hemoglobin, which carries oxygen from the lungs to the tissues in the body. Exposure even to small amounts of carbon monoxide reduces the amount of hemoglobin available for binding to oxygen and causes deprivation of oxygen to the body's tissues. The brain and heart are especially vulnerable to this action of carbon monoxide, since these systems depend on aerobic respiration for proper functioning (Blum, 1984).

Most of the cancer-causing substances in smoke are in tar, which is the material remaining after cigarette smoke is passed through a filter. Nicotine also has been traced as a source of heart attacks and the onset of cancer (USDHHS, 1987). A cigarette typically contains about 6–8 mg of nicotine (cigars yield 15 to more than 40 mg). When cigarettes are smoked and inhaled, about 10% of the nicotine is absorbed, compared to 2.5% to 5% as much when

"They don't get your wind"; "Kent, the one cigarette that can show you proof of greater health protection"; "Less 'tar' than all leading longs"
Camels ad, 1935; Kent ad, 1953; L&M ad, 1979, respectively
(Cited in Viscusi, 1992, pp. 38–39)

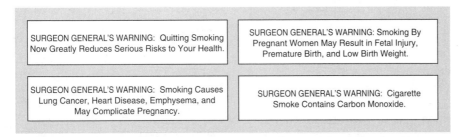

SURGEON GENERAL'S WARNING: Quitting Smoking Now Greatly Reduces Serious Risks to Your Health.

SURGEON GENERAL'S WARNING: Smoking By Pregnant Women May Result in Fetal Injury, Premature Birth, and Low Birth Weight.

SURGEON GENERAL'S WARNING: Smoking Causes Lung Cancer, Heart Disease, Emphysema, and May Complicate Pregnancy.

SURGEON GENERAL'S WARNING: Cigarette Smoke Contains Carbon Monoxide.

Figure 7-3   Four warnings that must appear on cigarette packages, according to a 1985 federal law. One warning per package appears, with each message rotated every three months. The contents of the messages are based on the *Reports of the Surgeon General on the Health Consequences of Smoking*.

smoke is drawn into the mouth and then exhaled. That virtually all cigarette smokers inhale is one reason other than sheer numbers that cigarette as opposed to cigar or pipe smoking has been traced as the major cause of diseases related to tobacco use.

Because of the importance of tar and nicotine content of cigarettes, until the mid-1980s the Federal Trade Commission (FTC) published statistics on the tar and nicotine yield of cigarette brands manufactured in the United States. The FTC used to conduct its own yield tests by using smoking machines and today reports the results of the same kind of tests conducted by tobacco companies, which the FTC requires them to do (Cotton, 1993).

The amount of tar and nicotine delivered in U.S. brand-name cigarettes has declined, as illustrated in Figure 7-4. Figure 7-4 shows that, from the late 1950s to the mid-1980s, the average delivery of tar and nicotine has gone down, although the rate of decline in tar seems higher than that of nicotine.

Reductions in delivery of tar and nicotine from a cigarette seem like a good thing, given what we said about their contribution to serious disease. Indeed, the American public perceives that low tar- and nicotine-yield cigarette brands are healthier (Cotton, 1993). However, an essential point throughout this discussion is that the measurement of tar and nicotine delivery is done by a smoking machine, which puffs consistently in the same controlled way regardless of the cigarette content. However, humans are not so standardized. When the nicotine content of a cigarette is reduced, smokers consciously or unconsciously either inhale the smoke more intensely or smoke more cigarettes (De Grandpre, Dickle, & Hughes, 1993). The result is exposure to similar amounts of toxic substances in the smoke from lower-yield and

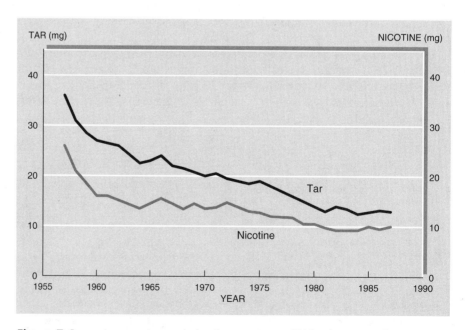

Figure 7-4   Average tar and nicotine content of U.S. cigarettes, 1957–1987. (Source: USDHHS, 1989, p. 88)

higher-yield cigarettes. This was confirmed empirically in a study of 298 smokers from New Mexico (Coultas, Stidley, & Samet, 1993). This is a critical finding, because risk of mortality from smoking goes up with increased exposure either by number of cigarettes smoked or by depth of inhalations. Therefore, any implication that low-yield nicotine and tar cigarettes are less hazardous is deceptive.

Diseases Linked to Cigarette Smoking

Cigarette smoking kills because it facilitates the development of coronary heart disease, cancer, and chronic obstructive lung disease. Heart disease is the single major killer in the United States, and people who smoke are at nearly twice the risk to contract it compared to nonsmokers. Cancers of the larynx, oral cavity, esophagus, bladder, pancreas, and kidney are associated with cigarette smoking. So associated that 30% of all cancer deaths are caused by it, as are 80% to 90% of all lung cancer deaths. Finally, 80% to 90% of chronic obstructive lung disease, such as emphysema, is caused by smoking. Fortunately, the risk of contracting these diseases falls with time away from cigarettes. If the smoker can manage to abstain for 10 years, his or her good health will be at the same risk as someone who has never smoked at all (USDHHS, 1987).

Many of the statistics on cigarette smoking and health in the United States were based on men who began the habit in a large way after World War I. Women increasingly took up smoking after World War II, and it was discovered that they soon fell prey to similar health damages (USDHHS, 1987). Perhaps the most startling indication of this change was that in 1987 lung cancer, a major killer related to smoking, replaced breast cancer as the leading cancer-related cause of death among women (Ernster, 1993).

Women also face health consequences of smoking that are unique to them. For example, women who smoke are at higher risk of cervical cancer, unwanted side effects of using oral contraceptives, and early menopause (Ernster, 1993). Furthermore, smokers who are pregnant incur a higher risk of spontaneous abortion, preterm births, low-weight babies, and fetal and infant deaths. If the infant is born healthy there still is risk, as nicotine is present in the mother's milk (USDHHS, 1987).

Other Tobacco Products and Health

The use of other tobacco products is not risk-free. Pipe and cigar smokers have higher death rates than do nonsmokers, but the differences are not as large as the comparisons we cited for cigarette smokers. Users of snuff and of other types of smokeless tobacco are more likely to get oral cancer and types of noncancerous oral disease.

Passive Smoking

It once was thought that smokers were harming only themselves. However, we know now that if you merely stay in the vicinity of people smoking, then you will absorb nicotine, carbon monoxide, and other elements of tobacco smoke,

Contemporary Issue
CIGARETTE SMOKING AND DEATH: WHO'S RESPONSIBLE?

Since the 1950s smokers have filed hundreds of cases against cigarette companies, claiming the companies are responsible for the smokers' poor health. Until the 1980s all of these cases had failed and the tobacco industry never paid a cent in damages. Their trump card was the 1965 Federal Cigarette Labeling and Advertising Act that took effect in 1966. (This is the same act that was extended to require the rotation of four warning labels on cigarette packages.) Federal courts had always claimed that this act preempted the tobacco industry from responsibility for the health consequences of smoking, at least for any smoking done on or after January 1, 1966. Furthermore, juries had tended to perceive that smokers were responsible for their own decisions regarding smoking.

Great attention was given to a smoker's suit filed in 1983 by a New Jersey woman. In 1988 a jury awarded $400,000 to the husband of the woman, who died in 1984 of lung cancer. This landmark decision was overturned in 1990 by an appeals court, which ruled that whether the woman had seen or believed tobacco industry advertisements before 1966 had not been proven. The woman's family continued to fight, and in a suit heard by the Supreme Court in June 1992 there was another watershed ruling. The Court argued that the 1965 law did not have preemptive effects but that a 1969 modification of the law did. However, the Court also ruled that smokers could file damage suits against tobacco companies if it could be proved that the companies intentionally concealed their own internal research findings showing the hazards of smoking, as has been suggested in U.S. Congressional hearings in Spring 1994. The first legal suit based on this latter ruling was filed in November 1992 by an Illinois man dying of lung cancer.

The New Jersey woman's family dropped their suit in November 1992 at least partly due to the great financial cost of pursuing it. But the family made a large impact on the legal battleground that will determine who owns what part of the responsibility for the effects of cigarettes on smokers' health. For example, in May 1994 both Mississippi and Florida planned legal action to hold tobacco companies liable for payments the states have made toward treating their residents' smoking-related diseases.

The implications of legal actions regarding the chronic effects of cigarette smoking are profound for the tobacco industry, for the consumer of tobacco products, and for our principles of choice and personal responsibility. For example, if tobacco companies are held liable for diseases that can be traced to use of their products, what does that imply for liability for the public's use of alcohol—another legal drug that could have chronic detrimental effects? What would the companies' liability imply about the principle that individuals have the freedom and responsibility of their actions?

although in lesser amounts than if you were actively smoking. However, because your body is the recipient of the toxins of another person's tobacco smoke, it is as if you were smoking passively.

Passive smoking is an active killer. One review of research on this topic suggests that passive smoking in households kills about 53,000 Americans a

The health message of this 1930s advertisement stands in stark contrast to current thinking.

year, mostly (74%) due to heart disease (Glantz & Parmley, 1991). The 53,000 figure places passive smoking as the third-leading preventable cause of death in the United States, behind active smoking and alcohol. In 1993 the Centers for Disease Control and Prevention released data showing how widespread is the exposure to tobacco smoke among Americans. The Centers' study showed that cotinine, a nicotine by-product, was in the blood of all of the first 800 individuals tested, whether or not they smoked! (The total sample size was 23,000, so a lot more people still had to be tested.) The age range of the first 800 people in the sample was 4–91, so young children were not spared the effects of passive smoke. Moreover, one study showed that the fetus is exposed to significant amounts of nicotine if the nonsmoking mother is regularly exposed to cigarette smoke during the gestation period (Eliopoulos, Klein, Phan, et al., 1994). The importance of these findings is that children whose parents smoke are more likely than children whose parents do not smoke to have bronchitis and pneumonia, as well as some impairment in pulmonary function (Bonham & Wilson, 1981).

Research findings on passive smoking resulted in the 1992 decision of the U.S. Environmental Protection Agency to designate tobacco smoke as a class A ("known human") cancer-causing agent (*The Lancet*, 1993). Such action is in accord with the increased restriction of smoking in public places (in some states, like California, smoking is banned in all public places) and raises the chances of litigation for health damages caused by passive tobacco smoking.

TREATMENT OF CIGARETTE SMOKING

In this chapter's last section we consider ways to stop smoking. Although stopping the use of other tobacco products also is an important topic, we again will focus on cigarette smoking because it accounts for the vast majority of tobacco use, and because it by far has been the major subject in the literature on ways to stop nicotine use.

Note that nicotine is the only drug for which we consider treatment outside of Chapter 16, where we review treatment of other drugs and their abuse. This is because such a large amount has been written on the subject compared to other nonalcohol drugs. Furthermore, treatments for stopping smoking have been at the center of health professionals' and the public's attention, due to the health hazards of smoking.

In reviewing nicotine's acute effects you began to see how a person easily could get into and keep the habit of tobacco use. In reviewing the health consequences of chronic tobacco use you may have wondered why anyone would continue to use tobacco products. Yet, of course, many people do continue to use such products despite wanting to quit; others find quitting easier.

Relapse
A term from physical disease, relapse means return to a previous state of illness from one of health. As applied to smoking, it means the smoker resumes smoking after having abstained for some amount of time.

Lichtenstein (1982) presented a useful summary of some of the possible determinants of people stopping smoking. These include health consequences, expense, social support for not smoking, self-mastery, aesthetics, and examples to others. Lichtenstein also summarized determinants of smoking **relapse,** which is a major problem in smoking treatment and in treatment of substance-use disorders in general. Smoking relapse determinants include nicotine withdrawal symptoms, stress and frustration, social pressure, alcohol use, and weight gain. We will examine how the determinants of stopping and resuming smoking have influenced the content of formal treatments and their long-term effectiveness. Before we get to that, there is the question of whether formal treatments of cigarette smoking are ever needed.

The Necessity of Formal Treatment

The survey studies we cited earlier in this chapter show the great trend of decline in smoking rates among U.S. adults from the 1960s to the early 1990s. It seems that about half of the living adults who have said they smoked have quit (USDHHS, 1989). We noted that most of these people stopped smoking on their own. This raises the question of whether formal treatments for smoking are necessary.

In answering this question there are a few points to consider. Although most people cease smoking without help, they tend to succeed only after multiple attempts. Perhaps you have heard of the comment attributed to Mark Twain: "Quitting smoking is easy; I've done it many times." Indeed, with or without formal treatment, success at stopping smoking is more likely with more previous tries at quitting. Another important statistic, which we discuss in more detail in Chapter 16, is the rate of "spontaneous remission." Briefly, this refers to the rate of "cure" (in other words, stopping smoking) during a given time period without any formal treatment. Although data on spontaneous remission are basic to evaluating treatment effectiveness, they unfortunately are extremely hard to collect. For cigarette smoking, Abrams and Wilson (1986) estimated that the rate of spontaneous remission ranges from 3% to 14%. Formal treatments have to do better than the rate of spontaneous remission in order to prove their worth.

Another set of statistics to consider in deciding whether formal treatments of smoking are necessary concern the economic and social costs of cigarette smoking; earlier we cited the figure of $72 billion in 1990. The financial figures do not begin to reflect the human suffering of patients and their families that goes with contracting cancer, heart disease, and other diseases associated with chronic tobacco use.

Add to this the finding of a 1991 study of men and women in three different communities that showed that quitting smoking, even at a later age of life, prolongs life. The increased longevity is due to a quick reduction in risk of major smoking-influenced illnesses (La Croix, Lang, Scherr, et al., 1991). Wynder and Hoffmann (1979) argued that if a smoking treatment resulted in a nicotine abstinence rate of 20% to 25% for one year after treatment ended, then that treatment would be worth its while from both health and economic standpoints.

Treatment Effectiveness

Programs for stopping smoking focus on controlling nicotine withdrawal symptoms, breaking the habitual motor behavior involved in smoking, and learning skills to cope with the emotions, thoughts, and situations in which smokers say they use cigarettes to help them. People who stop smoking permanently have learned these skills well, have incentives to abstain such as health, and have help in staying off cigarettes from family, friends, and others who care about them (Abrams & Wilson, 1986; Jones, 1987).

Abrams and Wilson (1986) divided stop-smoking programs into two types, minimal and full-treatment programs. The major difference between minimal and full programs is the amount of professional contact. Minimal programs do not involve the continual assistance of professionals or organizations and require only specific materials and occasional consultation. In contrast, full-treatment programs require ongoing contact with professional staff. Regardless of the type of treatment, the most efficient treatment goal is total abstinence from nicotine. Reduction of smoking to "controlled" amounts does not seem feasible for people who request treatment (Kenford, Fiore, Jorenby, et al., 1994).

Examples of minimal treatment programs include mass-media advertisements against smoking like those sponsored by the American Cancer Society, self-help books, and brief contacts with a physician in the private office or hospital setting. Results of studies of these types of treatments show quitting rates up to the mid-20% range. These outcomes are significant in view of the low costs and small amount of professional time required for their implementation. Accordingly, minimal treatment has become a major mode of smoking intervention in the 1990s (Curry, 1993; Shiffman, 1993). Such success should not be too surprising in view of the high percentage of former smokers who quit on their own. However, researchers have also shown minimal treatment programs do not work too well with the heavier, more nicotine-dependent smoker. These individuals are more likely to succeed in more intensive, full-treatment programs.

Most of the data we have on full treatment involve applying techniques to stop the smoking habit and changing how smokers think and feel about smoking as an effective method of gaining pleasure and relieving stress. The smoker usually is taught skills to help him or her handle settings associated with smoking. Such programs are called multicomponent behavioral treatments.

Behavioral treatments for smoking have averaged in the range of 25% to 35% abstinence rates at the end of six months to a year (Shiffman, 1993). However, the problem of resumption of smoking remains. Although these abstinence rates are significant, relapse is a major problem. If 35% of the smokers are abstinent at six months, 65% have relapsed.

You have seen that a major reason that smokers have such a problem staying off cigarettes is the craving they experience when they stop smoking. To the extent that craving is due to physical withdrawal, this implies that if nicotine could somehow be used in the treatment of smoking, there would be a better chance of quitting for good. Such a treatment has been developed in the form of chewing gum that contains nicotine (Jarvis, 1983). The use of this gum adds to one-year outcome success rates, especially in combination with behavioral treatment programs (Goldstein & Niaura, 1991). It seems nicotine gum reduces nicotine craving to some degree (West & Schneider, 1987), which gives the smoker more opportunity to strengthen ways other than smoking of coping with events and situations of everyday life. Fortunately, few patients have trouble with becoming dependent on the nicotine gum they were prescribed for treatment. Therefore, its use seems to be one safe way to handle the large problem of physical dependence on nicotine in the treatment of smoking.

Another nicotine-replacement method that has become popular is the nicotine patch. The idea is to control administration of nicotine transdermally by using a specially prepared patch, as we briefly described in Chapter 4. One reason for developing a transdermal patch was to combat some of the problems with using nicotine gum that reduce compliance with treatment, such as unpleasant taste and upset stomach if the gum is swallowed (Rose, 1991).

Studies of the longer term (one-year) smoking rates following treatment suggest that the patch combined with behavioral programs has success rates similar to those of nicotine gum combined with behavioral programs (Hughes, 1992; Hurt, Dale, Fredrickson, et al., 1994; Rose, 1991). Therefore, it seems that the nicotine patch may be an effective alternative nicotine-replacement method to nicotine gum for people who desire one. As it was designed to do, the nicotine patch may help success rates by reducing some nicotine withdrawal symptoms, such as irritability and difficulty concentrating. However, studies of this effect of the patch suggest that it does not substantially reduce smokers' overall craving for a cigarette (Rose, 1991).

"I'm telling you I wanted a cigarette so bad I cried. I was so nervous I could hardly carry on at work, and I couldn't hide it. After a while I would just shake. People said they couldn't see it, but I could feel it."

Person trying to stay off cigarettes
(Cited in Krogh, 1991, p. 71)

The finding that nicotine patch treatment reduced some of the specific symptoms of nicotine withdrawal but did not significantly reduce overall craving raises an important general point about nicotine-replacement treatment. Drug craving is extremely complex and is not only a product of biological factors such as physical withdrawal. Instead, craving also is a result of psychological, social, and environmental factors. In this context it is not startling that nicotine craving may be reduced only to a limited degree as a result of nicotine replacement. It also suggests a reason why nicotine-replacement treatments seem to work best when they are combined with behavioral programs. In this regard, behavioral programs for smoking help people to cope better with the determinants of continuing to smoke or of resuming smoking after stopping. Examples of such determinants include social pressure to smoke, general environmental cues that are strongly associated with smoking, and psychological states like stress and frustration (Lichtenstein, 1982). On the other hand, nicotine-replacement treatment alone gives people only nicotine as a way to cope with feelings and situations that are powerfully connected to smoking.

CONCLUSIONS

Nicotine is a strongly reinforcing drug to humans and can be quickly addicting. Nicotine does have some "adaptive" acute effects, such as improved sensory and cognitive functioning, but most attention has been paid to the health consequences of chronic nicotine use. As a result, the emphasis today is on how to stop the public from using nicotine in a damaging way. The best way to do this is by continuing the information campaigns that have resulted in an overall decline of the prevalence of smoking and other use of tobacco in the United States. Along these lines, programs aimed at youth who have not begun to use tobacco are the best bet, because once tobacco use starts it is hard to stop. Tobacco-use prevention programs with promise are being developed. However, a major counterforce to prevention programs is tobacco industry advertising. Tobacco companies in the United States spend almost $4 billion a year on advertising campaigns (and tobacco products cannot be advertised on television or radio). For both adolescents and adults, advertising strengthens the positive associations that go along with smoking and other tobacco use.

The importance of advertising cannot be overstated. Tobacco companies' targeting their ads to specific groups, such as youth, minorities, and women, has come under strong attack. In this regard, tobacco companies, especially cigarette producers, pair tobacco use with social ideals. For example, the "Joe Camel" ads have been alleged to attract youth with the suggestion that smoking is cool. Cigarette ads associate slim, attractive, successful females with smoking. Such an approach plays into the high demand in U.S. society for women to be slim, and into weight control as a major reason that girls begin and women continue to smoke (Ernster, 1993; Pierce, Lee, & Gilpin, 1994). Several years ago a new cigarette, Uptown, disappeared from the market shortly after its debut because of the uproar created over its obvious targeting of black consumers.

Contemporary Issue:
THE "SMOKELESS CIGARETTE"

An alternative "smokeless" cigarette has been developed. Although the manufacturer made no claims of less health risk to the smoker who uses the product, the smokeless cigarette did seem to alleviate some of the problems associated with passive smoking.

The smokeless cigarette first appeared on the market in 1987 with the product "Favor." However, Favor quickly fell into disfavor because the Federal Drug Administration decided it was a "drug delivery system" and should be regulated accordingly. This means the smokeless cigarette contraption could deliver drugs other than nicotine, such as crack. In this regard, the charcoal tip of the smokeless cigarette heats nicotine pellets, flavoring, and glycerol. The glycerol and heat combine to create an aerosol that is inhaled by the smoker (Page, 1988). It would seem to be a small step to replace nicotine pellets with chunks of crack cocaine. If the smokeless cigarette is viewed as a drug delivery system, then it would fall under regulation by the Food and Drug Administration instead of the Bureau of Alcohol, Tobacco, and Firearms, which regulates other nicotine products. Favor was then removed from the market and has not been heard of commercially since.

Then in 1988, another smokeless cigarette called "Premier" was test marketed. Premier was not really a cigarette at all, but just looked like one. Instead of burning leaf tobacco as with traditional cigarettes, the smokeless cigarette had a charcoal tip that heated a metal chamber filled with pellets of nicotine that were refined from leaf tobacco. The pellets were mixed with nutmeg for flavoring, and glycerol. When the glycerol was heated it formed an aerosol that the smoker inhaled as "smoke." Leaf tobacco was used in the chamber but only as insulation. The tobacco was never consumed.

Unfortunately for efforts at inventing alternatives to the traditional cigarette, the Premier efforts were also stymied. An essential problem was its bad odor and taste. One writer (a smoker) in *Vogue* magazine likened the odor to that of opening a grave on a warm day. A consumer in one of Premier's test market cities said using the product was similar to smoking a stick of plastic. These are not exactly the words that smokers of traditional cigarettes use to describe their tobacco pleasures.

Other problems arose, too. In January 1989 the American Medical Association (AMA) argued that Premier should be taken off the market and regulated by the FDA as a drug. In this regard, the AMA thought that similar to Favor, Premier actually is a nicotine delivery system.

The adversity proved to be too much for Premier, and in March 1989 the manufacturer decided to take it off the test market. The cost was about $325 million in product development and promotion. Although this is a substantial setback, the potential loss to the many people who still smoke would be greater if it caused the tobacco industry to stop trying to create new alternatives to the traditional cigarette.

Tobacco advertisers are attacked for the irony and questionable ethics of juxtaposing "cool," "successful," and "attractive" with a product that is incontrovertibly deadly. Though government has made major moves over the years to restrict tobacco advertising—in some North American, European, Asian, and African countries tobacco ads are totally banned (Wilkinson, 1986; *The Lancet*, 1993)—in the United States print ads for tobacco are abundant. The influences of such advertising on tobacco use is a vital research topic for now and the future.

Another direction of the future is toward the expansion of minimal treatments for smoking. Such treatments are the best way to capture the widest segment of the population who smoke. For example, new minimal treatments at work sites already have proved to be an effective way to help people to stop smoking. Furthermore, future research should continue to refine and strengthen full treatments for the heavy, dependent smoker. The combination of behavioral and pharmacological treatment seems to work best for these individuals. Improvements in their efficacy can be realized, for example, by discovering what combination of treatment components works best for different types of smokers (for example, Hughes, 1986). Finally, there probably always will be a percentage of people who simply do not want to stop smoking. Developing a less hazardous cigarette that such people will use would ease the serious health consequences of chronic tobacco use. The reduced-tar and -nicotine cigarettes dominating today's market are only part of the answer, because smokers compensate for the reduction to some degree by inhaling more deeply and by smoking more cigarettes.

summary

- Nicotine occurs naturally in only one source, the tobacco plant. The major commercial tobacco products are cigarettes, cigars, snuff, chewing tobacco, and pipe tobacco.

- Western Europeans discovered tobacco when they saw Native Americans in the New World smoking dried tobacco leaves. The Europeans seized the idea and spread it throughout Europe and Asia.

- Until about 1860, tobacco was widely believed to have medicinal properties. Nicotine's "medical cover" was blown when it was isolated in 1828 and shown to have addictive properties.

- Cigarette smoking is the most popular way to use tobacco.

- The prevalence of smoking among U.S. adults began to decline in 1965 and continued on that trend to 1992. A major reduction in the number of current smokers and an increase in the number of former smokers seem related to the U.S. Surgeon General's 1964 report, and subsequent publications, on the health consequences of cigarette smoking.

- Trends in overall prevalence of smoking in the past month vary according to age, gender, racial/ethnic identity, education, and employment status.

- Smoking among young people is an indirect indicator of smoking initiation. Smoking among 12–17-year-olds has been at an overall rate of about 10% since 1987.

- Smoking among high school seniors went from a high of 40% in 1976 to under 28% in 1992. The prevalence rates vary in a major way according to the respondents' college attendance plans.

- The use of smokeless tobacco products among youth has become a concern. The disparity in prevalence rates between males and females is extremely large.

- Nicotine is a cholinergic agonist that has biphasic (stimulant and depressant) action.

- Nicotine can be absorbed transdermally, through the oral, buccal, and nasal mucosa, the gastrointestinal tract, and the lungs.

- By inhalation the nicotine in tobacco smoke reaches the brain in seven seconds. Brain levels thus rise rapidly, but they fall rapidly, too, because nicotine is quickly distributed to other sites of action. Nicotine primarily is metabolized in the liver and eliminated mostly in urine.

- Functional tolerance to nicotine's effects is acquired quickly. Dispositional tolerance to nicotine also seems to develop.

- Nicotine induces physical dependence. In 1988 the U.S. Surgeon General's Office issued a report with the conclusion that nicotine is a physically addicting drug.

- Nicotine's acute effects include the CNS and ANS. It tends to have stimulant effects at lower doses but more depressant effects at higher doses.

- Despite its classification as a stimulant, users often perceive calming, relaxing effects of nicotine.

- Nicotine's body-weight suppressant effect is an important motivation for smoking, especially in women.

- Pharmacological, psychological, and social/ environmental factors combine to make nicotine a drug with high dependence liability. The major motivator in continuing tobacco use is nicotine.

- Smoking kills because of the smoker's chronic exposure to carbon monixide, tar, and nicotine in tobacco smoke.

- Cigarettes with reduced tar and nicotine levels are not "healthier," as smokers make up for the reduction either by smoking more cigarettes or by inhaling them more deeply.

- Major diseases linked to smoking are heart disease, chronic obstructive lung disease, and cancers of various types.

- In the last 25 years or so women have had smoking-related diseases similar to men. There also are smoking-related health risks that are unique to women.

- Because of the health consequences of passive smoking there has been a great increase in the banning and restriction of smoking in public places.

- Smoking treatment programs focus on stopping nicotine withdrawal symptoms, breaking the behavioral or habit part of smoking, and teaching stress-reduction skills.

- In general, treatment programs can be classified into two types—minimal and full programs. They differ primarily in the amount of contact the smoker has with treatment professionals.

- Quitting smoking is one thing; "staying quit" is another. A high rate of relapse follows smoking treatment.

- A major reason for relapse is that smokers may continue to crave nicotine long after they have stopped smoking.

- Two nicotine-replacement treatments that have been developed to combat the problem of craving—nicotine gum and the nicotine patch—seem to be most effective when used with behavioral treatments.

ANSWERS TO WHAT DO YOU THINK?

1. Tobacco was once thought to have major medical value.

T *From the time of Columbus until about 1860 tobacco was widely thought to be a panacea for medical problems.*

2. Throughout the age range, men have higher smoking rates than women do.

F *Although this once was true, smoking rates between men and women are now about equal.*

3. The prevalence of smokeless tobacco use among males is about three times that among females.

F *The discrepancy is at least 10 times; males use smokeless tobacco products far more than females do.*

4. Nicotine can be considered both a stimulant and a depressant.

T *Nicotine is called a biphasic drug because at lower doses it tends to act as a stimulant, but at higher doses it acts as a depressant.*

5. When using commercial tobacco products, the peak in blood level of nicotine is reached most quickly by using smokeless tobacco.

F *When using commercial tobacco products, the quickest way to reach the peak level for a dose of nicotine is by smoking.*

6. While psychological dependence is common, there have been no identified cases of physical dependence on nicotine.

F *Nicotine has been identified clearly as a drug on which users can become physically dependent.*

7. Nicotine's calming effects are a main reason for its use.

T *Even at doses associated with stimulant action in the body, users often perceive nicotine to have calming effects. Such effects are identified as major reasons for continuing to use nicotine.*

8. Nicotine plays a secondary role to learning and social factors in maintaining tobacco use.

F *Nicotine plays a substantial, and some think a major, part; learning and social factors are important, too.*

9. Health damage from cigarette smoking cost the U.S. economy about $25 billion in 1990.

F *The cost estimate provided by a Robert Wood Johnson Foundation study was $72 billion.*

10. Low-tar, low-nicotine cigarettes are healthier than cigarettes that do not have reduced tar and nicotine content.

F *Although theoretically this is true, in practice smokers tend to increase inhaling intensity or the number of cigarettes with cigarettes of reduced tar and nicotine content. Therefore, exposure to these compounds is similar to what it would be with cigarettes of nonreduced content.*

11. Despite the media hype, passive smoking actually poses a serious health risk to few Americans.

F *One study in 1991 provided an estimate that passive smoking in households kills about 53,000 Americans every year, mostly due to heart disease.*

12. A large portion of ex-smokers quit on their own.

T *Many people who quit smoking do so on their own, after three or four times. Self-quitters are thought to have been "lighter" smokers.*

8 Caffeine

WHAT DO YOU THINK?

True or False?

____ About half the world's population consumes caffeine regularly.

____ There are major subgroup differences in the United States in the amount of caffeine use.

____ In dose of caffeine consumed, young children have the highest exposure to caffeine after adults 18 years of age or older.

____ Caffeine is a drug that, when consumed, is distributed equally throughout the body.

____ Smokers tend to metabolize caffeine more slowly than do nonsmokers.

____ So many people use coffee and tea without apparent difficulty that it is obvious that people do not become physically dependent on caffeine.

____ Caffeine's stimulant effects seem to be its reinforcing properties in humans.

____ There is evidence that people can get intoxicated on caffeine.

____ Caffeine crosses the placenta and poses a danger to the health of the fetus.

____ Overall, caffeine seems to be a safe drug for everybody.

____ Caffeine has little medical value.

____ Caffeine's long-term effects on children are well-understood.

Caffeine, along with theophylline and theobromine, are three chemically related compounds that occur naturally in over 60 species of plants. These compounds are called the methylxanthines and are classified as alkaloids. An alkaloid is a compound that is of botanical origin, contains nitrogen, and is physiologically active (Levenson & Bick, 1977; Syed, 1976). Because of its overwhelming popularity, we will emphasize caffeine in our discussion.

We begin our review of caffeine by presenting the sources of caffeine and a brief history of its use. We then discuss current prevalence statistics. Following that we describe caffeine's pharmacological action, development of tolerance to and physical dependence on caffeine, and caffeine's acute and chronic effects. We conclude with a review of some of the therapeutic uses of caffeine and other major methylxanthine drugs.

SOURCES OF CAFFEINE

Most people take their caffeine orally, as is apparent in Table 8-1. This table includes the major sources of caffeine and their concentrations of the drug. Several features about sources of caffeine are highlighted by the table. First, there is a wide range of caffeine products that adults and children consume every day. Compounds synthesized to treat different medical problems also contain caffeine, even though the latter drug is not always of direct benefit in alleviating the problem symptoms. Finally, Table 8-1 does not contain another source of caffeine—illicit street drugs (Gilbert, 1984). For example, over-the-counter pain medications such as Anacin and Excedrin contain caffeine and frequently are used as filler to contaminate street drugs like heroin and cocaine.

HISTORY OF CAFFEINE USE

The plants that contain the methylxanthines have been used to make beverages popular with humans since ancient times. "Ancient" probably means at least back to the Stone Age (Rall, 1990). Many stories, some mythical, attempt to explain how these beverages were created. For example, coffee supposedly was discovered in Arabia by a holy man. It seems that goats in a herd had been jumping around at night instead of sleeping, apparently because they had been nibbling on the beans of the coffee plant. The holy man got a brilliant idea that beans from the same plant could help him endure his long nights of prayer. It was a small next step to the first cup of coffee (Blum, 1984).

Table 8-1 shows that caffeine is found in some of our most popular beverages and foods. In Chapter 7 we noted that during the time of Columbus, Europe knew nothing of these caffeine-containing substances. In fact, the only psychoactive substance that fifteenth-century Europeans did seem to know about was alcohol. However, this all changed with the ventures of the explorers and others from Europe. In Arabia, Turkey, and Ethiopia explorers found coffee. In China they found tea. In West Africa they found the kola nut. In Mexico and much of Central and South America they found the cacao plant, which is the source of chocolate. Other sources of teas were discovered in parts of North and South America. The travelers brought their discoveries home to Europe and then spread them across other continents.

As with other drugs, caffeine was not always well received by societies when it was introduced. For example, when the Mohammedans tried caffeine to stay awake during their long vigils, the orthodox priests were not pleased with the innovation. However, official punishments and attempts to kill coffee trees were not enough to stop coffee from becoming as popular among Arabian Moslems as tea is among the Chinese. Similar negative sanctions against coffee drinking in Egypt and Europe had as much success as the approach had in Arabia.

Caffeine, nicotine, and alcohol have been seen as having a greater effect on human civilization than have all other nonmedical psychoactive substances combined (Levenson & Bick, 1977). Caffeine stands out among these three drugs because of the ubiquity of its use around the world and because it is a "cradle to grave drug" (Kenny & Darragh, 1985, p. 278). That is, caffeine commonly is used nonmedically by young children and adults alike, which is true of no other psychoactive substance.

". . . The coffee habit had become so strong, that the people continued, notwithstanding all prohibitions, to drink it in their own houses. . . . it was drunk in particular places, with the doors shut, or in the back room of some of the shopkeepers' houses."

(Sixteenth-century text, cited in Greden & Walters, 1992, p. 358)

Table 8-1   Caffeine Concentration in Foods, Beverages, and Medications

Source	Concentration
Beverages	
Brewed coffee	100–150 mg/180 ml
Instant coffee	60–80 mg/180 ml
Decaffeinated coffee	3–5 mg/180 ml
Brewed tea	40–100 mg/180 ml
Pepsi-Cola	16 mg/240 ml
Coca-Cola	26 mg/240 ml
Mountain Dew	36 mg/240 ml
Dr Pepper	27 mg/240 ml
Canada Dry Ginger Ale	0
Food	
Milk chocolate	6 mg/oz
Cooking chocolate	35 mg/oz
Prescription Medications	
APCs (aspirin, Phenacetin, and caffeine)	32 mg/tablet
Cafergot	100 mg/tablet
Darvon compound	32 mg/tablet
Fiorinal	40 mg/tablet
Migral	50 mg/tablet
Over-the-Counter Preparations	
Anacin, aspirin compound, Bromo-Seltzer	32 mg/tablet
Aspirin	0
Tylenol	0
Cope, Easy–Mens, Empirin compound, Midol	32 mg/tablet
Vanquish	32 mg/tablet
Excedrin	60 mg/tablet
Pre Mens	66 mg/tablet
Bromoquinine	15 mg/tablet
Sinarest	30 mg/tablet
Dristan	30 mg/tablet
NoDoz	100 mg/tablet
ViVarin	100–200 mg/tablet

Note: Adapted with permission from a table in Sawyer, D.A., Julia, H. L., and Turin, A. C. (1982), Caffeine and human behavior: Arousal, anxiety, and performance effects. *Journal of Behavioral Medicine*, 5, pp. 415–439 (Plenum Press); and in Kenny, M., and Darragh, A. (1985), Central effects of caffeine in man, in S.D. Iverson (ed.), *Psychopharmacology: Recent Advances and Future Prospects*, pp. 278–288 (Oxford University Press). Also adapted from information in Clementz and Dailey (1988), and Greden and Walters (1992).

PREVALENCE OF CAFFEINE CONSUMPTION

Good estimates of caffeine consumption around the world are not nearly as available as prevalence estimates for other drug use, despite the ubiquity of caffeine use. Difficulty finding good worldwide estimates is a result of several factors. For one, since caffeine is consumed by using a number of different products, people find it hard, say in a survey, to provide accurate data on all their caffeine use over a time period. The surveys that have been done are, accordingly, expensive to conduct, and thus limited in numbers of respondents. Furthermore, it is hard to find good caffeine consumption survey data outside of North America and Europe (James, 1991). Another reason collecting good caffeine estimates is difficult is that how some products are prepared can make a difference in their caffeine content. One example is that coffee-brewing method affects caffeine content. For instance, there is higher caffeine content for boiled than for percolated coffee (D'Amicis & Viani, 1993).

Despite these problems, estimates of caffeine consumption have been derived, many based in a country's import figures for a given caffeine-containing product. Table 8-2 shows per-capita caffeine use estimates for the United States, Canada, the United Kingdom, and for comparison, the world. As you can see in Table 8-2, in the United States, caffeine consumption is over 200 mgs a day per capita (also see Hughes, Oliveto, Helzer, et al., 1992). The U.S. average almost triples the world average, and well over half is from coffee consumption. The dominant contribution of coffee also holds for Canada and the world. Europe has some heavy coffee-drinking countries. The Scandinavian countries—Finland, Sweden, Denmark, and Norway—are the world's top coffee consumers, for example. Austria's coffee consumption is at a similar level (D'Amicis & Viani, 1993).

Tea is the dominant source of caffeine in the United Kingdom, and the same is true for its close neighbor Ireland. Brazil is the world's leading producer of coffee (more than 25% of the total), but its citizens' primary caffeine source is maté, a type of tea that is grown in South America (James, 1991). The major producers and exporters of tea are China, India, and Sri Lanka, but the major consumers and importers (in absolute amounts) are the United States, the United Kingdom, and the countries that constituted the old Soviet Union (Gilbert, 1984).

Table 8-2 Estimates of Caffeine Use for the World, United States, Canada, and the United Kingdom, 1981–1982

		Per-Capita Consumption	
	Caffeine Source	*(grams/yr)*	*(milligrams/day)*
World	Coffee	14	38
	Tea	11	30
	Other	1	2
	Total	**26**	**70**
United States	Coffee	46	125
	Tea	13	35
	Soft drinks	13	35
	Cocoa	2	4
	Other	5	12
	Total	**79**	**211**
Canada	Coffee	47	128
	Tea	29	79
	Soft drinks	6	16
	Cocoa	1	3
	Other	5	12
	Total	**88**	**238**
United Kingdom	Coffee	32	84
	Tea	118	320
	Other	15	40
	Total	**165**	**444**

Note: "Other" category includes caffeine in medicines and other sources, such as yerba maté tea. Table adapted from Gilbert (1984), and published with permission from Alan R. Liss, Inc.

Cocoa is primarily produced in Africa, but the world's highest importer is the United States. Switzerland has the highest per-capita consumption of cocoa (James, 1991). Estimates of caffeine consumption from soft drinks are difficult to obtain outside of North America. In the United States, it has been estimated that the amount of caffeine consumed from soft drinks is equal to that from tea (Gilbert, 1984). From 1960 to 1982 in the United States caffeinated coffee consumption declined by about 40 percent while soft drink consumption more than tripled. Since the early 1980s the level of caffeinated coffee consumption has been stable (Greden & Walters, 1992). Therefore, whatever decline in caffeine consumption occurred from drinking less caffeinated coffee was compensated for to some degree by drinking more soft drinks. The contribution of soft drinks to total caffeine consumption is significant—one study showed that in 1962 one-third of the population said they had consumed soft drinks the day before, but in 1989 two-thirds said they had (Greden & Walters, 1992).

Caffeine consumption does not vary much in the United States among different subgroups of the population. One exception is age. In this regard, coffee consumption increases with age, until the elderly (60 years or more) years, when it declines somewhat. However, for "dose" of caffeine consumed,

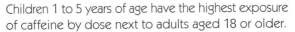

Children 1 to 5 years of age have the highest exposure of caffeine by dose next to adults aged 18 or older.

Contemporary Issue
CAFFEINE AND KIDS

Studies show that children all over the world regularly consume pharmacologically active amounts of caffeine. This pattern of use combines with our knowledge about the high degree of caffeine exposure in young children, because of their lower body weights, to raise serious concerns about children's use of caffeine. Despite the potential seriousness of this problem, little is known about caffeine effects in children. What research is available suggests that children are not more or less sensitive to caffeine's action in the body than are adults (James, 1991).

Children's use of caffeine is a major concern for several reasons. Caffeine is very popular among young people, for one reason. Second, caffeine exposure in children is high compared to that of adults. In addition, little is known about the long-term effects of children's caffeine use.

Given these circumstances would you, for example, require soft drink or candy makers to eliminate caffeine from their products? Children are major consumers of caffeine-containing soft drinks and chocolate. Would you require warning or caution labels on caffeine products, as are required for tobacco products and alcoholic beverages? Why or why not?

which takes into account body weight (see Chapter 4), children aged 1–5 have the highest exposure to caffeine next to adults aged 18 or older (Greden & Walters, 1992).

In summary, caffeine is consumed worldwide by people of all races and social classes. Generally, estimates are that about 90% of the world's population regularly consumes products containing caffeine, with coffee, tea, and soft drinks the most common sources (James, 1991). Trends in recent years in overall caffeine use are difficult to specify because of the measurement problems we referred to above. Nevertheless, there is no question that caffeine is the world's most preferred drug.

PHARMACOLOGY OF CAFFEINE

Sites of Action

For many years caffeine's effects were thought to be a result of the drug's inhibition of the enzyme phosphodiesterase. This enzyme breaks down cyclic AMP. Inhibiting phosphodiesterase results in the increased action of catecholamines which, as discussed in Chapter 3, are neurotransmitters. However, the phosphodiesterase theory fell out of favor following the realization that caffeine has such action only at doses much higher than the typical one required for pharmacological effects in humans, which is about 200 mg (Snyder & Sklar, 1984). The explanation for caffeine's acute effects most accepted now is the adenosine hypothesis. Adenosine is a chemical that the body produces and is an inhibitory neurotransmitter (see Chapter 3). Adenosine receptors are in the CNS and peripheral nervous systems. Adenosine acts to result in behavioral sedation, regulation of oxygen delivery to cells, dilation of cerebral and coronary blood vessels, and production of asthma (Julien, 1992, p. 135). Caffeine and the other methylxanthines occupy adenosine receptors and then block the action of that transmitter.

Pharmacokinetics

Absorption   Caffeine is rapidly absorbed from the gastrointestinal tract. The drug quickly reaches the brain, as it can pass the blood-brain barrier. The half-life of caffeine in the blood varies widely among people and ranges from about 2½ to 7½ hours (Blum, 1984; Leonard, Watson, & Mohs, 1987). Peak levels of caffeine after taking a dose of it occur in 15 to 45 minutes, depending on the source. For example, one study (Marks & Kelly, 1973) involved three healthy men who were given an average of 155 mg of caffeine in the form of Coca-Cola, tea, or coffee. The men's plasma levels of caffeine were then charted for two hours. The peak levels of caffeine were higher for tea and coffee and were reached within 30 minutes of ingestion. The peak for Coca-Cola was lower than that of the other two beverages and did not occur until about an hour passed. After two hours the plasma caffeine level for the cola was higher than for tea or coffee and still at a level comparable to its peak.

Distribution   Caffeine is equally distributed in total body water, and freely crosses the placenta to the fetus (Julien, 1992). Therefore, after consumption the concentration of caffeine is similar throughout the body.

Metabolism and Excretion   The liver does most of the metabolizing of caffeine. The drug is excreted almost entirely by the kidneys, less than 10% in pure form and the rest in metabolites. Very small proportions of caffeine also are excreted in the feces, saliva, semen, and breast milk. Of interest is the variance among people in caffeine metabolism and excretion from the body. For example, rates of these processes are slower in people who have been using caffeine over a shorter period of time (Leonard, Watson, & Mohs, 1987). Other differences in metabolism and excretion are caused by liver disease (it slows the process), pregnancy (slows), and use of oral contraceptives (slows). On the other hand, if you are a cigarette smoker you metabolize caffeine more quickly. One study showed that ex-smokers' blood levels of caffeine more than doubled over what they were when they drank the same amount of coffee before they quit smoking (Benowitz, Hall, & Modin, 1989). Other therapeutic drugs interact with caffeine to increase or decrease its metabolism and excretion.

TOLERANCE AND DEPENDENCE

Caffeine long was considered a strange drug because of its unorthodox potential for inducing tolerance and physical dependence (Gilbert, 1976). Evidence of a distinct caffeine withdrawal syndrome has been available for some time, but for tolerance the data have been far less clear. The usual picture for drugs is the reverse—they can induce tolerance without dependence, but rarely dependence without tolerance.

Caffeine Withdrawal

The caffeine withdrawal symptom most consistently reported is the headache. Other withdrawal symptoms have been documented in one of a series of studies by Goldstein and his colleagues (Goldstein, Kaizer, & Whitby, 1969). Some of the symptoms of caffeine abstinence their subjects reported were depression, decreased alertness, less contentment and relaxed mood, decreased activity and energy, greater sleepiness and drowsiness, and increased irritability. Currently it is thought that physical dependence on caffeine develops in from 6 to 15 days of consuming 600 mg of caffeine or more a day. Withdrawal can range from mild to severe in intensity and begins within 12 to 24 hours of cessation of caffeine use. It may last about a week (Griffiths & Woodson, 1988; Hughes et al., 1992).

Tolerance

The contradictions that abound in the experimental findings about tolerance to caffeine are probably a result of poor research methods, such as not specifying caffeine-use patterns in subjects (Curatolo & Robertson, 1987). In general, tolerance to caffeine's effects on renal function, sleep (see below) and other physiological functions probably does develop.

Confusion about caffeine tolerance also results from ignoring what may be differences among people in what is an "acceptable" level of caffeine. Differences between high and low caffeine users in the acute effects of a dose of caffeine in children and adults have been attributed to differences in degree of acquired tolerance. However, some better controlled studies offer another explanation: one reason people are heavier or lighter users is their individual ability to tolerate caffeine. This interpretation is always an alternative in studies that fail to specify long-term patterns of caffeine consumption in the experimental participants. The best way to do this would be to measure caffeine use and effects in the same people over a period of time.

ACUTE EFFECTS OF CAFFEINE

Caffeine's primary action is stimulation of CNS activity but, as we saw, it is distributed freely throughout the body. Such distribution is evidenced by caffeine's actions outside the CNS: contraction of striated muscle, including the heart; relaxation of smooth muscle, especially the coronary arteries, uterus and bronchi; diuretic effects on the kidneys; at higher doses, a stimulating effect on respiration; elevation of basal metabolism; and various endocrine and enzymatic effects (Levenson & Bick, 1977; Rall, 1990). Caffeine's effects on the body's systems provide good evidence for blockade of adenosine receptors as its mechanism of action, as caffeine's effects essentially are opposite to those of adenosine (Leonard, Watson, & Mohs, 1987).

Behavioral and Psychological Effects

"It makes the body active and alert . . . it banishes tiredness and cleanses the vital fluids and the liver . . . it eases the brain and strengthens the memory. It is especially good for sustaining wakefulness."

(English text, 1660, on the properties of tea, cited in Schivelbusch, 1992, pp. 83–84)

Mood   The CNS stimulation action of caffeine elevates mood. This was documented in a quote from a will of Dr. William Dunlap, who died in 1848. Dr. Dunlap wrote, "I leave John Caddle a silver teapot, to the end that he may drink tea therefrom to comfort him under the affliction of a slatternly wife" (cited in Gilbert, 1976, p. 77). The acute mood-elevating effects of caffeine account for much of the popularity that coffee and tea have as morning wake-up beverages. It also has been speculated that people who are afflicted with significant depression "medicate" themselves by using caffeine products. Caffeine may block adenosine's inhibition of cells in the brain that underlie alertness and upbeat mood (Konner, 1988).

Caffeine and Performance   Caffeine's effects on human task performance are complicated. Table 8-3 gives you a list of some of the major performance effects of caffeine. The table shows that the range of caffeine effects is wide, and many of them are in a stimulation direction. It should be noted that one of the major ways caffeine improves task performance is by decreasing fatigue and increasing vigilance, so that over time performance does not drop below what is typical for a person. Such action is in contrast to an effect that pushes performance above what is normal for a person. In addition, the complexity of caffeine's effects is illustrated in the choice reaction time task. Caffeine impairs the decision-making part of the task but improves the motor component. The drug's effects are different even for different components of the same task. You also will note there is some inconsistency in the findings

Caffeine's enhancing effects on the performance of various cognitive and motor tasks make it a popular drug in the workplace.

Table 8-3   Caffeine's Acute Effects on Human Performance

Performance Variable	Effect of Caffeine
Physical Endurance	
Bicycle ergometer	
—Fixed load	Increases
—Progressive load	No effect
Motor Skills	
Rapidity and accuracy	Decreases, higher doses
	Increases, lower doses
Eye-hand coordination	Decreases
Vigilance	
Visual	
—Night driving analogue	Increases
—Target scanning	
low coffee users	Decreases
high coffee users	No effect
Reaction Time	
Simple reaction time	Decreases (speeds up)
Choice reaction time	
—Decision time	Increases (slows down)
—Motor time	Decreases
Verbal Tests	
Graduate Record Exam Practice Test	
—Speed and accuracy	
extraverts	Increases, with higher doses
introverts	First increases, then decreases, with higher doses
Verbal Test, Time Stress	
Accuracy	
—Extraverts	Increases
—Introverts	Decreases
Verbal Test	
Accuracy	
—Low impulsives	Increases (in the a.m.), decreases (in the p.m.)
—High impulsives	Decreases (in the a.m.), increases (in the p.m.)

Note: Adapted with permission from Sawyer, D. A., Julia, H. L., and Turin, A. C. (1982), Caffeine and human behavior: Arousal, anxiety, and performance effects. *Journal of Behavioral Medicine*, 5, pp. 415–439 (published by Plenum Press).

about caffeine effects. This is probably due in part to the different methods experimenters have used. Another reason is that caffeine's effects depend not only on the drug's pharmacological action but also on the dose of the drug, the setting in which it is used, and the personality of the user. This is represented in Table 8-3 by findings such as in verbal test accuracy (the last entry in the table), which caffeine affects according to the personality of the subject ("impulsiveness") and the setting (time of day) (Sawyer, Julia, & Turin, 1982).

Overall, it seems that caffeine's acute effects at lower doses are what maintain the world's use of beverages such as coffee and tea (Griffiths & Woodson, 1988; James, 1991). Although caffeine's effects at low doses are not as intense as, say, cocaine, its reinforcing properties are strong enough to make it the world's most popular drug.

Interactions among Caffeine, Nicotine, and Alcohol

Caffeine, nicotine, and alcohol are the world's most popular drugs, and many people use them in combination (Koslowski, Henningfield, Keenan, et al., 1993). An important question, therefore, is what the interactive effects of these compounds are. It seems, for example, that smokers smoke fewer cigarettes after drinking coffee compared to when they have not had coffee. This effect is stronger for lighter caffeine users. And we have noted that another effect of nicotine is in excretion of caffeine from the body, which occurs more than 50% faster in smokers than in nonsmokers (Sawyer, Julia, & Turin, 1982).

Alcohol and caffeine interactions have been the subject of scientific investigations for nearly 80 years. As with other data on caffeine effects, this vast body of research has not greatly clarified the picture. Despite the age-old method of drinking black coffee to emerge from an alcoholic "drunk," caffeine does not seem to antagonize alcohol's CNS depressant effects. So what you get in giving black coffee to somebody who is drunk on alcohol is an energetic drunk. Some experimenters even have found that caffeine increases alcohol-related impairments (Kenny & Darragh, 1985).

One study (Lowe, 1988) suggests that everyday forgetting has something to do with the state-dependent effects of caffeine, nicotine, and alcohol in combination. In the first study, 24 men and women college undergraduates who were smokers and drinkers were given a moderate dose of vodka and smoked two cigarettes. They were exposed to a list of 19 items about a route on a map and then had to recall the items in successive tests until they achieved 14 correct items. On the day of their next session these subjects were randomly assigned to one of four drug conditions: alcohol and nicotine (control condition), alcohol and nicotine placebo, alcohol placebo and nicotine, or alcohol placebo and nicotine placebo. The subjects then were asked to recall as many of the 19 items as they could from their first experimental session. The results showed no recall decrement (Day 1–Day 2 score) for subjects who had alcohol and nicotine on both days. However, there were significant decreases in recall score for subjects in the other three groups. These "dissociative" or state-dependent effects seemed attributable to alcohol and, to a lesser extent, nicotine.

The next study by Lowe (1988) was the same as the first, except that 16 undergraduate coffee and alcohol drinkers participated, and caffeine was substituted for nicotine. The results of this study showed state-dependent effects for alcohol and caffeine. Because the major recall decrements occurred in people who had no caffeine the second day, even if they drank alcohol, it seems the state-dependence effect mostly was due to caffeine.

Acute Toxic Effects of Caffeine

Caffeine intoxication, or caffeinism, has received a lot of attention recently by health professionals. An example of a case of caffeinism will give you an idea of the phenomenon (adapted from Greden, 1974, pp. 1090–1091):

> A 27-year-old nurse requested an evaluation at an outpatient medical clinic because of lightheadedness, tremulousness, breathlessness, headache, and irregular heartbeat occurring sporadically about two to three times a day. The symptoms had developed gradually over a three-

DRUGS AND CULTURE
COFFEE AS THE BEVERAGE OF IDEALS

Many people today believe that coffee helps in sobering up after drinking too much alcohol. This belief, actually, is far from new, as it is at least as old as seventeenth-century western Europe. At that time, a book on beverages noted that "coffee sobers you up instantaneously, or in any event sobers up those who are not fully intoxicated" (cited in Schivelbusch, 1992, p. 35). Another facet of this belief is that coffee was regarded as an ideal beverage. In the nineteenth century, the poet-historian Jules Michelet praised coffee because it "heightens purity and lucidity" (cited in Schivelbusch, 1992, p. 35).

Coffee also was credited with other attributes during those years in Europe. In eighteenth-century England, for example, coffee was seen as an alternative to sex. To some people, coffee was a way that erotic arousal could be replaced by stimulation of the mind.

Of course, the ideas that coffee is a sobering agent and a displacer of erotic desires have long since been discredited scientifically, if not by personal experience. Yet the ideas, at least the sobering-up belief, persist. One hypothesis is that the origin of these enduring ideas is in the pharmacology of caffeine—a CNS stimulant—and in cultural and ideological factors that prevailed in Europe from the seventeenth to the nineteenth centuries (Schivelbusch, 1992). During that time more and more emphasis was being placed on achievement in an increasingly industrialized society, which caffeine's pharmacology is highly consistent with. Since coffee had been a popular drink anyway, it would seem like an ideal candidate to help foster the ideals of the time, and to show disapproval of behaviors thought to be inconsistent with them, such as alcohol use and sex.

Why coffee continues to be viewed by many as a sobering agent is open to discussion. Probably caffeine's CNS stimulant action gives a person the illusion of getting out of a drowsiness and lethargy that alcohol causes. Yet alcohol's CNS depressant action remains pretty much untouched.

week period. The nurse said there were no precipitating stresses. The physical exam was within normal limits, except that an electrocardiogram showed premature ventricular contractions.

At her final session with the evaluating internist the nurse was referred to an outpatient psychiatric clinic with the diagnosis of anxiety reaction, probably to fear that her husband would be transferred by the military to be stationed in Viet Nam. However, the nurse did not accept this diagnosis and searched for a dietary cause of her symptoms. After about ten days she had linked her symptoms to coffee consumption. With the recent purchase of a new coffee pot the nurse had been drinking ten to twelve cups of strong black coffee a day—more than 1000 mg of caffeine. She stopped drinking coffee, and within thirty-six hours virtually all of her symptoms disappeared, including the cardiovascular irregularities (Published with permission of American Psychiatric Press, Inc.).

Several points about this case illustration are worth noting. First, the symptoms occurred in the nurse apparently as a result of her consuming more than 1,000 mg of caffeine a day. However, as with other caffeine effects, people differ in how much caffeine they can ingest before experiencing symptoms of intoxication. For example, caffeinism has been reported following consumption of as little as 250 mg of caffeine in a day, which is not much more than the average for adults in the United States. Generally, ingesting caffeine at the rate of 600 mg a day greatly increases the chances of developing caffeinism (Kenny & Darragh, 1985).

Consuming more than 1,000 mg of caffeine increases the risk of experiencing even more severe toxic symptoms, including muscle twitching, rambling flow of thought and speech, cardiac arrhythmia, periods of inexhaustibility, and psychomotor agitation (American Psychiatric Association, 1987). Other symptoms that have been reported are ringing in the ears and seeing flashes of light. The lethal dose of caffeine when it is taken orally is about 10 grams for adults and 100 mg/kg for children (Leonard, Watson, & Mohs, 1987). The adult lethal dose is equal to about 75 cups of coffee, 125 cups of tea, 200 colas, or 100 NoDoz tablets. Reports of death due to caffeine overdose are rare. Much more common is people appearing for treatment of acute overexposure to caffeine. In fact, caffeinism may be viewed as a more extreme case of acute overexposure to caffeine (James, 1991). It should be kept in mind, however, that given the commonality of its use, caffeine overexposure seems to occur most infrequently.

"Sometimes, when I had drunk a lot of coffee, and the least little thing would startle me, I noticed quite clearly that I jumped before I had heard any noise."

(Lichtenberg, cited in Schivelbusch, 1992, inside front cover)

CHRONIC EFFECTS OF CAFFEINE USE

The chronic effects of caffeine have been studied primarily for major medical problems, and the research has produced some inconsistent findings. For example, a retrospective study (Infante-Rivard, Fernandez, Gauthier, et al., 1993) found a positive relationship between reported caffeine intake one month before and during pregnancy and loss of the fetus. In another, longitudinal study, however, no relationship was found between caffeine consumption during the first three months of pregnancy and damage to the fetus, including spontaneous abortion (Mills, Holmes, Aarons, et al., 1993). Research on other medical problems has suggested there is no relationship between caffeine consumption and cancer or myocardial infarction (Abbott, 1986; Grobbee, Rimm, Giovannucci, et al., 1990). Similarly, no clear evidence exists for a causal relationship between caffeine consumption and peptic ulcer (Council on Scientific Affairs, 1984).

In one study a positive relationship was discovered in postmenopausal women between amount of caffeinated coffee consumed lifetime and osteoporosis (Barrett-Connor, Chang, & Edelstein, 1994). In this study drinking two cups of coffee a day was associated with decreased bone mineral density, a measure of osteoporosis. However, the relationship between coffee and osteoporosis was eliminated in women who said they drank at least one glass of milk a day during the ages of 20–50.

Some studies have shown an association between serum cholesterol levels and quantity of caffeine consumption: as one level goes up, the other one also tends to. Level of serum cholesterol is related to atherosclerosis. The caffeine-cholesterol research illustrates the complexity of linking chronic drug use to medical problems and one reason why caffeine research in particular has yielded so many inconsistent findings. In this regard, when considering coffee intake as the source, the caffeine-cholesterol relationship seems to depend on how the coffee is brewed. It appears that when coffee is boiled, as is common, for example, in Norway, the caffeine-cholesterol link holds up. But it disappears if the coffee is made by drip-filtering (Bak & Grobbee, 1989; *Consumer Reports*, 1991).

Quantity of caffeine consumption seems to be associated with the occurrence of symptoms that are less major but are experienced more commonly. Abbott (1986) cited a survey of 4,558 Australians that concerned caffeine ingestion and the occurrence of indigestion, palpitations, tremor, headache, and insomnia. Respondents were more likely to report these symptoms the more caffeine they ingested (the average consumption for the sample was 240 mg a day).

In summary, based on the apparent infrequency of acute caffeine overexposure and on research on its chronic effects, caffeine is considered a relatively safe drug. For example, the American Medical Association's Council on Scientific Affairs (1984) recommended against labeling of caffeine products. However, because of the occurrence of more minor symptoms with higher levels of caffeine consumption (but still within the range of typical use patterns, as indicated above in the Australian study) it has been recommended that caffeine consumption be moderated. Furthermore, some individuals would particularly benefit by keeping their caffeine consumption at a low level. One example is people who suffer from certain psychiatric disorders characterized by high levels of anxiety (see Chapter 11). It appears, for instance, that people who have been diagnosed as having generalized anxiety disorder are hypersensitive to the effects of caffeine, and the drug may exacerbate the anxiety symptoms (Bruce, Scott, Shine, & Lader, 1992). You can connect this finding with the case study we cited that involved mistaking caffeinism for an anxiety reaction.

THERAPEUTIC USES OF CAFFEINE

Table 8-1 shows that caffeine is used in a variety of prescription and over-the-counter medications. Therefore, caffeine is very much a part of the medications used to treat a range of ailments. In fact, other methylxanthines also have therapeutic value. You can better appreciate this by looking at Table 8-4 listing the xanthine used to achieve a preferred pharmacological action. The differences among the xanthines in what effect is best produced is based on slight differences in their chemical structure. For example, aminophylline, a cardiac and bronchial dilator that contains theophylline, is used to treat both cardiac and bronchial asthma. Caffeine is the drug with the most presence, as it is part of a number of remedies for headaches and colds. Its mild stimulant properties help to counteract some of the side effects of medications for those ailments (Gilbert, 1976). Caffeine also is contained in appetite-suppressant medications for its diuretic effects (Snyder & Sklar, 1984).

Table 8-4   Methylxanthine Compounds and Desired Pharmacological Action

Desired Action	Preferred Compound
Cerebral stimulation	Caffeine (coffee)
Coronary dilation	Theophylline (tea)
Diuresis	Theobromine (cocoa)
Respiratory stimulant for premature infants	Caffeine

Note: This table is taken from Graham (1978). Products in parentheses are sources of the indicated compound. From *Nutrition Reviews*, 36 (1978):101. Used with permission of the International Life Sciences Institute-Nutrition Foundation.

CONCLUSIONS

Caffeine is an extremely important drug because of its widespread use. Overall, it also seems to be a relatively safe drug. However, despite the many years of research that have been devoted to caffeine, there still is a lot we have to learn about it. Probably the most essential research concerns developing better ways to obtain accurate measures of caffeine consumption. Such advances would stimulate answering important research questions. For example, we need to know more about the long-term effects of caffeine use in children, the development of tolerance to caffeine, and the prevalence of more minor symptoms of higher, but not extreme, levels of caffeine use. Another question is how caffeine affects people in special populations, such as those who are medically or psychiatrically ill.

Finally, Sawyer, Julia, and Turin (1982) made the excellent point that much of the research on caffeine has been done with healthy volunteers who have consumed only well-specified, single doses of caffeine. Little information exists on the cumulative effects, say during one day, of caffeine use on task performance. Such information is important, because that is the pattern of caffeine use that most people follow. Relatedly, caffeine effects in combination with other commonly used drugs need a lot more attention. Lowe's (1988) findings on state-dependent learning and alcohol, caffeine, and nicotine suggest that significant practical questions can be answered by such research.

summary

■ Caffeine and other methylxanthine drugs occur naturally in more than 60 species of plants. Caffeine is the world's most popular drug, and humans have used it since ancient times. Many everyday products that children or adults consume contain caffeine.

■ Overall, coffee is the major source of caffeine consumption, but for many countries tea is the dominant source. In the last 20 years soft drinks have risen to be another significant caffeine source.

■ Total caffeine consumption does not seem to vary by characteristics of people, except for age.

■ When considering body weight, children aged 1–5 have the highest exposure to caffeine after adults aged 18 or older.

- Caffeine's mechanism of action seems to be a blocking of adenosine receptor sites.

- Caffeine is rapidly absorbed from the gastrointestinal tract and is distributed throughout the body. Its half-life in the blood ranges from 2½ to 7½ hours.

- Caffeine is metabolized primarily in the liver and is virtually all excreted in the urine.

- A clear withdrawal syndrome has been identified for caffeine, but the evidence for the development of tolerance is not as strong.

- The acute effects of caffeine include diuresis, stimulation of the heart and CNS, relaxation of smooth muscles, and stimulation of gastric acid.

- Because caffeine, nicotine, and alcohol are used by many people in some combination, knowing how each of these drugs interacts with the other two is important.

- Acute caffeine intoxication is called caffeinism. Caffeinism is most likely to occur with a dose of 600 mg or higher. The symptoms are more severe the higher the dose.

- Overall it seems that caffeine is a relatively safe drug, but important research questions remain about long-term caffeine use and health.

ANSWERS TO WHAT DO YOU THINK?

1. About half the world's population consumes caffeine regularly.

F   *It is estimated that about 90% of the world's population consumes caffeine regularly.*

2. There are major subgroup differences in the United States in the amount of caffeine use.

F   *There are few subgroup differences in the amount of caffeine consumption, except for age.*

3. In dose of caffeine consumed, young children have the highest exposure to caffeine after adults 18 years of age or older.

T   *When body weight is taken into account, children aged 1–5 have the highest caffeine exposure after adults aged 18 or older.*

4. Caffeine is a drug that, when consumed, is distributed equally throughout the body.

T   *Since caffeine is equally distributed in total body water it has similar concentrations throughout the body.*

5. Smokers tend to metabolize caffeine more slowly than do nonsmokers.

F   *Studies show that smokers metabolize caffeine more quickly than do nonsmokers.*

6. So many people use coffee and tea without apparent difficulty that it is obvious that people do not become physically dependent on caffeine.

F   *There is a clearly identified caffeine withdrawal syndrome.*

7. Caffeine's stimulant effects seem to be its reinforcing properties in humans.

T   *Caffeine's acute effects of mood elevation and overall improvement in task performance seem to be reinforcing to humans.*

8. There is evidence that people can get intoxicated on caffeine.

T   *Acute caffeine intoxication, also called caffeinism, has been well-documented. It is most likely to occur when 600 mg or more of caffeine are consumed in a day.*

9. Caffeine crosses the placenta and poses a danger to the health of the fetus.

F   *The latest evidence is that typical doses of caffeine consumption by mothers pose little health risk to the fetus.*

10. Overall, caffeine seems to be a safe drug for everybody.

F   *Although, overall, caffeine is a relatively safe drug, there are some individuals who are advised to reduce its use. One example is people with anxiety disorders.*

11. Caffeine has little medical value.

F   *Caffeine, and the other methylxanthine drugs, are part of medications used to treat a variety of medical problems.*

12. Caffeine's long-term effects on children are well-understood.

F   *Despite the high consumption of caffeine in children, little is known about the chronic effects of their use of this drug. It is a major research area for the future.*

9 Alcohol

WHAT DO YOU THINK?

True or False?   ____   Humans have consumed alcohol since about 5000 to 6000 B.C.

____   In the United States of 1830, adults' average alcohol consumption was about five drinks a day.

____   The highest rates of heavy drinking, and greatest vulnerability to drinking problems, are in men between the ages of 40 and 45.

____   It is difficult to consume a lethal dose of alcohol.

____   If not treated properly, alcohol withdrawal syndrome can be fatal.

____   Alcohol is a drug that has no legitimate medical value.

____   If you drink a lot and black out, it means you have lost consciousness.

____   Alcohol causes violent behavior.

____   Alcohol improves sexual performance.

____   The cognitive deficits that seem to occur in some people as a result of years of heavy drinking are reversible.

____   The majority of alcoholics eventually develop cirrhosis of the liver.

____   Moderate drinking (1–3 drinks a day) is associated with reduced risk of heart disease.

In the preceding chapter we said alcohol, nicotine, and caffeine are the most popular psychoactive drugs. By far, of the three, alcohol has been known, manufactured, and used the longest. Most important, this drug has had profound influences on the societies around the world in which it is used. "Alcohol" actually refers to several substances, for example, isopropyl alcohol (rubbing alcohol), methyl alcohol (wood alcohol), and ethanol. Ethanol is the alcohol we drink, and in this text use of the word alcohol means ethanol unless otherwise specified.

In this chapter we give you an overview of the many facets of alcohol use. We begin with information on the major alcoholic beverages, how they are manufactured, and some history about the use of alcohol in human societies. We follow with a discussion of trends in consumption of alcohol in the United States, including a discussion of heavy drinking. We also explore more detailed information about alcohol use and patterns of alcohol consumption. With this general background we then examine the pharmacology of alcohol, including site of action, processing of the drug in the human body, and the development of tolerance and dependence. Then we examine the acute and chronic physiological, psychological, and social consequences of alcohol use in humans. The chapter ends with a discussion of the causes of alcohol dependence.

ALCOHOLIC BEVERAGES

Fermentation and Distillation

Alcohol virtually always is drunk in a form of the three major classes of alcoholic beverages: beer, wine, and hard liquor (also called distilled spirits). For their manufacture, all these beverages depend upon the process of fermentation, and hard liquor upon the further process of **distillation**. Fermentation begins when sugar is dissolved in water and exposed to air, which creates the perfect environment for living microorganisms called yeasts. In this environment

distillation
Process by which the heating of a fermented mixture increases its alcohol content.

A variety of alcoholic beverages is available to the interested consumer.

they multiply rapidly by eating the sugar, which is then converted to ethanol and carbon dioxide by the yeasts' metabolic processes. The carbon dioxide bubbles to the top of the mixture, leaving ethanol. As the number of yeasts grows, so does the percentage of ethanol, as much as 10 to 15%. At this highest point the yeasts cease their work. Therefore, fermented beverages will not have an alcohol content higher than 15%. Which kind of beverage results from fermentation depends on what sugar-containing substance is used. When grapes are used, the grape juice ferments to form wine. When grains are used, fermentation produces beer.

Distillation was developed to increase the ethanol content of fermented beverages. Distillation first involves heating a fermented mixture. Because alcohol has a lower boiling point than water, the steam emitted through boiling has a higher alcohol content than does the original fermented mixture. The vapor then is condensed through cooling, and the resulting liquid is higher in alcohol content than was the original fermented mixture. By repeating this cycle it is possible to raise the alcohol content of a beverage to progressively higher levels.

Expressing the Alcohol Content of a Beverage

In the United States alcohol percentage is denoted by volume. This is straightforward, so that 16 ounces of a beverage that is 50% ethanol contains 8 ounces of alcohol. Another way of expressing alcohol content is by weight, which is done, for example, in Britain.

proof
A term used to designate the proportion of alcohol in a beverage, by volume. Proof typically is used in reference to distilled spirits and equals twice the percentage of alcohol.

Another convention is the designation of alcohol content of a beverage by its **"proof."** Proof is used primarily with distilled spirits and is equal to twice the percentage of alcohol by volume. Accordingly, a beverage that is 43% alcohol by volume is 86 proof. This somewhat indirect way of expressing alcohol content comes from seventeenth-century England, where it was determined that a mixture that was 57% alcohol by volume, if poured over gunpowder, would cause its ignition in an open flame. The English still refer to their beverages as "over proof" (>57% alcohol by volume) or "under proof" (<57% alcohol by volume) (Becker, Roe, & Scott, 1975).

Table 9-1 is a summary of the essentials about the major types of alcoholic beverages commercially available. Varying the substances forming the base of the beverage and varying the alcohol concentration produce different types of alcoholic beverages.

HISTORY OF ALCOHOL USE

Humans have used alcohol for thousands of years. Keller (1979, p. 2822) reflected this fact in his comment that "in the beginning there was alcohol." The first nondistilled alcoholic beverages were made inadvertently, due to natural fermentation. For example, the first wines, which probably were drunk several thousand years ago, were likely made from fruit juice. The juices obtained from most types of fruit are contaminated with microbes, including yeasts, that constitute the flora on the fruit (Rose, 1977). Alcoholic fermentation results when the environmental temperature is right. Authorities believe the

Table 9-1   Major Kinds of Alcoholic Beverages, How They Are Made, and Alcohol Content

Beverage	How Made	Percent Alcohol (by vol.)
Beer (includes lager, ale, malt, stout)	Fermentation of carbohydrate extracted from barley malt (or rice or corn) by cooling with water. Product is boiled with hops, cooled, and fermented. Types of beer vary in malt, hops, and alcohol content	Lager = 3–6% others = 4–8%
Wine		
Red (table wine)	Fermentation of red grapes in skins	
White (table wine)	Fermentation of skinless grapes	Average 12%
Champagne	Same as white wine, with carbon dioxide	
Fortified (dessert) Wines	Ordinary table wines with alcohol content raised	Up to 20%
Distilled Spirits		
Brandy	Distilled from any sugar-containing fruit. Probably first to be produced commercially	About 40%
Whiskeys	Grains brewed with water to form a beer of 5–10% alcohol. Beer is distilled and aged in new or used charred oak barrels for two to eight years before blending	40–50%
Bourbon	From corn with rye and malted barley	
Scotch	Malted barley and corn	
Irish whiskey	Corn and malted and unmalted barley	
Rye whiskey	Rye and malted barley	
Other spirits		
Rum	Distilled from fermented molasses, aged about three years	40–75%
Gin	Distilled from any fermentable carbohydrate (barley, potato, corn, wheat, rye), flavored by a second distillation with juniper berries	35–50%
Vodka	Distilled from potato or almost any other carbohydrate source, kept free of flavors	35–50%

Note: Abstracted from Becker, C. E., Roe, R. L., and Scott, R. A. (1975). *Alcohol as a Drug.* New York: Medcom Press. Published with permission.

first beers were produced in Egypt as long ago as 5000 to 6000 B.C. Production of the first beers was similar to baking bread. An earthenware vessel filled with barley was placed in the ground until germination occurred. At that point the barley was crushed, made into a dough, and then baked until a crust was formed. This cake of dehydrated dough was soaked in water until fermentation was complete. The resulting product of acid beer was called "boozah." Distilled spirits were the last alcoholic beverages to be produced, but they are by no means recent entries on the scene. The earliest reference to distilled spirits appeared in China about 1000 B.C. Western Europe apparently does not have any record of distilled spirit production and consumption until about 800 A.D.

"I like alcohol. It is a powerful drug and, God knows, for some people a hellish one, but, if used carefully it can give great pleasure."

(62-year-old man, cited in Weil & Rosen, 1983, p. 190)

Since the beginning of its use, alcohol has been a double-edged sword to human societies. Alcoholic beverages have played, on the one hand, a part in important social occasions, such as births, religious ceremonies, marriages, and funerals. Such drinking was viewed as not harmful to individuals and as positive to societies. On the other hand, alcohol seemingly always has been consumed in excess by some, with consequent problems to the individual and to the society in which he or she lived. Such social consequences have been the source of repeated condemnations of alcohol by the clergy, prophets, physicians, and philosophers (Keller, 1979).

The two faces of alcohol were seen clearly when distilled spirits hit western Europe. Europeans sang the praises of this drug. For example, a French professor in the thirteenth century dubbed alcohol "aqua vitae," which means "water of life." The Danes expressed the same sentiment with their "akkevitt," the Swedes with their "akvavit." However, European societies also attributed many of their problems to alcoholic beverages, especially distilled spirits. For instance, the social problems in eighteenth-century England were represented in works of art such as Hogarth's "Gin Lane."

Colonial America adopted alcoholic beverages and many of the drinking customs from western Europe. One story has it the Pilgrims landed at Plym-

Eighteenth-century Europeans tended to attribute many of their social problems to alcoholic beverages, particularly distilled spirits.

outh Rock because they were out of alcohol. The dualistic nature of alcohol was manifested again in colonial America. The tavern was the center of town politics, business, trade, and pleasure. These Americans drank beer, wine, cider, and distilled spirits in considerable quantities. The practice of drinking was pervasive, as colonial American drinking showed no distinction among time, place, or person. The frequent practice of alcohol consumption coincided with positive attitudes toward it, as alcohol was viewed as fulfilling an array of physical, psychological, and social needs. The importance of alcohol to colonial Americans was represented in language. In 1737 Benjamin Franklin published a "Drinkers Dictionary," which included more than 235 terms to describe the drunkard. Included among these were "Loaded his cart," "Cock ey'd," "Moon-ey'd," "Tipsy," and "He carries too much sail" (Mendelson & Mello, 1985).

With such supporting attitudes and customs, Americans became known as a country of drunkards. In 1790 adult citizens of the young country annually drank six gallons of pure alcohol per capita, and by 1830 per-capita consumption had risen to seven gallons of alcohol. The latter computes to almost five alcoholic beverage drinks a day for each adult! With this kind of consumption, the ills of heavy drinking became more and more evident, especially in a society that was moving increasingly toward urbanization and industrialization. Accordingly, some people began to speak out against the ravages of alcohol, again mostly in reference to distilled spirits. The most influential among these critics, and a pillar of the Temperance Movement that was to gain strength in the nineteenth century, was the physician Benjamin Rush. Dr. Rush's 1785 treatise, "Inquiring into the effects of distilled spirits on the human body and mind," delineated the effects of distilled spirits on humans. It also was the basis of the idea that alcoholism is a disease.

In the nineteenth century, America expanded westward, and with that came the rise of the saloon. The word "saloon" comes from the French word *salon*, which refers to a public meeting place and entertainment hall. The saloon did serve a social function to the frontier people, but it quickly moved away from a center of civilized interchange to a reflection of the rural community of the American West (Mendelson & Mello, 1985). The first saloons were not exactly pictures of fine carpentry, as they could consist of structures as simple as a tent and a few barrels that made up the bar. The decor was the era's version of macho and might consist of pictures of naked women, famous boxers of the time such as John L. Sullivan, and famous events such as Custer's Last Stand (Mendelson & Mello, 1985). This decor was in tune with the typical clientele characteristics: aggressive men who were inclined to exploit other men, women, and nature. These explorers, soldiers, Native Americans, trappers, settlers, and cowboys had few of the attachments to family or community that might have helped to limit the occurrence of excessive drinking. Instead, their drinking in the saloon was characterized by the downing of large quantities of whiskey for the purpose of engaging in explosive behavior (Keller, 1979). The whiskey was plentiful and usually wretched—witness names for it such as "extract of scorpions" and "San Juan paralyzer."

Behavior associated with the saloon gave a rebirth to the Temperance Movement, which had been quieted somewhat by the American Civil War. The saloon was the focal scapegoat of the Temperance adherents and was blamed for social ills such as thievery, gambling, prostitution, and political corruption. The Temperance Movement also changed its stand from support of moderate use of nondistilled beverages to total abstinence from alcohol. The captains of industry of the late nineteenth and early twentieth centuries, such as John D. Rockefeller, Andrew Carnegie, and Henry Ford, supported the Temperance Movement. They believed that abstemious employees would be better employees. These industrial giants also gave money to supplement their moral support.

As World War I approached, the antialcohol drive had gained considerable financial, social, and political power. As mentioned in Chapter 2, this drive led to Prohibition and then to passage of the Volstead Act. The short life of Prohibition in the United States is well-known, and it was repealed nationally in 1933. However, part of this action was to leave much to the discretion of the states in regulating the sale and consumption of alcohol. In the stew of local laws that has evolved since, the American ambivalence about the use of alcoholic beverages is apparent. For example, some laws required the windows of drinking establishments be curtained, and others forbade it; some laws forbade women to drink standing at the bar, and others granted women the right to drink standing anywhere that a man could. The laws were consistent in their restriction of youths purchasing alcoholic beverages and in the channeling of alcohol tax revenue to local, state, and federal treasuries (Keller, 1979).

The public ambivalence about alcohol remains. This is reflected in the saying that "everybody enjoys a drink, but nobody enjoys a drunk." Still, there has been a general trend since the 1980s toward limitations of alcohol's use through change in social attitudes and tighter governmental controls. However, drinking remains a major part of many social rituals, and many people hail the benefits of moderate alcohol consumption. The negative consequences of excessive alcohol use are probably more apparent than ever because of activists with access to sophisticated communications techniques, yet they and government regulations are far from entirely successful in stopping or limiting alcohol consumption. This seems to be especially true among people who are alcohol dependent. We are still working to learn the greater part of the mystery of how alcohol problems develop, are maintained, and can be prevented and treated.

CONSUMPTION OF ALCOHOL AND HEAVY DRINKING IN THE UNITED STATES

In this section we consider trends in alcohol use in the United States. Because we covered data on prevalence of alcohol and other drug use in Chapter 1, we limit this discussion to trends we did not review earlier, including prevalence by specific alcoholic beverages and prevalence and correlates of heavy drinking.

The federal government compiles many statistics on the consumption of alcoholic beverages. One statistic, per-capita consumption, gives a good general summary of how much the "average" person in the United States drinks. Before we present this information, you should know that the population is all individuals (both drinkers and nondrinkers) at least 14 years old. Fourteen might seem young to some and is undoubtedly below the legal age for purchase of alcoholic beverages. It is used because survey data suggest that a substantial portion of 14-year-olds are drinking beverages containing alcohol. U.S. Census figures are used to estimate the number of people aged 14 and older for a given year in computing per-capita consumption. The quantity of alcohol part of the computation is based on beverage sales figures for each of the states. The quantities of different types of beverages (beer, wine, hard liquor) are translated to amount (in gallons) of pure alcohol according to standard alcohol equivalence formulas. For example, 12 ounces of regular domestic beer is computed as containing about .48 of an ounce or .045 gallons of pure alcohol. With these estimates, quantity of alcohol in gallons is divided by population number to yield per-capita alcohol consumption in gallons.

Figure 9-1 is the estimated per-capita consumption for all alcoholic beverages combined from 1935 to 1990 (Williams, Stinson, Clem, & Noble, 1992). One minor point to recognize in interpreting the information in Figure 9-1 is that until 1970, 15 was the lower age limit in computing population numbers. Figure 9-1 shows a few general trends. Per-capita consumption showed a constant increase from 1935, shortly after the end of Prohibition, into the 1940s. There also was a considerable increase in consumption from 1960 through the 1970s. Then, 1980 marked the beginning of a decline in consumption that was slightly reversed in 1990. In 1990 per-capita consumption was estimated at 2.46 gallons of alcohol. To give you some reference, 2.46 gallons of pure alcohol may be obtained in 656 12-ounce cans or bottles of regular domestic beer.

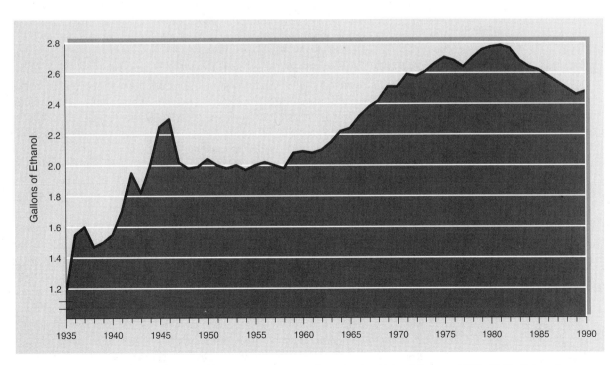

Figure 9-1   Per-capita consumption of alcohol in gallons in the United States, 1935–1990 (Taken from Williams et al., 1992, p. 4).

Combining data for all three types of alcoholic beverages masks some important differences, however. A more precise look at the per-capita consumption decline in the 1980s reveals that it was due to a reduction in the use of hard liquor. In fact, the Williams et al. (1992) report showed that the per-capita consumption of alcohol by drinking hard liquor fell by .28 gallons from 1977–1990. At the same time, consumption of alcohol in wine increased by .04 gallons and in beer, by .05 gallons.

Contemporary Issue
ENDS OF THE AGE SPECTRUM AND DRINKING

The U.S. national surveys of drinking patterns and practices have paid relatively little attention to the elderly (generally, age 65 or above) and no attention to young children. The reason in the case of the elderly probably is that this group has consistently shown a low prevalence of heavy drinking and drinking problems. Young children simply have not been sampled.

The same factors relating to low alcohol consumption and alcohol problems in the elderly recently have been thought to put them at higher risk of negative consequences when they do drink. One factor is an age-related decrease in physical tolerance for alcohol, so that smaller quantities can have considerable effects on an older person. Another factor is that many of the elderly are taking prescribed medications for medical problems that are synergistic with alcohol, again magnifying the effects of a given quantity of it. The higher risk of alcohol problems among the elderly who do drink is receiving a lot more attention than in previous years because of the increasing number of elderly: In 1983 the elderly were 11% of the U.S. population; in 2025 they are expected to be 17.2%. There also is research that shows a higher rate than once thought of alcohol-related hospitalizations among the elderly (Adams, Yuan, Barboriak, & Rimm, 1993). Accordingly, there is a strong need to learn about the development of drinking patterns and problems among the elderly, and any special needs for treatment of those individuals who do experience problems.

On the other end of the age range, knowledge of young children's drinking is limited at best. However, there has been some research on this age group's knowledge about alcohol and attitudes toward its use. For example, children as young as four years old can identify alcoholic beverages, and six-year-olds show some knowledge of the customs surrounding adult drinking. Unfortunately, much less is known about young children's actual alcohol consumption. There at least seems to be some local and national concern about it. For example, one newspaper report cited the National School Boards Association statement that local school boards were expressing increasing worry about the "spreading alcohol abuse" among children. Naturally, such reports alarm parents. The reason we know so little about the extent of children's drinking is that it is very difficult to study scientifically, say, by the survey methods that have been used to study adults' drinking. Can you think of some of the problems you would face if you wanted to research drinking among young children?

The data on per-capita alcohol consumption tell us how much the "average" drinker in the United States consumes. However, this statistic alone can be deceptive, because the average value masks the large amount of variation in drinking quantity and patterns among Americans. For example, as we saw in Chapter 1, national survey studies have shown consistently that drinking differs according to factors such as age, sex, and racial/ethnic background.

Essential to any discussion of alcohol is the rate of "heavy" drinking. Of course, what is "heavy" is open to wide interpretation and is highly dependent on the setting where the drinking occurs. From a public health point of view, however, what is called "heavy" is drinking that is associated with negative consequences such as accidents, job and family problems, and symptoms of dependence on alcohol (such as inability to cut down on drinking and memory loss associated with drinking). From that consideration what seems to be important is volume consumed on one drinking occasion, even if these occasions do not occur with great frequency (Midanik & Room, 1992).

Table 9-2 is a summary of data collected in the national survey of drug use conducted by the National Institute on Drug Abuse in 1992. The table presents reported "heavy" alcohol use—the type of consumption most highly associated with problems—in the 30 days preceding the interview. The data are highly consistent with earlier surveys and reveal, first, that current heavy drinking is by no means a rarity in the American population aged 12 and older. A total of 5% of the national sample reported such drinking in 1992. However, there are major differences hidden in that total percentage. Men reported a rate of heavy drinking almost four times higher than what women reported. Age also was a powerful factor, in that over 10% of 18–25-year-olds reported heavy drinking (remember the 5% overall rate). Again, gender within this age group is critical, as the rate for men was 16.2%, and for women 6.5%. Another striking difference in Table 9-2 is differences among the racial/ethnic groups among 18–25-year-olds. Whites reported a considerably higher rate (13.3%) than did either blacks (6.1%) or Hispanics (7.5%).

Table 9-2   Percentages of Individuals in Different Age, Gender, and Racial/Ethnic Groups Who Reported Heavy Alcohol Use in the Past Month, 1992

	Age				
	12–17	18-25	26–34	>34	Total
Sex					
Male	2.1	16.2	11.7	6.0	8.1
Female	.5	6.5	3.1	1.1	2.1
Race/Ethnicity					
White	1.4	13.3	7.7	3.3	5.1
Black	.5	6.1	6.6	4.9	4.5
Hispanic	1.5	7.5	7.4	5.1	5.6
Total	1.3	11.3	7.4	3.4	5.0

Note: "Heavy" alcohol use refers to drinking five or more drinks per occasion on five or more days in the past 30 days. Data based on 1992 national survey of drug use conducted by the National Institute on Drug Abuse.

(Source: U.S. Department of Health and Human Services, 1993.)

In summary, the data on prevalence of drinking patterns and problems show the average U.S. drinker consumes a considerable amount of alcohol during the course of a year. However, a number of personal, social, and environmental factors are associated with drinking patterns, including patterns that are associated with problems. Particularly vulnerable in this regard are young (18–25 years) men.

PHARMACOLOGY OF ALCOHOL

Sites of Action

Alcohol is a drug that depresses the CNS. Alcohol may exert such effects by dissolving in lipid membranes, which disturbs the normal chemical actions occurring there (Rall, 1990). That is, alcohol alters the cell membranes' anatomy by entering their internal structure. The result is reduced efficiency of conduction of neural impulses along axons, which reduces the action potential amplitude that reaches the synapse. As a consequence, neurotransmitter release and transmission of impulses across the synapse are inhibited (Julien, 1992, p. 75).

Recent research has been directed at testing the idea that alcohol acts on specific receptors, but the evidence on this possibility is not clear at this point. A prominent hypothesis in this regard is that alcohol acts on GABA-benzodiazepine receptors (for example, Rall, 1990). Actually, pinpointing a site of action or single mechanism of alcohol effects is difficult because the drug affects cell membranes, all neurochemical systems, and all endocrine systems (Abel, 1985). However, considerable knowledge does exist about the pharmacokinetics of alcohol.

Pharmacokinetics of Alcohol

Absorption   Because it provides calories, alcohol is formally classified as a food. However, unlike other foods, alcohol does not have to be digested before the body absorbs it. Nevertheless, alcohol must pass from the stomach to the small intestine in order for rapid absorption to occur. This by far is the most common way humans absorb alcohol. However, if alcohol is vaporized it can be absorbed through the lungs and subcutaneous sites (Ritchie, 1985).

As you saw in Chapter 4, the rate that a drug is absorbed varies widely among people, depending on individual differences in physiology and situational factors. Alcohol is no exception to this rule. The major factors influencing absorption are those that alter the rate of passing alcohol from the stomach to the intestines. In this regard, the drinker can considerably slow absorption by eating while drinking, since the presence of food in the stomach retards absorption. Milk is especially effective for slowing alcohol absorption. Another factor is the rate at which an alcoholic beverage is consumed, as faster drinking means faster absorption. Drinks with a higher concentration of alcohol, such as whiskey on the rocks, are absorbed more quickly than those of lower concentration, such as a highball. The food substances in beer slow its absorption. Carbonated beverages are absorbed more quickly than noncarbonated ones, which explains why people may feel a quick kick from a glass of champagne on an empty stomach, which they typically would not feel from drinking a comparable amount of table wine. Given these factors, the time between stopping drinking and the peak concentration of alcohol in the blood may range from 30 to 90 minutes (Rall, 1990).

Some people exhibit a reflexive action of the body that works to prevent the drinking of high quantities of alcohol. The pylorus, which is the muscular valve separating the stomach from the intestines, shuts when a large quantity of alcohol has been ingested. This action is called **pylorospasm** and prevents whatever is in the stomach from passing to the intestines. As long as alcohol stays in the stomach it will not be absorbed. Therefore, large amounts of alcohol may remain in the stomach unabsorbed when pylorospasm occurs. This mechanism is one of the natural defenses against an individual's becoming a very heavy drinker.

pylorospasm
The shutting of the pylorus valve that occurs in some people when they drink very large quantities of alcohol.

Distribution   After absorption the blood distributes alcohol to all of the body's tissues. Since alcohol is easily dissolved in water, the proportion of water in a tissue determines the concentration of alcohol in it. Blood is about 70% water and, therefore, gets a high concentration of alcohol. Muscle and bone contain smaller percentages of water and have correspondingly smaller percentages of alcohol.

Alcohol primarily affects the CNS, especially the brain. The concentration of alcohol in the brain approximates that in the blood, because of the brain's large blood supply and because alcohol freely passes the blood-brain barrier. Alcohol's LD 50 varies as a function of different factors. The average adult would reach alcohol's LD 50 by drinking about 25 **standard drinks** in an hour or so. A standard drink may be defined as half an ounce of alcohol, which is about the amount in an ounce of 90- to 100-proof whiskey, 12 ounces of 4% alcohol beer, or four ounces of table wine (12% alcohol).

standard drink
The alcohol equivalent in a drink of beer, wine, or distilled spirits. A standard drink equals a half-ounce of alcohol—about the alcohol content in 12 ounces of beer, 4 ounces of table wine, or 1 ounce of 90–100-proof whiskey.

Because all humans have the same proportions of the different tissues and water, it is possible to estimate the concentration of alcohol in the body from its concentration in the blood. The BAC, as the name implies, is the amount of alcohol in the bloodstream. It is expressed as a percentage of weight of alcohol per 100 units of blood volume (Sobell & Sobell, 1981). Typically, the ratio is expressed as milligrams (mg) of alcohol per 100 milliliters (ml) of blood. Therefore, one drop of alcohol, about 10 mg worth, in 1,000 drops of blood, about 100 ml, gives a BAC of .01% (100 ml of blood weighs about 100 gm). For your reference, as of August 1993, the legal level of intoxication in 44 of the 50 states was .10%; it was .08% in Oregon, California, Utah, Kansas, Vermont, and Maine; and now, since January 1, 1994, it became .08% in New Mexico, Florida, North Carolina, and New Hampshire as well. The legal level also is .08% in all of Canada. Alcohol's LD 50 is a BAC of .45%–.50%, although there have been case reports of people surviving BACs up to a little over 1.0 percent (Berild & Hasselbalch, 1981).

You can translate these numbers into an approximation of the number of drinks consumed over time. We emphasize approximation, because, as you saw above, the BAC that is reached depends in part on the different factors influencing absorption. However, knowing approximately what your BAC is at a given time can have practical value.

When a healthy 160-pound man consumes a standard drink, his BAC is raised by .02% to .03% within 45 to 60 minutes of drinking. Factors besides dose of alcohol determine the peak BAC that is reached. Again, the information in Chapter 4 will help you to understand this. Total body mass is a major factor, because alcohol is distributed both in muscle and fat. As a result, heavier people will reach a lower BAC than lighter ones after drinking the same amount of alcohol. Another factor is how much of a person's body consists of fat and muscle. Alcohol is soluble in fat, but is even more soluble in water. Everything being equal, a drink will result in a lower BAC for a leaner person than for the drinker with a higher percentage of body fat. This is the reason a woman would tend to reach higher BACs from drinking a given amount of alcohol than would a man of the same body weight: women tend to have a higher percentage of body fat than men do. Also, one study suggests women have less of the enzyme alcohol dehydrogenase in their stomachs than do men, preventing women from metabolizing as much alcohol in their stomachs. This results in more alcohol entering a woman's bloodstream and, eventually, the brain and other organs (Frezza, di Padova, Pozzato, Terpin, Baraona, & Lieber, 1990). This finding suggests that, for a man and a woman of equal weight, the same amount of alcohol affects the woman more.

Aspirin also may affect the amount of alcohol that is metabolized in the stomach. In a person who has recently eaten, if a moderate dose of aspirin is taken as drinking begins, the resulting BAC will be higher than it would be if the aspirin were not taken (Roine, Gentry, Hernández-Muñoz, et al., 1990). It seems that aspirin suppresses alcohol dehydrogenase in the stomach, so that less alcohol is metabolized there. The "recently eaten" part of this finding is important, because aspirin makes no difference when alcohol enters an empty stomach. In that circumstance, alcohol enters the intestines so rapidly that aspirin's effect on alcohol dehydrogenase has no time to have an effect.

Another variable that influences what peak BAC is reached is individual differences in the rate at which the body metabolizes alcohol. These and other reasons are why the following formula for computing BAC gives only an approximation.

The formula estimates the BAC that would result at a given time in our hypothetical 160-pound man who drank a given number of standard drinks. In the formula below, BAC = blood alcohol content, NSD = number of standard drinks, and NHD = number of hours since drinking began.

Estimated BAC = NSD × (.025%) − NHD × (.015%)

In the formula, NSD is multiplied by .025% because that is the midpoint of our estimated range of increase in BAC that results when our 160-pound drinker has a standard drink. The term NHD is multiplied by .015% because that is the BAC equivalent of the estimated hourly rate that the liver metabolizes alcohol (Rall, 1990). The metabolic rate is independent of body weight, unlike rise in BAC for a given amount of alcohol that is drunk.

Based on our approximation formula, a 160-pound man who drinks three 12-ounce regular beers in an hour will have a BAC of about .06%. That result would be adjusted up or down depending on the important factor of body weight; many conversion charts as illustrated in Figure 9-2 are available to make such corrections. Also, as discussed above, some adjustment up in the BAC would give a better estimate for women.

The estimation formula reflects that the BAC essentially depends on the dose of alcohol that is consumed and the time that it takes to drink it. Figure 9-3 shows the BAC-time relationship. The figure illustrates that the BAC rises quickly and then more gradually returns to zero after drinking stops. Therefore, time is an important factor in determining BAC. Time enters the formula

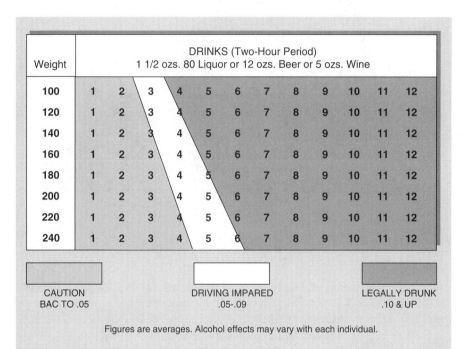

Weight	DRINKS (Two-Hour Period) 1 1/2 ozs. 80 Liquor or 12 ozs. Beer or 5 ozs. Wine											
100	1	2	3	4	5	6	7	8	9	10	11	12
120	1	2	3	4	5	6	7	8	9	10	11	12
140	1	2	3	4	5	6	7	8	9	10	11	12
160	1	2	3	4	5	6	7	8	9	10	11	12
180	1	2	3	4	5	6	7	8	9	10	11	12
200	1	2	3	4	5	6	7	8	9	10	11	12
220	1	2	3	4	5	6	7	8	9	10	11	12
240	1	2	3	4	5	6	7	8	9	10	11	12

CAUTION BAC TO .05	DRIVING IMPARED .05-.09	LEGALLY DRUNK .10 & UP

Figures are averages. Alcohol effects may vary with each individual.

KNOW YOUR LEGAL LIMIT

In Texas that means .10 of Blood Alcohol Content. If you are going to drive, don't drink more than two 12 oz. beers or two 1 oz. drinks or two 5 oz. glasses of wine in an hour. Another drink and you will have passed your legal limit. In any case, if you've been drinking at all, be careful!

CONOZCA SU LÍMITE LEGAL

En Tejas este seía, 10% de cantidad de alcohol en la sangre. Si Ud. piensa manejar, no tome más de 2 cervezas de 12 onzas o 2 copas de licor de una onza, o 2 vasos de vino de 5 onzas en una hora. Una bebida máz y Ud. se habrá pasado de su límite legal. De todos modos, si Ud. ha estado tomando, Itenga cuidado!

Tarrant Council on Alcoholism & Drug Abuse
(817)332-6329

Figure 9-2   This is one of the many conversion charts that are available to help you to approximate your blood alcohol concentration as a function of number of drinks, time, and your body weight.

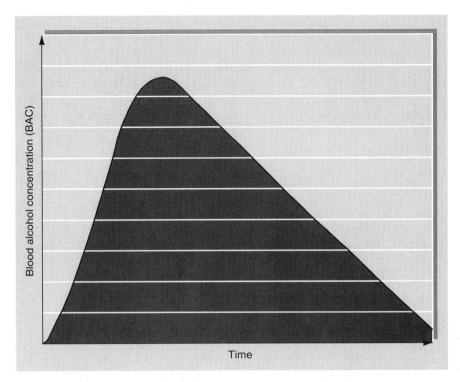

Y-axis: Blood alcohol concentration (BAC)

X-axis: Time

Figure 9-3   Blood alcohol concentration as a function of time.

independent of the number of standard drinks because of the way the liver metabolizes alcohol: generally, at a constant amount over a given time, regardless of the amount that is drunk.

For medical or legal purposes BAC is not estimated by formula but is measured by standardized procedures as precisely as possible. Blood and urine samples are taken frequently for medical and medical-legal reasons to measure BAC. For example, BACs of drivers killed in motor vehicle accidents often are determined by blood samples. A very prominent measurement of BAC is done by breath sample, because of the known ratio (1:2100) between the amount of alcohol in the lungs to the amount in the blood. Gas chromatography methods are used to obtain excellent estimates of BAC, so good they are considered legally admissible evidence. The police departments of many U.S. cities measure BAC by breath analysis. Gas chromatographic methods are expensive, however, and until recently this prohibited precise measurement of BAC in settings where it would be very useful, such as outpatient alcohol treatment programs. However, substantial improvements in electronic technology have made possible breath-testing devices that give good BAC estimates and cost only a few hundred dollars.

Metabolism and Excretion   More than 90% of the alcohol that is absorbed is metabolized by the body, mainly in the liver. (We saw earlier that the stomach also plays a part in metabolizing alcohol.) The small percentage of alcohol that is not metabolized is excreted in pure form through the kidneys and the

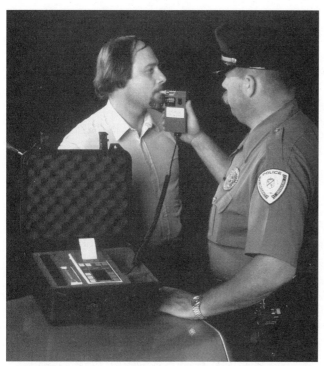

Blood alcohol concentration can be measured by breath analysis, as shown here.

lungs. When alcohol is metabolized in the liver, it is broken down to acetaldehyde by the enzyme alcohol dehydrogenase. This step is the basis of using the drug **disulfiram** (trade name Antabuse) in the treatment of alcohol dependence. We will have more to say about this in Chapter 16. Acetaldehyde eventually is broken down to carbon dioxide and water. At this point there is a release of energy, or calories (Julien, 1992). The carbon dioxide is excreted from the body through air exchange in the lungs, and the water is excreted in urine. Unlike other foods, such as proteins and carbohydrates, the rate that alcohol is metabolized is independent of the body's need for the calories it could provide or of the amount of alcohol consumed. The rate of alcohol oxidation is constant and averages about .35 ounces an hour.

Oxidation is the process by which the energy in foods is released in the form of heat and work. In this respect, alcohol liberates about 75 calories in each half-ounce. Therefore, one standard drink of whiskey has about 75 calories, because the calories in distilled spirits are only from alcohol content. However, beverages such as beer provide calories from foods such as proteins and carbohydrates as well as alcohol. A regular 12-oz 4% alcohol beer has about 150 calories, and a comparable amount of the commercial light beers has anywhere from 95 to 135 calories. Light beers have fewer calories primarily because they contain less alcohol.

Alcohol is notorious for being unaffected by attempts to hasten its removal from the body. Efforts such as vigorous exercise do nothing to speed up alcohol oxidation, except to the extent that exercise takes time and the

disulfiram
A drug that interferes with the metabolism of alcohol so that a person soon feels very ill if he or she drinks while on a regimen of disulfiram. The drug may be used as part of a treatment program for alcohol dependence.

individual does not drink while exercising. As noted in Chapter 8, the long-used intoxication "remedy" of black coffee, as a source of caffeine, also does nothing to hasten sobering up. However, because caffeine is a stimulant drug the individual may interpret such effects as decreased alcohol intoxication. In fact, little can be done to hasten sobriety except to wait for the liver to do its work in its own constant time.

TOLERANCE AND DEPENDENCE

Tolerance

Regular use of alcohol results to some degree in dispositional tolerance (see Chapter 5 for our detailed discussion of tolerance). Therefore, the drinker must consume greater quantities of alcohol in order to maintain a certain BAC. Dispositional tolerance can be reversed with a period of abstinence from alcohol.

Functional tolerance has a greater practical influence than does dispositional tolerance in altering how alcohol affects you with repeated use. There are both acute and protracted tolerances to alcohol. Because of acute tolerance, at a given BAC there are greater alcohol effects when the BAC curve is rising than there are at that same BAC on the descending limb of the curve. For example, at a BAC of .10% as it is ascending, an individual may show considerably impaired performance on tasks related to driving. However, if the BAC peaks at, say, .15% and then hits .10% as it is falling, the individual's performance on those same driving-related tasks would be improved although still probably far from its level with no alcohol in the blood. Of course, such improvement would make no difference to the police. A person with a BAC of .10% is legally drunk, and in some places beyond drunk, regardless of what direction the BAC is heading when it is measured. Acute tolerance is illustrated in Figure 9-4.

As with dispositional tolerance, the development of protracted tolerance requires that the individual drink greater amounts of alcohol in order to achieve an effect once achieved with less alcohol. Because protracted functional tolerance far outpaces dispositional tolerance, the person becomes more susceptible to serious health and other consequences of heavy alcohol consumption. For example, a person may drink high quantities of alcohol to achieve a mood change once reached with much less alcohol. But the BAC does not behave in the same way. Drinking large quantities of alcohol still will result in a high BAC. With higher BACs the body is more vulnerable to suffering alcohol's toxic effects, which we will review shortly. Similarly, a chronic heavy drinker may not feel drunk or even impaired at BACs greater than .10%, but he or she still is defined legally as drunk. Such a designation leaves a person liable to arrests for drunk driving and other alcohol-related charges.

As we noted in Chapter 5, there is cross tolerance between alcohol and other CNS depressant drugs. We also noted how this may cause difficulties for the anesthesiologist preparing a patient for surgery. Sometimes the problem is acute in the emergency room, where surgery must sometimes be performed immediately following a serious accident. You will see later how

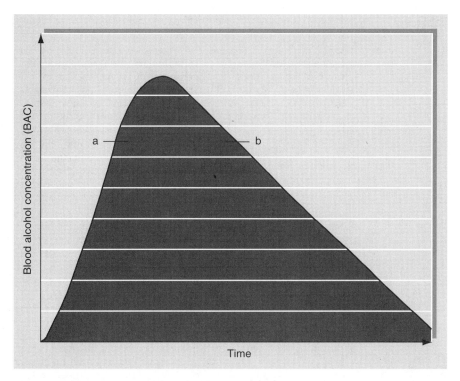

Figure 9-4   Acute tolerance to alcohol's effects—the effects of alcohol at (a) are greater than the effects at (b).

alcohol intoxication is associated with the occurrence of accidents and, as you might expect, the heaviest users (most tolerant) of alcohol are the people who are most likely to have the accidents (USDHHS, 1993a).

Alcohol also shows cross dependence to CNS depressant drugs. This means that taking one drug can suppress withdrawal symptoms in the other. So, for example, alcohol and the benzodiazepine drugs such as Valium and Librium show cross dependence. This phenomenon has proved valuable in managing withdrawal from alcohol in individuals who are physically dependent on it.

Physical Dependence

With chronic, abusive drinking some individuals develop physical dependence on alcohol. Symptoms of physical dependence can be severe. They may be classified into three phases, as outlined in Table 9-3. As you can see, a wide range of symptoms can appear and are associated with time of onset after drinking cessation, although there is some overlap among the symptoms in the different phases. You should note that not all people who are physically dependent on alcohol experience all three phases of symptoms. For example, Phase 2 symptoms probably appear least frequently, and individuals may go from Phase 1 to Phase 3 symptoms. Another important point: withdrawal symptoms may appear when the BAC is falling but still at a fairly

Table 9-3 Symptoms of the Alcohol Withdrawal Syndrome in Three Phases

Phase	Onset	Symptoms
1	As soon as a few hours after drinking stopped; BACs may still be >.00 percent.	Tremulousness (shakes), profuse perspiration, weakness, alcohol- and other drug-seeking. Also may include agitation, headache, anorexia, nausea and vomiting, abdominal cramps, high heart rate, and exaggerated and rapid reflexes. Visual and auditory hallucinations may follow in increased intensity. Hallucinations may also occur when the individual is severely intoxicated (called acute alcoholic hallucinosis).
2	When this occurs, it is within 24 hours of drinking cessation.	Grand mal seizures, ranging from one seizure to continuous severe seizure activity with little or no interruption.
3	About >30 hours after drinking cessation. Most protracted phase, may last 3–4 days. Commonly called delirium tremens (DTs).	Severe agitation, often appearance of confusion and disorientation. Almost continual activity. Very high body temperature and abnormally rapid heart beat. Terrifying hallucinations, may be visual, auditory, or tactile. Latter most often felt as bugs or little animals crawling on the skin. Hallucinations are accompanied by delusions, with high potential for violent behavior without medical management. Deaths during DTs still occur due to high fever, cardiovascular collapse, or traumatic injury.
End of withdrawal course	About 5–7 days after drinking stopped.	Exhaustion and severe dehydration.

Note: This table is based on information in Jacobs and Fehr (1987) and Wolfe and Victor (1971).

high level, such as .15%. The BAC needs not to have fallen all the way to zero for withdrawal to begin. Before its management by use of drugs associated with cross dependence with alcohol, alcohol withdrawal often ended in death. More recently less-severe alcohol withdrawal has been managed without the use of drugs (**social detoxification**) or with drugs in an outpatient setting.

The following account, based on a case described in the DSM-III *Case Book* (Spitzer, Skodol, Gibbon, & Williams, 1981, pp. 104–105), gives a good depiction of an individual experiencing alcohol withdrawal.

> The patient was a 43-year-old divorced carpenter. His sister reported that the patient had been drinking more than a fifth of cheap wine every day for the past five years. The patient also had not eaten well, maybe only one meal a day, and had relied on wine as his main source of nourishment. The patient stopped drinking three days ago, and the morning after he awoke with his hands shaking so badly that he could barely light a cig-

social detoxification
Treatment of alcohol withdrawal without the use of medicine.

arette. He also had a feeling of inner panic that made sleep almost impossible. A neighbor called the patient's sister in concern because he was not making any sense and seemed as if he could not take care of himself.

When he was examined at the hospital the patient alternated between superficial, chatty warmth and apprehension. He went back and forth from recognizing the doctor to thinking he was the patient's brother. Twice during the interview the patient called the doctor by his brother's name and asked him when he had arrived, apparently losing track of the interview. When the patient is at rest he shows a gross tremor and picks "bugs" off the bedsheets. The patient has no **orientation to time** and thinks that he is in the parking lot of a supermarket. The patient says that he is fighting against his feeling that the world is about to end in a holocaust. The patient is startled every few minutes, from what he says are sounds and sights of fiery car crashes. These perceptions apparently are retriggered by sounds of rolling carts in the hall. Memory testing is not possible because the patient's attention shifts too rapidly. (Published with permission of American Psychiatric Press.)

orientation to time
Awareness of temporal specification, such as time of day, the day of the week, or the year. Orientation to time is one of the functions assessed in a psychiatric exam.

THERAPEUTIC USES

Alcohol might have been thought to be the panacea for all of life's ills, but we now know its medical value is probably outdistanced by its social value (Ritchie, 1985). In fact, there was hint of this knowledge some time ago, based on a remedy for treating colds taken from an old English book: At first inkling of a cold, hang your hat on the bedpost, drink from a bottle of good whiskey until two hats appear, and then get into bed and stay there. The therapeutic value of alcohol in this case was in keeping the cold victim in bed.

But a recent study suggests that moderate drinking can help to resist getting a cold if you are exposed to a respiratory virus. A total of 391 healthy English men and women were exposed to one of five respiratory viruses; they were evaluated each of two days before, and each of six days after exposure. The findings of the study showed that the people who did not smoke cigarettes were less likely to become ill after virus exposure if they were moderate drinkers, defined as up to three to four drinks a day. Alcohol use did not influence the resistance of the smokers, who as a group were more prone than nonsmokers to develop respiratory illness following virus exposure (Cohen, Tyrrell, Russell, et al., 1993). The findings about the smokers were not surprising, but alcohol typically is thought to be a drug that suppresses the immune system responses. This may not be true in the case of fighting off the common cold, at least for moderate drinkers. Certainly more research on this topic appears warranted.

Alcohol also has other, better established therapeutic uses. For example, it is an ingredient in several legitimate medical products (Jacobs & Fehr, 1987). Because alcohol is an excellent solvent, small amounts are combined with other ingredients in making cough syrups and other products taken orally. Furthermore, alcohol is an ingredient in mouthwashes and shaving lotions. If the individuals like them, alcoholic beverages may be recommended in moderate amounts to convalescent or elderly patients to be taken before meals to stimulate appetite and digestion. Alcohol also is included in compounds created to treat skin problems. Because alcohol cools when it evaporates, ethanol sponges are used to treat fevers. In addition, alcohol is part of mixtures that serve as liniments (Rall, 1990). Finally, dehydrated alcohol may be injected close to nerves or sympathetic ganglia to relieve chronic pain that may occur, for example, in inoperable cancer (Ritchie, 1985).

ACUTE EFFECTS OF ALCOHOL

In this section we review both the acute and chronic effects of alcohol consumption. We first go over alcohol's many acute physiological, sensory-motor ("sensorimotor"), and psychological effects. We also discuss several topics of special societal concern related to alcohol's acute effects, including aggression, sexual behavior, and driving.

One point about alcohol's acute effects is that alcohol generally acts on the body as a depressant, and its acute effects are proportional to the magnitude of the BAC. Simply put, as the BAC increases, acute effects increase in number and intensity. However, how humans experience degree of **intoxication** and behave under different doses of alcohol often are modified by psychological and situational factors as well as alcohol dose and tolerance to this drug. For some behaviors these nondrug factors may even be more powerful determinants than drug factors of alcohol's acute effects.

intoxication
A transient state of physical and psychological disruption due to the presence of a toxic substance, such as alcohol, in the CNS.

Physiological Effects

Alcohol has several physiological effects occurring at lower doses.[1] For example, alcohol inhibits the secretion of the antidiuretic hormone, which causes increased urination. The effect happens when the BAC is rising but not when it is falling. Alcohol also reduces the amount of fat in the body that is oxidized. The acute effect of alcohol accumulates to result in long-term increased body fat and weight gain when alcohol is used in addition to normal food intake (Suter, Schutz, & Jequier, 1992). Commonly, such weight gain is called a "beer belly." Alcohol is a peripheral dilator and causes the skin to feel warm and turn red. A number of authors have cautioned against using alcoholic beverages in cold environments in order to warm up. This advice is counterintuitive to many drinkers, since they experience the warmth that occurs with peripheral dilation and know of the Saint Bernard and its keg of brandy rescuing victims in snow-covered mountains. However, alcohol's dilating effect on peripheral blood vessels causes some loss of body heat, and it was thought that such action would ultimately cause decreased protection against the cold. It turns out the problem is not a serious one, as experimental studies have shown alcohol does not significantly tilt the balance of the body's regulation of its temperature in cold environments.

An acute alcohol effect with wide practical application is that it increases gastric secretion, which is one basis for the American cocktail hour.

---

[1] Much of the discussion of alcohol's acute effects is based on Becker, Roe, and Scott (1975), Jacobs and Fehr (1987), McKim (1986), and Sobell and Sobell (1981).

The increase in gastric secretion stimulates the appetite. Unfortunately, at high doses alcohol harms the stomach mucosa and causes gastric distress. Nausea and vomiting may occur at BACs over .15%. Another physiological effect of alcohol when taken in high doses and when the BAC increases rapidly is a release of corticosteroids, which is part of the body's general reaction to stress. In this case the stressor is a high dose of alcohol, which is toxic to the body.

An important acute effect of alcohol is disruption of sleep patterns. Even at lower doses alcohol suppresses **REM sleep,** which is the stage of the sleep cycle when most dreaming occurs (REM stands for "rapid eye movements," which characterize this stage of sleep). When the dose is low, the REM suppression tends to occur only in the first half of the night, but in the second half REM time rebounds and increases. At larger doses of alcohol REM is suppressed throughout the night.

Alcohol impairs memory. Its acute effects are on short-term memory, and when high BACs are reached rapidly a **blackout** may occur. Blackouts are an individual's amnesia about events when drinking even though there was no loss of consciousness. For example, a person who had a lot to drink the night before may wake up and have absolutely no recollection of where he or she parked the car. Blackouts are thought to result from a failure in transfer of information in **short-term memory** to **long-term memory.** There also are grayouts, in which an individual can partially recall events occurring in full consciousness during a drinking occasion. Grayouts probably reflect state-dependent learning. Blackouts and grayouts do not happen consistently in the same individuals with a given dose of alcohol, and the factors specifically determining their occurrence have not been identified.

Every drinker probably has had at least one somewhat-delayed consequence of an episode of overindulgence—the hangover. Hangovers may be thought of as a minor withdrawal syndrome, because they are the body's readjustment to a nonalcohol state. Hangovers begin to appear about 4 to 12 hours after the peak BAC is reached and generally are not seen as a pleasant alcohol effect. Symptoms may include headache, dizziness, nausea, vomiting, increased heart rate, fatigue, and thirst. Furthermore, although the BAC is zero, hangovers are associated with a reduced ability to perform the complex skills required to drive a motor vehicle (Franck, 1983).

Remedies galore have been sought to cure the hangover. Perhaps the one heard most often is "hair of the dog that bit you," and in this case the dog is alcohol. It is true alcohol will erase its own hangover symptoms, just as drinking stops alcohol withdrawal symptoms. However, this solution is far from perfect, because all that is being accomplished is postponing the inevitable. Of course, a real danger in using alcohol in this way is that it is courting a pattern of frequent, heavy drinking, because alcohol is used to remove an unpleasant effect of drinking in high quantities. An ample number of studies have shown this effect to be highly reinforcing to humans and other animals alike. The only dependable and safe cure for hangover is time.

In discussing alcohol's acute effects it is important to reemphasize that it interacts synergistically with other CNS depressants. The point is worth repeating because of the dangerous effects of mixing alcohol and barbiturates— a common method of intended and unintended suicides. Alcohol and the

REM sleep
Acronym for "rapid eye movements," which are associated with dream activity and are one stage in a cycle of sleep.

blackout
A person's failure to recall events that occurred while drinking even though there is no loss of consciousness.

short-term memory
Memory for recent events. Short-term memory generally is thought to differ from long-term memory in several important ways.

long-term memory
Memory for remote events. According to one theory of memory, information enters long-term memory through short-term memory.

"Before I'd know it (while drinking), I'd be stumbling around, being loud and jovial, insensitive to pain. I'd feel great at the time, and I'd also know what was in store for me. And the next day I'd be totally out of action, feeling as if I'd been poisoned, which I guess I had. I got really scared one time when I woke up like that and couldn't remember anything of the night before."

(37-year-old man describing his drinking during college, cited in Weil & Rosen, 1983, p. 191)

benzodiazepines do not have the degree of suicide potential that alcohol and the barbiturates have, but there can be serious decrements in performance of skills essential to survival, such as driving a car or staying awake while driving a car. Similarly, marijuana and alcohol are frequently consumed on the same occasion, and there seems to be synergistic effects of these two drugs on skills related to driving (for example, Perez-Reyes, Hicks, Bumberry, Jeffcoat, & Cook, 1988). Antihistamines, which are available over the counter, also combine synergistically with alcohol. Another point about combining alcohol with other drugs: alcohol decreases the effects of certain prescribed medications, such as antibiotics, anticonvulsants, anticoagulants, and **monoamine oxidase (MAO) inhibitors.**

MAO inhibitors
Drugs used to treat depressions that inhibit the activity of the enzyme monoamine oxidase, which degrades the neurotransmitters of norepinephrine and serotonin.

Alcohol causes slight respiratory depression at lower doses, but this effect does not reach dangerous levels in healthy people unless very high doses are consumed. Higher doses also are associated with induction of sleep, stupor, and in extremely high doses, coma. In the overdose range of consumption, cardiovascular depression can occur. We earlier noted that a dose of alcohol can be lethal (LD 50 = BAC of .45–.50%), due to dysfunction of the more primitive areas of the brain controlling breathing and heartbeat.

Sensorimotor Effects

At moderate (.05%) to higher BACs alcohol has several different acute effects on the senses. Vision decreases in acuity, and taste and smell are not as sen-

Contemporary Issue
THE HANGOVER'S MANY CURES

Besides the "hair of the dog that bit you," several other supposed hangover cures have made the circuit among drinkers. Here are some of them, as listed by Carroll and Miller (1986).

1. Take megadoses of vitamins, so your body will have the strength to ward off the hangover.
2. Take tranquilizers.
3. Inhale pure oxygen to quicken the body's oxidation of alcohol.
4. Exercise.
5. Eat a big breakfast.
6. Drink a repulsive concoction, so the disgusting taste will help you to forget the hangover.
7. Ignore your hangover.
8. Stay in bed and lie still.

Some of these purported remedies sound as though they were created by people desperately suffering from hangovers. None of them has a basis in medical science or practice. Hangovers are "cured" in only two ways: time, or not getting too intoxicated in the first place.

sitive. Pain sensitivity decreases when the BAC is in the .08 to .10% range. Simple reaction time begins to slow significantly at a BAC of .10%. An example of a simple reaction time task is to press a key as quickly as possible when a single light on a panel shines. In complex reaction time, subjects are required to integrate two or more stimuli and then respond to them as quickly as possible. An example is to press a key when a white and red light shine but not to press it when only the white light shines. Complex reaction time may be impaired for both speed and accuracy at BACs of .05% or even lower.

Alcohol strongly affects body sway, which is measured by asking the subject to stand steady with his or her eyes closed. The body's deviation from a "steady state" is then recorded. At a BAC of .06% body sway is impaired by about 40%. At a high BAC, we see alcohol's effect on body sway manifested as staggering and, eventually, as an inability to walk independently at all. The sensitivity of body sway to alcohol is the source of the "walk a straight line" test police use to decide whether a suspect is drunk. Alcohol's influence on body sway is due to its effects on balance controls in the inner ear. This also is the reason why the room may spin when the party goer lies down and closes his or her eyes to sleep after a night of heavy drinking.

Alcohol impairs psychomotor skills. In tasks designed to measure these skills, subjects are required to make controlled muscular movements to adjust or position a machine or some mechanism on an experimental apparatus in response to changes in speed or direction of a moving object (for example, Levine, Kramer, & Levine, 1975, p. 288). A common example is the pursuit rotor task, in which the subject must keep a stylus on a target that moves circularly on an automated disk.

Psychomotor task performance on the average shows deterioration at BACs of about .03% and higher (Levine et al., 1975). These tasks commonly require relatively fine motor dexterity. At high BACs, .15% or more, there is clear abnormality in gross motor functions, like standing or walking. At these levels, alcohol has impaired the brain centers responsible for motor activity and balance to such a degree that the neural messages are not being sent to the muscles.

Alcohol and Driving Ability

Sensorimotor skills constitute a major part of driving ability. During the early 1980s there was an enormous increase in public awareness of drinking and driving a motor vehicle. Probably most influential in opening the public's eyes and ears about drunk driving were citizens' organizations such as Mothers Against Drunk Driving (MADD) and Students Against Drunk Driving (SADD). These movements contributed to and were strengthened by the more conservative attitudes toward alcohol and drug use that marked the 1980s in the United States. Part of this trend was increased enforcement of stricter legal penalties for driving under the influence (DUI) of alcohol (or other drugs). One example, in well over half of the United States, is mandatory jail sentences. Jail may be a consequence even for a first DUI offense.

The center of attention about the dangers of alcohol use has been motor vehicles, particularly cars. There is ample cause for concern. Motor vehicle crashes are the most common nonnatural cause of death in the United States; they are the leading cause of death overall of people aged 5–34 (USDHHS,

"In Amarillo, Texas, I participate in a community coalition dedicated to fighting drunken driving and underage drinking. Our motto: All it takes is everyone. Only community-wide efforts around the country can defeat the problem of alcohol abuse."
(Ms. Bernadette Teichmann, USA *Today*, August 30, 1993, p. 11A)

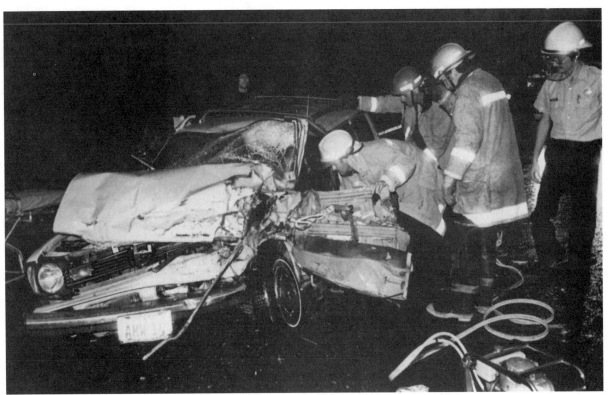

Motor vehicle accidents are the single most common nonnatural cause of death in the United States.

1987, 1990). Alcohol is implicated as a causal factor in traffic fatalities, but statistics are not conclusive, because we have only correlational studies. The argument for alcohol as cause is strengthened, however, by data on the relationship between relative risk of involvement in a traffic accident (fatal or not) and BAC. At a BAC of .05% the risk is about twice the likelihood when the BAC is zero. At a BAC of .10%, the risk triples from that at a BAC of zero. At a BAC of .15% it is about seven times, and at a BAC of .20%, the risk balloons to more than 20 times (Harvard, 1977).

The case for alcohol as a causal factor in traffic fatalities becomes even more solid with experimental data on how alcohol affects performance on tasks requiring psychomotor skills and an integration of sensory information. An example, called a "divided attention" task, would be combining the pursuit rotor and complex reaction time tasks into one experimental task. Subjects would be required to keep the stylus on target (pursuit rotor) while they are simultaneously responding to the two light stimuli on a panel (complex reaction time). Driving a car requires the same motor control and sensory integration abilities that would be necessary to complete such a divided attention task. Alcohol impairs performance on divided attention tasks at BACs of .05% or lower. In fact, this is one basis of the recommendation of several groups, such as the American College of Emergency Physicians, the Associates for the Advancement of Emergency Medicine, and the American Medical Association, that the legal level of intoxication be uniform across the United States at a BAC of .05%. Currently, as we have noted, some states have moved to lower their legal level of intoxication from .10% to .08%. In many states, arrest still is possible at BACs below their respective legal levels of intoxication for "driving while impaired."

Alcohol seems to be, therefore, a primary factor raising the risk of involvement in fatal and nonfatal motor vehicle accidents. Other factors interact with alcohol to affect risk, and two of the more important ones are gender and age. Young drivers are far more likely to be involved in alcohol-related accidents. For example, one study showed that in 1980 18-year-olds constituted 2.2% of the driver population and drove 2% of the total number of miles traveled. Yet they were involved in 5.5% of the alcohol-related accidents. By comparison, 45–54-year-olds drove nine times as many miles as the 18-year-olds but had only one and one-third as many alcohol-related accidents. It also appears young people are put at increased risk for alcohol-related fatal accidents at lower BACs than are older drivers. In a study comparing five different age groups of drivers involved in fatal motor vehicle accidents, 16–19-year-olds were measured as having a much lower BAC than did drivers in the older age groups. One explanation for this finding is that younger people have less experience in both drinking and driving (USDHHS, 1987). This means driving is not as well-learned a skill in younger people and is more likely to be disrupted at a given BAC. Furthermore, younger people would tend to show less protracted tolerance in general at a given BAC because of their shorter period of use of alcoholic beverages.

Young males (≤ 25 years old) seem to be the group most likely to be intoxicated, driving, and in traffic accidents. This supports the consistent finding in surveys that young men are the ones most likely to drink heavily (say, five or more drinks) on an occasion. Data published in 1983 show that 38% of the young men drivers who were involved in fatal accidents had a BAC of .10% or higher, compared to 30% for all other age and gender groups (USDHHS, 1987). Young men are more likely to be legally intoxicated and the drivers in fatal accidents because of their tendency to drink heavily on occasion, and because they drive a relatively higher percentage of miles on weekend nights, when all drivers are most likely to be intoxicated.

In summary, motor vehicle accidents continue to be an extremely serious problem in the United States, and alcohol seems to play a major part in them. It appears that continued vigilance both by law enforcement personnel and by citizens' groups such as MADD is essential for sustained progress on the drunk-driving problem. The drivers' perception that DUI arrest and conviction are highly likely consequences for driving while legally intoxicated is particularly important for stemming the DUI problem (USDHHS, 1987). A major part of prevention efforts (Chapter 17) aimed at adolescents and young adults also must continue to be repeated as reminders about the facts and dangers in driving under the influence of alcohol or other drugs.

Psychological Effects

Alcohol combines with other factors to change emotion and mood. Different people report a range of psychological effects at a given BAC, and the same drinker may report different effects at a BAC on different occasions. The influences of nondrug factors, particularly situational and cognitive variables (for example, expectancies and attitudes), are perhaps most powerful in this domain. The person's mood state before he or she started to drink also is an important factor.

At lower BACs, drinkers report feeling elated and friendly when the BAC is rising, but when it is falling common reports are anger and fatigue. Other reports when the BAC is rising have been expansiveness, joviality, relaxation, and self-confidence. The importance of nondrug factors is accented in the finding that during the ascending phase of these same BACs other subjects have reported feeling hostile, depressed, and withdrawn. When BACs go above .10%, drinkers commonly become more labile, as the drinker may abruptly change from friendly to hostile. Often the level of frustration tolerance is lowered.

Alcohol's effects on thinking and perception are less influenced by nondrug factors and more by BAC. Alcohol significantly impairs short-term memory at BACs over .05%. At a BAC of .05% the ability to estimate time is impaired. Drinkers seem to overestimate time passage at a BAC of .05%. So, they might estimate a time passage of 8 minutes to be 12 minutes. The ability to estimate distance (depth perception) also is disrupted at lower BACs, as are attention and concentration. At higher BACs these cognitive effects are intensified and are compounded by more disorganized thinking.

Alcohol and Behavior

Among alcohol's effects, those that affect interpersonal behavior are of great social interest. As the word implies, "interpersonal" means between people. The interpersonal behaviors of sex and aggression in combination with alcohol have garnered the greatest interest and concern.

Alcohol and Aggression   Aggression is behavior that is intended to harm a person who would prefer not to receive such treatment (Bushman & Cooper, 1990). Violence is a type of aggression that is a major social concern. As you saw in Contemporary Issue Box 1-3, studies suggest that when people commit violent crimes they tend to be under the influence of alcohol. Violent crimes include murder or attempted murder, manslaughter, rape or sexual assault, robbery, assault, and others, such as kidnapping, purse snatching, hit-and-run driving, and child abuse. These findings also hold for Canada and western Europe (Collins, 1981). The co-occurrence of alcohol use and violent crime is especially prevalent among men aged 18 to 30 years, who have a relatively high rate of both heavy drinking and criminal activity. Another problem of national concern is physical abuse of spouses (predominantly husbands abusing wives), and alcohol has been estimated to be involved (offender or victim) in 25 to 50% of spouse abuse incidents (Collins, Guess, Williams, & Hamilton, 1980).

National statistics not only show associations between alcohol and violence toward others, but also violence toward the self. For example, suicide is one of the three leading causes of death (the other two are homicide and accidental death) among males 15 to 34 years old and one of the 10 leading causes of death among all persons 34–54 years old. One study of the causes of violent death centered on 3,400 individuals who had had their BACs tested at the time of their deaths. Among those people who died by suicide, 35% had been drinking alcohol when they took their lives (USDHHS, 1987).

During the late 1980s national attention was directed at alcohol and behavior at baseball games and other professional sports events and at fraternities. In both cases aggressive behavior was the focus, and alcohol was singled out as a major culprit. One example is the fans' rowdy reactions during an April 1988 game at Cincinnati's Riverfront Stadium, when an umpire made a call unfavorable to the home team Reds. Alcohol was viewed by league officials to be at the heart of the "deterioration" of the situation. This and similar events led many major league baseball teams to adopt restricted alcohol sales (primarily beer) policies, and even to have alcohol-free sections in the stands, similar to smoke-free areas in public places. Alcohol also has been identified as a major problem in the behavior of members of fraternities on college campuses. For example, misconduct and violence against property and persons that some fraternities are known for have been highly correlated with the occurrence of popular frat functions such as beer bashes.

The consistency of the co-occurrence of drinking and violent behavior tempts the conclusion that alcohol causes such behavior. However, data such as government statistics are only descriptive and correlational and cannot be the bases of valid causal statements about alcohol and aggression. Nevertheless, the adult drinking public believes alcohol does indeed cause aggression. A consistent finding in many studies of beliefs about the effects of alcohol is that it increases power and aggression (Brown, Christiansen, & Goldman, 1987). Perhaps these beliefs underlie officials' statements that alcohol causes disorderly conduct at ballparks and fraternities.

Of course, aggressive behavior is a highly significant social concern, and it is important to find the reasons for the association between drinking and the occurrence of violent behavior. A traditional explanation is the disinhibition theory, which was first proposed in the early twentieth century. This theory holds that alcohol releases behavior normally inhibited by society, such as aggression and sex, as a result of its depressant action on the brain. Essentially, the theory suggests that whatever anxieties about the social consequences of behavior such as aggression that we have learned vanish as a result of alcohol's pharmacological action. So, people who have been drinking should be more aggressive than people who have not.

Controlled laboratory experiments involving human subjects do not support the disinhibition theory, however. Some studies have shown a correlation between alcohol and aggression that has been discovered in epidemiological studies. However, this was not a simple matter of alcohol's pharmacological action, as disinhibition theory predicts. Rather, alcohol combines with situational factors, such as social pressure and threat of retaliation (Adesso, 1985). Furthermore, drinkers' expectancies about alcohol and aggression also seem to contribute to aggression, sometimes considerably more than actually drinking alcohol does.

It seems, therefore, that alcohol does not simply cause aggression, despite the beliefs of some public officials and the general population. Instead, aggression is a complex social behavior affected by the characteristics of the aggressor and situational factors, only one of which is alcohol consumption. Theories about aggression must accommodate this complexity to be useful.

Alcohol and Sex   For about 500 years Shakespeare probably has been the author most frequently cited on the acute effects of alcohol on human sexual

Contemporary Issue
THE BALANCED PLACEBO DESIGN

Because of placebo effects (see Chapter 5) experimental studies of drug effects in humans and other animals usually include a placebo control group. In studies of alcohol effects in humans, this involves telling subjects they are drinking an alcoholic beverage when, in fact, they are not given one. Instead they are given a nonalcoholic drink resembling the alcoholic beverage in every way except alcohol content. So, in the traditional placebo group design everybody in two groups of subjects is told he or she will drink an alcoholic beverage, but only one group's beverage actually contains alcohol. Studies following this design have varied in their success of making the alcoholic and placebo beverages indistinguishable on cues such as taste and smell and, therefore, in the validity of their findings. How do you think failure to make the alcohol and placebo beverages indiscriminable would affect the interpretation of results of a study?

A significant advance in studying the effects of drugs on human behavior was made over 30 years ago in what has been named the balanced placebo design (BPD). The design has helped a lot to advance knowledge about alcohol and aggression and sex, among other human behaviors. The BPD involves adding two groups to the traditional two-group placebo group design. The subjects in each of the two additional groups are told they will not receive a drug, and in one group they get the drug and in the other they do not. Therefore, comparisons are possible with a group of subjects who believe they are not getting, and do not get, a drug (sober control group). It also is possible to make comparisons with a group of subjects who believe they are not receiving a drug but do really get one. The advance that the design offers is that we can separate a pure drug effect, an "expectancy" (about drug actions) effect, and their interaction. Under the best conditions of control the traditional placebo design provides a comparison of drug plus expectancy and expectancy conditions, which permits conclusions about drug action. The BPD seems much better suited than the traditional placebo design for studying the complexity of drugs and human behavior.

Table 9-4   Balanced Placebo Designs

		Beverage Received	
		Alcohol	Placebo
Beverage Told	Alcohol	Group 1	2
	Placebo	3	4

Outline of the balanced placebo design in studying alcohol effects. The traditional design includes groups 1 and 2 only.

response. The specific reference is from *Macbeth*, Act 2, Scene 2: "It [alcohol] provokes and unprovokes; it provokes the desire, but it takes away from the performance." It turns out that the results of recent experimental studies are in part consistent with Shakespeare's observations.

Alcohol and sexual response in men and women has been a favorite subject of writers for thousands of years. Much of the writing has been like Shakespeare's comments, based on informal personal observations. As regards male sexual response, the folklore leads to dose-dependent conclusions. Alcohol has been thought to be an aphrodisiac in men at lower doses but an impediment to sexual performance at higher doses. An example is a quote of the Greek poet Euenas, from the fifth century B.C.

> The best measure of wine is neither much nor very little;
> For 'tis the cause of either grief or madness.
> Then too, 'tis most suited for the bridal chamber and love.
> And if it breathe too fiercely, it puts love to flight.
> And plunges men in a sleep, neighbor to death.
> (Quoted by Abel, 1985)

There have been efforts at systematic study of human sexual response to a dose of alcohol, but only in the past 20 years or so has it been possible to do well-controlled research on this topic. The significant breakthroughs have been the invention of the penile strain gauge to measure penile erectile response and the photoplethysmograph to measure vaginal blood volume and pressure. These advances have paved the way to experimental study of human sexual response and alcohol.

Experimental studies of men have consistently shown that, at BACs between .05% and .10%, alcohol pharmacologically retards sexual arousal. When the BAC climbs over .10%, erection and ejaculatory competence are inhibited or eliminated. Importantly, these findings have been repeated in samples of nonproblem-drinker college students and in alcoholics. Alcohol does not stimulate men's libido, especially at moderate or higher BACs.

At lower BACs alcohol effects are not as dominant. It appears that cognitive factors, such as expectancies about alcohol effects, may work to increase men's libido. Indeed, studies of alcohol expectancies suggest the drinking public generally believes alcohol enhances sexual experience (Brown et al., 1987). Consistent with this finding, balanced placebo design studies suggest men's sexual arousal is increased when they believe they are drinking a dose of alcohol that brings them to a BAC less than .05%. Alcohol itself, however, has no effect on measured arousal at such BACs, which coincides with many other studies of the pharmacology of alcohol (Abel, 1985). Another characteristic of the drinker that seems to affect his sexual arousal at BACs below .05% is personality. One study showed increased sexual response was especially evident in subjects who thought they were drinking alcohol and who scored high on a measure of guilt about sex (Lang, Searles, Lauerman, & Adesso, 1980).

A reasonable conclusion about the acute effects of alcohol on male sexual response is that, similar to aggression, the disinhibition theory falls far short of explaining the information that is available. Rather, social and psychological factors seem to be important determinants of sexual response in men at low BACs and often work to increase libido. However, the pharmacology of alcohol begins to dominate at BACs greater than .05% and causes a decrease in arousal and sexual competence.

The folklore about the acute effects of alcohol on sexual behavior in women is that it promotes promiscuity. For example, Chaucer wrote in his "The Wife of Bath's Tale":

> After wine, I think mostly of venue for just
> as it's true that cold engenders hail a liquor
> mouth must have a liquorous tail. Women
> have no defense against wine as lechers know
> from experience.

Previous nonexperimental studies, as well as studies of alcohol expectancies that we cited earlier, suggest that alcohol increases sexual arousal in women and that women believe alcohol has that effect. The recent experimental evidence is that, as in men, women's physiological sexual response decreases with increasing alcohol dose. However, unlike men, women continue to perceive increased sexual arousal and sexual pleasure even as the physiological indexes of their response and arousal are declining. It seems that Shakespeare's observation most clearly applies to women, even though he was referring to men. It also is important not to conclude that the disinhibition theory accounts for the data on alcohol effects in women. Despite their perceived increased sexual arousal when they drink, whether women act on such perception depends on characteristics in the drinking setting and what the drinker has learned is acceptable sexual behavior in that setting. Therefore, again, a theory about the acute effects of alcohol on women's sexual behavior should incorporate social and psychological factors as well as the pharmacology of alcohol.

To conclude this section, Table 9-5 provides a summary of the acute effects of alcohol at different BACs. The table succinctly shows how pervasive alcohol's effects are. It is essential to remember, however, that the effects listed for given BACs are what might be observed in the "typical" drinker. Alcohol effects are notorious for their variability among people and in the same person on different drinking occasions. And, as our discussion of alcohol and aggression and sex most clearly illustrated, situational and psychological factors also influence what behaviors occur in people when they drink, as well as the effects they perceive alcohol is having on them.

EFFECTS OF CHRONIC HEAVY DRINKING

Chronic, heavy use of alcohol may have numerous physiological and psychological effects. All of the effects involve increased dysfunction, and some may be fatal. Some chronic alcohol effects are caused directly by alcohol's toxicity to the body, such as damage to the liver. Other effects are indirectly related to long-term abusive drinking. For example, Wernicke's disease, which involves impaired cognitive functioning, is caused by nutritional deficiencies that tend to occur in people dependent on alcohol (Jacobs & Fehr, 1987).

Table 9-5   Typical Acute Effects of Alcohol Associated with Different Ascending Blood Alcohol Concentrations (BACs)

BAC (%)	Effects
.01–.02	Slight changes in feeling; sense of warmth and well-being.
.03–.04	Feelings of relaxation, slight exhilaration, happiness. Skin may flush, mild impairment in motor skills.
.05–.06	Effects become more noticeable. More exaggerated changes in emotion, impaired judgment, and lowered inhibitions. Coordination may be altered.
.08–.09	Reaction time increased, muscle coordination impaired. Sensory feelings of numbness in cheeks, lips, and extremities. Further impairment in judgment. As of January 1994 the legal level of intoxication is .08% in 10 of the United States.
.10	Definite deterioration in motor coordination and reaction time. Person may stagger and slow speech. Legal level of intoxication in most of the United States.
.15	Major impairment in balance and movement. Large increase in reaction time. Large impairment in judgment and perception.
.20	Difficulty staying awake; substantial reduction of motor and sensory capabilities; slurred speech, double vision, difficulty standing or walking without assistance.
.30	Confusion and stupor. Difficulty comprehending what is going on; possible loss of consciousness (passing out).
.40	Typically unconsciousness; sweatiness and clamminess of the skin. Alcohol has become an anesthetic.
.45–.50	Circulatory and respiratory functions may become totally depressed. LD 50 in humans.

Chronic, heavy drinking is difficult to define precisely. Suffice it to say that many of alcohol's long-term effects take years to become evident. And, heavy drinkers vary greatly in their susceptibility to alcohol-related impairments.

A standard for what is heavy, or at least "unsafe" drinking, has been proposed. However, long-term drinking of a given quantity of alcohol affects different drinkers in different ways, both in number and severity of symptoms. Furthermore, the standard could vary according to what risk (for example, occurrence of liver disease, pancreatitis, or brain damage) we are concerned about (Bradley, Donovan, & Larson, 1993). Nevertheless, it is useful to have a guide to what is a "safe" level of alcohol consumption for the average drinker. One estimate is to set the safety level at an upper limit of three drinks a day for men and two drinks a day for women (Babor, Kranzler, & Lauerman, 1987).

Table 9-6 includes the major effects of chronic heavy drinking on body systems. As you can see in the table, alcohol can be highly toxic to the human body and cause extensive damage to it in a variety of ways. Two prominent body systems that alcohol harms are the brain and the liver. We will look at alcohol's chronic effects on these systems in more detail. Alcohol's chronic effects extend to human reproductive functioning, which has to do with alcohol's altering the functioning of the hypothalamic-pituitary-gonadal endocrine axis and with the fetal alcohol syndrome (FAS).

Table 9-6   The Effects of Chronic, Heavy Drinking on Body Systems

System	Effects
Central Nervous System	Specific and general impairment in cognitive functioning
Liver	Minor, reversible (with abstinence) damage to irreversible, sometimes fatal damage
Cardiovascular	Increased mortality from coronary heart disease, and increased risk for cardiovascular diseases in general; alcohol-induced wasting of the heart muscle (alcohol cardiomyopathy)
Endocrine	Affects secretion of hormones in different hormone hierarchies, or "axes." Examples are hypothalamic-pituitary-adrenal axis, and the hypothalamic-pituitary-gonadal axis
Immune System	Increased susceptibility to several infectious diseases
Gastrointestinal	Causes gastritis and increases risk of pancreatitis
Multiple	Increased risk of contracting the following cancers: oral cavity, tongue, pharynx, larynx, esophagus, stomach, liver, lung, pancreas, colon, rectum

Note: The information in this table is based on USDHHS (1987) and Jacobs and Fehr (1987).

Alcohol and Brain Functioning

The acute effects of alcohol on memory and other cognitive functioning are manifest at moderate BACs and are reversible. However, alcohol affects these same functions in the long term in some people if it is drunk long enough and heavily enough. Such chronic effects occur in degrees of severity, evidenced as mildly impaired performance on **neuropsychological tests** to severe, irreversible brain structural and functional damage shown as severe memory impairment in Korsakoff's Syndrome (Charness, 1993; Parsons, 1986).

neuropsychological tests
Formal ways of measuring behavioral functions that may be impaired by brain lesions.

The average alcohol-dependent individual who has been studied, when abstinent from alcohol or other psychoactive drugs, performs more poorly than nonalcoholic control groups on tests of abstracting, problem solving, memory, learning, and perceptual-motor speed. Recent reviews have shown about 60% of the individuals who have been tested show such impairments, which suggests that characteristics of the drinkers also influence their vulnerability to alcohol's effects on brain function. A major one is the individual's drinking history. While the evidence is mixed, in general the longer a person drinks and the higher the quantity that is consumed, the greater the impairment in cognitive functioning.

Fortunately, with long-term abstinence from alcohol most alcohol-related neuropsychological impairment once evident can be virtually reversed, with only mild deficits left compared to control subjects. This conclusion is based on studies that involved following subjects' test performance during periods of abstinence lasting from one month to five years (Parsons, 1986; Parsons & Leber, 1982). The reversibility of cognitive deficits may be due to several factors. These include increased cerebral blood flow, better nutrition, and some recovery of brain atrophy (Mello, 1987; Nace & Isbell, 1991; USDHHS, 1990). The more recent findings on changes in the brain and recovery of cognitive function are the result of technology that allows noninvasive study of brain structure and activity, such as computerized tomography (CT).

Wernicke-Korsakoff Syndrome This severe CNS disorder is the result of combining extreme nutritional deficiency, specifically Vitamin B_1 or thiamine, and chronic heavy drinking. Basically there are two diseases. Wernicke's disease is characterized by confusion, loss of memory, staggering gait, and an inability to focus the eye (Sobell & Sobell, 1981; USDHHS, 1987, 1990). In the absence of permanent brain damage, Wernicke's disease is reversible by giving the patient Vitamin B_1.

Korsakoff's Syndrome may have a nutritional component to it but is most directly due to alcohol. It is associated with damage to brain structure and most affects memory. In this regard, there are serious impairments in short-term memory and learning. Because of these dysfunctions there often is considerable confusion and **confabulation.** There also is a lesser degree of impairment in memory for events in longer-term memory. The following case, based on one discussed in the DSM-III *Case Book* (Spitzer, et al., 1981, pp. 56–57), gives a good illustration of some of the major symptoms of Korsakoff's Syndrome.

confabulation
A fabrication about events, when asked questions concerning them, because of an inability to recall.

> The patient was a 40-year-old man who in the interview claimed to be an accountant. He said that he had some business troubles and had come to the hospital to get help. His story was coherent, but there was a lack of consistency and details to it. As regards his hospitalization, the patient said that he had been in for only a few days but a few minutes later he said several weeks. He could not recall his doctor's name.

> Formal testing showed that the patient could not recall the names of three objects that he had seen five minutes earlier, or repeat a story that was told to him. However, the patient could perform simple calculations, define words and concepts, and find similarities and differences among objects and concepts. The patient's medical record showed that he had a long history of alcohol dependence and had been living in a nursing home for the last three years until he was admitted to the hospital a week ago. He was admitted after several incidents of his wandering from the nursing home and being returned there by police. (Published with permission of American Psychiatric Press.)

Alcohol and the Liver

As the major metabolic site of alcohol the liver is highly vulnerable to alcohol's toxic effects. The damage that alcohol can cause to the liver occurs in three ways: fatty liver, alcohol hepatitis, and cirrhosis. Fatty liver is characterized by fat accumulating in the liver and is the earliest, most benign effect of alcohol's effects on the liver. This condition is reversible with abstinence from alcohol, and there is no evidence that it is a precurser of cirrhosis. Alcohol hepatitis is more serious and involves the inflammation and death of liver cells. Often jaundice occurs because of the accumulation of bile. This condition is reversible with abstinence and medical treatment, but can cause death if it is severe enough and not treated. Liver hepatitis can be caused by means other than heavy drinking. Evidence of such drinking must be obtained in order to diagnose alcohol hepatitis.

The most serious and life-threatening of alcohol's liver assaults is cirrhosis. Alcohol dependence is the leading cause of cirrhosis, which in turn is

 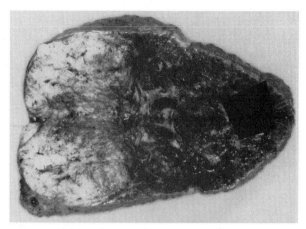

A cirrhotic liver (left) is compared with a healthy human liver (right).

the ninth-leading cause of death in the United States (USDHHS, 1990). Drinking must be prodigious and long-term for someone to develop cirrhosis. For example, one survey showed that people with alcohol dependence who developed cirrhosis drank an average of 13 drinks a day for about 20 years! It did not matter what beverage form alcohol was consumed in. It should be noted that a minority of individuals who are alcohol-dependent develop cirrhosis—between 10% and 20%.

For those who do get cirrhosis, the condition is not reversible, and only half are still alive five years after the initial diagnosis is made. Cirrhosis is a chronic inflammatory disease of the liver involving cell death and the formation of scar tissue. It may or may not be preceded by alcohol hepatitis. Death results from cirrhosis because the liver fails to metabolize various toxins, such as ammonia, and these toxins accumulate in the body.

Alcohol and Reproductive Functioning

Both men and women suffer impaired reproductive functioning as a result of chronic, heavy drinking. In men, such drinking affects the male sex hormones, reflexive responses of the nervous system relating to sexual performance, and sperm production. First, there often is gynecomastia (formation of breasts in men), which is a result of alcohol's altering the balance of the female sex hormone, estrogen, and the male sex hormone, testosterone. The shifting in balance is due to alcohol's damage to the liver and resorption of estrogens into the blood. Another result of changing the balance in the sex hormones is a loss in sexual desire. Along with a loss in desire is a drop in sexual performance, manifested as ejaculatory incompetence and impotence. These latter effects are due to alcohol's inhibition of reflexive responses in the nervous system. Finally, chronic heavy drinking may result in hypogonadism and eventual sterility. There is also some possibility that sperm production is so impaired that defective offspring could be conceived (Abel, 1985; Mello, 1987).

As with most alcohol effects, we know a lot less about the chronic effects of alcohol on reproductive functioning in women. The little scientific information available suggests alcohol dependence in women is associated with dysfunction of the ovaries, disruption of the luteal phase of fertilization, and amenorrhea (cessation of the menstrual period) (Mello, 1987; USDHHS, 1990). A household survey suggests that a woman does not have to be diagnosed as having alcohol dependence to experience impaired sexual function related to alcohol use. A survey of more than 900 women living in households showed a positive correlation between alcohol consumption and the occurrence of different menstrual disorders (Wilsnack, Klassen, & Wilsnack, 1984).

Fetal Alcohol Syndrome

In this section we discuss a chronic alcohol effect that does not focus on a specific body system or on the drinker. Rather, it focuses on the fetus and what alcohol consumption may do to it if its mother drinks during pregnancy. A characteristic set of symptoms appearing in some newborns of mothers who drink during pregnancy has become known as the fetal alcohol syndrome (FAS). FAS falls in to the class of alcohol **teratology**. Teratology is defined in biology as the study of monsters or deformities. The FAS actually has been written about since the time of Aristotle but only recently has it received the attention of scientists. Since 1973 the literature on it has grown geometrically.

teratology
In biology, the study of monsters, or distortions in growth.

The FAS refers to gross physical deformities that were identified in 11 very young children who had severely alcohol-dependent mothers who drank during pregnancy. These deformities were described in a 1973 clinical report and include the following: small eyes and small eye openings, drooping eyelids, underdeveloped midface, skin folds across the inner corners of the eyes (which were abnormal in this sample of 11 white children), underdevelopment of the depression above the upper lip, and a small head circumference.

This child was diagnosed as fetal alcohol syndrome affected.

Furthermore, abnormal creases in the palm were reported, along with abnormalities in the joints. Some of the children had cardiac defects, benign tumors consisting of dilated blood vessels, and minor ear abnormalities. A 10-year follow-up of these children showed low-normal to severely retarded intellectual functioning, physical deformities similar to those originally reported, and the development of additional physical problems.

Although estimates vary, it seems that FAS occurs in the range of 1 to 3 of every 1,000 live births (USDHHS, 1990). In thinking about these statistics it is essential to remember that there is great individual variability in the effects on the fetus of prenatal exposure to alcohol. In this regard, the rate of FAS is much lower than is the rate of women who abuse alcohol while they are pregnant. Furthermore, rates of FAS vary with the population in question. For example, rates of FAS seem to be much higher among Native American or black mothers of low socioeconomic status, who have been the participants in most FAS studies conducted in the United States, than they are among white, middle-class mothers.

The amount of variability in rates of FAS begins to tell of the complexity in conducting human studies of this serious public health problem. For one reason, it is extremely difficult to get accurate self-reports among pregnant women about their drinking; this seems to be particularly true for women who are heavier, problem drinkers (why do you think this is the case?). In addition, since FAS can be detected only after a child is born, postpartum environmental or other factors cloud an interpretation of what part prenatal alcohol exposure played in the resulting FAS. It sometimes even is difficult to determine if alcohol was the only prenatal substance that may have resulted in FAS. For example, there is the possibility of other drug use during pregnancy, and this would be most likely to occur among the heaviest drinkers (Erenhart, 1991). When other drugs are taken during pregnancy they may harm the fetus in ways similar to alcohol.

Everybody wants to know what is the "safe" level of drinking during pregnancy. As our brief discussion of FAS suggests, no simple answer is available. Actually, it is best to think of FAS as the most severe result of a continuum of effects of prenatal exposure to alcohol. Subtle behavioral or cognitive effects may be observed on the other end of the continuum. In addition, it seems that each abnormality of outcome may have its own yardstick of amount of alcohol exposure, and of timing of exposure (Jacobson, Jacobson, Sokol, et al., 1993; USDHHS, 1990).

Although a straightforward answer regarding safe drinking during pregnancy is not available, there is one rule to go by. FAS or milder degrees of abnormality in newborns have not been observed without prenatal exposure to alcohol or other drugs. Therefore, the safest course remains the most conservative: If you are pregnant, do not use alcohol or other drugs.

Concluding this section on the chronic effects of heavy alcohol consumption puts in relief alcohol as a double-edged sword. On the one side, the economic costs of alcohol abuse to the United States are tremendous—remember the estimate of $99 billion for 1990 that we cited in Chapter 1. When a major part of this vast sum is broken down by some of the social consequences that contribute to it, then alcohol's costs may become more real to you. We already discussed how alcohol is implicated in traffic accidents and violence. Its abuse also is associated with accidental falls, drownings, fires, and burns, the occurrence of traumatic injuries like broken bones, and crime and family violence (spouse abuse, child abuse) (USDHHS, 1990).

The other side of the sword is the economic gain afforded by alcohol, not to mention the high regard many people have for it as a social and psychological booster. Economically, the alcoholic beverage industry creates and maintains a lot of jobs, and contributes a lot of revenue to governments. For example, one estimate is that in 1981 retail sales of alcohol in the United States were $40 billion, and $170 billion worldwide (Cavanagh & Clairmonte, 1985).

So, perhaps you can see why there seems to be never-ending discussion about how to regulate alcohol, with opinions ranging from reinstating Prohibition to freer use. What arguments on each side can you think of? What policy do you think you would end up with if given the responsibility to write one?

Moderate Drinking and Health

As we suppose you are convinced at this point, long-term, heavy use of alcohol could seriously damage the body. But what about long-term abstinence from alcohol and long-term lighter drinking? In the last 15 years or so, a number of studies have been reported that suggest the moderate drinkers turn out the healthiest, followed by the abstainers, and dead last are the heavy drinkers. "Health" is measured by risk of cardiovascular disease and mortality (Knupfer, 1987).

The surprise here, of course, is that drinking can be healthy. The first question is, what is "moderate"? Generally, it has been defined as one to three drinks a day. How could such drinking possibly aid health? One hypothesis is that light alcohol consumption increases the production of high-density lipoproteins (HDLs), which take damaging cholesterol away from artery walls (Gaziano, Buring, Breslow, et al., 1993). Alcohol could have this effect by its effect on the liver—it increases the activity of the liver, and the liver produces the protein that envelops HDL particles.

Many experts have concluded that moderate drinking could be associated with lower risk of coronary disease (Riman, Giovannucci, Willett, et al., 1991). However, there is not unanimity on this subject. One reason is how the relevant studies have been done. A big question is whether many "light/moderate daily drinkers" exist. In this respect, most light drinkers do not drink every day, and most people who drink every day do not drink lightly. Another major point is that more than twice as many of the people who were classified as abstainers in the studies were poor as compared to wealthy. It is well-known that people with low incomes have worse health (Knupfer, 1987). It seems safe to conclude that there is considerable support for the moderate drinking-health hypothesis but that the evidence is not flawless. And it is essential to remember that much of the research has centered on coronary heart disease. However, there also is research suggesting that moderate drinking is associated with higher risk of breast and colon cancer (Friedman & Klatsky, 1993). In any case, it may be a while before alcohol is available at your local health food store. As we have learned, alcohol, especially in heavy quantities, is toxic to many organs of the body.

The French Paradox   The moderate drinking-health hypothesis relates to a recent finding that has been called the French paradox, or the co-occurrence of a diet high in saturated fats and a low incidence of coronary heart disease (Frunkel, Kanner, German, Parks, & Kinsella, 1993). This biological paradox is called French because it was first identified among people who live in Touraine, France. Again, we are talking about moderate drinking, and the focus is on red wine—the French consume wine in relatively high amounts. The equivalent of 1–2 4-ounce glasses of wine a day is associated with the improved health effects (Renaud & deLorgerd, 1992).

A few hypotheses have appeared in the literature to explain the French paradox. One is that coronary heart disease is reduced because beyond its beneficial effects of reducing atherosclerosis, alcohol in red wine inhibits platelet aggregation. Blood platelets are associated with the process of blood clotting. Reduction in platelet aggregation is correlated with reduced risk of coronary disease, and is the basis for advising the use of aspirin to help prevent heart disease (Renaud & deLorgerd, 1992). Note that this hypothesis continues to target alcohol as the trigger of health benefits. Red wine is specified because the French drink a considerable amount of it. Another explanation of the French paradox that has appeared does not target alcohol. Instead, the **phenolic compounds** in red wine have been specified as the main benefactors of reduced risk of heart disease (Frunkel et al., 1993). According to this hypothesis, the nonalcoholic phenolic compounds inhibit oxidation of low-density lipoproteins (LDLs), the ones that cause atherosclerosis. Oxidation of LDLs seems to be associated with the occurrence of atherosclerosis.

The French paradox raises the surprising possibility that a therapeutic use of alcohol in the future may be listed for prevention of heart disease. However, before that happens, we have a lot to learn about the French paradox, and about the relationship between "moderate" alcohol use and health in general. In the meantime, the red wine vintners are enjoying the debates.

phenolic compound
Compounds contained in or derived from phenol, a compound produced from coal tar.

THE DEVELOPMENT OF ALCOHOL ABUSE AND DEPENDENCE

The national survey data we covered in this chapter and in Chapter 1 showed that well over 60% of Americans drink alcohol, and that a minority of them drink heavily. Some of the heavy drinkers develop problems with alcohol to different degrees. When they do, the effects on themselves, their families, and their society are devastating. Accordingly, this question has preoccupied many for many years: How do alcohol abuse and dependence develop, or, what is their etiology? In this last section we briefly present what approaches to the question have been taken and describe the current thinking.

Traditional Approaches to Etiology

Until recently researchers and clinicians alike usually sought a single-factor explanation of what causes alcohol problems. Theories frequently outpaced data to evaluate them and could be classified as biological, psychological, or sociological.

Contemporary Issue
IS ALCOHOL DEPENDENCE A DISEASE?

Periodically, controversy flares over whether alcohol dependence is a disease. It happened again in 1988, following a Supreme Court decision denying two veterans an extension of their Veterans Administration (VA) education benefits. The Court's decision coincided with publication of a book by University of California philosopher Herbert Fingarette challenging the position that alcohol dependence is a disease.

Disease can be defined broadly, but in the strict medical sense it refers to a clearly identified, physical process that is pathological. A critical feature of the definition is that once a disease is contracted, the afflicted individual has no control, or is not responsible, for the disease running its course. Typically, when alcohol dependence is called a disease the traditional medical model of disease is the referent.

Treatment providers and other citizens fought long and hard in the early twentieth century to get alcohol dependence acknowledged as a disease in order to take "treatment" of alcohol dependence out of the legal system and into the medical profession. The campaign has been more than successful. In 1957 the American Medical Association formally recognized alcohol dependence as a disease and still does. Other professional organizations that do include the American Hospital Association, American Academy of Pediatrics, American Dental Association, American College Health Association, American Chiropractic Association, the United States Congress, and the U.S. Surgeon General. Public opinion polls consistently have shown that a large majority of Americans say they believe that alcohol dependence is a disease.

The controversy is whether the symptoms we call alcohol dependence are not more accurately thought of as a result of behavior that is learned and voluntary rather than as a manifestation of some disease process. The question is based on research and clinical findings over the last 30 years (see Chapter 16) that have sparked much discussion in scientific journals and that are the foundation of Fingarette's book.

The question is not just an academic one. It has large implications for how alcohol-dependent people are given treatment, for one thing. In this respect, the dominant position among U.S. treatment professionals, as well as Alcoholics Anonymous, is that alcohol dependence is a disease. It also has great legal ramifications. The two veterans argued unsuccessfully that they should have an extension of the time to take advantage of their benefits because they were "afflicted" with alcoholism within the usual benefit period. The gist of their argument was that because alcoholism is a disease they should not be punished for having something they have no control over. The VA instead asserted alcoholism is the result of "willful misconduct."

With this example, what do you suppose some of the ramifications might be of adherence to a strict position that alcohol dependence is the result of a biological disease process?

Biological approaches have waxed and waned in popularity over the years (Roebuck & Kessler, 1972). Such theories hold the common premise that there is a physiological or structural anomaly that causes the individual to become alcohol-dependent. Earlier single-factor biological approaches, which have not received experimental support, have included hypotheses that the source of the structural deficit was metabolic, glandular, due to body chemistry, or due to an allergic condition. The most prevalent position among U.S. treatment providers is that alcohol dependence is a physical disease (see nearby Contemporary Issue Box). Although the source of the disease process is not specified, disease model adherents use the process of a physical disease, such as a fever, as an analogy in order to understand alcohol dependence. As a result, the disease model is classified as a biological model.

Biological explanations of alcohol problems have regained popularity among scientists because of the findings suggesting there is a genetic predisposition at least to some "types" of alcohol dependence (Kendler, Heath, Neale, et al., 1992; Schuckit, 1987). The evidence comes primarily from family, twin, and adoption studies. In summary, family studies show that sons and daughters of alcohol-dependent parents are four times more likely to develop the disorder themselves, relative to people whose parents are not alcohol-dependent. In addition, studies of twins show there is greater likelihood that both members of identical twin pairs have alcohol dependence ("concordance") than is the likelihood of concordance in fraternal twins. The significance of this finding is that identical twins are genetic matches, whereas members of fraternal twin pairs have 50% of their genes in common. Another finding pertains to adopted children of alcohol-dependent parents. These studies show that the development of alcohol problems in the offspring is far more influenced by having an alcoholic parent than by the adoptive home environment. This conclusion is especially strong for males. Based on this body of research, the argument for a biological predisposition to alcohol dependence has gained considerable strength.

Psychological explanations of etiology have centered on finding the "alcoholic personality," which means a psychological trait or set of traits that predispose someone to become alcohol-dependent. Failure to find such a high-risk profile has not been due to lack of trying, as evidenced by the number of publications on the topic. However, some recent, well-designed studies have suggested that presence of an "antisocial personality" (the personality identified with convicted criminals, as one group) and ego weakness, which is manifested by impulsivity, intensity of mood, unstable self-esteem, and alternating dependence on and independence from others, could be psychological factors that predispose to alcohol dependence (Donovan, 1986). In Chapter 5, we also discussed some earlier research on psychological characteristics that may predispose an individual to alcohol dependence.

Sociological models of etiology were proposed partly in response to the failure to discover the unique alcoholic personality. The models are supported by findings of cross-cultural differences in drinking patterns (MacAndrew & Edgerton, 1969), as well as the demographic factors that you have seen are correlated with drinking patterns and problems. Studies that take them into account have shown consistently that sociological factors help to explain the development of alcohol dependence.

DRUGS AND CULTURE
ALCOHOL AND THE JAPANESE

One of many countries that lend support to sociological/cultural theories of alcohol use is Japan. Dr. Dwight Heath, a cultural anthropologist at Brown University, noted in a 1984 article that in Japan, as in many countries, alcohol consumption increased steadily after World War II. Patterns of drinking also showed some major changes. For example, men who worked together often drank together nightly while having loud parties. This contrasted sharply with the more traditional social-religious drinking contexts of the Japanese. The changes triggered predictions of increasing alcohol abuse and dependence, but the expectations never were realized.

A major reason the negative consequences of drinking did not occur on a large scale was cultural. In Japan, and in Asia in general, moderate alcohol use is valued and excessive drinking is not. Alcohol still is linked to social and religious rituals, customs that tend to discourage an individual's abuse of alcohol. According to Heath, alcohol dependence is relatively rare in Asia.

Another part of the reason the Japanese did not develop an epidemic of alcohol problems may be biological. The phenomenon of importance here is the "Oriental flushing response." This is a physical reaction that occurs with drinking alcohol; it consists of cutaneous flushing and sometimes other symptoms, including palpitations, tachycardia, perspiration, and headache. The reaction is called Oriental because it occurs in Asians but not in people of other races. It appears to be due to a deficiency in aldehyde isozyme. This deficiency leads to a buildup of acetaldehyde when drinking, as alcohol metabolism is disrupted. The acetaldehyde causes the flushing response. The important point is that Oriental flushing is assumed to be unpleasant to most people and thus may serve as a biological limit-setter on amount of alcohol that is drunk on an occasion (Kitano, 1989).

Not all Asians show the Oriental flush, and of those who do, they show it to different degrees (Higuchi, Parrish, Dufour, et al., 1992). However, this biological reaction, coupled with cultural customs for alcohol use in the Japanese, provides an excellent example of how different types of factors work together to influence alcohol use.

"Biopsychosocial" Approaches to Etiology

Although there are bright spots in each type of single-factor explanation, each alone ultimately fails to explain how alcohol abuse and dependence develop. For example, a minority of children of alcoholic parents become alcohol-dependent themselves. What happens to the rest? A set of psychological characteristics may be associated with developing alcohol dependence, but those same characteristics could be correlated with other outcomes. Demographic factors are correlated with drinking problems, but the factors themselves are often associated with biological and psychological variables, too. It seems that single-factor researchers design their studies so one type of factor, say, psychological, is emphasized and other types are underplayed or not represented at all. Indeed, the fact that there are seeds of support for each type of approach, but not strong support for any one alone, suggests that multiple types of factors influence the development of alcohol dependence. At least among scientists this is the most current thinking: Alcohol, as well as drug dependence, is caused and maintained by a combination of biological, psychological, and sociological factors (for example, Galizio & Maisto, 1985). As we will discuss further in Chapter 16 on treatment, the three types of factors together in "shorthand" are called biopsychosocial.

What this means in practice is that scientists and practitioners alike cannot hope to understand alcohol dependence unless they consider together all the types of influencing variables. A good example is some of the exciting research that has been done with nonalcohol-dependent sons of alcoholics. One finding is from electrophysiological studies of the brain that show preadolescent sons of alcoholics may have a deficit that is expressed as a lesser ability to focus on stimuli in the environment. This difference from boys who do not have alcohol-dependent parents is presumably inherited and cannot be a consequence of the subject's own drinking. In theory, such a deficit could increase the risk of developing alcohol dependence because of, say, a decreased ability to discriminate degree of intoxication when drinking moderately. Additionally, discrimination deficits could affect performance of various cognitive tasks and how the individual relates to other people (Schuckit, 1987). Whether risk actually is translated into alcohol dependence, however, depends in large part on how the environment (say, the family and school systems) "reacts" to any deficit in discrimination.

Saying that multiple factors combine to cause alcohol dependence is, after all, an extension of a theme we have followed since Chapter 1, that human experience and behavior under the influence of drugs can be understood only by considering multiple types of factors in combination. The research suggests that the same thinking should be applied to understanding alcohol dependence.

summary

- Alcohol virtually always is drunk in the form of three major classes of alcoholic beverages, which are beer, wine, and hard liquor (also called distilled spirits).

- Alcoholic beverages are produced through fermentation and distillation.

- The alcohol content of a beverage may be expressed by volume or by weight.

- The proof of an alcoholic beverage refers to its percentage of alcohol content.

- People have used alcohol for thousands of years, but societies always have viewed alcoholic beverages as mixed blessings.

- In the United States, per-capita alcohol consumption increased from the end of Prohibition into the 1940s. There was another increase from 1960 into the 1970s. In 1980 a decline in consumption began that was slightly reversed in 1990.

- Overall consumption figures mask beverage differences. Consumption of hard liquor fell considerably from 1977 to 1990, while consumption of beer and wine increased slightly during that same time.

- Social and environmental factors, such as urban vs. rural residence, sex, age, and racial/ethnic background are associated with alcohol consumption rates. The same is true for the prevalence of heavy drinking.

- Alcohol is a drug that depresses the CNS. It may exert such effects by dissolving in lipid membranes.

- The GABA receptors are one locus that is being studied as a specific neural site of alcohol's action in the body. However, identifying a specific receptor mechanism is difficult, because alcohol's effects on the body are so diffuse.

- Alcohol is a food primarily absorbed from the small intestine. The rate of alcohol absorption can vary widely according to a number of physiological and situational factors.

- Following its absorption alcohol is distributed to all of the body's tissues. Blood gets an especially high concentration of alcohol.

- Alcohol primarily affects the CNS, particularly the brain. The LD 50 for alcohol is a BAC of .45 to .50%.

- It is possible to get an approximation of current BAC by using a simple equation that includes alcohol dose and time. Other factors that influence BAC are percentage of body fat, gender, and rate of alcohol metabolization.

- Breath analysis is a very practical, precise way of measuring the BAC.

- The body metabolizes over 90% of the alcohol it absorbs, primarily in the liver.

- The liver metabolizes alcohol at a constant rate of about .35 ounces of alcohol an hour, and little can be done to quicken the pace.

- Alcohol use leads to some degree of dispositional tolerance and, more important, to both acute and protracted functional tolerance.

- Chronic, heavy use of alcohol can lead to physical dependence on it. The alcohol withdrawal syndrome is a serious medical problem that can result in death if not treated properly.

- Alcohol has few direct medical uses, but is an ingredient of several legitimate medical products.

- Alcohol's acute action is evident in a wide variety of physiological, sensorimotor, and behavioral effects. In general, as the BAC increases, acute effects increase in number and intensity. However, how humans experience degree of intoxication and behave under different doses of alcohol are modified by psychological and situational factors as well as alcohol dose and tolerance to this drug.

- Sensorimotor skills, which alcohol impairs, make up a major part of driving motor vehicles.

- Alcohol seems to be a major contributor to fatal and nonfatal automobile accidents. Gender and age combine with alcohol to influence risk of involvement in an automobile accident.

- Stemming the drunk-driving problem seems to be a matter of sustained attention and action by law enforcement and citizens' action groups. Drivers' perceptions that arrest and conviction are likely consequences of drunk driving also are important.

- Alcohol and sex and aggression are major topics of social interest and concern. To understand alcohol's association with aggressive behavior it is necessary to take into account characteristics of the aggressor and situational factors, only one of which is alcohol.

- Alcohol's effects on sexual behavior are similarly complex. It is necessary to know the physiological basis of alcohol's effect on sexual function, as well as include situational and psychological factors, in order to explain alcohol's effects on sexual behavior.

- Histories of chronic, heavy drinking are associated with damage to most of the body's organs and systems. Two of the most prominent ones are the liver and the brain.

- A chronic effect of alcohol is impairment in memory and other cognitive functions. Some of these effects are virtually reversible with abstinence from alcohol. However, when there is structural damage to the brain, as in Korsakoff's Syndrome, the effects are permanent.

- As the major metabolic site of alcohol, the liver is vulnerable to the chronic effect of heavy alcohol use. Three liver disorders that are attributable to drinking are fatty liver, alcohol hepatitis, and cirrhosis. The first two disorders are reversible with abstinence; cirrhosis, a leading killer in the United States, is not.

- Chronic, heavy drinking is associated with impaired sexual functioning in both men and women.

- A mother's drinking during pregnancy may result in fetal alcohol syndrome (FAS) in the newborn child. The FAS consists of gross physical deformities that are identifiable at birth. FAS is associated with continued physical problems, as well as subaverage intellectual functioning, later in childhood.

- The idea that moderate alcohol consumption is associated with lowered risk of cardiovascular disease and mortality has some research support but remains a topic of spirited debate.

- The development of alcohol dependence remains an unsolved problem. It does seem that "single cause" theories are inadequate to explain the etiology of alcohol dependence. Instead, it is necessary to incorporate biological, psychological, and sociological factors.

ANSWERS TO WHAT DO YOU THINK?

1. Humans have consumed alcohol since about 5000 to 6000 B.C.

T *Humans indeed have consumed alcohol since about 5,000 to 6,000 years before the time of Christ.*

2. In the United States of 1830 adults' average alcohol consumption was about five drinks a day.

T *Americans in the early nineteenth century were prodigious consumers of alcohol.*

3. The highest rates of heavy drinking, and greatest vulnerability to drinking problems, are in men between the ages of 40 and 45.

F *The highest rates are in younger men, ages 18 to 25.*

4. It is difficult to consume a lethal dose of alcohol.

F *It is all too easy. The LD 50 of alcohol in humans is about equal to drinking a fifth (25.3 oz) of whiskey in an hour. This is not too hard to do, and it has been*

done with dire consequences during events such as fraternity hazings.

5. If not treated properly, alcohol withdrawal syndrome can be fatal.

T *Because of the availability of drugs that show cross dependence with alcohol, medical management of alcohol withdrawal is generally straightforward. Nevertheless, it is a serious medical condition; if not treated properly or at all alcohol withdrawal can be fatal.*

6. Alcohol is a drug that has no legitimate medical value.

F *Although alcohol is hardly the elixir people once thought it was, it does have legitimate therapeutic uses, such as being a component of compounds in medicines taken orally or applied externally.*

7. If you drink a lot and black out, it means you have lost consciousness.

F Blackouts refer to a memory loss for events that occur while under the influence of a drug (in this case, alcohol). The drinker was fully conscious when the nonrecalled events happened.

8. Alcohol causes violent behavior.

F Alcohol is correlated with the occurrence of violent behavior, but cognitive, social, and environmental factors must also be used to explain the alcohol-violence association.

9. Alcohol improves sexual performance.

F Pharmacologically, alcohol impairs sexual performance, particularly when BACs reach .05% and beyond. However, people may perceive that the use of alcohol is associated with greater sexual arousal and better sexual performance.

10. The cognitive deficits that seem to occur in some people as a result of years of heavy drinking are reversible.

T At least when there is not severe structural damage to the brain as in Korsakoff's Syndrome, much of the cognitive deficits that may occur are reversible with prolonged abstinence from alcohol.

11. The majority of alcoholics eventually develop cirrhosis of the liver.

F This certainly is true for some chronically heavy drinkers, but only a minority of them, about 10% to 20%.

12. Moderate drinking (1–3 drinks a day) is associated with reduced risk of heart disease.

T This actually is not a straightforward true or false answer. Although experts disagree on interpretation of the data, there is some evidence that moderate use of alcohol is correlated with reduced risk of heart disease.

10 Depressants

WHAT DO YOU THINK?

True or False?   ____ Nitrous oxide (laughing gas) is no longer used by the medical profession.

____ The effects of a moderate dose of a barbiturate drug resemble those of alcohol.

____ Withdrawal from depressant sleeping pills can trigger rebound insomnia.

____ Withdrawal from barbiturates is similar to alcohol withdrawal.

____ Benzodiazepines (Valium) are one of the most commonly prescribed drugs in America.

____ Benzodiazepines are a common street drug, commonly known as "bennies."

____ Overdose of benzodiazepines was the cause of the suicide death of Marilyn Monroe.

____ The main depressant drugs (barbiturates, benzodiazepines, and alcohol) all act by vastly different physiological mechanisms and on different areas of the body.

____ Depressant drugs may show cross-tolerance with cocaine.

____ Alcohol in combination with other depressant drugs is the leading cause of drug overdose deaths in the United States.

____ Nitrous oxide (laughing gas) can cause nerve damage.

____ Inhalant abuse is a rare phenomenon among young people.

Barbiturates
Depressant drugs formerly used as sleeping pills. Currently used in anesthesia and treatment for epilepsy.

Anxiolytic
Anxiety-reducing.

Sedative-hypnotic effects
The ability of some drugs to produce a calming effect and induce sleep.

General anesthesia
The reduction of pain by rendering the subject unconscious.

Although alcohol is the prototypical depressant drug (see Chapter 9), many other drugs can depress the central nervous system and behavior. These include a variety of different chemical agents, but especially the **barbiturates,** the benzodiazepines, a number of nonbarbiturate sedatives, and the general anesthetics (see Table 10-1). These drugs are often classified according to their most common medical uses, but such a classification can be misleading. For example, benzodiazepines such as diazepam (Valium) and chlordiazepoxide (Librium) are often labeled as **anxiolytic** (antianxiety) drugs. Although moderate doses of these compounds do indeed relieve anxiety and are widely used for this purpose, in larger doses benzodiazepines produce **sedative-hypnotic effects** (that is, they induce sleep), and now are prescribed widely as sleeping pills. Barbiturates, on the other hand, often are called sleeping pills and can certainly be effective in this regard. In lower doses barbiturates, too, are anxiolytic, and if the dose is high enough these and other depressants can produce surgical anesthesia. All depressant drugs (including alcohol) can relieve anxiety at low dose levels, produce intoxication at a moderate level, induce sedation and sleep at still higher levels, produce **general anesthesia** at very high dose levels, and eventually lead to coma and death. Due to differing potency, duration of action, and safety,

Table 10-1   Representative Depressant Drugs

Generic Name	Brand Name	Slang Name
Hypnotics		
Barbiturates		
Pentobarbital	Nembutal	Yellow jackets
Secobarbital	Seconal	Reds
Amobarbital	Amytal	Blues, Amys
Phenobarbital	Luminal	
Chloral Hydrate		
Methaqualone	Quaaludes	Ludes
Ethchlorvynol	Placidyl	
Zolpiden	Ambien	
General Anesthetics		
Halothane	Fluothene	
Nitrous oxide		
Minor Tranquilizers (*anxiolytics*)		
Benzodiazepines		
Chlordiazepoxide	Librium	
Diazepam	Valium	
Flurazepam	Dalmane	
Alprazolam	Xanax	
Lorazepam	Ativan	
Oxazepam	Serax	
Temazepam	Restoril	
Clorazepate	Tranxene	
Triazolam	Halcion	
Nonbarbiturates, Nonbenzodiazepines		
Meprobamate	Equanil	
Hydroxyzine	Vistaril, Atarax	
Ethinamate	Valmid	
Buspirone	BuSpar	

some depressants are used for specific purposes more often than others (for example, nitrous oxide is used almost exclusively for anesthesia). The benzodiazepines are currently the most important class of drugs for treatment of anxiety and sleeping disorders.

EARLY HISTORY

Perhaps the first of the depressant compounds other than alcohol to be used was the gas nitrous oxide, discovered by Joseph Priestly and synthesized by Humphrey Davy in 1776. These English scientists were the first to note that inhalation of nitrous oxide produced a short period of intoxication similar to drunkenness. Since the euphoric state produced by nitrous oxide often results in laughter and giggling, it came to be known as laughing gas (Brecher, 1972). Although Davy and others experimented with the gas for recreational purposes, its use in medicine was to be long delayed by one of the most famous stories in the history of medicine.

The story begins in Hartford, Connecticut, in 1845 where a young dentist named Horace Wells attended an exhibition of the effects of laughing gas. People paid admission to sniff nitrous oxide or just to watch others. One of the users apparently tripped and was badly cut during the exhibition, and

Wells noticed that he seemed to feel no pain despite the severe injury. As a dentist, Wells immediately realized the possible uses of such a drug. Dentistry and other surgeries were immensely painful during this era due to the lack of anesthetic agents. Wells then experimented with nitrous oxide and discovered that teeth could be pulled without pain. After proclaiming his discovery, Wells was invited to demonstrate his procedure at the Massachusetts General Hospital in Boston. There, before a prestigious group of physicians, Wells placed a patient under anesthesia. However, Wells had not studied the drug well enough to reliably establish dosages and the patient awakened during surgery screaming in pain. Wells was laughed out of the amphitheater by the skeptical scientists, and the use of nitrous oxide as an anesthesia was set back many years. Today nitrous oxide is widely used in dentistry and some types of surgery.

The next phase in the history of depressants also involved the search for an effective anesthetic. William Morton was a Boston dentist and medical student who was familiar with Wells' blunder, but Morton learned of another drug that he believed might be a better choice as an anesthetic: ether. Ether is a highly flammable liquid that vaporizes at room temperature. When the fumes are inhaled, they produce a state of intoxication. After conducting some initial experiments with ether, Morton asked permission to demonstrate its use as a general anesthetic. In 1846, just a year after Wells' failure, Morton gave his demonstration at Massachusetts General Hospital. A large crowd gathered to observe and possibly to laugh at the brash young student who claimed to have developed a method for eliminating surgical pain. Smith, Cooperman, and Wollman (1980) describe the events that followed:

> Everyone was ready and waiting, including the strong men to hold down the struggling patient, but Morton did not appear. Fifteen minutes passed,

William Morton successfully used ether inhalation to render a patient unconscious in the first public demonstration of surgical anesthesia.

and the surgeon, becoming impatient, took his scalpel and turning to the gallery said, "As Dr. Morton has not arrived I presume he is otherwise engaged." While the audience smiled and the patient cringed, the surgeon turned to make his incision. Just then Morton entered . . . [the surgeon] said "Well, sir, your patient is ready." Surrounded by a silent and unsympathetic audience, Morton went quietly to work. After a few minutes of ether inhalation, the patient was unconscious, whereupon Morton looked up and said "Dr. Warren, *your* patient is ready." The operation was begun. The patient showed no sign of pain, yet he was alive and breathing. The strong men were not needed. When the operation was completed, Dr. Warren turned to the astonished audience and made the famous statement "Gentlemen, this is no humbug" (pp. 258–259).

Morton had just accomplished the first public demonstration of surgical anesthesia and had revolutionized the practice of surgery. The use of ether as an anesthetic quickly became widespread, and it is still occasionally used today along with newer anesthetics such as halothane, related gases, and barbiturates.

BARBITURATES

History and Development

A number of depressant drugs were introduced in the nineteenth century, including chloroform, chloral hydrate, and paraldehyde, but the next truly significant development was the introduction of the barbiturates in 1862. The first barbiturate was developed in that year in the Bayer laboratories in Munich, Germany. Barbiturate compounds are synthesized using, among other things, chemicals found in urine, and some say Bayer gave the drugs their name to honor a woman named Barbara who provided the urine samples (Barbara's urates?). Others claim the name came from the fact that the discovery took place on St. Barbara's Day (Dundee & McIlroy, 1982). We may never know, but regardless of how they were named the class of depressant drugs called barbiturates now includes more than 2,000 different compounds (although only about 50 are currently available in the United States). Because so many barbiturates have been developed custom dictates that both generic and brand names of these drugs end with the suffix "-al." A few representative barbiturates are listed in Table 10-1. The effects of these various barbiturates are generally similar, differing primarily in potency and duration of action. Thus, pentobarbital and secobarbital are considered potent and short-acting (duration of action two to four hours), while amobarbital is intermediate (six to eight hours) and phenobarbital longer-acting (eight to ten hours). Barbiturates, similar to benzodiazepines, are thought to act by influencing inhibitory neurotransmission, a mechanism of action we discuss later in this chapter. In general, barbiturates with a rapid onset and short duration of action are used as anesthetics today (e.g., pentobarbital) while those with slower onset and longer duration of action are preferred for the treatment of epilepsy (e.g., phenobarbital).

*"You can get roaring drunk on
'barbs.'"*

(Brecher, 1972)

Barbiturates were first introduced into general medical practice in 1903 when barbital was marketed under the brand name of Veronal. They soon became popular as a treatment for anxiety and as the first "sleeping pills" (Brecher, 1972). Use of barbiturates continued to increase until the 1960s, but has declined markedly in the years since. There are a number of reasons for the rise and fall of barbiturate use. Of the various afflictions experienced by people in the twentieth century, sleeping disorders and anxiety problems are among the most common. Thus, any drug offering relief from anxiety or promising sleep to the insomniac has potential for tremendous popularity and commercial success. The barbiturates do have the capacity to induce sleep and to relieve anxiety, and this accounts for their ascendance. However, there are a number of problems with barbiturate use discussed below that were unknown to consumers and physicians at first. These led to the decline of barbiturate use in the past 20 years.

Physiological and Psychological Effects of Barbiturates

All of the barbiturates possess the properties of central nervous system depressants. Thus, in moderate doses they produce a drunken euphoric state. Similar to alcohol, barbiturates may produce a loss of motor coordination, a staggering gait, and slurred speech. Loss of emotional control and behavioral disinhibition are also characteristic effects. Sedation and sleep are produced by increased doses, and higher doses produce surgical anesthesia. Physiological effects include respiratory depression, which is responsible for most of the overdose deaths associated with barbiturates. In addition, some depression of heart rate, blood pressure, and gastrointestinal activity is noted at higher doses.

Medical Uses of Barbiturates

As noted above, the barbiturates once were used extensively as sedative-hypnotic drugs, but except for certain specialized uses they now have been replaced by the safer benzodiazepines. Short-acting barbiturates still are used to produce anesthesia. Other current uses include emergency treatment of convulsions and prevention of seizures in certain types of epilepsy (Harvey, 1985).

Tolerance, Dependence, and Adverse Effects of Barbiturates

One major reason for the movement away from medical use of barbiturates involves tolerance and dependence. Tolerance develops fairly rapidly to many of the effects of the barbiturates. Thus, while a given dose may be effective at inducing sleep for a while, if the drug is used regularly the patient soon may require a higher dose in order to sleep. If doses escalate too much and regular use persists, the patient will experience an abstinence syndrome when he or she attempts to withdraw from barbiturates. The symptoms of the barbiturate withdrawal syndrome are essentially similar to those of alcohol—shakes, perspiration, confusion, and in some cases full-blown delirium tremens (DTs) (see Chapter 7)—but convulsions and seizures are more likely to occur in barbiturate withdrawal (Harvey, 1985). As with alcohol, the severity of barbiturate withdrawal depends upon the extent of use. Mild symptoms such as **rebound insomnia** (see below) and anxiety may occur after brief use of barbiturates, while life-threatening convulsions occur only after heavier usage.

Many people became dependent on barbiturates even though the drugs were used only under medical supervision. Suppose someone is in crisis, say, after the death of a spouse or other loved one. A physician may prescribe a sleeping pill to help the person rest during the crisis. After a few weeks the patient may feel emotionally ready to sleep without the drug—and indeed may be. But the first night he or she attempts to sleep without the barbiturate the person may have a great deal of trouble because one of the features of barbiturate withdrawal is rebound insomnia (Mendelson, 1980). That is, after chronic use of barbiturates, abstinence produces insomnia, even in someone who was untroubled with insomnia previously.

A related problem involves the type of sleep experienced while under the influence of barbiturates and after heavy use of sleeping pills. Barbiturates do induce sleep, but similar to alcohol, they reduce the amount of time spent in the rapid eye movement or REM stage of sleep. This may account in part for the "hungover" feeling some people report after sleeping with the aid of a drug. Although they get enough hours of sleep, it may not be "high quality" sleep. A further problem is that when subjects try to sleep without a pill after taking drugs for several nights, they may experience **REM rebound.** That is, they spend more time in REM than normal. Often accompanying REM rebound are vivid dreams and nightmares with nocturnal awakening. So even if the tired patient is able to get to sleep without drugs during barbiturate withdrawal, he or she may awaken early in the morning and not be able to get back to sleep. There may be other factors involved, but it is clear that once dependence on sleeping pills has developed, considerable time must pass before normal sleep patterns return (Mendelson, 1980). All of these factors make it easy to understand why dependence on drugs such as barbiturates for sleeping so often develops. Such dependence is certainly a feature limiting the usefulness of these and other depressants in the treatment of sleep disorders.

An additional problem with the barbiturates is the risk of fatal drug overdose. The lethal dose of many barbiturates is fairly low compared to the effective dose in inducing sleep, and accidental overdoses have been a problem. This is particularly evident when barbiturates are taken in combination with alcohol or other depressant drugs, because these drugs potentiate one another (Harvey, 1980). Barbiturates often were prescribed to persons suffering from depression because sleeping disorders are a common symptom of clinical depression. Because there is a risk that severely depressed patients may attempt suicide, having a prescription for barbiturates could make it more likely the attempt will succeed. Barbiturates have been the lethal drug in many suicides, including celebrated cases such as that of Marilyn Monroe.

Barbiturates (particularly the short-acting barbiturates) produce a euphoric state similar to alcohol intoxication. As a result, barbiturates became significant recreational drugs on the street during the 1950s and 1960s. An estimated 5 billion doses of barbiturates entered into the illicit market in 1969 alone (Brecher, 1972)! Clearly, barbiturates were causing some major

Rebound insomnia
Inability to sleep produced as a withdrawal symptom associated with some depressant drugs.

REM rebound
An increase in the rapid eye movement or REM stage of sleep when withdrawing from drugs that suppress REM time.

societal problems, and the quest was on for safer drugs to relieve anxiety and induce sleep.

QUAALUDES AND OTHER NONBARBITURATE SEDATIVES

Several nonbarbiturate sedatives were introduced in the 1950s and 1960s as possible alternatives for the treatment of anxiety and sleep disorders. Meprobamate (Equanil), ethchlorvynol (Placidyl), and glutethimide (Doriden) have all been used in this way, but each seemed to possess the same undesirable properties as the barbiturates. One important candidate as an alternative to barbiturates was methaqualone, first marketed under the brand names Quaalude and Sopor in 1965. Although some thought methaqualone would be much safer because it was not a barbiturate, this did not prove to be true. It quickly became evident that methaqualone was quite toxic at high doses, especially when taken in combination with alcohol. In addition, dependence develops rapidly to methaqualone, with abstinence symptoms similar to those produced by alcohol and barbiturates. Thus, medical enthusiasm for methaqualone was quickly dampened. However, because it produces a pronounced state of "drunkenness" and developed a reputation as a sexual enhancer, methaqualone became a major street drug in the 1970s and was sometimes known as "Disco-biscuits" or "Ludes." Very little research is available about the true effects of methaqualone on sexuality. Anecdotal data are mixed: some users report a disinhibition they find enhances sexual experience, but others report it interferes with sexual behavior (Abel, 1985). Actually, given the similarity in pharmacology between methaqualone and other depressants such as alcohol, it would be surprising if there were any major differences in the way these drugs affect sexual behavior (see Chapter 7). In any case, the abuse problems with methaqualone and other nonbarbiturate sedatives far outweigh their medical benefits, and currently these drugs are rarely used for management of sleep problems or anxiety. In fact, methaqualone has become a Schedule I drug and is no longer produced for medical use. A major reason these drugs and the barbiturates have lost favor has been the widespread acceptance of the benzodiazepines as the treatment of choice in these disorders.

BENZODIAZEPINES AND THE TREATMENT OF ANXIETY

The Problem of Anxiety

Antianxiety drugs, also known as anxiolytics and tranquilizers, are intended to treat the physiological and psychological symptoms of anxiety. It is difficult to provide a complete definition of anxiety, given the wide array of phenomena it encompasses. However, anxiety is frequently experienced as some or all of the following four categories of symptoms: (1) motor tension (for example, shakiness, muscle tension, restlessness), (2) autonomic hyperactivity (for example, sweating, pounding heart, stomach tightness, flushing), (3) apprehensive expectation (such as anxiety, fear, rumination), and (4) vigilance (for example, impatience, hyperattentiveness, insomnia) (APA, 1980). Clinicians frequently speak of two types of anxiety. The first is a trait or characterological anxiety, in that the person seems to experience his or her anxiety practically all the time. The second is a more transient state, called situational anxiety, wherein the anxiety is much greater at some times than at others, when the person may not even feel anxious at all. A related type of anxiety is panic attacks, which are recurrent and unpredictable periods of intense fear and impending doom (APA, 1987). These attacks frequently include sweating, palpitations, dizziness, and difficulty in breathing. A case illustration of panic attacks from Spitzer et al. (1989) follows.

> Mindy Markowitz is a stylishly dressed, 25-year-old art director who is seeking treatment for "panic attacks" that have occurred with increasing frequency over the past year, often two or three times a day. These attacks begin with a sudden intense wave of "horrible fear" that seems to come out of nowhere, sometimes during the day, sometimes waking her from sleep. She begins to tremble, is nauseated, sweats profusely, feels as though she is gagging, and fears that she will lose control and do something crazy, like run screaming into the street.
>
> Mindy remembers first having attacks like this when she was in high school. She was dating a boy her parents disapproved of, and had to do a lot of "sneaking around" to avoid confrontations with them. At the same time, she was under a lot of pressure as the principal designer of her high school yearbook, and was applying to Ivy League colleges. She remembers that her first panic attack occurred just after the yearbook went to press and she was accepted by Harvard, Yale, and Brown. The attacks lasted only a few minutes, and she would just "sit through them." She was worried enough to mention them to her mother; but because she was otherwise perfectly healthy, she did not seek treatment.
>
> Over the eight years since her first attack, Mindy has had them intermittently, sometimes not for many months, sometimes, as now, several times a day. There have also been extreme variations in the intensity of the attacks, some being so severe and debilitating that she had to take a day off from work.
>
> Apart from her panic attacks and a brief period of depression at 19, when she broke up with a boyfriend, Mindy has always functioned extremely well, in school, at work, and in her social life. She is a lively, friendly person who is respected by her friends and colleagues both for her intelligence and creativity and for her ability to mediate disputes.
>
> Even during the times that she was having frequent, severe attacks, Mindy never limited her activities. She might stay home from work for a day because she was exhausted from multiple attacks, but she never associated the attacks with particular places. (Published with permission of American Psychiatric Press, Inc.)

Before the twentieth century, however, the common palliative for anxiety symptoms was drinking alcohol, perhaps the oldest known means of sedation.

Contemporary Issue
BENZODIAZEPINES: PRESCRIPTION CAVEATS

The invention of the benzodiazepine drugs was an advance in the treatment of anxiety and of alcohol withdrawal. The popularity of the benzodiazepines as prescription drugs, however, brought concerns that they were being overprescribed. The major concern was that the benzodiazepine drugs are physically addicting, and that freely prescribing these drugs was solving one problem, for example, severe anxiety, by inducing another, benzodiazepine dependence.

The concern is particularly acute if a physician is treating a person who has a history of alcohol or other drug problems. For example, not too long ago some physicians recommended treating people who were alcohol-dependent with benzodiazepines to relieve emotional distress. It was reasoned that, rather than using alcohol to relieve distress, it would be better to use a benzodiazepine drug. Now that the potential for developing physical dependence on the benzodiazepines is much more widely recognized, few physicians recommend prescribing benzodiazepines to people as substitutes for alcohol.

When treating people who have a history of alcohol or drug dependence there is the added problem of benzodiazepine abuse potential. These drugs have psychoactive properties that are reinforcing and thus are candidates for abuse. For people who have a history of drug or alcohol problems the risk of abuse is higher than in people who have no such history. For example, one study compared the effects of a benzodiazepine drug on alcoholic men who had abstained from alcohol for up to 72 hours to the effects in nonalcoholic men. The study showed that the pharmacokinetics (absorption, distribution, and metabolism) of the drug did not differ in the two groups, but that the alcoholics liked the effects of the drug more. "Liking" the drug was measured with a questionnaire that correlates with drug-use liability (Ciraulo, Barnhill, Greenblatt, et al., 1988).

Data such as these sometimes leave the physician in a dilemma. Although few prescribe benzodiazepines to alcoholics as substitutes for alcohol, the drugs may have treatment value for, say, alcoholics who have a major anxiety problem such as panic disorder. It is for such cases that the anxiolytic drug BuSpar has been invented. BuSpar's special feature is that it seems as effective as the benzodiazepines in treating major anxiety problems, but it is not likely to be abused. (See the Contemporary Issue Box on BuSpar.)

The problem in prescribing benzodiazepines accents the general point that the pros and cons of using any drug as part of treatment must be considered carefully. This principle is especially important in drug treatment of people who are or have been alcohol—or drug—dependent.

For much of this century, into the 1950s, anxiety was treated primarily through the use of bromide salts (which were available without prescription) and barbiturates. The latter decreased anxiety symptoms through a generalized and nonspecific depression of all body tissues, but more crucially the central nervous system and the cardiovascular system. By the 1930s scientists were discovering that the use of the bromides had unwanted cumulative effects and could produce toxic delirium (Hollister, 1983). Barbiturates, such as phenobarbital, were used then more frequently as an anxiolytic agent. However, as noted earlier, it gradually became clear these drugs were physically addictive, with users developing tolerance and exhibiting a severe withdrawal reaction when drug use ceased. As a result, efforts were directed at developing an anxiolytic medication that would effectively treat the anxiety but not be physically addicting. The first in the desired group of nonbarbiturate sedatives was meprobamate, but again it was found that a severe withdrawal syndrome was associated with discontinuing its use after some period of time on the drug. The world was still looking for a safer anxiolytic.

Development of the Benzodiazepines

In the late 1950s, scientists working at Roche Laboratories synthesized a new group of compounds known as the **benzodiazepines.** Animal tests with these drugs showed sedative, anticonvulsant, and muscle-relaxant effects similar to those of the barbiturates. An additional feature was that they produced a "taming" effect in monkeys. Even more intriguing, these drugs showed very low toxicity: The lethal dose is sufficiently high that it is difficult to achieve. The first of the benzodiazepines, Librium (chlordiazepoxide), was first marketed in 1960, and was closely followed by the introduction of its more potent cousin, Valium (diazepam) in 1963 (see Sternbach, 1983). These two drugs quickly came to dominate the market as treatments for anxiety and insomnia. By the 1970s, they were among the best-selling drugs in America with 100 million prescriptions written for benzodiazepines in 1975 alone (Harvey, 1980). Today because of widespread concern about dependence, particularly on Valium, and the over-prescription of these drugs, the use of Valium and Librium is down. However there are a number of new benzodiazepines (see Table 10-1) and these are finding increasing favor such that the overall prescriptions for benzodiazepines are down only slightly.

Mechanisms of Action

As has been noted, the depressant drugs share many traits. Alcohol, barbiturates, nonbarbiturate sedatives, and, of course, benzodiazepines all have very similar effects when equated for dose. In addition, cross-tolerance occurs between these drugs. They also potentiate one another. Cross-dependence also occurs between these drugs, because an appropriate dose of any depressant can be used to reduce the withdrawal symptoms produced by any other. In fact, benzodiazepines are commonly used to withdraw alcoholics from alcohol. Thus, substantial evidence indicates a common mechanism of action for depressant drugs (Breese, Frye, Vogel, Mann-Koepke, & Mueller, 1983).

By the 1970s, evidence had begun to accumulate that GABA, the brain's major inhibitory neurotransmitter, might provide the common link (Costa, Guidotti, & Mao, 1975; Ticku, Burch, & Davis, 1983). The problem arose when there was no direct evidence that any of the depressant drugs bound to the GABA receptor site. Then, in 1977, two independent laboratories reported

"Valium is . . . a leveler. It evens things out silently, quietly. No rush. No thrill. No charge."

(Gordon, 1979)

Benzodiazepines
Currently the most widely prescribed anxiolytic drugs.

the discovery of binding sites for benzodiazepines (Mohler & Okada, 1977; Squires & Braestrup, 1977), and it was subsequently shown that although specific to benzodiazepines, these receptors are part of what is now called the GABA-benzodiazepine receptor complex (Dykstra, 1992). Apparently, the normal neural inhibition produced by GABA is greatly enhanced when there is activity at the benzodiazepine receptor. In addition, a third receptor in the system has been identified that responds to barbiturates (Dykstra, 1992). It appears both barbiturates and benzodiazepines act by enhancing neural inhibition in the GABA system, although they act at different receptor sites.

Another exciting discovery has been the development of new drugs that are antagonists at the benzodiazepine receptor. These drugs block or reverse the effects of Valium or other benzodiazepines, but may themselves produce effects. However, the effects of these antagonists (or inverse agonists, as they are called by some) are to produce convulsions and anxiety—effects just opposite those of benzodiazepine agonists such as Valium. For example, Dorow, Horowski, Paschelke, Amin and Braestrup (1983) working with a compound known as FG-7142, noted it produced panic attacks and terror in three humans who were administered the drug. Research with animals seems to confirm FG-7142 produces fear or anxiety (File, Pellow, & Braestrup, 1985). It is now hoped research on this and related compounds may reveal important secrets about the neurochemistry of anxiety. After all, these benzodiazepine receptors must be in our brains for a reason, and it seems unlikely they were waiting in mammalian brains for the discovery of benzodiazepines. More likely, benzodiazepines (or their antagonists) are mimicking some natural neurotransmitter regulating fear and anxiety (see review by Hommer, Skolnick, & Paul, 1987).

When taken orally, benzodiazepines generally are absorbed slowly and have a long duration of action. Considerable variability exists in duration of action, however, and this accounts for different uses for and effects of the different benzodiazepines. Table 10-2 shows the half-life for some of the widely used benzodiazepines (the time required for half of the drug to be metabolized). The longer acting benzodiazepines such as Valium are considered most useful when it is desirable to maintain the patient at a constant level of drug over an extended period, for example, when an individual is suffering from an anxiety reaction. The short- and moderate-duration benzodiazepines

Table 10-2   Kinetic Classification of Benzodiazepines

Type	Half-Life (hours)
Long Half–Life	
Flurazepam (Dalmane)	40–250
Diazepam (Valium)	30–200
Intermediate Half–Life	
Alprazolam (Xanax)	6–20
Lorazepam (Ativan)	10–20
Oxazepam (Serax)	5–15
Short Half–Life	
Triazolam (Halcion)	1.5–5

are more useful for treating insomnia when it is desirable to have the drug effects wear off by morning.

Psychotherapeutic Uses for Benzodiazepines

A number of reasons exist for the commercial success of the benzodiazepines. First, they are effective at relieving anxiety and inducing sleep. In fact, it is sometimes claimed benzodiazepines are uniquely effective as anxiolytic agents. It is true they relieve anxiety in animal studies and in humans at doses that do not produce motor impairment (ataxia) or pronounced sedation. In animals anxiolytic action is tested by determining the ability of a drug to increase rates of punished responding (see Chapter 5). Animals (typically rats) are trained to press a lever to produce food or water reinforcement. Then, during some periods, lever-pressing is punished by electric shock. During other periods no shock is delivered. Normally, rats will show decreased rates of lever-pressing in the punished component. When benzodiazepines are given to animals trained with such procedures, the rates of lever-pressing in the punished component go up almost to baseline levels at doses that do not affect the unpunished component. The clinical efficacy of various benzodiazepines measured in humans is correlated closely with these antipunishment actions, and for this reason the facilitation of punished responding is viewed as an excellent animal model of human anxiety. In fact, novel anxiolytic drugs have been discovered on the basis of antipunishment effects on this animal model. While other depressant drugs also show antipunishment effects, none is as selective in this regard as benzodiazepines. This is one reason for considering benzodiazepines as possessing some unique anxiolytic actions.

"You can get drunk on them [benzodiazepines and other minor tranquilizers]; you can become addicted to them; and you can suffer delirium tremens when they are withdrawn."

(Brecher, 1972)

The potent anxiolytic actions of benzodiazepines occur at doses producing few serious side effects. Although drowsiness may occur when taking benzodiazepines, it is less of a problem than was true of other depressant drugs. Because the lethal dose is so high, suicide and accidental overdose is far less of a problem with benzodiazepines than with other depressant drugs. However, benzodiazepines do interact to potentiate alcohol and other depressant drugs, and fatal overdoses are not uncommon with such drug combinations (see Contemporary Issue Box). So benzodiazepines, although not nearly as toxic as depressants such as barbiturates or methaqualone, are not without overdose risk.

Benzodiazepines also are used for purposes other than anxiety management. For example, benzodiazepines are frequently used to medically manage withdrawal from alcohol. Alcohol and benzodiazepines have some effects in common so that tapering from alcohol is made easier through the use of benzodiazepines. In addition, benzodiazepines have anticonvulsant properties. Benzodiazepines also are used as an anesthetic for minor procedures such as dental surgery and as a treatment for muscle spasms and seizures.

Tolerance, Dependence, and Misuse of Benzodiazepines

Tolerance develops to benzodiazepines, and there is cross-tolerance between them and other depressants. However, tolerance to benzodiazepines develops

Contemporary Issue
DEPRESSANT DRUGS AND POTENTIATION

All of the depressant drugs reviewed to this point tend to potentiate one another. That is, the effects of the drugs when combined are greater than would be expected from the individual doses considered alone. Such effects are among the most dangerous aspects of drug use. The vast majority of drug overdose deaths are due not to overdose of a single drug—but rather to smaller doses of more than one drug taken in lethal combination. Alcohol, barbiturates, nonbarbiturate sedatives, (Quaaludes, meprobamate), and benzodiazepines all interact with one another to produce additive effects. They interact with heroin and other opiate drugs to produce additive effects as well. Many deaths attributed to heroin overdose actually involve heroin taken in combination with alcohol or other depressant drugs (see Chapter 12), and the largest number of drug overdose deaths in America every year involves alcohol taken in combination with other depressants, according to the National Institute on Drug Abuse. Such a combination of depressants killed Elvis Presley, and it kills thousands of others every year.

A further problem with additive effects involves cases in which lower doses are consumed. Consider a young woman who is given a prescription for Valium to help her weather a family crisis. Suppose after taking her Valium she

Elvis Presley died of a combination of depressant drugs.

goes out with some friends for dinner and has a couple of beers. Perhaps under normal conditions she could tolerate this much alcohol without impairment, but taken in combination with the Valium, she may find herself quite intoxicated. If she attempts to drive home after such a drug combination, the loss of motor co-ordination may prove fatal. Combinations of alcohol with another depressant are thought to be responsible for many highway deaths above and beyond alcohol alone (O'Hanlon & De Gier, 1986). Never combine depressant drugs with alcohol or one another.

---

slowly, and fairly high doses are needed for tolerance to develop. The abstinence syndrome associated with benzodiazepine withdrawal is encountered infrequently because heavy use of benzodiazepines is necessary for withdrawal symptoms to occur. When it does occur, it is similar to that of alcohol and barbiturates, but not nearly as severe. Most benzodiazepines are very long-acting drugs with half-lives of more than a day and active metabolites persisting still longer (Greenblatt, Shader, Abernethy, Ochs, Divoll, & Sellers, 1982). Thus, abstinence symptoms may not appear for several days or even more than a week, and may persist for up to four weeks. The main symptoms are rebound insomnia, anxiety, tremors, sweating, and occasionally more serious problems such as seizures (Salzman, 1992). One of the problems in interpreting benzodiazepine withdrawal is differentiating abstinence symptoms from symptoms the drug was suppressing when it was present. For example, a great deal of controversy about Valium was stirred by the autobiographical book and movie I'm Dancing as Fast as I Can by Barbara Gordon (1979). Gordon was a successful professional who was maintained by her psychiatrist on very high doses of Valium. When she decided to quit Valium, her physician told her to simply stop taking the drug, rather than tapering her off the drug. This was certainly a poor decision. Gordon describes her withdrawal symptoms vividly:

> ". . . By early afternoon I began to feel a creeping sense of anxiety. But it was different from my usual bouts of terror. It felt like little jolts of electricity, as if charged pins and needles were shooting through my body. My breathing became rapid and I began to perspire.
>
> . . . My scalp started to burn as if I had hot coals under my hair. Then I began to experience funny little twitches, spasms, a jerk of a leg, a flying arm, tiny tremors that soon turned into convulsions" (p. 51).

She was unable to leave her own house, much less work. Her relationships with her lover and other friends deteriorated, and eventually she required hospitalization for several months. Nevertheless, her symptoms persisted even beyond this time. Thus, the novel is a moving description of anxiety disorder, although perhaps not a very typical description of Valium withdrawal. As we noted, although there are some very persistent withdrawal symptoms (Smith & Wesson, 1983), it is difficult to differentiate long-lasting withdrawal from the reemergence of previous anxiety symptoms. Thus, Barbara Gordon's experience may illustrate a case where the severity of her symptoms was revealed only when the drug, which had masked them, was removed.

Benzodiazepines do turn up on the street but far less frequently than barbiturates or methaqualone did in their day. In general, the potential for abuse of benzodiazepines is considered to be less than that for other depressants (Cappell, Sellers, & Busto, 1986). Laboratory animals will self-administer benzodiazepines, but they are only moderately potent reinforcers and are less preferred than barbiturates (Ator & Griffiths, 1987; Griffiths, Lukas, Bradford, Brady, & Snell, 1981). Griffiths and his associates also have investigated benzodiazepine self-administration in human volunteers with histories of sedative abuse. In double-blind laboratory studies these researchers have shown humans will self-administer benzodiazepines, and prefer them to placebo, but similar to nonhumans, prefer barbiturates (Griffiths, Bigelow, Liebson, & Kaliszak, 1980). When different benzodiazepines were compared, it was shown that the more potent drugs with a rapid onset of action, such as Valium, were preferred to less potent compounds with slower onset of action such as oxazepam (Griffiths, McLeod, Bigelow, Liebson, Roache, & Nowowieski, 1984; Griffiths, McLeod, Bigelow, Liebson, & Roache, 1984).

Tolerance, dependence, and abuse are associated with the benzodiazepines, but the problems produced are far milder than those connected with other depressant drugs. However, over the years a number of other problems associated with benzodiazepine use have emerged.

Contemporary Issue
HALCION: TRANQUILITY OR TURMOIL?

Halcion (triazolam) is a short-acting benzodiazepine that was placed on the American market by Upjohn in 1983, primarily for use as a sedative/hypnotic (sleeping pill). The drug was named after the phrase "halcyon days," which refers to a period of calm and tranquility. By the early 1990s Halcion was providing tranquility for millions of Americans and was the best-selling sleeping pill in the world. Its use by former President George Bush when he could not sleep was widely documented. So Upjohn was riding the crest of an enormously profitable drug. But then a series of negative reports about Halcion surfaced through the media. There were reports of patients who were on Halcion developing depression and paranoia, and a case of a Salt Lake City woman who shot her mother eight times while under the influence of Halcion. This case received extensive publicity, perhaps because the murder charges were eventually dropped ("the drug made me do it"), and she received an out-of-court settlement after suing Upjohn (Goode, 1993). In the midst of this adverse publicity, Halcion was pulled off the market in Great Britain and the Netherlands.

So is Halcion really that bad? Psychiatric side effects, of the sort attributed to Halcion, do develop very rarely to other benzodiazepines as well, although generally only when excessively high doses are used chronically. Chronic administration of any benzodiazepine is questionable medical practice, especially if high doses are used. There have been a number of studies comparing side effects of Halcion with those of other benzodiazepines with mixed results (e.g.,

Roache et al., 1990). However, to keep the Halcion controversy in perspective, one must keep in mind that millions of patients worldwide have used the drug without notable side effects. Perhaps the key point is that although benzodiazepines, including Halcion, are safer than their predecessors, they can produce all the adverse side effects of other depressant drugs if abused.

Adverse Effects of Benzodiazepines

As with other depressants, the main adverse effects of benzodiazepines involve drowsiness and motor impairment. Although even these side effects are rare with benzodiazepines alone (see Cappell, Sellers, & Busto, 1986, for a review), they may become particularly problematic when benzodiazepines are taken, as often they are, in combination with alcohol or other depressant drugs (see the nearby Contemporary Issue Box).

A problem more recently recognized indicates benzodiazepines may interfere with the storage of memories, a phenomenon called **anterograde amnesia.** Thus, when an individual is wakened by a phone call from sleep induced by benzodiazepines, he or she may fail to remember the events discussed during the call. The drug may be present in sufficient dose the next morning such that the patient forgets what he or she had for breakfast or what was read in the morning paper. These are examples of benzodiazepine-induced amnesia, and evidence is mounting that it is a common problem particularly with some of the popular benzodiazepines such as triazolam (Halcion) and alprazolam (Xanax) (Salzman, 1992). This type of effect is not unique to benzodiazepines. After all, alcohol is known to produce the more dramatic memory loss of the blackout (see Chapter 9). Barbiturates and methaqualone also produce blackouts, suggesting that some type of memory deficit may be characteristic of any depressant drug.

Other adverse effects are occasionally reported with benzodiazepines, especially after chronic use, but despite the high frequency of use of these drugs, reports of toxicity are extraordinarily rare (Cappell, Sellers, & Busto, 1986; Salzman, 1992). Nonetheless there is considerable interest in newly developed non-benzodiazepine antianxiety drugs that may be effective with even fewer side effects, such as buspirone (BuSpar—see the accompanying Contemporary Issue Box).

Anterograde amnesia
Loss or limitation of the ability to form new memories.

USE AND ABUSE OF DEPRESSANT DRUGS

Over the years a host of different depressant drugs have been used and abused in American society and around the world. Currently the benzodiazepines have become the drugs of choice in the treatment of insomnia and anxiety disorders. There is no doubt these drugs relieve an enormous amount of the human suffering associated with these ailments. There also is no doubt the benzodiazepines do so with far less toxicity and risk of dependence than their predecessors, the barbiturates and other sedatives. But there is considerable

Contemporary Issue
BUSPAR—AN ALTERNATIVE FOR ANXIETY

We have noted in the text that all of the drugs used to treat anxiety disorders cause side effects of some sort. Thus, the search for safer antianxiety drugs has been a major goal of psychopharmacology. Recently a new drug was brought to the market by Bristol-Myers called "BuSpar" (generic name, buspirone). Buspirone's chemical structure and activity are very different from any of the traditional anxiolytic drugs but, in spite of the differences, it appears to relieve anxiety symptoms much like the benzodiazepines. No withdrawal symptoms have been reported following chronic use of buspirone, and it is considered to have very low abuse potential. For example, animals will not self-administer buspirone, and humans report no intoxication or euphoria after taking it. Virtually no sedation or motor impairment has been shown during buspirone treatment, and it does not produce synergistic effects with alcohol or other depressant drugs. Simply put, buspirone seems to relieve anxiety without producing any of the undesirable side effects of the other anxiolytic drugs. Buspirone is a new drug, and more research is needed to determine whether it really works as well as the benzodiazepines, and whether it may produce side effects that have yet to be determined. We still do not know exactly what is responsible for buspirone's anxiolytic actions. BuSpar appears to affect the serotonin neurotransmitter system, and unlike benzodiazepines does not show direct action on the GABA system. Regardless of how BuSpar works, the increase in prescriptions for it suggests that we are entering a new era in the treatment of anxiety disorders (see Tunnicliff, Eison, & Taylor, 1991).

debate about the wisdom of benzodiazepine treatment as the *sole* treatment for anxiety disorders, especially as a chronic or long-term treatment. Most benzodiazepines are prescribed not by psychiatrists whose specialty is the treatment of psychological disorders, but instead by general practitioners who have no special training in such matters. Thus, tranquilizers may be used to treat the symptoms of anxiety disorders, but do not really help the patient learn to cope with problems. Taking a sleeping pill may help you sleep on the nights you take one, but pills do not make one's relationship with one's spouse any better, or improve one's job situation, or change any of the stressors that may be causing the insomnia in the first place. In fact, a hidden danger occurs when the use of drugs masks these symptoms and allows the person to function under less than optimal environmental conditions. Whether and when this is a desirable state of affairs may be a value judgment, but we believe it is tremendously important for potential consumers of benzodiazepines (according to statistics that include most of us) to recognize these drugs do not *cure* anxiety or affect its causes, but merely mask these symptoms. When symptom control is considered appropriate as a goal by the physician and patient these drugs can do a great deal of good.

The term "inhalants" is used to describe a number of different compounds related more by their method of administration than by their pharmacology. Some categories of inhalants such as the medical anesthetics (halothane, nitrous oxide) are true depressant drugs, and that is why inhalants are treated in this chapter. However, it should be noted that inhalants include a wide variety of products with widely varying pharmacologies, including glue, paint, butane gas, correction fluid, and many others (see Table 10-3 for a more detailed list). Perhaps the only thing all these products really have in common is the ability to produce a dizzy euphoria upon inhalation.

"You can put a supply (of glue to sniff) in your pocket, and nobody can tell."

(Cohen, 1977)

In the 1992 survey of America's high school seniors and eighth graders one of the most surprising statistics was the widespread abuse of inhalants. Among eighth graders, 9.5% reported that they used inhalants, up by .5% from 1991. Although fewer 12th graders reported inhalant use (6.2%), the use of inhalants, called "huffing" or "bagging," is clearly one of the major forms of dangerous drug use among young people today.

Because of the bewildering variety of substances associated with inhalant abuse, it is difficult to characterize the hazards completely. There have been a number of reports of deaths due to cardiovascular collapse or suffocation related to inhalation of butane, toluene, and gasoline (Garriott, 1992; Johns, 1991). Chronic use of inhalants has been linked to a variety of medical problems including brain damage (Pryor, 1990).

The nitrite inhalants—amyl, butyl, and isopropyl nitrite (see Table 10-3)—represent a group of inhalant drugs that deserve special mention. Amyl nitrite dilates coronary arteries when inhaled and was once prescribed to

Table 10-3   Common Inhalants and the Chemicals They Contain[1]

Inhalant Class	Product	Chemicals
Adhesives	Airplane glue	toluene, ethyl acetate
Aerosols	Spray paint	butane, propane, fluorocarbons
	Hair spray	butane, propane
	Fabric spray	butane, trichloroethane
Anesthetics	Nitrous oxide	
	Halothane	
Cleaning agents	Spot remover	xylene, chlorohydrocarbons
	Degreaser	tetrachloroethylene
Solvents	Nail polish remover	acetone
	Paint thinner	petroleum distillates
	Correction fluid	trichloroethylene
	Gasoline	
Gases	Fuel gas	butane, isopropane
	Lighter fluid	butane
Food products	Whipped cream	nitrous oxide
	Whippets	nitrous oxide
Nitrites	Locker Room, Rush, Poppers	isoamyl, butyl, or isopropyl nitrite

[1]Based on Sharp (1992).

patients suffering from angina in the form of ampules that were crushed or popped before inhalation—hence the slang name "poppers" or "snappers." Nitrites also dilate cerebral blood vessels, producing a brief period of euphoria and dizziness. These products are sometimes sold over the counter as room deodorizers under brand names like "Rush" and "Locker Room" (nitrites smell a little like dirty athletic socks . . .). Nitrites have been widely used for recreational purposes, particularly in the gay community. Both gay and heterosexual users report that "poppers" inhaled during sexual activity prolong and intensify orgasm. A number of side effects have been noted from these drugs, including headache, tachycardia, eye problems, and rare sudden deaths (Bruckner & Peterson, 1977; Rosenberg & Sharp, 1992).

DRUGS AND CULTURE
EPIDEMIOLOGY OF INHALANT ABUSE

In a review of the literature on inhalants, Barnes (1979) noted that Native American youth showed the highest rates of inhalant abuse. Since that time numerous studies have investigated the patterns of inhalant abuse in various subcultures in the United States and other countries. The findings have consistently shown high rates of abuse among Native Americans, Indian youth of Central and South America, and Hispanic youth living in poor areas of large cities (barrios). Oetting and Webb (1992) have argued that the common feature among these people is their low socioeconomic status. The American Indian reservation and the barrio are places where "unemployment, low education, poverty, and prejudice are endemic" (Oetting & Webb, 1992, p. 61). Perhaps the link between "huffing" and low socioeconomic status is simply that inhalants can be obtained so cheaply and easily. As one young man put it: "If you're broke, there's always gasoline!" (Cohen, 1977).

Contemporary Issue
NITROUS OXIDE—NO LAUGHING MATTER

As you have seen, use of nitrous oxide (laughing gas) is scarcely a new phenomenon—in fact it was one of the first depressant drugs to be used for medical and recreational purposes. But, it has become a "hot" drug once again, and as the nearby photo depicts, is often dispensed in doses consisting of a "balloonfull." Vendors filling balloons with nitrous oxide from canisters have become a familiar sight at concerts and some "head" shops. The gas also is available in cartridges (whippets) designed for use as a propellant for food and beverages (such as whipped cream). The recent boom in popularity may in part be due to the ready availability of nitrous oxide.

The effects of inhaling nitrous oxide involve a short-lived state of intoxication described by most users as a pleasant euphoria, and as the drug's nickname implies, often accompanied by giggling and giddy laughter. However, in controlled studies not all subjects enjoyed the effects of nitrous oxide, which they reported as producing significant levels of confusion, feeling high, and stimulation, but paradoxically, also depression (Dohrn, Lichtor, Finn, Uitvlugt, Coalson, Rupani, de Wit, & Zacny, 1992).

Adverse effects reported from nitrous oxide use have included nausea, vomiting, and headache. In addition, heavy chronic use has occasionally been reported that appears to resemble the sort of dependence that develops with other depressant drugs. With heavy use, more severe problems, including numbness of the extremities and permanent peripheral nerve damage, have been reported. There have also been some reports of death by asphyxiation from using large amounts in a poorly ventilated space (Garriott, 1992; Hutchens & Miederhoff, 1989; Rosenberg & Sharp, 1992).

A child "huffing," or inhaling the fumes from glue.

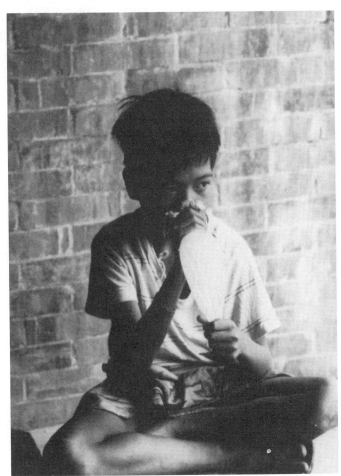

summary

- All depressant drugs (including alcohol) produce similar effects. At low doses they relieve anxiety, while at moderate doses they induce sleep, and at higher doses produce general anesthesia, and eventually, coma and death.

- The first depressants to be discovered were drugs used for general anesthesia such as nitrous oxide and ether. Modern surgery would not be possible without this development.

- The development of the barbiturate drugs led to use of depressants as sleeping pills and as treatment of anxiety symptoms and epilepsy.

- Limitations in the use of barbiturates became apparent when a number of adverse effects of barbiturate use were discovered. These include rapid development of tolerance, severe withdrawal symptoms, high risk of overdose, and high abuse potential.

- A number of barbiturate-like compounds have been developed (such as methaqualone or Quaaludes), but these possess the same undesirable effects as the barbiturates.

- The discovery of benzodiazepines revolutionized the medical use of depressant drugs because they relieve anxiety with fewer side effects than previous depressants.

- Benzodiazepines and other depressant drugs are believed to act at the GABA receptor site in the central nervous system.

- The anxiolytic effects of benzodiazepines are more selective than those of other depressants because they relieve anxiety at doses that produce minimal sedation and motor impairment.

- Although less problematic than barbiturates, benzodiazepines may produce tolerance and dependence, and withdrawal symptoms may occur.

- A variety of compounds can produce intoxication through inhalation.

ANSWERS TO WHAT DO YOU THINK?

1. Nitrous oxide (laughing gas) is no longer used by the medical profession.

F   *Nitrous oxide is still widely used in dentistry and some types of surgery.*

2. The effects of a moderate dose of a barbiturate drug resemble those of alcohol.

T   *Barbiturate effects closely resemble those of alcohol, as do most depressant drugs.*

3. Withdrawal from depressant sleeping pills can trigger rebound insomnia.

T   *Insomnia and REM sleep rebound occur after use of barbiturates or benzodiazepines to induce sleep.*

4. Withdrawal from barbiturates is similar to alcohol withdrawal.

T   *Delirium tremens-like effects characterize withdrawal from all depressants.*

5. Benzodiazepines (Valium) are one of the most commonly prescribed drugs in America.

T   *A recent survey revealed that four different benzodiazepines (Valium, Dalmane, Ativan, and Tranxene) are among the top 30 most commonly prescribed drugs in America.*

6. Benzodiazepines are a common street drug, commonly known as "bennies."

F   *"Bennies" are a type of amphetamine, while benzodiazepines are considered a depressant. Also, although benzodiazepines do turn up on the street, their prevalence is less widespread than other depressant drugs.*

7. Overdose of benzodiazepines was the cause of the suicide death of Marilyn Monroe.

F   *Benzodiazepines have a very high LD 50. Highly toxic barbiturates were the fatal drugs for Marilyn Monroe.*

8. The main depressant drugs (barbiturates, benzodiazepines, and alcohol) all act by vastly different physiological mechanisms and affect different areas of the body.

F   *Substantial evidence indicates a common mechanism of action for depressant drugs. GABA is one of the primary inhibitory neurotransmitters of the brain, and many depressants are thought to act through this system.*

9. Depressant drugs may show cross-tolerance with cocaine.

F   *Depressant drugs show cross-tolerance with other depressant drugs, such as barbiturates or alcohol.*

10. Alcohol in combination with other depressant drugs is the leading cause of drug overdose deaths in the United States.

T   *Alcohol and other depressant drugs produce strong potentiation.*

11. Nitrous oxide (laughing gas) can cause nerve damage.

T   *Heavy use of nitrous oxide has been linked to peripheral neuropathy.*

12. Inhalant abuse is a rare phenomenon among young people.

F   *Inhalants are among the most widely abused drugs.*

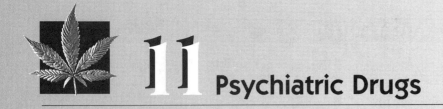

11 Psychiatric Drugs

WHAT DO YOU THINK?

True or False?

____   One of the first successful attempts to treat symptoms of mental illness with psychotropic drugs occurred in the 1840s when Moreau used cannabis to treat both depressed and manic patients.

____   Since the 1950s, the number of hospitalized psychiatric patients has decreased significantly.

____   In the United States, psychiatric drugs are prescribed for about 10 to 15% of the population each year.

____   The prevalence of psychiatric medication is twice as high among men as among women.

____   Psychiatric drugs are rarely abused.

____   As with most drugs, the age group least likely to misuse psychiatric drugs is the elderly.

____   Most psychiatric medications are administered intravenously, where direct transport in the bloodstream occurs.

____   Schizophrenia is one of the most common psychiatric disorders in the United States.

____   Stimulants are often used to treat chronic depression.

____   Because antidepressants are absorbed rapidly, their effects are often immediate.

____   Lithium, a natural alkaline metal, is often used to treat manic attacks.

____   Most psychiatric drugs pose little or no threat to the fetus and may be used safely during pregnancy.

Psychoactive substances have been used to treat mental illnesses for centuries. In fact, many of the substances described in this text, such as alcohol, cannabis, and opium, have at one time or another been used as treatments for mental illness. In some cases the motivation to administer psychopharmacological agents to the mentally ill has simply been to subdue them. More typically today medications are intended to provide persons with some relief and ideally with the opportunity to function better within their environments.

The development, testing, and distribution of psychotherapeutic drugs, as described in Chapter 5, is today a major worldwide industry. In the United States alone more than 200 million prescriptions are processed yearly for the lawful use of psychotherapeutics, including, for example, antidepressants, stimulants, and sedative-hypnotics. In any given year, approximately 10 to 15% of the general population is given a prescription for some psychoactive drug, usually an antianxiety agent.

In the present chapter, we provide an overview of the use of psychiatric drugs in this country. Following a brief historical overview, we discuss some epidemiological features of what are called **psychotropic** drugs. The term psychotropic describes those drugs that have a special or unique effect on the mind or mental functioning. Mechanisms of drug action are discussed, and an overview of three major classes of psychiatric drugs provided: antipsychotics, antidepressants, and antimanic or mood-stabilizing drugs. (A fourth major class of psychiatric drugs includes the antianxiety agents, which were discussed in Chapter 10.) We supplement this material with case examples so you have a feeling for the problems or disorders these drugs are intended to relieve.

Psychotropic
Any substance that exerts a special or unique action on psychological functioning.

HISTORICAL OVERVIEW

The roots of psychopharmacology began in the nineteenth century, when a science of chemistry was developing, and the field has undergone an immense amount of growth since, especially during the twentieth century. The actual coining in 1920 of the term *psychopharmacology* is attributed to David Macht, an American pharmacist (Caldwell, 1970).

The Pre-Chlorpromazine Era

In the nineteenth century, society had very little understanding of mental illness. Although as early as the 1800s several compendia of treatments and psychopharmacological agents existed (especially in England, France, and Germany) for mental illnesses, the proposed remedies were mostly speculative and without scientific support. Many of the approaches used were actually quite cruel, including bloodletting, hot irons, flogging, revolving chairs, starvation, and sneezing powder (Spiegel & Aebi, 1983). Nevertheless, this period was marked by the efforts of some to attempt to understand and treat, or in some cases "cleanse," those with mental illness. The efforts of Emil Kraepelin, Phillip Pinel, and J. E. Esquirol were particularly noteworthy. These scientists were involved in the development of a classification system of mental illnesses. They believed that a scientific understanding and categorizing of mental illnesses was a prerequisite to the identification of effective treatments.

One of the more systematically studied drugs in this period was cannabis. In the 1840s, the French physician Jacques-Joseph Moreau de Tours was working at a mental hospital in Paris. He theorized that treatment should "substitute symptoms of mental illness with similar but controllable drug-induced symptoms" (Caldwell, 1978, p. 16). Moreau used cannabis and found gaiety and euphoria to be among its effects. He decided to give cannabis to two depressed hospital patients to see if it would produce similar results in them. These patients did indeed respond to the cannabis, appearing happy and becoming talkative. Moreau also found **manic** patients given the cannabis subsequently calmed down and relaxed. Unfortunately, the effects of the cannabis tended to be temporary.

The first half of the twentieth century was characterized by further attempts to use drugs and other therapies to treat mental illness. For example,

Manic
Relating to mania, a mood disturbance that typically includes hyperactivity, agitation, excessive elation, and pressured speech.

Early psychiatric hospitals did not have the advantage of psychiatric drugs to treat mentally ill patients. This drawing depicts a mentally ill patient during the early 1800s.

Narcoleptic
A state characterized by brief but uncontrollable episodes of sleep.

Neuroses
A term that in common usage describes any nonpsychotic emotional disturbance, pain, or discomfort beyond what is appropriate in the conditions of one's life.

Psychosurgery
Surgery that entails the cutting of fibers connecting particular parts of the brain or the removal or destruction of areas of brain tissue with the goal of modifying severe behavioral or emotional disturbances.

tests on the effectiveness of giving amphetamines to depressed and **narcoleptic** patients were conducted, and carbon dioxide inhalation procedures were used in the treatment of illnesses referred to as the psychoses and the **neuroses.** Also used in the treatment of psychosis were antihistamines, insulin shock, and **psychosurgery.** Electroshock therapy was used in treating severe depression (a procedure still used today). Finally, in 1949, an Australian physician named John Cade discovered that the alkali metal lithium successfully moderated manic conditions, although concerns regarding toxic reactions to it prevented its approval for use in the United States until 1970. Lithium remains a mainstay in the treatment of bipolar illnesses today.

Despite the many efforts, the collective impact of these advances on the treatment of mental illness was modest at best. In fact, the total positive impact of this progress pales in comparison to the successes experienced in the use later of another drug, chlorpromazine. To the extent psychopharmacology is defined as the use of psychotropic medications to restore and maintain some degree of mental health, then the true coming of age for psychopharmacology was in Paris in 1951.

The Age of Chlorpromazine

The roots of chlorpromazine as a psychiatric medication extend to its initial use in general surgery. It was synthesized by Paul Charpentier in 1950. Chlorpromazine was used as an anesthetic: it decreased patients' anxiety associated with surgical preparations and prevented shock during surgery. This work in surgery was conducted primarily by Henri Laborit, and it was his observation of chlorpromazine's calming effects that led him to suggest its potential use in psychiatry. This application was initially tried at Val-de-Grace, a military hospital in Paris. Agitated psychotic patients appeared calm following administration of chlorpromazine. In addition, the patients' thoughts appeared to become less chaotic, and the patients were less excitable. Notably, the patients did not exhibit any loss in consciousness. Instead, they showed a disinterested and detached demeanor, or what Deniker (1983) has called "the syndrome of psychomotor indifference" (p. 166).

Chlorpromazine has had a profound effect on the field of psychiatry. As described by Caldwell (1978):

> By May 1953, the atmosphere in the disturbed wards of mental hospitals in Paris was transformed: straightjackets [*sic*], psychohydraulic packs and noise were things of the past! Once more, Paris psychiatrists who long ago unchained the chained, became pioneers in liberating their patients, this time from inner torments too, and with a drug: (chlorpromazine). It accomplished the pharmacologic revolution of psychiatry—then and there (p. 30).

Word of the successful use of chlorpromazine spread rapidly, and its adoption spread throughout Europe and to the United States and the rest of the world. The effects following introduction of chlorpromazine in the United States were just as dramatic. Since 1955, the number of hospitalized psychiatric patients in the United States has lowered significantly. In 1955 the figure was 600,000, and today there are approximately 150,000 hospitalized psychiatric patients, despite an overall increase in the general population. Of course, other factors have contributed to today's lower figure (for example, the development of other psychotropic drugs and the movement toward deinstitutionalizing psychiatric patients), but the starting point was chlorpromazine.

The decades following the introduction of chlorpromazine witnessed much growth in the field of psychopharmacology. The next major event was the appearance of reserpine in 1954. This drug, similar to chlorpromazine, was originally used in the treatment of another medical disorder (arterial hypertension), and the physicians using the drug noted symptoms of indifference in their patients. Because of this effect, reserpine was given to psychiatric patients. The drug yielded positive effects overall, but its action often took several weeks to be apparent (see Deniker, 1983), and patients using the medication often appeared depressed. Thus, reserpine never achieved the popularity of chlorpromazine.

Other advances in the field included progress in antianxiety (or anxiolytic) medications, such as meprobamate (which also was used as a muscle relaxant), and in antidepressant medications, such as monoamine oxidase inhibitors (MAOIs) and tricyclic antidepressants. Another drug receiving renewed attention was LSD. Because of the psychotic-like effects produced by LSD, efforts were made to use LSD-created effects as a model for studying psychoses. Researchers used LSD to create a "model psychosis" to study (to date with limited success) possible etiological factors contributing to mental illness. It also enabled them to treat the LSD-created symptoms with psychiatric drugs.

In retrospect, the 1950s were a frontier period for psychopharmacology. Much growth was experienced, and advances in the field continue to be made (although none with quite the impact and significance of chlorpromazine, which remains widely used today). These advances have also had a profound effect on the face of mental illness today. As noted, psychopharmacology contributed to decreases in the numbers of hospitalized psychiatric patients. Unfortunately, there have been downsides to this deinstitutionalization. While psychiatric medications often ameliorate primary symptoms associated with a disorder, this does not necessarily mean that social coping skills or general "life skills" will simultaneously materialize or reappear. Thus, some form of continuing care is often warranted. It had been expected that a variety of outpatient psychiatric services would be available to serve the needs of the discharged chronically mentally ill, but that has not been the case (Flynn, 1985). As a result, a number of patients once under psychiatric care are now without such services. It also has been argued that this is one of the factors contributing to the increased incidence of homeless people, many of whom suffer from psychiatric illnesses.

EPIDEMIOLOGY

It is estimated that approximately 15% of the U.S. population (around one in seven persons) experience some form of mental disorder in any given year. Most of these persons are experiencing symptoms associated with one of three problems: anxiety states, depression and affective disorder, or alcohol-related dysfunction. In addition, it is estimated an additional 15% of the population seek clinical services for various symptoms (for example, stress, depression, anxiety) that cut into their life-functioning effectiveness, even though they may not meet the diagnostic criteria for a particular disorder. These mental-health difficulties taken together account for around 15% of the total health-care expenditures yearly in this country.

The symptoms associated with mental health disorders frequently are treated through the use of prescription medications. Each year 10 to 15% of the general population receive a prescription for some psychotropic drug, usually an antianxiety agent (see Chapter 10). (Antidepressant and antipsychotic medications account for a small fraction of the total number of prescriptions provided.) And considerable relief is reported: national surveys suggest approximately three-fourths of patients receiving these medications report some degree of symptomatic relief. Many of the most commonly prescribed drugs are benzodiazepines—minor tranquilizers used in the treatment of anxiety and tension (see Chapter 10).

There are several important findings about the people who use psychotropic medications. One is that the prevalence of psychiatric medication use is about twice as high among women as among men. A second trend is for psychotropic drug use to increase with age, a tendency seen more dramatically among men. Additionally, greater use of psychotropics is found among those who live alone, those with more education, and those with higher income levels (Wells, Kamberg, Brook, Camp, & Rogers, 1985).

While most psychiatric medications are used as prescribed, the nonprescribed use and abuse of psychiatric drugs is a significant problem. Abuse of prescription drugs can take many forms, ranging from patients who exceed recommended dosages to the street sale of pharmaceuticals (Weiss & Greenfield, 1986). Prescription drugs sold on the street are diverted from legal distribution through thefts from drugstores or pharmaceutical companies, the pilfering of supplies by hospital or clinic employees, and the altering or forging of prescriptions. Estimates indicate that prescriptions for one and a half billion drug dosage units are written each year in the United States, and that several hundred million of these units are diverted to street or other illicit use (OSMJ, 1986). The consequences of prescription drug abuse are immense. For example, prescription drug use is implicated in significant numbers of injuries and deaths, drug-related emergency room cases, and drug-related deaths.

The drugs most often abused or misused in Western cultures are depressants and stimulants. While people of all age groups have been known to misuse prescription drugs, it is an especially notable problem among the elderly. The elderly use approximately a third of the drugs taken yearly in the United States while accounting for a much lesser proportion of the population. It is not uncommon to see the elderly use prescribed medications in combination with each other, with over-the-counter drugs (see Chapter 15), or with alcohol. (The use of multiple prescription drugs is not always intentional, because doctors sometimes provide prescriptions to the elderly without being aware of other prescription medications they already are using.)

Over the years both legislative and medical association efforts have been implemented to monitor and control the availability and access to prescribed medications. Most legal guidelines are consolidated within the Comprehensive Drug Abuse Prevention and Control Act of 1970 and the Controlled Substances Act of 1971 (see Chapter 2). In particular these acts mandate explicit procedures for the distribution and dispensing of prescription medications. Most psychotropic medications are under federal control and require a prescription for use.

Several information-gathering networks have been established to monitor the distribution and use (legal and otherwise) of drugs overall, including psychotropic drugs. Two of these, the Client-Oriented Data Acquisition Process (CODAP) and the Drug Abuse Warning Network (DAWN), are operated under federal supervision. CODAP entails the collection of information on drug use among persons entering drug-abuse treatment programs. DAWN uses reports from emergency rooms and medical examiners' offices to produce yearly statistics on morbidity and mortality associated with drug use. Both of these systems permit a monitoring of trends in drug use and consequences. The usefulness of this information, of course, is a direct function of the accuracy with which the original data are gathered in the field.

Another system, focused more on prescription drug abuse, is the Prescription Abuse Data Synthesis (PADS). It was developed by the American Medical Association and operates at the state level. PADS serves to identify the ways in which prescription drug diversions occur. The program also yields information on which prescription drugs are most in demand for illicit use in which states.

Before leaving the discussion on prescription drug abuse, it should be noted that a variety of over-the-counter substances with psychoactive properties are also subject to abuse. These include, for example, nonprescription hypnotics that contain antihistamines, nonprescription cold and allergy products, laxatives, nonprescription stimulants, and diet pills. These are described in more detail in Chapter 15.

MECHANISMS OF ACTION

As you recall from Chapter 3, our thoughts, emotions, and behavior can be reduced to the actions of neurons or nerve cells, which in turn are largely dependent on the chemical reactions central to communication between neurons. According to a physical/medical model, mental illness is a consequence of dysfunctional brain chemistry, and this serves as the basis of drug treatments in psychiatry. Therefore, psychiatric medications are designed to operate on these dysfunctional nerve cell communications so that specific biological changes occur.

Remember, neurotransmitter action entails the chemical transmission of messages between nerve cells in the central nervous system and the receptors throughout the system. Psychoactive medications can affect the neurotransmitter/receptor system in a number of ways (Gitlin, 1990), including the following:

- by binding directly to the receptor site, serving as a receptor agonist (stimulates the receptor) or receptor antagonist (blocks the neurotransmitter)
- by causing the release of more neurotransmitters, increasing the effect on the system
- by blocking the reuptake of neurotransmitters back into the presynaptic neuron, allowing the chemicals more time in the synapse
- by changing the number of receptor sites or the sensitivity of the receptors
- by altering the metabolism of the neurotransmitter, changing the amount available for release
- by altering the enzymatic degradation of the neurotransmitter

While psychotropic drugs can modify virtually any stage of synaptic action, they most generally affect three main processes: transmitter-receptor binding, reuptake of transmitters, and the manufacture of receptors (Lickey & Gordon, 1983). In each case, the mode of functioning of the nerve cell is changed.

The biological action of the drug occurs during tissue penetration and localization. When taken orally (as most psychiatric medications are), the drug is absorbed in the gastrointestinal tract and modified in the liver before being transported in the bloodstream. When administered IV or IM, direct transport in the bloodstream occurs. Drug distribution occurs primarily through the water phase of blood plasma, and the drug's arrival at the intended site(s) of action will vary as a function of the blood flow within the organ and the rate at which the drug can cross the lipoprotein membrane (Boulenger & Lader, 1982; Lader, 1976). The drug arrives fairly rapidly at those organs richly blood perfused, such as the heart, brain, and liver (Poling, 1986). Drugs not bound to plasma protein cross the lipoprotein membranes with most ease and progress toward the intended sites of action. Most psychiatric medications are highly lipid-soluble and thus diffuse fairly easily through the gastrointestinal wall, the blood-brain barrier, and cell membranes (Potter, Bertilsson, & Sjoquist, 1981). Medications can enter the brain via blood transport. The drug arrives at its final sites by passing from small arteries to the capillaries, and then through the capillary walls to the extracellular fluid (Lader, 1976). It is in the extracellular fluid that the drug diffuses and impacts on the cells it affects.

As we noted, orally administered medications are processed through the liver before being transported in the bloodstream to sites of action. This is referred to as hepatic "first pass" metabolism, or presystemic metabolism, and drugs can vary significantly in the extent to which they are metabolized in the liver before even reaching systemic circulation. (For example, it has been found that about 80% of an oral dose of chlorpromazine is metabolized in the first pass in the liver, leaving about 20% to exert the intended drug action.) The resultant metabolites can be inactive or active, and if active either therapeutic or toxic (Potter et al., 1981). In some cases the metabolites can be more active than the originally administered drug (as in the case of chloral hydrate, a sleeping medication).

Drug elimination involves metabolic and excretory processes. Drug metabolism occurs most commonly in the liver through oxidation. Less-prevalent metabolic processes include reduction and hydrolysis. Excretion of most psychotropic drugs occurs primarily through the kidneys.

CLASSES OF DRUGS AND THEIR ACTIONS

Psychiatric drugs, similar to other drugs, can be classified along a variety of dimensions, such as chemical structure, clinical actions, or sites of action (see Chapter 1). However, the most common classification used in psychiatry, and the one we will use, is by therapeutic usage. This classification yields four basic categories: antipsychotics, antidepressants, antimanic medications, and antianxiety agents. In the following sections we will describe representative psychotropics for the first three of these classifications (the antianxiety agents were described in Chapter 10).

Antipsychotics

As you will recall, the introduction of antipsychotic medications in the 1950s represented a major turning point in the treatment of severe psychiatric disorders, especially schizophrenia. "Schizophrenia" is a term that encompasses an array of psychotic disorders that can include a variety of disturbances in areas of functioning such as language, thought, affect, perception, and behavior. These disturbances, depending on the type of schizophrenia, could include distortions of reality (such as delusions and hallucinations), profoundly blunted mood, and withdrawn or bizarre behavior. The symptoms that are most likely to respond to antipsychotic medications are agitation, mania, hallucinations, delusions, fury, and accelerated and disorganized thinking processes (Magliozzi & Schaffer, 1988). It is estimated that schizophrenia affects approximately 1% of people over a lifetime, and the rate appears to be slightly higher among men than women (Lewine, 1988). Sometimes an individual will have previously or concurrently experienced a significant depressive or manic episode, in which case a diagnosis of schizoaffective disorder might be given, reflecting the presence of symptoms of schizophrenia and a major affective disorder.

To a lesser extent, these drugs also have been used in the treatment of mania, **agitated depression,** toxic (such as drug-induced) psychoses, emotionally unstable personalities, and psychoses associated with old age. Antipsychotic medications are also known as **neuroleptics** or major tranquilizers (the latter a term used much less frequently now). The term "neuroleptic" is derived from the Greek meaning "to clamp the neuron" (Snyder & Largent, 1989). "Antipsychotics" is the term more commonly used in the United States, with "neuroleptics" used in Europe. The terms are used interchangeably in this discussion. The major antipsychotic drugs are listed in Table 11-1.

The basic—but oversimplified—notion regarding antipsychotic medications is that they primarily affect the reticular activating system, the limbic system, and the hypothalamus. The effects on the reticular activating system generally moderate spontaneous activity and decrease the patient's reactivity to stimuli. The action within the limbic system serves to moderate or blunt emotional arousal. These actions are thought to produce the drug's dramatic effects on schizophrenic or agitated behavioral patterns. Because of these effects, antipsychotics remain the major approach to the drug treatment of schizophrenia. Below is a case example of clinical **paranoid schizophrenia.** The case is taken, with slight modification, from the DSM-III-R *Case Book* (Spitzer, Gibbon, Skodol, Williams, & First, 1989).

"Sometimes people are taking away parts of my body and putting them back. Sometimes I think they are going to kill me."

(22-year-old schizophrenic describing his thoughts and feelings, *Time,* July 6, 1992)

Agitated depression
Depressed mood accompanied by a state of tension or restlessness. Person shows excessive motor activity, as he or she may, for example, be unable to sit still, pace, wring the hands, or pull at his or her clothes.

Neuroleptic
Tranquilizing drugs used to treat psychoses. Another term for neuroleptic is major tranquilizer.

Paranoid schizophrenia
A type of schizophrenia distinguished by systematic delusions or auditory hallucinations related to one theme.

Table 11-1   Representative Antipsychotic Medications

	Generic Name	Trade Name
Phenothiazines		
	Chlorpromazine	Thorazine
	Prochlorperazine	Compazine
	Trifluoperazine	Stelazine
	Fluphenazine	Prolixin
	Thioridazine	Mellaril
Nonphenothiazines		
	Haloperidol	Haldol
	Thiothixene	Navane
	Loxapine	Loxitane
	Clozapine	Clozaril
	Molindone	Moban

Mr. Simpson is a forty-four-year-old, single, unemployed, white man brought into the emergency room by the police for striking an elderly woman in his apartment building. Mr. Simpson had been continuously ill since the age of twenty-two. During his first year of law school, he gradually became more and more convinced that his classmates were making fun of him. He noticed that they would snort and sneeze whenever he entered the classroom. When a girl he was dating broke off the relationship with him, he believed that she had been "replaced" by a look-alike. He called the police and asked for their help to solve the "kidnapping." His academic performance in school declined dramatically, and he was asked to leave and seek psychiatric care.

Mr. Simpson got a job as an investment counselor at a bank, which he held for seven months. However, he was getting an increasing number of distracting "signals" from co-workers, and he became more suspicious and withdrawn. It was at this time that he first reported hearing voices. He was eventually fired, and soon thereafter was hospitalized for the first time, at age 24. He has not worked since.

Mr. Simpson has been hospitalized 12 times, the longest stay being eight months. However, in the past five years he has been hospitalized only once, for three weeks. During the hospitalizations he has received various antipsychotic drugs. Although medication has been prescribed on an outpatient basis, he usually stops taking it shortly after leaving the hospital. Aside from twice-yearly lunch meetings with his uncle and his contacts with mental health workers, he is isolated socially. He lives on his own and manages his own financial affairs, including a modest inheritance. He reads the Wall Street Journal daily. He cooks and cleans for himself.

Mr. Simpson maintains that his apartment is the center of a large communication system that involves all three major television networks, his neighbors, and apparently hundreds of "actors" in his neighborhood. There are secret cameras in his apartment that carefully monitor all his activities. When he is watching TV, many of his minor actions, such as getting up to go to the bathroom, are soon directly commented on by the announcer. Whenever he goes outside, the "actors" have all been warned to keep him under surveillance. Everyone on the street watches him. His neighbors operate two different "machines"; one is responsible for all of his voices, except the "joker." He is not certain who controls this voice, which "visits" him only occasionally, and is very funny. The other voices, which he hears many times each day, are generated by this machine, which he sometimes thinks is directly run by the neighbor whom he attacked. For example, when he is going over his investments, these "harassing" voices constantly tell him which stocks to buy. The other machine he calls "the dream machine." This machine puts erotic dreams into his head, usually of "black women."

Mr. Simpson describes other unusual experiences. For example, he recently went to a shoe store 30 miles from his house in the hope of getting some shoes that wouldn't be "altered." However, he soon found out that, like the rest of the shoes he buys, special nails had been put into the bottom of the shoes to annoy him. He was amazed that his decision concerning which shoe store to go to must have been known to his "harassers" before he himself knew it, so that they had time to get the altered shoes made up especially for him. He realizes that great effort and "millions of dollars" are involved in keeping him under surveillance. He sometimes thinks this is all part of a large experiment to discover the secret of his "superior intelligence." (Published with permission of American Psychiatric Press, Inc.)

Although several theories address the action of antipsychotics, the predominant theory is the dopamine hypothesis. This theory is based on the observation of amphetamine-induced psychosis, which serves as a pharmacological model of schizophrenic behavior. The symptoms evidenced in this model psychosis are readily ameliorated through the use of neuroleptic drugs. Further, it appears that most amphetamine-induced psychotic behavior is mediated through increased release of dopamine in the brain. Thus, there are two core components to the dopamine theory: (1) Psychosis is induced by increased levels of dopaminergic activity and (2) most antipsychotic drugs block postsynaptic dopamine receptors (Baldessarini, 1985; Hollister, 1983). Unfortunately, it is not certain what leads to this dopaminergic overactivity in the first place.

It is believed that although antipsychotic medications block norepinephrine, serotonin, and acetylcholine, their primary action is as central dopamine antagonists (Gelenberg, 1991). That is, these drugs block central dopamine receptors and thus inhibit dopaminergic neurotransmission in the brain. The postsynaptic receptor blockade in the limbic system is thought to produce the reduction in schizophrenic symptoms.

The preceding represents the predominant beliefs regarding the actions of antipsychotic medications. This thinking, however, probably is best viewed as tentative, because much research is ongoing in an effort to identify the precise mechanisms of action that account for the effects of antipsychotic medications. Nevertheless, while the precise mechanisms underlying the actions of neuroleptics remain to be isolated, current knowledge does point to at least some role for dopamine in the modulation of psychotic behaviors (Snyder & Largent, 1989).

Although the antipsychotics have produced many positive effects in the treatment of mental disorders, their use is not without significant side effects. Antipsychotics also affect the **extrapyramidal** tract by blocking postsynaptic receptors in the basal ganglia, and these actions produce among the most profound of side effects associated with antipsychotics. Chief among the acute side effects are motor disturbances, which, taken together, give the appearance of a Parkinsonian syndrome. Persons with Parkinson's disease are typified by tremor, blank rigidity, gait and posture changes, and excessive salivation. Extrapyramidal symptoms are the most apparent motor disturbances, primarily **dyskinesia** (disordered movements) and **akinesia** (slowness of movement and underactivity). These symptoms result from the drug's effects on the extrapyramidal system. These are experienced acutely by more than 30% of patients receiving antipsychotics (Mackay, 1982). Autonomic side effects of antipsychotics are a result of the drug's actions on the hypothalamus. These side effects of antipsychotics tend to be dose-related: a greater

Extrapyramidal
Outside the pyramidal tracts, with origin in the basal ganglia. These cell bodies are involved with starting, stopping, and smoothing out movements.

Dyskinesia
Disordered movements.

Akinesia
Slowness of movement and underactivity.

degree of side effects is associated with higher doses of the antipsychotic medication.

The most common side effect associated with long-term use of antipsychotics is another extrapyramidal complication known as **tardive dyskinesia.** Tardive dyskinesia, which typically can be seen after two years or more of antipsychotic drug use, is characterized most often by repetitive involuntary movements of the mouth and tongue (often in the form of lip smacking), trunk, and extremities. Most cases of tardive dyskinesia are preceded by the Parkinson symptoms described earlier. The current estimates are that tardive dyskinesia occurs among 15–25% of treated patients (Gitlin, 1990), and many if not most of the tardive dyskinesia symptoms are permanent. The effects are seen more among women than men. Efforts to control or eliminate these effects include reducing the dose of the drug, which sometimes reduces the side effect and still provides some relief from the psychotic symptoms, administering medications designed to treat the side effects symptomatically (for example, benztropine [trade name Cogentin] or trihexyphenidyl [trade name Artane]), or instituting what are called "drug holidays," during which the patient is off medication to provide a physiological break from the use of the drug.

Although great strides have been made in the pharmacological treatment of psychotic disorders, concerted efforts in this area are continuing with several emphases. One focus is on developing neuroleptics providing symptom relief but acting through different mechanisms. The hope is to avoid or minimize the side effects (especially tardive dyskinesia) of current antipsychotic medications. A second emphasis is on developing neuroleptics which not only diminish the obvious symptoms such as hallucinations but also alleviate some less-visible symptoms, such as emotional withdrawal. New drugs are being investigated (see Contemporary Issue Box on "wonder drugs"). Some of these new drugs being studied do not appear to exert their effects by blocking dopamine receptors. These issues are discussed in more detail by Snyder and Largent (1989) and Gitlin (1990).

Tardive dyskinesia
An extrapyramidal complication characterized by involuntary movements of the mouth and tongue, trunk, and extremities. Tardive dyskinesia is a side effect of long-term (two or more years) use of antipsychotic drugs.

Contemporary Issue
"WONDER DRUGS": THE CASES OF PROZAC AND CLOZARIL

Every so often a psychotherapeutic drug enters the marketplace with such fanfare and potential that it is given the label "wonder drug." Sometimes these drugs live up to their early expectations, sometimes they do not.

Two psychiatric medications that have come onto the marketplace in recent years have been placed in the category of "wonder drugs." The first is the antidepressant Prozac (generic name, fluoxetine), and the second is Clozaril (generic name, clozapine), an antipsychotic medication. Both appear to offer great potential for the treatment of psychiatric disorders.

Prozac has received, by far, the greater amount of attention. Introduced in 1987, Prozac was the most prescribed antidepressant medication in the United

States by the early 1990s, and now is the world's top-selling antidepressant. One of the major advantages of Prozac is that it appears to have fewer and less-severe side effects than many of the previously available antidepressants. (Its actual efficacy in the treatment of depression does not appear to be greater than that of the tricyclics.) Although chemically unrelated to the tricyclic antidepressants, Prozac's mechanisms of action are similar to those of the tricyclics. As such, the drug acts to block neurotransmitter reuptake. However, while most of the tricyclics generally block the reuptake of both serotonin and norepinephrine, Prozac works exclusively on serotonin. (This is the case as well with two more recent antidepressants: sertraline [trade name Zoloft] and paroxetine [trade name Paxil].)

The major attractive feature of Clozaril for the treatment of psychotic and schizophrenic disorders is that it has yielded antipsychotic efficacy among patients who have not responded to other antipsychotics, such as haloperidol. In addition, Clozaril appears to produce a minimal degree of acute extrapyramidal side effects, and may be the only antipsychotic that does not produce tardive dyskinesia.

Clozaril is a member of the dibenzodiazepine class of drugs and is chemically related to loxapine, another antipsychotic. Clozaril, however, has greater serotonergic, adrenergic, and histaminergic blocking activity, relative to its dopamine-blocking effects. The drug may have its greatest impact among patients who have been chronically hospitalized for psychotic conditions, particularly patients who have been unresponsive to other drugs. However, as with all medications, Clozaril has side effects. The most significant concern with Clozaril is the occasionally seen side effect of agranulocytosis, a destructive condition in which the bone marrow stops producing white blood cells, opening the door to infection. If undetected, agranulocytosis results in death, so a very close monitoring of the patient is required. Agranulocytosis is observed in around 1–2% of patients placed on clozapine over a one-year period (Gitlin, 1990).

The ultimate roles of Prozac in the treatment of depression and of Clozaril in the treatment of psychotic conditions are not yet known. And each drug has had its share of controversies. There have been allegations, and associated lawsuits, claiming that Prozac can cause irrational or violent behavior and suicidal tendencies. The manufacturer of Clozaril has been widely criticized for the high price tag for a one-year supply of the drug (over $4,000, excluding the necessary monitoring blood tests), placing the drug out of reach of many who might otherwise benefit from it. Nevertheless, the prospects for each drug are promising, although the long-term outcomes still remain to be determined.

Antidepressants

Depression is among the most common psychiatric disorders in the United States. Approximately 8–10% of the population in the United States will experience a major depressive episode in their lifetimes. Depressions vary in severity, duration, and frequency of occurrence, and the most common symptoms contributing to what has been characterized as a depressive syndrome (as opposed to cases where a person might feel sad or blue) include dysphoric mood, loss of interest, disturbances in appetite and weight, sleep disturbance, fatigue, withdrawal, thoughts of suicide, and difficulties in concentration. Depressions frequently are classified either as **endogenous,** in which symptoms tend to be chronic and associated with genetic constitutional factors, or **exogenous,** in which symptoms are thought to be in response to some situation or event (Cooperrider, 1988). The average age for onset of a first depressive episode traditionally has been in the late 30s or early 40s, although such depressions are being seen more and more frequently among younger people. Further, the length of time for a depressive episode is variable, although periods of six months are common. Around 50% of the people who experience a major depressive episode do not have a recurrence of the illness (Coryell & Winokur, 1982).

The case below, excerpted from Spitzer et al. (1989), is an example of major depression rated as moderately severe.

> Connie is a 33-year-old homemaker who separated from her husband three months previously. She has a 4-year-old son, Robert.
>
> Connie left her husband, Donald, after a five-year marriage. Violent arguments between them, during which Connie was beaten by her husband, had occurred for the last four years of their marriage, beginning when she became pregnant with Robert. During their final argument, about

Endogenous
Developed from within. When applied to depression, the term means that depressive symptoms seem to be due to genetic factors.

Exogenous
Developed from without. When applied to depression, the term mean that depressive symptoms seem to be in reaction to a particular situation or event.

Common symptoms of depression are dysphoric mood, loss of interest, sleep disturbance, withdrawal, and difficulties in concentration.

Connie's buying an expensive tricycle for Robert, her husband had held a loaded gun to Robert's head and threatened to shoot him if she didn't agree to return the tricycle to the store. Connie obtained a court order of protection that prevented Donald from having any contact with her or their son. She took Robert to her parents' apartment, where they are still living.

Connie is an only child, and a high school and secretarial school graduate. She worked as an executive secretary for six years before her marriage and for the first two years after, until Robert's birth. Before her marriage Connie had her own apartment. She was close to her parents, visiting them weekly and speaking to them a couple of times a week. Connie had many friends whom she also saw regularly. She still had several friends from her high school years. In high school she had been a popular cheerleader and a good student. In the office where she had worked as a secretary, she was in charge of organizing office holiday parties and money collections for employee gifts.

During their first year of marriage, Donald became increasingly irritable and critical of Connie. He began to request that Connie stop calling and seeing her friends after work, and refused to allow them or his in-laws to visit their apartment. Connie convinced Donald to try marital therapy, but he refused to continue after the initial two sessions.

Despite her misgivings about Donald's behavior toward her, Connie decided to become pregnant. During the seventh month of the pregnancy, she developed thrombophlebitis and had to stay home in bed. Donald began complaining that their apartment was not clean enough and that Connie was not able to shop for groceries. He never helped Connie with the housework. He refused to allow his mother-in-law to come to the apartment to help. One morning when he couldn't find a clean shirt, he became angry and yelled at Connie. When she suggested that he pick some up from the laundry, he began hitting her with his fists. She left him and went to live with her parents for a week. He expressed remorse for hitting her and agreed to resume marital therapy.

At her parents' and Donald's urging, Connie returned to her apartment. No further violence occurred until after Robert's birth. At that time, Donald began using cocaine every weekend and often became violent when he was high.

In the three months since she left Donald, Connie has become increasingly depressed. Her appetite has been poor, and she has lost ten pounds. She cries a lot and often wakes up at five in the morning, unable to get back to sleep. Ever since she left Donald, he has been calling her at her parents' home and begging her to return to him. One week before her psychiatric evaluation, Connie's parents took her to their general practitioner. Her physical examination was normal, and he referred her for psychiatric treatment.

When seen by a psychiatrist in the outpatient clinic, Connie is pale and thin, dressed in worn-out jeans and dark blue sweater. Her haircut is unstylish, and she appears older than she is. She speaks slowly, describing her depressed mood and lack of energy. She says that her only pleasure is in being with her son. She is able to take care of him physically, but feels guilty because her preoccupation with her own bad feelings prevents her from being able to play with him. She now has no social contacts other than with her parents and her son. She feels worthless and blames herself for her marital problems, saying that if she had been a better wife, maybe Donald would have been able to give up the cocaine. When asked why she stayed with him so long, she explains that her family disapproved of divorce and kept telling her that she should try harder to make her marriage a success. She also thought about what her life would be like trying to take care of her son while working full time and didn't think she could make it. (Published with permission of American Psychiatric Press, Inc.)

Although stimulants once were used as a treatment for depression, their effectiveness was limited, especially among persons with severe depressions. Today stimulants are rarely used for depression. Instead, two central classes of antidepressant medications are prescribed; both act in a manner different from stimulants, which produce a euphoria that does not generally occur with the antidepressants (Cooperrider, 1988). The first are the cyclic antidepressants. Historically these were referred to as the tricyclic antidepressants (Cooperrider, 1988) because of their three-ring chemical structure nucleus. However, newer antidepressants have had more varied chemical structures and have been identified as heterocyclic antidepressants. We will use the term cyclic when referring to these antidepressants generally, and the term tricyclics when referring to that specific group of antidepressants. In the second class of antidepressants are the monoamine oxidase inhibitors (MAOIs).

Table 11-2   Representative Antidepressant Medications

	Generic Name	Trade Name
Cyclic Antidepressants		
	Fluoxetine	Prozac
	Imipramine	Tofranil, Imavate, Antipress
	Amitriptyline	Amitril, Elavil
	Desipramine	Norpramine
	Nortriptyline	Aventyl, Pamelor
	Doxepin	Sinequan, Adapin
	Protriptyline	Vivactil
	Amoxapine	Asendin
	Trimipramine	Surmontil
	Clomipramine	Anafranil
	Bupropion	Wellbutrin
	Maprotiline	Ludiomil
	Trazodone	Desyrel
	Sertraline	Zoloft
	Paroxetine	Paxil
MAOIs		
	Tranylcypromine	Parnate
	Isocarboxazid	Marplan
	Phenelzine	Nardil

Note: The most frequently prescribed antidepressant drug is fluoxetine (Prozac) (see associated Contemporary Issue Box).

The cyclics are used much more than the MAOIs in the treatment of depression in the United States; in Europe they are used about equally. Representative antidepressant medications are listed in Table 11-2.

Both the cyclics and MAOIs were available in the late 1950s. As with other psychiatric medications, their potential antidepressant effects were discovered serendipitously. The tricyclics initially were being investigated as antipsychotic agents, while the MAOIs initially were used in the treatment of tuberculosis. In both cases antidepressant effects were noted by investigators. It was observed, for example, that some tuberculosis patients treated with an MAOI showed an energized state. The cyclics and MAOIs represent the current mainstays of biological treatments for depression.

Before discussing the cyclics and MAOIs in more detail, it is necessary to discuss the postulated biochemical hypotheses for depression. It is believed that depression results from a deficiency in biogenic amines—specifically catecholamines and serotonin—which act as central nervous system neurotransmitters (see Chapter 3). According to the catecholamine hypothesis, depression is a result of a deficiency in catecholamines (particularly norepinephrine) at varied neuron receptor sites in the brain. The cyclics are believed to block the reuptake of norepinephrine from the synaptic cleft. Thus, there results a greater concentration of norepinephrine in the synaptic cleft, alleviating the hypothesized neurotransmitter deficiency. This cyclic-mediated process is thought to occur in the amygdala and reticular formation areas of the midbrain.

The catecholamine theory is derived in large part from observations of the effects of the antipsychotic agent reserpine, discussed earlier in the historical overview. Patients given reserpine often exhibit a depressed appearance. Further, reserpine was found to deplete brain concentrations of norepinephrine. Thus, there was the suggestion that such depletions were causally related to depression.

The serotonin hypothesis, the other central theory regarding antidepressant action, postulates that depression is the result of a deficiency of the neurotransmitter serotonin in the brain stem (Gelenberg & Schoonover, 1991; Kalus, Asnis, & van Praag, 1989). Persons who are depressed have reduced levels of serotonin and chemicals involved in its metabolism in their cerebrospinal fluid. As in the case with the catecholamine norepinephrine, the cyclics have been found to prevent the uptake of serotonin (Cooperrider, 1988).

While the cyclics block the uptake of amines, MAOIs prevent the breakdown of the neurotransmitters. As described by Cooperrider (1988), the enzyme monoamine oxidase metabolizes a variety of neurotransmitters, including norepinephrine and serotonin. MAOIs inhibit this degradation process and thus enhance the availability of the transmitter within the neuron. Thus, the actions of the cyclics and MAOIs each are consistent with the hypothesis that decreased brain catecholamine activity causes depression, and that these antidepressants (using different mechanisms) reverse this process by raising catecholamine activity in the brain (McNeal & Cimbolic, 1986).

Taken together, the cyclics and MAOIs each appear to enhance the functional activity of one or more neurotransmitters. But our understanding of the mechanisms remains clouded. One finding contributing to our lack of

DRUGS AND CULTURE
THE RIGHT TO REFUSE PSYCHIATRIC MEDICATIONS

As you are aware, countries and cultures vary considerably in the extent to which they tolerate freedom of speech and various other forms of behavioral expression. Not surprisingly, this often predicts the extent to which mentally ill patients (however defined) will have any say in how they are treated. In some cultures, the response to behaviors viewed as "different" or "mentally ill" is to subdue the person, through incarceration, restraints, drugs, or some combination of these interventions. In other cultures, treatment might include a more collaborative approach in which the patient discusses his or her problems with a counselor or works with a psychiatrist in trying different drugs to see how they work.

The United States has a long constitutional history of endorsing the rights of the individual. But how far should this privilege extend? For example, should a person voluntarily or involuntarily admitted to a psychiatric facility have the opportunity to refuse psychotropic drugs? For many years it was the case that people hospitalized for psychiatric treatment had little if any say in whether drugs would be administered, based in part on the assumption that they had no expertise in the area of psychiatric medications and that being hospitalized to begin with suggested some impairment in functioning and thus the ability to make decisions.

This issue has been addressed in a number of court cases over the years. In one case, seven Boston State Hospital patients filed suit to stop the (nonemergency) administration of medications without their first being able to provide their informed consent. Relatedly, the patients claimed the right to refuse medication. The psychiatrists faced a dilemma. On the one hand, they knew by experience certain drugs were able to significantly relieve emotional distress. On the other hand, some of these drugs had unpleasant side effects, and patients understandably might want to avoid these.

The court decided in favor of the patients. It ruled patients should be presumed (whether voluntarily or involuntarily admitted to the hospital) competent to accept or refuse psychotropic medications. The court added that when a patient was not deemed competent, the decision on whether to use medications needed to be made by a court-appointed guardian.

Is this the final word? No, probably not. Other cases are bound to come up, and could yield different rulings. In the late 1960s, for example, doctors in two states were successfully sued for not giving medications to committed patients who refused the drugs (see Gutheil, 1980). Furthermore, the practical implication of the Boston State Hospital case may not arise very often for the simple reason that hospitalized psychiatric patients do not frequently raise the issue of refusing their medications.

understanding is that the effects noted above occur within hours, although the therapeutic antidepressant action can take days or weeks to be experienced by the patient. Therefore, current theories regarding the actions of antidepressants probably best are viewed as tentative.

The cyclics and MAOIs are absorbed readily through the gastrointestinal tract. The cyclics are administered only rarely through injection, and MAOIs always are taken orally. Following absorption is the development of relatively high concentrations of the drugs in especially the brain, but also in other organs. After absorption, the antidepressant pharmacokinetics resemble those of the antipsychotics, especially chlorpromazine (Baldessarini, 1985). More is known of the absorption and distribution of the cyclics than of the MAOIs, in part because of the difficulty in isolating MAOI metabolites (Tyrer, 1982). Metabolism for each occurs primarily in the liver, with most excreted through the urine.

Despite the rapid absorption of antidepressant medications, one disadvantage (noted above) in their use is that clinical action frequently takes two to three weeks to be apparent in the patient's functioning. Unfortunately, it is during this initial period of use when most of the undesired side effects of antidepressants are experienced, and many patients terminate their use of the antidepressants because they experience the side effects in the absence of rapid symptom relief. The most common side effects of the cyclics are drowsiness and a variety of anticholinergic effects such as dry mouth, constipation and difficulty in urinating, blurred vision, orthostasis (dizziness upon standing up), and tachycardia. The most common side effects of the MAOIs are drowsiness, dry mouth, dizziness, and fatigue. In addition, MAOI use is associated with two other unwanted effects. The first is temporary low blood pressure when changing position (such as from sitting to standing) and the second is impaired sexual functioning. Men may experience impotence and difficulty in ejaculating, and women may report orgasmic inhibition. The use of MAOIs also requires several dietary restrictions. Most significant among these is avoiding substances which contain tyramine, such as most cheeses and some alcoholic beverages (especially Chianti wine). MAOIs and tyramine interact to cause potentially severe hypertensive reactions. Finally, a concern in the use of antidepressants is their potential for lethal use. Overdosing on cyclics can result in coma, respiratory difficulties, and a variety of cardiac problems. Accordingly, the patient's potential for suicide has to be assessed in order to prescribe most of the cyclics safely. MAOIs do not produce intoxicating effects, and overdosing on them is not common.

The therapeutic effects of antidepressants are impressive once the lag time has passed. The cyclics in particular show marked alleviation of depressive symptoms. MAOIs also have strong supportive treatment effectiveness rates when compared to placebos, although the positive outcomes are not as dramatic as with the cyclics. Also, MAOIs, when compared directly to cyclics, tend to be not as effective. This has led to a tendency, in the United States at least, for the cyclics to be a treatment of choice for most depressions, with MAOIs used when the cyclics do not produce desired results.

While the above drugs remain the mainstay in the treatment of depressive disorders, others continue to be developed (Gitlin, 1990). Trazodone (trade name Desyrel) and fluoxetine (trade name Prozac) (see Contemporary

Issue Box), both released in the 1980s, are examples. Trazodone has selective serotonergic effects but no apparent effect on norepinephrine reuptake. Fluoxetine is a potent serotonin reuptake inhibitor. Two others are bupropion (trade name Wellbutrin), released in 1989, and clomipramine (trade name Anafranil), released in 1990. Bupropion's actions are not fully understood, since it does not significantly impact on either norepinephrine or serotonin. Clomipramine, used for decades in Europe, has strong serotonergic effects. Such serotonergic effects also characterize two other antidepressants released in the 1990s: sertraline (trade name Zoloft) and paroxetine (trade name Paxil).

"What we're going to find out about the brain is mind-boggling. Every time a new drug is found another disease disappears, and makes one very curious about what other diseases have a biological basis."

(Drug therapist Dr. Paul Wender, *Newsweek*, March 26, 1990)

Mood-Stabilizing Drugs

The most specific treatment for the mood disorders of mania and bipolar disorder is lithium. Mania is a state in which there are pronounced elevations in mood and increased activity. Symptoms of a manic episode typically might include the following: increased talkativeness, flight of ideas or racing thoughts, grandiosity, decreased need for sleep, and excessive involvement in behaviors that can produce negative consequences (such as buying sprees or sexual indiscretions) (APA, 1994). While these symptoms may seem to describe someone who is "happy-go-lucky" or "pleasantly high," their occurrence and severity generally are profound and significantly disrupt the person's functioning. For persons with this disorder, the first manic episode generally occurs in their 20s or 30s, although there are exceptions in both directions. The natural course of an untreated manic episode is generally around a couple of months. Manic attacks generally are a component of what is called bipolar, or manic-depressive, disorder; periodic episodes of depression often are experienced by these individuals as well. The following case (Spitzer et al., 1989) illustrates the manic component of bipolar disorder. The case is an example of the development of manic symptoms late in life.

> A wealthy, 72-year-old widow is referred by her children, against her will, as they think she has become "senile" since the death of her husband 6 months previously. After the initial bereavement, which was not severe, the patient had resumed an active social life and become a volunteer at local hospitals. The family encouraged this, but over the past three months have become concerned about her going to local bars with some of the hospital staff. The referral was precipitated by her announcing her engagement to a 25-year-old male nurse, to whom she planned to turn over her house and a large amount of money. The patient's three sons, by threat and intimidation, have made her accompany them to this psychiatric evaluation.
>
> Initially in the interview the patient is extremely angry at her sons and the psychiatrist, insisting that they don't understand that for the first time in her life she is doing something for herself. She then suddenly drapes herself over the couch and asks the psychiatrist if she is attractive enough to capture a 25-year-old man. She proceeds to elaborate on her fiancé's physique and sexual abilities and describes her life as exciting and fulfilling for the first time. She is overtalkative and repeatedly

refuses to allow the psychiatrist to interrupt her with questions. She says that she goes out nightly with her fiance to clubs and bars and that although she does not drink, she thoroughly enjoys the atmosphere. They often go on to an after-hours place and end up breakfasting, going to bed, and making love. After only three or four hours' sleep, she gets up, feeling refreshed, and then goes shopping. She spends about $700 a week on herself and gives her fiance about $500 a week, all of which she can easily afford. (Published with permission of American Psychiatric Press, Inc.)

Lithium is an alkaline metal readily available throughout nature and is found in the form of silicate in such rocks as petalite, lepidolite, and spodumene (Tyrer & Shaw, 1982). (Most of the lithium used in the United States is mined in North Carolina.) Its mood-stabilizing properties were discovered in the 1940s. An Australian physician, John Cade, was giving research animals lithium in an attempt to decrease uric acid-induced kidney damage. In the course of his work, he observed a calming effect on the animals and speculated that lithium might be useful in humans as a mood attenuator (Baldessarini, 1985; Sack & De Fraites, 1977). Cade administered lithium to a sample of manic patients and observed positive responses. Subsequent research eventually led to lithium's approval for clinical use in the United States in 1970, although it was in clinical use in Europe several years prior. Although lithium may have some value in treating other psychiatric disorders (such as depression, some schizophrenias, alcoholism, impulsive-aggressive behaviors, and movement disorders), it is approved in the United States only in the treatment of manic episodes and prophylactically to prevent the recurrence of manic episodes. There is strong evidence that lithium is effective with these two indications. Lithium probably is, incidentally, the only drug in psychiatry for which there is effective prophylaxis against disease recurrence (Fieve, 1976; Sack & De Fraites, 1977).

As with the antidepressants discussed earlier, the major biological theory regarding mania concerns the monoamine neurotransmitters. In depression there was a hypothesized underactivity of neurotransmitters, and the hypothesis for mania is that there exists an increased functional activity of the neutrotransmitters. Within these hypotheses, the central focus is on catecholamines and serotonin. At the presynaptic level, lithium appears to enhance reuptake of serotonin and norepinephrine. Lithium also appears to decrease dopamine and norepinephrine effects at the postsynaptic receptors (Gitlin, 1990). Importantly, lithium serves to normalize the mood of manic patients, not just offset mania through sedation.

The most common preparations of lithium salts are carbonates (lithium carbonate, or Li_2CO_3), which are prepared in tablet form. In terms of pharmacokinetics, lithium, which is taken orally, is absorbed completely from the gastrointestinal tract (primarily the small intestine) and distributed throughout the system. The lithium is distributed in the body water and is not metabolized. Excretion occurs almost entirely by the kidneys, with between 90 and 95% eliminated through urine.

Despite its success in the treatment of mania, there are cautions which must be taken into account prior to and during lithium use. Several of these considerations pertain to lithium's therapeutic index, or safety margin. In this regard, the difference between the therapeutic and toxic levels is small. When the therapeutic range is exceeded, at least several of the following symptoms might be observed: drowsiness, blurred vision, ataxia, confusion, cardiac irregularities, and even seizures and coma. Some deaths have been reported. Thus, lithium use requires close medical supervision. Also, pretreatment medical work-ups are specifically geared toward ruling out cardiovascular problems or renal disease. Cardiac problems are a concern because toxic effects can cause cardiac irregularities, which could then exacerbate preexisting cardiovascular problems. Renal functioning must be satisfactory so that the lithium is efficiently excreted. If it is not, lithium will accumulate in the body. Finally, there are several side effects associated with lithium use, including gastrointestinal problems such as nausea, diarrhea, fine hand tremor, urinary frequency, and dry mouth. However, these side effects often decrease within a period of weeks.

While lithium remains the major drug used in the treatment of mania, other drugs are available when lithium is not tolerated by the patient or when the patient does not respond to the lithium. The most frequently used alternative is carbamazepine (trade name Tegretol), better recognized as an antiepileptic drug. Chemically related to the tricyclic antidepressants, carbamazepine has been shown to be effective with patients with rapid-cycling manic depressive episodes. Other alternatives to lithium that are available are clonazepam (trade name Klonopin) and valproic acid (trade name Depakene), another anticonvulsant drug.

PSYCHOTROPIC DRUGS AND PREGNANCY

No psychotropic medication is totally safe for use during pregnancy, and all carry FDA warnings regarding use when the patient is pregnant. As a result, a judgment needs to be made between the health of the mother on the one hand, and the risks to the unborn child on the other. The approach most recommended is that psychotropics not be used during pregnancy unless absolutely necessary, and only after nondrug interventions, such as counseling, have been tried first.

There are several reasons why psychotropic drug use during pregnancy is potentially unsafe. Certainly on one level, the risks to the mother are at least the same as when she is not pregnant. However, the risks are increased when one considers the variety of physical changes that occur during pregnancy, including alterations in metabolism and endocrine, renal, and cardiac changes (Kerns & Davis, 1986). These and other changes create an environment in which absorption, distribution, and excretion of the drug can occur. For example, one effect of antipsychotic medication on the mother is lowered blood pressure, which can compromise the placental blood flow to the fetus.

Risks are also faced by the fetus, particularly **teratogenic** effects, long-term effects on neurobehavioral functioning, and direct toxic effects of the drug. This is especially the case during the first trimester of pregnancy, when the most important fetal development occurs. Three points should be kept in

Teratogenic
Producing abnormalities in the fetus.

mind (Kerns & Davis, 1986). First, all classes of psychotropic drugs cross the placenta. Second, drug effects can change the blood flow within the placenta, influencing the transport and nutritive functions of the placenta. Third, the fetus, compared to an adult, has greater cardiac output and a greater proportion of blood flow to the brain. This results in a greater exposure of the drug to the brain.

The effects of psychotropic drugs on the fetus are not well-established. Most of the research has been conducted, for obvious reasons, on animals rather than humans. And the work involving humans, usually follow-up studies on women who used these drugs during pregnancy and their offspring, is hard to interpret. For example, many of the pregnant women who use psychotropic medications have used more than one drug and many have used other substances as well, such as alcohol or cigarettes: Nevertheless, there are indications that, although not well-established, various teratogenic, neurobehavioral, and toxic consequences can and do occur when psychotropics are used during pregnancy. Perhaps the most widely recognized effect is when lithium is used during the first trimester of pregnancy. Such use is associated with a significant teratogenic risk of cardiovascular system impairment.

summary

- Psychotropic medications are prescribed in hopes of providing mentally ill persons some relief and ideally the opportunity to function better within their environments.

- Early efforts to deal with mental illness included a variety of speculative approaches, many of which were cruel. These included bloodletting, hot irons, flogging, and starvation.

- Later on, in the mid-1800s, cannabis was studied as a treatment for depression and mania.

- During the first half of the 1900s, amphetamines were used in the treatment of depression and narcolepsy and carbon dioxide in the treatment of various psychotic and neurotic conditions.

- In 1949, the Australian physician John Cade discovered the benefits of lithium in the treatment of mania, and lithium remains a mainstay in the treatment of that disorder today.

- The greatest advance in psychopharmacology was the use, starting around 1950, of the drug chlorpromazine as an antipsychotic medica-

tion. A host of other drugs was introduced in the years following, including antianxiety medications (including meprobamate, a muscle relaxant) and antidepressant medications (including the tricyclic antidepressants and monoamine oxidase inhibitors).

- About 15% of the U.S. population experience some form of mental disorder in any given year. Most of the persons are experiencing symptoms associated with anxiety, depression, or alcohol abuse.

- More than 200 million prescriptions for the lawful use of psychotherapeutics are written yearly. Approximately 10 to 15% of the general population in any given year are given a prescription for a psychoactive agent, usually an antianxiety agent.

- Psychotropic drug use is more likely among women, older persons, persons living alone, the more educated, and those with higher income levels.

- The illicit use of prescription medications is a serious problem. Prescription drugs are a factor in a large number of drug-related emergency room cases and drug-related deaths. Information-gathering networks, such as the Client-Oriented Data Acquisition Process (CODAP) and Drug Abuse Warning Network (DAWN), have been established to monitor the distribution and use (legal and otherwise) of drugs overall, including psychotropic drugs.

- Psychotropic drugs can affect the neurotransmitter/receptor system in a number of ways. The prominent processes are by binding directly to the receptor site, serving as a receptor agonist or antagonist; by causing the release of more neurotransmitters; by blocking the reuptake of neurotransmitters back into the presynaptic neuron; by changing the number of receptor sites or the sensitivity of the receptors; by altering the metabolism of the neurotransmitter; and by altering the enzymatic degradation of the neurotransmitter.

- As with other drugs, psychiatric drugs can be classified in different ways. The most common way is by therapeutic use, and there are four major categories: antipsychotics, antidepressants, antianxiety agents, and mood-stabilizing drugs.

- Antipsychotic medications, also known as neuroleptics or major tranquilizers, are used to treat schizophrenia and other disorders, such as mania, agitated depression, toxic psychoses, emotionally unstable personalities, and psychoses associated with old age. These medications primarily affect the reticular activating system, the limbic system, and the hypothalamus.

- The dopamine hypothesis is the most accepted explanation of the action of antipsychotic medications. Two core elements of the dopamine hypothesis are: psychoses are induced by increased levels of dopaminergic activity; most antipsychotic drugs block postsynaptic dopamine receptors.

- Tardive dyskinesia is a major side effect of long-term use of antipsychotic drugs. It is most characterized by repetitive involuntary movements of the mouth and tongue, trunk, and extremities.

- Depression is one of the most common psychiatric disorders in the United States. Depression often is classified as one of two major types—endogenous or exogenous.

- Two major classes of antidepressant medications now are prescribed, cyclic antidepressants and monoamine oxidase inhibitors (MAOIs). In the United States, cyclics are prescribed more frequently than the MAOIs.

- Antidepressant medication treatment of depression follows from the biochemical hypothesis of the disorder. The hypothesis is that depression results from a deficiency in two biogenic amines—catecholamines and serotonin—which act as CNS neurotransmitters.

- Lithium is the major drug used in treating the mood disorders of mania and manic-depressive illness. Lithium is the only psychiatric drug that is an effective prophylaxis against disease recurrence.

- Use of lithium is based in the biological theory that bipolar disorder results from an overactivity of the neurotransmitters in the brain. Lithium appears to enhance reuptake of serotonin and norepinephrine at the presynaptic, and to decrease dopamine and norepinephrine effects at the postsynaptic receptors.

- No psychotropic drug is totally safe for use during pregnancy. The best approach is that psychotropic drugs be given to a pregnant woman only when necessary, and when nondrug therapies, such as counseling, have been tried and have failed.

- Psychotropic drug use during pregnancy poses a health risk to the mother and to the fetus. Although the experimental evidence is not solid, the fetus may face various teratogenic, neurobehavioral, and toxic consequences of its mother's use of psychotropic medications during pregnancy.

ANSWERS TO WHAT DO YOU THINK?

1. One of the first successful attempts to treat symptoms of mental illness with psychotropic drugs occurred in the 1840s when Moreau used cannabis to treat both depressed and manic patients.

T   *Depressed patients treated with cannabis became more talkative and happy, while manic patients calmed down and relaxed. Unfortunately, these effects were temporary.*

2. Since the 1950s, the number of hospitalized psychiatric patients has decreased significantly.

T   *The introduction of chlorpromizine was the starting point of this trend. Other factors contributing to the decrease in hospitalized psychiatric patients include the development of other psychotropic drugs and the movement toward deinstitutionalization.*

3. In the United States, psychiatric drugs are prescribed for about 10 to 15% of the population each year.

T   *Antianxiety agents are the most commonly prescribed psychiatric drug.*

4. The prevalence of psychiatric medication is twice as high among men as among women.

F   *The use of psychiatric medication is twice as high among women as among men.*

5. Psychiatric drugs are rarely abused.

F   *The nonprescribed use and abuse of psychiatric drugs are a significant problem.*

6. As with most drugs, the age group least likely to misuse psychiatric drugs is the elderly.

F   *The elderly are the age group most likely to misuse psychiatric drugs.*

7. Most psychiatric medications are administered intravenously, where direct transport in the bloodstream occurs.

F   *Most psychiatric medications are taken orally, are absorbed in the gastrointestinal tract, and are modified in the liver before being transported in the bloodstream.*

8. Schizophrenia is one of the most common psychiatric disorders in the United States.

F   *Schizophrenia affects only about 1% of the population.*

9. Stimulants are often used to treat chronic depression.

F   *Although stimulants were once used as a treatment for depression, their effectiveness is limited. Antidepressant medications are generally used to treat depression.*

10. Because antidepressants are absorbed rapidly, their effects are often immediate.

F   *Despite the rapid absorption, the effects of antidepressant medications take two to three weeks to become apparent.*

11. Lithium, a natural alkaline metal, is often used to treat manic attacks.

T   *Although lithium may have some value in treating other disorders, its use in the United States is approved only for treatment of manic episodes.*

12. Most psychiatric drugs pose little or no threat to the fetus and may be used safely during pregnancy.

F   *In the case of many psychotropic drugs taken during pregnancy, the fetus faces the risk of teratogenic effects, long-term effects on neurobehavioral functioning, and the direct toxic effects of the drug. Therefore, it is most often recommended that psychotropic drugs not be used during pregnancy unless absolutely necessary.*

12 Opiates

WHAT DO YOU THINK?

True or False?

____ Opium comes from a plant called *Cannabis sativa*.

____ Morphine is one of the active ingredients in opium.

____ Heroin was first made illegal by the 1965 Drug Abuse Control Amendments.

____ Use of "dirty" needles is now one of the major causes of AIDS.

____ Most designer heroin compounds are less potent than pure heroin.

____ The opiates are among the most powerful analgesic drugs.

____ Heroin enhances sexual desire and activity.

____ Opiate drugs show cross-dependence with alcohol.

____ Heroin withdrawal is much like alcohol withdrawal.

____ Veterans of the Vietnam War had a high rate of heroin addiction and were unable to kick the habit when they returned to the United States.

____ The effects of opiates can be potentiated by alcohol.

____ The expression "cold turkey" comes from the goosebumps seen in addicts withdrawing from heroin.

As indicated in historical overviews in earlier chapters, psychoactive drugs can be two-edged swords in their great potential for improving the human condition on one hand, and their capacity to cause destruction to individuals and society on the other. No group of drugs captures this paradox more dramatically than the class of drugs we call opiates, which includes opium, morphine, heroin, and a number of related compounds. Opiate drugs have been used for many centuries to relieve pain and, when introduced to Europe, were hailed by physicians as a godsend. One of the first European physicians to use opium to relieve pain and suffering in his patients, Thomas Sydenham, wrote in 1680: "Among the remedies which it has pleased Almighty God to give man to relieve his sufferings, none is so universal and so efficacious as opium" (cited in Gay & Way, 1972, p. 47). Even today opiate drugs remain the most potent painkillers available to physicians, yet we now recognize the other edge of the opiate sword—the ability of opiates to produce severe dependence. Heroin is viewed as the prototypic addictive drug, and illegal use and traffic in heroin is a major international problem. Thus, many of the concerns in general regarding psychoactive drugs emerge in bold relief in a consideration of opiates.

EARLY HISTORY OF THE OPIATES

Opium comes from *Papaver somniferum*, one of the many species of the poppy plant. The opium poppy is native to the Middle East in the areas that border the Mediterranean Sea, but it is now cultivated extensively throughout Asia and the Middle East. Contrary to the experiences of Dorothy in *The Wizard of Oz*, however, simply walking through a poppy field will not cause sleep or euphoria. Rather, to experience the active drug effects, special procedures must be followed. The petals fall after the poppy blooms, leaving a round seedpod the size of an egg. If the seed pod is scored lightly with a knife, a milky white sap is secreted. After drying, this sap forms a thick, gummy, brown substance that is called **opium.** Opium effects may be obtained by consuming the substance orally or by smoking it. The use of such crude opium preparations is truly an ancient practice. There is evidence that opium was cultivated and used as long as 6,000 years ago by the Sumerian and Assyrian civilizations. The ancient Egyptians had discovered medical uses for opiates 3,500 years ago, as documented in the "Therapeutic Papyrus of Thebes" (Scott, 1969). Opium also was used for a variety of medical purposes by the Greek and Roman civilizations. The great Greek physician, Galen (A.D. 130–201) noted the following uses for opium:

> "(opium) . . . resists poison and venomous bites, cures chronic headache, vertigo, deafness, epilepsy, apoplexy, dimness of sight, loss of voice, asthma, coughs of all kinds, spitting of blood, tightness of breath, colic, the iliac poison, jaundice, hardness of the spleen, stone, urinary complaints, fevers, dropsies, leprosies, the troubles to which women are subject, melancholy and all pestilences" (Scott, 1969, p. 111).

Opium
The dried sap produced by the poppy plant.

Opium exudes from incisions of the poppy *Papaver somniferum*.

Analgesia
Pain relief produced without a
loss of consciousness.

Although this quote may seem more a testament to the ignorance of medical problems of this age, certainly the remarkable **analgesic** (pain-relieving) properties of opium must have made it at least seem helpful for many disease states. In fact, opiate drugs do have special cough-suppressant and antidiarrhea properties in addition to their analgesic actions and are used in modern medicine for these purposes.

The use of opium for medical and recreational purposes became widespread among the Islamic peoples of the Middle East. This may have been because the Koran's explicit prohibition of the use of alcohol and some other drugs did not include opiate use (Latimer & Goldberg, 1981). To this day use of opiates is less censored than alcohol among Muslims. Arab traders spread the use of opium to India and China by the ninth century, and it was in China that the practice of smoking opium developed. Dependence on opium was first recognized as a problem in China as well with the first edict against opium issued in 1729. But there were already so many opium addicts in China that the demand remained very high. In spite of the ban on importing opium into China, British ships continued to trade opium grown in India for Chinese tea, and this activity was the basis for the "Opium Wars" between China and Great Britain in the middle of the nineteenth century (see Chapter 2).

Opium dependence was a serious problem in China by the beginning of the nineteenth century, but it was not yet seen as such in Europe or America. Although opium was readily available in the form of Laudanum, a beverage containing opium, and various patent medicines, it almost always was taken orally (a practice called opium eating, even though it was really opium drinking) rather than smoked. It was used mostly for medical purposes. There were a number of developments during the century bringing the addictive properties of opiate drugs to the awareness of Western societies. As noted in Chapter 2, opium preparations were readily available and completely legal in nineteenth-century Europe and the United States. It was probably only a matter of time before the pleasurable properties of opium led to widespread use for nonmedical reasons. The pleasures of opium were brought to public awareness in a book written by the British poet Thomas de Quincey, *Confessions of an Opium Eater*, published in 1822. De Quincey's book praised the effects of opium and included several famous quotes including: ". . . thou hast the keys of Paradise, O just, subtle and mighty opium!" (Scott, 1969, p. 52). Westerners were slow in recognizing that "eating" opium could prove just as addictive as smoking it, but as the use of opium, fueled by tomes such as de Quincey's, became more widespread, so did concern about the drug. By the late 1800s opium use had spread throughout society affecting such noted literary and scientific figures as Elizabeth Barrett Browning, Samuel Coleridge, William Halstead, Walter Scott, and Percy Shelley, to name a few. It was becoming recognized that opium dependence was not limited to the Chinese.

Pharmacological developments added to the problems. In 1803 the German pharmacist F. W. Serturner developed the process which allowed the separation of morphine from opium. Morphine is the major active chemical in opium (codeine is another opiate drug found in opium) and is about 10 times more potent than crude opium. Serturner experimented with morphine and was so impressed with the blissful, dreamlike state it induced that he named the chemical after Morpheus, the Greek god of dreams. Morphine became

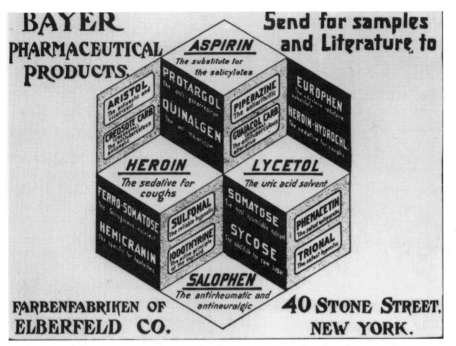

Patent medicines of the 19th century frequently contained opiates such as heroin.

widely available in the middle 1800s, and with the concomitant development of the hypodermic syringe, injected morphine became a major dependence problem in Europe and the United States. Because of the rapid and potent pain-relieving properties of injectable morphine, it became the treatment of choice during periods of recovery from severe wounds. However, withdrawal from the morphine was often more difficult than recovery from the wound. As noted in Chapter 2, morphine dependence was so common among soldiers on both sides during the Civil War in America that it was often called "Soldier's Disease." In 1874 British chemist Alder Wright published experiments describing the production of a new chemical compound based on an alteration of morphine: diacetylmorphine. Wright's discovery went unnoticed until 1898 when the great German pharmacologist Heinrich Dreser (who also discovered aspirin—see Chapter 15) rediscovered the compound and noted that it was almost 10 times more potent than morphine. Because this new compound was so powerful it was viewed as a new treatment with "heroic" possibilities and was christened **heroin.** Heroin was used immediately as a cough suppressant and pain-reliever. Not until many years later was it recognized that heroin was even more likely than morphine to produce dependence.

Heroin
Heroin is produced by chemically processing morphine. It is more potent than morphine, and has become the major opiate drug of abuse.

OPIATE USE IN THE TWENTIETH CENTURY

The growing awareness of the danger and pervasiveness of opiate dependence led to a number of legal changes reviewed in detail in Chapter 2. In the

United States these culminated in the 1914 Harrison Act. Of course, the Harrison Act did not eliminate completely nonmedical use of opiates and, in fact, marked the origin of drug crime in America. Illegal opiate use meant smuggling of opium and heroin into the country, escalating prices, and a change in the type of person who became or remained addicted to opiates. The Harrison Act placed control of opiate drugs in the hands of physicians, and the determination of whether an addict had a valid medical need for opiates was exclusively the physician's decision. However, several legislative interpretations ruled a physician must not prescribe opiates unless doses could be shown to be decreasing over time (1915), that opiates must not be prescribed to addicts (1917), and in 1924 that heroin might not be prescribed at all (Kramer, 1972). The legitimate channels for obtaining drugs now were blocked for many addicts, so they turned to a growing black market to maintain their addiction.

There have been many changes in opiate use since the Harrison Act. One major change involved the demographics of opiate use. Opiate addiction cut across social classes in the pre-Harrison Act era. A wealthy middle-aged woman was as likely to be an opiate addict as anyone, but she would be addicted to Laudanum purchased at her drugstore. When opiates became illegal, their use became focused in large cities where organized crime provided a source. In addition, users tended more and more to be young, poorly educated persons of lower socioeconomic status (Latimer & Goldberg, 1981), which is still the case. Finally, the more potent heroin has come to be the addict's drug of choice. Although there was widespread use of opiates by American GIs during the Vietnam War, that made only a small change in these demographic patterns. As reviewed in Chapter 1, current survey data reveal heroin and other opiate use is relatively infrequent among high school and college students. For example, less than 1% of American high school seniors reported any heroin use during any of the past 10 years (Johnston, O'Malley, & Bachman, 1991). Although many different opiate drugs are prescribed for pain today, and certainly some users become dependent upon them, the major opiate problem in the United States today relates to heroin use, and that problem is usually centered in the inner cities.

A huge criminal apparatus for producing and supplying heroin was spawned in the wake of the Harrison Act. Today opium largely is grown in the Middle East (Afghanistan, Pakistan, Iran) or Southeast Asia (Laos, Myanmar [formerly called Burma], and Thailand), and Mexico (Inciardi, 1992). From Europe or Mexico the heroin is smuggled into the United States. Most of the opium grown for legitimate medical purposes is cultivated in India or Australia. Street heroin is adulterated or cut many times as it changes hands on the way from the importer to those who sell to individual users. Heroin remains a large and important source of revenue and helps supply recruits for organized crime. It has been noted that most heroin addicts must get involved in criminal activity in order to support their habit. At first the cost of heroin may appear relatively low to the addict who uses the drug occasionally for "kicks." But in the words of an addict interviewed by Smith and Gay (1972): "It's so good, don't even try it once." Many users find that they take the drug more and more frequently, and since tolerance develops rapidly to heroin and other opiates, higher doses are soon required to produce the desired effect.

Soon the cost of maintaining the growing habit virtually forces the addict to engage in criminal activities. Here is another interview with a street addict from San Francisco:

> (Heroin) . . . is the mellowest downer of all. You get none of the side effects of speed and barbs. After you fix, you feel the rush, like an orgasm if it's good dope. Then you float for about four hours; nothing positive, just a normal feeling, nowhere. It's like being half asleep, like watching a movie; nothing gets through to you, you're safe and warm. The big thing is, you don't hurt. You can walk around with rotting teeth and a busted appendix and not feel it. You don't need sex, you don't need food, you don't need people, you don't care. It's like death without permanence, life without pain.
>
> For me, the only hard part is keeping in H, paying my connection, man. I know these rich cats who can get good smack and shoot it for years and nothing happens, but me, you know, it's a hustle to stay alive. I run about a $100, $150-a-day habit, so I have to cop twice that much to keep my fence happy . . . (Luce, 1972, p. 145).

Heroin addiction is a hard way to live for a number of other reasons. Addicts are at great risk for disease and death from AIDS, hepatitis, and other needle-borne diseases from sharing contaminated needles (see the

A user prepares to inject heroin.

Contemporary Issue Box). Current estimates place the number of heroin addicts in the United States in the vicinity of 500,000 (Inciardi, 1992), and recent reports suggest that heroin use may be on the rise (*Time*, 1993). Although the number of heroin addicts is small relative to the extent of alcoholism or nicotine dependence, it poses significant societal risks. Risk of overdose or complications from contaminated street heroin is always present. The National Institute on Drug Abuse (NIDA) estimates heroin overdose is responsible for more than 1,000 deaths every year. With the death toll from needle-borne disease, heroin addiction remains a very serious social problem.

Contemporary Issue
FATAL ATTRACTION: INTRAVENOUS DRUG USE AND AIDS

The National Institute on Drug Abuse estimates 900,000 Americans are regular intravenous (IV) drug users, and that another 200,000 inject drugs at least occasionally. The majority of these IV drug users are heroin addicts, but many inject cocaine or methamphetamine. They may be young or old, black or white, male or female, but one thing they have in common is that they are at great risk for developing Acquired Immune Deficiency Syndrome—AIDS. In the early 1980s male homosexuals were the major group at high risk for AIDS, but drug-related AIDS cases have risen so sharply in the past few years that they now account for one-third of all new AIDS cases. Recent reports indicate that 24% of all current AIDS cases in the United States are thought to have contracted the virus through IV drug use. When women are considered separately the problem is even more striking: 55% of female AIDS cases were related to IV drug use (Rathus, Nevid, & Fichner-Rathus, 1993). The magnitude of the problem is considerable now, and likely to get worse. A recent study of IV drug users (Dasgupta et al., 1993) in New York City found that more than half were infected with the human immunodeficiency virus (HIV). Moreover, it is not just the users who are involved. Heterosexual spread of the virus is occurring and the babies born of HIV-positive mothers will usually develop AIDS as well.

An ironic aspect of this tragedy is that it is so avoidable. IV drug users are at risk for AIDS only because of the common practice of sharing needles. By using a needle contaminated with the blood of someone with HIV, direct blood-to-blood transmission occurs, which involves a very high risk of infection. If sterile needles were used, this risk would be eliminated. Health care workers are striving to send the message out to IV drug users that they should avoid sharing needles, or clean them with bleach if sharing is necessary. New York City has even developed a needle exchange, where clean needles are given to users in exchange for dirty ones. However, in most areas in the country, hypodermic syringes are controlled legally and remain difficult for addicts to obtain. In addition, sharing needles has become part of the "culture" for users. IV drug use often occurs in "shooting galleries," places where people gather to inject and enjoy the effects of the drug. A single needle may be used to deliver dozens of injections in such a place, unbeknownst to the users. Unless these practices can be stopped, the desire to use IV drugs will remain a fatal attraction.

Another development involving opiate drug use is the disturbing availability of "designer" heroin. Designer heroin is produced illicitly by chemists who design or develop chemical analogues to heroin. These new compounds are untested, but usually produce effects similar to those of heroin or other opiates. Until recently they had the advantage to the dealer of not being controlled under federal law, because in some cases they are compounds that are new to science. Most of the designer heroin compounds are derivatives of the powerful opioid, fentanyl. The problem with these fentanyl derivatives (often sold on the street as China White) is that they may be 10 to 1,000 times more potent than heroin. Thus, the risk of overdose death is greater. Numerous overdoses are now being attributed to designer heroin (Kirsch, 1986). Another example of problems caused by a designer heroin was noted earlier (see Chapter 3). A synthetic opiate known as MPPP when improperly synthesized yields a compound called MPTP. MPTP is metabolized in the brain to a toxic chemical: MPP+, which kills cells in the substantia nigra, and produces a neurological disorder that closely resembles Parkinson's disease. Thus designer heroin compounds are often far more dangerous than heroin. As noted in Chapter 2, to control the development and spread of designer drugs, Congress enacted legislation called the Controlled Substance Analogue Act of 1986.

ABSORPTION, DISTRIBUTION, METABOLISM, AND EXCRETION

Opiate drugs may be taken into the body in a variety of ways. Most are readily absorbed from the gastrointestinal tract, although the effect of a given dose is greater if it is injected intravenously. Most opioids also are absorbed through the nasal mucosa and lungs. Thus, opium often is smoked, and heroin frequently is taken intranasally. Opiates are also absorbed after intramuscular or subcutaneous administration. On the street, for example, heroin may be injected intravenously ("mainlining") or subcutaneously ("skin-popping").

Once in the bloodstream, opioids are distributed throughout the body with accumulations in the kidneys, lungs, liver, spleen, digestive tract, and muscles as well as the brain. With some opiates, such as morphine, only a small amount penetrates the blood-brain barrier. In fact, the main difference between morphine and the more potent drug, heroin, is that heroin is more lipid-soluble and thus more readily penetrates the blood-brain barrier. Once in the brain, heroin is converted to morphine. So heroin is essentially a more effective package for delivering morphine to the brain than morphine itself.

Most opiate drugs are rapidly metabolized in the liver and excreted by the kidneys. Excretion of opiates is fairly rapid, with 90% excretion within a day after taking the drug. However, traces of morphine may remain in urine for two to four days after use (Hawks & Chiang, 1986).

MECHANISMS OF OPIATE ACTION

One of the most exciting developments in the neurosciences was the discovery in the 1970s of the neural mechanisms of action of opiate drugs. Research on this topic led to the discovery of a class of brain chemicals called the endorphins, which apparently function as neurotransmitters. It is now believed the effects of heroin, morphine, and other opiate drugs are produced by triggering activity in the brain's endorphin systems (Dykstra, 1992). We will review the events leading to these discoveries and consider how these new developments have helped us understand the effects of opiate drugs.

One of the first events was the discovery by chemists in the 1960s that making a rather slight change in the morphine molecule resulted in a chemical that did not produce any of the standard opiate drug effects (pain relief, euphoria), but instead reversed or blocked the effects of morphine and other opiate drugs. This compound is called **naloxone (Narcane)** and may be described as an opiate antagonist. When naloxone is given to a patient suffering from an overdose of heroin or morphine, it will reverse completely the effects of those drugs. If naloxone is given to someone who then takes heroin, the heroin has no effect. Obviously naloxone has practical applications in the treatment of opiate overdose, but it also has theoretical implications. Since naloxone's chemical structure is similar to morphine, it seemed to researchers the two drugs might be acting at some common brain receptor site and that morphine's action at that site was blocked by the naloxone. In the early 1970s, two researchers at Johns Hopkins University in Baltimore, Candace Pert and Solomon Snyder, reported they had discovered brain receptors

Naloxone (Narcane)
A brief-acting opiate antagonist.

Acupuncture analgesia may be produced by endorphin release.

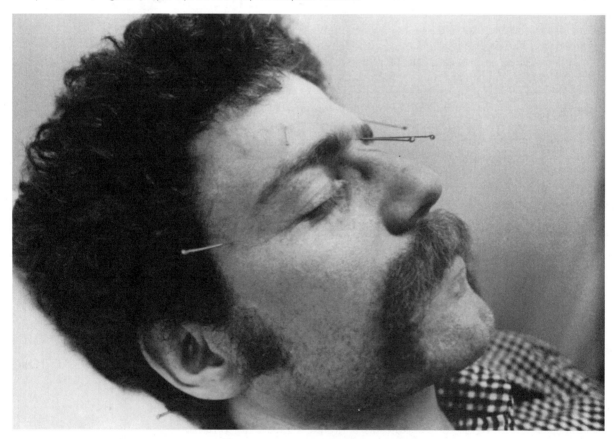

that responded selectively to opiate drugs, and these were dubbed "opiate receptors" (Pert & Snyder, 1973). The existence of opiate receptors was of great interest. One might reasonably wonder why there would be neurons in the brain that responded to such drugs. Did nature somehow intend us to be heroin addicts? Neuroscientists had a different notion. They believed the presence of such receptors must mean there existed natural brain chemicals with morphine-like structure and properties. The search was on for the "brain's own opiates," and in 1975 several such chemicals were discovered (Snyder, 1989). Although there appear to be several morphine-like substances found in the brain (beta-endorphin, enkephalin, and dynorphin are the most important compounds), these complex peptide molecules are referred to collectively as endorphins, a contraction of endogenous morphine.

The scientific questions emanating from the discovery of the endorphins have focused on just why the brain is endowed with its own morphine: what do endorphins do? Much of this ongoing work has started with the premise that because opiate drugs apparently mimic endorphin activity by stimulating the opiate or endorphin receptor sites in the brain, then endorphins might share many properties with opiate drugs, such as pain relief and production of pleasure. Probably the most clearly established function of endorphins is as part of a natural pain-relief system. Current thinking is that after certain kinds of pain or stress, endorphins are released and analgesia or pain relief occurs (Snyder, 1989). This may help explain why under certain circumstances, such as on the battlefield or in athletic events, a person may sustain severe injury, but at least for a time not feel pain. Pain relief produced by acupuncture is probably related to endorphin release, because naloxone can reverse acupuncture-induced analgesia (Han & Terenius, 1982). Because the major action of naloxone is to block the endorphin receptors, naloxone-reversible analgesia is strong evidence that the acupuncture needles are triggering the release of endorphins and relieving pain through this system.

Similarly, vigorous exercise has been shown to result in increased release of endorphins and it is possible that some of the positive effects of exercise on mood, such as the so-called "runner's high," are related to endorphin effects (Farrell & Gustafson, 1986; Steinberg & Sykes, 1985). In fact, some researchers seriously have proposed that the "addiction" to exercise some people seem to develop may occur through the same brain mechanisms as heroin addiction (Davis, 1984)! Can we become addicted to our own brain chemicals?

TOLERANCE AND DEPENDENCE

Many researchers believe that research on endorphins ultimately may help us to understand the phenomena of addiction to opiates and perhaps other drugs as well. One problem with opiate drugs is, of course, that tolerance develops to many of their effects when they are taken regularly. A related problem exists after tolerance has developed. Abstinence from opiates produces dramatic and unpleasant withdrawal symptoms (more detail later in this chapter). There is good reason to believe tolerance and withdrawal symptoms produced by opiate drugs are related to activity at the endorphin receptors.

One piece of supporting evidence is that naloxone can precipitate withdrawal in opiate-dependent subjects (Wei, Loh, & Way, 1973). Thus, if a heroin addict is administered a dose of naloxone she or he immediately will begin to experience withdrawal symptoms, even if she or he has just shot up heroin! Another line of evidence comes from studies showing that if chronic morphine administration always is paired with naloxone, neither tolerance nor withdrawal symptoms develop (Hendrie, 1985). Thus, activation of the endorphin receptors seems to be involved in some way with tolerance to and dependence on opiate drugs. There are several theories for just how this might work, but it is suspected that chronic use of opiates may alter the production of endorphins or the number of available receptor sites, and that these changes are in some way responsible for tolerance and abstinence phenomena (Snyder, 1989).

MEDICAL USE OF OPIATE DRUGS

The major medical use of opiate drugs is for their analgesic or pain-relieving effects. As noted above, opiates have been used for this purpose for centuries and remain the most potent and selective pain-relievers known to medicine. Unlike the depressant-type anesthetic drugs discussed earlier, opiate analgesics are described as relieving pain without causing unconsciousness. After receiving moderate doses of opiates, patients remain conscious and still are able to report painful sensations, but do not suffer from the pain.

The other major drugs that possess such analgesic properties are the over-the-counter painkillers: aspirin, acetaminophen, and ibuprofen (see Chapter 15). Table 12-1 shows some of the major opiate drugs used as analgesics, along with their potency and their duration of action. Recall that potency refers to the dose required for a drug to produce a given effect. In Table 12-1, potency is given relative to an effective dose of morphine. For example, heroin has a value of four in Table 12-1. This means that if 8 mg of morphine were required to relieve pain in a given patient, only 2 mg of heroin would be required. In other words, heroin is four times as potent as morphine. Mor-

Table 12-1   Comparison of the Major Opiate Drugs

Generic Name	Brand Name	Potency	Duration (hrs) of Action
Morphine		1	4–5
Heroin		4	3–4
Hydromorphone	Dilaudid	5	4–5
Codeine		.1	4–6
Oxycodone	Percodan	.75	4–5
Methadone	Dolophine	1	24–48
Meperidine	Demerol	.1	2–4
Propoxyphene	Darvon	.05	6
Fentanyl	Sublimaze	80	1–3
Pentazocine	Talwin	.2	2–3

Note: Potency estimates are presented relative to an effective dose of morphine (1). Table is based in part on Jaffe and Martin (1985).

phine is the prototypic opiate analgesic and is the standard by which others are measured. It is used primarily when pain is very severe. As we have noted, although heroin is more potent than morphine, it is not used medically in the United States because it is a Schedule I drug. It is, however, used in other countries (see nearby Contemporary Issue Box).

When pain is less severe, drugs less potent than morphine may be used. Thus, codeine, propoxyphene (Darvon), oxycodone (Percodan), and pentazocine (Talwin) often are prescribed for pain (see Table 12-1). Finally, there are some opiates even more potent than heroin: fentanyl is 80 times as potent. Fentanyl is used primarily to produce anesthesia. In general, opiate drugs are the most potent and effective drugs available to medicine in the treatment of

Contemporary Issue
HEROIN AND PAIN RELIEF

One risk of using opiate drugs for pain relief is addiction. To reduce this, less potent opiates are used whenever possible and treatment is as brief as possible. However, when pain is severe and chronic, as with terminal cancer patients, tolerance inevitably develops, and higher doses of more potent drugs must follow if the patient's pain is to be relieved. Ultimately, high doses of morphine may be the only way of relieving the patient's suffering. Eventually even this may not be enough. In Great Britain, physicians then may use the potent opiate, heroin. In fact, a preparation called Brompton's cocktail, composed of heroin and cocaine, is administered sometimes to the terminally ill in Great Britain (Jaffe & Martin, 1985). However, because heroin is a Schedule I drug, it may not be administered by doctors in the United States.

Should physicians in the United States be permitted to administer heroin? One argument against this is that, because of its potency, heroin is more addicting than morphine. However, in the cases of the severe pain of the terminally ill patient, addiction seems somewhat irrelevant. Besides, patients normally are receiving doses of morphine that are high and frequent enough that they certainly are addicted to morphine by the time heroin treatment is begun. Heroin is converted to morphine in the brain, and thus morphine is the active chemical in producing pain relief in both cases (heroin is more potent because it penetrates the blood–brain barrier more efficiently). One could accomplish the same degree of pain relief by giving higher and higher doses of morphine. But terminal cancer patients often become very thin, and with repeated injections may lose tone in their veins. Thus, it may become difficult to administer enough morphine solution to be effective. Here is where the more potent heroin can be of value, because less solution is required. Moving heroin to Schedule II would make it possible for physicians to elect to administer heroin but should not make it any more difficult to control heroin addiction. Yet the move remains controversial, perhaps because it is seen as a softening of the heroin laws. A potential solution may come with the development of more potent opiate drugs that have not yet acquired the stigma associated with heroin.

pain. The limitations of their use as analgesics are primarily the tendency of these drugs to produce tolerance and dependence. Tolerance and dependence develop for all these drugs, although some, such as pentazocine (Talwin), for example, are thought to possess less abuse liability than others. It is hoped safer analgesic drugs will be developed as more is learned about endorphins and their ability to produce natural analgesia.

There are other medical uses for opiate drugs. Opiates have a constipating effect that can be a problem for addicts but is of value in treating diarrhea. Opiates still are used to treat coughs. The drug most commonly used for this purpose is dextromethorphan, which is a synthetic opiate with no analgesic or addictive properties, but is an effective cough suppressant (Jaffe & Martin, 1985). A final medical use for opiates such as methadone is in the treatment of heroin addicts in withdrawal and in maintenance programs designed to help addicts stay off heroin (see Chapter 17).

ACUTE PSYCHOLOGICAL AND PHYSIOLOGICAL EFFECTS OF OPIATES

There are a number of acute effects of opiate drugs in addition to analgesia. Subjective reports of the euphoria produced by opiates include drowsiness, body warmth, and a heavy feeling of the limbs (Jaffe & Martin, 1985). William S. Burroughs describes the feeling in his autobiographical novel *Junky*: "Morphine hits the backs of the legs first, then the back of the neck, a spreading wave of relaxation slackening the muscles away from the bones so that you seem to float without outlines, like lying in warm salt water" (Burroughs, 1953, p. 7). The pleasure experienced under the influence of opiates seems to interfere with other interests on the part of the user. Burroughs described it as follows: "Junk short circuits sex. The drive to nonsexual sociability comes from the same place sex comes from, so when I have an H(eroin) or M(orphine) shooting habit I am non-sociable. If someone wants to talk, O.K. But there is no drive to get acquainted" (Burroughs, 1953, p. 124). In fact, there is good evidence that opiate drugs reduce sexual drive or interest, and in males, often produce impotence (Abel, 1985). Consistent with Burroughs's anecdotal reports, laboratory studies also show opiates impair social interactions (Meyer & Mirin, 1975). After smoking opium or taking other opiate drugs, vivid dreamlike experiences are often reported. These are the basis for the expression "pipe dreams."

The acute physiological effects of opiate drugs resemble those of depressant drugs, but there are some differences. Like depressants, opiates cause respiratory depression and lowered body temperature, but the effects of opiates on heart rate are complex (Jaffe & Martin, 1985; Mayer, 1987). Nausea and vomiting often occur immediately after taking opiates. Perhaps the most visible sign of opiate drug use is the pupillary constriction caused by opiates. This effect is so pronounced in overdose that "pinpoint pupils" may be used as a diagnostic sign of opiate poisoning. When a high dose of heroin is fatal, the immediate cause is usually respiratory failure. However, the lethal dose of heroin is surprisingly high. As Brecher (1972) has noted, many street overdose victims are found on autopsy to have injected less than would be expected to be lethal. Many of these cases involved not simply an overdose of heroin, but a lethal drug interaction between heroin and alcohol or another depressant drug. Opiates and depressant drugs potentiate one another (Ho & Allen, 1981). This synergy can often be lethal and many of the most publicized "heroin" overdoses actually involve synergy, such as the death of Janis Joplin in 1970:

> The quart bottle of Southern Comfort (whiskey) that she held aloft on-stage was at once a symbol of her load, and her way of lightening it. As she emptied the bottle, she grew happier, more radiant and more freaked out. . . . Last week on a day that superficially at least seemed to be less lonely than most, Janis Joplin died on the lowest and saddest of notes. Returning to her Hollywood motel room after a late-night recording session and some hard drinking with friends at a nearby bar, she apparently filled a hypodermic needle with heroin and shot it into her left arm. The injection killed her. (*Time*, quoted by Brecher, 1972, p. 113).

We now recognize the alcohol was as responsible for her death as was the heroin.

CHRONIC EFFECTS OF OPIATES

The effects are somewhat different when opiate drugs are taken chronically. As noted, tolerance develops to opiates, so the effects are generally diminished unless the user escalates the dose, which often occurs. Figure 12-1 shows the pattern of opiate intake in a human and a rhesus monkey studied under laboratory conditions of continuous drug availability (Henningfield, Lukas, & Bigelow, 1986). Each graph shows the drug intake plotted over days in the experiment. The human data come from an experiment in which a volunteer with an extensive drug-abuse history was studied under laboratory conditions and could regulate his daily intravenous morphine dose. Note the gradual increase in dose chosen by the subject over time. For the first month the subject never administered more than 500 mg/day. By the fourth month, however, he frequently took more than 1,000 mg. Also note the bottom panel of Figure 12-1, which reveals a very similar pattern of heroin self-administration by monkeys that could obtain intravenous heroin by pressing a lever. Clearly the emergence of tolerance to the rewarding consequences of opiate drugs is a phenomenon of great generality.

The motives for continued use of opiates over time may change. While repeated use is initially motivated by a desire to reexperience the pleasant rush associated with the drug, addicts report with continued use that taking the drug does not make them nearly as high as before. However, they continue to use the drug in order to avoid the unpleasant symptoms of abstinence. Thus, the processes maintaining heroin use change from positive to negative reinforcement. The withdrawal symptoms associated with opiate dependence may appear after only one to two weeks of chronic use of heroin, morphine, or a synthetic opiate drug. The symptoms become more severe with longer-term use of higher doses. Early indications of withdrawal begin

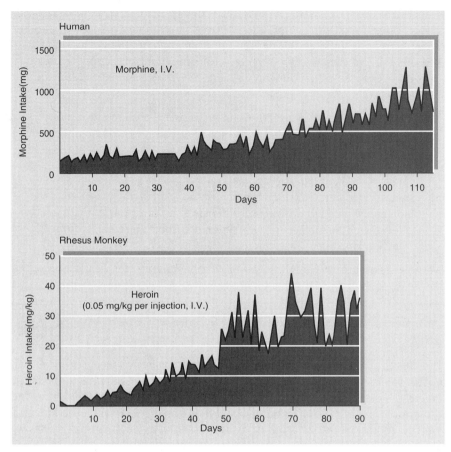

Figure 12-1   Similar patterns of opioid intake in a human and a rhesus monkey under conditions of continuous drug availability. Each graph shows the amount of drug taken over consecutive days. The human data are replotted from an experiment in which a volunteer with a history of drug abuse was permitted to self-regulate his intravenous morphine intake. The animal data are from a study in which lever-press responses by rhesus monkeys produced intravenous injections of heroin (Elsmore, Fletcher, & Sodetz, unpublished raw data—from Henningfield, Lukas, & Bigelow, 1986).

"I have seen life measured out in eyedroppers of morphine solution. I experienced the agonizing deprivation of junk sickness, and the pleasure of relief when junk-thirsty cells drank from the needle."

(Burroughs, 1953)

8 to 12 hours after the last dose and include flu-like symptoms such as runny nose, tearing, sweating, irritability, and tremor. As time passes these symptoms become more severe, and others appear, including pupil dilation, anorexia, and piloerection (goosebumps). This last symptom leaves the addict looking a bit like a plucked turkey and may be the basis for the expression "going cold turkey." These symptoms continue to worsen and reach a peak after about 48 to 72 hours. At this time heart rate and blood pressure are elevated, and the addict experiences severe flu-like symptoms such as nausea, diarrhea, sneezing, excessive sweating, and pain in the bones. In addition, the addict may show spastic movements of the arms and legs that may appear similar to kicking. This is thought to be the basis for the expression "kicking

the habit." Other somewhat bizarre symptoms, which apparently indicate a rebound of the addict's sexual system, include spontaneous erection and ejaculation in men and orgasm in women. The loss of fluids and failure of the addict to eat or drink much during withdrawal can leave the addict physically and emotionally drained and occasionally can be fatal (Jaffe & Martin, 1985).

It is worth noting that a suitable dose of any opiate drug (but not depressant drugs) will reverse the abstinence symptoms and restore a feeling of well-being to the addict. Hospital detoxification procedures take advantage of this fact by treating addicts in withdrawal with low doses of a synthetic opiate drug such as methadone. The dose of methadone given is sufficient to reduce the severity of the addict's withdrawal symptoms, but not enough to produce much of a high. Gradually over a period of several weeks the dose of methadone is tapered off, until finally the addict shows no further signs of physical dependence. If physical withdrawal symptoms were the only factors maintaining heroin addiction, detoxification would be a cure. However, after detoxification procedures, there is an estimated relapse rate of 90% within two years after leaving the hospital, and most of these relapses occur during the first six months after detoxification (Hunt & Odoroff, 1962). Thus, returning an addict to the environment in which she or he became addicted is most likely to result in relapse, even if physical withdrawal symptoms are not problems.

That heroin (and other drug) addiction depends on more than just physical withdrawal symptoms is illustrated nicely by the heroin addiction epidemic that failed to occur. During the early 1970s as the Vietnam War was

DRUGS AND CULTURE
OPIATE USE IN CHINA

Use of opium has long been associated with China. As noted in Chapter 2, it is estimated that several million Chinese were addicted to opium in the mid-1800s during the "Opium Wars" with the British. Opium smoking in the United States was popularized by Chinese laborers who established "opium dens" in the Chinatowns of the American West. Although Chinese government officials had long sought to reduce opium use, more extreme strategies were employed after 1949 when the Communist party came into power. The draconian approaches involve public executions of drug dealers after mass-sentencing rallies in large sports stadiums. Addicts may be sent to labor camps without trial for up to three years. Yet in parts of China use of opiate drugs persists. The Kunming province is on the trade routes that deliver heroin from Myanmar (formerly Burma), and apparently heroin remains available and widely used. Ironically, the one thing that has clearly changed since the 1800s is the method of opiate administration: instead of smoking opium, the current fashion is injection of heroin (*The Economist*, Vol. 320, 1991).

drawing to a close, heroin addiction rates were very high among returning American soldiers, with some estimates as high as 21%. These soldiers were required to go through a detoxification before their return to the United States, but given a 90% relapse rate one would have expected most would return to heroin use after returning home. Thus, an epidemic of heroin addiction in the States was expected. However, follow-up studies showed that very few did relapse (less than 15%), illustrating clearly that environmental and psychosocial factors associated with Vietnam were apparently responsible for the development of the dependence. Upon returning to the United States, Vietnam veterans found heroin far less available. That, added to the change in life style and social environment accompanying their return to the United States, apparently eased the pressures leading to their initial dependence (Robins, Helzer, & Davis, 1975). However, the radical change in environment from Vietnam to the United States cannot be duplicated in the typical treatment setting. This is one reason it is so difficult to treat heroin addiction, although a number of different types of treatment have been developed. These are reviewed in Chapter 17.

summary

- Opium is produced from the sap of the poppy plant and it has been used for medicinal purposes for centuries.

- In the nineteenth century the major active agent in opium, morphine, was isolated. More potent than opium, morphine was prized for its analgesic effects, but also became a major addiction problem.

- Heroin was developed as an alternative to morphine, but soon became the addict's drug of choice. While opiate drugs remained important in medicine, after the passage of the 1914 Harrison Act, heroin became a major criminal drug.

- Opiate drugs act in the brain by mimicking endorphins, natural neurotransmitters that are involved in the regulation of pain and pleasure.

- The major medical use for opiate drugs involves the treatment of severe pain.

- Opiates depress respiration, lower body temperature, and cause pupillary constriction. They induce a pleasurable euphoria in addition to pain relief.

- Regular use of opiates results in tolerance and an abstinence syndrome characterized by flu-like symptoms and intense drug craving. However, heroin addiction is more complex than simple avoidance of withdrawal symptoms.

ANSWERS TO WHAT DO YOU THINK?

1. Opium comes from a plant called *Cannabis sativa*.

   F   *Opium comes from the poppy plant, Papaver somniferum.*

2. Morphine is one of the active ingredients in opium.

   T   *Morphine and codeine are chemicals directly derived from opium.*

3. Heroin was first made illegal by the 1965 Drug Abuse Control Amendments.

F *All opiates were brought under legal control by the 1914 Harrison Act.*

4. Use of "dirty" needles is now one of the major causes of AIDS.

T *In more than one-third of all new AIDS cases, the use of contaminated needles is suspected as the source of infection.*

5. Most designer heroin compounds are much less potent than pure heroin.

F *Designer heroin compounds may be 10 to 1,000 times more potent than pure heroin. Thus, the risk of overdose is greater.*

6. The opiates are among the most powerful analgesic drugs.

T *The principal medical use for opiates is to relieve pain.*

7. Heroin enhances sexual desire and activity.

F *Heroin inhibits sexual arousal.*

8. Opiate drugs show cross-dependence with alcohol.

F *Alcohol does not eliminate the symptoms of opiate withdrawal.*

9. Heroin withdrawal is much like alcohol withdrawal.

F *Opiate withdrawal does not include delirium tremens, but rather is characterized by flu and cold symptoms.*

10. Veterans of the Vietnam War had a high rate of heroin addiction and were unable to kick the habit when they returned to the United States.

F *Most vets were able to quit using heroin when they returned to their home environment.*

11. The effects of opiates can be potentiated by alcohol.

T *Alcohol and other depressant drugs act synergistically with heroin and other opiates, and these combinations are often fatal.*

12. The expression "cold turkey" comes from the goosebumps seen in addicts withdrawing from heroin.

T *The resemblance is thought to be the basis for that expression.*

13 Marijuana

WHAT DO YOU THINK?

True or False?   ____   The cannabis plant was raised for its psychoactive properties by the settlers at Jamestown and, later, by George Washington.

____   The Eighteenth Amendment, prohibiting the use of alcohol, had the paradoxical effect of increasing the prevalence of marijuana use in the United States.

____   Criminal penalties in the United States for the possession and use of marijuana have increased steadily since the 1960s.

____   Data recently gathered both in national household surveys and in annual surveys of high school seniors demonstrate a sharp decrease in the prevalence of marijuana use since 1979.

____   The marijuana smoked in the United States today is more potent than that smoked 10 years ago.

____   Drug effects following oral ingestion of marijuana last longer than when the drug is smoked.

____   Tolerance to cannabis has been well-documented in humans.

____   Marijuana has been used effectively to treat glaucoma and the nausea and vomiting associated with chemotherapy for cancer.

____   Marijuana use often causes long-term damage to the cardiovascular system.

____   One consequence of cannabis intoxication is the impairment of short-term memory.

____   The most commonly reported emotional effects of cannabis use are suspiciousness and paranoid ideation.

____   An area of concern regarding marijuana use is that it often causes the user to be aggressive and violent.

Cannabis sativa, more commonly known as marijuana, is a hemp plant that grows freely throughout the world. The cannabis plant most commonly is known today as a potent psychoactive substance, but for many years it was harvested primarily for its fiber. These strong hemp fibers were employed in the production of rope, clothes, and ship sails. Although used for several centuries in other parts of the world for its mind-altering properties, it was not until the first third of this century that its psychoactive properties were recognized in the United States. After that, the hemp plant has been more often harvested for its psychoactive effects.

The term "marijuana" is thought to be based on the Portuguese word *mariguango*, which translates as "intoxicant." Marijuana, incidentally, is not the same as hashish, although both are derived from the *cannabis sativa* plant. Marijuana is the leafy top portion of the plant. Hashish is made from the dust

The marijuana plant.

of the resin that is produced by the hemp plant to protect it from the sun and heat and to maintain hydration. Plants growing in warmer climates will produce greater amounts of the resin, which generally has stronger psychoactive effects.

We begin this chapter with a historical overview of the drug and its use through the centuries. This is followed by a section on the epidemiology of current marijuana use. Next we provide information on absorption, distribution, metabolism, and excretion; mechanisms of action; and tolerance and dependence. Following this is an overview of the medical and psychotherapeutic uses of marijuana. The chapter's final sections concern the physical, psychological, and social/environmental effects of marijuana.

HISTORICAL OVERVIEW

According to Ernest Abel in his book *Marihuana: The First Twelve Thousand Years* (1980), the earliest known evidence of the use of cannabis occurred more than 10,000 years ago during the Stone Age. Archeologists at a Taiwanese site

"[The Scythians] have discovered other trees that produce fruit of a peculiar kind, which the inhabitants, when they meet together in companies, and have lit a fire, throw on the fire, as they sit round in a circle; and that by inhaling the fumes of the burning fruit that has been thrown on, they become intoxicated by the odor, just as the Greeks do by wine; and that the more fruit that is thrown on the more intoxicated they become, until they rise up to dance and betake themselves to singing."

(Herodotus commenting on marijuana use by the Scythians, a nomadic central Asian barbarian group, cited in McKenna, 1992)

have discovered pots made of fibers presumed to be from the cannabis plant. The earliest known references to the use of cannabis for its pharmacological properties are attributed to Shen Nung about 2800 B.C. Shen Nung was a mythical Chinese emperor and pharmacist who purportedly shared with his subjects knowledge of the medicinal uses of cannabis. It has been speculated cannabis was used in this period in China for its sedative properties, treating pain and illness, countering the influences of evil spirits, and its general psychoactive effects (Abel, 1980; Nahas, 1973).

Cannabis use gradually spread from China to surrounding Asian countries. Of particular note was its adoption in India, where cannabis served a religious function. The *Atharva Veda*, one of the oldest books of Hinduism, includes it as one of the five sacred plants (Aldrich, 1977). This provided the plant with the protection and reverence engendered by cultural or religious acceptance.

The use of cannabis as an intoxicant was not evident outside China and India during these ancient times. Not until much later did cannabis use spread to the Middle East and then later to North Africa. It was during this expansion that hashish was first identified. The use of hashish dates to around the tenth century among the Arabs, and to the eleventh century in Egypt (Abel, 1980).

The use of cannabis for its intoxicating effects appears to have been centered in these parts of the world for an extended period of time. It was not until the nineteenth century that the Western world began to be exposed to cannabis, primarily through written descriptions of the hashish experience. This exposure typically occurred through either medical writings or the popular press. The use of cannabis was introduced to Great Britain primarily by William O'Shaughnessy, an Irish physician. In India he observed the medical applications of cannabis and described them in his writings. Suggestions regarding the use of cannabis were described in France by Dr. Jacques Moreau, a physician who thought it could be used in the treatment of mental illness (Bloomquist, 1971). Subsequently, the use and effects of cannabis were described in much detail in the works of a number of French authors. Perhaps

DRUGS AND CULTURE
GAUTIER'S EXPERIENCES AT THE HASHISH CLUB

As noted in the main text, the Frenchman Theophile Gautier in the 1840s wrote in graphic detail of his experiences using hashish. These drug-use descriptions are of interest to us today for several reasons. For example, they provide an opportunity to observe the similarities that exist in the marijuana experience then and now, at least as described by those who write of their experiences. In addition, these descriptions provide the opportunity to observe the use of drugs in different cultures. In the present case, the user is a French hashish user, the setting is a club in Paris, and the time is the mid-nineteenth century.

The hashish used by Gautier and his friends was contained in a sweetmeat (a food rich in sugar, such as candied or crystallized fruit) called Dawamesc, which they ate at the Paris hotel that housed *Le Club des Hachichins* (The Hashish Club). The drug-laced sweetmeat was eaten before dinner. After dinner, sitting in a large drawing room, Gautier described the drug effects as follows:

> After several minutes, my companions had vanished, one after another, leaving no trace other than their shadows on the walls, which were soon absorbed like the brown stains that water makes on sand, fading as they dry.
>
> As I was no longer conscious, from that time on, of what others were doing, you now must be content with a relation of my simple personal impression.
>
> Solitude reigned in the drawing room, which was studded with only a few dubious gleams; all of a sudden, a red flash passed beneath my eyelids, innumerable candles burst into light and I felt bathed in a warm, clear glow. I was indeed in the same place, but it was as different as a sketch is from a painting: everything was larger, richer, more gorgeous. Reality served as a point of departure for the splendors of the hallucination. (Gautier, 1844; quoted from Solomon, 1966, p. 126)

This period was followed by a state Gautier labeled "fantasia," after which *al-kief* was experienced:

> I was in that blessed state induced by hashish which the Orientals call al-kief. I could no longer feel my body; the bonds of matter and spirit were severed; I moved by sheer willpower in an unresisting medium.
>
> Thus I imagine the movement of souls in the world of fragrances to which we shall go after death. A bluish haze, an Elysian light, the reflections of an azure grotto, formed an atmosphere in the room through which I vaguely saw the tremblings of hesitant outlines; an atmosphere at once cool and warm, moist and perfumed, enveloping me like bath water in a sort of enervating sweetness. When I tried to move away, the caressing air made a thousand voluptuous waves about me; a delightful languor gripped my senses and threw me back upon the sofa, where I hung, limp as a discarded garment.
>
> Then I understood the pleasure experienced by the spirits and angels, according to their degree of perfection, when they traverse the ethers and the skies, and how eternity might occupy one in Paradise. (Gautier, 1844; quoted from Solomon, 1966, pp. 130–131).

Al kief later was replaced by a nightmarish stage in which Gautier felt fear, fury, and aspects of paranoia, then, finally, around five hours after entering The Hashish Club, the drug effects ended:

> The dream was at an end.
>
> The hashisheen went off, each in his own direction, like the officers in *Marlborough Goes to War*.
>
> With light steps, I went down the stairs that had caused me so much anguish, and a few moments later I was in my room, in full reality; the last vapors raised by the hashish had vanished. (Gautier, 1844; quoted from Solomon, p. 135)

most notable was Theophile Gautier, who was introduced to cannabis by Moreau. Gautier graphically described his initiation into *Le Club des Hachichins* (The Hashish Club), which was centered in 1840s Paris in the exclusive Hotel Pimodan. The hashish consumed was contained in a sweetmeat called Dawamesc. Gautier's descriptions of the drug effects were graphic (some excerpts from his writings are highlighted in a nearby Drugs and Culture Box). His descriptions of the hashish experiences included elements of mystery, intrigue, joy, ecstasy, fear, and terror.

Despite what appeared to some as attractive features of cannabis and hashish, the use of this drug did not immediately become extensive in Europe. In fact, widespread use of cannabis for its psychoactive properties in Europe did not occur until the 1960s when it was reintroduced by, among others, tourists from the United States (Bloomquist, 1971).

Cannabis in the New World

The presence of cannabis in the New World dates to 1545, when it was brought to Chile by the Spaniards. In the North American colonies, the cannabis plant was raised for fiber by the Jamestown settlers in Virginia in 1611. Not long after, this hemp product was firmly entrenched as a basic staple crop, and was cultivated by George Washington, among many others. Cannabis was harvested in New England starting in 1629; it remained a core U.S. crop until after the Civil War. The center of this hemp production was Kentucky, where it was a major crop product for decades.

Despite its widespread presence, the marijuana plant was relatively unknown as a mind-altering substance. However, there was some recognition of its uses beyond the fiber component. Following the lead of European doctors, American physicians used cannabis in the 1800s as a general, all-purpose medication (Nahas, 1973). The most commonly used preparation was Tilden's Extract of Cannabis Indica, an Indian hemp plant produced in East Bengal. By the 1850s marijuana was listed in the *United States Pharmacopeia*, a listing of legitimate therapeutics; it remained listed until 1942. The cannabis extract also was listed in the less-select *National Formulary*.

Cannabis was consumed for recreational purposes only to a limited degree during this period, and descriptions of its psychoactive effects were not common. One notable exception was the publication in 1857 of the book *The Hasheesh Eater*. Written by Fitz Hugh Ludlow, this volume details his cannabis-eating experiences over a four-year period beginning at around age 16. Ludlow lived in the town of Poughkeepsie, north of New York City in the Hudson River Valley. He spent much of his time with a friend named Anderson, an **apothecary,** and often engaged in personal experimentation with the varied substances in Anderson's drugstore. One day Anderson pointed out to Ludlow a new arrival: a marijuana extract from Tilden and Co. Ludlow began experimenting with the substance. At first, he experienced no immediate drug effects but after several hours described the onset of effects as follows:

> Ha! what means this sudden thrill? A shock, as of some unimagined vital force, shoots without warning through my entire frame, leaping to

Apothecary
A pharmacist.

my fingers' ends, piercing my brain, startling me till I almost spring from my chair.

I could not doubt it. I was in the power of the hasheesh influence (Ludlow, p. 20).

Ludlow continued his experimenting, graphically describing the varied cannabis effects. For example, in a chapter titled "The Kingdom of the Dream," he began by noting:

The moment that I closed my eyes a vision of celestial glory burst upon me. I stood on the silver strand of a translucent, boundless lake, across whose bosom I seemed to have been just transported. A short way up the beach, a temple, modeled like the Parthenon, lifted its spotless and gleaming columns of alabaster sublimely into a rosy air—like the Parthenon, yet as much excelling it as the godlike ideal of architecture must transcend that ideal realized by man (Ludlow, p. 34).

In his writings, Ludlow also identified two "laws of the hasheesh operation." The first was that "after the completion of any one fantasia has arrived, there almost invariably succeeds a shifting of the action to some other stage entirely different in its surroundings" (pp. 36–37). The second law was that "after the full storm of a vision of intense sublimity has blown past the hasheesh-eater, his next vision is generally of a quiet, relaxing, and recreating nature" (p. 37).

The 1920s marked a wider use of cannabis. Edward M. Brecher, in The Consumers Union Report on *Licit and Illicit Drugs* (1972), attributes this increase in use to alcohol prohibition. He writes, "Not until the Eighteenth Amendment and the Volstead Act of 1920 raised the price of alcoholic beverages and made them less convenient to secure and inferior in quality did substantial commercial trade in marijuana for recreational use spring up" (p. 410). In New York City, for example, a number of marijuana **tea-pads** (estimated at more than 500 in Harlem alone) were opened in the early 1920s. These "tea-pads" were generally located in a room or apartment. As described by the 1944 LaGuardia Commission:

The "tea-pad" is furnished according to the clientele it expects to serve. Usually, each "tea-pad" has comfortable furniture, a radio, victrola or, as in most instances, a rented nickelodeon. The lighting is more or less uniformly dim, with blue predominating. An incense burner is considered part of the furnishings. The walls are frequently decorated with pictures of nude subjects suggestive of perverted sexual practices. The furnishings, as described, are believed to be essential as a setting for those participating in smoking marihuana (p. 10).

The commission went on to note that:

The marihuana smoker derives greater satisfaction if he is smoking in the presence of others. His attitude in the "tea-pad" is that of a relaxed individual, free from the anxieties and cares of the realities of life. The "tea-pad" takes on the atmosphere of a very congenial social club. The smoker readily engages in conversation with strangers, discussing freely his

Tea-pad
Historically, a place where people gathered to smoke marijuana. The site could be anywhere from a rented room to a hotel suite.

"*Prolonged use of marihuana frequently develops a delirious rage which sometimes leads to high crimes, such as assault and murder. Hence marihuana has been called the "killer drug." The habitual use of this narcotic poison always causes a very marked mental deterioration and sometimes produces insanity.*"

(Excerpt from a 1936 pamphlet entitled *Marijuana or Indian Hemp and Its Preparations*, distributed by the International Narcotic Education Association)

pleasant reactions to the drug and philosophizing on subjects pertaining to life in a manner which, at times, appears to be out of keeping with his intellectual level. . . . A boisterous, rowdy atmosphere did not prevail and on the rare occasions when there appeared signs indicative of a belligerent attitude on the part of a smoker, he was ejected or forced to become more tolerant and quiescent (p. 10).

The origins of the practice of smoking marijuana in this country in the early part of this century are not clear, but most agree that one of the earliest introductions was through Mexican laborers crossing the border into the United States. The greatest extent of use was found in New Orleans also in the early 1920s. In fact, New Orleans was a central dispensing arena for marijuana as late as the 1930s. The marijuana could be sent up the Mississippi River to a number of river ports, and then further distributed throughout the country. According to Nahas (1973), marijuana was available in the larger cities by 1930, although its use was primarily limited to black Americans, not infrequently jazz musicians.

Public concern over the use of marijuana was small during this period, with one notable exception. In 1926, a series of articles was printed in two New Orleans newspapers. These articles sensationally "exposed" the "menacing" presence of marijuana, and attributed a number of crimes and heinous acts to use of the drug. Although many of these lurid reports were ridiculous and fabricated, a Louisiana law mandating a maximum penalty of $500 fine and/or six months imprisonment for conviction of possession or sale of marijuana was passed the next year. However, this law had little effect on the sale or use of marijuana in New Orleans, except for a possible moderate increase in the price of a marijuana cigarette (Brecher, 1972).

Despite the fact that marijuana had not threatened to enter the mainstream of American life, additional governmental and legal action continued into the next decade. Much of this activity was promoted by Harry J. Anslinger, who in 1932 became director of the Federal Bureau of Narcotics. Anslinger was convinced marijuana represented a major threat to the safety and well-being of the country. He successfully encouraged many states to restrict the trafficking and use of marijuana. In 1930, only 16 states had statutes prohibiting the use of marijuana; by 1937, virtually all states had such statutes.

Anslinger's efforts culminated in the 1937 passage of the Marijuana Tax Act. The act did not officially ban marijuana. Rather, the bill acknowledged the medicinal uses of marijuana and permitted the prescription of marijuana following payment of a license fee of $1 per year. However, any other possession or sale of marijuana was strictly outlawed. Punishments for violation could be quite strong: a $2,000 fine, five years' imprisonment, or both. Anslinger's efforts overall were successful in reducing *legal* dispersement of marijuana, as in the following year only 38 physicians paid the $1 license fee to prescribe marijuana (Brecher, 1972). Further, Anslinger's efforts set the stage for progressively stricter penalties for marijuana sale or possession in the ensuing years. Throughout the 1960s judges often had the option of sentencing a user or seller of marijuana to life imprisonment. A second offense of selling marijuana to a minor in Georgia could be punished by death. Since 1970, however, the penalties for marijuana possession and use have been moderated significantly during the gradual decriminalization for possession of small amounts or use of the substance. Whether this trend continues during the ongoing emphasis on "zero tolerance" and the "war on drugs" remains to be seen.

Committee Reports on Marijuana

Several comprehensive reports on the use of marijuana and its effects have appeared during the past century. One of the earliest was the Indian Hemp Drugs Commission Report released in 1894. The committee preparing the report included four British and three Indian commissioners. A second report was the 1933 Panama Canal Zone Military Investigations, which spanned the period 1916–1929. A third, and one of the most widely known investigations, was the LaGuardia Commission Report published in 1944. Because the conclusions reported by these three commissions were similar, we will focus on the LaGuardia findings.

The LaGuardia Commission Report was created by the New York Academy of Medicine at the request of New York City Mayor Fiorello LaGuardia. This study, second in scope only to the Indian Hemp Drugs Commission, was a truly multidisciplinary report. It included coordinated input by physicians, psychologists, pharmacologists, and sociologists. Data were gathered on marijuana use and effects in "tea-pads" as well as in laboratory settings. The general finding of the study was that marijuana use was not particularly harmful to the user or to society at large. The report failed to find evidence for the claim that aggression, violence, and belligerence were common consequences of marijuana smoking. This was not intended to suggest, however, that marijuana did not induce psychoactive effects. A number of individual changes were noted, including in more extreme form "mental confusion and excitement of a delirious nature with periods of laughter and of anxiety" (p. 216).

These report findings were consistent with those of commission reports published earlier. Subsequent reports also have mirrored these basic conclusions. These investigations include the 1968 Baroness Wootton Report from Great Britain, the 1970 Interim Report of the Canadian Government's LeDain Commission, and the First Report of the National Commission on Mental Health and Drug Abuse (titled Marihuana: A Signal of Misunderstanding) in 1972. More recent reports in this country, such as the Ninth Report to the United States Congress on Marijuana and Health (1982) and Drug Abuse and Drug Abuse Research (1984, the first in a series of triennial reports to Congress), both prepared by the National Institute on Drug Abuse, have likewise not provided markedly discrepant findings, although they are much more cautious in describing nonnegative effects of marijuana use.

"*A person may be a confirmed smoker for a prolonged period, and give up the drug voluntarily without experiencing any craving for it or exhibiting withdrawal symptoms.*"

(Excerpt from the 1944 LaGuardia Commission Report)

EPIDEMIOLOGY

Marijuana remains the most frequently used illicit drug in the United States. Its use rose dramatically throughout the 1960s and 1970s, followed by steady decreases until into the early 1990s. However, there was an increase in marijuana use by high school seniors in 1993.

Data gathered as part of a National Institute on Drug Abuse (NIDA) National Household Survey in 1991 revealed that almost 68 million Americans (33% of the population) have used marijuana at least once in their lives. The lifetime (ever used) prevalence rates were 13% for youths (ages 12–17), 51% for young adults (ages 18–25), and 33% for older adults (ages 26+).

These and other data from the survey are shown in Figure 13-1. The first trend you will notice is the drop, since the 1979 survey through 1991, in lifetime, annual (used in the past year), and current (used in the last 30 days) use for the youth and young adult populations. The greatest changes occurred among young adults. Between 1979 and 1991, lifetime prevalence for the young adult group dropped from 68% to 51%, annual prevalence from 47% to 25%, and current use from 35% to 13%. The findings for older adults (those over age 25) were different. Annual and current prevalence rates (approxi-

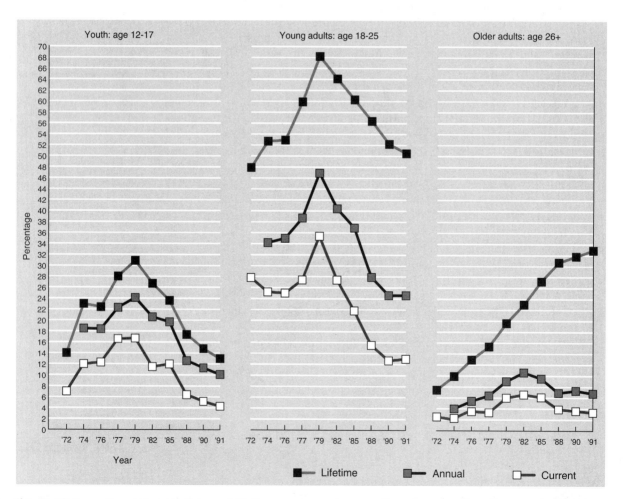

Figure 13-1 Trends in prevalence of lifetime use, annual use, and current use of marijuana or hashish for youths, young adults, and older adults (from National Household Survey on Drug Abuse, 1991, NIDA, Division of Epidemiology and Statistics Analysis).

mately 7% and 3%, respectively, in 1991) have been relatively stable since 1979. The lifetime prevalence rate for the older adult group is steadily increasing, probably the result of the aging of individuals who had used marijuana in previous years.

Several other findings from the household surveys in the 1990s are noteworthy. First, males in general were more likely to have used marijuana than females. The only exception was for persons aged 12–17, where males and females were about equally likely to have used marijuana in their lifetimes,

Contemporary Issue
MARIJUANA AS A GATEWAY TO OTHER DRUG USE

The gateway or "stepping-stone" theory of drug use posits that the use of licit and illicit substances follows a predictable pattern. This theory of stages received considerable attention in the 1960s and 1970s during debates on the legalization of marijuana. Opponents of legalization, including the then-Federal Bureau of Narcotics, argued that marijuana use was the first step on a path leading to heroin addiction. As it turns out, research by Johnson (1973) and others has shown that the vast majority of marijuana users do not go on to become heroin addicts.

Nevertheless, substance use does appear to follow a pretty uniform sequencing of drugs. One of the earliest studies (Kandel, 1975) found that alcohol use among high school students was a necessary stepping stone between nonuse of drugs and use of marijuana. This finding was replicated in research conducted at the New York State Research Institute on Addictions (Welte & Barnes, 1985; Windle, Barnes, & Welte, 1989). They have found that high school students (white, black, and Hispanic) tend to use drugs in the following sequence: alcohol, marijuana, and the so-called "hard drugs" (such as cocaine, crack, other hallucinogens, and heroin). In a recent study, Kandel and Yamaguchi (1993) found that crack users almost always previously had used marijuana. Indeed, only 10% of high school crack users had not previously used marijuana. Alder and Kandel (1981) have found that similar patterns in the sequencing of drug use occur among adolescents in Israel and France.

It is important to keep a couple of things in mind in interpreting these "stepping-stone" data. First, and perhaps most important, not everyone who uses alcohol will subsequently use marijuana, and not everyone who uses marijuana will subsequently use other illicit drugs. Second, persons who start using marijuana after previously using alcohol typically do not stop using alcohol. Instead, both substances can be part of the person's drug-use repertoire.

Keeping these cautions in mind, the studies mentioned above have implications for persons working in the areas of prevention and drug policy. As an example (and you probably can imagine others), these studies suggest that people who do not use marijuana for the most part will not use "hard drugs" such as cocaine or heroin. As such, prevention efforts focused on not using marijuana potentially will decrease the pool of marijuana users who will subsequently use other drugs.

past year, and past month. Second, marijuana use showed some variation according to race/ethnicity. Lifetime marijuana prevalence was higher among whites (34%) than Hispanics (30%); the rate for blacks was 32%. Lifetime marijuana use also was more common among whites for each of the age groups except for those aged 35 and older, where use was somewhat more common among blacks. There were few significant differences among the racial/ethnic groups for use in the past year or past month. A third finding concerned frequency of use. The percentages of persons who reported using marijuana 100 times or more (among those who had used it at least once) were 14% for those aged 12–17 years of age, 21% for the 18–25 age group, 27% for the 26–34 age group, and 20% for those over 34 years of age. Finally, the survey revealed that current marijuana users, compared to those not currently using the substance, are more likely to be current users of other drugs. As an example, 28% of current young adult marijuana users also were current users of drugs other than marijuana and 11% were current users of cocaine.

The reasons for the decline in marijuana use in the national household surveys have not been specified. However, the decreases probably reflect to some degree economic factors, growing concerns about health and fitness, and concerns over possible negative effects of drug use in general.

The decreases in marijuana use shown in the national household surveys also appeared—until recently—in the annual surveys of high school seniors. As you can see in Figure 13-2, the percentages of seniors ever using, using in the past month or year, or using daily for the past month all had been dropping from around 1979 until 1992. However, the 1993 high school seniors data revealed that marijuana was making a comeback, at least among high school seniors. As shown in Figure 13-2, marijuana use increased significantly

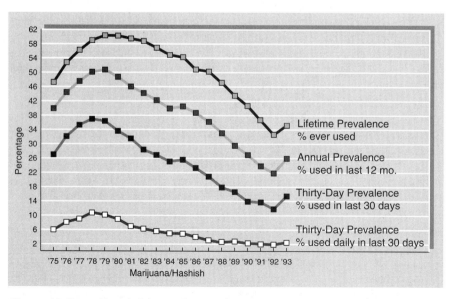

Figure 13-2   Trends in prevalence of marijuana use among high school seniors from 1975 to 1993 (from Johnston, O'Malley, and Bachman, 1994).

in 1993. For example, the number of high school seniors who used marijuana in the last 30 days jumped from 11.9% in 1992 to 15.5% in 1993. The percentage of seniors using marijuana daily in the past month increased from 1.9% to 2.4% during that same period. In attempting to account for these notable increases in marijuana use, the authors of the survey pointed to indications that attitudes and beliefs about drugs were beginning to "soften" among high school students. In this regard, they reported that students were believing less strongly about the dangers associated with the use of drugs and about their personal disapproval of using them. It will be of interest to see if the upswing in marijuana use is reflected in future national household surveys and if the increases are maintained in subsequent surveys of high school seniors.

METHODS OF USE

Marijuana and hashish have been administered in a number of ways in their use as psychoactive agents. For example, they were ingested in India centuries ago in liquid and food form. Further, it has been reported that psychoactive effects of marijuana can be experienced through the chewing of marijuana leaves. However, the most common procedure for ingesting cannabis in this country has been and remains smoking, typically in cigarette (**joint**) form. Inhalation through cigarette form is also the most efficient method for absorption of cannabis.

Joint
A hand-rolled marijuana cigarette.

ACTIVE INGREDIENTS

The first chemical analysis of cannabis apparently was performed by Tscheep in 1821 (Mechoulam, 1973). Since then studies have shown cannabis to be a complex plant. More than 400 individual chemical compounds have been identified in the plant. Approximately 60 of these chemicals, collectively called **cannabinoids,** are unique to the cannabis plant. Continued research will probably identify additional cannabis chemical compounds and cannabinoids.

Despite years of study, not until 1964 was the principal psychoactive agent in cannabis isolated. This substance has been labeled **delta-9-tetrahydrocannabinol,** but is more commonly known as Δ-9-THC or simply THC. The THC compound was first reported by Gaoni and Mechoulam (1964), two researchers working in Israel. Research since 1964 has shown that the Δ-9-THC cannabinoid accounts for the vast majority of known specific pharmacological actions of marijuana. Although THC is the prime psychoactive agent in cannabis, other cannabinoids, such as cannabidiol and cannabinol, can be biologically active and can modify THC effects. However, they tend not to be psychoactive in and of themselves.

Cannabinoids
A general term to describe the more than 60 chemical compounds present in cannabis. One of these cannabinoids is delta-9-tetrahydrocannabinol (better known as THC).

Delta-9-tetrahydrocannabinol
The principal active cannabinoid in marijuana responsible for the experienced psychoactive effects.

Potency of Cannabis

The strength of cannabis varies considerably, and most of the marijuana grown in the United States has a THC content that is lower than that grown in many overseas countries. Marijuana smoked in the United States today is much stronger than that used as recently as a decade ago. It often contains potencies in the range of 13–15% (frequently in sinsemilla, a high-potency seedless variety of marijuana), and sometimes reaches 30%. Similar variations and increasing average potencies have been found as well for hashish. A third form of cannabis is **hash oil,** a concentrated liquid marijuana extract derived from the cannabis plant using solvents. This oil has been available on the streets for a number of years, and is quite potent relative to the marijuana leaf material or resin. Estimates are that hash oil can contain as much as 60% THC.

Hash oil
A potent distillate of marijuana or hashish. It first appeared in the United States in 1971, and can contain up to 60% THC.

ABSORPTION, DISTRIBUTION, METABOLISM, AND EXCRETION

The absorption of THC depends primarily on the mode of consumption. The most rapid and efficient absorption of marijuana occurs through smoking. This inhalation results in absorption directly through the lungs, and the onset of the THC action begins within minutes. Assessments of blood plasma reveal that peak concentrations occur approximately 30 to 60 minutes later. The drug effects can be experienced for around two to four hours.

Several factors can influence the amount of THC absorbed through smoking. One important variable, of course, is the potency of the cannabis being smoked. Only about half of the THC available in a marijuana cigarette is present in the smoke, and the amount ultimately absorbed into the bloodstream is probably less. Another variable is the amount of time the inhaled smoke is held in the lungs; the longer the smoke is held, the more time for absorption of the THC. Another factor influencing intake is the number of persons sharing the cigarette because more smokers may decrease the amount of marijuana available to any one user.

Oral ingestion of marijuana is much slower and relatively inefficient. The onset of action is longer than when smoked, taking as long as one hour. The marijuana is absorbed primarily through the gastrointestinal tract, and peak plasma levels can be delayed for as long as two to three hours following ingestion. An important difference from absorption through smoking is that blood containing orally ingested marijuana goes through the liver before going to the brain. The liver processes or clears much of the THC so that lesser amounts have the opportunity to exert action in the brain. However, the drug effects following oral ingestion can be experienced for longer periods of time, generally four to six hours. It is estimated that the dose needed to create a comparable high when orally ingested is three times greater than that needed when smoking.

Using peak plasma THC levels to assess cannabis effects can be misleading because the psychoactive cannabinoids are highly lipid-soluble; that is, the cannabinoids are lipids, which means they are almost entirely insoluble in water. The cannabinoids instead are a dark, viscous oil-like substance. Plasma levels of THC decrease rapidly because the THC is deposited in the tissues of various organs, particularly those containing fatty material. Assessments of organs following cannabis ingestion reveal marked concentrations of THC in the brain, lungs, kidneys, and liver. Thus, even when blood levels of THC are zero, the levels of THC in other organs can be substantial. Also, THC is capable of crossing the placental barrier and reaching the fetus.

As noted above, THC is carried through the bloodstream and deposited within various organs. The THC is then over time metabolized to less-active products. Although this process occurs primarily in the liver, it can occur in other organs as well. The THC metabolites are excreted slowly through the feces and urine. Approximately half of the THC is excreted over several days, and the remainder by the end of about a week. However, some metabolites of the THC, a number of which may still be active in the system, can be detected in the body at least 30 days following ingestion of a single dose and, following chronic use, in the urine for several weeks.

MECHANISMS OF ACTION

The primary psychotropic actions of marijuana occur in the brain and are a result of the drug's effect on neurotransmitters. Much of the research in this area (typically performed with animals) has focused on the effects of marijuana on the chemical transmitter acetylcholine. THC in relatively small doses has been shown to decrease the turnover in acetylcholine, particularly in the hippocampus (Domino, Donelson, & Tuttle, 1978), resulting in a decrease in neurotransmitter activity. In addition, THC facilitates release of the neurotransmitter serotonin. While specification of the drug action remains speculative, important advances are occurring. Foremost among these has been recent research on an apparent THC receptor in the brain. Scientists in the late 1980s reported the presence of a selective binding site for cannabinoid drugs (Devane et al., 1988). Their research also opened a door to new efforts to study pathways in the brain that may be involved in cannabinoid actions and to search for chemicals produced by the body that normally would interact with the identified receptor. More recently, a research team (Devane et al., 1992) identified a naturally occurring chemical in the body (named "anandamide" from the Sanskrit word for bliss) that binds to the same receptors on brain cells as do cannabinoids. Researchers in the future will be using the compound anandamide to study how the cannabinoid receptors affect functions such as memory, movement, hunger, and pain, which are affected by marijuana use.

Tolerance and Dependence

Tolerance to cannabis has been well-documented with animal species (for example, Agurell et al., 1986, and Harris, Dewey, & Razdan, 1977). However, the evidence for tolerance to cannabis in humans is less clear, with some studies indicating tolerance and others not. Some of the discrepancies in the studies with humans can be attributed to the dose of marijuana and duration of use being studied. Tolerance is more likely to occur with higher doses used over longer periods of time. This is typically seen in controlled laboratory settings, where the doses and frequencies of use studied are generally much greater than those reported by marijuana users in the general population. The mechanisms by which tolerance occurs are still unknown.

Physical dependence on cannabis is unusual. To date, no significant withdrawal syndrome has been identified. There does not seem to be any clustering of withdrawal indicators as has been identified for other substances, such as alcohol or heroin. Jones (1980) has noted that aspects of dependence with heavy sustained use have been described. These aspects generally entail motor symptoms, such as sleep disturbance, nausea, irritability, and restlessness. It has been argued by some that these symptoms are more reflective of a psychological dependence or withdrawal from the use of the drug. Nevertheless, as in the case of tolerance, physical dependence apparently is uncommon. When seen, it has been associated with quite high doses of marijuana taken over extended periods of time. Nevertheless, some people do become physically dependent on marijuana, and the mechanisms accounting for this remain unclear.

MEDICAL AND PSYCHOTHERAPEUTIC USES

Cannabis has a long history of use for medical and health purposes, with the earliest documentation attributed to Shen Nung in the twenty-eighth century B.C. As we noted earlier, Shen Nung purportedly recommended the use of cannabis to his people for its medicinal benefits. The earliest physical evidence for the use of marijuana as a medicine recently was uncovered by Israeli scientists who found residue of marijuana with the body of a young woman who apparently died in childbirth 1,600 years ago. The discoverers suggested that the marijuana was used to speed the birth process and to ease the associated pain. Indications that cannabis had been used during childbirth previously had been found in Egyptian papyri and Assyrian tablets (Martin et al., 1993). More systematic uses of cannabis as a therapeutic agent did not occur until the 1800s. For example, the Paris physician Jacques Moreau used cannabis in the mid-1800s to treat mental illnesses. (Recall that it was Moreau who supplied the cannabis used by Gautier at Le Club des Hachichins.) Much greater legitimization of the medical use of marijuana was provided by Dr. William O'Shaughnessy, the Irish physician who in an 1838 treatise described the use of cannabis for a number of problems, including rheumatism, pain, rabies, convulsions, and cholera.

Cannabis also was used widely in the United States for a number of complaints. It was recognized as a therapeutic drug well into the 1900s. At that time, the cannabis extract was listed for varying periods of time in the United States Pharmacopeia, the National Formulary, and the United States Dispensatory. In the Dispensatory, for example, cannabis was recommended for neuralgia, gout, rheumatism, rabies, cholera, convulsions, hysteria, mental depression, delirium tremens, and insanity.

Decline in the medicinal use of cannabis in this century is the result of two factors. The first was the advances made in medicine and the discovery of more specific knowledge regarding various diseases and their treatments. The second factor was the Marijuana Tax Act of 1937. This legislation markedly decreased prescribed medicinal uses of marijuana.

The therapeutic uses of marijuana today are much more circumscribed. For the most part synthetic products (such as Levontradol, Nabilone, and Marinol) that chemically resemble the cannabinoids have been used in current treatment efforts (see Ungerleider & Andrysiak, 1985). These synthetics are used because they provide the active elements of THC in a more stable manner. Synthetics also can provide better solubility. Unfortunately, a downside to the synthetics is the absence of the rapid effect experienced when marijuana is smoked. When synthetic THC is taken orally, it is broken down prior to entering the bloodstream and absorption thus is delayed.

There has been a recent resurgence in efforts to legalize marijuana for medicinal purposes. Much of this effort has been spurred by an increased use of marijuana by AIDS patients who claim that marijuana reduces the nausea and vomiting caused by the disease and because it stimulates appetite, thus helping them to regain weight lost during their illness. An off shoot of these efforts has been the establishment of "cannabis clubs" in several major cities in the United States. These organizations purchase marijuana in bulk and provide it (free or at cost) to patients with AIDS, cancer, and other diseases. The cannabis club in San Francisco operates fairly openly, and is shielded by a city law that makes medicinal marijuana use a low priority for its police force.

A resolution of the debate over legalizing marijuana for medicinal purposes is not likely in the near future. In the meantime, there are several disorders—especially glaucoma and nausea—for which cannabis is prescribed in synthetic form, and we will describe these briefly in the following sections.

Glaucoma

Glaucoma is a generic term used to denote ocular diseases involving increases in intraocular pressure. This pressure damages the optic nerve and represents the leading cause of blindness in the United States. Over 2 million Americans over age 35 have developed glaucoma, and an estimated 300,000 new cases are diagnosed yearly. While drug and surgical interventions are available, their effectiveness is variable.

Cannabis has been shown to decrease intraocular pressure, although patients have experienced side effects regardless of whether the cannabis was administered orally, through injection, or by smoking (Hepler & Petrus, 1976). These side effects have included increased heart rate, decreased blood pressure, and psychological effects. Some of these effects dissipate with extended exposure to the cannabis.

The mechanisms through which the cannabis reduces intraocular pressure have not been determined. Cohen and Andrysiak (1982) suggested cannabis dilates the vessels that drain excess fluids from the eyeball. This draining is thought to prevent fluid buildup and the resultant pressure that causes optic nerve damage.

Clinical research on the potential benefits of cannabis as a treatment for glaucoma is continuing, with two emphases. The first is on developing synthetic formulas that reduce side effects. The second emphasis is on modes of application. Particular attention is being given to developing a topical preparation that could be applied directly onto the eye.

Nausea and Vomiting

Cannabis and THC synthetics have been used to counter the nausea and vomiting frequently associated with chemotherapies (and some radiation treatments) for cancer. These side effects, which can last for several hours or

"Our research behind the decision [to not legalize marijuana for medicinal purposes] stands five feet tall. Marijuana doesn't have accepted medical uses."

(Bill Ruzementi, DEA official, USA *Today*, October 1, 1993)

"All we're asking is for the DEA to get the hell out of the way so a medicine proven effective can be used."

(John Morgan, professor of pharmacology at City University of New York Medical School, USA *Today*, October 1, 1993)

even several days, often are not ameliorated by traditional antiemetic medications. Researchers in the 1970s began more systematic study of the antinausea and antivomiting effects of THC (usually administered orally) and results were favorable. This research, incidentally, followed anecdotal reports by chemotherapy patients that their private use of marijuana had reduced the aversive side effects of their treatments.

Positive outcomes have continued to emerge in subsequent research. Further, there are indications that children undergoing cancer chemotherapy may particularly benefit from administration of orally administered high doses of cannabinoids (see Martin et al., 1993). More recent studies have included the use of THC synthetics, such as Nabilone. The main drawback to the use of cannabis and THC synthetics has been the resultant mental effects, which have been viewed by some patients as uncomfortable and disorienting. Nevertheless, many patients undergoing chemotherapy find the THC side effects an acceptable price for reductions in the chemotherapy side effects. Research in this area perhaps will be enhanced by the 1986 decision by the Drug Enforcement Administration to reclassify synthetic THC as a Schedule II drug, which means some medical value is recognized. The synthetic previously had been classified as a Schedule I drug, meaning it was a prohibited substance with no recognized medical benefit. Marijuana not in synthetic form remains a Schedule I drug.

Other Uses

Cannabis and THC synthetics have been used to a much lesser extent in the treatment of pain, muscle spasticity, convulsant activity, insomnia, hypertension, asthma, and depression. However, the data in support of these uses have been equivocal. More research is needed to identify the utility of cannabis in medical treatment of these and other disorders.

PHYSIOLOGICAL EFFECTS

Although cannabis can produce a number of physiological effects, most of these actions are different for different users, not only in strength or intensity of the effect but also in duration. In general, the acute physiological effects of marijuana in a healthy individual are not dramatic. In fact, the LeDain Commission (1972) reported the "short-term physiological effects of a typical cannabis dose on normal persons are generally quite benign, and are apparently of little clinical significance."

The most commonly experienced effects are cardiovascular. Predominant among these is injection of the conjunctiva, or bloodshot eyes. This effect, a result of vasodilation, is most obvious around one hour after smoking, and it is generally dose-related. Although some cite a concomitant dilation of the pupil, research does not support this claim. It appears more likely the dilation is a consequence of smoking the marijuana in a darkened room. There does, however, tend to be a cannabis-induced sluggish reaction to light.

The second most common cardiovascular effect is an increase in heart rate and pulse rate (Kelly, Foltin, & Fischman, 1993). Both of these effects are present for around one hour, and each appears to be dose-related. The peak heart rate occurs around 20 minutes after smoking. In addition to these effects, blood pressure tends to become slightly to moderately elevated. No evidence indicates that these effects create any permanent damage within the normal cardiovascular system (Institute of Medicine, 1982).

Another general effect following cannabis use is a generalized decrease in motor activity. The only real exception to this is the loquacious behavior of many following smoking. Some users also report drowsiness. Relatedly, cannabis use also can have a marked effect on sleep stages, tending in part to decrease the total REM sleep achieved. However, this effect typically occurs only with higher doses of cannabis.

A number of other effects have also been reported, but they tend to be minor and/or infrequent, and often variable from person to person. These other effects include (but are not limited to) the following: dry mouth, thirst, fluctuations in respiration and body temperature, hunger or "the munchies" (peaking about two to three hours after smoking), nausea, and headache and/or dizziness.

Longer-Term Effects

Data on the longer-term effects of marijuana unfortunately are sparse and difficult to interpret. The research that has been conducted has been focused on four central systems: respiratory, cardiovascular, immune, and reproductive.

Respiratory System   Little controlled research exists regarding the long-term effects of smoking cannabis. Proper lung functioning seems to be altered as a consequence of smoking cannabis, but much of this impairment, such as airway obstruction, appears to reverse following abstinence from smoking. Marijuana cigarettes contain more tar than tobacco cigarettes. Additionally, cannabis tar contains greater amounts of cancerous agents than does tobacco tar (Jones, 1980). This is particularly noteworthy since marijuana smokers (in an effort to maximize the effects of the drug) inhale deeply and hold the smoke in their lungs. The long-term consequences unfortunately are not known. One difficulty in specifying these effects is that cannabis smokers frequently also smoke cigarettes, and separating the effects of each substance is difficult. Nevertheless, the possibility of irreversible lung damage due to marijuana smoking remains.

Cardiovascular System   The vast majority of cardiovascular effects associated with cannabis smoking were described earlier in this section as short-term (or acute). No evidence shows smoking marijuana to produce deleterious cardiovascular effects among healthy individuals. The acute effects produced (for example, increased heart rate) are, however, potentially dangerous among persons with existing cardiovascular problems, such as abnormal heart functioning or atherosclerosis.

Immune System   Although some of the research on this topic has been contradictory, apparently cannabis poses no significant long-term threat to the immune system. Thus, although cannabis can act as an immunosuppressant and decrease resistance to some viruses and bacteria, its clinical significance remains questionable. The mechanism through which this immune dysfunction occurs has not yet been defined.

Reproductive System   Studies using lower animal species and humans suggest cannabis does disrupt the reproductive system in both males and females. For example, chronic marijuana use has been associated with decreases in the number of sperm and sperm motility among men. The potential effects of these disruptions on fertility are difficult to specify (Institute of Medicine, 1982). Frequent use of cannabis by women may produce nonovulatory menstrual cycles, in which menstruation is not preceded by the release of an ovum. As in the case of males, the delayed effects of these disruptions on fertility are not known. In their review, Ehrenkranz and Hembree (1986) concluded that disruptions in reproductive function, at least in males, are not obvious, although subtle alterations may be operative.

Of more concern are possible teratogenic effects. The active agents present when marijuana is smoked readily cross the placental barrier, exposing the fetus to the array of cannabinoids. Although few data are available for humans, it does not appear that major birth malformations result. However, this does not mean significant effects cannot occur. The use of marijuana by pregnant women is associated with increased risk of premature birth, short body length, and lower infant birth weight (e.g., Day & Richardson, 1991; Fried, 1986). In addition, Jones (1980) has noted the presence of tremor, startle responses, and altered visual responses in newborn infants whose mothers used marijuana during pregnancy. The functional impact of these latter effects has not been determined, in part because it has been difficult to specify the durability of these postpartum effects and because cannabis-using women who are pregnant frequently also smoke tobacco and use alcohol. Nevertheless, the prudent advice is not to use cannabis during pregnancy.

Summary of Long-Term Effects   It appears the majority of effects associated with marijuana use are more acute than chronic, and that longer-term effects tend to be reversible with termination of drug use. However, significant exceptions may occur. The smoking of marijuana may be found to be linked to various respiratory disorders, including cancer. Most of the negative effects found are correlated with higher doses and frequency of use than that described by most cannabis smokers in this country. Nevertheless, these indications are tentative and await confirmation through the conduct of more systematic and controlled research.

PSYCHOLOGICAL EFFECTS

Although cannabis can produce the varied effects previously noted, most marijuana users use the drug in order to experience the psychological effects, some of which users report consistently, and some of which are more idiosyncratic. The psychological effects generally experienced by marijuana users can be divided into three domains: behavioral, cognitive, and emotional.

Drug paraphernalia stores, better known as "head shops," have long been popular with marijuana users. This shop owner is standing amidst a wide selection of pipes.

Some cannabis effects, especially those associated with the "marijuana high" that users describe, are learned. This learning process has been described in detail by Becker (1953, 1963). According to Becker, the first step is mechanical, in which the smoker learns to inhale the smoke and hold it in the lungs to maximize intake and absorption. The second step is to learn to perceive the effects that are created by the cannabis. These effects can be physical as well as psychological. The final step described by Becker is learning to label these effects as pleasant. The existence of this learning process accounts largely for the frequent finding that experienced users are more sensitive to cannabis effects than novice smokers.

Behavioral Effects

The most common behavioral effect is a generalized decrease in psychomotor activity and decrements in some domains of psychomotor performance. These effects appear to be dose-related, with more pronounced changes associated with greater amounts of marijuana taken in. The general decrease in motor activity appears to be pervasive, and the state is described as being associated with feelings of relaxation and tranquility. The only exception to this effect appears to be speech, as marijuana use is associated with the presence of rapid or slurred speech, circumstantial talk, and a loquaciousness. These effects in speech often are observed more in the early smoking phase, followed by the more traditional relaxation.

Although relaxation and a sense of well-being are the usual response to cannabis, some users first experience a stage in which they feel excited and restless. However, fairly soon, these users virtually always experience transition into the relaxation stage. Furthermore, despite feeling relaxed, users sometimes also feel the senses are markedly keener. Many users, for example, describe more intense perceptions of touch, vision (especially in perceiving colors), hearing, and smell. However, the research cited to support these reports is not strong. Finally, other research has shown a decreased sensitivity to pain during marijuana intoxication.

Concomitant with the feelings of relaxation and decreased motor activity is a generally subtle impairment in some areas of psychomotor performance. There do appear to be dose-related dysfunctions in motor coordination, signal detection, and the ability to monitor a moving object. The data on reaction time are not conclusive. Taken together, these findings have implications for driving a motor vehicle after using cannabis. Laboratory studies involving the use of a driving simulator have revealed detrimental effects of marijuana on driving skill. Some of these impairments may be cognitively mediated. Klonoff (1974) found that drivers under the influence of marijuana showed impairment in judgment and concentration along with other general driving skills. Others have suggested that some of the detriments in driving skill may be due to decreased vigilance and thus less awareness of peripheral stimuli. Therefore, it would appear psychomotor impairment can be caused by cannabis, and that this impairment becomes more apparent in tasks where thinking and concentration are necessary.

The influence of marijuana on sexual behavior and functioning is not fully understood, but it appears its effects vary considerably from user to user. Some report that sexual pleasures are more intense and enjoyable when using marijuana, but others describe instead a disinterest in sex. Those who report increased sexual pleasure when smoking probably are responding to the enhanced sensory sensitivity that frequently accompanies marijuana use. The drug itself produces no known specific physiologic response that stimulates sexual drive or performance. However, long-term or heavy use of marijuana has been associated with temporary impotence among men and temporary decreases in sex drive among women.

Cognitive Effects

Two primary cognitive consequences of cannabis intoxication have been documented. The first is impaired short-term memory and the second is the perception that time passes more slowly.

The impairment in short-term memory seen following cannabis use can occur with intake of a fairly low dose. Further, the degree of impairment increases rapidly with the complexity of the memory task. This effect has been observed with various types of stimuli, such as word lists and conversational materials.

The mechanisms of marijuana's effects on memory have not been specified, but several possibilities have been identified by Paton and Pertwee (1973). The first cause simply may be that the user is not motivated to attend to or to retrieve the material presented. Although this hypothesis is plausible, indications suggest subjects in these experiments perceive the tasks administered as a challenge and respond actively to the task demands. A second possibility is that the perceptual changes created by cannabis produce a "curtain of interference" that blocks or hinders intake or retrieval of material. The third hypothesis proposed by Paton and Pertwee (1973) is that marijuana creates a decreased ability to concentrate and attend to the material presented. This mechanism was advocated by Abel (1971) and by DeLong and Levy (1974). These latter researchers have proposed a model of attentional processes as a central key in understanding the cognitive effects of cannabis. Finally, cannabis drug action may interfere with the neurochemical processes operative in memory and retrieval operations. The exact factor, or set of factors, remains unknown, but it is likely they will in some manner operate in concert to affect short-term memory.

Altered perceptions of the passage of time is the second common cognitive effect of cannabis. This is perhaps best described in statements like "a few minutes seemed to pass like hours." The effect has been noted in both surveys and in the experimental literature. However, the time distortion is not as pronounced in the research reports as it is in more subjective self-reports provided by marijuana users.

Other cognitive effects of marijuana have been reported, but not as consistently as those already described. One effect is that cannabis decreases the ability to attend and concentrate, making the user easily distracted. Many users report that cannabis produces racing thoughts and "flight of ideas," in which various (and sometimes seemingly random) ideas "fly" in and out of mind. Another perception sometimes reported is of enhanced creativity. This especially has been noted by artists such as writers and painters, but no research evidence supports these claims. Finally, some cannabis users describe occasional feelings of "unreality" (see Hollister, Richards, & Gillespie, 1968) and the attachment of increased meaning to events or objects not previously perceived as important.

Emotional Effects

Positive emotional changes following cannabis intake are cited frequently as key motivators to smoke marijuana. A number of alterations in mood can occur; however, there is some uncertainty regarding the extent to which these are direct drug effects. A host of nonpharmacological factors can contribute to the drug effects experienced (Adesso, 1985; Zinberg, 1984). Chief among these nondrug influences are past experiences with cannabis, attitudes about the drug, expectancies regarding the drug use consequences, and the situational context of drug use. These factors, taken in conjunction with the dose of THC absorbed, must be considered in understanding the emotional changes attributed to the drug.

Contemporary Issue
AMP: ANOTHER FORM OF MARIJUANA

There is seemingly no end to the number of ways in which a drug can be used or abused. Sometimes the effects of a drug will be much more pronounced when taken, for example, intravenously versus orally. Sometimes the way a substance is prepared will have an effect on how and what effects are experienced. One dramatic example of changing the preparation of a psychoactive substance is the drug known as AMP. AMP is marijuana soaked in formaldehyde and dried before being smoked. It is a preparation first described in the clinical literature in 1985 by Ivan Spector, a physician at Baylor College of Medicine in Texas.

According to Spector, who provided case examples of patients seeking treatment following smoking AMP, these users showed some profound psychiatric effects and impairments. Several of them reported they "immediately felt as if a transparent field has been placed between them and their surroundings." Among the symptoms associated with AMP intoxication are a slowed sense of time, memory impairment, disorientation, paranoid thoughts, anxiety, confusion, disordered thought and difficulties in reality testing, and tremor. Physiological components in the response to AMP intake include elevated blood pressure, hypersalivation, tachycardia, and psychomotor excitement.

It may be instructive to describe one of the cases seen by Spector. A 35-year-old woman, called Ms. D., was presented for treatment three days after smoking AMP. She felt anxious, was tremulous, was salivating excessively and sweating, and her heartbeat was racing. All of this followed closely the actual AMP smoking. Several hours later she exhibited psychomotor retardation, secluded herself, reported she could not think well and lost all motivation, and described paranoid thoughts. Ms. D. also described hallucinations in which she saw blood on the walls. After three days, many of these complaints disappeared, with the exception of the anxiety and tremulousness. She was treated with an antianxiety medication, and the discomfort cleared within several days.

Ms. D.'s scenario was similar to those of the other AMP users described in the report, and there are two conclusions we can offer. One is that any given drug can be prepared in ways that markedly influence its effect on the user. A second conclusion is that drug users sometimes may be in a situation in which the drug they are using is not quite what they thought it was. Some AMP users have reported they were given AMP by friends who told them it was only marijuana.

The typical emotional response to cannabis is a carefree and relaxed state. This feeling has been described in various ways; the adjectives commonly used have included euphoric, content, happy, and excited. It frequently includes laughter and loquaciousness, and takes on the character for some of a dream-like state. Most generally, the response is viewed as pleasant and positive. It appears the degree of response is positively correlated with the dose.

It is noteworthy that negative emotional feelings, such as anxiety or dysphoria, are more common than might be expected. Additionally, a variety of somatic consequences have been experienced. Primarily, these include headache, nausea, and muscle tension; less frequently reported are suspiciousness and paranoid ideation.

It has been reported that around a third of marijuana users at least occasionally experience some of these negative effects; however, the effects can be transitory. A user may fluctuate between experiencing these negative feelings and the more positive states described earlier. Also, the negative effects often are reported more by inexperienced cannabis users.

SOCIAL AND ENVIRONMENTAL EFFECTS

There are three hypothesized social/environmental consequences of cannabis use that have received attention: the role of marijuana in enhancing interpersonal skills, the effect of cannabis on aggression and violence, and the role of marijuana use in what has been called the **amotivational syndrome.**

Amotivational syndrome
A term used to describe a loss of effectiveness and reduced capacity to accomplish conventional goals as a result of chronic marijuana use.

Many young users of marijuana have said they use the drug because it enhances their social skills and allows them to be more competent in social situations. Although insufficient data are available to evaluate it fully, this claim has not been supported by the available research. Rather, what seems to occur is that the user is either (a) more relaxed in the situation and thus perceives less anxiety or (b) interprets his or her behavior differently while under the influence of marijuana. In any event, it does not appear marijuana significantly enhances competence in social situations.

A long-standing claim regarding cannabis use, dating in this country to the 1920s newspaper articles in New Orleans cited above, is that marijuana causes the user to be aggressive and violent. However, the overwhelming conclusion drawn from the available data, including surveys, laboratory investigations, and field studies, is that cannabis use is not causally related to increases in aggression (see Institute of Medicine, 1982). When aggression is observed, it probably is more a function of the beliefs and characteristics of the individual drug user (Cherek, Roache, Egli, Davis, Spiga, & Cowan, 1993). In fact, levels of aggression actually decrease following cannabis use.

The third, and perhaps most controversial, social/environmental consequence of cannabis use is the amotivational syndrome. The term was independently used in the late 1960s by McGlothlin and West (1968) and Smith (1968) to describe the clinical observation "that regular marijuana use may contribute to the development of more passive, inward turning, amotivational personality characteristics" (McGlothlin & West, 1968). The list of behaviors proposed as part of the syndrome include apathy, decreased effectiveness, lost ambition, decreased sense of goals, and difficulty in attending and concentrating. Further, based on case reports, the phenomenon was most likely to be seen among younger users who were using marijuana daily or heavily.

Although there does not seem to be much question that the clustering of these characteristics occurs in some marijuana users, the causal influence of cannabis is not clear (Brick, 1990). Also, there is some debate about just how commonly the syndrome occurs, with some citing it as a fairly infrequent occurrence (NIDA, 1982). In addition, anthropological investigations of heavy cannabis users in other countries generally have not found the presence of the amotivational syndrome (for example, Carter, 1980; Carter & Doughty,

1976; Comitas, 1976; Page, 1983), and recent laboratory studies on cannabis use in humans have not supported the hypothesized syndrome (Foltin, Fischman, Brady, Kelly, Bernstein, & Nellis, 1989; Foltin, Fischman, Brady, Bernstein, Capriotti, Nellis, & Kelly, 1990). Further, survey studies do not always find the differences between marijuana users and nonusers that would be expected if marijuana caused this clustering of effects. Also, the amotivational syndrome has been seen in youths who do not use marijuana and is often not seen in other daily users of marijuana. Thus, it would seem that both pre-existing personality characteristics as well as some drug effects *together* probably account for the clustering labeled as the amotivational syndrome, when it occurs.

summary

- The plant *cannabis sativa* is more commonly known as marijuana. It once was harvested primarily for its fiber, but now is most often grown for its psychoactive effects.

- Marijuana is the leafy top portion of the plant, and hashish is the resin produced by the plant to protect it from the sun.

- The use of cannabis for its intoxicating effects appears to have been centered in Asia, the Middle East, and North Africa for an extended period of time before Europe was exposed to these effects in the nineteenth century.

- Cannabis in the New World dates to 1543, when it was brought to Chile by the Spaniards. The cannabis plant was raised in the U.S. colonies for its fiber.

- Several influential reports have appeared on the use of marijuana and its effects, including the 1894 Indian Hemp Drugs Commission Report and the 1944 LaGuardia Commission Report. Such reports have tended to find marijuana use overall is not particularly harmful to society at large.

- Marijuana is the most frequently used illicit drug in the United States, although there have been decreases in the extent of its use over the last decade.

- The most common and efficient procedure for ingesting cannabis is smoking.

- The principal psychoactive agent in cannabis, isolated in 1964, is delta-9-tetrahydro-cannabinol, more commonly known as Δ-9-THC or simply THC.

- The potency of cannabis varies widely. Most of the marijuana grown in the United States has a lower THC content than that imported from overseas. THC potency for marijuana smoked in the United States frequently is around 13–15%. Values for hashish and hash oil are higher, with hash oil containing up to 60% THC.

- The onset of THC action occurs within minutes of inhalation, and peak concentrations occur around 30 to 60 minutes later. The effects usually are experienced for around two to four hours. Most of the THC metabolites are excreted slowly, approximately half within several days and the remainder by the end of about a week. However, some metabolites can be detected in the body for up to and beyond 30 days.

- The main actions of marijuana occur in the brain and are a result of the drug's effect on neurotransmitters. While specification of the drug action remains speculative, recent advances include work on an apparent THC receptor in the brain.

- Tolerance, when it occurs, is most likely when high doses are used over extended periods of time. Physical dependence on cannabis is rare.

- Cannabis has long been used for medicinal and psychotherapeutic purposes. Today it is mostly used in the treatment of glaucoma and to reduce nausea and vomiting associated with cancer chemotherapies.

- The acute effects of marijuana generally are benign. These effects include bloodshot eyes, increased heart rate and pulse rate, and decreased motor activity.

- Research on long-term effects of marijuana is sparse. Some effects associated with long-term marijuana use appear to be reversible with termination of its use. There may be significant exceptions, such as the possible association between marijuana and lung cancer.

- Psychological effects of cannabis include decreased psychomotor activity, happy feelings and relaxation, impaired short-term memory, and altered time perception.

- Marijuana has not been shown to enhance social skills or to induce aggression or violence.

- The data on an "amotivational syndrome" due to cannabis use are mixed. It appears both preexisting personality characteristics as well as drug effects together account for what has been labeled the amotivational syndrome.

ANSWERS TO WHAT DO YOU THINK?

1. The cannabis plant was raised for its psychoactive properties by the settlers at Jamestown and, later, by George Washington.

F *Although they did cultivate the cannabis plant, it was for use of its fiber component and not for its psychoactive properties.*

2. The Eighteenth Amendment, prohibiting the use of alcohol, had the paradoxical effect of increasing the prevalence of marijuana use in the United States.

T *As the price of alcoholic beverages rose and the quality of these products declined during the Prohibition era, commercial trade in marijuana "sprang up."*

3. Criminal penalties in the United States for the possession and use of marijuana have increased steadily since the 1960s.

F *The penalties have been moderated significantly over this period, including the gradual decriminalization for possession of small amounts of marijuana. Throughout the 1960s, judges had the option of sentencing a user or seller to life in prison.*

4. Data recently gathered both in national household surveys and in annual surveys of high school seniors demonstrate a sharp decrease in the prevalence of marijuana use since 1979.

F *While the prevalence of marijuana use generally has decreased since the late 1970s, the most recent data*

on high school seniors showed significant increases in marijuana use.

5. The marijuana smoked in the United States today is more potent than that smoked 10 years ago.

T *It is many times more potent today.*

6. Drug effects following oral ingestion of marijuana last longer than when the drug is smoked.

T *Although the onset of action is slower and up to three times as much marijuana is needed to create a comparable high, the drug effects following oral ingestion last four to six hours compared to from two to four hours when smoked.*

7. Tolerance to cannabis has been well-documented in humans.

F *Although tolerance to cannabis has been well-documented with animals, the evidence for tolerance in humans is less clear. Some studies have indicated tolerance and some have not.*

8. Marijuana has been used effectively to treat glaucoma and the nausea and vomiting associated with chemotherapy for cancer.

T *Cannabis and THC synthetics have been used for both of these medical purposes. Research on these medical uses has increased since 1986, when the*

Drug Enforcement Administration reclassified synthetic THC as a Schedule II drug.

9 Marijuana use often causes long-term damage to the cardiovascular system.

F *Although marijuana use does cause short-term increases in heart rate and pulse rate, no evidence shows marijuana smoking to produce deleterious cardiovascular effects in healthy individuals. The acute effects may be dangerous to individuals with preexisting cardiovascular problems.*

10. One consequence of cannabis intoxication is the impairment of short-term memory.

T *This impairment is a common consequence of marijuana use and can occur with intake of a fairly low dose. The degree of impairment increases rapidly with the complexity of the task.*

11. The most commonly reported emotional effects of cannabis use are suspiciousness and paranoid ideation.

F *The typical emotional response to cannabis is a carefree and relaxed state. Paranoia and suspiciousness are reported less frequently and are reported more by inexperienced cannabis users.*

12. An area of concern regarding marijuana use is that it often causes the user to be aggressive and violent.

F *The overwhelming conclusion drawn from available data is that cannabis use is not causally related to increases in aggression. In fact, levels of aggression actually decrease following cannabis use.*

14 Hallucinogens

WHAT DO YOU THINK?

True or False?   ____   Unlike other classes of drugs, most hallucinogens are derived from synthetic compounds.

____   Hallucinogenic compounds were commonly used in the early 1900s throughout Europe and America.

____   The hallucinogenic properties of LSD were discovered by accident.

____   LSD was once used in psychotherapy.

____   Federal law mandates that anyone using LSD more than five times is declared legally insane.

____   Use of LSD, even once, is likely to cause permanent chromosome damage and subsequent birth defects.

____   Ecstasy (MDMA) produces vivid visual hallucinations.

____   Ecstasy has been shown to cause brain damage in nonhumans.

____   Hallucinations experienced under the influence of drugs such as LSD are very similar to those experienced by schizophrenics.

____   Dependence develops very easily to hallucinogens such as LSD.

____   Reports of LSD flashbacks are now considered an urban myth.

____   Phencyclidine (PCP or angel dust) was originally used as an animal tranquilizer.

OVERVIEW

One of the most fascinating, but also confusing, classes of drugs is the group called hallucinogens. These drugs are fascinating because they can alter consciousness in profound and bizarre ways. They are, at the same time, confusing because there are so many different drugs that act in a variety of ways as hallucinogens, and because these drugs have been named and classified in many different ways over the years. Originally called "phantastica" by Lewin (1964), hallucinogens have gone through dozens of name changes. Some researchers have used the term "psychotomimetics" because of the belief these drugs mimic the symptoms of functional psychoses such as schizophrenia. This usage is rare today because it is now clear that, although intriguing similarities exist, the effects of hallucinogens differ in a variety of ways (to be considered later) from natural psychosis. During the 1960s, advocates of hallucinogen use referred to them as "psychedelics," a term coined by one of the early LSD experimenters, Humphrey Osmond. Osmond defined psychedelic as "mind-expanding or mind-revealing" (Stevens, 1987), but whether LSD or other hallucinogens actually possess such properties is controversial at best, and we avoid the term for that reason.

The end result is that we are left with the term hallucinogen, but this term, too, is more than a bit misleading. It does focus attention on hallucinations and other alterations in perception, and indeed the drugs in this category generally do produce sensory disturbances or alterations that can be considered hallucinogenic. However, that is certainly not the only effect these drugs produce. Hallucinogens exert profound effects on mood, thinking processes, and physiological processes as well. Hallucinogens alter nearly all aspects of psychological functioning and the phrase "altered state of consciousness" describes these drugs better than any we have considered.

An additional complexity is that there are more than 90 different species of plants, and many more synthetic agents, that can be used to produce these kinds of effects (Siegel, 1984). In order to simplify this complex group of drugs we divide them on the basis of their effects and mechanisms of action into four different subgroups to be treated separately.

The first, and historically most important group, is referred to as the **serotonergic hallucinogens.** This category includes the synthetic compound lysergic acid diethylamide (LSD) and related drugs, such as **mescaline** (from the peyote cactus) and **psilocybin,** from certain mushrooms. These drugs all produce vivid visual hallucinations and a variety of other effects on consciousness. Recent experiments suggest that, despite differing chemical structures, these drugs also have in common the action of influencing serotonergic transmission in the brain (Pierce & Peroutka, 1990; Titeler, Lyon, & Glennon, 1988).

The second class of hallucinogens includes **MDA** and **MDMA** (ecstasy), referred to as the **methylated amphetamines.** As the name suggests these drugs are structurally related to amphetamine (as is mescaline), but produce alterations in mood and consciousness with little or no sensory change. They are thought to act like amphetamine and cocaine on dopamine and norepinephrine synapses, although they apparently influence serotonin as well (Commins et al., 1987).

A third class of hallucinogens, called the **anticholinergic hallucinogens,** is less familiar to most people and includes drugs such as atropine and scopolamine found in plants such as the mandrake, henbane, belladonna, and Jimson weed. These drugs produce a dreamlike trance in the user from which he or she awakens with little or no memory of the experience. The drugs in this class act on cholinergic synapses of the brain (Grinspoon & Bakalar, 1979).

Finally, a fourth class of hallucinogens includes phencyclidine (PCP or angel dust) and the related compound ketamine. These are often referred to as the **dissociative anesthetics** because of their ability to produce surgical anesthesia while the individual remains at least semiconscious. PCP is thought to act through a receptor that influences activity of the excitatory amino acid neurotransmitter, glutamate (Johnson & Jones, 1990).

Serotonergic hallucinogens
A class of drugs including LSD and drugs with similar effects and mechanisms of actions.

Mescaline
An LSD-like hallucinogen found in the peyote cactus.

Psilocybin (sihl-oh-SIGH-bin)
An LSD-like hallucinogen found in mushrooms.

Methylated amphetamines
A class of drugs including MDA and MDMA (ecstasy).

Anticholinergic hallucinogens
A class of drugs including atropine and scopolamine.

Dissociative anesthetic
A class of drugs including PCP and ketamine.

SEROTONERGIC HALLUCINOGENS: LSD AND RELATED COMPOUNDS

Early History

Table 14-1 shows some of the major drugs thought to obtain their hallucinogenic properties by altering serotonin function in the brain. LSD is the prototypic hallucinogen of this class, but drugs with effects similar to those of LSD

Table 14-1   Serotonergic Hallucinogens

Drug	Botanical Source	Area Found	Other Names
Lysergic acid diethylamide (LSD)	Synthetic, but derived from the ergot fungus	Ergot native to Europe	Acid, many others
Ibogaine	Iboga plant: *Tabernanthe iboga*	Africa	—
Psilocybin	Mushrooms of genus *Psilocybe*, *Conocybe*, *Panaeolus*, and *Stropharia*	Throughout the world	Teonanacatl
Dimethyltryptamine (DMT)	Virola tree *Virola calophylla* and other species	South America	Yakee, Yopo
Mescaline	Peyote cactus *Lophophora williamsii*	Mexico and Southwest U.S.	Peyote
Harmaline, Harmine	Ayahuasca vine *Banisteriopsis caapi* *Banisteriopsis inebrians*	South America	Yagé
Ergine, Isoergine	Morning glory seeds: *Rivea corymbosa* *Ipomoea violacea*	Throughout the world	Ololuiqui

were used long before LSD was synthesized. As you can see in Table 14-1, LSD-like hallucinogens can be found in a wide variety of plants. The hallucinogenic properties of these plants were primarily discovered and used by the Indian peoples of Central and South America (an exception is ibogaine, which was discovered and used by tribal peoples of Africa). The uses to which these hallucinogenic plants were put have been reconstructed by historians and anthropologists and are worth some consideration here.

When the Spanish *conquistadores* began to explore and colonize Mexico and other parts of Central and South America, they encountered new civilizations with customs and religious practices unfamiliar to Europeans. Among these practices was the use of hallucinogenic plants in religious ceremonies. One of the earliest documentations of these practices was by Fernando Hernandez, the royal physician to the king of Spain (Stewart, 1987), who in 1577 studied the plants used by the Aztecs and noted the use of peyote cactus (referred to as peyotl) (see nearby Drugs and Culture Box), psilocybe mushrooms (called teonanacatl), and morning glory seeds (called ololuiqui). Although each of these plants contains a different drug, all are capable of producing vivid visual hallucinations, and the Indians took the visions produced by them as oracles that could reveal the future and solve other mysteries, help in decision making, and aid the medicine man or shaman in healing the sick.

The hallucinogenic compounds in the morning glory (ergine and isoergine) are similar to, but far less potent than, LSD, and besides producing their hallucinogenic effects cause severe nausea and vomiting, a factor that has limited their current use.

The Aztec and Mayan peoples called the psilocybe mushrooms "teonanacatl" which means "flesh of the gods," and as one might guess from that name, the mushrooms were viewed as sacred. Mushroom icons found in

Psilocybin comes from mushrooms such as this *Psilocybe cubensis*.

Mayan ruins dating back to more than 1000 B.C. suggest the use of the sacred mushroom is an ancient practice (Schultes, 1976). One Spanish writer, de Sahagun in the 1500s, described the use of mushrooms by Aztecs as follows:

> These mushrooms caused them to become intoxicated, to see visions and also to be provoked to lust. . . . They ate the mushrooms with honey and when they began to feel excited due to the effect of the mushrooms, the Indians started dancing, while some were singing and others weeping. . . . Some Indians who did not care to sing, sat down in their rooms, remaining there as if to think. Others, however, saw in a vision that they died and thus cried; others saw themselves eaten by a wild beast; others imagined that they were capturing prisoners of war; others that they were rich or that they possessed many slaves; others that they had committed adultery and had their heads crushed for this offense. . . . (quoted by Schlieffer, 1973, p. 19).

This may be the first description of hallucinogenic drug effects capturing the range of experiences different individuals may have after taking the drug. As with the morning glory, use of sacred mushrooms persists in parts of Mexico today with rituals for healing and divination (Schultes, 1976).

In South America a number of different hallucinogenic plants traditionally have been used in much the same way as peyote and psilocybin were to the north. Hallucinogens called harmaline and harmine are found in the bark of the vines B*anisteriopsis caapi* and B. *inebrians*. These plants are known as Ayahuasca or Caapi by natives of the western Amazon area of Brazil, Colombia, Peru, Ecuador, and Bolivia. Local names for the drink made from the bark of these vines are yagé, pinde, and dapa. These plants are used in healing

"Rotating kaleidoscopes . . . kaleidoscopes moving horizontally . . . weeds, lots of yellow weeds multiplying, embellished with colors . . ."
(Siegel, 1992, description of peyote vision)

Mescaline comes from the peyote cactus, *Lophophora williamsii.*

ceremonies, initiation rites, and other rituals. They are said by the natives to provide the user with telepathic powers, but there is no scientific support for this claim (Schultes, 1976). Also widely used in South America for their hallucinogenic properties are various species of the Virola tree (*Virola calophylla, V. calophylloidea,* and *V. theiodora*) of Brazil, Colombia, and Venezuela. The bark of these trees is taken as a snuff that contains the potent hallucinogen dimethyltryptamine (DMT). Virola snuff is taken by some Amazon tribes in a funeral ritual in which the powdered bones of the deceased are consumed along with the snuff (Schultes, 1976).

Recent History

Despite the long history of hallucinogenic drug use, these drugs had virtually no impact on mainstream European or American culture until the 1960s when an explosion of hallucinogen use occurred. The history of the "psychedelic movement" began in Basel, Switzerland, where Albert Hofmann, a chemist working in Sandoz Laboratories, discovered LSD in 1938. Hofmann was studying derivatives of ergot, a fungus that infests grain and occasionally caused outbreaks of disease (St. Anthony's Fire) in medieval Europe when infected bread was eaten. Ergot derivatives have medical use in the treatment of migraine headache and in effecting uterine contractions during pregnancy, and this accounted for Sandoz' interest. Hofmann eventually synthesized a number of compounds involving lysergic acid, the 25th of which was lysergic acid diethylamide—abbreviated LSD-25 on the bottle. LSD was given several preliminary animal tests and, not showing any commercially interesting properties, was shelved. It stayed unknown until 1943 when Hofmann decided to reexamine its properties. During a laboratory experiment, Hofmann appar-

DRUGS AND CULTURE
PEYOTE

Peyote may have been the most widespread hallucinogenic drug in the New World. This is surprising considering the peyote cactus is limited in range to a relatively small area of northern Mexico and southwestern Texas. The Aztecs used peyote in their rituals and de Sahagun noted "Those who eat or drink it see visions either frightful or laughable . . ." (Stewart, 1987, p. 19). Peyote, like ololiuqui and sacred mushrooms, was forbidden to the Indians by the Spaniards, who regarded its use for religious purposes as blasphemous. Thus, the use of all these agents persisted only "underground," and little is known of them before the twentieth century. However, intriguingly, the peyote religion apparently spread widely during the eighteenth and nineteenth centuries, becoming a religion uniting most Indian tribes in western Mexico and the United States.

The southwestern tribes gathered peyote by cutting the cactus at the soil-line, leaving the root intact. The cactus was sliced and dried into hard "buttons." These buttons could be transported great distances without losing their potency, and indeed they found their way to Native American tribes living throughout the west and as far north as Minnesota and Wisconsin. The ritual itself was (and is) almost identical regardless of the tribe studied. The all-night ceremony takes place in a large tepee where the participants sit in a circle around a fire. Peyote buttons are eaten and peyote tea is drunk. Tobacco is smoked in the form of cigarettes or a pipe. The night is spent chanting, singing, and praying, and later on, in discussing and interpreting the peyote-induced visions. These ceremonies are still conducted today by some Native American people much as they were many centuries ago (Stewart, 1987). Until recently, use of peyote by members of the Native American Church was exempted from U.S. drug laws. However, in 1990 the Supreme Court ruled that states may ban the religious use of peyote without violating the constitutional right of free religious exercise. This ruling in turn is being challenged, but the future of legal religious use of hallucinogens is in doubt.

---

ently spilled a small amount of LSD on his hand where it was absorbed. Thus Hofmann became the first person to experience the effects of LSD. He described his experiences as follows:

> I was forced to interrupt my work in the laboratory in the middle of the afternoon and proceed home, being affected by a remarkable restlessness, combined with a slight dizziness. At home I lay down and sank into a not unpleasant intoxicated-like condition, characterized by an extremely stimulated imagination. In a dreamlike state, with eyes closed . . . I perceived an uninterrupted stream of fantastic pictures, extraordinary shapes with intense, kaleidoscopic play of colors (Hofmann, 1980, p. 15).

Hofmann decided the bizarre experience must have been due to contact with LSD, and decided to test that hypothesis with an experiment. He reasoned that LSD must be very potent to have produced such effects through an accidental exposure, and measured out for oral administration 250 micrograms— a minute amount by standards of drugs known at that time. What Hofmann could not have known is that LSD is *so* potent that this dose was at least twice as potent as the normal effective dose (25–125 micrograms).

After taking the drug Hofmann noted in his journal: "Beginning dizziness, feeling of anxiety, visual distortions, symptoms of paralysis, desire to laugh" (Hofmann, 1980, p. 16). At this point Hofmann was overcome by the drug and could no longer write. He asked his assistant to escort him home, and he later wrote the following about his LSD trip:

> On the way home, my condition began to assume threatening forms. Everything in my field of vision wavered and was distorted as if seen in a curved mirror. . . . Finally we arrived at home safe and sound, and I was just barely capable of asking my companion to summon our family doctor and request milk from the neighbors . . . as a nonspecific antidote for poisoning.
>
> My surroundings had now transformed themselves in more terrifying ways. Everything in the room spun around, and assumed grotesque, threatening forms. They were in continuous motion, animated, as if driven by an inner restlessness. The lady next door, whom I scarcely recognized, brought me milk. . . . She was no longer Mrs. R., but rather a malevolent, insidious witch with a colored mask . . . (Hofmann, 1980, p. 16–17).

Later, as the intensity of the drug effects began to subside, Hofmann reported enjoying the hallucinations and altered thought processes. After he recovered and made his report to Sandoz, many other experiments followed.

Sandoz began to distribute LSD to psychologists and psychiatrists for use as an adjunct to psychotherapy. The theory was that the drug would break down the patient's normal ego defenses, and thus facilitate the psychotherapy process. Psychiatrists were encouraged to try LSD themselves so they would better understand the subjective experience of schizophrenia. The idea was that LSD was psychotomimetic—mimicked psychosis.

By the early 1960s many people had tried LSD, and it was beginning to generate some publicity. One user was movie star Cary Grant, who said in an interview that his LSD psychotherapy changed his whole life and brought him true peace of mind. Another famous user, Henry Luce, head of Time, Inc., said he talked to God under LSD's influence. The British author Aldous Huxley, who earlier had tried peyote and written a book about his experiences (Huxley, 1954), promoted LSD and other hallucinogenic drugs as leading to the next step in human evolution! But the most influential of the early LSD users were Harvard psychologist Timothy Leary and the writer Ken Kesey.

Leary and his Harvard associate Richard Alpert (who later became known as religious writer Baba Ram Dass) had taken LSD and other hallucinogens and become convinced of the psychological and spiritual value of these drugs. What began as legitimate experiments, including work on the possible beneficial effects of hallucinogens on prison inmates, began to look suspiciously like LSD parties involving Harvard faculty, students, and an assortment of celebrities and intellectuals. At some point, Leary had stepped out of his role as a scientist and had become the leader of a social and religious movement. Calling himself "High Priest," Leary claimed LSD was a ticket to a trip to spiritual enlightenment. He exhorted an entire generation to "Turn on. Tune in. Drop out" (Stevens, 1987). Leary left Harvard under duress in 1963, but continued to proselytize for LSD and in fact became a media celebrity. Harassment by law enforcement officials continued to increase Leary's eminence, and he became viewed as something of a martyr, winning new converts as a curious nation heard more and more about the wonders of LSD.

On the west coast, LSD was popularized by Ken Kesey, celebrated author, and his "merry pranksters." Kesey is the author of *One Flew Over the Cuckoo's Nest*. As recounted by Wolfe (1969), Kesey's "acid tests" were large parties where hundreds of people would be "turned on to LSD" in a single night. LSD began to make an impact on the emerging hippie subculture, particularly through the music of groups like the Grateful Dead, Jefferson Airplane, Jimi Hendrix, and others whose music became known as "acid rock." Eventually the Beatles became part of the movement and the surreal images of songs such as "Lucy in the Sky with Diamonds" had the entire Western world talking about, if not using, LSD. By the late 1960s LSD had become the most controversial drug in the world. As many as 2 million people had tried LSD in the United States, but the positive statements about LSD had become counterbalanced by increasing negative publicity. LSD was claimed to cause chromosome damage—users were said to be likely to have mutant children. It was said to cause insanity, suicide, acts of violence, and homicidal behavior (Stevens, 1987). All of this controversy led to a decline in LSD use in the 1970s and 1980s, but perhaps equally important was a loss of faith in the LSD mystique, the recognition that spiritual enlightenment produced by LSD was a false hope. As Hunter S. Thompson put it in his chronicle of the era:

> This was the fatal flaw in Tim Leary's trip. He crashed around America selling consciousness expansion without ever giving a thought to the grim meat-hook realities that were lying in wait for all the people who took him too seriously. . . . Not that they didn't deserve it: No doubt they all Got What Was Coming To Them. All those pathetically eager acid freaks thought they could buy Peace and Understanding for three bucks a hit. But their loss and failure is ours, too. What Leary took down with him was the central illusion of a whole life-style that he helped to create . . . a generation of permanent cripples, failed seekers, who never understood the essential old-mystic fallacy of the Acid Culture: the desperate assumption that somebody—or at least some *force*—is tending that Light at the end of the tunnel." (Thompson, 1971, pp. 178–179.)

The use of LSD did not vanish, but did decline through the 1980s, reaching a low in 1990 (Johnston, O'Malley, & Bachman, 1991). However, a variety of indicators suggest that LSD use, along with other hallucinogens, is on the rise again. Recent media reports have emphasized the use of LSD and MDMA (ecstasy—see below) in the "Rave" subculture. The protracted parties or concerts that are sometimes referred to as raves typically last many hours and

The Rave scene has been associated with an increased use of LSD and ecstasy.

often are associated with laser light shows, "technomusic," vigorous dancing, and "headbanging." A recent edition of CBS' 48 *Hours* called the rave scene "more like the 60s than the 60s," and emphasized the increased use of LSD and ecstasy that has accompanied the movement. The National Institute on Drug Abuse has reported recent indicators that support the notion that LSD use is rising with findings of increased LSD availability, increased frequency of self-reported use, and an increased frequency of emergency room admissions involving LSD (Mathias, 1993).

Mechanisms of Action of LSD-like Drugs

The mechanisms by which LSD and related drugs are capable of producing—in such small doses—such dramatic effects as visual hallucinations and alterations of consciousness remain enigmatic, but there is increasing consensus that an important aspect involves the alteration of activity of brain systems mediated by the neurotransmitter serotonin. The first bit of evidence was suggested by the chemical structures of some of the major hallucinogens. LSD, psilocybin, harmaline, and most of the other drugs in Table 12-1 are classified according to their chemical structure as indolealkylamines (Nichols & Glennon, 1984). That chemical structure is shared by the naturally occurring transmitter serotonin. The structural similarity led to the notion that LSD and related compounds might act by mimicking serotonin, and thus activate serotonin receptors in the brain. This hypothesis has now received considerable support. For example, it has been shown that LSD and the other hallucinogenic indolealkylamines bind to serotonin receptors, and that the potency of serotonin binding correlates strongly with the potency of the drug as a hallucinogen (Glennon, Titeler, & McKenny, 1984; Titeler, Lyon, & Glennon, 1988; Pierce & Peroutka, 1990).

One problem with the above analysis is mescaline. Mescaline's chemical structure is quite different from the others. In fact, mescaline has a structure far more similar to amphetamine than LSD. For this reason, it has often been classified as having a different mechanism than LSD. However, unlike amphetamine (and the methylated amphetamines like MDA—see the following), mescaline produces vivid visual hallucinations virtually identical in form to those of LSD. Further evidence for a common mechanism of action between LSD and mescaline comes from studies on tolerance. Tolerance to all the effects of LSD develops fairly rapidly. The same is true for mescaline. In addition, there is cross-tolerance between LSD, mescaline, and other drugs of this class (Jacobs, 1987). Finally, recent data suggest that mescaline (or perhaps one of mescaline's metabolites) also binds to the serotonin receptor (Appel & Rosencrans, 1984; Davis, 1987; Jacobs, 1987).

As we noted in Chapter 3, serotonin is distributed widely in the brain. This may account for the many and various effects of LSD-like hallucinogens. Serotonin is thought to play an important role in mood, which is consistent with the powerful emotional effects of these drugs. The precise areas of the brain responsible for the hallucinogenic actions of these drugs, however, remain a mystery.

Pharmacokinetics of LSD-like Drugs

As we have noted above, the effects of all of the hallucinogens that act upon serotonin receptors are quite similar. However, these drugs differ widely in potency, duration of action, and other pharmacokinetic variables. LSD is the most potent of the class, with oral doses of as little as 25 micrograms producing effects. Street doses range from about 75 to 250 micrograms and are prepared by placing a small amount of LSD solution on paper (blotter) or in a gel (windowpane) or in a tablet (Stock, 1986a). LSD is rapidly absorbed and subjective effects are usually noted within 20 to 60 minutes after consumption. The drug is distributed throughout the body and readily penetrates the blood-brain barrier. The effects of LSD persist for 8 to 12 hours, and the drug is rapidly metabolized and eliminated from the body. Even the most sensitive techniques can detect LSD or its metabolites in urine for no more than 72 hours after use (Hawks & Chiang, 1986). Although the hallucinogens found in morning glory seeds (ergine and isoergine) are quite similar to LSD, they are far less potent—perhaps 5 to 10% as strong as LSD (Grinspoon & Bakalar, 1979).

Psilocybin normally is taken orally by either eating the mushrooms or drinking a brew containing them. It is difficult to specify doses because the amount of psilocybin varies depending on the species of mushroom, among other things. Typically, 5 to 10 g of mushrooms are taken, containing 10 to 20 mg of psilocybin. Thus, psilocybin is about 1% as potent as LSD. The duration of action is about four to six hours. As is true of virtually all of the serotonergic hallucinogens, tolerance develops to psilocybin, and it shows cross-tolerance with other members of the family (Grinspoon & Bakalar, 1979).

Mescaline is normally taken by consumption of peyote buttons, as described above. Usually 5 to 20 buttons are eaten, delivering about 200–800 mg of mescaline. Mescaline is about 1/3000 as potent as LSD, with 200 mg considered an effective dose. Duration of action is about 8 to 12 hours.

Less information is available about the other serotonergic hallucinogens, but most are similar to the above. One noteworthy exception is dimethyltryptamine (DMT), which is usually taken by using the bark of the Virola as a snuff or by smoking it. Its effects begin within minutes of use, but persist for only about 30 minutes.

Psychotherapeutic Uses

LSD and the related hallucinogens historically have been thought to have two applications in psychotherapy, but neither is well-accepted today. One notion was that LSD produced a model psychosis, and that the psychotherapist would benefit from having experiences similar to those of the patient. It is true that hallucinations, unusual affective reactions, and loss of reality contact are characteristic of both schizophrenia and hallucinogenic experiences. But there also are important differences. For example, the hallucinations experienced under the influence of LSD are primarily visual in nature, while those of schizophrenics are usually auditory (Anderson, 1980). So the subjective experiences of the psychotic are certainly not identical to those of the hallucinogen user. However, an intriguing similarity is that chlorpromazine and the other antipsychotics used in the treatment of schizophrenia are effective antagonists of LSD effects. Thus, hallucinogens may yet provide clues about the biochemistry of mental disorders.

Paradoxically, the other major application of hallucinogens has been as an adjunct to psychotherapy. The general idea was that the therapist would be able to learn important information when the patient was using LSD, and that the patient would be better able to gain insight into his or her condition because LSD could break down ego defenses. Many extravagant claims have been made about the benefits of LSD for mental health and spiritual development, but the use of LSD in psychotherapy gradually has declined. Although one important reason for this was the political climate, another was that most therapists thought the potential risks of LSD outweighed the benefits. In fact, it never has been demonstrated scientifically that the use of LSD is superior to placebo as an adjunct to psychotherapy. Some therapists think these drugs deserve further evaluation as possible psychotherapeutic agents (Grinspoon & Bakalar, 1979, 1983), but the current controversy has shifted to the related drugs MDA and MDMA (see page 354).

Effects of Serotonergic Hallucinogens

The physiological effects of LSD and related hallucinogens are generally similar to those of amphetamine and cocaine. That is, they are sympathomimetic. Thus, the effects include pupil dilation, increased heart rate and blood pressure, increased body temperature, and increased sweating (Grinspoon & Bakalar, 1979).

The psychological effects are more difficult to characterize. Experiences with hallucinogens are tremendously variable between individuals and, for a single individual, may vary from one experience to the next. Common to all the serotonergic hallucinogens are profound changes in visual perception, although there is some consistency in the types of visual changes that occur. Many were summarized by Albert Hofmann in his account of his first LSD trip described earlier. Hofmann added:

> Kaleidoscopic fantastic images surged in on me, alternating, variegated, opening, and then closing themselves in circles and spirals, exploding in colored fountains, rearranging and hybridizing themselves in constant flux. It was particularly remarkable how every acoustic perception, such as the sound of a door handle or a passing automobile, became transformed into optical perceptions. Every sound generated a vividly changing image, with its own consistent form and color (Hofmann, 1980, p. 19).

The spiral explosions and vortex patterns described by Hofmann have been noted by Siegel (1992) to be among the most common forms in hallucinogenic experiences. Siegel calls them *form constants* because they are reported so frequently. Another form constant noted by Siegel is the lattice pattern—a checkerboard-like pattern that appears in an otherwise plain surface. The experience described by Hofmann of sensing a sound stimulus as a visual one is called **synesthesia,** and it has been reported by others as well. Other visual effects are flashing lights, increased brightness and intensity of colors, the experience of trails or plumes around objects, and the sense of movement in stable objects (for example, the wall breathes or moves rhythmically).

However, there is a good bit more to the "trip" than just a light show. Other perceptions may be altered. Mood is extremely labile, and bizarre cognitive experiences occur (Stevens, 1987). Some examples of such experiences are given in the nearby Contemporary Issue Box. Although the descriptions recounted in the box are quite different, they do reveal some similarities. All are characterized by strong affect, although the nature of the emotional state varies. All involve "magical" thinking and, particularly in the last two, events are fraught with cosmic significance. If the visions are terrifying (as in the second quote) the subject may behave in a psychotic manner—and this is usually referred to as a bad or bum trip. The insights, enlightenments, and beliefs that occur and seem so significant during the trip often turn out to be trivial or false afterwards. For example, subjects are often convinced they possess telepathic or clairvoyant abilities under the influence of the drug, but when tested, these abilities are not present. Nonetheless, it is easy to see how such experiences must have led prescientific cultures to attach mystical and religious significance to hallucinogens.

Synesthesia
An effect sometimes produced by hallucinogens characterized by the perception of a stimulus in a modality other than the one in which it was presented (for example, a subject may report "seeing" music).

Adverse Effects of Serotonergic Hallucinogens

An important part of the LSD controversy revolves around the adverse effects stemming from its use. One of the major concerns about LSD use involved the claim that it produced chromosome damage—that those who used the drug, male or female, would stand a high risk of having deformed children.

Contemporary Issue
DESCRIPTIONS OF SUBJECTIVE EFFECTS OF LSD

Many attempts have been made to describe the effects and experiences produced by LSD. Such accounts are remarkably diverse, often confusing, and sometimes contradictory, yet there are some common features. The following are vivid recollections given by well-known LSD users, illustrating the variety of the experience:

> I looked into the glass of water. In its swirling depths was a vortex which went down the center of the world and the heart of time. . . . A dog barked and its piercing howl might have been all the wolves in Tartary. . . . At one moment I would be a giant in a tiny cupboard, and the next, a dwarf in a huge hall (Humphrey Osmond on mescaline—quoted by Grinspoon & Bakalar, 1979, p. 100).

> I was lying on my back on the floor. Then the room itself vanished and I was sinking, sinking, sinking. From far away I heard very faintly the word "death." I sank faster, turning and falling a million light years from the earth. The word got louder and more insistent. It took shape around me, closing me in.
> "DEATH . . . DEATH . . . DEATH." I thought of the dread in my father's eyes in his final hours. At the last instant before my own death I shouted, "No." Absolute terror, total horror (Lingeman on LSD—quoted by Grinspoon & Bakalar, 1979, p. 112).

> Now a series of visions began. The imagery appeared to synchronize with the phonograph music. . . . I envisioned myself at the court of Kubla Khan . . . at a concert being held in an immense auditorium . . . in some futuristic utopia . . . at Versailles . . . at a statue of Lincoln. . . . I felt myself engulfed in a chaotic, turbulent sea. . . . There were a number of small boats tossing on the raging sea . . . [I was] in one of these vessels . . . we came upon a gigantic figure standing waist-deep in the churning waters . . . His facial features were graced by an unforgettable look of compassion, love, and concern. We knew that this was the image of God. We realized that God, too, was caught in the storm (Krippner on psilocybin—quoted by Grinspoon & Bakalar, 1979, pp. 100–101).

This concern was based on a study that found LSD produced chromosome breaks in white blood cells artificially cultured in the laboratory. The study raised fears that LSD also might damage human gametes (Cohen & Marmillo, 1967). However, breaking chromosomes in white cells in a test tube under high doses of LSD has not been shown to be relevant to *in vivo* conditions. After considerable research into this question, there is no convincing evidence that LSD (or any other serotonergic hallucinogen) increases birth defects in offspring when taken in normal doses. Although in high doses some risk is possible, LSD is no more likely to cause birth defects than aspirin under ordinary circumstances (Grinspoon & Bakalar, 1979; Long, 1972). As with most drugs, however, there is risk of fetal damage if taken by pregnant women (Grinspoon & Bakalar, 1979).

Some of the other adverse effects of LSD and related hallucinogens are more cause for concern. An important problem has been acute panic or paranoid reactions to the drug. These bad trips can leave individuals in an acute psychotic state during which they may harm themselves or others. The frequency of bad trips is difficult to estimate, but was high enough in the 1960s to lead to the widespread development of walk-in crisis centers where victims could be brought for reassurance (talking the subject down), and if necessary, hospital referral. Bad trips appear to be less frequent today perhaps because more is known about how to prevent them. The psychological state of the user and the environmental setting are important. For example, one of the few documented LSD-suicides took place after a man was administered LSD without his knowledge in an experiment conducted by the CIA in the 1950s (Grinspoon & Bakalar, 1979). Being exposed to the drug without foreknowledge is apparently quite frightening and disturbing. Individuals seem to be less likely to have bad trips if they are aware and frequently reminded that they are under the influence of a drug. A calm and comfortable setting and low doses of LSD are thought to reduce the frequency of bad trips as well, although bad trips may occur even under the best of circumstances (Brecher, 1972).

Another problem associated with LSD-like hallucinogens is a phenomenon known as the **flashback.** Flashbacks involve a sudden, unexpected reexperience of some aspect of a hallucinogenic trip that occurred weeks, months, or years before. Although, as with bad trips, it is difficult to estimate the frequency of flashbacks, in one study 53.5% of LSD users reported flashbacks (Abraham, 1983). Most subjects did not find these flashbacks to be terribly disturbing, but 12.9% sought clinical help for the problem. Although little is known about the causes of flashbacks, they tend to be precipitated by anxiety, fatigue, marijuana, or sudden changes in the environment such as emergence into darkness (Abraham, 1983).

Flashback
A sudden recurrence of an LSD-like experience.

LSD also has been linked to long-term psychiatric disorders. Perhaps the most publicized and horrifying example is Charles Manson and his "family." The Manson family used LSD heavily, but it is unclear what role, if any, the drug played in the development of their psychopathology and subsequent mass murders. When confronted with a psychotic individual who has used LSD, it is difficult to determine whether LSD caused the psychosis, or whether the person was psychotic to begin with and LSD made the symptoms more flagrant. To complicate matters further, most users of LSD who are diagnosed as psychotic have extensive histories with other drugs as well, and the role these other drugs may have played is rarely certain. It generally is agreed hallucinogens may precipitate or exacerbate psychosis or emotional disturbance in certain vulnerable individuals (Bowers, 1977; Smith & Seymour, 1985). Other adverse effects have been associated with LSD use. For example, there have been rare, but disturbing, reports of permanent visual disturbances induced by LSD in humans (Kaminer & Hrecznyj, 1991). LSD has also been reported to produce long-term or permanent alterations in brain chemistry and behavior in laboratory animals (King & Ellison, 1989). Thus, while the problems associated with LSD do not include drug dependence, it is, nonetheless, a potentially dangerous drug.

METHYLATED AMPHETAMINES

Overview

The recent controversy over designer drugs has focused a great deal of attention on the drugs in this category, particularly MDMA, better known as ecstasy. MDMA is one of a group of drugs known as methylated amphetamines because of their chemical structures (there are dozens of drugs in this category, but the more well-known variations are presented in Table 14-2). These drugs are often categorized with the serotonergic hallucinogens, and indeed, their chemical structures resemble that of mescaline. In addition they influence serotonin transmission (but also norepinephrine and dopamine—Commins et al., 1987). DOM not only resembles mescaline in structure, but also produces similar effects, including visual hallucinations. However, the others (MDA, MDMA, DOET) are different from the serotonergic hallucinogens reviewed above in that they produce few or no visual hallucinations. In drug-discrimination studies, laboratory animals identify MDA, MDMA, and DOET with amphetamine and discriminate them from LSD. Similar observations are reported by humans (Boja & Schecter, 1987; Oberlender & Nichols, 1988). The effects of MDA and MDMA seem to be primarily a mild euphoria accompanied by openness and lack of defensiveness. These properties led some psychotherapists to advocate the use of these drugs, particularly MDMA, as an adjunct to therapy. Thus, there is growing sentiment to consider these drugs as belonging to a unique category among hallucinogens. However, on the less positive side, there are reports suggesting that these drugs may damage serotonergic neurons in the brain (de Souza, Errol, Battaglia, & Insel, 1990).

History and Epidemiology

DOM was first reported on the street in the late 1960s, when its potent hallucinogenic effects and very long duration of action (as long as 24 hours) led to many bad trips. MDA also surfaced on the street about this time, but it had a better reception. It was referred to as Mellow Drug of America because it is less intense and has fewer perceptual effects than LSD. It also was called the

Table 14-2   Methylated Amphetamines

Chemical Name	Abbreviation	Street Names
2,5-dimethoxy-4 methylamphetamine	DOM	STP
3,4-methylenedioxyamphetamine	MDA	Love Drug, Mellow Drug of America
3,4-methylenedioxymethamphetamine	MDMA	Ecstasy, XTC, Adam
N-ethyl-3,4-methylenedioxyamphetamine	MDE	Eve

Love Drug, because users reported positive feelings toward others and great empathy as part of the experience. Use of MDA declined along with the LSD in the 1970s while MDMA began to increase in popularity, peaking in the mid-1980s. In 1976 it was estimated 10,000 doses of MDMA were used on the street during the year. In 1985 the Drug Enforcement Agency (DEA) estimated 30,000 doses were distributed per month in one Texas city alone (Stock, 1986b). What accounted for this enormous increase? Publicity about the therapeutic benefits of MDMA made it attractive (Sound familiar? Remember Timothy Leary . . .). It did not hurt public relations for the drug to pick up the nickname "ecstasy." Finally, until 1985 MDMA was a legal drug. Although MDA was a Schedule I drug, its close relative MDMA had not been classified under the schedule system. Thus, dealers preferred the low risks associated with the designer drug, ecstasy. However, in the face of the explosive rise in MDMA use, coupled with animal research implicating the drug with brain damage, the Drug Enforcement Agency classified MDMA as Schedule I in 1985 on an emergency basis (Barnes, 1988). As soon as MDMA was controlled, dealers began to distribute DOET, which is a similar drug that also is now controlled by the Designer Drug Act of 1986 (Boja & Schecter, 1987). These decisions have been controversial, because they effectively banned further psychiatric

Ecstasy is ". . . like LSD without the hallucinations."

(*Time*, Vol. 141, No. 6, 1993)

Contemporary Issue
TROUBLE WITH ECSTASY

The research necessary to determine the value of MDMA in psychotherapy may never be done because of recent evidence that the drugs in this family may produce long-term damage of certain brain structures. The report sounding the alarm (Ricaurte et al., 1985) showed that after several administrations of high doses of MDA, rats had a depletion of serotonin apparently caused by degeneration of serotonergic neuron terminals. These effects were apparent as long as two weeks after treatment and Ricaurte and others speculated the effects might prove to be permanent. Similar results now have been reported for MDMA at fairly low doses and in several species including primates (see de Souza et al., 1990; Kosten & Price, 1992). Whether these neurons ever recover from the toxic effects of the drugs is unknown. As noted in Chapter 3, serotonin is a neurotransmitter modulating sleep and is thought to be deficient in depressive disorders. Therefore, depletion of serotonin could lead to serious problems. Whether MDMA and MDA will produce these neurotoxic effects in humans at moderate dose levels is unknown at the present.

There have been reports of long-term neuropsychiatric problems in ecstasy users (McCann, Ridenour, Shaham, & Ricaurte, 1993; McCann & Ricaurte, 1991) but the role of ecstasy in producing these effects is controversial (Grob et al., 1992). Until this issue is resolved, the possibility of therapeutic applications of MDMA will remain uncertain. Acute toxic reactions to MDMA, which include some deaths due to kidney failure, have also been reported (Randall, 1992).

testing of MDMA and related compounds. As of this writing the drug is in a legal limbo: the answers to some of the questions about its therapeutic potential and neurotoxicity will determine where MDMA winds up in our legal system (see Kosten & Price, 1992; Liester et al., 1992).

Effects of Methylated Amphetamines

The effects of MDMA, MDA, and DOET are similar enough to be discussed together (DOM effects are like those of mescaline or LSD and are not considered further). These drugs are usually taken orally, but can be injected or absorbed intranasally (snorted). They are absorbed rapidly and have a duration of action of about six to eight hours. At effective doses (75–150 mg for MDMA; 50–150 mg for MDA; 1–2 mg for DOET) these drugs produce clear sympathomimetic effects, including increased heart rate, blood pressure, and pupil dilation. Additional physical effects include muscle tension, jaw-clenching (bruxism), appetite suppression, and insomnia—effects remarkably similar to those of amphetamine (Davis, Hatoum, & Waters, 1987; Grinspoon & Bakalar, 1979). The psychological effects claimed for these drugs are euphoria, increased emotional warmth, lowered defensiveness and increased communicative ability (Kirsch, 1986; Liester et al., 1992; Peroutka, 1987). Hallucinations are uncommon or absent at ordinary doses. These properties led some psychiatrists to advocate use of these drugs as an adjunct to psychotherapy, but as yet there is no convincing evidence supporting the value of MDMA (or any others of this class) in psychotherapy (Kirsch, 1986).

ANTICHOLINERGIC HALLUCINOGENS

Atropine
An anticholinergic hallucinogen found in certain plants.

Scopolamine
An anticholinergic hallucinogen found in certain plants.

Atropine and **scopolamine** are drugs that block acetylcholine receptors in the brain. Although used in low doses for medical purposes, these drugs can produce hallucinogenic effects in high doses. They are found in a number of plants known throughout the world and have a long history of use. Hundreds of years B.C., plants containing scopolamine and atropine were used by the ancient Greeks at the oracle of Delphi. In the Middle Ages such plants were included in the infamous witches' brews. Plants such as belladonna, also called the deadly nightshade (*Atropa belladonna*), mandrake (*Mandragora officinarum*), henbane (*Hyoscyamus niger*) of Europe, and Jimson weed (*Datura stramonium*), and other plants of the Datura genus from the New World, have been eaten for their hallucinogenic properties (Schultes, 1976). Although these drugs are no longer in use for witchcraft, Datura is allegedly one of the ingredients in Zombie powder in Haiti (Davis, 1988).

Anticholinergic hallucinogens produce a variety of physiological effects, including dry mouth, blurred vision, loss of motor control, and increased heart rate and body temperature. They can be fatal due to respiratory failure at doses only slightly higher than the effective dose (Grinspoon & Bakalar, 1979). The psychological experience appears to be a dreamlike trance or stupor. The user appears delirious and confused, but may be able to describe visions if asked. A unique feature of the drugs of this class is that memory of the experience is very poor and subjects may be unable to recall details of any of the experiences. This may be one of the reasons these drugs are rarely seen on the street today.

One additional plant to be discussed in this section is the fly agaric mushroom (*Amanita muscaria*). Fly agaric contains several different hallucinogenic chemicals, including muscarine, which is a cholinergic agonist, and muscimole, a hallucinogen that may be similar to the LSD-like drugs. Although rarely used today, the mushroom is worth noting because it may represent the earliest form of hallucinogen use. Fly agaric grows through much of Europe and Asia and it may have been the mysterious "Soma" described in the Indian Rig-Veda more than 2,000 years ago. The Rig-Veda describes the rather bizarre practice of recycling the drug effect by drinking the urine of the intoxicated individual. Muscimole is the only hallucinogen known that passes through the system into the urine unchanged (Wasson, 1979). The effects of the mushroom are somewhat unique among hallucinogens. Users of the fly agaric typically fall into a stupor for several hours during which they experience visions, and later experience intense euphoria and energy accompanied by visual hallucinations (Wasson, 1979).

DISSOCIATIVE ANESTHETIC HALLUCINOGENS

History

The final class of hallucinogens to be considered is a large group, but only two of its members, **phencyclidine** (PCP, angel dust) and its close analogue, **ketamine,** have been used enough to warrant discussion here. PCP was synthesized in 1956, and because it had pronounced tranquilizing effects it was tested as an anesthetic. With animals it produced a general anesthesia that left the animal conscious but not feeling pain, even during surgery. However, in clinical trials with humans, some patients experienced hyperexcitability, delirium, and visual disturbances. Thus, PCP was abandoned for human use, although it was marketed as a veterinary anesthetic and tranquilizer under the brand name Sernyl (Linder, Lerner, & Burns, 1981). Little more was heard about PCP until the late 1960s, when it began to appear as a "rip-off" drug sold under the guise of being THC, MDA, or mescaline. Although PCP got a bad reputation on the street during this time, it emerged in the 1970s as a street drug of preference. Sold under a variety of names, including angel dust, hog, horse tranquilizer, and lovely, it was often taken by sprinkling the powder on a cigarette or joint and smoking it. Although PCP also is effective orally and can be injected, smoking remains the most popular route of administration. By the early 1980s some surveys were finding that more than 20% of America's high school students had tried PCP. Because of the high frequency of dangerous side effects, PCP has become a notorious drug. PCP use has declined in recent years. Johnston, O'Malley, and Bachman (1991) found that about 1% of America's high school seniors reported using PCP. However, because of its hazards, PCP remains a serious social concern. Although PCP is no longer widely used in veterinary medicine, a similar drug, ketamine, is commonly used, and there are recent reports of ketamine abuse.

Phencyclidine
A dissociative anesthetic.

Ketamine
A dissociative anesthetic.

Pharmacokinetics of PCP

PCP's mechanism of action is poorly understood, but appears to involve interaction with receptors for the excitatory amino acid, glutamate (Johnson & Jones, 1990). PCP is absorbed rapidly after smoking or injection with peak blood concentrations noted within 5 to 15 minutes after smoking. In contrast, peak concentrations are reached two hours after oral administration. The drug remains in the system unmetabolized for more than two days, and PCP is detectable in urine for several weeks after a single use (Hawks & Chiang, 1986).

Effects of PCP

The effects of PCP are relatively unique. A moderate dose (1–10 mg) produces feelings of euphoria and numbness resembling alcohol intoxication. Speech may be slurred and generally there is motor discoordination. The subject may be catatonic and rigid with a blank stare, or may be aggressive and hyperactive. There is profuse sweating, heart rate and blood pressure may be increased, and there are rapid, jerky eye movements called nystagmus (Linder et al., 1981; Young et al., 1987). Subjects often report blurred vision or double vision, but rarely visual hallucinations. Rather there are changes in perception of body image—distortions of the tactile senses. Consider these descriptions from PCP users:

> It's weirdly hallucinogenic. It makes you go, boy that's steep stairs I have to climb there, that you realized you climb in five minutes you know, and stuff, and it actually feels like you're going to float off the couch and stuff, you know. Your arm is over somewhere. I can remember like crawling down the stairs because the only thing that I trusted was my fingers and my knees. . . .
>
> The most frequent hallucination is that parts of your body are extremely large or extremely small. You can imagine yourself small enough to walk through a keyhole, or you can be lying there and all of a sudden you just hallucinate that your arm is twice the length of your body (from Feldman, Agar, & Beschner, 1979, p. 133).

These effects normally last from four to six hours, but are quite variable and, particularly after high doses, may persist for days or weeks. Overdoses (more than 20 mg) may result in seizures, prolonged coma, and sometimes death from respiratory failure (Carroll, 1990). PCP is extremely likely to produce bad trips. These may occur in 50% to 80% of PCP users (Young, Lawson, & Gacono, 1987). Toxic psychosis produced by PCP is often characterized by paranoia and violence and may persist for several days. Additionally, PCP frequently precipitates long-term psychotic episodes and depressions that last 7 to 30 days or more. Talking the subject down from a PCP bad trip generally is unsuccessful. Physical restraint and intensive medical care are often necessary. PCP is far more likely than other hallucinogens to produce medical or psychiatric complications. In many cities, PCP is responsible for more psychiatric emergencies than any other drug, and in some hospitals PCP psychoses exceed schizophrenia and alcoholism as a cause of psychiatric admission (McCarron, 1986; Young, Lawson, & Gacono, 1987).

summary

- Hallucinogens are a group of drugs with the capacity to alter perceptual, cognitive, and emotional states.

- Hallucinogens may be divided into four classes: serotonergic hallucinogens, the methylated amphetamines, anticholinergic hallucinogens, and dissociative anesthetics.

- Serotonergic hallucinogens include drugs such as LSD, psilocybin, and mescaline. Psilocybin comes from mushrooms of the Psilocybe genus and mescaline from the peyote cactus. These drugs have a long history of use by early Indian peoples for religious purposes.

- LSD is a synthetic compound. Its hallucinogenic properties were discovered by the Swiss chemist Albert Hofmann, but it was made popular by counterculture figures such as Timothy Leary and Ken Kesey.

- LSD and the other drugs in this class affect serotonergic neurons. They are sympathomimetic drugs as well.

- The psychological effects of these drugs are diverse, but include visual hallucinations, alterations of mood and thought, and dreamlike visions.

- Many adverse effects have been linked to LSD and other drugs in this class, including acute psychotic reactions (bad trips), flashbacks, and long-term psychological deficits.

- Methylated amphetamines include drugs such as MDA and MDMA (ecstasy). These drugs are sympathomimetic and produce many other effects similar to LSD, but generally do not produce visual hallucinations.

- Anticholinergic hallucinogens include atropine and scopolamine, which are chemicals found in plants such as the deadly nightshade, mandrake, Jimson weed, and henbane. These drugs produce a semisleep state characterized by vivid visions and very poor memory of the experience later.

- Phencyclidine (PCP) and ketamine are classified as dissociative anesthetic hallucinogens. They produce a potent intoxication in moderate doses and complete surgical anesthesia with higher doses. Violent psychotic reactions appear to be fairly common with PCP.

ANSWERS TO WHAT DO YOU THINK?

1. Unlike other classes of drugs, most hallucinogens are derived from synthetic compounds.

F *There are more than 90 different species of plants, in addition to many more synthetic agents, that can be used to produce hallucinogenic effects.*

2. Hallucinogenic compounds were commonly used in the early 1900s throughout Europe and America.

F *Although hallucinogens were used for centuries by Indians of South and Central America, these drugs*

had virtually no impact on mainstream European or American culture until the 1960s.

3. The hallucinogenic properties of LSD were discovered by accident.

T *Albert Hofmann of Sandoz Laboratories in Switzerland accidentally discovered the effects of LSD when he spilled some on himself and it was absorbed through the skin.*

4. LSD was once used in psychotherapy.

T   *Although LSD was used by psychologists and psychiatrists, its benefits were never successfully defended.*

5.   Federal law mandates that anyone using LSD more than five times be declared legally insane.

F   *Although there is concern about long-term psychiatric effects of chronic LSD use, no such law exists.*

6.   Use of LSD, even once, is likely to cause permanent chromosome damage and subsequent birth defects.

F   *LSD should be avoided by pregnant women, but otherwise has not been shown to cause birth defects.*

7.   Ecstasy (MDMA) produces vivid visual hallucinations.

F   *Ecstasy rarely produces true hallucinations.*

8.   Ecstasy has been shown to cause brain damage in nonhumans.

T   *Long-term destruction of serotonergic terminals has been associated with ecstasy.*

9.   Hallucinations experienced under the influence of drugs such as LSD are very similar to those experienced by schizophrenics.

F   *The hallucinations experienced under the influence of LSD are primarily visual in nature, while those of schizophrenics are usually auditory.*

10.   Dependence develops very easily to hallucinogens such as LSD.

F   *The problems associated with LSD do not include drug dependence, but it is, nonetheless, a potentially dangerous drug.*

11.   Reports of LSD flashbacks are now considered an urban myth.

F   *Heavy users of LSD sometimes report vivid flashbacks.*

12.   Phencyclidine (PCP or angel dust) was originally used as an animal tranquilizer.

T   *Phencyclidine and the related compound ketamine are still widely used for nonhuman anesthesia.*

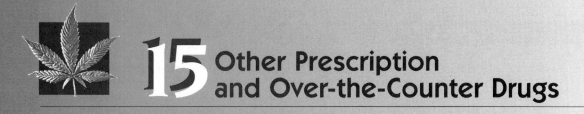

15 Other Prescription and Over-the-Counter Drugs

WHAT DO YOU THINK?

True or False?

_____ Birth control pills contain synthetic forms of one or both of the female sex hormones.

_____ One of the risks associated with use of birth control pills is an increased chance of lung cancer.

_____ Anabolic steroids are synthetic forms of testosterone.

_____ Anabolic steroids are generally taken because of the high they produce.

_____ Acne, baldness, and liver damage are all side effects associated with steroid use.

_____ GRAS is a common street name for marijuana.

_____ Aspirin relieves pain through action on the endorphins, much in the same way that the pain-relieving effects of opiates are produced.

_____ Many over-the-counter diet pills contain low doses of amphetamines.

_____ Antitussive agents are used to suppress coughing.

_____ Antihistamines are common ingredients in over-the-counter cold remedies.

_____ Antihistamines are the major ingredients in many over-the-counter sleeping aids.

_____ Caffeine is a common ingredient in over-the-counter stimulant preparations.

OVERVIEW

We have discussed the major traditional classes of psychoactive drugs: stimulants, depressants, and hallucinogens. However, there are other drugs of importance with psychoactive properties that do not fit neatly into the categories of earlier chapters. In this chapter we review some of these. We first discuss some significant prescription drugs, including birth control pills and anabolic steroids. Next we consider the wide array of drugs that do not require a prescription to purchase: the over-the-counter drugs. These primarily include analgesics (such as aspirin), antihistamines and other cold and allergy medications, diet pills, and sleeping aids.

OTHER PRESCRIPTION DRUGS

Birth Control Drugs

The first birth control pill became available in the early 1960s, and since that time "the pill" has had a profound impact on our culture. It is probably no accident that the so-called sexual revolution of the late 1960s coincided with the widespread availability of the pill. Today it is estimated that 60 million women worldwide and 10 million in the United States use the birth control pill, making it the most widely used form of contraception (Katchadourian, 1989).

The most common form of the birth control pill is the **combination pill,** which consists of synthetic forms of two female sex hormones, **progesterone** and **estrogen.** With some forms of the combination pill (multiphasic) the amount of synthetic progesterone or estrogen varies depending on where the woman is in the menstrual cycle. The combination birth control pill works by suppressing ovulation (release of a mature egg from the ovary). It is taken daily for 21 days, then removed for seven days, during which a period of menstruation should occur. Most birth control pills contain placebo or vitamin pills to be taken during the seven off-days to help the woman stay in the habit of taking a pill each day.

Basically the pill works by "tricking" the woman's brain into responding as if she were already pregnant. When a woman is pregnant, she no longer ovulates. The hypothalamus and pituitary gland are responsible for regulating ovulation. When circulating levels of estrogen and progesterone are high (as in the case of pregnancy or use of the birth control pill), these structures do not release the hormones that are necessary to prepare the ovaries to release an egg, and thus ovulation is prevented.

To keep circulating levels of estrogen and progesterone continually high enough to inhibit ovulation, the woman using the birth control pill must faithfully remember to take a pill every day at approximately the same time of day. If she misses a pill, it is important to take it as soon as possible. If she misses more than one pill, her levels of circulating estrogen and progesterone may have dropped sufficiently low to allow ovulation to occur (Rathus, Nevid, & Fichner-Rathus, 1993). Used properly, the combination pill is one of the most reliable forms of birth control available with a failure rate of between 0.5% to 3%, much lower than most alternatives (Katchadourian, 1989—see Table 15-1 and nearby Contemporary Issue Box). The pill has other advantages over other contraception methods as well. Because it does not require taking precautions just before or after intercourse, it permits more spontaneity than other approaches. A disadvantage of the pill compared to condoms, of course, is that the pill does not prevent the spread of sexually

Combination pill
Birth control pill containing synthetic forms of both female sex hormones: progesterone and estrogen.

Progesterone (proh-JEST-er-own)
One of the female sex hormones that are involved with the regulation of ovulation and the menstrual cycle.

Estrogen (ESS-troh-jen)
One of the female sex hormones involved in the regulation of ovulation and the menstrual cycle.

Table 15-1   Comparison of Contraceptive Methods

Method	Failure Rate in Typical Users
Vasectomy	<0.2%
Norplant	<1%
Combination Birth Control Pill	3%
Progestin Only Pill	3%
IUD	6%
Condom	10%
Diaphragm + spermicide	10%
Condom + spermicide	5%
Withdrawal	25%
Rhythm, Body Temperature	20–30%
Chance	90%
Abstinence	?

Contemporary Issue
WHAT KIND OF BIRTH CONTROL IS BEST?

Perhaps the question most college women have when reading about the pill is whether it is the best method of contraception. But, it is impossible to evaluate the pill without considering the other available methods. Table 15-1 shows the failure rates for various methods of birth control in typical users. The difference between these various techniques often amounts to error in their proper use. Failure is minimized with surgical procedures such as vasectomy. But, in addition to the possible complications of surgery, this procedure may be irreversible. Thus, this procedure is uncommon among young people. Notice that birth control pills are the most effective techniques not requiring surgery. The drawbacks of the pill are the side effects noted in the text. The intrauterine device (IUD) is also highly effective and is a very popular technique. But the IUD also can produce side effects. The most common are irregular bleeding and pelvic pain. More serious complications are less common but may include greater risk of pelvic inflammatory disease, uterine perforation, and complications if pregnancy should occur when the IUD is in place. There are a variety of "barrier" techniques that are used by women, including the diaphragm and the contraceptive sponge. These devices involve blocking the cervical opening and when used with a spermicide produce acceptable failure rates. A disadvantage of these methods is the repeated insertion and removal of the device that some women find problematic.

Recently the condom has gained favor as a method of birth control. The reason is the protection that condoms may provide against sexually transmitted disease. With the current concern about AIDS, condoms should be recommended to most couples. However, unless used properly (and reliably), condoms may have a high failure rate, as Table 15-1 shows. As you will also note in Table 15-1, techniques such as withdrawal and rhythm have a common side effect: pregnancy! Then, of course, there is abstinence . . .

transmitted disease. In addition, there are a number of side effects of the combination pill.

One of the more serious concerns is the increased risk of blood clots in users of the combination pill. Such blood clots can produce stroke or heart attacks, and indeed women over 40 show an increased risk of heart attack when they take the combination pill. This risk is greatly increased if the woman is also a cigarette smoker. Mood changes, including severe depression, are often reported by women on the pill (it is, after all, a psychoactive drug). Other side effects experienced by some women include high blood pressure, benign liver tumors, and gall bladder disease, although the risk of these and many other reported side effects is controversial (see Rathus et al., 1993, for a review).

In an effort to minimize the side effects due to estrogen, an alternative form of birth control pill has been developed containing only small amounts of synthetic progesterone (progestin). The **progestin pill** is sometimes called

Progestin pill
Birth control pill containing only progestin—a synthetic progesterone.

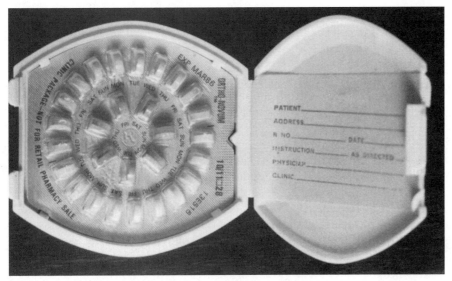

The most common type of birth control pill (the combination pill) works by suppressing ovulation.

the minipill. It is thought to work somewhat differently from the combination pill in that it may not always block ovulation. Rather, the major effect of the progestin is to alter the cervical mucus medium in such a way as to block sperm entry. A limitation of the progestin pill is that it is less effective than the combination pill, although it is still more reliable than other reversible methods (see Table 15-1).

A new development in birth control is a technique called a contraceptive implant, primarily known as the brand name, Norplant. Norplant is a device that is surgically implanted under the skin of a woman's arm and releases low, continuous doses of progestin into the bloodstream for as long as five years. This technique was approved for use in the United States in 1990, and has gained in popularity since then. An obvious advantage is that the woman need not worry about remembering to take pills or use other forms of contraception for years after the implant, which involves only minor surgery. Norplant has an extremely low failure rate (<1%, see Table 15-1), and the effects are reversible when the device is removed or exhausted. Side effects related to Norplant reported thus far are minimal, but include irregular menstrual bleeding. Norplant and similar drugs may eventually replace the birth control pill as the most popular means of contraception (Rathus et al., 1993).

When considering the potential side effects of birth control pills and other methods of contraception, it is important to keep things in perspective. Although there are risks associated with use of the pill, they are lower than the risks involved in pregnancy and delivery.

Anabolic Steroids

Background   On a sunny day in September, 1988 in Seoul, Korea, the world of sports was changed forever. Ben Johnson ran the 100-meter dash in a time

Anabolic steroids
Tissue-building drugs, which produce masculinizing effects as well.

Testosterone
The male sex hormone. Anabolic steroids are basically synthetic versions of testosterone.

of 9.79 seconds to win the Olympic gold medal and break the world record. Johnson had become the world's fastest human—of all time. Then just two days later, after traces of the **anabolic steroid** stanozolol were found in Johnson's urine sample, he was stripped of his record and his medal and left the games in disgrace. The reverberations in the sports world are still being felt, and perhaps more significantly, Johnson's scandal has opened the eyes of the public to a little understood and potentially very dangerous new drug epidemic: steroid abuse.

Anabolic steroids are synthetic drugs resembling the male sex hormone **testosterone.** In addition to its role in determining male sexual characteristics such as facial and chest hair (androgenic or masculinizing effects), testosterone helps build body tissues and repair damaged tissue. Such bodily construction processes are called anabolic effects. These anabolic effects also can be attained by taking synthetic testosterone for certain medical problems, or for improving athletic performance or body-building. The clinical uses for anabolic steroids include treatments for testosterone deficiency, some types of anemia, breast cancer, osteoporosis, and arthritis. The efficacy of anabolic steroids in these medical situations is controversial, and the drugs are not ex-

Ben Johnson won the 100-meter dash in world record time at the 1988 Olympic Games in Seoul, Korea, but was stripped of his victory after testing positive for anabolic steroids.

tensively used (Colby & Longhurst, 1988). Most commonly, anabolic steroids are obtained illicitly and used for the purpose of body-building or otherwise enhancing athletic performance.

Although most people are becoming aware only recently of the use of anabolic steroids, the drugs, in fact, have been around for a long time. They were first developed in Nazi Germany in the 1930s, allegedly to help create an army of supermen (Marshall, 1988). The first known use of anabolic steroids in athletics is reported to have been by Russian weight-lifters and some female athletes in the early 1950s. By the late 1950s, they were being tested by American athletes as well (Wade, 1972). By the 1968 Olympics, steroids were in widespread use. Consider this testimony given by Harold Connelly, Olympic gold medalist in the hammer throw, before a Senate committee:

> It was not unusual in 1968 to see athletes with their own medical kits, practically a doctor's bag in which they would have syringes and all their various drugs. . . . I know any number of athletes on the 1968 Olympic team who had so much scar tissue and so many puncture holes on their backsides that it was difficult to find a fresh spot to give them a new shot (Hecht, 1985, p. 270).

It was not until 1976 that the International Olympic Committee ruled steroids could not be used by athletes. Urine testing was used to enforce this policy. After that time a great many athletes have tested positive and have been banned from the games, but certainly the Ben Johnson case has been the most notorious.

Estimates on the contemporary use of steroids by athletes vary widely. Olympic hurdler Edwin Moses had this to say about the scene at the 1988 Seoul Olympics: ". . . drug use definitely is rampant. In Seoul we had a community of people ravaged by steroids and other banned substances. My educated guess is that at least 50% of the athletes in the high-performance sports such as track and field, cycling, and rowing would be disqualified if they weren't so adept at beating the tests" (Moses, 1988, p. 57). There was less overt evidence of steroid use at the 1992 Olympic games, although some athletes were disqualified. However, it is generally agreed that many athletes are able to use steroids but discontinue use prior to the competition to avoid detection. Some are less successful: Ben Johnson was readmitted to World Track and Field after the 1992 games, but once again tested positive for steroid use in 1993 and has now been banned for life. Some estimates place the number of weight-lifters and body-builders who use steroids as high as 90%. Perhaps even more disturbing were the findings of a recent national survey of high school seniors that reported 6.6% of the male students sampled had taken or were taking steroids. Of those using steroids, just over 47% reported they used them to improve athletic performance, but many (over 26% percent) reported using the drugs for cosmetic benefits (Buckley et al., 1988). Apparently "getting big" has become so important that many young people are willing to take the risk of using steroids to achieve the larger muscles and better definition they believe are associated with these drugs. Therefore, we consider in some detail the available data on how steroids work and the side effects that may follow their use.

Actions of Anabolic Steroids   There are a number of different anabolic steroids, including ethylestrenol, methandrostenolone, nandrolone, oxandrolone, ometh- olone, and stanozolol (brand names include Dianabol, Anavar, and Winstrol). These drugs may be taken orally or injected (see Table 15-2). In the Buckley study, 38% of the steroid users reported injecting steroids, while the remain- der took the drugs only orally. The metabolism and elimination of steroids is quite variable. Steroids can be detected reliably in urine for between 4 and 14 days after use, but there are reports of positive urine tests as long as 13 months after use of nandrolone (Marshall, 1988).

One of the most ironic features of the widespread use of steroids among athletes is that medical researchers have had great difficulty determining whether they produce performance benefits. It is clear that at puberty male testes increase testosterone output resulting in the increase in muscle mass and strength characteristic of males at that age. However, this does not nec- essarily mean supplemental testosterone would result in further gains in a normal male. There have been a number of studies of the effects of anabolic steroids on weight gain, strength, and performance. Some of these have shown improvement in subjects taking steroids, but others have not (Lamb, 1983). Even in the studies where enhanced performance is shown, the effects were generally rather small. Yet athletes persist in believing anabolic steroid regimens (combined with training) increase lean muscle mass, strength, and other measures of performance. Performances such as that of Ben Johnson and physiques such as the ones shown in the nearby photos tend to support those claims. Why then have the body-building effects of steroids been so dif- ficult to demonstrate in laboratory studies? Lamb (1983) suggests that the reason is that the doses used in laboratory studies are much lower than those actually used by athletes and body-builders. As Lamb pointed out, re- searchers are unable to administer higher doses because of the risks it poses to their subjects. Indeed, athletes who take high doses of anabolic steroids may be paying a high price for the enhanced performance.

Side Effects of Anabolic Steroids   There are a number of physical side effects associated with anabolic steroid use. Perhaps the most commonly reported are acne, balding, and reduced sexual desire. In men, there is often atrophy of the testes and a related decline in sperm count and enlargement of the breasts. It seems ironic but many male steroid users have to take special drugs to prevent breast growth! These effects are usually reversible. In fe-

Table 15-2   Anabolic Steroids

Drug	Trade Name	Administration
Ethylestrenol	Maxibolin	oral
Methandrostenolone	Dianabol	oral
Oxandrolone	Anavar	oral
Stanozolol	Winstrol	oral
Nandrolone	Androlone, Durabolin Nandrolin	injection
Methandriol	Anabol, Durabolic, Methabolic, Steribolic	injection

Do they or don't they? Only their pharmacist knows for sure.

males, there are pronounced masculinizing effects from steroid use, and many of these effects are irreversible. They include growth of facial and chest hair, baldness, deepening of the voice, breast shrinkage, clitoral enlargement, and menstrual irregularities. Another cause for concern is that steroid use often results in changes in cholesterol levels that may increase the risk of heart disease. Damage to liver function is also common and can include an increased risk of liver cancer (Friedl, 1990; Goldman & Klatz, 1992). The late National Football League All-Pro, Lyle Alzado, attributed his inoperable brain cancer to heavy steroid use. However, whether steroids play a causal role in this and other types of cancer is controversial (Friedl, 1990). Additional problems can occur when steroids are used by children and adolescents, such as premature bone fusion causing stunted growth (Rogol et al., 1990). Alteration of normal pubertal development is also a risk in young people. Cause for alarm exists in the finding of Buckley et al. (1988) that more than 4% of their sample began using steroids at 16 years of age or younger.

In addition to the physical side effects of steroids, a number of psychological effects of these drugs exist. Most users report a mild euphoria during

"Steroids make the athlete more aggressive and in some sports that is seen as an advantage."
(Al Oerter, four-time Olympic gold medalist in discus)

periods of steroid use, and increased energy levels also are noted. Withdrawal symptoms and dependence associated with steroid use have also been described (Yesalis et al., 1990). Less desirable are reports of increased irritability and aggressiveness, sometimes leading to violent behavior. Mood swings and even psychotic reactions have been reported. Pope and Katz (1988) reported a study of 41 body-builders and football players who had used steroids. Nine of the subjects (22%) experienced emotional disturbance associated with steroid use, and five (12%) developed psychotic reactions during their steroid regimens. One of the subjects studied deliberately drove a car into a tree at 40 mph. Another described becoming irritated at a driver in front of him who had left his blinker on. At the first stoplight, he jumped out of his car and punched out the other car's windshield!

The use of steroids by athletes will continue as long as athletes believe their competition is using them. Better testing methods are needed, but perhaps more important would be regular tests. The current procedures allow athletes to discontinue the drugs prior to an important event in order to avoid a positive urine test. Such procedures could reduce cheating sharply. But what of the thousands of young men (and women) who are *not* Olympic-caliber athletes who are taking steroids to improve their performance at the high school or college level or to just "get big"? Steroids may represent one of the major drug-abuse problems facing the country today, and most drug education programs do not even discuss them. Clearly there is a need to make the public aware of the potential dangers of steroid abuse.

OVER-THE-COUNTER DRUGS

About Over-the-Counter Drugs

The Federal Food and Drug Administration (FDA) divides drugs into two categories: those requiring a prescription from a physician to purchase (such as the psychiatric drugs discussed in Chapter 9, and the birth control pills and anabolic steroids just described), and those considered safe enough to dispense without a prescription. These drugs are often referred to as over-the-counter (OTC) drugs. The FDA was charged by the 1962 Kefauver-Harris amendment with regulating and reviewing OTC drugs—no small task when you consider there were over 300,000 products on the market! Rather than focus on specific brands, the FDA has organized the ingredients found in these products, and divided them into the categories shown in Table 13-3. As shown, a wide range of ailments is treated by OTC drugs. The FDA created panels to study these ingredients and to evaluate them on two major criteria: safety and efficacy. The panel's final reports were presented in 1985; then those drugs authorized as OTC drugs must meet the standard of "Generally Recognized as Safe" or GRAS, and "Generally Recognized as Effective" or GRAE. Drugs not meeting these criteria are removed from OTC products. However, it should be noted that safety and efficacy are relative terms. Some OTC drugs can be hazardous, and some are of very limited efficacy.

In addition to reviewing the ingredients of OTC drugs, some of the FDA panels reviewed prescription drugs and, on the grounds that some were rela-

Table 15-3   FDA Classification of OTC Drugs

1. Antacids	13. Analgesics
2. Antidiarrheal products	14. Antitussives
3. Sunscreens	15. Eye products
4. Dandruff products	16. Dental products
5. Bronchodilators	17. Emetics
6. Stimulants	18. Antiperspirants
7. Cold remedies	19. Antimicrobials
8. Skin preparations	20. Hemorrhoidal products
9. Laxatives	21. Sedatives and sleep aids
10. Antiemetics	22. Allergy drugs
11. Vitamin and mineral products	23. Contraceptive products
12. Oral hygiene products	24. Weight-control products

tively safe and effective, recommended they be made available without prescription. The pain-reliever ibuprofen and some antihistamines, such as diphenhydramine, are examples of drugs previously available only by prescription. They are available now over the counter.

Of the many categories of drugs noted in Table 15-3 we focus on those with psychoactive properties—analgesics, diet pills, cold and allergy medications, stimulants, and sedatives.

Analgesics

In Chapter 12 we discussed the use of opiate drugs in the treatment of pain. But the use of opiates for pain relief is usually reserved for severe cases.

Over-the-counter drugs are considered safe enough to dispense without a prescription.

**Acetylsalicylic acid
(ah-SEAT-ill-sal-iss-ill-ik)**
Chemical name for aspirin.

Many effective painkillers are available over the counter. The most widely known and used is aspirin. **Acetylsalicylic acid** (aspirin) is closely related to a chemical found in the bark of the willow and other trees (salicylic acid). Willow bark was used in the treatment of painful conditions and fever by the ancient Greeks and by Native Americans. Salicylic acid was isolated and used as a pain-reliever in Europe, but it causes severe stomach distress. It was not until the late nineteenth century that acetylsalicylic acid was synthesized and named aspirin by the Bayer company of Germany. Aspirin has come to be one of the most important drugs known to medicine. It is marketed under the brand names Anacin, Bufferin, and Excedrin to name just a few, and more than 10,000 tons of aspirin are consumed every year (Julien, 1992).

Aspirin is analgesic (produces pain relief without unconsciousness), antipyretic (reduces fever), and antiinflammatory (reduces swelling). It is thought to accomplish these effects by a mechanism quite different from opiate analgesia. Aspirin (and other OTC painkillers) act by blocking the production and release of **prostaglandins,** chemicals that are released by the body at sites of pain. These chemicals are thought to enhance certain kinds of pain—dull pain and aches, such as headache. Indeed, aspirin is not very effective with sharp pains or with stomach pain. It is, however, very effective with muscle aches, headaches, and soreness due to inflammation such as arthritis (Grogan, 1987).

**Prostaglandins
(pross-tah-GLAND-inz)**
Naturally occurring chemicals blocked by aspirin and related analgesics.

Aspirin is not without some adverse effects, though. It frequently causes stomach irritation and bleeding and is contraindicated in persons who have stomach problems. Aspirin may be related to a rare and dangerous disease called Reye syndrome. Reye syndrome occurs only in children treated with aspirin for flu or chicken pox, and involves severe vomiting, disorientation, and sometimes, coma, brain damage, or death. Thus aspirin should be avoided by children with these diseases. Aspirin is also an anticoagulant and may prolong bleeding under certain circumstances. However, this same mechanism may be useful in the prevention of strokes and heart attacks (Steering Committee of the Physicians Health Study Research Group, 1988).

**Acetaminophen
(ah-seat-ah-MIN-ah-fen)**
Aspirin-like analgesic.

An effective analgesic drug useful for people with stomach problems is **acetaminophen.** This drug, marketed under brand names such as Datril and Tylenol, reduces fever and produces analgesic effects, but does not cause stomach irritation. However, acetaminophen is not a potent antiinflammatory drug, and in high doses may cause liver problems. It is worth noting that an overdose of acetaminophen is a more serious problem than one with aspirin. Both drugs are leading causes of poisonings in children. As few as 10 Extra-Strength Tylenol can be lethal to a child (Grogan, 1987). It is important to keep these and all drugs out of the reach of children.

Ibuprofen (ih-BYOU-proh-fen)
Aspirin-like analgesic.

Another widely used OTC painkiller is **ibuprofen.** Ibuprofen was exclusively a prescription drug (Motrin) until 1984, when the FDA approved it for OTC use. Now it is marketed under brand names such as Advil and Nuprin, and has captured a large share of the OTC painkiller market. Ibuprofen has analgesic effects similar to aspirin, but it is more potent. Ibuprofen also is a particularly effective antiinflammatory drug. However, like the other OTC pain-relievers, ibuprofen can produce side effects, including stomach irritation, and in high doses, liver and kidney damage.

Appetite Suppressants

We discussed in Chapter 5 the use of amphetamines and related drugs in weight control. There are dozens of OTC preparations taken to suppress appetite. Some are essentially high-fiber or some type of food replacement low in calories. Others (Dexatrim, Appedrine) contain an anorectic drug called **phenylpropanolamine** or PPA (often in combination with caffeine). Often an ingredient in "look-alike" stimulant pills (see nearby Contemporary Issue Box), PPA has a chemical structure similar to amphetamine. It is only a mild stimulant and does not produce euphoria. It does have anorectic properties, but it has not been demonstrated to be effective in long-term weight control (Grogan, 1987).

Phenylpropanolamine (feen-ill-proh-pan-OH-lah-meen) A mild stimulant with decongestant and appetite-suppressant properties (PPA).

PPA also serves as a decongestant and is found in OTC cold and allergy medication. PPA also has a number of undesirable side effects, such as elevated blood sugar levels, hypertension, heart palpitations, rapid heart beat, insomnia, headache, nausea, and anxiety. Geraldine Ferraro, who ran for vice president of the United States in 1984, testified on OTC diet pills before the House of Representatives Subcommittee on Health and Long-Term Care (cited in Hallowell, 1987, p. 133). Ferraro, referring to her use of diet pills to lose weight, said:

> I can recall . . . my heart started beating very fast and I cleaned my house as if I was . . . the white tornado . . . I'd be up very early in the morning and I couldn't sleep at night . . . I decided I didn't want to become a

Contemporary Issue
SIDE EFFECTS FROM OVER-THE-COUNTER DRUGS?

OTC drugs are so widely used in our society that most of us do not think of them as drugs. We walk into the supermarket or convenience store and buy cold or pain medication without really recognizing we are buying potent psychoactive drugs. Yet these drugs can produce side effects. There simply is no drug that is completely safe. As noted earlier, even drugs as innocuous as aspirin and acetominophen can be toxic if taken in overdose levels.

Some OTC drugs may possess abuse potential as well. For example, appetite suppressants such as PPA are potent enough stimulants that they are frequent ingredients (usually along with caffeine) in "look-alike" stimulant preparations. Look-alike drugs are made to closely resemble a controlled substance, usually a prescription amphetamine, but actually contain only OTC products. Such look-alikes often are misrepresented as amphetamine, and sold on the street. These compounds may be taken in high enough doses that dangerous side effects occur.

Finally, some OTC drugs, particularly antihistamines used in cold preparations or sleeping aids, cause fatigue and may potentiate the effects of alcohol or other depressant drugs. These sedatives should not be taken in combination with other drugs, and driving should be avoided after exposure to them.

nervous wreck, so I stopped taking them . . . and immediately . . . the symptoms stopped.

Thus, PPA side effects can cause some relatively severe problems. In view of the limited effectiveness of OTC diet preparations and their potential for causing problems, some criticize the FDA's approval of PPA preparations (e.g., Grogan, 1987).

Cold and Allergy Medications

The common cold is common enough that its victims spend $1.3 billion on OTC cold remedies in the United States every year. OTC cold and allergy medications contain a variety of different ingredients. These include analgesics, such as aspirin or acetaminophen, which are of value in reducing aches, pain, and fever. In addition, many OTC cold preparations include PPA because of its decongestant properties. An alternative decongestant is **pseudoephedrine** (Sudafed), which is as effective as PPA but has fewer side effects. Cold remedies also may include expectorants, which help to break up phlegm so that it may be coughed up. **Guaifenesin** is the most common expectorant. **Antitussive** agents actually suppress coughing and are often included in cold and cough formulations (dextromethorphan is an example).

Other common ingredients in OTC cold and allergy preparations are **antihistamines.** These compounds actually are more effective in the treatment of hay fever and related allergic reactions. Many allergic symptoms are caused by the release of a naturally occurring chemical called histamine. As the name suggests, antihistamines act by blocking histamine. Commonly used antihistamines include diphenhydramine and chlorpheniramine maleate. However, antihistamines produce a number of side effects limiting their usefulness. Drowsiness and fatigue are probably the most significant. It can be very hard to stay awake after taking antihistamines, and in fact, diphenhydramine is the major ingredient in most OTC sleeping aids. Other side effects include thickening of mucus secretions, blurred vision, dizziness, dry mouth and nose, and sweating (Grogan, 1987).

Pseudoephedrine (soo-doh-eff-EHD-rin)
An over-the-counter (OTC) decongestant.

Guaifenesin (guay-FEN-eh-sin)
An OTC expectorant.

Antitussives
Cough suppressant drugs.

Antihistamines
Common OTC drugs with decongestant effects.

Over-the-Counter Stimulants and Sedatives

We already have discussed the ingredients in OTC stimulants. They are basically caffeine and/or PPA. OTC stimulants include popular brands such as No-Doz and Vivarin. They certainly will induce mild central nervous system stimulation, but one No-Doz, for example, contains about as much caffeine as a cup of coffee, so the user should expect about that effect. More information on the side effects of caffeine is in Chapter 8.

As we noted, the major ingredient in OTC sleeping aids is an antihistamine, diphenhydramine. Because fatigue is a common side effect of antihistamines, they sometimes can help people suffering from insomnia. However, other side effects associated with antihistamines (for instance, dry mouth, dizziness, and nausea) may limit their use as sleeping aids. In addition, the problems associated with using prescription sleeping pills may apply to these drugs, too, as discussed in Chapter 10.

summary

- The combination birth control pill consists of synthetic versions of the two female sex hormones, estrogen and progesterone.

- Although highly effective at reducing risk of pregnancy, the birth control pill has been linked to a number of side effects, including increased risk of heart attack and stroke.

- Anabolic steroids are generally synthetic versions of the male sex hormone testosterone, and are used to promote the development of muscle mass and to enhance athletic performance.

- Side effects associated with anabolic steroids include masculinizing effects in women, liver damage, acne, hair loss, and emotional disturbance.

- Three major analgesic drugs are available without prescription: aspirin, acetaminophen, and ibuprofen.

- Aspirin relieves pain, reduces fever, and is also antiinflammatory. Its side effects include stomach irritation and bleeding. The effects of ibuprofen are similar.

- Acetaminophen is also a potent analgesic drug, but it lacks the antiinflammatory effects of aspirin. However, it also is less likely to cause stomach irritation.

- Phenylpropanolamine (PPA) is a drug used in over-the-counter appetite suppressants and cold preparations.

- Other ingredients of nonprescription cold and allergy medications include pseudoephedrine, guaifenesin, dextromethorphan, and antihistamines.

- The antihistamine compound diphenhydramine also is used as the major ingredient in nonprescription sleeping pills.

ANSWERS TO WHAT DO YOU THINK?

1. Birth control pills contain synthetic forms of one or both of the female sex hormones.

T *Combination birth control pills contain synthetic estrogen and progesterone, while the progestin pill contains only synthetic progesterone.*

2. One of the risks associated with use of birth control pills is an increased chance of lung cancer.

F *An increased risk of blood clots is associated with birth control pills.*

3. Anabolic steroids are synthetic forms of testosterone.

T *Anabolic steroids mimic the action of the male sex hormone.*

4. Anabolic steroids are generally taken because of the high they produce.

F *Although steroids may produce a high, they are generally taken to increase muscle mass.*

5. Acne, baldness, and liver damage are all side effects associated with steroid use.

T *There are a number of other potential side effects as well.*

6. GRAS is a common street name for marijuana.

F *GRAS stands for "Generally Recognized as Safe."*

7. Aspirin relieves pain through action on the endorphins, much in the same way that the pain-relieving effects of opiates are produced.

F *The pain-relieving effects of aspirin are produced by blocking prostaglandin release.*

8. Many over-the-counter diet pills contain low doses of amphetamines.

F   *Many diet pills contain phenylpropanolamine (PPA). Although PPA has a chemical structure similar to amphetamines, it is only a mild stimulant and does not produce euphoria.*

9. Antitussive agents are used to suppress coughing.

T   *Antitussives are used to suppress coughing.*

10. Antihistamines are common ingredients in over-the-counter cold remedies.

T   *Antihistamines relieve nasal congestion and related symptoms.*

11. Antihistamines are the major ingredients in many over-the-counter sleeping aids.

T   *The major ingredient in sleeping aids is diphenhydramine, an antihistamine.*

12. Caffeine is a common ingredient in over-the-counter stimulant preparations.

T   *Caffeine and PPA are both commonly used.*

16 Treatment of Substance-Use Disorders

WHAT DO YOU THINK?

True or False?   ____   The process of change of a problem behavior seems to be different for everyone.

____   Treatment is needed to change patterns of alcohol and drug abuse or dependence.

____   Alcoholics Anonymous was created over 100 years ago, and its influence predominantly is in the United States.

____   It is generally agreed that substance-use disorders are caused by psychological problems.

____   Assessment typically is thought to be essential to good treatment.

____   The only goal of any importance in alcohol and drug treatment is a reduction of substance use.

____   Abstinence from alcohol is a mandatory goal of alcohol treatment.

____   Methadone maintenance seems to be an effective treatment for heroin dependence.

____   Today there are good reasons for rigid boundaries between what we call alcohol treatment and drug treatment.

____   People with major psychiatric problems are rarely seen in settings where alcohol and drug treatment are provided.

____   Relapse is such a long-standing problem in alcohol and drug treatment that there must be little we can do about it.

____   Professional treatment for substance-use disorders is freely available to anyone who wants it.

Treatment
Planned activities designed to change some pattern of behavior(s) of individuals or their families.

Now that we have covered the most commonly used psychoactive substances we are ready to address the question, "what is done for people whose use becomes abuse or dependence?" The question pertains to **treatment,** or planned activities designed to change some pattern of behavior(s) of individuals or their families. In this chapter we are concerned with patterns of substance use. We emphasize psychological and behavioral treatments (also called interventions), as opposed to medical treatments, although some examples of the latter are discussed.

Because the information about treatment is large both in volume and variety, it will be useful to have a model to guide us through this chapter. Figure 16-1 illustrates our model of what might occur in the course of treatment, from the point that an alcohol or drug problem is recognized through outcome, or result that is attributed to treatment. In this case the essential outcome of interest is change in alcohol or other drug-use patterns.

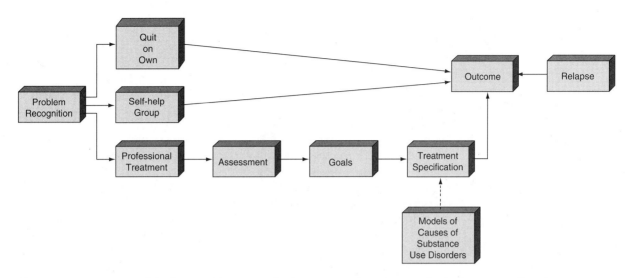

Figure 16-1   A model of events that occur in the course of treatment of substance-use disorders

You should read Figure 16-1 from left to right. In order for any treatment to happen there has to be recognition of a problem. That recognition may come from the individual himself or herself, or it may come first from other sources (family, friends, legal system, employer) in the individual's environment. In spite of this external feedback about a problem, the individual still may not be convinced that he or she actually does have a problem and needs to change. This complex decision point typically is summarized by terms such as a person's motivation to change, or commitment to change.

With problem recognition, if change is initiated, it typically happens in one of three ways. A person may decide to change his or her substance use without any kind of help. You saw in Chapter 7 that many ex-smokers stopped without help. The same applies to people with alcohol or other drug problems, though as with smoking, it may take a few tries to do so (Sobell, Sobell, Toneatto, & Leo, 1993). This phenomenon has been called **spontaneous remission.**

Another option that the individual may choose is self-help groups, such as Alcoholics Anonymous. A third possibility is that individuals go into some kind of professional treatment. Note that frequently individuals may combine self-help group attendance with professional treatment activities.

If the person initiates professional treatment, some type of assessment of his or her problem usually occurs first. That assessment leads to specification of treatment goals, which contribute to placement in a specific treatment setting or activity. The content and structure of treatments are influenced by models and theories of alcohol and drug problems, reflected by the broken arrow in Figure 16-1.

The result, or outcome, of these change options is of primary interest. Outcomes can take a variety of forms, especially over the course of a long period of time. When considering change in alcohol and other drug use, as is true for nicotine use, individuals may relapse after some time of substance-use problem reduction or resolution. If that happens, the person "goes back" to any of the preceding points in Figure 16-1, including back to the step of considering whether the person has any degree of commitment to change.

"One way or another, with professional help or without, with friendly advice from uncle or neighbor or without it, with constant nagging from wife or husband or without it, the individual . . . makes a decision [to change]."

(Orford, 1980, cited in Orford, 1985, p. 272)

Spontaneous remission
Resolution of a problem without the help of formal treatment.

With this framework we can begin our presentation on treatment of the substance-use disorders. As we essentially will follow Figure 16-1, we start with a discussion of problem recognition and motivation to change.

MOTIVATION TO CHANGE

"We must use the carrot and stick of the criminal justice system to demand that drug-dependent offenders become involved in treatment."

(Lee Brown, director of the U.S. Office of National Drug Control Policy, cited in *The Alcoholism Report*, 1993, 21 (6), p. 6)

Terms like motivation have been around as long as human behavior has been observed and interpreted. Motivation to change has been considered essential if there is any hope that a treatment for a behavioral or psychological problem will be effective. In the substance-use disorders, motivation to change is discussed often and sometimes heatedly. For example, it frequently is asserted that the major barrier to change is the person's denial that he or she has any problem at all with alcohol or drugs. Denial may persist even in the face of evidence of a problem that is blatant to everybody but the person with the problem.

As much discussed as motivation has been, it has not been as fruitful as we might expect it to be in helping us to understand change in behavior like alcohol and drug use. Part of the problem is there have been many different ways to define a motivation to change and to measure it when conducting research. A relatively recent solution to this problem that has proved productive in addictions (smoking, alcohol, and other drug use) research is to look at "readiness" (or commitment) to change instead of grappling with the abstract idea of motivation. There have been several attempts to do this, but the one that has achieved the greatest influence is the stage of change model (Prochaska, DiClemente, & Norcross, 1992). This model is thought to apply to people who change on their own or who use outside resources to change. In the most recent version of this model, there are five stages: precontemplation, contemplation, preparation, action, and maintenance. A person may cycle through the stages to various points for a number of times before problem resolution is maintained. You can connect this idea to what we said about self-quitters "quitting" smoking or drinking several times before it seems permanent, and about the difficult problem of relapse.

To briefly describe the stages of change, people in the precontemplation stage are not aware of the problem or, if they are, have no interest in change. Precontemplators are those who often are said to be in "denial." It appears that progression in the change cycle requires acknowledgement of the problem, its negative consequences, and an accurate evaluation of change possibilities and how they might occur (e.g., with or without professional treatment). Contemplators vacillate between the pros and cons of their problem behavior, and between the pros and cons of making changes in it. So, they are deciding whether to change, but have taken no steps to do so. People in the preparation stage are on the edge of taking action to change and may have made a try in the recent past. In order to progress, a commitment to take action and to set goals is needed. Individuals in the action stage already are engaged in explicit activities to change. Maintenance, the last stage, involves the continued use of behavior-change activities for up to three years after the action stage has begun. After that time the problem might be considered resolved. People are thought to progress through each of these stages in the process of change. The rate of progression and the amount of recycling may differ from person to person or from problem to problem for a given person, but going through the stages applies generally. We should add here that identification of a person's stage is problem-specific. That is, for example, a person's stage of change for his or her drinking may not be indicative of stage of change for smoking.

What this all means for us is that stage of change helps us to identify a person's perception of the problem and readiness to change it. These factors may help us to determine the timing and content of treatment, or if self-help groups or professional treatment are needed at all. Moreover, it may tell us what needs to be done to move the change process forward. For example, although coming to one's own conclusion that change is needed is the most effective foundation of long-term changes, external (to the individual) pushes to change (for example, from spouse or employer) may help the person to progress from the precontemplation to a later stage that is characterized by more internally based desire to change.

With problem recognition and a source of motivation to change the next point is a decision about how change will occur. We consider in turn problem resolution on one's own, the use of self-help groups, and the use of professional treatment services.

CHANGE WITHOUT FORMAL TREATMENT

We do not have sufficient space here to discuss the research on spontaneous remission of alcohol and other drug-use problems, but suffice it to say that it happens. In fact, it is generally agreed that more people with such problems resolve them on their own than with the use of self-help groups or professional treatment. How such changes are initiated is of interest and has been studied most extensively with alcohol problems. The best study methodologically of this question to date was reported by Sobell et al. (1993). Most of the people these researchers studied (57%) said their change was the result of a process of weighing the benefits and costs of continuing their current alcohol-use pattern. When the disadvantages seemed to grow in number and importance, change occurred. Notice how similar this is to what people in the contemplation stage are thought to do. Another sizable proportion of study participants (29%) reported that change was immediate, and they either could not recall what triggered the change, or said it was a major event, such as a serious alcohol-related health problem.

> "The one thing I could never do is go to a formal rehab; for me to have to ask somebody else to help with a self-made problem, I would rather drink myself to death."
>
> (Individual who resolved his alcohol problem on his own, cited in Tuchfeld, 1981, p. 631)

The most important point to take from this extremely brief discussion is that spontaneous remission occurs and apparently occurs often. How often has not been determined; to specify the prevalence would be extremely costly and complex. Nevertheless, even with our limited knowledge of it, the phenomenon of change without treatment has taught us a lot about change processes in general, including change that occurs with the use of treatment sources. We turn next to one of those resources—self-help groups.

SELF-HELP GROUPS

Peer self-help groups are a major part of the treatment of the substance-use disorders. According to Emrick, Lassen, and Edwards (1977), members of peer self-help groups perform therapeutic functions, but do not have professional credentials. A member of a peer self-help group could have training pertinent to conducting therapy, but such credentials are not used in performing self-help group functions. Members of these groups all have some identified problem that is the focus of the group's therapeutic activity. This is the basis of using the term "peer self-help," to distinguish from groups in which therapeutic agents (the group leader, for example) are not identified as having the same problems as the clients. Therefore, through the peer self-help group participants both give and receive help with their problems.

Although the peer self-help movement does not use professionally defined methods to help participants with their problems, it does not mean professionals are shunned. In fact, the professional community is welcome to join with the peer self-help group in achieving common goals in helping people alleviate their problems (for example, Alcoholics Anonymous, 1972). The reasons are the complementary functions that professionals and the self-help group serve with each other. In practice, professionals working in the treatment of alcohol and drug problems often use the relevant self-help groups (such as Alcoholics Anonymous for alcohol problems and Narcotics Anonymous for other drug problems) in a professionally run rehabilitation program and as part of aftercare planning. Indeed, many alcohol- and drug-treatment programs are organized around principles of peer self-help groups.

In discussing treatment of the psychoactive substance-use disorders it is important to review peer self-help groups because of their popularity and influence in the treatment of alcohol and other drug-use disorders. Peer self-help also has been a popular treatment of choice for other addictive behaviors: there are Weight Watchers and TOPS (Taking Off Pounds Sensibly) for treatment of obesity, Smokers Anonymous for treatment of cigarette smoking, and Gamblers Anonymous for treatment of compulsive gambling. One national survey estimates that in 1990 close to 1.5 million people in the United States used self-help groups for addiction or other mental health problems (Regier, Narrow, Rae et al., 1993).

In this section we briefly describe the peer self-help movement organized for helping individuals identified as alcoholic—Alcoholics Anonymous (AA). Because of space limitations we cannot describe in detail the major self-help groups for the treatment of drug problems, called Narcotics Anonymous (NA). However, NA is analogous to AA, and what we know about AA can be applied readily to NA.

Emrick et al. (1977) called AA the prototypic self-help group, because it is the oldest, established in 1935. It has been the basis for development of other self-help movements for treatments in other problem areas. The AA movement began when an alcoholic surgeon (Dr. Bob) and an alcoholic stockbroker (Bill W.) helped each other to maintain sobriety. They spread from its Ohio origin their idea that alcoholics needed to help each other. Today AA is an international organization. A few alcohol self-help groups such as Alateen and Alanon have been derived from AA. Alateen's purpose is to help teenagers who have an alcoholic parent. Alanon generally is organized for spouses and others close to the alcoholic.

The bases of the AA "program" are self-help recovery through following the Twelve Steps and group participation. The core of AA is the model of recovery outlined in the Twelve Steps, which are listed in Table 16-1. There are a few features of the Twelve Steps important to point out. The first step states AA absolutely dismisses the notion that alcoholics can control their drinking or can ever reach that position. The beginning of recovery occurs when the alcoholic admits to himself or herself a powerlessness over alcohol, that without alcohol a return to health is possible and that with it the downward spiral to self-destruction continues. Another point causing much controversy is the frequent reference to God in the Twelve Steps. An immediate reaction to this is that AA is only for alcoholics who accept Western religious beliefs. However, AA takes pains to accent the phrase "God as He is understood," which means each person may interpret "God" or "Higher Power" as he or she wishes. The importance of referring to a Supreme Being is to emphasize that alcoholics have lost control over alcohol and of their lives and must enlist the assistance of a greater power in recovery. A final point is that the Twelve Steps recovery program is oriented toward action, both in self-examination and change and in behavior toward others.

The Twelve Steps are a guide designed for people to follow largely by themselves on the road to **recovery.** The Steps are bases of recovery, but there are other parts to the AA program. One of these is group participation. Two major types are discussion meetings and speakers' meetings. In discussion meetings the chairperson of the group tells his or her personal history of alcoholism and recovery from it, and then the meeting is opened for members' discussion of alcoholism and related matters. In a speakers' meeting a couple of members recite their personal histories of alcoholism and recovery. In open speakers' meetings, anyone who is interested may attend. Closed meetings are for alcoholics only.

Recovery
In the addictions field, this term means changes back to health in physical, psychological, spiritual, and social functioning. It generally is believed that recovery is a lifetime process that requires total abstinence from alcohol and nonprescribed drugs.

Table 16-1   The Twelve Steps of Alcoholics Anonymous

1. We admitted we were powerless over alcohol—that our lives had become unmanageable.
2. Came to believe that a Power greater than ourselves could restore us to sanity.
3. Made a decision to turn our will and our lives over to the care of God *as we understood* Him.
4. Made a searching and fearless moral inventory of ourselves.
5. Admitted to God, to ourselves, and to another human being the exact nature of our wrongs.
6. Were entirely ready to have God remove all these defects of character.
7. Humbly ask Him to remove our shortcomings.
8. Made a list of all persons we had harmed, and became willing to make amends to them all.
9. Made direct amends to such people wherever possible, except when to do so would injure them or others.
10. Continued to take personal inventory and when we were wrong promptly admitted it.
11. Sought through prayer and meditation to improve our conscious contact with God *as we understood* Him praying only for knowledge of His will for us and the power to carry that out.
12. Having had a spiritual experience as the result of these steps, we tried to carry this message to alcoholics, and to practice these principles in *all* our affairs.

The Twelve Steps reprinted with permission of Alcoholics Anonymous World Services, Inc. Alcoholics Anonymous is a program of recovery from alcoholism. Other self-help programs address other addictions. Any opinions about either the steps or AA are those of the authors.

One purpose of group meetings is to aid recovery through peer identification and learning from the experience of others. Building social relationships that do not revolve around alcohol represents an entirely new social life. The importance of forming sober social relationships may be seen in various AA functions such as "Sober Anniversaries" (the first day of a member's current episode of continuous sobriety) and "Sober Dances" (dances without alcohol or drugs).

Other major activities in the AA program are "Twelfth Stepping" and sponsorship. Twelfth Stepping refers to the twelfth of the Twelve Steps and involves members reaching out to other alcoholics in a time of need. Pertinent activities include helping an active alcoholic begin the AA program or helping a current AA member return to sobriety after he or she has begun drinking again. Sponsorship is similar to Twelfth Stepping, but there are important differences. First, sponsorship involves a stable one-to-one relationship between a member with more sobriety (the sponsor) and one with less (the sponsoree). To quote, "the process of sponsorship is this: An alcoholic who has made some progress in the recovery program shares that experience on a continuous, individual basis with another alcoholic who is attempting to attain or maintain sobriety through AA" (Alcoholics Anonymous, 1983, p. 5). Another important difference is that the sponsor helps the person in a variety of ways that may include taking the newer member's "inventory" (looking at what is behind a person's behavior) when asked, guiding an individual to AA literature, such as the *Big Book* and *Twelve Steps and Twelve Traditions*, and explaining the AA program to family and others close to the sponsoree. Therefore, the sponsor-sponsoree relationship is in many ways more varied and more enduring than that involved in Twelfth Stepping. AA members view both types of activities as essential to their continued sobriety.

What has been described for AA is directly applicable to Narcotics Anonymous (NA). NA's organization and program of recovery is derived directly from AA's, including the use of the Steps of Recovery Program, group meetings, and the sponsor-sponsoree relationship. As the name implies, NA evolved with concentration on helping people addicted to opiate drugs, usually heroin. However, people who identify their primary problem as addiction to drugs of any type other than alcohol use NA instead of AA.

In summary, the AA program of recovery has been the cornerstone of a self-help movement that has been of value to many and that is reaching increasing numbers of people. It is worth mentioning again that both AA and NA may be, and are, used alone as programs of treatment. However, many members of these organizations began treatment or concurrently are receiving treatment from professional sources.

Additional Self-Help Groups

We have spent so much space on AA and its "relatives" because they are by far the most prevalent and influential self-help treatments for alcohol- and drug-use disorders. Perhaps stimulated by AA's success, other types of self-help groups for alcohol and drug problems have been organized. One important example is Women for Sobriety (WFS), which began in 1975 (WFS, 1985). WFS groups are now available throughout the United States and in other countries as well.

WFS is in agreement with AA that alcohol- and drug-use disorders are a progressive illness. Complete abstinence from these substances is required to arrest the illness, but it cannot be cured. Also similar to AA, WFS members meet in groups (weekly) that are led by a moderator. The WFS "program" that is the core topic of the discussion groups consists of 13 statements about spiritual and emotional change and growth.

So far it is not clear why WFS required a new name, since it seems like a slight variant of AA. However, the focus of WFS is what is seen to be the special psychological and social needs and concerns that women face in achieving and maintaining sobriety—a focus that does not in general exist in AA. As such, WFS suggests that its program alone may be used to maintain sobriety, used in conjunction with professional services, or used in conjunction with AA.

Another self-help group is Rational Recovery. Like any other alcohol or drug treatment that has been developed, AA does not work well for everybody. Rational Recovery (RR) is an alternative-to-AA, self-help group that started in 1986 and that is rapidly gaining in acceptance and popularity. The major "bible" RR is called *The Small Book* (Trimpey, 1992)—a name to contrast with the AA "bible" called *The Big Book*. Based on the philosophy of **humanism** and on Albert Ellis's system of psychotherapy called rational emotive therapy, RR contrasts sharply with AA. Alcohol- and drug-use disorders are not viewed as the result of a disease process but of "consistently bad" personal decisions (Trimpey, 1990). RR is presented as a system of beliefs about alcohol and drug problems rather than as a step program. The emphasis of RR is on personal responsibility and control over the use of alcohol and drugs rather than on a lack of control as in AA. There also is an emphasis on the self as the agent of change, rather than on a "higher power" and the AA group.

Humanism
A system of thought and culture that emphasizes human interests instead of the natural world or religion.

RR members meet in usually twice-a-week discussion groups that may or may not have a lay coordinator present. All groups have an "advisor" available for special problems that may arise, such as acute psychiatric distress in a member. Members are expected to attend RR groups for six months to one year, when recovering is typically seen as ended (in contrast to AA, which says that recovering lasts a lifetime). Of course, if an individual leaves an RR group but wishes to return, he or she always is welcome back. RR groups may be used alone in making and maintaining changes in alcohol and drug use, or used following some more intensive treatment, such as inpatient care, for example. Like AA, RR emphasizes the importance of the goal of abstinence from alcohol and drugs.

The last self-help group we will discuss is "SOS," which stands for Secular Organizations for Sobriety or, as an alternative, Save Our Selves. It is another self-help support group that began in 1986 as an alternative to AA. As in Rational Recovery, the SOS alternative has no emphasis on spirituality or higher powers in staying sober. Instead, individuals are viewed as in charge of making rational decisions about their use of alcohol and drugs. SOS's popularity is increasing rapidly, and as of 1990 had over 200 sites in the United States where groups meet, with the number of members increasing. SOS also is international, with groups in Canada, Europe, and Australia (American Health Consultants, 1990; Secular Organizations for Sobriety, 1990).

Like AA and RR, SOS uses peer support group meetings as the vehicle to staying sober. Groups generally have 10–12 members and meet weekly for 1–1½ hours, but other procedures are possible, as the parent organization is flexible regarding the scheduling and format of individual support group meetings. These meetings have a rotating leader, who is a group member. Groups are free, but members may make donations to sustain the group financially.

The core principle of SOS is that sobriety—abstinence from alcohol and drugs—is maintained "one day at a time," an expression well-known to AA members. The "Sobriety Priority Program" is the philosophy that underlies SOS, with these major points: (1) acknowledgment of one's addiction as a disease and a habit; (2) acceptance of one's problem; (3) placement of sobriety as the number one priority, separate from other problems or concerns in life. These three points may be viewed as analogous to AA's Twelve Steps. In SOS, groups are seen as a safe place where members can discuss their concerns and ways that they stay sober. It appears that no limit is placed on how long a person may stay in a group or on the number of meetings that he or she attends.

To conclude this section, self-help groups are an extremely important resource that people use to change patterns of alcohol or other drug use. Self-help groups may be used alone or in conjunction with professional treatment services, which is our next topic. Before we go into our discussion of what happens in such treatment, it is important for you to know something about the ideas (models and theories) behind it. You saw this to some degree in our review of self-help groups, and how beliefs about the causes of alcohol and drug problems greatly influenced the content of the self-help group and what participation in it involved. The same is true for professional treatments.

MODELS OF SUBSTANCE-USE DISORDERS

In Chapter 9 we discussed at length how many different models and theories have been championed about the causes (another term is etiology) of alcohol dependence. These conceptual views have: spanned biological, psychological, and social/environmental domains of variables; tended to be heavy on one of the three variable domains and light or silent on the other two; and often explained something about the development of alcohol dependence but not everything. The same conclusions could be drawn about theories of the development of dependence on drugs other than alcohol. For example, a book that Lettieri, Sayers, and Pearson (1980) edited on "selected" contemporary theories of drug abuse covered 43 theories. The collection cut across the disciplines of the biological and behavioral/social sciences.

"Society and its agencies have always had a consistent response, in that in the same breath they are able to say the homeless alcoholic is 'sad, mad, and bad.'"

(Cook, 1975, cited in Orford, 1985, p. 292)

In order to make learning about these models and theories easier, we summarized them by use of five major categories (there are specific variations within the categories): moral model, American Disease model, biological model, social learning model, and sociocultural model. Each of these classes of models has implications for designing treatment of the substance-use disorders. Our discussion is based heavily on a chapter by Miller and Hester (1989).

Five Model Categories

The first category is the moral model, in which individuals are seen as personally responsible for problems they may incur from their use of drugs and alcohol. That is, the development of a substance-use disorder is seen as the product of a series of personal decisions or choices to use those substances in a way that is harmful. This perspective implies that choices other than to use alcohol and drugs were available to the person but not taken. Depending on the variation of the model, treatment consists either of spiritual or legal (e.g., jail) intervention.

The American Disease model is especially important because of its great prevalence and prominence in the United States. It also is the foundation of Alcoholics Anonymous and other self-help groups. In the American Disease model (it is called American because it is not nearly as popular in other countries) alcohol and drug dependence are viewed as products of a progressive, irreversible disease. The disease is described as a merging of physical, psychological, and spiritual causes. The treatment that follows from the disease model is to identify people who have the disease, confront them with it, help them to accept that they have it, and persuade them to abstain from alcohol and other drugs.

In the biological model dependence on alcohol or other drugs is viewed as the result of genetic or physiological processes. Theories about how the pharmacological action of drugs themselves in the brain can lead to dependence also fall under the biological umbrella. The treatment most clearly implied from biological models is to advise biologically-at-risk people of their risk for disorder development status, and perhaps to counsel those who are at risk to avoid alcohol and other drugs altogether.

Social learning theory is a position that alcohol and drug disorders are the result of complex learning that results from an interaction of the person with his or her environment. Situations and psychological processes are most important. For example, harmful substance-use patterns may develop from direct experiences in using alcohol and drugs, from modeling the behavior of other individuals when they drink or use drugs in a harmful way, from false beliefs about the powers of alcohol and drugs in helping to get through difficult times, or from a failure to learn ways to cope with stress without alcohol or drug use. Treatment follows straightforwardly from this conception: Arrange the person's environment so that nonabuse of psychoactive substances is reinforced and abuse is not, or is punished (Higgins, Delaney, Budney, et al., 1991); display individuals ("models") engaging in desirable alcohol-use patterns (use of psychoactive drugs other than for medical purposes never is viewed positively by the greater society); teach facts about the actions of alcohol and drugs on the body and how humans experience their effects; and teach nondrug ways to cope with stress.

According to the sociocultural model, subcultures and societies shape alcohol- and drug-use patterns and consequences. Examples might include norms and rules that a subculture has for alcohol use (such as when it is appropriate, as at adult dinner parties, and when it is not, as at work), and laws about substance use (such as what drugs are legal and what drugs are not). The treatment that follows from this perspective is interventions that affect large groups of people or society in general. For example, taxation of beverage alcohol is an effort in part to control its availability and accessibility. Another example of a sociocultural intervention is the classification of drugs by "schedule" status (see Chapter 2).

You can see that the five major categories of models and theories of substance-use disorder reflect a wide array of perspectives. You also might notice that, in general, models fitting under a category do not overlap much with models fitting under other categories. A summary of the five categories of models and their implications for treatment is presented in Table 16-2.

Biopsychosocial Model

If no one model or theory of causes of substance-use disorders proves adequate, as is the case, some way of proceeding with treatment design must occur. We could be atheoretical in our efforts, but that approach tends not to be too productive. Instead, we can combine the disciplines (biological/ medical-psychological-social/environmental) into one perspective. As you saw in Chapter 9, the term "biopsychosocial" reflects an attempt to take into account simultaneously three major variable domains that are known to influence human health and behavior. You will recognize again that this combined perspective follows from the theme of the drug experience and its determinants that we have articulated and developed since the first chapter of this text.

It is no secret that taking a biopsychosocial perspective of the causes of the substance-use disorders is taking on a new level of complexity. But drugs and human behavior is a complex subject that requires complex analysis for its understanding. Because of its complexity and recency, the biopsychosocial viewpoint is just that, a viewpoint, at this time—it is not precise or developed enough to be called a theory. However, our premise is that this perspective has been providing and will continue to provide a guide for the kind of research that will lead to explanations of the causes of the substance-use disorders.

Table 16-2   Summary of Five Major Categories of Models of the Causes of Substance-Use Disorders, and Their Implications for Treatment

Model	Cause(s)	Treatment
Moral	The making of personal choices to use alcohol and drugs in a harmful way, when other choices could have been made.	Punish legally or intervene spiritually.
American Disease	Substance-use disorders are progressive, irreversible diseases that are the products of a mix of physical, psychological, and spiritual causes.	Identify those with the disease, confront them with it, and persuade them to abstain from drugs and alcohol.
Biological	Genetic or physiological processes.	Advise people at risk for problems of their risk status. Counsel those at risk to avoid alcohol and drugs entirely.
Social Learning	Complex learning, based on an interaction of the individual with his or her environment.	Arrange environment to reinforce nonabuse of substances; do not reinforce, or punish, abuse; provide models of appropriate substance use; debunk myths about alcohol and drugs; teach nondrug alternatives for coping with stress.
Sociocultural	Subcultures and societies shape alcohol and drug-use patterns.	Intervene in ways that affect large groups or society in general (e.g., drug-use laws and alcohol taxes).

Note: Information in this table is adapted from a chapter by Miller and Hester (1989). See text for more detailed discussion of the models.

PROFESSIONAL TREATMENT: ASSESSMENT AND GOALS

When individuals go to professionals for help to change their substance use a process of assessment and treatment goal setting typically is initiated. Actually, models of etiology influence this part of the treatment experience as they do treatment content. We also should note that discussing assessment and goals here is not meant to imply they are not relevant for self-change or self-help groups. Although no systematic, formally structured assessment occurs in these latter contexts, some type of appraisal has occurred, however unsystematic or subtle, that a problem exists. Furthermore, goals are set that define the desired end of the change process. Again, such goals may not be explicitly documented or articulated, but they direct change. Note how this general concept of the need to set goals to direct change is incorporated in the stages of change model.

"Wouldn't stick to goals if they were forced on me; you have to make up your own mind."

(Patient involved in "Guided Self-Change" Treatment, cited in Sobell & Sobell, 1993, p. 159)

An overarching assumption of professional settings is that good assessment underlies good treatment. When we say assessment in this context we mean use of mostly formal (e.g., standard psychological tests), but sometimes informal (e.g., casual observation of a patient's behavior on a treatment unit), procedures to measure some aspect of a person's functioning. Assessment of persons appearing for drug and alcohol treatment may include several different procedures.

Measuring qualities or characteristics of a person in order to design treatment means that treatment is tailored to the person. This is the same as matching the treatments to the individual. Matching concerns decisions about what treatment choices are preferred for different groups of individuals to produce the best results. Along these lines, a major task of assessment and matching is to help define or specify treatment goals. Treatment goals refer to the purposes or aims of a treatment, which in general are to "get better." However, that is too general to be of much use in guiding a treatment. We can be more specific. For example, in drug and alcohol treatment everybody agrees that the person's use of drugs and alcohol must change. In the United States that typically means a change to complete abstinence from these substances, although we will see there has been some controversy over whether all individuals require a goal of total abstinence from alcohol.

There may be goals of alcohol and drug treatment besides a person's substance use. For a few examples, it may be important for changes to occur in an individual's family, work, and social functioning. This is because in virtually all people who appear for substance-abuse treatment, their use of alcohol or other drugs has affected other parts of their lives. Those changes in turn may affect a person's use of alcohol and drugs. It is important to see that the influences of substance use on different areas of life, and the reverse, are consistent with a biopsychosocial model. Substance use may be affected by multiple and varied factors, and the use of psychoactive substances may have multiple and varied consequences. These consequences may in turn affect future substance use.

How these multiple influences work in the development, maintenance, and change in substance use tends to be different for each person. As a result, a person's goals for treatment must be tailored to his or her specific, unique circumstances. Professionals working in drug and alcohol treatment call this "individualizing" treatment goals.

"We're all allowed to deal with the issue of drinking the way each of us wants to. If a guy wants to reduce his drinking, so let him try. AA stands for unconditional abstinence only, but with us everyone makes his own program. I do recommend abstinence for all of those who have reached an advanced stage of alcoholism. That way you certainly get away with less distress and damage."

(Member of the Tampere A-guild, a Finnish self-help organization, cited in Alasuutari, 1992, p. 130)

Abstinence or Moderation?

Before leaving the topic of treatment goals it is important to discuss a specific question about goals relating to alcohol use. Traditionally, and still predominantly in the United States and Canada, the assumption is that the goal of treatment for alcohol problems is abstinence from alcohol. This applies to self-help treatments as well as to professional treatment service; indeed, AA and other self-help groups are adamant that abstinence is essential to long-term improved functioning for the person. However, there have been a number of reports in the literature both on self-change and on treatment that individuals identified as alcohol abusers or alcohol dependent do modify their alcohol use to a stable, moderate level.

Findings such as these have created and still create heated controversy. The controversy stems from the disease model of alcohol problems, which implies that lifelong abstinence is the only safe course toward amelioration of alcohol problems. The need for abstinence is not questioned in the treatment of other drug problems, however. It is likely that abstinence from nonprescribed use of drugs is the only acceptable goal because the drugs are illegal, and society has a strong reaction against illicit drug use.

The question of moderation as a drinking goal is of more than academic importance. Knowledge about different drinking outcomes would help to increase our understanding of the causes and course of alcohol problems, and to improve the results of our treatment efforts through better individualization of treatment goals. We do know that moderate drinking outcomes happen, but knowledge beyond that is more sketchy. It seems to make the most sense to frame this question the same way we framed treatment goals in general above—they should reflect the individual's specific, unique circumstances.

Research does help somewhat in telling us what are the best "circumstances" for a goal of moderate drinking. Overall, it seems that less severe alcohol dependence (in DSM-IV terms, or in terms of physical dependence on alcohol), a belief in the individual that moderate drinking is possible, younger age, employment, and psychological and social stability provide the "backdrop" that suggests the feasibility of a moderate drinking outcome (Rosenberg, 1993). However, some of these factors are not static (such as beliefs about moderate drinking) and it would be essential to monitor them closely over time to make maintained moderate drinking most likely.

It seems that moderate drinking outcomes will continue to stimulate debate and research for years to come. The best result of this activity would be better understanding of the course of alcohol problems and the creation of better treatment service delivery.

Once assessment and specification of treatment goals have been accomplished, the next step is to make the best use of that information to place an individual in the best treatment environment to meet his or her needs. Two levels of such matching may be considered—the treatment setting and the services that are delivered within a setting. We turn now to review both of these, first for alcohol treatment and then for other drug treatment. We also will comment on how effective alcohol and drug treatment are. When we say drug treatment, we refer to treatment for drugs of abuse, such as the opiates, stimulants, and depressant drugs. Nicotine is not covered in this chapter, since we discussed treatment of nicotine dependence in Chapter 7.

ALCOHOL TREATMENT SETTINGS AND SERVICES

The settings and services of treatment for alcohol problems could be classified in a number of ways. We use the classification that Armor, Polich, and Stambul published in their well-known 1976 Rand Corporation study of alcoholism treatment in the United States.

Armor et al. (1976, p. 102) identified the general treatment settings of hospital setting, intermediate setting, and outpatient setting. Within each of these settings specific treatment services are offered. Inpatients in the hospital setting live there for the duration of their treatment, and the organization of patient care is similar to that given to persons hospitalized for physical problems. For example, nurses play a large role in treatment, and much weight is given to the medical aspects of alcohol problems. On the other hand, a good deal of the specific alcohol rehabilitation methods followed in hospital-based programs are **psychological** in origin. The emphasis of these nonmedical treatment methods is on learning about the self and the environment we live in, how they alter the course of alcohol problem development, and how a person can change both the self and his or her environment to produce desired changes in psychoactive substance use. (Similar treatment methods are followed in inpatient "free-standing" alcohol programs. These programs do not operate within the hospital setting and typically are "for profit," that is, they need to make a profit to stay in business.) Partial hospital care occurs in the hospital setting, but the patient[1] is not in the setting for 24 hours a day. Typically, treatment programs of this type are designed for six- to eight-hour schedules, usually in the daytime or evening hours. The last type of service in the hospital setting is detoxification, mainly involving the medical management of alcohol withdrawal symptoms. Care mostly consists of the management of medications given to treat withdrawal, although counseling is available, especially referral to additional treatment services.

Within the intermediate setting are halfway house services. Halfway houses usually are designed as **milieu treatment** settings. (In milieu treatment the organization and structure of a setting are designed to be therapeutic.) These settings are at the patients' residence during treatment. Other treatment services usually available include **counseling, psychotherapy,** and a strong orientation toward use of self-help groups, usually Alcoholics Anonymous (AA). A quarterway house is similar to a halfway house except, as the name implies, it is more structured and allows residents less independence than is accessible to halfway house residents. (Similarly, less structured versions of halfway houses have been called three-quarterway houses.) Finally, the intermediate setting also includes residential care, consisting of living quarters, but little other treatment.

Psychological treatment
Treatments geared to changing emotions, thoughts, or behavior without the use of medications or other physical or biological means.

Milieu treatment
Treatment in which the organization and structure of a setting are designed to change behavior.

Counseling
In alcohol and drug treatment, counselors are specially trained professionals who perform a variety of treatment activities, including assessment, education, and individual, marital, or family counseling.

Psychotherapy
Typically, a conversation between a specially trained individual (therapist) and another person (or family) that is intended to change patterns of behavior, thoughts, or feelings in that person.

[1]In the treatment of psychiatric disorders, including the addictions, there is inconsistency among professionals in their use of the words "patient" or "client" to refer to individuals presenting themselves for treatment. What underlie this disagreement are beliefs about the utility of a medical model as a guide to understanding the psychiatric disorders. In addition, often what term is chosen depends on the setting of treatment. For example, individuals in hospital inpatient settings are more likely to be referred to as patients, as compared to persons receiving treatment in outpatient clinics. In this chapter we have used the terms patient and client as synonyms to refer to an individual who is in formal treatment for his or her alcohol or drug problems.

The outpatient setting is perhaps the most idiosyncratic of the three Armor et al. (1976) described. Two general distinctions of treatment services are made: individual and group. In individual treatment, the patient works with a professional in a one-to-one relationship. Similarly, "individual" couples or families also may work with a professional in a planned course of treatment. In contrast, group treatment usually involves 5 to 10 individuals joined together in regular sessions and led by a professional. In such treatment, much of what helps group members to change theoretically stems from the way group members interact with each other and form relationships. The leader's job is to guide this process and to keep group members on productive tracks of discussion. Groups often are organized around specific themes governing the types of people who join the group and what they discuss. Examples are adults whose parents were alcoholic, and ways to prevent a recurrence (relapse) of alcohol problems once they are treated. Other groups are general and have only the theme of maintaining abstinence from substance use. Individual and group alcohol treatment is conducted by a range of workers with mental health training. There are "paraprofessionals," who are people working in direct patient care and not possessing a formal degree. Then there are the professionals who are physicians (typically psychiatrists), clinical psychologists, social workers, clinical nurse specialists, and certified alcohol (or other drug) counselors. Actually, people in any of the professional disciplines also may earn certification as an alcohol and drug counselor.

Outpatient care also varies in intensity. That is, some patients may have program contact only monthly or less, with little structure in schedule, and other outpatient programs may be similar to what we described above for the partial hospital setting. When such programs are not in the hospital context, they typically are called day (or evening) treatment programs.

It is somewhat artificial to describe setting for treatment of alcohol (and, for that matter, drug) abuse in discrete categories, because a treatment episode for many people involves participation in more than one treatment setting. For example, a common course of treatment includes detoxification from alcohol and later referral to an inpatient or outpatient treatment program. Or, an individual may begin treatment by completing an inpatient intensive rehabilitation program and then engage in outpatient treatment as part of an **aftercare** plan. Other combinations are possible, each suited to the person's needs.

Categories of treatment settings and services can give only an outline of actual treatment activities occurring in alcohol programs. It is difficult to characterize alcohol programs except in the broadest terms. In alcohol programs, what is called individual or group counseling or psychotherapy can refer to many specific activities. They can occur in any of the treatment settings described, with some settings having greater latitude than others. For example, the smallest range of treatment activities is in settings devoted primarily to detoxification. In contrast, outpatient or inpatient treatment programs can include many different activities that are called treatment. These may include medical care to a limited degree and pharmacotherapy.

To give an idea of the many treatment activities used, Maisto and Nirenberg (1986) studied the use of treatment procedures in inpatient alcoholism treatment programs funded by the Veterans Administration (VA) (now called

Aftercare
In alcohol and drug treatment, this term usually refers to therapeutic activities following completion of a formal treatment program.

the Department of Veterans Affairs). In this study a detailed questionnaire was sent to the directors of the VA alcoholism treatment programs. One survey question concerned patients' use of different treatment "components." The directors' responses to this questionnaire item confirmed the impression that there is great variation in what constitutes treatment of alcohol (and drug) problems. No fewer than 48 different program components were reported by at least one of the 72 directors. Each component had been used in the last three months by at least some of their patients. Any of the treatment program components could be offered in combination. Again, it should be remembered that Maisto and Nirenberg's study addressed only VA inpatient alcoholism treatment programs. It is possible that if there were more variety in the types of treatment settings sampled, there would have been reports of even greater variety of treatment activities.

Pharmacological Treatment

Although our discussion of alcohol treatment has emphasized nonmedical interventions, drugs frequently are used in the treatment of alcohol problems. This practice is known as pharmacotherapy. In discussing pharmacotherapy it is important to distinguish between detoxification and post-detoxification treatment. Detoxification of people who are physically dependent on alcohol often involves the use of drugs in the medical management of withdrawal, although there are drug-free approaches to detoxification. These latter approaches, as noted in Chapter 9, are called "social detoxification," in which a person's withdrawal is monitored by professional staff in a treatment setting, but no drugs are administered, if at all possible. There is little controversy about using drugs in managing acute withdrawal. However, there are some disagreements over the use of chemicals in treatment activities subsequent to detoxification.

The first type of pharmacotherapy for alcohol problems uses compounds that alter the metabolism of alcohol if it is consumed. Peachey and Annis (1985) reviewed these compounds, which they called the alcohol-sensitizing drugs. The most popular of these are disulfiram (trademark Antabuse) and carbimide (trademark Temposil). Antabuse has been in use in the United States since 1948. Temposil, on the other hand, is not available in the United States and is used less frequently overall than Antabuse. In any case, use of both agents in treatment is based on similar assumptions regarding the psychological effects of their chemical action.

The chemical action of alcohol-sensitizing drugs results in an increase in the blood level of acetaldehyde after alcohol consumption (see Chapter 9 on the metabolizing of alcohol). The consequence of the heightened acetaldehyde depends on how much alcohol is drunk. For people on therapeutic doses of disulfiram or carbimide, one or two drinks will produce flushing, tachycardia (excessively rapid heartbeat, usually a pulse rate of over 100 per minute), tachypnea (excessively rapid respiration), sensations of warmth, heart palpitations, and shortness of breath. These effects usually last about 30 minutes and are not life-threatening. However, if larger quantities of alcohol are consumed, the reaction may include intense palpitations, dyspnea (difficult or labored breathing), nausea, vomiting, and headache, all of which may last more than 90 minutes. In some people this more severe reaction has induced shock, loss of consciousness, or death due to myocardial infarction (Peachey & Annis, 1985, p. 202).

The unpleasant effects of drinking while on a regimen of the alcohol-sensitizing drugs are why such drugs are used in treatment. The assumption is that fear of experiencing the unpleasant effects will deter a person from drinking and will have the concurrent result of building a learned aversion to alcohol based on the imagined negative consequences of drinking. If a person on disulfiram or carbimide tests out the effects of drinking, the same learned aversion will proceed more rapidly because of the addition of experiencing direct, as well as imagined, negative consequences. The learned aversion to alcohol underlies eventual avoidance of it and, with the cessation of drinking, improvements in other areas of functioning such as job and family that often are impaired with abusive drinking patterns.

Alcohol-sensitizing drugs virtually always are used as part of a treatment program that includes other treatment components. When they first were available for treatment, these drugs were perceived as magic pills that would revolutionize alcoholism treatment and make it a simple matter of medical management. Unfortunately, such hopes soon were dashed by research findings and an increasing awareness of the complexity of alcohol abuse and dependence.

A second type of pharmacotherapy for alcohol problems is based in biological theories of etiology, which focus on abnormalities or changes in brain chemistry as causes or consequences of substance abuse. Such theories imply that a correction of the abnormal brain chemistry is essential to alleviating the substance-use problem. Applying this implication to pharmacotherapy has not extended, for the most part, much beyond animal research.

One exception is the use of naltrexone to reduce craving in alcoholic men. As you will see below, naltrexone is an opiate antagonist that has been used to treat opiate dependence but it recently has been applied to the treatment of alcohol dependence. Volpicelli, Alterman, Hayashida, and O'Brien (1992) found that male alcoholics who were administered naltrexone as part of their treatment following detoxification experienced less craving for alcohol and fewer instances of more severe (longer duration, or higher quantity) drinking episodes, if they drank at all during the 12-week evaluation period. These results were essentially repeated and extended in a study of male and female alcoholics (O'Malley, Jaffe, Chang, et al., 1992).

The results of these two studies were interpreted as showing that taking naltrexone results in less craving for alcohol, and thus fewer periods of severe drinking, by blocking opioid receptors in the brain. That is, it is hypothesized that drinking alcohol triggers craving through its stimulation of the opioid receptors. By blocking that stimulation less craving for alcohol is experienced.

As interesting as these findings are, there are some problems with them. First, there has been a recent failure to replicate the findings in a pilot study of treatment of patients with alcohol- and cocaine-use disorders (Carroll, Ziedonis, O'Malley et al., 1993). Second, the interpretation of the original findings is open to question. It is debatable that naltrexone reduces craving, since it does not reduce craving for opiates. In fact, it may increase craving for opiates. Therefore, if naltrexone does result in reduced alcohol consumption—and the failure to replicate the original findings casts some doubt on that—then the mechanism likely is something other than a reduction in craving.

Effectiveness of Alcohol Treatment

At this point, after reading about a variety of settings and methods that fall into the category of alcohol treatment, you probably are wondering whether any of the effort is worth it. That is, you probably are wondering about the effectiveness of alcohol treatment. When we talk about treatment effectiveness, we refer to the relationship between participation in some treatment and achieving some treatment goal. Therefore, treatment effectiveness centers on if and how treatment participation causes different outcomes. Evaluations of the effectiveness of treatment are called **treatment outcome research.**

Treatment outcome research
Research designed to show a causal relationship between undergoing a treatment and some physical, psychological, or social change.

In this section we will not cover detoxification services, as they are not considered rehabilitation. Rather, they should be viewed as effective in managing safe alcohol withdrawal, but not in providing rehabilitation beyond that. Similarly, pharmacotherapies are not evaluated separately since they predominantly are administered in the context of at least one (and usually several) other psychological or social treatment component.

In discussing the effectiveness of treatment it is essential to take into account the rate of spontaneous remission of alcohol problems. As you might guess, in order to show a treatment is worth its cost, one thing that must be demonstrated is that it helps significantly beyond the rate of spontaneous remission. This reasoning is sound, but it is extremely difficult to determine just what are the rates of spontaneous remission. In this regard, people who resolve their problems without treatment are the ones with whom clinicians and researchers are least likely to have contact. Professionals instead tend to see people who are referred to a formal treatment setting. We noted earlier in this chapter that making a credible effort to determine the prevalence of spontaneous remission of alcohol problems would be highly complex and costly.

Despite this problem, estimates of spontaneous remission have been made for alcohol abuse, mostly through studies of people who entered a formal treatment program but who dropped out of it prematurely and could say they received "no treatment." Another method to estimate spontaneous remission involves rates of improvement in "no treatment" or similar control groups in treatment outcome studies. The estimates of spontaneous remission of alcohol problems that have been made vary with the definition of remission, the comparison groups used, and the length of the interval during which functioning is measured. Miller and Hester (1980) suggested the spontaneous remission (abstinence or improvement in drinking patterns) in one year for untreated alcohol abusers is 19%, while Emrick (1975) calculated 13% for abstinence and 28% for abstinence plus "improved."

As you can tell from this discussion about spontaneous remission and treatment outcome, the main criterion considered is drinking behavior, even though earlier you saw that other criteria could be used. That said, questions about the effectiveness of alcohol treatment have been studied for well over 50 years. It is impossible here to cite the findings for specific treatment approaches, but some general conclusions can be offered. First is that there is not a single alcohol treatment type or setting that is consistently better than others, but staying in any kind of treatment increases the chances of long-term improvement, even with rates of spontaneous remission taken into account (McKay, Murphy, & Longabaugh, 1991; USDHHS, 1993).

Some may find little positive in this overall conclusion about the effectiveness of alcohol treatment. However, these findings should not be taken lightly. Studies have shown that the amount of money saved in, say, health care and business expenses as a result of improvements in people undergoing treatment is greater than the amount of money the treatment costs. Similarly, research completed by insurance companies suggests that substance abusers (and their families) use significantly fewer health care services after treatment than before. This shows the benefits of alcohol treatment in financial terms; the more important, but more difficult to measure, gains in human welfare are considerable.

The downside of the conclusion about alcohol treatment effectiveness is that it does not leave us with much of a guideline in placing a person in a specific treatment based in our assessment and the person's goals for change. However, alcohol treatment research has advanced in the last 15 years to some emphasis in patient-treatment matching, and this seems to be a productive future direction for the field. Although our knowledge about matching still is not too sophisticated there is some research to inform us about matching patients to some treatment settings and services. For example, inpatient or residential treatment settings may be best reserved for individuals whose alcohol problems are more severe, or who have other drug problems, or who have less social stability (for example, not employed, not married, not living in a permanent residence), or who have psychiatric disorders. For other individuals outpatient treatment likely will do just as well as inpatient and at far less cost. Another example is the finding that psychotherapy works best if a patient's conceptual level (defined by preference for rules, dependence on authority, and abstractness of thinking) is matched to his or her therapist's (McKay et al., 1991).

It would seem that accumulation of findings such as these will take alcohol treatment to a level of more efficient service delivery. A reason to think that this can be realized is provided by Miller's (1992) identification of several specific alcohol treatment techniques (such as marital and family therapy, and therapy called "community reinforcement," based on learning principles of arranging the environment to reinforce nonabusive drinking and to punish abusive drinking) that show "promise." In a considerable portion of the well-done outcome studies these and several other techniques were related to better outcomes compared to other treatments or to some type of control group. These promising treatment techniques and approaches would seem to be the best candidates for patient-treatment matching outcome research.

Effectiveness of Self-Help Treatment for Alcohol Problems

What we said above about treatment effectiveness was pertinent to professional services. Because of its importance, self-help group treatment also should be evaluated. Almost all of the research on this question concerns AA, and we will focus on that organization.

Contemporary Issue
BRIEF INTERVENTIONS FOR ALCOHOL PROBLEMS

Traditional ideas about alcohol treatment have been challenged in the last five years or so by increased awareness and discussion of "brief" interventions for alcohol problems. What is called brief is relative to typical alcohol treatment. Brief interventions average 1–3 sessions in number, and each session lasts up to 45 minutes, but often less time is spent in a session. These averages are far less than what happens in traditional alcohol treatment. Brief interventions have been applied in several different settings, but perhaps the most important is the general medical care setting. In this regard, patients in that setting tend to have higher rates than the general population of unidentified alcohol problems of varying degrees of severity, because of the correlation between heavy alcohol use and physical problems. Accordingly, if some type of intervention could be done in these settings to thwart the development of more severe alcohol problems, then there is the potential to save society billions of dollars.

Brief interventions, which can be something as simple as feedback about the consequences of heavy alcohol use for a person (for example, "you have some liver problems, and we can trace it to your drinking") along with advice to cut down or stop drinking, are based on the idea that alcohol problems exist on a continuum of severity and that interventions can occur at any point along that continuum. The research has shown that for the most part brief interventions have been used with people who have mild to moderate alcohol problems, and are effective compared to no treatment in reducing alcohol consumption to below "risk" levels. There is some speculation about who is most helped by brief interventions, and why they work. These clearly are topics for future research.

The findings about brief interventions have great practical implications for alcohol treatment providers, and for saving society a lot of money and suffering. They also have implications for theories of the causes of alcohol problems. For example, what do you think disease or biological model adherents might say about brief interventions?

As important a question as it is, how effective AA is can be difficult to answer. One reason for the difficulty is the AA emphasis on anonymity of its members. The principle of anonymity is a major part of the "Twelve Traditions" of AA, which are a set of principles or guidelines adopted in 1950 for the operations of AA (Leach & Norris, 1977). The twelfth tradition, anonymity, "is the spiritual foundation of our traditions, ever reminding us to place principles before personalities." This tradition is strictly adhered to in AA groups and makes outcome research very difficult to do, because it often requires identification of those receiving treatment.

Despite the difficulties associated with the systematic evaluation of AA, some research has been done. In his review of research related to AA's effectiveness, Emrick (1989) concluded: (a) it is not possible to predict who will affiliate with AA, except that it seems that people who have more severe alcohol problems are more likely to join; (b) among people who do join AA, it is not clear who will do well and who will not; (c) people who go to AA before, during, or after receiving other forms of treatment do as well as, if not better than people who do not volunteer to go to AA; (d) AA participation is associated with relatively high abstinence rates, but with average overall improvement in drinking rates; (e) people who achieve abstinence seem to participate in AA more than those who moderate their drinking or who continue to drink at a problem level (Emrick, 1989, pp. 48–49).

Emrick's (1989) review makes a few major points about AA. First is that AA seems to help some people, but not all people. So, making blanket referrals to AA as part of a treatment plan, which is common, is not warranted. With the growth of groups such as Rational Recovery and Secular Organizations for Sobriety other self-help options are available. Of course, currently we have no evaluation research on these alternative groups, but studies are in progress. It is essential that researchers do matching research aimed at discovering which individuals fit best with which self-help group participation.

As difficult as it is, it is important to try to do well-controlled treatment outcome research on self-help groups. Emrick (1989) cited a few such studies on AA, but they involved individuals who were mandated by the legal system to attend treatment. These are not the best patient population for evaluation of a treatment's effectiveness, because of their often dubious commitment to change. Controlled treatment outcome studies on self-help groups would go a long way toward helping clinicians to use such groups in ways that are best for their patients.

OTHER DRUG TREATMENT SETTINGS AND SERVICES

There is a wide array of treatment services for drug abusers. Allison and Hubbard (1985, p. 1322) noted, "Treatment programs may involve outpatient, residential, or day care and may take place in a hospital, clinic, mental health center, prison, or group home environment. Treatment may be drug-free or use chemical aids. Counseling, job training, physical health care, and a variety of other services may or may not be part of the treatment program. The staff may be highly trained professionals or the program may be of the self-help type."

The traditional classification of drug-abuse treatments includes detoxification, methadone maintenance, residential, and outpatient. (We discuss methadone maintenance in the section on pharmacotherapy for drug abuse.) Similar to alcohol treatment, the primary goal of detoxification is a medically managed withdrawal from physical dependence on drugs. Managing detoxification often involves the use of medications, but could be drug-free. As with alcohol withdrawal treatment, detoxification services may include some counseling directed in part at guiding the patient to additional treatment services.

Residential treatment is known more commonly as the therapeutic community (TC). Drug TCs are run mostly by ex-addicts, who work as peer counselors and administrators. There is heavy reliance on self-help groups. The TC is a highly structured residential program, especially at the beginning of treatment, and clients gain more responsibilities and independence as they progress through the program by meeting certain requirements. In TCs there

A treatment group is in progress in a program for drug abuse.

also is an emphasis on group counseling and therapy, which often is confrontational. One well-known example of a drug TC is Phoenix House in New York City.

The final drug abuse treatment modality is outpatient. In the outpatient setting, there may or may not be a policy prohibiting pharmacotherapies. Similar to alcohol treatment, outpatient drug treatment is the most varied of the treatment types and includes a wide range of programs and services. The most salient features of outpatient treatment are that it is not residential and drugs are not used in treatment. Almost half of the drug abusers in treatment receive their treatment in this setting.

Treatment of Nonopiate Drug Abusers

In general, the classification of drug abuse treatment refers to services that have been available for the treatment of heroin abuse. In this regard, the great expansion in drug abuse treatment services over the last 25 years largely was due to public alarm over increasingly widespread use and abuse of heroin, with its highly visible and well-publicized negative social effects. For example, a sharp increase in violent crime in some urban areas, such as the more recent experience with crack use, was attributed to heroin use. However, in recent years there has been an increase in the numbers of individuals appearing for drug abuse treatment who primarily abuse drugs other than alcohol or the opiates. For example, in 1977 33.4% of the clients admitted to drug abuse treatment programs were nonopiate abusers, and this proportion had increased to 54.9% by 1980 (USDHHS, 1984). This trend continued through the 1980s with the high number of people presenting themselves for treatment of cocaine dependence. As with the abuse of heroin and alcohol, nonopiate abusers may appear in treatment settings other than those designed specifically to treat the substance-use disorders. These include hospital emergency rooms, physicians' offices, or general psychiatric treatment settings. They currently also appear in settings traditionally created for the heroin abuser, such as the therapeutic community. In general, little is known about any unique problems and characteristics of nonopiate drug abusers that might be important for their treatment, although there has been some discussion of this question (Washton, 1990).

Contemporary Issue
FACTORS INFLUENCING THE EXPANSION OF DRUG TREATMENT

Currently political and social forces are contributing to the increased demand for drug treatment, just as these same forces pushed the growth of treatment of heroin abuse. This recent trend reaffirms the importance of social and political factors in how U.S. society deals with alcohol and other drug use.

In 1986 the surge in demand for drug treatment, particularly in the residential or inpatient setting, arose from two major sources: crack and AIDS. These worked in a political climate that was strongly in favor of eradicating drugs and drug abuse.

As you saw in Chapter 6, crack is the highly addictive, cheaper form of cocaine. People who start using it are quickly hooked on it, and in the mid-1980s people from a wide range of social classes became addicted to crack. The variety of people affected, along with social consequences such as large increases in drug-related criminal activity and flagrant selling of crack in public places, lighted the public's torch for getting crack abusers off the streets and into treatment. Further, the media devoted much time to the crack epidemic, just as they have to other diseases or medical problems in the past.

The AIDS scare has sent drug abusers, particularly heroin abusers who take their drugs intravenously, to treatment programs to help them stop their drug abuse. The reason: fear of catching the deadly disease of AIDS through the use of contaminated needles. The fear of AIDS sent addicts looking for treatment when it is unlikely they otherwise would have done so. Again, the media attention to AIDS and the general public alarm and fears about AIDS supported the increased demands for more accessible drug treatment. These two examples show how political and social forces, and not only an actual increase in drug use or in the valuing of a drug-free society, affect the demand for drug and alcohol treatment.

Pharmacotherapy of Other Drug Problems

Methadone maintenance is the pharmacotherapy for drug abuse that has received the most attention—probably more than any other type of drug-abuse treatment, for that matter—from researchers and the popular press. The attention centers on the conflict in treating dependence on a chemical substance (heroin, an opiate) with another opiate (methadone). Proponents of this approach say that if the heroin addict's desire for heroin is prevented by methadone, he or she will be more likely to break out of the destructive life style associated with drug addiction and then engage in rehabilitation leading to a socially acceptable and productive way of living. The major opposition to methadone treatment is that it perpetuates the individual's dependence on an opiate drug.

Methadone maintenance treatment typically involves administration of a daily, prescribed dose of methadone in order to block the addict's cravings for heroin. Usually, methadone maintenance programs are outpatient so that the individual may pursue activities that build to a socially productive life. Furthermore, many programs (and state or federal regulations) require patients to receive some kind of counseling while enrolled in methadone maintenance,

Methadone maintenance remains a controversial treatment for opiate dependence.

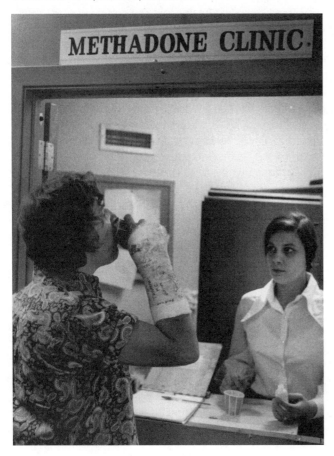

and patients are required to adhere to a formal set of rules for continued participation in methadone maintenance treatment.

As you might have guessed, one of the problems with the use of methadone is its potential for abuse. That is, addicts may use their methadone in nonprescribed ways just as they used heroin. One way that methadone programs have tried to handle this problem is to require the patient to swallow the methadone dose on the program premises while being observed by the medical staff. In fact, one measure of a person's progress in a program is whether he or she comes to the clinic less often than daily to get the methadone dose. That is, as progress is made, the person may earn the privilege of taking two to several days' worth of methadone home at a time. Another way to handle the problem of compliance is to administer **levo-alpha-acetyl-methadol (LAAM),** which is similar in pharmacological action to methadone but has longer-lasting effects. The advantage of a longer-lasting methadone substitute is that patients are more likely to comply with the regimen for taking the drug.

**Levo-alpha-acetylmethadol
(LAAM)**
A drug used in treating heroin addiction that is similar in action to methadone but has longer-lasting effects.

Contemporary Issue
DRUG TREATMENT AND THE LEGAL SYSTEM

For a long time the legal system has been a major force in getting abusers of alcohol, and especially other drugs, into some type of treatment. Recently, drug treatment programs within the prison system have become increasingly important due to a political climate that since the 1980s has favored using prison as a deterrent to drug involvement. As a consequence, many individuals who abuse illicit drugs have wound up in prison.

There has been recognition that some type of drug treatment might be beneficial for these individuals. Actually, the idea is not new, as California began such programs for heroin addicts over 30 years ago. Prison-based drug treatment programs have been based on the TC model of care, or have been outpatient nonmethadone treatment combined with parole supervision. For younger (adolescents, young adults) and first-time offenders, a recent phenomenon is "boot camp" treatment and "shock incarceration." These are prison-based interventions that are conducted in settings that are segregated from older or more chronic offenders. The "prison sentences" of three to six months typically involve military structure and strenuous physical exercise. How much goes on of what traditionally is called drug treatment varies widely in these settings.

The research on prison-based drug treatment is of highly uneven quality. In a few well-controlled studies of such programs, it seems that, as with other drug treatment settings, length of retention in treatment and good connections between program and community are associated with better outcomes. There is virtually no good experimental research in the boot camp or shock incarceration programs to inform us about their effectiveness.

Prison-based drug treatment, perhaps more so than drug treatment in general, is influenced by political forces. How do you think such forces affect the content of prison-based drug treatment? How might they affect its evaluation?

Methadone maintenance involves replacing one opiate, say, heroin, with another, methadone. Another pharmacotherapy for heroin use involves blockade of opiate receptors by the use of naltrexone, which we discussed in the section on alcohol treatment. Naltrexone is used most commonly with patients who have been maintained for long periods on methadone and then choose to become drug-free. The naltrexone may help these patients bridge the gap between methadone maintenance and a drug-free life. Naltrexone works, theoretically, because the abused opiate cannot achieve its effect in the brain. The result is that the individual loses a major reason for using the opiate—its psychoactive effects.

Along these lines, buprenorphine, a mixed opiate agonist-antagonist, is a drug that blocks the effects of heroin and has been used in treatment. Buprenorphine has a lower potential for abuse than does methadone. More-over, one study showed that rhesus monkeys greatly reduced cocaine self-administration when given buprenorphine compared to saline injections (Mello, Mendelson, Bree, & Lukas, 1989). Since buprenorphine has been found safe for human use, the Mello et al. study implies that this compound may be an effective pharmacotherapy for people who abuse cocaine. This idea has been pursued (Crosby, Halikas, & Carlson, 1991; Stimmel, 1991).

A final pharmacotherapy for drug abuse involves the use of antidepressant medication, such as **desipramine** in treatment of cocaine abusers (Annis, 1987). Similar in concept to using naltrexone to treat alcoholics, antidepressants are thought to alter neural transmission in the brain so that the cocaine abuser does not experience the extreme drug cravings and depression that tend to be part of cocaine withdrawal. These reactions seem to be a big reason why people dependent on cocaine have such a hard time stopping its use or staying "straight" if they do manage to stop (also see Chapter 6).

Desipramine
An antidepressant medication.

Effectiveness of Drug Treatment

Research on the effectiveness of drug treatment does not have a history that is nearly as long as that for alcohol, but in the last 25 years a number of good studies have appeared. Our summary of what is known about drug treatment effectiveness, like that of alcohol treatment, will exclude detoxification and pharmacotherapy, for the same reasons. The exception to this is our summary of the findings on methadone maintenance.

The literature on drug treatment effectiveness has profited by the completion of several large, multisite (i.e., different programs), multimodal (i.e., different settings, like outpatient and methadone maintenance) studies (Ball, Meyers, & Friedman, 1988; DeLeon, 1984; Hubbard, Marsden, Rachal, et al., 1989), and reviews of treatment research (Institute of Medicine, 1990b). Compared to the literature on alcohol there is less attention in this literature given to individual treatment techniques or services. Instead, research tends to be centered on the treatment settings, as we have organized them in this chapter. The exception, of course, is methadone maintenance, for which the setting essentially is equivalent to the specific service.

Table 16-3 presents a summary of the major conclusions about methadone maintenance, therapeutic community, and outpatient drug treatment. There are several points to emphasize in the table. First is that conclusions

Table 16-3   Summary of Effectiveness for Methadone Maintenance, Therapeutic Community, and Outpatient Drug Treatment

Setting	Conclusions
■ Methadone Maintenance	■ Associated with reduced drug use and criminal behavior compared to no treatment, detoxification alone, or methadone treatment terminators ■ Associated with higher retention rates for heroin addicts compared to other treatments ■ Treatment is cost-effective
■ Therapeutic Community	■ Drug use and criminal behavior end while in residence; associated with a more productive life following discharge if there was sufficient length of stay (at least several months) in residence ■ High treatment attrition rates ■ Treatment is cost-effective
■ Outpatient	■ Associated with improved functioning compared to no treatment or detoxification only ■ Benefits of treatment greater with longer involvement in treatment ■ Treatment is cost-effective for people who stay in treatment longer than six months

Note: Adapted from information in Institute of Medicine (1990b)

about treatment are based not only on drug use, but also on correlated events such as social productivity and criminal behavior. The research on drug treatment reflects society's interest not only in whether a person has stopped illicit drug use, but also in whether social disruption and disorder have stopped, too. With that said, Table 16-3 shows that, overall, the three major drug settings seem to be associated with improved functioning, if the person stays in treatment. Unfortunately, dropping out of drug treatment is a chronic problem that is difficult to solve. One of methadone maintenance's great advantages in this regard is that it is correlated with better treatment retention. Similarly, if people stay in drug treatment, it is cost effective. That is, society gets more back from the reduced drug use and gain in social and financial productivity that are associated with treatment than it pays to deliver the treatment services.

The overall summary of drug treatment effectiveness is encouraging, but we should add there is considerable individual variation in patient outcomes. This leads to identifying a big gap in this treatment literature, which pertains to patient-treatment matching research. Although there have been several excellent studies of matching patients to drug treatment (e.g., McLellan, Luborsky, Woody, et al., 1983), more studies guided by the matching question would advance drug treatment.

Effectiveness of Drug Self-Help Treatment

Unfortunately, there is little that we can say on this topic because, as we noted earlier, virtually all the research on self-help groups has concerned AA. We know essentially nothing about the effectiveness of drug self-help groups

DRUGS AND CULTURE
"SPECIAL POPULATIONS" AND ALCOHOL
AND DRUG TREATMENT

In Chapter 1 we examined substance use prevalence by gender and racial-ethnic subgroups. The idea behind doing this is that any subgroup differences in prevalence likely are due to biological or, more prominently, social and cultural factors that distinguish the subgroups. This same idea can be applied to assessment and treatment, although research on "special populations" (that is, subgroups) has lagged far behind other treatment research. Treatment research on special populations is important, because subgroup differences can influence assessment and diagnosis, treatment accessibility and content, and treatment retention.

To cite several examples, studies show that for adolescents, assessment of social factors in substance use, such as patterns of use and attitudes about use that peers have, is critical. Similarly, social skills training to resist peer pressure to use substances may be an emphasis in treatment. For the elderly, sensitive assessment and diagnostic practices incorporate knowledge about the interaction of alcohol and prescribed medications, and the interaction of alcohol with the aging body. In women, substance use problems tend to develop faster than they do in men and tend to be more strongly related to psychological and familial variables. Failure to use this information would preclude sensitive diagnosis and effective treatment. For all defined subgroups, learned aspects of substance use underlie beliefs and expectations about its effects and attitudes toward its use in different situations. Without sensitivity to these group differences assessment and treatment would not be adequate.

Special population differences could be viewed as corollaries of the idea that patient-treatment matching improves treatment. How? What models of the etiology of the substance-use disorders seem most flexible to you in incorporating gender and racial-ethnic differences?

"The advantages of ethnically oriented programs appear not so much that something particularly efficacious happens in treatment, but rather the attraction to treatment is greater when one can join peers in a familiar setting."

(Joseph Westermeyer, professor of psychiatry, cited in Institute of Medicine, 1990a, p. 372)

like Narcotics Anonymous or Cocaine Anonymous because the research simply has not been done. However, like AA, drug self-help groups are popular and their effectiveness is an important research question.

SPECIAL TOPICS IN ALCOHOL AND DRUG TREATMENT

In this section we discuss three topics that we feel are important and that apply both to alcohol and drug treatment. The first is treatment of the poly-substance abuser, or the person who uses more than one drug. We then briefly review the treatment of dual-diagnosis patients, especially regarding how such treatment involves the use of psychotropic medication. The last topic is relapse (see Figure 16-1), which has challenged alcohol- and drug-treatment providers for many years.

Treatment of the Polysubstance Abuser

The traditional and common way of viewing treatment implies that someone called an alcohol abuser or alcoholic does not have trouble with or does not abuse other drugs. Similarly, the traditional view gives the impression that people called drug abusers have no patterns of abusive alcohol use. However, it may be a mistake to designate programs as either alcohol treatment or drug treatment.

For example, Sokolow, Welte, Hynes, and Lyons (1981) reported a survey of multiple substance use among patients arriving for treatment at New York state-funded alcoholism rehabilitation programs. The total sample of 1,340 men and women selected for this study represented wide ranges in age and educational background. Most (57.3%) of the patients were between 31 and 50 years old. In addition to their alcohol use, which was their reason for beginning treatment, patients were asked about their licit and illicit use in the past 30 days of minor and major tranquilizers, sedatives, amphetamines, antidepressants, opiates, hallucinogens, marijuana, and cocaine.

Almost half of the patients reported use of at least one of the other-than-alcohol drugs during the 30 days before their treatment began. About 20% of these patients used combinations of the drugs. The single drug class reported most frequently was the tranquilizers (12.7% of the patients), which is notable because tranquilizers are cross tolerants with alcohol and are the drugs most abused by those identified as alcoholics. We should also note that people identified as drug abusers often abuse alcohol, too, according to Carroll, Malloy, and Kenrick (1977). Significantly, during the 1980s treatment personnel showed an accelerated recognition of multiple substance use in their patients (Gottheil, 1990; Rawson, 1990–1991).

Studies of multiple substance use have important implications for treatment. As we have said, the strong tendency has existed to develop programs centered on alcohol treatment or drug treatment, implying major differences in treatment. The differences sometimes became real in practice. Furthermore, some treatment providers strongly object to treating substance abuse other than what has been identified as the patient's primary substance of abuse. Such reactions have been found especially in alcohol programs and restrict treatment, given the prevalence of multiple substance use. In this respect, two points quickly emerge about treatment effects. First, if treatment programs concentrate only on, for example, alcohol use, the abuse of other drugs may result in poorer, shorter-lasting **treatment effects** than if the person's substance-use patterns were treated in a more unified way. Another point is that people seeking alcohol or drug treatment who are multiple substance abusers may have more severe social, legal, and psychiatric difficulties than those in treatment whose patterns of abuse are limited to single drug categories (Carroll et al., 1977). Beginning treatment with more severe problems predicts poorer functioning following treatment. So, failing to ad-

Treatment effects
The result of experiencing a treatment, usually measured in different areas of functioning, such as substance use, family functioning, and vocational functioning.

dress patterns of multiple substance use because of program philosophy and policy could mean inadequate treatment planning.

Treatment of multiple substance abusers relates to more general questions about treatment. One of these is the need to view substance use as part of a person's total pattern of behavior in order to achieve an understanding of drug and alcohol use. Those who take this approach suggest effective treatment planning can occur only if connections are made among all of a person's different problems. Similarly, some clinicians and researchers believe addictive behavior patterns have a lot in common with what causes them, what maintains them, and how they are treated. It is thought these commonalities should underlie treatment programming instead of the traditional emphasis on single addiction patterns. According to this viewpoint, behaviors identified as addictive, including, for example, alcohol and other drug abuse, overeating, and compulsive gambling, have common factors that may be addressed in "generic" treatment programs to the improvement of any one or more of the problem areas troubling a person. The DSM-IV recognizes this approach in addressing the psychoactive substance-use disorders as a diagnostic class rather than addressing alcohol and other drug diagnoses in a nonintegrated way. Nonetheless, it should be remembered that the properties of the various drugs of abuse vary, as might the characteristics of the users, and there is no guarantee that a program that works well for alcoholics would be successful with heroin addicts.

Alcohol- and drug-treatment programs have not been designed according to a more integrated look at alcohol and drug use. Although there is research on the combined treatment of abusers of alcohol and other drugs suggesting that the approach has promise, combined treatment has not been accepted widely (Beidler, 1991).

Treatment of Dual-Diagnosis Patients

A topic of increasing importance for alcohol- and drug-treatment providers in the last decade is patients who have major psychiatric problems to go along with their substance-use problems. Such patients have been called dual-diagnosis patients. Dual-diagnosis patients, as you might imagine, typically have more complex and extensive treatment needs than do patients without psychiatric problems, and dual-diagnosis patients tend to do more poorly in and following treatment.

Psychotropic medication may be part of treatment of alcohol or drug abuse when a person has an alcohol or drug problem and another psychiatric disorder. These psychiatric disorders include depression and manic depression, especially among alcoholics. A relationship exists between alcohol or drug abuse and disorders characterized by a high degree of anxiety, and the **personality disorders,** particularly what is commonly called **sociopathy.** Psychotropic agents usually are used in the treatment of alcohol or drug abuse on the premise that patients use alcohol and other drugs to **self-medicate.** This means the individual acts as his or her own physician and self-prescribes alcohol and other drugs to lessen troubling psychological symptoms such as anxiety or depression. When used, psychotropic agents

Personality disorders
Long-standing patterns of behavior that frequently create distress for the individual due to their personal or social consequences. These patterns are usually recognizable from adolescence or earlier.

Sociopathy
A type of personality disorder characterized by a lack of concern for social obligations or rules, a lack of feelings for others, and a tendency toward violence.

Self-medication
The idea that some people prescribe their own medication, in the form of alcohol or illicit drugs, to alleviate psychological difficulties such as anxiety or depression.

generally are administered in combination with nonmedical techniques in treating the substance-use disorder.

Considerable controversy still exists over the use of psychotropic agents as part of alcohol- or drug-treatment services. The primary objection is that the use of drugs in treating a person who abuses drugs is tantamount to inducing a dual (the drug the person entered treatment for and the prescribed drug) dependency (Diesenhaus, 1982). In some cases this opposition is ideological rather than based on scientific evidence, such as in the outright rejection by some drug therapeutic communities of using medication as part of treatment. More objectively, the value of using medication in treating alcohol or drug abuse varies with the purpose of use and the individual being treated.

Relapse

Any discussion of alcohol and drug treatment would be incomplete without including relapse. Defining and measuring relapse is not as simple as you might think, but in concept it means the reappearance of some problem after

Settings such as taverns that are associated with a person's heavy use of alcohol in the past may pose a risk to the person of relapsing to heavy drinking after a period of abstinence from or moderate use of alcohol.

a period of its remission. With physical diseases such as cancer, which are where the term relapse comes from, its measurement is much more straight-forward. However, you have seen that arriving at a definition of alcohol and drug problems that has general consensus is no easy matter. This difficulty carries through to defining relapse, as reflected by the different operational definitions of relapse that have been used in research on this topic.

In spite of these complexities in definition, relapse has been studied ex-tensively in the addictions field for the last 20 years or so. You might remem-ber that we mentioned the problem of relapse in Chapter 7 when we discussed the treatment of smoking. Actually, alcohol- and drug-treatment providers have grappled with the problem of relapse for much longer than that, and today many people refer to alcohol and other drug abuse and dependence as "chronic re-lapsing conditions." The classic paper by Hunt, Barnett, and Branch (1971) il-lustrates this point. Their review of the literature at that time showed that about 70% of individuals treated for alcohol, tobacco, or heroin abuse in abstinence-oriented programs had returned to their primary substance use by the time they were out of treatment for three months. Today the problem is the same, and much treatment research is directed at discovering ways to help individu-als maintain the changes they might make as a result of completing treatment.

The research on relapse and the substance-use disorders has generated several models and theories that were created to explain it. Table 16-4 sum-marizes six models and theories of relapse. As you can see, the models and theories make few distinctions among different drugs in the mechanisms of relapse. Another point is the emphasis on relapse precipitants, or the events immediately preceding the relapse. Events more removed from the immedi-ate relapse environment are given less attention. Examples of these are the social support a person has for nonproblem substance use, the period of time a person has been unemployed, and the level of tension among mem-bers of a family. Finally, the models and theories can be divided into two gen-eral categories—psychological and biological. The psychological theories emphasize cognitions, while the biological theories emphasize learned moti-vation to use drugs and cravings.

At this point no one theory of relapse has emerged as superior to the others, so it would make sense to look across the theories to discern what may be the important ingredients of relapse. First is the internal (e.g., mood) and external (e.g., drinking setting) stimulus conditions that precede relapse. Cravings to use drugs also are important. Two types of expectancies may be relevant to relapse. The first is a person's beliefs about the effects of a drug in a given situation, and the second is a person's *self-efficacy*, which is an indi-vidual's estimation that he or she can successfully enact a behavior in a given situation. Finally, a person's coping responses or skills may be important in relapse.

Research and theory about relapse have generated treatment applica-tions. These are known as relapse prevention methods. Relapse prevention methods first have focused on assessment of "high risk" situations, or those situations associated with abuse of alcohol or drugs in the past. High-risk sit-uations may center on negative moods such as anxiety or depression, posi-tive mood, the presence of people the patient used to drink with, or some

"Patient living alone, no job, com-plained of feeling bored and use-less; could see no reason why he should not take a drink." "Patient reported that everything was going so well for him that he wanted to celebrate by having a drink."

(Reasons given by two patients for their alcohol-use relapse following treatment, cited in Marlatt & Gordon, 1985, p. 74)

Table 16-4   Summary of Major Models and Theories of Relapse

Model/Theory	Mechanism(s) of Relapse
■ Cognitive-behavioral model (Marlatt & Gordon, 1985)	■ Interaction between "high risk" (for substance use) and the individual's self-efficacy to cope with those situations without substance use determines relapse. Expectations about the utility of drugs and alcohol in a situation also are important.
■ Person-situation interaction model (Litman, 1986)	■ Relapse is determined by an interaction among three factors: situations that the individual perceives as threatening ("high risk"), availability of an adequate repertoire of coping strategies, and the individual's perception of the effectiveness of available coping strategies.
■ Self-efficacy and outcome expectancies (Annis, 1986; Rollnick & Heather, 1982)	■ Initial substance use occurs from the mislabeling of negative affect and negative physical states as craving. After first substance use, expectations of control over such use decreases, along with self-efficacy. This process leads to a more severe relapse.
■ Opponent process (Solomon, 1980)	■ Through conditioning, formerly neutral internal and external stimuli become connected with various "A" and "B" states. Reexposure or reexperiencing these states may increase the individual's motivation to use drugs following a period of abstinence.
■ Craving and loss of control (Ludwig & Wikler, 1974)	■ Internal and external stimuli associated with drug withdrawal are labeled as craving. Drugs are sought as a way to relieve craving.
■ Urges and craving (Tiffany, 1990, 1992; Wise, 1988)	■ Drug use and drug urges and cravings have occurred enough times to be "automatic cognitive processes." In the abstinent substance abuser, these processes can be triggered by various internal and external stimuli. Relapse may occur if an adequate "action plan" not to use drugs, a nonautomatic cognitive process, is impeded or not used. Wise adds that use of one drug may trigger urges to use another—a result of action in the brain.

Note: Adapted in part from Donovan and Chaney (1985)

combination of internal and external precipitants. When high-risk situations have been identified the next step is to look at the person's ways to cope with the situation without resorting to undesired levels of substance use, and his or her self-efficacy to do so. Coupled with this is an examination of the person's beliefs about how alcohol or drug use would help in different situations. For example, a person may believe that at a party, drinking would help a great deal in talking with the other people present. Assessment of these elements then determines what might be done in treatment: teaching alternative coping skills to substance use (for example, using communication skills instead of alcohol to help a person enjoy a party), improving self-efficacy, or educating the person about the actual effects of alcohol and drugs. In practice, all of these elements typically are covered, and there is a correlation among them. For example, teaching a person a coping skill may elevate his or her self-efficacy about using that skill.

You can see that much of what is done in relapse prevention work follows from psychological models of relapse. The major method following from the biological models is cue exposure. This method essentially involves presenting (exposing) the person with cues (e.g., bottle of favorite brand of whiskey, drug-use paraphernalia like a syringe) that might elicit cravings to use a substance, without allowing its actual use. With repeated exposure, the cravings theoretically reduce in number and intensity. So, as a person's repeated association of these "stimulus conditions" with drug use resulted in the stimuli eliciting a strong desire to use drugs or alcohol, repeated pairing of the stimuli with nonuse of substances will decrease the power of the stimuli to elicit cravings.

The work on relapse has stimulated substantial advances in alcohol and drug treatment. However, it also brings up an important point about relapse research and prevention, and about treatment more generally. What has been absent to a large degree in theories of relapse is more serious study of conditions in the "broader backdrop" of relapse, such as the person's social environment (family functioning, job satisfaction) or general level of stress (recent job change, recent divorce). Immediate relapse precipitants obviously are important, but so are these more remote factors. In fact, we know this from research in the long-term effects of alcohol and drug treatment, which seems highly relevant to relapse. Perhaps it would help to understand this more easily if you do not think of alcohol or drug treatment as a specific entity that "acts on" a person to produce some lasting outcome. Instead, treatment is one event in the life of a person who is trying to change the way he or she uses alcohol or drugs. Furthermore, the person and the treatment interact in a social context that strongly contributes to the course of change.

"The treatment setting of prime significance for recovery from alcohol (and other drug problems) is not a hospital, a clinic, a doctor's or minister's office, a social agency or a jail, or any other specialized institution or place. The prime setting of significance is the social, interpersonal setting of—daily life. And, equally important, it is that setting through time."

(Bacon, 1973, cited in Orford, 1985, p. 246)

MODELS OF CAUSES AND TREATMENT METHODS

So far we have presented a lot of information about alcohol and drug treatment, although space limits prevented us from going into any great detail. But in the level of discussion that we did present you may have noticed the influence of each of the models of causes that we reviewed at the beginning of this chapter. There are several instances we can cite. Placing substance-abuse treatment programs in the hospital setting—a common practice—is broadly based in a disease model of thought. Indeed, the great achievement that came years ago with wide acceptance of the disease model was to take treatment of alcohol and drug problems out of the legal system (moral model) and into the hands of physicians and medical settings—an apparently more useful means of rehabilitation of addicted persons.

Another example is Alcoholics Anonymous, rooted in both the disease and moral models. Pharmacological treatments, like methadone maintenance, are most clearly linked to the biological model. Within most settings of treatment, psychological and social interventions occur that are consistent with the social learning and sociocultural models. The most explicit example of this merging of models is the community reinforcement approach (Higgins et al., 1991; Hunt & Azrin, 1973). As noted, this approach centers on rearranging the person's environment to reinforce nonabuse of substances and not to reinforce, or to punish, substance abuse.

We can trace individual parts of alcohol and drug treatment to a particular model of etiology, but in virtually all treatment programs what is offered combines practices that are derived from two or more of the causes models. This is the result in part of the many clinical, social, political, and economic forces that influence substance-abuse treatment programs and that affect their evolution. However, another force is the current scientifically based thought that the substance-use disorders are multifaceted problems, and so treatment must touch on the person's biological, psychological, and social make-up. This thinking is implemented in the sometimes-seeming stew of activities that constitute many treatment programs.

So far we have discussed treatment freely, that is, free of concerns of how available or accessible it is. We conclude this chapter by discussing this all-important question, especially as it pertains to economic forces and alcohol and drug treatment.

ECONOMIC FACTORS IN ALCOHOL AND DRUG TREATMENT

An issue of great controversy and consequence that is not likely to be resolved soon is the influence of health insurance coverage on whether a person gets treatment and, if so, what kind (Holder & Blose, 1991). A brief history of the role of finances and insurance will help you to appreciate the current controversy (Rawson, 1990–1991).

In the early 1970s, alcohol and drug treatment was not in the mainstream of psychiatry, clinical psychology, and social work. By 1990, alcohol and drug treatment was a central concern. The change was due mostly to cocaine, AIDS, and adjustments in health care financing.

In the mid to late 1970s, interest in drug treatment had been quelled considerably because the heroin scare of the 1960s and early 1970s had quieted down. At the same time, 28-day inpatient programs became the standard of alcohol treatment because of agreements between care providers, typically hospitals and health insurance companies. These 28-day programs proliferated during the 1980s with legislation passed in many states that required insurers to cover alcohol and drug treatment. The cost to the insurance company was high—the price of completing an inpatient program varied, but it always was in the thousands of dollars. The term "chemical dependence" treatment was spawned in the 1980s because the 28-day programs now also were accommodating high numbers of individuals who abused drugs other than alcohol, especially cocaine. Treatment availability and accessibility (with an expanding economy) were rising rapidly. Another force in the treatment expansion was a social-political climate that encouraged people with alcohol and drug problems to get into treatment.

Therefore, by the late 1980s, treatment was accessible in an unprecedented way, at least for those with health insurance or independent wealth. Typically, this is viewed as good. But a counterforce was operating. With increased expansion of and expectations for alcohol and drug treatment, employers' health insurance premiums were rising quickly. Quietly at first in the unbounded economy of the mid-1980s, then loudly as the economy recessed, came "managed" mental health and alcohol- and drug-treatment services. Managed care is a movement based in the goal of limiting the costs of health care, including alcohol and drug treatment. The term "cost-effectiveness" became popular vocabulary—is the benefit of a treatment worth what it costs?

Cost consciousness has led to a far more restricted use of inpatient alcohol and drug treatments, at least those that are paid for by health insurers. When such inpatient stays are covered, they are often for much fewer than 28 days. Instead, outpatient treatment is the insurer's preference. This policy is based on research that suggests that, on average, inpatient treatment is no more effective than the much cheaper outpatient treatment (Miller & Hester, 1986).

It seems that the trend to less inpatient and more outpatient care will continue. Many treatment providers, however, are concerned that this prescription for care is based too much on money and not enough on proven differences (or lack thereof) in treatment benefits. Some treatment providers ask, what does a lack of difference in benefits overall tell us? What is outpatient treatment anyway? (We saw earlier in this chapter that what constitutes outpatient alcohol and drug treatment is highly variable.) Is the finding of no difference true for everybody? When is the more structured, more intense inpatient treatment indicated, and when is it not? These and similar questions became more salient for alcohol treatment in a report of a study by Walsh, Hingson, Merrigan et al. (1991). A total of 227 individuals who were newly identified as alcohol abusers were randomly assigned to one of three treatments through their employee assistance program (thus, all these people had jobs). The treatments were compulsory inpatient treatment, compulsory AA attendance, or choice of treatment option. Two years after treatment the three groups did not differ in measures of job performance. However, a major finding was that, overall, the cost of treatment for the compulsory inpatient group was only 10% more than it was for the AA and choice groups (remember that AA is free). The small cost difference was particularly true for study participants who had used cocaine in the six months before they began treatment. The overall cost results occurred because the choice and AA groups had a much higher inpatient treatment admission rate during the two-year follow-up period than did the group who initially received compulsory inpatient care. One implication of the small cost difference that was confirmed during the follow-up assessments was that at least for some of the time after treatment, the compulsory inpatient group had less use of alcohol and drugs than did the other two groups.

In summary, finances and insurance have played and do play a major part in the accessibility of alcohol and drug treatment and in what treatment options are available. As the Walsh et al. (1991) research illustrates, we have a lot to learn about the effects of the strong current trend toward less intense, less expensive treatment. And we have focused in this discussion on people who rely on health insurance to pay for part or all of their health care. A serious concern is individuals who do not have health insurance—an increasingly common problem in the United States. For them, because of decreased availability of publicly funded treatment, getting any professional care at all may be impossible. This is a significant point when you remember that overall, completing alcohol and drug treatment is associated with improved functioning in multiple areas. And, of course, how the final version of national health insurance in the United States will cover alcohol and drug treatment is anybody's guess right now, although it does appear as if some type and level of coverage will be available.

summary

- Readiness or commitment to change is an important consideration in treatment. One model of this process is the stages of change model.

- As with nicotine dependence, people with substance-use disorders change these problem behaviors on their own quite frequently. This is known as spontaneous remission of the substance-use patterns.

- The self-help groups Alcoholics Anonymous and Narcotics Anonymous are major resources in helping people with alcohol- and drug-use disorders, respectively.

- Other self-help groups, presented as alternatives to AA, also are becoming more popular. Two examples are Rational Recovery and Secular Organizations for Sobriety.

- The model of etiology of alcohol- and drug-use disorder that a treatment is based on affects its design. We review five types of models in this chapter: the moral model, the American Disease model, the biological model, the social learning model, and the sociocultural model.

- The biopsychosocial model of etiology addresses the inadequacy of single-factor models by combining the major types of factors that seem to influence the development of alcohol- and drug-use disorders.

- Treatments have aims, or goals. In alcohol and drug treatment, goals typically follow from a thorough assessment and refer to a person's use of alcohol and drugs, and to other areas of life functioning.

- It has been standard practice to specify abstinence from alcohol or other drugs as the major

outcome goal for a treatment. However, there are some who argue that moderate, nonproblem use of alcohol is a reasonable outcome goal for some patients.

- Alcohol treatment can be classified broadly into three categories of settings: hospital, intermediate, and outpatient. Within each of these settings a wide variety of services may be offered.

- Pharmacological treatment of alcohol problems includes medication to manage withdrawal from alcohol, alcohol-sensitizing drugs, and drugs to manage alcohol craving.

- Overall, no one treatment for alcohol problems seems to be superior to others, but staying in treatment is associated with better outcomes. It would seem that individual treatments may be more effective if they are matched to patients' characteristics.

- It has proved difficult to conduct controlled outcome research on self-help groups. What research has been done suggests that AA helps some people, but not everybody.

- Settings of drug treatment traditionally have been defined by treatment of heroin abuse, but abusers of other drugs now also appear in most of these settings. Traditionally drug treatment settings include detoxification, methadone maintenance, residential, and outpatient. As with alcohol treatment, a wide variety of treatment services may be offered in a setting.

- Since the 1980s there has been an upsurge in the treatment of nonopiate drug abusers. However, treatments for drug use other than the opiates have not been well-specified.

- Pharmacotherapy of drug problems includes management of drug withdrawal, replacing one opiate (e.g., heroin) with another one that is less addictive (methadone), and prescribing compounds to reduce drug craving.

- Research shows that staying in methadone maintenance, residential, and nonmethadone outpatient drug treatment is associated with reduced substance use and a more socially productive life style. Drug treatment research would benefit from more studies of patient-treatment matching.

- Treatment providers have found increasing numbers of their patients are multiple-substance abusers. This has caused a change in the thinking that drug and alcohol treatment are independent efforts. Rather, there is increasing recognition of the need for settings that can accommodate multiple-substance users, and for understanding common aspects of the addictive behaviors.

- There has been a major increase in recognition that individuals who show up for alcohol or drug treatment may have major psychiatric disorders. One approach to treating these individuals is to use psychotropic medications.

- The challenging problem of relapse has received a lot of research attention in the last 20 years. This work has resulted in treatment applications called relapse prevention.

- Financial factors, especially health insurance coverage, have had and are having great influence on the type and accessibility of alcohol and drug treatment.

ANSWERS TO WHAT DO YOU THINK?

1. The process of change of a problem behavior seems to be different for everyone.

F *According to one model, called the stages of change, self-change and change resulting from treatment can be characterized by progression through discrete steps or stages.*

2. Treatment is needed to change patterns of alcohol and drug abuse or dependence.

F *Research shows "spontaneous" remission of the substance-use disorders occurs, and it seems to be the most common way that change in problem substance use occurs.*

3. Alcoholics Anonymous was created over 100 years ago, and its influence predominantly is in the United States.

F *Alcoholics Anonymous was created in 1935 and its influence spans the world.*

4. It is generally agreed that substance-use disorders are caused by psychological problems.

F *Psychological theories are one type of explanation of etiology of the substance-use disorders, but there also are biological and sociocultural theories. A theory that incorporates all three theories seems to have the best chance of providing an adequate explanation of etiology.*

5. Assessment typically is thought to be essential to good treatment.

T *It is virtually universal in professional treatment contexts that assessment of the individual precedes any formally defined treatment activities.*

6. The only goal of any importance in alcohol and drug treatment is a reduction of substance use.

F *Substance use goals indeed are important, but goals relating to other areas of life functioning, like psychological or occupational, also are important.*

7. Abstinence from alcohol is a mandatory goal of alcohol treatment.

F   *Although the predominant assumption in U. S. and Canadian treatment programs is that abstinence is mandatory, there is evidence that certain individuals can modify their drinking patterns to stable, moderate, nonproblem use.*

8.   Methadone maintenance seems to be an effective treatment for heroin dependency.

T   *You might not think this is true given all the controversy surrounding methadone maintenance. However, a lot of research has shown that staying in methadone treatment results in reduced opiate use and other related problem behaviors such as criminal activity.*

9.   Today there are good reasons for rigid boundaries between what we call alcohol treatment and drug treatment.

F   *With increasing numbers of individuals who abuse more than one substance, the reasons for segregating at least some settings of alcohol and drug treatment have become less compelling.*

10.   People with major psychiatric problems are rarely seen in settings where alcohol and drug treatment are provided.

F   *Individuals with major psychiatric disorders do appear for alcohol or drug treatment. The frequency of such dual-diagnosis patients varies with the treatment setting.*

11.   Relapse is such a long-standing problem in alcohol and drug treatment that there must be little we can do about it.

F   *Relapse is a long-standing problem, but as a result of research and theory over the last 20 years or so, methods to prevent relapse have been developed and are in use.*

12.   Professional treatment for substance-use disorders is freely available to anyone who wants it.

F   *Treatment is as available today as it ever has been, but there still are major economic barriers that come between treatment and some of the people who need and want it. Therefore, treatment is not always accessible.*

17 Prevention of Substance Abuse

WHAT DO YOU THINK?

True or False?

____ Primary prevention includes interventions to treat persons who are beyond the early stages of substance abuse or dependence.

____ One strength of the sociocultural model of prevention is its emphasis on reducing the physical problems associated with alcohol consumption.

____ Raising the price of alcohol relative to disposable income and limiting the hours of operation for bars are examples of prevention strategies based on the distribution of consumption model.

____ The proscriptive model of prevention, which involves prohibiting the availability of drugs and promoting abstention from use, has proven to be the most effective of the three major models of prevention.

____ The "zero tolerance" policy of drug prevention was designed to hold drug users responsible for their role in drug trafficking.

____ The main proponents of warning labels for alcoholic beverages have been the manufacturers of these beverages.

____ Research evidence indicates that mass media prevention strategies do not result in significant changes in patterns of alcohol or drug use.

____ The primary goal of affect-oriented prevention programs is to increase the individual's knowledge base regarding drugs and alcohol.

____ Research evidence suggests that resistance-oriented prevention programs, such as Project DARE, have been successful in training students in drug-refusal skills.

____ The focus of most workplace prevention programs is primary prevention.

____ One disadvantage of workplace prevention programs is their cost.

____ The idea of holding people who serve alcohol responsible for the patrons' behavior if they become intoxicated is a recent development in drinking moderation strategies.

The preceding chapters include a great amount of information on alcohol and drugs, their actions and their use and abuse. The previous chapter concerned the treatment of problems associated with substance use. This brings us to our final chapter, which focuses on the prevention of substance-use problems.

It may seem a bit curious that preventing drug misuse is discussed in the last and not the first chapter of a text such as this. After all, you might say, if the focus of society and government were on prevention, might not material on drug abuse be unnecessary? Unfortunately, professionals and funding sources historically have not made prevention a high priority. The reasons for this are not certain, but two possibilities stand out. One is that past prevention efforts have tended to yield at best only modest influences in changing patterns of drug use. A second reason is that current, ongoing substance abuse is dramatically visible, and thus receives a more rapid response in personnel and financial resources. Whether this approach is shortsighted is a question that is often and strongly debated.

While prevention traditionally has received less attention than treatment, we nevertheless are now in a period where prevention research and development have been on the rise. Probably the strongest contributing factor to this increased focus on prevention is that substance use has contributed to the spread of AIDS. Intravenous drug users are the second-largest group of persons to have contracted AIDS in the United States and in Europe. Furthermore, being under the influence of drugs in some cases may lead to decisions to engage in unsafe sexual practices, increasing the risk of HIV transmission. Accordingly, federal and state resources have been increasingly used over the past decade to fund projects designed to prevent substance use.

Despite the lesser emphasis that traditionally has been placed on prevention relative to treatment (even during this current period of increased attention to prevention), most would agree that prevention efforts should—indeed must—be an important component of any comprehensive approach to substance abuse. In this chapter, we first provide an overview of definitions of prevention. The major models of prevention and their implications then will be discussed. We also provide examples of several types of prevention projects and their outcomes. The chapter closes with some comments on the prospects for future work in prevention.

DEFINING PREVENTION

Prevention in this context pertains, broadly, to the avoidance or alleviation of problems associated with substance use. This relatively straightforward proposition opens the door to a variety of potential goals for prevention efforts. For example, the goal of prevention efforts aimed at illegal drug use generally is to stop its occurrence. However, an alternative or additional goal of such activities might be to minimize the effects of any illegal drug use that does occur (a harm-reduction approach; see Drugs and Culture Box later in this chapter). As such, the approaches chosen for implementation probably would be different. Therefore, in speaking of prevention, it is important to identify what is being prevented, whether it be onset of use, continued use, negative effects on society, health problems, or something else.

Prevention of substance abuse traditionally has been divided into three types of intervention. The first is **primary prevention,** which pertains to the avoidance of substance abuse before it has a chance to occur. For example, one goal of primary prevention would be precluding the initial use of a substance. Never starting to use a drug, it is argued, means that you will not have any problems with it. This thinking in part underlies the "Just Say No" advertising effort used to encourage young persons to turn down invitations to use drugs. Another goal of primary prevention for some substances might be the development of responsible attitudes and/or substance-use behaviors. The best example of this would be responsible drinking behaviors. A number of

Primary prevention
Attempts to avoid substance use or abuse before it has a chance to occur.

posters and television spots have emphasized the need not to, for example, drive after drinking or to let friends drive drunk.

Secondary prevention
Interventions designed to prevent substance-use problems just as the early signs of abuse begin to appear.

"It's easier to stop a moving bus than to stop doing drugs. Don't start and you won't have to stop."
(Poster being displayed in buses, subways, and bus shelters by the Partnership for a Drug-Free Greater New York)

Tertiary prevention
Refers to treatment interventions with persons well beyond the early stages of substance abuse or dependence.

Secondary prevention refers to interventions applied when substance-use problems already have begun to appear. This type of prevention is analogous to early treatment in that interventions are used when problems are first surfacing. Secondary prevention frequently is used in the legal system response to substance misuse. For example, persons arrested for driving under the influence of alcohol often are referred to alcohol education courses designed to decrease the likelihood of the person drinking and driving again. Similarly, in some parts of the country educational programs are used with youthful offenders first arrested for drug possession. In each case the emphasis is on nipping the problem in the bud, just as it first appears. Central to such efforts, of course, is the early identification of these drug problems.

The third form of prevention, called **tertiary prevention,** includes interventions used in treating persons who are beyond the early stages of substance abuse or dependence. The goals of tertiary prevention essentially are to terminate use of the substance and thus avoid further deterioration in the person's functioning. Tertiary prevention and substance-abuse treatment (see Chapter 16) are comparable activities, and prevention efforts are more appropriately viewed as being either primary or secondary in nature. In the remainder of this chapter we accordingly emphasize primary and secondary prevention activities.

MODELS OF PREVENTION

Over years of much debate and some research, three major prevention models have evolved. In reading about these models, you will notice the philosophy underlying each model has diverse implications for what approaches would be recommended to prevent substance-use problems.

Sociocultural Model

The sociocultural, or social science, framework to understanding prevention posits that social norms directly influence the use and abuse of psychoactive substances. This model primarily has been used in efforts to prevent alcohol abuse, although the model also has implications for the prevention of other substance abuse, which we describe later in this section. When applied to drinking behavior, the model, according to Blane (1976), consists of three basic components:

- an emphasis on the culture's normative structure
- a need to integrate drinking into socially meaningful activities
- a focus on providing for the gradual socialization of drinking behavior

As you can see, prevention efforts derived from this model involve influencing the entire climate of drinking within the culture.

One of the strongest proponents of the sociocultural model is Rupert Wilkinson, who argues that alcohol use can be affected by planned policy measures. Wilkinson notes identifiable patterns of alcohol consumption exist that

Posters are widely used to communicate messages about the dangers of alcohol and drug abuse. Sometimes these posters deal with specific drugs and are directed at specific groups that might be at risk for drug use. This poster focuses on inhalants and is directed at Native American youths and young adults. Copies of similar posters are available from the U.S. Office of Substance Abuse Prevention, P.O. Box 2345, Rockville, MD 20852.

correspond to low rates of problematic drinking, and that these patterns can be used as guides for ingraining altered drinking patterns within the culture.

In his 1970 seminal work, Wilkinson identified five proposals for modifying drinking patterns culturally. At the forefront is the need to have within the culture a low level of emotionalism about drinking and at the same time a lack of ambivalence about alcohol use. Emotionalism surrounding drinking, according to Wilkinson, merely creates tension and produces an environment in which discussion and change in drinking behavior cannot occur. A more measured and nonreactive approach will have the added benefit of reducing societal ambivalence about drinking and thus provide more clarity about drinking norms.

A second tenet of Wilkinson's sociocultural model is that there must be a distinction between drinking per se and drunkenness. The notion here is that acceptable drinking and unacceptable drinking (drunkenness) both should be clearly defined. Unfortunately, arriving at such definitions is not easy. Wilkinson's third point is that after identifying what drunkenness is, there should be firm taboos on its occurrence.

A fourth and central theme is that drinking should be integrated into a broader social context. That is, alcohol consumption should not be the focus of activity at any given gathering, but instead should be adjunctive to other activities.

Finally, Wilkinson proposes that society should allow the serving of alcohol only when food also is available. The belief here is that when food is available, alcohol consumption will not necessarily be the sole focus of activity. Furthermore, food slows the absorption of alcohol and potentially reduces the rate of drunkenness.

Taken together, these proposals designate acceptable and unacceptable forms of drinking, and thus clearly identify desired patterns of responsible drinking. These patterns of drinking then should be integrated into routine family and other social activities. It is noteworthy that the goal of the sociocultural approach is not the cessation of drinking but rather changes in social norms regarding drinking. Therefore, the approach is not a prohibitionist strategy, and some have argued that a fault of the sociocultural approach is that it may encourage drinking.

A major criticism of the sociocultural model is that it may not be widely applicable. Many countries, such as the United States and Canada, have diverse cultures and subcultures, and customs and values that fit one of them may not be amenable to or be accepted by another. A second criticism is that the sociocultural approach, while emphasizing moderate consumption, fails to account for the value and pleasure many people attach to heavier drinking. A third concern with the model is that it assumes attitudinal changes in the culture will result in the desired behavioral changes. However, there is no specification of the mechanisms by which that change will occur, and past research has provided no strong indication that attitudinal change even leads to behavioral change. Finally, it is argued that the sociocultural model does not adequately take into consideration physical problems associated with alcohol consumption (for example, cancers, liver, and stomach ailments). In fact, some think that use of the sociocultural model may result in a greater prevalence of such physical problems, even if social problems are eliminated, simply by virtue of widespread use of alcohol (Blane, 1976; Nirenberg & Miller, 1984; Skirrow & Sawka, 1987).

Despite these concerns, the sociocultural model remains influential in the United States. Indeed, this approach probably is the dominant strategy currently being used (Skirrow & Sawka, 1987). When it is applied, the strategy has a broad scope. Examples of its applications include the advertising and education approaches to the problem of driving after drinking.

The sociocultural model has been applied predominantly in the context of alcohol-use problems, but it also has been a cornerstone to many prevention efforts geared toward problems associated with other drug use. As noted earlier, an example would be the "Just Say No" campaign, which encourages people nationwide, but particularly young people, to refuse offers or temptations to use drugs. Another example is the advertising efforts of the Partnership for a Drug Free America. The partnership's campaign, which focuses on marijuana, cocaine, and crack, seeks to decrease the social acceptance of drug use among young people and alert users or potential users to the risks of using drugs. Most of its communications are presented on television. To date, the effectiveness of these programs has not been documented. Further, they may be limited in scope in that they are geared toward youth of middle

"There is still a misguided notion that people can experiment with drugs with impunity. But we can't predict who will go on to develop dependence, and neither can the individual. It's essential that we get a consistent message across to young people that experimentation has its great risks."

(Dr. Charles Schuster, National Institute on Drug Abuse Addiction Research Center, *The Journal*, October 1993)

This poster is one in a series produced by Partnership for a Drug-Free America. It notes that American businesses lost billions of dollars to drugs and that many companies are now using drug tests. The advertisement warns college graduates that using drugs could cost them their jobs.

and upper socioeconomic status who have limited exposure to drugs. The only major difference between use of the sociocultural model with drugs as opposed to alcohol is that the former application keys on inculcating in society a norm of no use, as opposed to responsible use.

Distribution of Consumption Model

The second major model of prevention is the distribution of consumption approach. This model has been studied predominantly in the context of prevention or reduction of alcohol problems, although in recent years some effort has been directed at extending it to other drugs (see Skirrow & Sawka, 1987). The model is based on research showing a fairly consistent statistical distribution of alcohol consumption across cultures. The pioneering work in the development of the model was conducted by the French mathematician Sully Ledermann in the 1950s. The model's visibility was enhanced greatly by its endorsement a number of years later for the prevention of alcohol problems by an international group of scholars (Bruun, Edwards, Lumio, Makela, Pan, Popham, Room, Schmidt, Skog, Sulkunen, & Oesterberg, 1975).

There are three central propositions of the distribution of consumption model (Rush & Gliksman, 1986; Schmidt & Popham, 1978). The first is that the proportion of heavy alcohol users in a given population is positively correlated with the mean level of alcohol consumption in that population. That is, the number of heavy drinkers in a society increases with the society's per-capita consumption. Given this relationship, it is predicted that a decrease in average alcohol consumption within a given culture would be accompanied by a corresponding decrease in the proportion of heavy alcohol consumers.

The second proposition of the distribution of consumption model is that heavy alcohol consumption increases the probability of negative alcohol-related consequences, such as mental/emotional, physical, and social problems. Should the population's mean consumption increase, and thus raise the number of heavy drinkers, a corresponding increase in these negative consequences would be anticipated.

Finally, the model's third proposition is that societies should attempt to reduce the negative consequences of alcohol consumption by restricting the availability of alcohol. It is assumed that restricting alcohol availability, especially but not exclusively through procedures designed to raise the price of alcohol relative to disposable income, will lower per-capita consumption and correspondingly the damages associated with alcohol use. Other approaches could include limiting the hours that bars and taverns can be open, controlling retail sales of alcohol, and raising the minimum drinking age.

Although it is a well-regarded approach to prevention, the distribution of consumption model has its critics. Some think the model is purely descriptive and does not provide any insights into the reasons people drink or how a person's drinking environment may contribute to drinking behavior. Skog (1985) has addressed this problem in more detail, and noted that sociocultural variables such as the drinking environment actually can be incorporated in the distribution of consumption model. Whitehead (1975) has gone further in his discussion of the ways in which the sociocultural and distribution of consumption models might be used together. Of more concern to critics is that "normal" drinkers in a population may react differently to efforts to reduce or restructure alcohol availability than "heavy" or "alcoholic" drinkers (Nirenberg & Miller, 1984). Again, the concern is that sociocultural and psychological variables are not included in the distribution of consumption model. For example, differences between normal drinkers and alcohol abusers may be crucial in predicting drinking behavior, with alcohol abusers perhaps less likely to respond to price increases and other policies designed to decrease per-capita consumption. Relatedly, there may be a point at which these policies on restructuring alcohol use have no benefit. If, for example, the price of alcohol rises too much, the result may be an increase in bootlegging and home production of alcohol and in the mystique surrounding alcohol use (Skirrow & Sawka, 1987). As you can see, the task of reducing per-capita consumption is very complex.

Proscriptive Model

This third prevention model is the most basic in principle. It takes a moral stance in addressing substance-use problems. The guiding theme is that if there is no use of the substance, there can be no problem. If a person does use the substance, that use is not seen as a societal problem but instead as a product of a person's character flaw. As such, the goals of the proscriptive model are (a) prohibition of availability and (b) abstention from use (Skirrow & Sawka, 1987).

The proscriptive model has been applied to both alcohol and other drug use. The most important application to alcohol use was during Prohibition in the United States from 1921 to 1932. However, the model has been applied

Contemporary Issue
ZERO TOLERANCE FOR DRUGS

Among the more recent applications of the proscriptive model of drug-abuse prevention has been the "zero tolerance" policy implemented by some states and federal agencies. The theme behind the approach is that there will be no tolerance of any drugs in any amount in any place at any time. The goal of the policy is to attack the "demand side" of the drug-abuse problem and thus hold drug users accountable for their role in drug trafficking.

Under the policy, which was prominently reported in the news services in the late 1980s and early 1990s, cars, boats, luxury yachts, and other private property were seized when even the smallest amount of a substance was found. During one one-month period alone, the Coast Guard confiscated 27 boats. One yacht, the *Ark Royal*, was seized when Coast Guard officials found some marijuana seeds and two stems in a dresser drawer and in a trash can. On another yacht, Coast Guard inspectors found one twenty-eighth of an ounce of marijuana. The two yachts, which frequently were chartered out, were returned to their owners after fines and seizure costs were paid. These, however, were just the more celebrated cases. Smaller amounts of private property, such as cars and luggage, also have been confiscated, and many of these cases remain in the judicial system.

Some government officials during that period felt the zero tolerance policy should have been expanded. Edwin Meese III, attorney general of the United States in Ronald Reagan's administration, called for drug testing of all workers across the country, with any positive test findings to result in termination of employment. According to Meese, this zero tolerance policy in drug testing was an "absolute necessity" to reduce drug problems. Meese felt that the fear of losing one's job would be a strong deterrent to drug use. Other observers have noted that constitutional questions surrounding such tests, especially when administered by the government, likely will preclude their widespread use.

Do you think the zero tolerance policy has had an effect on drug use or the overall drug problem? Former officials of the Reagan and Bush administrations believe their policies have led to decreased substance use. However, many others are not so optimistic. They note that arresting only a small percentage of those using drugs simply clogs the legal system—even if most of them plead guilty to the charges! These same observers subscribe more to the approach of focusing on drug producers and drug traffickers.

National policies such as the zero tolerance approach are, of course, a function of decisions made by senior government officials, and it will be of interest to study over time the strategies implemented by the Clinton administration. Clinton has indicated a desire to devote greater resources to reducing demand for drugs through prevention and treatment interventions. The effects of this strategy, in concert with other approaches to reducing drug use and abuse, will be closely watched.

"Drug users must be seen as human beings and not as criminals."
(Pat Erickson, criminologist with the Toronto Addiction Research Foundation, *The Journal*, October 1993)

more consistently in the context of drug use. There has been for decades a strong proscriptive approach to drug use, generally focused on marijuana and heroin and more recently on cocaine. The proscriptive model in the 1930s and 1940s was most evident in films and newspaper and magazine articles geared toward mass audiences. Sensationalized stories about marijuana-induced crime sprees commonly were found in newspapers, and similar themes are evident in films from that era, such as *Reefer Madness*, *Assassin of Youth*, and *Marijuana: Weed with Roots in Hell*. Then, as now, the key to such campaigns has been that "good" people do not use drugs (Skirrow & Sawka, 1987).

Although the proscriptive model remains popular with some, it has not resulted in any significant contribution to the prevention of substance-abuse problems. It is well-known that Prohibition was less than successful in alleviating problems associated with alcohol use, and other substance-use problems also have continued. Perhaps the major difficulty with the model is that it is too simple to tackle a problem that is complex.

CURRENT TOPICS IN PREVENTION

Prevention efforts are being implemented on a number of fronts, and in this section we provide an overview of several contemporary topics and programs in primary and secondary prevention. (You will notice that the majority of these prevention activities are derived predominantly from the sociocultural model.) We preface this section by highlighting the most noteworthy trends in prevention activities today. They are:

- increasing focus on having family (especially parental) involvement in prevention programs
- including attention to resistance-skills development, specifically the development of strategies to use in avoiding pressures to use drugs
- developing programs in conjunction with more broad-based communitywide strategies. For example, a school-based intervention now might be presented in conjunction with messages being communicated through mass media outlets.
- identifying subgroups of individuals most at risk for alcohol and other drug misuse and developing programs specifically for them. Examples include inner-city youths, Native American youths, and minority youths.
- focusing attention on the "gateway" drugs. While almost all programs emphasize abstinence from all illegal substances, some programs have been focusing on not initiating use of tobacco, alcohol, and marijuana in particular. These are viewed as "gateway" drugs, in that use of these substances typically precedes use of the so-called "harder drugs" such as cocaine, heroin, and LSD.
- increasing attention on programs designed to minimize risk or negative consequences associated with any substance use that does occur. These risk-reduction programs do not sanction drug use, but instead seek to minimize the negatives associated with such use for the individual and for society.

You will observe these trends in many of the programs described below.

Education and Mass Media Efforts

By far the most common and pervasive approaches to substance-misuse prevention have been education and **mass media** efforts. Traditionally, these programs have been geared toward adolescents and young adults, two of the more visible groups at risk for substance abuse. More recently, there have been efforts to extend these interventions to children.

Mass media
Communications designed for widespread distribution, such as advertisements, films, and printed materials.

The school system has been touted as an ideal setting for providing educational materials on substance use and misuse. Indeed, most states now require the inclusion of education about alcohol and other drugs in the school curricula, although the state laws unfortunately have not been translated in any systematic way into comprehensive instructional programs. Further, in the past programs were hampered by the tendency for teachers to have not been sufficiently trained in alcohol and drug education materials. However, major improvements have occurred in recent years, and programs have been gradually becoming more and more systematized.

What happens when alcohol and drug education courses are implemented? The results have been mixed. The general outcome is that students presented with educational materials do increase their knowledge about the topics covered. However, there has not been much of an indication that

Contemporary Issue
WARNING LABELS FOR ALCOHOLIC BEVERAGES

A form of education/mass media intervention directed at preventing alcohol-related problems is the placement of warnings at alcohol sales outlets and on alcoholic beverage containers. The idea behind the strategy is analogous to why labels are placed on cigarette packages.

For years, efforts to pass legislation to require alcohol warning labels had been unsuccessful, despite the endorsement of approximately 100 health and public interest groups. However, such legislation became law in 1989. A bill passed by Congress now requires this warning on all alcohol beverage containers:

> Government Warning: 1) According to the Surgeon General, women should not drink alcoholic beverages during pregnancy because of the risk of birth defects. 2) Consumption of alcoholic beverages impairs your ability to drive a car or operate machinery and may cause other health problems.

Alcohol producers are less than supportive of warning labels. They argue that the information on the containers is common knowledge and unlikely to produce changes in drinkers' behavior. Accordingly, research is needed to determine whether warning labels have a durable effect on drinking behavior, but early indications are that these labels are noticed by consumers and do increase awareness about alcohol-related risks (Mazis, Morris, & Swasy, 1991; Scammon, Mayer, & Smith, 1991). More basic, however, to the reservations of alcohol producers is the issue of product liability. Some producers fear the use of the labels will open the door to lawsuits for drinkers' previous use of alcohol. On the other hand, argue proponents of the labeling, not placing the labels now, at a time when there is more research in support of the warnings, may result in an even greater number of lawsuits later.

The passage of the national labeling legislation goes beyond policies that already had been in place on a smaller scale in several cities. Since 1983, New York City, Philadelphia, Washington, D.C., and Columbus, Ohio, among others, passed city ordinances requiring posting of a sign where alcohol is sold indicating the relationship between drinking during pregnancy and the incidence of birth defects. And not all alcohol producers are against warning labels. For more than 20 years, Walter Stephen Taylor, a winemaker at Bully Hill Vineyards in upstate New York, has been placing warning labels on his products. He also has testified at congressional hearings in favor of such labeling.

patterns of substance use change (Bangert-Drowns, 1988; Cellucci, 1984; Schaps, DiBartolo, Moskowitz, Palley, & Churgin, 1981). Indeed, in some cases (e.g., Engs, 1977; Kinder, Pape, & Walfish, 1980; Stuart, 1974) students receiving the education program have actually been found in the short run to escalate their drug use! However, these findings should be viewed with caution until more systematic research on education programs has been conducted, especially research on the long-term effects of these interventions.

Tentatively, though, increased knowledge about alcohol and other drugs does not necessarily translate into modifications in their use.

One factor that may contribute to these discouraging results is the age at which youths receive exposure to the intervention. As a result of data indicating that young children have already begun to form concepts about intoxication, drinking behavior, and alcohol effects (Jahoda & Cramond, 1972), more attention is being placed on educational materials geared toward children in early elementary school. Preparing materials for that level of development may be more successful than trying to modify beliefs at a later age when they are more firmly established. An example is research on smoking beliefs and behavior. Chen and Winder (1986) wanted to determine the best time to apply a smoking intervention program. They surveyed over 500 6th, 9th, and 12th graders in a Massachusetts school system. The results showed that students are likely to respond best to a smoking educational program around the sixth grade. There were several reasons for this conclusion. One is that fewer 6th graders (6.5%) described themselves as occasional or regular smokers than did 9th (21%) or 12th (32%) graders. Sixth graders also reported much less peer pressure to smoke than the 9th or 12th graders, less knowledge about smoking and its effects, and less familiarity about their parents' attitudes regarding smoking. In addition, there were indications that many of the 6th graders surveyed were planning to smoke within the following five years. Consequently, the use of an education program with these sixth-grade students would appear to hold the most promise for engendering attitudes against personal smoking.

A related trend in the area of prevention education has been the use of parents serving as teachers of their children. According to DuPont (1980), a former director of the National Institute on Drug Abuse, "It is ironic that after a decade of parent put-downs that we are today rediscovering that parents, who were written off as ignorant and meddlesome at best and as 'the problem' at worst, are now 'the solution' to drug problems" (p. 2). While this statement might be overstating the point, it does appear that parents can be an important—perhaps crucial—element in prevention activities. Much of this growing emphasis on parents during the last decade derives from the view that substance use is a family concern. These parent-focused programs seek to enhance family communication about alcohol and other drugs, to have parents model or foster either abstinence or responsible use of accepted substances (generally alcohol), and to encourage abstinence from other substances (Botvin & Botvin, 1992; Kimmel, 1976). One such program, called "The Power of Positive Parenting," includes a curriculum designed to make parents aware of the profound influence their behavior has on their children's (Richmond, 1977). Children, especially in their preschool years, turn primarily to their parents when looking for models of appropriate behavior. The program aims to make parents aware of the ways they influence their children's beliefs about drugs and to help them determine what constitutes "responsible modeling" of, for example, drinking behavior.

Educational efforts also have been implemented in broader scope using mass media technology. Mass media in this context refers to "communication through television, radio, newspapers, billboards, films, and printed materials designed for widespread distribution" (Hewitt & Blane, 1984, p. 282), although television and radio are the most frequently used vehicles for these messages. Because mass media campaigns often involve frequent presentations of a relatively brief message (for example, a 15-second television spot), developers of these campaigns generally will create a slogan that unites the material within the various spots. Slogans of some recent campaigns include "Just Say No" for drugs and "Know When to Say When" and "Friends Don't Let Friends Drive Drunk" for alcohol. Most of the campaigns in recent years regarding alcohol abuse have focused on decreasing the incidence of driving under the influence.

While research on mass media campaigns has not yielded a clear picture of their effects, it appears the programs do succeed in raising knowledge levels and increasing awareness about the use of drugs (Blane, 1988; Botvin & Botvin, 1992). Of particular note is the finding that campaigns on drunk driving pretty consistently yield changes in knowledge level (for example, knowing the legal definition of intoxication). As with other prevention approaches, attitude change has been found less consistently. There is no evidence, however, that significant changes in patterns of alcohol or drug use are occurring as a function of these mass media strategies. These approaches will more likely be successful if they are directed at particular substance-using groups.

Taken together, education and mass media approaches continue to command the majority of resources available for prevention. Their benefits appear to be primarily in the areas of knowledge and, to a lesser extent, attitude change. Their effectiveness is likely to increase as a function of better tailoring of campaign messages and efforts to target these campaigns to particular populations of drug users. And, of course, more work is needed to increase the likelihood that these approaches will result in actual changes in substance use.

Affect-Oriented Programs

Many prevention programs, and particularly those geared toward youth, incorporate what is called an "affective" component. This affective feature typically involves **values clarification** and decision making. Values clarification activities include self-exploration, life-values assessment, and strategies for fulfilling needs that are part of those values (Hewitt, 1982). These programs provide students with general strategies for making life choices and for applying these techniques to situations that involve alcohol or other drugs. The goal of the affect-oriented material overall is to have participants be aware of their own feelings and attitudes regarding drugs, so they can deal effectively with drug-use situations according to their individual value structures.

The logic behind the use of an affective component is that thoughts, feelings, attitudes, and values regarding alcohol and drugs can be just as important in drug-use situations as knowledge, and perhaps more so. As yet, we do not know the extent to which affect-oriented programs are beneficial. As with educational programs, there has not been much well-designed research on the effects of affect-oriented interventions. The research that has been conducted does suggest, though, that such interventions do help to clarify personal views on substance use. Popular in the 1970s and 1980s, these programs are used less frequently today, although some components of the

Values clarification
A frequent component of affect-oriented prevention programs, it typically involves exploration of one's own needs and beliefs regarding drugs.

affect-oriented programs have been incorporated in modified forms in contemporary programs.

Alternative Behaviors and Resistance-Skills Training

In recent years there has been a significant growth in prevention programs that focus on developing alternatives to drug use or on developing skills to recognize and resist drug-use pressures.

In terms of developing alternatives to drug use, the objective is to provide the opportunity to engage in various productive activities (e.g., sports, vocational training, hobbies) that are as or more appealing than drug use. While in theory this strategy seems to make sense, evaluations of these programs have not revealed any particular benefits in terms of substance-use behavior (Botvin & Botvin, 1992).

Resistance-skills training interventions, on the other hand, have shown more promise. As described by Flay (1985), these interventions often include some combination of the following informational and skills-building strategies:

- Developing problem-solving and decision-making skills
- Developing cognitive skills for resisting interpersonal and media-based (e.g., prodrinking or prosmoking) drug-use messages
- Increasing self-awareness and self-esteem
- Learning nondrug-use skills for dealing with anxiety and stress
- Enhancing interpersonal skills such as the ability to initiate a conversation
- Developing assertiveness skills such as the ability to express displeasure and anger and to communicate needs
- Drawing the relationship between drug use and health concerns

Typically in these programs, participants learn to be aware of social influences that lead to drug use and to use skills to resist these influences. For example, participants will be exposed to strategies for refusing drugs when they are offered to them by peers. Often the programs will include peer leaders or co-leaders. In summarizing the evaluation of resistance-skills training, Botvin and Botvin (1992) note some positive indications, especially in the area of cigarette smoking.

One of the better-known resistance-oriented programs in use today is Project DARE (Drug Abuse Resistance Education). (Two other programs are "Quest: Skills for Living" and "Here's Looking at You 2000." However, neither has been sufficiently studied yet in terms of effectiveness.) The Project DARE curriculum typically is targeted at fifth- and sixth-grade elementary school students before they enter junior high school. The program is based on the assumption that schoolchildren must be educated to recognize the dangers of substance use and to resist subtle as well as direct pressures to use drugs. Accordingly, the program is designed to train students to recognize and resist peer and other influences to experiment with drugs. The curriculum includes between 15 and 20 modules, each led by a law enforcement officer and lasting 45–60 minutes. Modules focus on topics such as refusal skills, risk assessment, decision making, interpersonal and communication skills, critical thinking, and alternatives to substance use. Evaluations of Project DARE

"We talk about high-risk youth and families in the U.S., but I do not know of any continent that is not threatened by drug and alcohol abuse or misuse or any country not affected. We have youth at risk on a worldwide basis, families at risk on a worldwide basis. We have communities and institutions at risk on a worldwide basis, and we have nations at risk."

(Dr. Benson Bateman, president of Human Resources Development Institute, *The Journal*, May 1993)

One of the best known resistance-oriented programs in drug use prevention is Project DARE (Drug Abuse Resistance Education). The program typically is targeted at fifth and sixth grade elementary school students.

programs have been positive in the context of successfully training students in the use of refusal skills (Pellow & Jengeleski, 1991), although longer-term evaluations of subsequent drug use are lacking.

Worksite Programs

Substance-use problems among employees can be costly for employers. The costs can be seen in lost production, accidents, absenteeism, and thefts to support drug habits. Indeed, the total cost to the U.S. economy attributable to substance abuse is estimated at over $144 billion a year, with approximately 60% due to alcohol abuse and the remainder to other substance abuse (Rice, 1991). As such, it makes sense to some employers to provide the opportunity for early identification and intervention when an employee begins to show impairments due to drug use. Although part of the employer's motivation may be humanitarian, a central incentive frequently is to avoid losses in company productivity.

There are several potential advantages to worksite prevention programs. One is their service to adults who still are functioning relatively well. As Nathan (1984) notes, they still have their jobs and are more likely to be physically, psychologically, and economically healthy compared to those who already have lost jobs because of their substance abuse. Thus, they may be in a better position to respond to prevention opportunities. Other advantages, according to Nathan (1984), are that the company employees are a captive audience, making it easier to direct prevention-related messages to them. Relatedly, employees do not have to travel outside the company to see or hear

Contemporary Issue
SERVER INTERVENTIONS

Holding people who serve alcohol to patrons or guests responsible for the patrons' behavior if they become intoxicated is not a new idea. Its roots are in what are referred to as dram shop (an old English term for taverns) laws. These laws, which in various forms are active and being upheld in courts today, have two implications. The first is that servers of alcohol, whether a bartender or the host of a private dinner party, can in some circumstances be held liable for the actions of intoxicated patrons or guests. The second implication, important in the context of prevention, is that servers and hosts can contribute to preventing alcohol-related problems through their decisions not to serve alcohol to persons who are intoxicated. Indeed, the premise of model legislation for a uniform dram shop law is the prevention of alcohol-related injuries, deaths, and other damages (Mosher & Colman, 1986).

This model legislation has been enacted in several states and introduced in a number of others. Part of the legislation identifies several practices that businesses and hosts may be able to use in preventing or limiting their liability in serving alcohol, such as encouraging patrons or guests not to become intoxicated if they consume alcohol, providing nonalcoholic beverages and food, and promoting the use of safe transportation alternatives to preclude the intoxicated drinker from driving home. These guidelines very much are derived from a sociocultural framework of drug misuse in that they seek to prevent alcohol-related problems by modifying the context of the drinking by encouraging safer drinking practices.

One important outcome of the dram shop legislation is that a variety of education and training programs have been developed to help alcohol servers and hosts to detect intoxication and to stop serving alcohol to a person who appears intoxicated. There are indications that these programs can have a positive effect (e.g., Geller, Russ, & Delphos, 1987), but there are obstacles to their implementation, especially in business situations. For example, one frustrating experience occurred in working with alcohol servers in Atlantic City, New Jersey, gambling casinos (Nathan, 1984; Nathan & Niaura, 1987). Nathan and his colleagues were asked to provide information on how to detect intoxication among patrons and how to stop serving them drinks (most of which were served free to the patrons if they were at a gambling table). Although servers did acquire these skills, the program eventually broke down because casino owners resisted allowing their servers to cut off intoxicated patrons who still were gambling. Thus, servers were in a true bind. According to Nathan and Niaura (1987), servers would refuse drinks to an intoxicated patron and avoid legal liability, but at the same time they might antagonize their employer if the patron stopped gambling!

---

these messages. Finally, an employer implementing a program that benefits employees may improve employee morale, thus improving work performance.

One disadvantage to employers of worksite programs is their cost. Despite the possible payoff of enhanced employee functioning, some company executives are skeptical of the effectiveness of prevention programs, or do not think program benefits outweigh program costs. Another problem is employees' concerns about confidentiality. Employees may hesitate to identify themselves as having problems with alcohol or other drugs for fear of being dismissed from their positions. A worksite prevention and intervention program is unlikely to be effective without stringent guidelines to protect the confidentiality of those the program is intended to help.

Prevention and intervention efforts, when they do occur, can take several forms. Primary prevention might include the use of posters and mailings providing educational material on drug problems. Some companies have used films and outside speakers to increase awareness of these problems. These strategies, which generally heighten awareness of substance use and its effects, also are intended to set the stage for employees who are abusing alcohol or drugs to decide to start treatment. This treatment phase represents a second tier of the prevention effort. It can take several forms. Frequently it involves the employee meeting with an on-site counselor. These counselors typically operate through what has been called an employee assistance program, or EAP. The counselor will either work with the employee on the substance-use problem in that setting or arrange for the employee to participate in an outside treatment setting (e.g., inpatient treatment, sessions with an outside counselor). Either separately or as part of either of these two treatment options, the counselor could encourage the employee to begin attending self-help groups, such as Alcoholics Anonymous or Cocaine Anonymous.

While worksite programs have become increasingly prevalent in industrial settings (Lewis, 1991), their effectiveness rarely is evaluated. In addition, most current programs focus on secondary rather than primary prevention (e.g., identifying alcohol or drug abusers and arranging for treatment). Nathan (1984), in reviewing worksite programs, noted that "when prevention efforts are undertaken, they are usually a small, ineffective afterthought grafted onto a treatment program" (p. 404). Thus, as with the national scene, prevention efforts in the workplace appear to be a low priority.

Programs for College Students

Abuse of alcohol—whether chronic or sporadic—long has been a problem on college campuses. Studies on collegiate drinking practices have consistently documented a higher prevalence of alcohol use than in the general population, and an apparent increase in the number of alcohol-related problems over the course of the past 20 years. Problems associated with drinking in college students include relationship difficulties, driving under the influence, involvement in arguments or fights, vandalism and other property destruction, and lowered grades. Both male and female drinkers are candidates to experience such problems related to alcohol. Estimates are that up to one-quarter of student drinkers can be considered problem drinkers, in that at least some degree of negative consequence is associated with their use of alcohol (Berkowitz & Perkins, 1986; Saltz & Elandt, 1986).

Colleges have taken various approaches in attempting to curtail problematic uses of alcohol, and we describe two well-known programs. The first, implemented at the University of Massachusetts at Amherst, has a primary prevention focus, and the second, at the University of Washington at Seattle, is a secondary prevention strategy.

The program at the University of Massachusetts was intended as a university-wide strategy "to create a campus environment that encouraged responsible use of beverage alcohol and discouraged irresponsible drinking behaviors" (Kraft, 1984, p. 328). The program was viewed mostly as a primary prevention strategy—that is, to educate people about alcohol use *before* problems arise. The logic behind this approach, as with the educational strategies described earlier, is that knowledge will translate into an ability to avoid alcohol problems. The program included three forms of prevention effort. The first, called extensive educational activity, was used to enhance awareness about alcohol and its use. Information was disseminated by use of posters, radio and newspaper advertisements, and pamphlets. The second form of intervention involved intensive approaches, which included small discussion groups, classes, and workshops on a variety of topics related to alcohol use and abuse. The final form of intervention—community development actions—keyed on the identification of and response to the specific alcohol-related needs of special groups of students, such as black and Latino students and women. Other community actions included liaison with the management of the local campus pub to arrange for service of food and non-alcoholic beverages, and in-service training workshops for staff members of the university's health services center.

DRUGS AND CULTURE
HARM-REDUCTION SOCIAL POLICIES

Countries vary widely in their social policies regarding substance use. You have read elsewhere in this book about the "war on drugs" and "zero-tolerance" policies being utilized in the United States. This policy is in striking contrast to another social policy strategy—called harm reduction or harm minimization—being implemented in some other countries, particularly Britain and the Netherlands. Harm-reduction policies focus on decreasing the negative consequences of drug use for the individual and the community, even if they in the interim endorse continued but safer drug use. According to Diane Riley at the Canadian Centre on Substance Abuse, "Harm reduction establishes a hierarchy of goals, with the more immediate and realistic ones to be achieved as first steps toward risk-free use or abstinence. It is a pragmatic approach, which recognizes that abstinence may be neither a realistic nor a desired goal for some, especially in the short term."

Two examples of harm-reduction policies have been described by Riley (1993). The first was in Merseyside in Britain. Health clinics have collaborated with pharmacists and police officials to establish a "comprehensive approach [to drug abuse] involving prescription of drugs, provision of clean syringes and helping rather than criminalizing drug users." Among the reported benefits of the Merseyside collaboration: low incidence of HIV in drug users, continued employment for many drug abusers, and a decrease in theft and robbery crimes.

A second example is from Amsterdam, which sought to reduce drug-use harm by providing medical and social services to persons continuing to use drugs. Among the strategies used were decreased police attention to marijuana possession and use and mobile methadone distribution stations. Prison terms apply only to dealers of hard drugs.

While the policy of harm-reduction has not been fully embraced in the United States (see Marlatt, Larimer, Baer, & Quigley, 1993), there are examples of some such strategies being implemented. First is the introduction of methadone maintenance programs throughout the country in the 1960s. These programs were implemented in part to reduce crime rates among heroin users. A second strategy, more recently implemented, is needle-exchange programs, designed to reduce the risk of HIV transmission among drug abusers. However, both of these strategies have had their vocal opponents. This recently has been the case for needle-exchange programs, despite research indicating that intravenous drug users participating in such programs do not show an increase in the number of injections and that there has not been an associated increase in the number of addictions. A broad-based harm-reduction approach to the problems of drug use in the United States is not foreseen in the near future.

The University of Massachusetts project is an example of a coordinated effort to use a variety of interventions to prevent alcohol problems. In contrast to most projects, where only a unidimensional educational program is used, the Massachusetts program was multifaceted. Subsequent evaluation of the program's effects has been both encouraging and disappointing. On the positive side, it was found that the program, using its variety of approaches, had significant saturation—that is, a large number of the students came into contact with the program components, whether that contact was seeing a program poster, hearing a radio spot on drinking, or attending a workshop on alcohol. There also was evidence of increased awareness and knowledge about drinking. However, as with the majority of programs aimed at modifying knowledge or attitudes regarding alcohol, changes in actual alcohol use or alcohol-use problems were not apparent.

The program at the University of Washington has been developed by Alan Marlatt and his colleagues (Baer, Kivlahan, Fromme, & Marlatt, in press; Kivlahan, Coppel, Fromme, Williams, & Marlatt, in press; Kivlahan, Marlatt, Fromme, Coppel, & Williams, 1990). In contrast to the Massachusetts program, Washington's prevention approach focuses on skills training. In this regard, their program includes four central components:

- training in blood alcohol level monitoring to acquire knowledge about specific alcohol effects
- development of coping skills to use in situations associated with risky or heavy drinking
- modifying expectations regarding alcohol use and alcohol effects
- development of stress management and other life-management skills

As you can see, the "skills" that the University of Washington program is designed to impart can be used to avoid problematic uses of alcohol.

Results from the University of Washington program have been impressive and encouraging. For example, from before to after the eight-week program, students in the skills-training program showed decreases on three measures of alcohol consumption: number of drinks per week, peak blood alcohol level reached per week, and hours per week with a blood alcohol level exceeding .055% (recall that a level of .10% is considered legally intoxicated in most of the United States). These decreases were not observed in students who only participated in an assessment phase or who only attended an alcohol education class that emphasized alcohol effects. Most important, the changes observed among the students receiving the skills-training program were still evident 12 months after the intervention (Baer et al., in press). Although it will be important to see if these differences in response to the program continue over longer periods of time, the degree of change maintained through 12 months is impressive.

CLOSING COMMENTS ON PREVENTION

Prevention of alcohol and drug abuse is a topic that almost everyone acknowledges as being central to any coherent response to alcohol and drug problems in this country. Unfortunately, it is an area that has been allocated meager resources, at least in comparison to the monies spent annually in the treatment of alcohol and drug abuse. Although past efforts at prevention, especially education and mass media approaches, have increased relevant knowledge, they have had much less effect on alcohol and drug use. Especially critical in future research on prevention will be the design and evaluation of programs for specific cultural subgroups, the creation of programs geared toward the specific developmental levels of children and teenagers, parental involvement programs, and programs aimed at providing alternatives to alcohol and drug use. However, full exploration of these possibilities requires more resources from state and federal agencies compared to what has been available so far.

summary

- Most would agree that prevention efforts should be an important component of any comprehensive approach to substance abuse, but professionals and funding sources have not made prevention efforts a high priority.

- Prevention traditionally has been divided into three types of intervention: primary, secondary, and tertiary.

- Primary prevention refers to efforts focused on avoiding substance use or abuse before it occurs.

- Secondary prevention involves early interventions designed to address substance abuse just as problems are beginning to appear.

- Tertiary prevention, which actually is more treatment than prevention, includes intervention used to treat persons beyond the early stages of substance abuse.

- The sociocultural model of prevention, probably the dominant approach applied in the United States, posits that social norms directly influence substance use. Prevention efforts derived from this model involve influencing the entire climate of drinking within a culture.

■ Another major prevention model is the distribution of consumption approach, which posits (1) that the proportion of heavy drinkers in a culture is positively related to the mean level of alcohol consumption, (2) that heavier alcohol consumption increases the probability of alcohol problems, and (3) that societies should attempt to reduce the negative consequences of drinking by reducing alcohol consumption across the culture.

■ A third model of prevention is the proscriptive approach, which focuses on prohibiting availability of substances and emphasizes abstention from drug use.

■ The most common substance-abuse prevention interventions have included education and use of mass media. Most states now require the inclusion of alcohol and drug education in school curricula.

■ Alcohol and drug education courses generally have been shown to increase knowledge levels, but have not been as successful in changing substance-use patterns.

■ In recent years there has been an increasing use of parents in education prevention programs, especially in prevention programs focused on children.

■ Mass media campaigns appear to succeed in raising levels of knowledge and awareness about drugs. Changes in attitudes and actual drug-use behavior have not been found as consistently.

■ Prevention programs using a resistance-training approach have been receiving much attention in recent years. These programs focus on training young people to recognize and resist pressures to use drugs.

■ Prevention programs are sometimes located at worksites, where the goal is to identify drug abusers and to intervene when drug problems interfere with job performance. These programs, when established, generally concentrate more on secondary than on primary prevention.

■ A variety of prevention programs, generally focused on alcohol use, have been established on college campuses.

■ The full potential of prevention interventions has not yet been tested. But before this potential can be assessed, more resources from state and federal agencies will be needed.

ANSWERS TO WHAT DO YOU THINK?

1. Primary prevention includes interventions to treat persons who are beyond the early stages of substance abuse or dependence.

F *Primary prevention refers to the avoidance of substance abuse before it has the chance to occur. Tertiary prevention involves treatment of individuals already engaged in substance abuse.*

2. One strength of the sociocultural model of prevention is its emphasis on reducing the physical problems associated with alcohol consumption.

F *This model has been criticized for not adequately taking into account these physical problems. Some believe that use of the sociocultural model may result in a greater prevalence of such problems.*

3. Raising the price of alcohol relative to disposable income and limiting the hours of operation for bars are examples of prevention strategies based on the distribution of consumption model.

T *This model posits that the proportion of heavy drinkers in a given population increases with the mean level of alcohol consumption in that population. Therefore, methods to lower per-capita consumption should lead to a decrease in the prevalence of heavy drinking.*

4. The proscriptive model of prevention, which involves prohibiting the availability of drugs and promoting abstention from use, has proven to be the most effective of the three major models of prevention.

F *This model has not resulted in any significant contribution to the prevention of substance abuse. One example of this type of approach was Prohibition, which was less than successful in alleviating problems associated with alcohol use.*

5. The "zero tolerance" policy of drug prevention was designed to hold drug users responsible for their role in drug trafficking.

T *According to this policy, there would be no tolerance of any drugs in any amount at any place at any time. Under this policy, private property such as cars and yachts was seized if the smallest quantity of a drug was found.*

6. The main proponents of warning labels for alcoholic beverages have been the manufacturers of these beverages.

F *Most alcohol manufacturers have opposed these labels. They feel that the information on these labels is common knowledge and that the labels may open the door to lawsuits associated with drinkers' previous use and abuse of alcohol.*

7. Research evidence indicates that mass media prevention strategies do not result in significant changes in patterns of alcohol or drug use.

T *Although evidence suggests that these programs do succeed in raising knowledge levels and increasing awareness about the use of drugs, there is no evidence that changes in patterns of use are occurring.*

8. The primary goal of affect-oriented prevention programs is to increase the individual's knowledge base regarding drugs and alcohol.

F *The goal of affect-oriented material is to help participants be aware of their own feelings and attitudes regarding drugs so they can deal effectively with drug-use situations according to their individual value structures.*

9. Research evidence suggests that resistance-oriented prevention programs, such as Project DARE, have been successful in training students in drug-refusal skills.

T *Resistance-oriented prevention programs have been found to effectively teach students drug-refusal skills. However, research concerning long-term patterns of subsequent drug use is lacking.*

10. The focus of most workplace prevention programs is primary prevention.

F *Most current programs focus on secondary rather than primary prevention. Prevention efforts are typically grafted onto treatment programs.*

11. One disadvantage of workplace prevention programs is their cost.

T *Many executives are skeptical of the efficacy and cost-effectiveness of these programs despite the potential of enhanced employee productivity.*

12. The idea of holding people who serve alcohol responsible for the patrons' behavior if they become intoxicated is a recent development in drinking moderation strategies.

F *This idea has its roots in what are referred to as dram shop (old English for "tavern") laws. Various forms of these laws have been enacted in several states and are being considered in many others.*

Appendix

INFORMATION AND TREATMENT RESOURCES

National and Regional Organizations Providing Substance Abuse Information

Al-Anon or Alateen
P.O. Box 182
Madison Square Station
New York, New York 10159-0182

Alcohol and Drug Abuse Education
   Program
U.S. Department of Education
400 Maryland Avenue N.W.
Room 4145, MS6411
Washington, D.C. 20202

Alcohol and Drug Problems Association
   of North America
Hall of States
444 North Capitol Street N.W.
Washington, D.C. 20001

Alcoholics Anonymous
P.O. Box 459
New York, New York 10163

American Alcohol and Drug Information
P.O. Box 10212
Lansing, Michigan 48901-0212

American Council on Alcohol Problems
6955 University Avenue
Des Moines, Iowa 50311

Americans for Non-Smokers Rights
2054 University Avenue
Suite 500
Berkeley, California 94704

Boost Alcohol Consciousness Concerning
   the Health of University Students
(BACCHUS)
c/o Campus Alcohol Information Center
124 Tigert Hall
University of Florida
Gainesville, Florida 32611

Central States Institute of Addictions
Addiction Materials Center
120 W. Huron Street
Chicago, Illinois 60610

Children of Alcoholics Foundation
P.O. Box 4185
Grand Central Station
New York, New York 10163

Citizens for Safe Drivers Against Drunk
   Drivers and Other Chronic Offenders
5632 Connecticut Avenue N.W.
P.O. Box 42018
Washington, D.C. 20015

Co-Dependents Anonymous
P.O. Box 5508
Glendale, Arizona 85312-5508

Distilled Spirits Council of the
   United States
1250 I Street N.W.
Suite 900
Washington, D.C. 20005

Families in Action National Drug
   Information Center
3845 North Druid Hills Road
Suite 300
Decatur, Georgia 30033

Just Say No Foundation
1777 North California Boulevard
Walnut Creek, California 94596

Licensed Beverage Information Council
425 13th Street N.W.
Suite 1300
Washington, D.C. 20004

Mothers Against Drunk Drivers (MADD)
669 Airport Freeway
Hurst, Texas 76053

Narcotics Anonymous
P.O. Box 9999
Van Nuys, California 91409

National Association for Children of
   Alcoholics
P.O. Box 421691
San Francisco, California 94142

National Association of Women in
   Alcoholism and Other Drug
   Dependencies
700 Dimmick Drive
Los Angeles, California 90065

National Clearinghouse on Alcohol and
   Drug Information*
P.O. Box 2345
Rockville, Maryland 20852

National Black Alcoholism Council
417 South Dearborn Street
Suite 1000
Chicago, Illinois 60605

National Council on Alcoholism
12 West 21st Street
7th Floor
New York, New York 10010

National Organization for the Reform of
   Marijuana Laws
2001 S Street N.W.
Suite 640
Washington, D.C. 20009

Office on Smoking and Health
Technical Information Center
5600 Fishers Lane
Room 116
Rockville, Maryland 20857

Remove Intoxicated Drivers (RID)
P.O. Box 520
Schenectady, New York 12301

Rutgers Center of Alcohol Studies
P.O. Box 969
Piscataway, New Jersey 08854

Stop Teenage Addiction to Tobacco
   (STAT)
P.O. Box 50039
Palo Alto, California 94303

Students Against Drunk Driving (SADD)
Box 800
Marlboro, Massachusetts 01752

United States Brewers Association, Inc.
1750 K Street N.W.
Washington, D.C. 20006

Up Front Drug Information
5701 Biscayne Boulevard
Suite 602
Miami, Florida 33137

Women for Sobriety, Inc.
Box 618
Quakerstown, Pennsylvania 18951

STATE AND TERRITORIAL LISTING OF ORGANIZATIONS

Alabama

Alabama Department of Mental
   Health/Mental Retardation
P.O. Box 3710
200 Interstate Park Drive
Montgomery, Alabama 36193

Alaska

Alaska Council on Prevention of Alcohol
   and Drug Abuse
7521 Old Seward Highway
Anchorage, Alaska 99518

*The NCADI is the U.S. federal clearinghouse for information and services on alcohol and other drugs. It is the largest, most comprehensive resource on alcohol and drug information in the world. Most of its materials (for example, pamphlets, booklets, posters, fact sheets, directories, resource lists, and so on) and services are free to the public.

American Samoa

Department of Human Resources
Social Services Division
Government of American Samoa
Pago Pago, American Samoa 96799

Arizona

Office of Community Behavioral Health
Arizona Department of Mental Health
411 North 24th Street
Phoenix, Arizona 85008

Arkansas

Office on Alcohol and Drug Abuse
    Prevention
P.O. Box 1437
400 Donaghey Plaza N.
7th and Main Streets
Little Rock, Arkansas 72203-1437

California

State of California
Department of Alcohol and Drug
    Programs
111 Capitol Mall, Room 250
Sacramento, California 95814-3229

Colorado

Colorado Alcohol and Drug Abuse
    Division
4210 East 11th Avenue
Denver, Colorado 80220

Connecticut

Connecticut Clearinghouse
334 Farmington Avenue
Plainville, Connecticut 06062

District of Columbia

Washington Area Council on Alcoholism
    and Drug Abuse
1232 M Street N.W.
Washington, D.C. 20005

Delaware

The Resource Center of the YMCA of
    Delaware
11th and Washington Streets
Wilmington, Delaware 19801

Florida

Florida Alcohol and Drug Abuse
    Association
1286 North Paul Russell Road
Tallahassee, Florida 32301

Georgia

Department of Human Resources
Division of Mental Health
878 Peachtree Street N.E.
Room 319
Atlanta, Georgia 30309

Guam

Department of Mental Health and
    Substance Abuse
P.O. Box 9400
Tamuning, Guam 96911

Hawaii

Hawaii Substance Abuse Information
    Center
200 North Vineyard Boulevard
Room 603
Honolulu, Hawaii

Idaho

Health Watch Foundation
1076 North Cole Road
Boise, Idaho 83704

Illinois

Prevention Resource Center Library
901 South 2nd Street
Springfield, Illinois 62704

Indiana

Indiana Prevention Resource Center for
    Substance Abuse
840 State Road, 46 Bypass
Room 110
Indiana University
Bloomington, Indiana 47405

Iowa

Iowa Substance Abuse Information
    Center
Cedar Rapids Public Library
500 First Street S.E.
Cedar Rapids, Iowa 52401

Kansas

Kansas Alcohol and Drug Abuse Services
Department of Social and Rehabilitation
   Services
300 S.W. Oakley
Topeka, Kansas 66606

Kentucky

Drug Information Service for Kentucky
Division of Substance Abuse
275 East Main Street
Frankfort, Kentucky 40621

Louisiana

Bureau of Criminal Justice and
   Prevention
Office of Prevention and Recovery from
   Alcohol Abuse
2744-B Wooddale Boulevard
Baton Rouge, Louisiana 70805

Maine

Maine Alcohol and Drug Abuse
   Clearinghouse
Office of Alcoholism and Drug Abuse
   Prevention
State House Station #11
Augusta, Maine 04333

Maryland

Alcohol and Drug Abuse Administration
Department of Health and Mental Hygiene
201 West Preston Street
4th Floor
Baltimore, Maryland 21201

Massachusetts

Massachusetts Information and Referral
   Service
675 Massachusetts Avenue
Cambridge, Massachusetts 02139

Michigan

Michigan Substance Abuse and Traffic
   Safety Information Center
925 East Kalamazoo
Lansing, Michigan 48912

Minnesota

Minnesota Prevention Resource Center
2829 Verndale Avenue
Anoka, Minnesota 55303

Mississippi

Mississippi Department of Mental Health
Division of Alcoholism and Drug Abuse
1101 Robert E. Lee Building
9th Floor
239 N. Lamar Street
Jackson, Mississippi 39207

Missouri

Missouri Division of Alcohol and Drug
   Abuse
1915 Southridge Drive
Jefferson City, Missouri 65109

Montana

Department of Institutions
Chemical Dependency Bureau
1539 11th Avenue
Helena, Montana 59620

Nebraska

Alcohol and Drug Information
   Clearinghouse
Alcoholism Council of Nebraska
215 Centennial Mall South
Room 412
Lincoln, Nebraska 68508

Nevada

Bureau of Alcohol and Drug Abuse
505 East King Street
Suite 500
Carson City, Nevada 89710

New Hampshire

New Hampshire Office of Alcohol and
   Drug Abuse Prevention
6 Hazen Drive
Concord, New Hampshire 03301

New Jersey

New Jersey Department of Health
Division of Narcotic and Drug Abuse
   Control
129 East Hanover Street
Trenton, New Jersey 08625

New Jersey Division of Alcoholism
Training, Prevention, and Education Unit
129 East Hanover Street
Trenton, New Jersey 08625

New Mexico

Health and Environment Department
Substance Abuse Bureau
1190 St. Francis Drive
Harold Runnles Building, Room 3350
Santa Fe, New Mexico 87504-0968

New York

Prevention/Intervention Group
194 Washington Avenue
Albany, New York 12210

Narcotic and Drug Research, Inc.
Resource Center
11 Beach Street
2nd Floor
New York, New York 10013

North Carolina

North Carolina Alcohol/Drug Resource
   Center
G5
1200 Broad Street
Durham, North Carolina 27705

North Dakota

Division of Alcoholism and Drug Abuse
Department of Human Services
1839 East Capitol Avenue
Bismarck, North Dakota 58501

Ohio

Bureau of Drug Abuse and Bureau
   on Alcohol Abuse and Alcoholism
   Recovery
170 North High Street
3rd Floor
Columbus, Ohio 43266-0586

Oklahoma

Oklahoma State Department of Mental
   Health
P.O. Box 53277
Oklahoma City, Oklahoma 73152

Oregon

Oregon Drug and Alcohol Information
   Center
235 North Graham
Portland, Oregon 97227

Pennsylvania

Pennsylvania Department of Health
Department of Health Programs
P.O. Box 2773
Harrisburg, Pennsylvania 17105

Puerto Rico

Department of Anti-Addiction Services
Apartado 21414-Rio Piedras Station
Rio Piedras, Puerto Rico 00928-1414

Rhode Island

Rhode Island Division of Substance
   Abuse
Substance Abuse Administration Building
Cranston, Rhode Island 02920

South Carolina

South Carolina Commission on Alcohol
   and Drug Abuse
The Drug Store Information Clearinghouse
3700 Forest Drive
Suite 300
Columbia, South Carolina 29204

South Dakota

Department of Health
Division of Alcohol and Drug Abuse
523 East Capitol
Joe Foss Building Room 125
Pierre, South Dakota 57501

Tennessee

Division of Alcohol and Drug Abuse
   Services
Tennessee Department of Mental Health
706 Church Street
4th Floor
Nashville, Tennessee 37216

Texas

Texas Commission on Alcohol and Drug
   Abuse Resource Center
1705 Guadalupe
Austin, Texas 78701-1214

Utah

Division of Substance Abuse
120 North 200 West
4th Floor
P.O. Box 4550
Salt Lake City, Utah 84145-0500

Vermont

Office of Alcohol and Drug Abuse
    Programs
103 South Main Street
Waterbury, Vermont 05676

Virgin Islands

Division of Mental Health, Alcoholism,
    and Drug Dependency
P.O. Box 1117
St. Croix, Virgin Islands 00821

Virginia

Office of Substance Abuse Services
State Department of Mental Health and
    Mental Retardation
P.O. Box 1797
109 Governor Street
Richmond, Virginia 23214

Washington

Washington State Substance Abuse
    Coalition
14700 Main Street
Bellevue, Washington 98007

West Virginia

Division of Alcohol and Drug Abuse
State Capitol
1800 Westington Street E.
Room 451
Charleston, West Virginia 25305

Wisconsin

Wisconsin Clearinghouse
University of Wisconsin-Madison
1245 East Washington Avenue
Madison, Wisconsin 53701

Wyoming

Division of Community Programs
Office of Substance Abuse
351 Hathaway Building
Cheyenne, Wyoming 82002-0710

SOME PROFESSIONAL JOURNALS FOCUSING ON SUBSTANCE ABUSE TOPICS

These are available at most university and medical school libraries.

Addiction
Addictive Behaviors
Advances in Alcohol and Substance Abuse
Alcohol
Alcoholism: Clinical and Experimental Research
Alcoholism Treatment Quarterly
American Journal of Drug and Alcohol Abuse
Contemporary Drug Problems
Drug and Alcohol Dependence
Drugs and Society
International Journal of the Addictions
Journal of Chemical Dependency Treatment
Journal of Drug Educations
Journal of Drug Issues
Journal of Substance Abuse Treatment
Journal of Studies on Alcohol
Pharmacology, Biochemistry and Behavior
Psychology of Addictive Behaviors
Psychopharmacology

Glossary

A

Absorbed. Drugs are absorbed, or entered into, the bloodstream (Chapter 4).

Acetaminophen (ah-seat-ah-MIN-ah-fen). Aspirin-like analgesic (Chapter 15).

Acetylcholine (ass-it-teel-KOLE-een). A neurotransmitter found both in the brain and in the parasympathetic branch of the autonomic nervous system (Chapter 3).

Acetylsalicylic Acid (ah-seat-ill-sal-iss-ill-ik). Chemical name for aspirin (Chapter 15).

Action Potential. The electrical impulse along the axon that occurs when a neuron "fires" (Chapter 3).

Acute Tolerance. A type of functional tolerance that occurs within a course of action of a single drug dose (Chapter 5).

Addiction. In reference to drugs, overwhelming involvement with use of a drug, getting an adequate supply of it, and a strong tendency to resume use of it after stopping for a period (Chapter 1).

Addictive Personality. The hypothesis of a personality structure common to all people with substance abuse disorder (Chapter 5).

Aftercare. In alcohol and drug treatment, this term usually refers to therapeutic activities following completion of a formal treatment program (Chapter 16).

Agitated Depression. Depressed mood accompanied by a state of tension or restlessness. Person shows excessive motor activity, as he or she may, for example, be unable to sit still, pace, wring the hands, or pull at his or her clothes (Chapter 11).

Agonist (AG-o-nist). A substance that occupies a neural receptor and causes some change in the conductance of the neuron (Chapter 3).

Akinesia. Slowness of movement and underactivity (Chapter 11).

Alzheimer's Disease (ALLZ-hi-merz). One of the most common forms of senility among the elderly, Alzheimer's disease involves a progressive loss of memory and other cognitive functions (Chapter 3).

Amotivational Syndrome. A term used to describe a loss of effectiveness and reduced capacity to accomplish conventional goals as a result of chronic marijuana use (Chapter 13).

Amphetamine. A central nervous system stimulant whose actions are similar to those of the naturally occurring adrenaline (Chapter 2).

Anabolic Steroids. Tissue-building drugs, which produce masculinizing effects as well (Chapter 15).

Analgesia. Pain relief produced without a loss of consciousness (Chapter 12).

Anorectic Effects. Causing one to lose appetite—suppression of eating (Chapter 6).

Antagonism. The diminished or reduced effect of a drug when another drug is present (Chapter 4).

Antagonist. A substance that occupies a neural receptor, but blocks normal synaptic transmission (Chapter 3).

Anterograde Amnesia. Loss or limitation of the ability to form new memories (Chapter 10).

Anticholinergic Hallucinogens. A class of drugs including atropine and scopolamine (Chapter 14).

Antihistamines. Common OTC drugs with decongestant effects (Chapter 15).

Antitussives. Cough suppressant drugs (Chapter 15).

Anxiolytic. Anxiety-reducing (Chapter 10).

Apothecary. A pharmacist (Chapter 13).

As a Function of. A term expressing causality. In graphing functional relationships between two variables, changes in one variable (in this case, drug effect) resulting from changes in another (in this case, drug dose) are represented (Chapter 4).

Atropine. An anticholinergic hallucinogen found in certain plants (Chapter 14).

Attention Deficit Disorder. A disorder of childhood with features such as greater than normal amount of activity, restlessness, difficulty concentrating or sustaining attention, and impulsivity (Chapter 5).

Autonomic Nervous System. Part of the PNS, the autonomic nervous system or ANS has two branches: the sympathetic and parasympathetic (Chapter 3).

Avoirdupois. Something sold or measured by weight based on the pound of 16 ounces (Chapter 2).

Axon. A long cylindrical extension of the cell body of the neuron. The axon conducts an electrical charge from the cell body to the axon terminals (Chapter 3).

Axon Terminal (or Terminal Button). Enlarged button-like structures that occur at the end of axon branches (Chapter 3).

B

Barbiturates. Depressant drugs formerly used as sleeping pills. Currently used in anesthesia and treatment for epilepsy (Chapter 10).

Basal Ganglia (BAY-sell GANG-lee-ah). Forebrain structures important for motor control. The basal ganglia include the caudate nucleus, the putamen, and the globus pallidus (Chapter 3).

Behavioral Pharmacology. The specialty area of psychopharmacology that concentrates on drug use as a learned behavior (Chapter 5).

Behavioral Tolerance. Adjustment of behavior through experience using a drug to compensate for its intoxicating effects (Chapter 5).

Benzodiazepines. Currently the most widely prescribed anxiolytic drugs (Chapter 10).

Beta-Blockers. Drugs that block beta-adrenergic receptors of the sympathetic system and thus act to relieve high blood pressure (Chapter 3).

Bioavailability. The portion of the original drug dose that reaches its site of action, or that reaches a fluid in the body that gives it access to its site of action (Chapter 4).

Blackout. A person's failure to recall events that occurred while drinking even though there is no loss of consciousness (Chapter 9).

Blood-Brain Barrier. A term given to the system that "filters" the blood before it can enter the brain (Chapter 3).

Brand Name. The commercial name given to a drug by its manufacturer (Chapter 5).

C

Cannabinoids. A general term to describe the more than 60 chemical compounds present in cannabis. One of these cannabinoids is delta-9-tetrahydrocannabinol (better known as THC) (Chapter 13).

Cannabis Sativa. The Indian hemp plant popularly known as marijuana; its resin, flowering tops, leaves, and stem contain the plant's psychoactive substances (Chapter 2).

Causal Relationship. There is a causal relationship between variables if changes in a second variable are due directly to changes in a first variable (Chapter 5).

Central Nervous System. The brain and the spinal cord comprise the central nervous system or CNS (Chapter 3).

Cerebellum (sair-ah-BELL-um). Hindbrain structure important in motor control and coordination (Chapter 3).

Chemical Name. The name given to a drug that represents its chemical structure (Chapter 5).

Combination Pill. Birth control pill containing synthetic forms of both female sex hormones: progesterone and estrogen (Chapter 15).

Computerized Axial Tomography (CAT). The CAT scan is a technique for developing a three-dimensional X-ray image of the brain (Chapter 3).

Confabulation. A fabrication about events, when asked questions concerning them, because of an inability to recall (Chapter 9).

Conflict Paradigm. A research procedure that concerns the effects of a drug on a behavior that has a history of both reinforcement and punishment (Chapter 5).

Control. In research, control means to be able to account for variables that may affect the results of a study (Chapter 4).

Control Group. In an experiment, the control group is the reference or comparison group. The control group does not receive the experimental manipulation or intervention whose effect is being tested (Chapter 5).

Cortex. The cerebral cortex or cortex is the outermost and largest part of the human brain (Chapter 3).

Counseling. In alcohol and drug treatment, counselors are specially trained professionals who perform a variety of treatment activities, including assessment, education, and individual, marital, or family counseling (Chapter 16).

Crack. A freebase cocaine produced by mixing cocaine salt with baking soda and water. The solution is then heated, resulting in brittle sheets of cocaine that are "cracked" into small, smokeable chunks or "rocks" (Chapter 6).

Craving. A term that has been variously defined in reference to drug use. Typically it refers to a strong or intense desire to use a drug (Chapter 1).

Cross Tolerance. Tolerance to a drug or drugs never taken that results from protracted tolerance to another drug or drugs (Chapter 5).

D

Delta-9-Tetrahydrocannabinol. The principal active cannabinoid in marijuana responsible for the experienced psychoactive effects (Chapter 13).

Dendrite. Spiny branch-like structures that extend from the cell body of a neuron. Dendrites typically contain numerous receptor sites and are thus important in neural transmission (Chapter 3).

Desipramine. An antidepressant medication (Chapter 16).

Diffusibility. A more diffusible substance is more easily entered into, or "receptive" of another (Chapter 4).

Dispositional Tolerance. An increase in the rate of metabolizing a drug as a result of its regular use (Chapter 5).

Dissociative Anesthetic. A class of drugs including PCP and ketamine (Chapter 14).

Dissolved. A drug is dissolved by converting it from solid to liquid by mixing the drug with a liquid (Chapter 4).

Distillation. Process by which the heating of a fermented mixture increases its alcohol content (Chapter 9).

Distribution. Drugs are distributed, or transported, by the blood to their site(s) of action in the body (Chapter 4).

Disulfiram. A drug that interferes with the metabolism of alcohol so that a person soon feels very ill if he or she drinks while in a regimen of disulfiram. The drug may be used as part of a treatment program for alcohol dependence (Chapter 9).

Dopamine (DOP-ah-meen). A neurotransmitter found in the brain (Chapter 3).

Drug. Broadly defined as any chemical entity or mixture of entities, not required for the maintenance of health, that alters biological function or structure when administered (Chapter 1).

Drug Abuse. Any use of drugs that causes physical, psychological, legal, or social harm to the individual user or to others affected by the drug user's behavior (Chapter 1).

Drug Discrimination Study. A research procedure that primarily concerns the differentiation of drug effects (Chapter 5).

Drug Dosage. Measure of the quantity of drug consumed (Chapter 1).

Drug Effect. The action of a drug on the body. Drug effects are measured in different ways (Chapter 1).

Drug Expectancy. A person's anticipation of or belief about what he or she will experience upon taking a drug (Chapter 5).

Drug Potency. The dose of a drug that yields its maximal effect (Chapter 4).

Dyskinesia. Disordered movements (Chapter 11).

E

Effective Dose. The percentage of individuals who show a given effect of a drug at a given dose (Chapter 4).

Electroencephalography (EEG). Technique used to measure electrical activity in the brain (Chapter 3).

Endogenous. Developed from within. When applied to depression, the term means that depressive symptoms seem to be due to genetic factors (Chapter 11).

Endorphins (en-DORE-finz). Neurotransmitters found in the brain that are mimicked by opiate drugs (Chapter 3).

Enzyme Breakdown. One process by which neurotransmitters are inactivated. Chemicals called enzymes interact with the transmitter molecule and change its structure so that it no longer is capable of occupying receptor sites (Chapter 3).

Estrogen (ESS-troh-jen). One of the female sex hormones involved in the regulation of ovulation and the menstrual cycle (Chapter 15).

Exogenous. Developed from without. When applied to depression, the term means that depressive symptoms seem to be in reaction to a particular situation or event (Chapter 11).

Extrapyramidal. Outside the pyramidal tracts, with origin in the basal ganglia. These cell bodies are involved with starting, stopping, and smoothing out movements (Chapter 11).

F

Feedback. In this context, in a series of events, what happens in a later event alters those preceding it (Chapter 4).

Fermentation. A combustive process in which yeasts interact with the sugars in plants, such as grapes, grains, and fruits, to produce an enzyme that converts the sugar into alcohol (Chapter 2).

Flashback. A sudden recurrence of an LSD-like experience (Chapter 14).

Forebrain. The largest part of the human brain, the forebrain includes the cerebral cortex, thalamus, hypothalamus and the limbic system (Chapter 3).

Formication Syndrome. Symptoms of itching and feeling as if insects were crawling on skin caused by cocaine and ampthetamine (Chapter 6).

Freebase. A substance may be separated, or "freed," from its salt base. The separated form of the substance is thus called "freebase" (Chapter 4).

Functional Tolerance. Decreased behavioral effects of a drug as a result of its regular use (Chapter 5).

G

GABA. Short for gamma-amino-butyric acid, a neurotransmitter found in the brain (Chapter 3).

General Anesthesia. The reduction of pain by rendering the subject unconscious (Chapter 10).

Generalizable. Applicability of a research finding from one setting or group of research participants to another (Chapter 5).

Generic Name. The general name given to a drug that is shorter (and easier for most people to say) than its chemical name (Chapter 5).

Grain. As a measure, a unit of weight equal to .0648 of a gram (Chapter 1).

Group Design. A type of experimental design in which groups (as compared to individual cases) of subjects are compared to establish experimental findings (Chapter 5).

Guaifenesin (guay-FEN-eh-sin). An OTC expectorant (Chapter 15).

H

Half-Life. The amount of time that must pass for the amount of drug in the body to be reduced by half (Chapter 4).

Hash Oil. A potent distillate of marijuana or hashish. It first appeared in the United States in 1971, and can contain up to 60% THC (Chapter 13).

Hashish. Produced from the resin that covers the flowers of the cannabis hemp plant. This plant resin generally contains a greater concentration of the drug's psychoactive properties (Chapter 2).

Heroin. Heroin is produced by chemically processing morphine. It is more potent than morphine, and has become the major opiate drug of abuse (Chapter 12).

Hindbrain. The lower part of the brain including the medulla, pons, and cerebellum (Chapter 3).

Hippocampus (hip-poe-KAMP-us). A structure of the limbic system thought to be important in the formation of memories (Chapter 3).

Homeostasis. A state of equilibrium or balance. Systems at homeostasis are stable; when homeostasis is disrupted, the system operates to restore it (Chapter 5).

Humanism. A system of thought and culture that emphasizes human interests instead of the natural world or religion (Chapter 16).

Hyperactive Children. Disorder of childhood involving restlessness, inability to be attentive, and disruptive behavior. Today referred to as "attention-deficit hyperactivity disorder" (Chapter 6).

Hypothalamus (HIGH-poe-THAL-ah-muss). Forebrain structure that regulates eating, drinking, and other basic biological drives (Chapter 3).

I

Ibuprofen (ih-BYOU-proh-fen). Aspirin-like analgesic (Chapter 15).

Inferior Colliculi (ko-LICK-you-lie). Midbrain structures that control sound localization (Chapter 3).

Initial Sensitivity. The effect of a drug on a first-time user (Chapter 5).

Interact. An interaction occurs between two drugs if the effects of one drug are modified by the presence of another (Chapter 4).

Intoxication. A transient state of physical and psychological disruption due to the presence of a toxic substance, such as alcohol, in the CNS (Chapter 9).

J

Joint. A hand-rolled marijuana cigarette (Chapter 13).

K

Ketamine. A dissociative anesthetic (Chapter 14).

Kindling. Repeated exposure to a stimulus may lower the brain's threshold for seizures. This effect, which is produced by electrical stimulation or by cocaine, is called kindling (Chapter 6).

Korsakoff's Syndrome. A disorder characterized by memory loss and psychotic behavior related to heavy use of alcohol and malnutrition (Chapter 3).

L

L-Dopa (el-DOPE-ah). A chemical precursor of dopamine used in the treatment of Parkinson's disease (Chapter 3).

Lethal Dose. The percentage of individuals who are killed by a given dose of a drug within a specified time (Chapter 4).

Levo-Alpha-Acetylmethadol (LAAM). A drug used in treating heroin addiction that is similar in action to methadone but has longer-lasting effects (Chapter 16).

Limbic System. Forebrain structures including the amygdala, hippocampus, and others (Chapter 3).

Long-Term Memory. Memory for remote events. According to one theory of memory, information enters long-term memory through short-term memory (Chapter 9).

M

Magnetic Resonance Imaging (MRI). This technique creates a high-resolution, three-dimensional image of the brain (Chapter 3).

Manic. Relating to mania, a mood disturbance which typically includes hyperactivity, agitation, excessive elation, and pressured speech (Chapter 11).

MAO Inhibitors. Drugs used to treat depressions that inhibit the activity of the enzyme monoamineoxidase, which degrades the neurotransmitters of norepinephrine and serotonin (Chapter 9).

Mass Media. Communications designed for widespread distribution, such as advertisements, films, and printed materials (Chapter 17).

Maximal Effect. The most intense, or peak, level of a drug effect (Chapter 4).

Medial Forebrain Bundle. Pathway that is rewarding when stimulated. Thus it is often referred to as the pleasure center (Chapter 3).

Medulla Oblongata (meh-DULL-ah ah-blong-GOT-ah). The lowest hindbrain structure of the brain, the medulla is important in the regulation of breathing, heart rate, and other basic life functions (Chapter 3).

Mescaline. An LSD-like hallucinogen that is found in the peyote cactus (Chapter 14).

Metabolism. The process by which the body breaks down matter into more simple components and waste (Chapter 4).

Methylated Amphetamines. A class of drugs including MDA and MMDA (ecstasy) (Chapter 14).

Midbrain. Includes the inferior and superior colliculi (Chapter 3).

Milieu Treatment. Treatment in which the organization and structure of a setting are designed to change behavior (Chapter 16).

Monoamine (mon-o-AM-mean). A class of chemicals characterized by a single amine group. This class includes neurotransmitters: norepinephrine, dopamine, and serotonin (Chapter 3).

Morphine. A derivative of opium that is best known as a potent pain-relieving medication (Chapter 2).

Myelin (MY-a-lin). A fatty white substance that covers the axons of some neurons (Chapter 3).

N

Naloxone (Narcane). A short-acting opiate antagonist (Chapter 12).

Narcoleptic. A state characterized by brief but uncontrollable episodes of sleep (Chapter 11).

Narcotic. A central nervous system depressant that contains sedative and pain-relieving properties (Chapter 2).

Neuroleptic. Tranquilizing drugs used to treat psychoses. Another term for neuroleptic is major tranquilizer (Chapter 11).

Neuromuscular Junction. Junction between neuron and muscle fibers where release of acetylcholine by neurons causes muscles to contract (Chapter 3).

Neuron (NUR-on). The individual nerve cell that is the basic building block of the nervous system (Chapter 3).

Neuropsychological Tests. Formal ways of measuring behavioral functions that may be impaired by brain lesions (Chapter 9).

Neuroses. A term that in common usage describes any non-psychotic emotional disturbance, pain, or discomfort beyond what is appropriate in the conditions of one's life (Chapter 11).

Neurotransmitters. Chemical substances stored in the axon terminals that are released into the synapse when the neuron fires. Neurotransmitters then influence activity in post-synaptic neurons (Chapter 3).

Nicotine Poisoning. A consequence of nicotine overdose, characterized by palpitations, dizziness, sweating, nausea, or vomiting (Chapter 7).

Norepinephrine (nor-ep-in-EFF-rin). A neurotransmitter found in the brain and involved in activity of the sympathetic branch of the autonomic nervous system (Chapter 3).

O

Opium. The dried sap produced by the poppy plant (Chapter 12).

Opium Poppy. A plant cultivated for centuries, primarily in Eurasia, for opium, a narcotic that acts as a central nervous system depressant (Chapter 2).

Orientation to Time. Awareness of temporal specification, such as time of day, the day of the week, or the year. Orientation to time is one of the functions assessed in a psychiatric exam (Chapter 9).

Over-the-Counter (OTC) Drugs. Drugs that can be legally obtained without medical prescription (Chapter 1).

P

Paradoxical. Contrary to what is expected. A paradoxical drug effect is one that is opposite in direction to what is expected, based on the drug's chemical structure (Chapter 5).

Paranoid Schizophrenia. A type of schizophrenia distinguished by systematic delusions or auditory hallucinations related to one theme (Chapter 11).

Parasympathetic Branch. The branch of the ANS that is responsible for lowering heart rate, blood pressure, and so on (Chapter 3).

Parkinson's Disease. A disease that primarily afflicts the elderly and involves a progressive deterioration of motor control (Chapter 3).

Peripheral Nervous System. Sensory nerves, motor nerves, and the autonomic nervous sytem comprise the peripheral nervous sytstem or PNS (Chapter 3).

Personality Disorder. Long-standing patterns of behavior that frequently create distress for the individual due to their personal or social consequences. These patterns are usually recognizable from adolescence or earlier (Chapter 16).

Peyote (pay-YO-tea). A cactus plant, the top of which (a "button") is dried and ingested for its hallucinogenic properties (Chapter 2).

Pharmacodynamics. The branch of pharmacology that concerns the biochemical and physiological effects of drugs and their mechanisms of action (Chapter 4).

Pharmacokinetics. The branch of pharmacology that concerns the absorption, distribution, biotransformation, and excretion of drugs (Chapter 4).

Pharmacology. The scientific study of drugs; concerned with all information about the effects of drugs on living systems (Chapter 1).

Phencyclidine. A dissociative anesthetic (Chapter 14).

Phenolic Compound. Compounds contained in or derived from phenol, a compound produced from coal tar (Chapter 9).

Phenylpropanolamine (feen-ill-proh-pan-OH-lah-meen). A mild stimulant with decongestant and appetite suppressant properties (PPA) (Chapter 15).

Placebo. In pharmacology, refers to a chemically inactive substance (Chapter 1).

Placebo Control. A type of control originating in drug research. Placebo subjects are of the same makeup and are treated exactly like a group of subjects who receive a drug, except that placebo subjects receive a chemically inactive substance (Chapter 5).

Polydrug Use. The same person's regular use of more than one drug (Chapter 1).

Pons (pahnz). Hindbrain structure important in the control of sleep and wakefulness (Chapter 3).

Positron Emission Transaxial Tomography (PETT or PET). The PET scan is a technique used to measure activity in selected brain regions (Chapter 3).

Prevalence. The general occurrence of an event, usually expressed in terms of percentage of some population. Another common statistic in survey studies is incidence, or the number of first-time occurrences of an event during some time period (Chapter 1).

Primary Prevention. Attempts to avoid substance use or abuse before it has a chance to occur (Chapter 17).

Progesterone (proh-JEST-er-own). One of the female sex hormones that are involved with the regulation of ovulation and the menstrual cycle (Chapter 15).

Progestin Pill. Birth control pill that contains only progestin—a synthetic progesterone (Chapter 15).

Prohibition. The legislative forbidding of the sale of a substance, as in the alcohol Prohibition Era in the U.S., 1920–1933 (Chapter 2).

Proof. A term used to designate the proportion of alcohol in a beverage, by volume. Proof typically is used in reference to distilled spirits and equals twice the percentage of alcohol (Chapter 9).

Prostaglandins (pross-tah-GLAND-inz). Naturally occurring chemicals blocked by aspirin and related analgesics (Chapter 15).

Protracted Tolerance. A type of functional tolerance that occurs over the course of two or more drug administrations (Chapter 5).

Pseudoephedrine (soo-doh-eff-EHD-rin). An OTC decongestant (Chapter 15).

Psilocybin (sihl-oh-SIGH-bin). An LSD-like hallucinogen found in mushrooms (Chapter 14).

Psychoactive. Pertaining to effects on mood, thinking, and behavior (Chapter 1).

Psychological Dependence. The emotional state of craving a drug either for its positive effect or to avoid negative effects associated with its abuse (Chapter 1).

Psychological Set. An individual's knowledge, attitudes, expectations, and other thoughts about an object or event, such as a drug (Chapter 1).

Psychological Treatment. Treatments geared to changing emotions, thoughts, or behavior without the use of medications or other physical or biological means (Chapter 16).

Psychology. The scientific study of behavior (Chapter 1).

Psychopharmacology. The subarea of pharmacology that concerns the effects of drugs on behavior (Chapter 1).

Psychosis. A severe mental disorder whose symptoms include disorganized thinking and bizarre behavior (Chapter 5).

Psychosurgery. Surgery which entails the cutting of fibers connecting particular parts of the brain or the removal or destruction of areas of brain tissue with the goal of modifying severe behavioral or emotional disturbances (Chapter 11).

Psychotherapy. Typically, conversation between a specially trained individual (therapist) and another person (or family) that is intended to change patterns of behavior, thoughts, or feelings in that person (Chapter 16).

Psychotropic. Any substance that exerts a special or unique action on psychological functioning (Chapter 11).

Punisher. A consequence of behavior that suppresses or decreases its likelihood (Chapter 5).

Pylorospasm. The shutting of the pylorus valve that occurs in some people when very large quantities of alcohol are consumed (Chapter 9).

Q

Qualitative. The kind, as opposed to quantity, of effect (Chapter 4).

R

Rebound Insomnia. Inability to sleep produced as a withdrawal symptom associated with some depressant drugs (Chapter 10).

Receptor Sites. Specialized structures located on dendrites and cell bodies for neurons which are activated by neurotransmitters (Chapter 3).

Recovery. In the addictions field, this term means changes back to health in physical, psychological, spiritual, and social functioning. It generally is believed that recovery is a lifetime process that requires total abstinence from alcohol and nonprescribed drugs (Chapter 16).

Reinforcer. A consequence of behavior that increases its likelihood (Chapter 5).

REM Rebound. An increase in the rapid eye movement or REM stage of sleep when withdrawing from drugs that suppress REM time (Chapter 10).

REM Sleep. Acronym for "rapid eye movements," which are associated with dream activity and are one stage in a cycle of sleep (Chapter 9).

Relapse. A term from physical disease, relapse means return to a previous state of illness from one of health. As applied to smoking, it means the smoker resumes smoking after having abstained for some amount of time (Chapter 7).

Reticular Activating System. Pathway running through the medulla and pons that regulates alertness and arousal (Chapter 3).

Reuptake. Another process by which neurotransmitters are inactivated. Neurotransmitter molecules are taken back up into the axon terminal that released them (Chapter 3).

Reverse Tolerance. Increased sensitivity to a drug with repeated use of it (Chapter 5).

Route of Drug Administration. The way that drugs enter the body (Chapter 1).

S

Scopolamine. An anticholinergic hallucinogen found in certain plants (Chapter 14).

Secondary Prevention. Interventions designed to prevent substance use problems just as the early signs of abuse begin to appear (Chapter 17).

Sedative-Hypnotic Effects. The ability of some drugs to produce a calming effect and induce sleep (Chapter 10).

Self-Administration Study. A study that involves testing whether research participants will "give themselves" a drug (Chapter 5).

Self-Medication. The idea that some people prescribe their own medication, in the form of alcohol or illicit drugs, to alleviate psychological difficulties such as anxiety or depression (Chapter 16).

Serotonergic Hallucinogens. A class of drugs including LSD and drugs with similar effects and mechanisms of action (Chapter 14).

Serotonin (sair-o-TONE-in). A neurotransmitter found in the brain (Chapter 3).

Short-Term Memory. Memory for recent events. Short-term memory generally is thought to differ from long-term memory in several important ways (Chapter 9).

Side Effects. Effects of a drug other than those of central interest. Used most often in reference to the other-than-therapeutic effects of medications, such as the side effect of drowsiness for antihistamines. Note that what are considered a drug's side effects depends on what specifically the drug is being used for (Chapter 4).

Social Detoxification. Treatment of alcohol withdrawal without the use of medicine (Chapter 9).

Sociopathy. A type of personality disorder that is characterized by a lack of concern for social obligations or rules, a lack of feelings for others, and a tendency toward violence (Chapter 16).

Solubility. The ease with which a compound can be dissolved or entered into a solution (Chapter 4).

Solvent. A substance, usually a liquid or gas, that contains one or more intoxicating components. Examples include glue, gasoline, and nonstick frying pan sprays (Chapter 2).

Speakeasy. A slang expression used to describe a saloon operating without a license. The term was popularly used during Prohibition (Chapter 2).

Spontaneous Remission. Resolution of a problem without the help of formal treatment (Chapter 16).

Standard Drink. The alcohol equivalent in a drink of beer, wine, or distilled spirits. A standard drink equals a half-ounce of alcohol, which is about the amount in 12 ounces of beer, 4 ounces of table wine, or 1 ounce of 90–100 proof whiskey (Chapter 9).

State-Dependent Learning. Learning under the influence of a drug is best recalled when in the same "state" (Chapter 6).

Stimulant Psychosis. Paranoid delusions and disorientation resembling the symptoms of paranoid schizophrenia caused by prolonged use or overdose of cocaine and/or an amphetamine (Chapter 6).

Substantia Nigra (sub-STAN-sha NIE-gruh). Literally, "black substance," this basal ganglia structure is darkly pigmented. The substantia nigra produces dopamine. Damage to this area produces Parkinson's disease (Chapter 3).

Superior Colliculi. Midbrain structures that control visual localization (Chapter 3).

Suspended. A drug is suspended in solution if its particles are dispersed in solution but not dissolved in it (Chapter 4).

Sympathetic Branch. Branch of the ANS that is activated during emotional arousal and is responsible for such physiological changes as increased heart and respiratory rate, increased blood pressure, and pupil dilation (Chapter 3).

Sympathomimetic. Term applied to drugs such as cocaine and amphetamine which produce the physiological effects of sympathetic activity (Chapter 3).

Synapse (SIN-naps). The junction between neurons (Chapter 3).

Syndrome. In medicine, a number of symptoms occurring together and characterizing a specific illness or disease (Chapter 1).

Synergism. Used here to mean any enhancing drug interaction (Chapter 4).

Synesthesia. An effect sometimes produced by hallucinogens characterized by the perception of a stimulus in a modality other than the one in which it was presented (e.g., a subject may report "seeing" music) (Chapter 14).

T

Tardive Dyskinesia. An extrapyramidal complication characterized by involuntary movements of the mouth and tongue, trunk, and extremities. Tardive dyskinesia is a side effect of long-term (two or more years) use of antipsychotic drugs (Chapter 11).

Tea-Pad. Historically, a place where people gathered to smoke marijuana. The site could be anywhere from a rented room to a hotel suite (Chapter 13).

Teratogenic. Producing abnormalities in the fetus (Chapter 11).

Teratology. In biology, the study of monsters, or distortions in growth (Chapter 9).

Tertiary Prevention. Refers to treatment interventions with persons well beyond the early stages of substance abuse or dependence (Chapter 17).

Testosterone. The male sex hormone. Anabolic steroids are basically synthetic versions of testosterone (Chapter 15).

Thalamus (THAL-ah-muss). Forebrain structure that organizes sensory input (Chapter 3).

Therapeutic Index. A measure of a drug's utility in medical care, it is computed as a ratio (LD 50/ED 50) (Chapter 4).

Tolerance. Generally, a diminished drug effect with its continued use (Chapter 1).

Treatment. Planned activities designed to change some pattern of behavior(s) of individuals or their families (Chapter 16).

Treatment Effects. The results of experiencing a treatment, usually measured in different areas of functioning, such as substance use, family functioning, and vocational functioning (Chapter 16).

Treatment Outcome Research. Research designed to show a causal relationship between undergoing a treatment and some physical, psychological, or social change (Chapter 16).

V

Values Clarification. A frequent component of affect-oriented prevention programs, it typically involves exploration of one's own needs and beliefs regarding drugs (Chapter 17).

Vesicles (VES-ik-ulls). Tiny sacs located in axon terminals that store neurotransmitters (Chapter 3).

W

Withdrawal. A definable illness that occurs with a cessation or decrease in use of a drug (Chapter 1).

References

Chapter 1

A

American Psychiatric Association (1987). *Diagnostic and statistical manual of mental disorders*. (3rd edition—rev.). Washington, DC: Author.

B

Blum, K. (1984). *Handbook of abusable drugs*. New York: Gardner Press, Inc.

G

Goldman, A. (1971). *Ladies and gentlemen, Lenny Bruce!* New York: Random House.

H

Helzer, J. (1993). Personal communication, January.

J

Jacobs, M. R., & Fehr, K. O'B. (1987). *Drugs and drug abuse: A reference text* (2nd edition). Toronto: Addiction Research Foundation.

K

Krogh, D. (1991). *Smoking: The artificial passion*. New York: W.H. Freeman & Co.

M

Mendelson, J. H., & Mello, N. K. (1985). *Alcohol: Use and abuse in America*. Boston: Little, Brown & Co.

N

Nathan, P. E. (1991). Substance use disorders in the DSM-IV. *Journal of Abnormal Psychology*, 100, 356–361.

R

Rice, D. P., Kelman, S., Miller, L. S., & Dunmeyer, S. (1990). *The economic costs of alcohol and drug abuse and mental illness: 1985*. San Francisco: Institute for Health and Aging.

Rinaldi, R. C., Steindler, E. M., Wilford, B. B., & Goodwin, D. (1988). Clarification and standardization of substance abuse terminology. *Journal of the American Medical Association*, 259, 555–557.

U

U.S. Department of Health and Human Services (1993a). *Preliminary estimates from the 1992 National Household Survey on Drug Abuse: Selected excerpts*. Washington, DC: Substance Abuse and Mental Health Services Administration.

U.S. Department of Health and Human Services (1993b). *National Household Survey on Drug Abuse: Highlights 1991*. Washington, DC: Substance Abuse and Mental Health Services Administration.

W

World Health Organization (1981). Nomenclature and classification of drugs and alcohol-related problems: A WHO memorandum. *Bulletin of the World Health Organization, 59,* 225–242.

Z

Zinberg, N. E. (1984). *Drug, set, and setting.* New Haven, CT: Yale University Press.

Chapter 2

A

Aaron, P., & Musto, D. (1981). Temperance and prohibition in America: A historical overview. In M. H. Moore & D. R. Gerstein (Eds.), *Alcohol and public policy.* Washington, DC: Academy Press.

B

Blum, K. (1984). *Handbook of abusable drugs.* New York: Gardner Press.

Brecher, E. M. (1972). *Licit and illicit drugs.* Boston: Little, Brown & Co.

Brecher, E. M. (1986). Drug laws and drug law enforcement: A review and evaluation based on 111 years of experience. *Drugs and Society, 1,* 1–27.

C

Clinger, O. W., & Johnson, N. A. (1951). Purposeful inhalation of gasoline vapors. *Psychiatric Quarterly, 25,* 557–567.

Cohen, S. (1981). *The substance abuse problems.* New York: Haworth Press.

G

Goode, E. (1972). *Drugs in American society.* New York: Alfred A. Knopf.

Government Printing Office (GPO). (1972). *Drug abuse: Games without winners.* Washington, DC: Author.

H

Hofmann, F. G. (1975). *A handbook on drug and alcohol abuse.* New York: Oxford University Press.

L

Lender, M. E., & Martin, J. K. (1982). *Drinking in America.* New York: The Free Press.

M

Mellaart, J. (1967). *Catal Huyuk: A neolithic town in Anatolia.* New York: McGraw-Hill.

Morgan, H. W. (1981). *Drugs in America: A social history, 1800–1980.* Syracuse: Syracuse University Press.

N

Nahas, G. G. (1973). *Marijuana—Deceptive weed.* New York: Raven Press.

O

O'Brien, R., & Cohen, S. (1984). *The encyclopedia of drug abuse.* New York: Facts on File, Inc.

W

Whitaker, B. (1987). *The global connection: The crisis of drug addiction.* London: Jonathan Cade.

Chapter 3

B

Bradford, H. F. (1986). *Chemical neurobiology: An introduction to neurochemistry.* New York: W. H. Freeman and Co.

C

Carlson, N. R. (1991). *Foundations of physiological psychology,* (4th edition). Boston: Allyn and Bacon, Inc.

Carpenter, W. T., & Buchanan, R. W. (1994). Schizophrenia. *The New England Journal of Medicine, 330,* 681–690.

Cooper, J. R., Bloom, F. E., & Roth, R. H. (1991). *The biochemical basis of neuropharmacology* (6th edition). New York: Oxford Press.

Crow, T. J., & Deakin, J. F. W. (1979). Monoamines and the psychoses. In K. Brown & S. J. Cooper (Eds.), *Chemical influences on behavior* (pp. 503–533). London: Academic Press.

D

Dackis, C. A., & Gold, M. S. (1985). New concepts in cocaine addiction: The dopamine depletion hypothesis. *Neuroscience and Biobehavioral Reviews, 9,* 469–477.

Dykstra, L. (1992). Drug action. In J. Grabowski & G. R. VandenBos (Eds.), *Psychopharmacology: Basic mechanisms and applied interventions* (pp. 59–96). Washington: American Psychological Association.

G

Goeders, N. E., Dworkin, S. I., & Smith, J. E. (1986). Neuropharmacological assessment of cocaine self-administration into the medial prefrontal cortex. *Pharmacology, Biochemistry, and Behavior, 24,* 1429–1440.

J

Johanson, C. E. (1992). Biochemical mechanisms and pharmacological principles of drug action. In J. Grabowski & G. R. VandenBos (Eds.), *Psychopharmacology: Basic mechanisms and applied interventions* (pp. 11–58). Washington: American Psychological Association.

K

Kramer, P. (1993). *Listening to Prozac*. New York: Viking Press.

Kruk, Z. L., & Pycock, C. J. (1979). *Neurotransmitters and drugs*. Baltimore: University Park Press.

L

Logue, A. W. (1991). *The psychology of eating and drinking* (2nd edition). New York: W. H. Freeman and Co.

M

Markey, S. P., Castagnoli, N., Trevor, A. J., & Kopin, I. J. (Eds.) (1986). *MPTP: A neurotoxin producing a Parkinsonian syndrome*. Orlando, FL: Academic Press.

O

Olds, J., & Milner, P. (1954). Positive reinforcement produced by electrical stimulation of septal area and other regions of rat brains. *Journal of Comparative and Physiological Psychology, 47*, 419–427.

S

Snyder, S. H., Burt, D. R., & Creese, I. (1976). Dopamine receptor of mammalian brain: Direct demonstration of binding to agonist and antagonist states. *Neuroscience Symposia, 1*, 28–49.

W

Wise, R. A. (1989). The brain and reward. In S. J. Cooper & J. M. Liebman (Eds.), *The neuropharmacological basis for reward* (pp. 377–424). Oxford: Clarendon Press.

Chapter 4

A

Abel, E. L. (1985). *Psychoactive drugs and sex*. New York: Plenum Press.

B

Bangert-Drowns, R. L. (1988). The effects of school-based substance abuse education: A meta-analysis. *Journal of Drug Education, 18*, 243–264.

Benet, L. Z., Mitchell, J. R., & Sheiner, L. B. (1990). General Principles. In A. G. Gilman, T. W. Rall, A. S. Nies, & P. Taylor (Eds.), *Goodman and Gilman's The pharmacological basis of therapeutics* (8th edition) (pp. 1–2). New York: Pergamon Press.

Benet, L. Z., Mitchell, J. R., & Sheiner, L. B. (1990a). Pharmacokinetics: The dynamics of drug absorption, distribution, and elimination. In A. G. Gilman, T. W. Rall, A. S. Nies, & P. Taylor (Eds.), *Goodman and Gilman's The pharmacological basis of therapeutics* (8th edition) (pp. 3–32). New York: Pergamon Press.

B

Botvin, G. J., & Botvin, E. M. (1992). School-based and community-based prevention approaches. In J. H. Lowinson, P. Ruiz, & R. B. Millman (Eds.), *Substance abuse: A comprehensive textbook* (2nd edition) (pp. 910–927). Baltimore: Williams & Wilkins.

C

Clark, W. G., Brater, D. C., & Johnson, A. R. (Eds.) (1988). *Goth's medical pharmacology* (12th edition). St. Louis: The C.V. Mosby Co.

F

Flay, B. R. (1985). What we know about the social influences to smoking prevention: Review and recommendations. In C. Bell & R. Battjes (Eds.), *Prevention research: Deterring drug abuse among children and adolescents* (pp. 67–112). Rockville, MD: National Institute on Drug Abuse.

H

Hilts, P. J. (1993). Needle exchanges defended in study. The *Pittsburgh Post-Gazette*, October 1, p. A-8.

J

Jacobs, M. R., & Fehr, K. O'B. (1987). *Drugs and drug abuse* (2nd edition). Toronto: Addiction Research Foundation.

Johanson, C. E. (1992). Biochemical mechanisms and pharmacological principles of drug action. In J. Grabowski & G. R. VandenBos (Eds.), *Master lecture series. Psychopharmacology: Basic mechanisms and applied interventions* (pp. 11–58). Washington, DC: American Psychological Association.

K

Kivlahan, D. R., Marlatt, G. A., Fromme, K., Coppen, D. B., & Williams, E. (1990). Secondary prevention with college drinkers: Evaluation of an alcohol skills training program. *Journal of Consulting and Clinical Psychology, 58*, 805–810.

L

Leavitt, F. (1982). Drugs and behavior (2nd edition). New York: John Wiley & Sons.

Lewis, J. A. (1991). Alcohol abuse prevention in industrial settings. In B. Forster & J. C. Salloway (Eds.), *Preventions and treatments of alcohol and drug abuse* (pp. 137–152). Lewiston, NY: Edwin Mellen Press.

M

Marlatt, G. A., Larimer, M. E., Baer, J. S., & Quigley, L. A. (1993). Harm reduction for alcohol problems: Moving beyond the controlled drinking controversy. *Behavior Therapy, 24*, 461–504.

Mazis, M. B., Morris, L. A., & Swasy, J. L. (1991). An evaluation of the alcohol warning label: Initial survey results. *Journal of Public Policy and Marketing*, 10, 229–241.

Miller, N. S. (1991). The pharmacology of alcohol and drugs of abuse and addiction. New York: Springer-Verlag.

P

Pellow, R. A., & Jengeleski, J. L. (1991). A survey of current research studies on drug education programs in America. *Journal of Drug Education*, 21, 203–210.

R

Rice, D. P. (1991). Estimates of economic costs of alcohol and drug abuse and mental illness: 1985–1988. *Public Health Reports*, 106, 280–292.

Ross, E. M., & Gilman, A. G. (1985). Pharmacodynamics: Mechanisms of drug action and the relationship between drug concentration and effect. In A. G. Gilman, L. S. Goodman, T. W. Rall, & F. Murod (Eds.), *Goodman and Gilman's The pharmacological basis of therapeutics* (7th edition) (pp. 35–48). New York: Macmillan Publishing Co.

S

Scammon, D. L., Mayer, R. N., & Smith, K. R. (1991). Alcohol warnings: How do you know when you have had one too many? *Journal of Public Policy and Marketing*, 10, 214–228.

Schleifer, S. J., Delaney, B. R., Tross, S., & Keller, S. F. (1991). AIDS and addiction. In R. J. Francis & S. I. Miller (Eds.), *Clinical textbook of addictive disorders* (pp. 299–319). New York: The Guilford Press.

W

Wester, R. C., & Maibach, H. I. (1983). Cutaneous pharmacokinetics: 10 steps to percutaneous absorption. *Drug Metabolism Reviews*, 14, 169–205.

White, J. M. (1991). *Drug dependence*. Englewood Cliffs, NJ: Prentice Hall.

Y

Young, A. M., & Herling, S. (1986). Drugs as reinforcers: Studies in laboratory animals. In S. R. Goldberg & I. P. Stolerman (Eds.), *Behavioral analysis of drug dependence* (pp. 9–68). Orlando: Academic Press.

Chapter 5

B

Baldessarini, R. J. (1985). *Chemotherapy in psychiatry: Principles and practice* (rev. ed.). Cambridge, MA: Harvard University Press.

Barnes, G. E. (1979). The alcoholic personality: A re-analysis of the literature. *Journal of Studies on Alcohol*, 40, 571–634.

Barrett, R. J. (1985). Behavioral approaches to individual differences in substance abuse. In M. Galizio & S. A. Maisto (Eds.), *Determinants of substance abuse: Biological, psychological, and environmental factors* (pp. 125–175). New York: Plenum Press.

Becker, H. (1963). *Outsiders*. New York: The Free Press.

Bozarth, M. A. (Ed.). (1987). *Methods of assessing the reinforcing properties of drugs*. New York: Springer-Verlag.

Brecher, E. M. (1972). *Licit and illicit drugs*. Boston: Little, Brown & Co.

Budney, A., Higgins, S. T., Delaney, D. D., Kent, L., & Bickel, W. K. (1991). Contingent reinforcement of abstinence with individuals abusing cocaine and marijuana. *Journal of Applied Behavior Analysis*, 24, 657–665.

C

Carlin, A. S., Bakker, C. B., Halpern, L., & Post, R. D. (1972). Social facilitation of marijuana intoxication: Impact of social set and pharmacological activity. *Journal of Abnormal Psychology*, 80, 132–140.

Cicero, T. J. (1980). Alcohol self-administration, tolerance, and withdrawal in humans and animals: Theoretical and methodological issues. In H. Rigter & J. Crabbe, Jr. (Eds.), *Alcohol tolerance and dependence* (pp. 1–50). Amsterdam: Elsevier/North-Holland Biomedical Press.

Colpaert, F. C. (1987). Drug discrimination: Methods of manipulation, measurement, and analysis. In M. A. Bozarth (Ed.), *Methods of assessing the reinforcing properties of drugs* (pp. 341–372). New York: Springer-Verlag.

Cox, W. M. (1986). *The addictive personality*. New York: Chelsea.

Crowley, T. J. (1981). The reinforcers for drug abuse: Why people take drugs. In H. Shaffer & M. E. Burglass (Eds.), *Classic contributions in the addictions* (pp. 367–381). New York: Brunner/Mazel.

F

Fisher, L. M. (1992, October 6). New drugs by process of elimination. *The New York Times*, pp. D1, D13.

G

Goldstein, J. W., & Sappington, J. T. (1977). Personality characteristics of students who became heavy drug users: An MMPI study of an avant garde. *American Journal of Drug and Alcohol Abuse*, 4, 401–412.

Griffiths, R. R., & Woodson, D. P. (1988). Reinforcing properties of caffeine: Studies in human and laboratory animals. *Pharmacology, Biochemistry, and Behavior, 29,* 419–427.

H

Henningfield, J. E., Lukas, S. E., & Bigelow, G. E. (1986). Human studies of drugs as reinforcers. In S. R. Goldberg & I. Stolerman (Eds.), *Behavioral analysis of drug dependence* (pp. 69–122). Orlando, FL: Academic Press.

Higgins, S. T., Delaney, D. D., Budney, A. J., Bickel, W. K., Hughes, J. R., Foerg, F., & Fenwick, J. W. (1991). A behavioral approach to achieving initial cocaine abstinence. *American Journal of Psychiatry, 148,* 1218–1224.

Hinson, R. E. (1985). Individual differences in tolerance and relapse: A Pavlovian conditioning perspective. In M. Galizio & S. A. Maisto (Eds.), *Determinants of substance abuse: Biological, psychological, and environmental factors* (pp. 101–124). New York: Plenum Press.

Hull, J. G., & Bond, C. F. (1986). Social and behavioral consequences of alcohol consumption: A meta analysis. *Psychological Bulletin, 99,* 347–360.

J

Jacobs, M. R., & Fehr, K. O'B. (1987). *Drugs and drug abuse* (2nd edition). Toronto: Addiction Research Foundation.

Johanson, C. E., & Uhlenhuth, E. H. (1978). Drug self-administration in humans. In N. A. Krasnegor (Ed.), *Self-administration of abused substances: Methods for study* (NIDA Research Monograph 20, pp. 68–87). Washington, DC: U.S. Government Printing Office.

K

Kalant, H., LeBlanc, A. E., & Gibbins, R. J. (1971). Tolerance to, and dependence on, some nonopiate psychotropic drugs. *Pharmacological Reviews, 23,* 135–191.

Koob, G. F., & Bloom, F. E. (1988). Cellular and molecular mechanisms of drug dependence. *Science, 242,* 715–723.

M

MacAndrew, C., & Edgerton, R. B. (1969). *Drunken comportment.* Chicago: Aldine.

McCarty, D. (1985). Environmental factors in substance abuse: The microsetting. In M. Galizio & S. A. Maisto (Eds.), *Determinants of substance abuse: Biological, psychological, and environmental factors* (pp. 247–282). New York: Plenum Press.

McKercher, P. L. (1992). Pharmaceutical research and development. *Clinical Therapeutics, 14,* 760–764.

Mello, N. K., & Griffiths, R. R. (1987). Alcoholism and drug abuse: An overview. In H. Y. Meltzer (Ed.), *Psychopharmacology: The third generation of progress* (pp. 1511–1514). New York: Raven Press.

N

Nurnberger, J. I., Jr. (1987). Pharmacogenetics of psychoactive drugs. *Journal of Psychiatric Research, 21,* 499–505.

O

Orcutt, J. D. (1987). Differential association and marijuana use: A closer look at Sutherland (with a little help from Becker). *Criminology, 25,* 341–358.

P

Pliner, P., & Cappell, H. (1974). Modification of affective consequences of alcohol: A comparison of social and solitary drinking. *Journal of Abnormal Psychology, 89,* 224–233.

S

Sher, K. J. (1987). Stress response dampening. In H. T. Blane & K. E. Leonard (Eds.), *Psychological theories of drinking and alcoholism* (pp. 227–271). New York: The Guilford Press.

Sher, K. J., & Levenson, R. W. (1982). Risk for alcoholism and individual differences in the stress-dampening effect of alcohol. *Journal of Abnormal Psychology, 91,* 350–368.

Solomon, R. L., & Corbit, J. D. (1974). An opponent-process theory of motivation: I. Temporal dynamics of affect. *Psychological Review, 81,* 119–145.

Spiegel, R., & Aebi, H. (1983). *Psychopharmacology.* New York: John Wiley & Sons.

T

Tabakoff, B., & Hoffman, P. L. (1988). Tolerance and the etiology of alcoholism: Hypothesis and mechanism. *Alcoholism: Clinical and Experimental Research, 12,* 184–186.

Tyrer, P. J. (1982). Evaluation of psychotropic drugs. In P. J. Tyrer (Ed.), *Drugs in psychiatric practice.* London: Butterworths.

V

Vuchinich, R. E., & Tucker, J. A. (1988). Contributions from behavioral theories of choice to an analysis of alcohol abuse. *Journal of Abnormal Psychology, 97,* 181–195.

W

Walters, P. G. (1992). FDA's new drug evaluation process: A general overview. *Journal of Public Health and Dentistry, 52,* 333–337.

Y

Young, A. M., & Herling, S. (1986). Drugs as reinforcers: Studies in laboratory animals. In S. R. Goldberg &

I. Stolerman (Eds.), *Behavioral analysis of drug dependence* (pp. 9–68). Orlando, FL: Academic Press.

Z

Zinberg, N. E. (1984). *Drug, set, and setting*. New Haven: Yale University Press.

Zuckerman, M. (1979). *Sensation seeking: Beyond the optimal level of arousal*. New York: John Wiley & Sons.

Chapter 6

A

Abel, E. L. (1985). *Psychoactive drugs and sex*. New York: Plenum Press.

Aigner, T. G., & Balster, R. L. (1978). Choice behavior in rhesus monkeys: Cocaine versus food. *Science, 201*, 534–535.

Allen, D. F. (1987). History of cocaine. In D. F. Allen (Ed.), *The cocaine crisis* (pp. 7–15). New York: Plenum Press.

Ashley, R. (1975). *Cocaine: Its history, uses, and effects*. New York: Warner.

B

Bozarth, M. A., & Wise, R. A. (1985). Toxicity associated with long-term intravenous heroin and cocaine self-administration in the rat. *Journal of the American Medical Association, 254*, 81–83.

Brecher, E. M. (1972). *Licit and illicit drugs*. Boston: Little, Brown & Co.

Byck, R. (Ed.) (1974). *Cocaine papers by Sigmund Freud*. New York: Stonehill Publishing Company.

C

Caldwell, J., Croft, J. E., & Sever, P. S. (1980). Tolerance to the amphetamines: An examination of possible mechanisms. In J. Caldwell & S. J. Mule (Eds.), *Amphetamines and related stimulants: Chemical, biological, clinical and sociological aspects* (pp. 131–146). Boca Raton, FL: CRC Press.

D

Dackis, C. A., & Gold, M. S. (1985). New concepts in cocaine addiction: the dopamine depletion hypothesis. *Neuroscience and Biobehavioral Reviews, 9*, 469–477.

Davis, J. M., & Schlemmer, R. F. (1980). The amphetamine psychosis. In J. Caldwell & S. J. Mule (Eds.), *Amphetamines and related stimulants: Chemical, biological, clinical, and sociological aspects* (pp. 161–174). Boca Raton, FL: CRC Press.

E

Ellinwood, E. H. (1980). Neuropharmacology of amphetamines and related stimulants. In J. Caldwell &

S. J. Mule (Eds.), *Amphetamines and related stimulants: Chemical, biological, clinical, and sociological aspects* (pp. 69–84). Boca Raton, FL: CRC Press.

F

Fischman, M. W. (1984). The behavioral pharmacology of cocaine in humans. In J. Grabowski (Ed.), *Cocaine: Pharmacology, effects and treatment of abuse*. Research Monograph 50, National Institute on Drug Abuse, Washington, DC.

Fischman, M. W., Schuster, C. R., Javaid, J., Hatano, Y., & Davis, J. (1985). Acute tolerance development to the cardiovascular and subjective effects of cocaine. *Journal of Pharmacology and Experimental Therapeutics, 235*, 677–682.

Foltin, R. W., & Fischman, M. W. (1992). The cardiovascular and subjective effects of intravenous cocaine and morphine combinations in humans. *Journal of Pharmacology and Experimental Therapeutics, 261*, 623–632.

Foltin, R. W., & Fischman, M. W. (1993). Self-administration of smoked cocaine by humans. In L. Harris (Ed.), *Problems of Drug Dependence, 1992*. Research Monograph 132 (p. 63). National Institute on Drug Abuse, Washington, DC.

G

Gawin, F. H. (1991). Cocaine addiction: Psychology and neurophysiology. *Science, 251*, 1580–1586.

Goeders, N. E., Dworkin, S. I., & Smith, J. E. (1986). Neuropharmacological assessment of cocaine self-administration into the medial prefrontal cortex. *Pharmacology, Biochemistry, and Behavior, 24*, 1429–1440.

Grinspoon, L., & Bakalar, J. B. (1976). *Cocaine: A drug and its social evolution*. New York: Basic Books Inc.

H

Hawks, R. L., & Chiang, C. N. (1986). *Urine testing for drugs of abuse*. Research Monograph 73, National Institute on Drug Abuse, Washington, DC.

Higgins, S. T., & Stitzer, M. L. (1988). Time allocation in a concurrent schedule of social interaction and monetary reinforcement: effects of d-amphetamine. *Pharmacology, Biochemistry, and Behavior, 31*, 227–231.

Hughes, C. E., & Branch, M. N. (1991). Tolerance to and residual effects of cocaine in squirrel monkeys depend on reinforcement-schedule parameter. *Journal of the Experimental Analysis of Behavior, 56*, 345–361.

I

Inciardi, J. A. (1992). *The war on drugs* II. Mountain View, CA: Mayfield Publishing Co.

Inciardi, J. A., Lockwood, D., & Pottieger, A. E. (1993). *Women and crack-cocaine*. New York: Macmillan Publishing Co.

J

Jones, R. T. (1984). The pharmacology of cocaine. In J. Grabowski (Ed.), *Cocaine: Pharmacology, effects and treatment of abuse*. Research Monograph 50 (pp. 34–53). National Institute on Drug Abuse, Washington, DC.

Jones, R. T. (1987). The psychopharmacology of cocaine. In A. M. Washton & M. S. Gold (Eds.), *Cocaine: A Clinician's Handbook* (pp. 55–72). New York: Guilford Press.

K

Katz, J. J., Terry, P., & Witkin, J. M. (1992). Comparative behavioral pharmacology and toxicology of cocaine and its ethanol-derived metabolite, cocaine ethyester (cocaethylene). *Life Sciences*, 50, 1351–1361.

Kennedy, J. (1985). *Coca exotica*. Cranbury, NJ: Associated University Presses, Inc.

Kirsch, M. M. (1986). *Designer drugs*. Minneapolis: CompCare Publications.

Koob, G. F., & Bloom, F. E. (1988). Cellular and molecular mechanisms of drug dependence. *Science*, 242, 715–723.

L

Laties, V. G., & Weiss, B. (1981). The amphetamine margin in sports. *Federation Proceedings*, 40, 2689–2692.

M

Mortimer, W. G. (1901). *Peru: History of coca "The divine plant" of the Incas*. New York: J. H. Vail.

N

National Institute on Drug Abuse. (1991). *Annual Emergency Room Data: 1990*. National Institute on Drug Abuse, Washington, DC.

Newsweek (1993). Death on the spot: The end of a drug king. December 12, pp. 18–20.

Newsweek (1989). A tide of drug killing. January 16, pp. 44–45.

O

Overton, D. A. (1985). Contextual stimulus effects of drugs and internal states. In P. D. Balsam & A. Tomie (Eds.), *Context and learning* (pp. 357–384). Hillsdale, NJ: Lawrence Erlbaum Associates.

P

Perez-Reyes, M., DiGuiseppi, S., & Ondrusek, G. (1982). Freebase cocaine smoking. *Clinical Pharmacology and Therapeutics*, 32, 459–465.

Petersen, R. C. (1977). History of cocaine. In R. C. Petersen & R. C. Stillman (Eds.), *Cocaine: 1977*. Research Monograph 13 (pp. 17–34). National Institute on Drug Abuse, Washington, DC.

Post, R. M. (1977). Progressive changes in behavior and seizures following chronic cocaine administration: Relationship to kindling and psychosis. In E. H. Ellinwood & M. M. Kilbey (Eds.), *Cocaine and Other Stimulants* (pp. 353–372). New York: Plenum.

R

Rapoport, J. L., Buchsbaum, M. S., Zahn, T. P., Weingartner, H., Hudlow, C., & Mikkelsen, E. J. (1978). Dextroamphetamine: Cognitive and behavioral effects in normal prepubertal boys. *Science*, 199, 560–563.

S

Safer, D. J., Allen, R. P., & Barr, E. (1975). Growth rebound after termination of stimulant drugs. *Journal of Pediatrics*, 86, 113–116.

Seigel, R. K. (1984). Changing patterns of cocaine use: Longitudinal observations, consequences and treatment. In J. Grabowski (Ed.), *Cocaine: Pharmacology, effects, and treatment of abuse*. Research Monograph 50 (pp. 92–110). National Institute on Drug Abuse, Washington, DC.

Seigel, R. K. (1985). New patterns of cocaine use: Changing doses and routes. In N. J. Kozel & E. H. Adams (Eds.), *Cocaine use in America: Epidemiological and clinical perspectives*. NIDA Research Monograph 61, pp. 204–220.

Singer, L., Farkas, K., & Kleigman, R. (1992). Childhood medical and behavioral consequences of maternal cocaine use. *Journal of Pediatric Psychology*, 17, 389–406.

Sorer, H. (1992). *Acute cocaine intoxication: Current methods of treatment*. Research Monograph 123, National Institute on Drug Abuse, Washington, DC.

W

Washton, A. M. (1987). Cocaine: Drug epidemic of the '80's. In D. F. Allen (Ed.), *The cocaine crisis* (pp. 45–64). New York: Plenum Press.

Weiss, R. D., & Mirin, S. M. (1987). *Cocaine*. Washington, DC: American Psychiatric Press, Inc.

Wise, R. A. (1984). Neural mechanisms of the reinforcing action of cocaine. In J. Grabowski (Ed.), *Cocaine: Pharmacology, effects, and treatment of abuse*. Research Monograph 50 (pp. 15–33). National Institute on Drug Abuse, Washington, DC.

Woodward, B. (1984). *Wired: The short life and fast times of John Belushi*. New York: Pocket Books.

Chapter 7

A

Abrams, D. B., & Wilson, G. T. (1986). Habit disorders: Alcohol and tobacco dependence. In A. J. Frances & R. E. Hales (Eds.), *American Psychiatric Association*

Annual Review (Vol. 5) (pp. 606–626). Washington, DC: American Psychiatric Press, Inc.

B

Benowitz, N. L., Porchet, H., Sheiner, L., & Jacob, P. (1988). Nicotine absorption and cardiovascular effects with smokeless tobacco use: Companion with cigarettes and nicotine gum. *Clinical Pharmacology and Therapeutics*, 44, 23–28.

Blum, K. (1984). *Handbook of abusable drugs.* New York: Gardner Press.

Bonham, G., & Wilson, R. (1981). Children's health in families with cigarette smokers. *American Journal of Public Health*, 71, 290–293.

Brecher, E. M. (1972). *Licit and illicit drugs.* Mount Vernon, NY: Consumers Union.

C

Chen, Y., Horne, S. L., & Dosman, J. A. (1993). The influence of smoking cessation on body weight may be temporary. *American Journal of Public Health*, 83, 1330–1332.

Cotton, P. (1993). Low tar cigarettes come under fire. *Journal of the American Medical Association*, 270, 1399.

Coultas, D. B., Stidley, C. A., & Samet, J. M. (1993). Cigarette yields of tar and nicotine and markers of exposure to tobacco smoke. *American Review of Respiratory Disease*, 148, 435–440.

Curry, S. J. (1993). Self-help interventions for smoking cessation. *Journal of Consulting and Clinical Psychology*, 61, 790–803.

D

DeGrandpre, R. J., Dickle, W. K., Hughes, J. R., & Higgins, S. T. (1992). Behavioral economics of drug self-administration, III. A reanalysis of the nicotine regulation hypothesis. *Psychopharmacology*, 108, 1–10.

E

Edwards, D. D. (1986). Nicotine: A drug of choice? *Science News*, 129, 44–45.

Eliopoulos, C., Klein, J., Phan, M., Knie, B., Greenwald, M., Chitayat, D., & Koren, G. (1994). Hair concentrations of nicotine and cotinine in women and their newborn infants. *Journal of the American Medical Association*, 271, 621–623.

Ernster, V. L. (1993). Women and smoking. *American Journal of Public Health*, 83, 1202–1203.

G

Gilbert, R. M. (1976). Caffeine as a drug of abuse. In R. J. Gibbins, Y. Israel, H. Kalant, R. E. Popham, W. Schmidt, & R. G. Smart (Eds.), *Research advances in alcohol and drug problems* (Vol. 3) (pp. 49–176). New York: John Wiley & Sons.

Gilbert, R. M. (1984). Caffeine consumption. *Progress in Clinical Biological Research*, 158, 185–213.

Glantz, S. A., & Parmley, W. W. (1991). Passive smoking and heart disease. *Circulation*, 83, 1–12.

Goldstein, M. G., & Niaura, R. (1991). Nicotine gum. In J. A. Cocores (Ed.), *The clinical management of nicotine dependence* (pp. 181–195). New York: Springer-Verlag.

Gritz, E. R., Ksir, C., & McCarthy, W. J. (1985). Smokeless tobacco use in the United States: Present and future trends. *Annals of Behavioral Medicine*, 7, 24–27.

H

Hughes, J. R. (1993). Pharmacotherapy for smoking cessation: Unvalidated assumptions, anomalies, and suggestions for future research. *Journal of Consulting and Clinical Psychology*, 61, 751–760.

Hughes, J. R., Grist, S. W., & Pechacek, T. F. (1987). Prevalence of tobacco dependence and withdrawal. *American Journal of Psychiatry*, 144, 205–208.

Hughes, J. R., Hatsukami, D. K., Mitchell, J. E., & Dahlgren, L. A. (1986). Prevalence of smoking among psychiatric outpatients. *American Journal of Psychiatry*, 143, 993–997.

Hurt, R. D., Dale, L. C., Fredrickson, P. A., Caldwell, C. C., Lee, G. A., Offord, K. P., Langer, G. G., Marusic, Z., Neese, L. W., & Lundberg, T. G. (1994). Nicotine patch therapy for smoking cessation combined with physician advice and nurse follow-up. *Journal of the American Medical Association*, 271, 595–600.

J

Jaffe, J. H. (1990). Drug addiction and drug abuse. In A. G. Gilman, T. W. Rall, A. S. Nies, & P. Taylor (Eds.), *The pharmacological basis of therapeutics* (8th edition) (pp. 522–573). New York: Pergamon Press.

Jarvis, M. (1983). The treatment of cigarette dependence. *British Journal of Addiction*, 78, 125–130.

Johnston, L. D., O'Malley, P. M., & Bachman, J. G. (1993). *National survey results on drug use from monitoring the future study, 1975–1992.* Washington, DC: U.S. Government Printing Office.

Jones, R. T. (1987). Tobacco dependence. In H. Y. Meltzer (Ed.), *Psychopharmacology: The third generation of progress* (pp. 1589–1595). New York: Raven Press.

Julien, R. M. (1992). *A primer of drug action* (6th edition). New York: W. H. Freeman & Co.

K

Kenford, S. L., Fiore, M. C., Jorenby, D. E., Smith, S. S., Wetter, D., & Baker, T. B. (1994). Predicting smoking cessation. Who will quit with and without the nicotine patch. *Journal of the American Medical Association*, 271, 589–594.

Klesges, R. C., Meyers, A. W., Klesges, L. M., & La Vasque, M. E. (1989). Smoking, body weight, and their effects on smoking behavior: A comprehensive review of the literature. *Psychological Bulletin*, 106, 204–230.

Krogh, D. (1991). *Smoking: The artificial passion*. New York: W. H. Freeman & Co.

L

LaCroix, A. Z., Lang, J., Scherr, P., Wallace, R. B., Cornoni-Huntley, J., Berkman, L., Curb, D., Evans, D., & Hennekens, C. H. (1991). Smoking and mortality among older men and women in three communities. *New England Journal of Medicine*, 324, 1619–1625.

Lichenstein, E. (1982). The smoking problem: A behavioral perspective. *Journal of Consulting and Clinical Psychology*, 50, 804–819.

P

Page, L. (1988). Arizona 'smokeless' cigarette to be withdrawn. *American Medical News*, 31, 1:33.

Pierce, J. P., Lee, L., & Gilpin, E. A. (1994). Smoking initiation by adolescent girls, 1944 through 1988. *Journal of the American Medical Association*, 271, 608–611.

R

Rose, J. E. (1991). Transdermal nicotine and nasal nicotine administration as smoking cessation treatments. In J. A. Cocores (Ed.), *The clinical management of nicotine dependence* (pp. 196–207). New York: Springer-Verlag.

Russell, M. A. H. (1976). Tobacco smoking and nicotine dependence. In R. J. Gibbins, Y. Israel, H. Kalant, R. E. Popham, W. Schmidt, & R. G. Smart (Eds.), *Research advances in alcohol and drug problems* (Vol. 3) (pp. 1–47). New York: John Wiley & Sons.

S

Schelling, T. C. (1986). Economics and cigarettes. *Preventive Medicine*, 15, 549–560.

Schivelbusch, W. (1992). *Taste of paradise*. New York: Pantheon Books.

Sesser, S. (1993). Opium war redux. *The New Yorker*, LXIX, pp. 78–82, 84–89.

Shiffman, S. (1993). Smoking cessation treatment: Any progress? *Journal of Consulting and Clinical Psychology*, 61, 718–722.

Shopland, D. R., & Brown, C. (1985). Changes in cigarette smoking prevalence in the U.S., 1955 to 1983. *Annals of Behavioral Medicine*, 7, 5–8.

Stewart, G. C. (1967). A history of the medical use of tobacco. *Medical History*, 11, 228–268.

T

Taylor, P. (1990). Agents acting at the neuromuscular junction and autonomic ganglia. In A. G. Gilman, T. W. Rall, A. S. Nies, & P. Taylor (Eds.), *The phar-macological basis of therapeutics* (8th edition) (pp. 166–186). New York: Pergamon Press.

The Lancet (1993). Controlling the weed in public (Editorial). *The Lancet*, 341, 525–526.

U

U.S. Department of Health and Human Services (1987). *Smoking, tobacco, and health. A fact book*. Rockville, MD: U.S. Public Health Service.

U.S. Department of Health and Human Services (1989). *Reducing the health consequences of smoking: 25 years of progress*. Rockville, MD: U.S. Public Health Service.

U.S. Department of Health and Human Services (1993a). *National Household Survey on Drug Abuse: Highlights 1991*. Washington, DC: Substance Abuse and Mental Health Services Administration.

V

Viscusi, W. K. (1992). *Smoking: Making the risky decision*. New York: Oxford University Press.

W

West, R. J., & Russell, M. A. H. (1985). Nicotine pharmacology and smoking dependence. In S. D. Iverson (Ed.), *Psychopharmacology: Recent advances and future prospects* (pp. 303–314). Oxford: Oxford University Press.

West, R., & Schneider, N. (1987). Craving for cigarettes. *British Journal of Addiction*, 82, 407–415.

Wilkinson, J. (1986). *Tobacco: The facts behind the smoke screen*. Middlesex, England: Penguin Books.

Wynder, E. L., & Hoffmann, D. (1979). Tobacco and health: A societal challenge. *The New England Journal of Medicine*, 300, 894–903.

Z

Zusy, A. (1987). For smokers, ways to quit are many, but the goal is elusive. *The New York Times*, July 15, pp. C1, C10.

Chapter 8

A

Abbott, P. J. (1986). Caffeine: A toxicological overview. *The Medical Journal of Australia*, 145, 518–521.

American Psychiatric Association (1987). *Diagnostic and statistical manual* (3rd edition—rev.). Washington, DC: Author.

B

Bak, A. A., & Grobbee, D. E. (1989). The effect on serum cholesterol levels of coffee brewed by filtering or boiling. *New England Journal of Medicine*, 321, 1432–1437.

Barrett-Connor, E., Chang, J. C., & Edelstein, S. L. (1994). Coffee-associated osteoporosis offset by daily milk consumption. *Journal of the American Medical Association, 271,* 280–283.

Benowitz, N. L., Hall, S. M., & Modin, G. (1989). Persistent increase in caffeine concentrations in people who stop smoking. *British Medical Journal, 298,* 1075–1076.

Blum, K. (1984). *Handbook of abusable drugs.* New York: Gardner Press.

Bruce, M., Scott, N., Shine, P., & Lader, M. (1992). Anxiogenic effect of caffeine in patients with anxiety disorders. *Archives of General Psychiatry, 49,* 867–869.

C

Clementz, G. L., & Dailey, J. W. (1988). Psychotropic effects of caffeine. *AFP, 37,* 167–172.

Consumer Reports (1991). Coffee and cholesterol: Hold that second cup? *Consumer Reports,* January, 40.

Council on Scientific Affairs (1984). Caffeine labeling. *Journal of the American Medical Association, 252,* 803–806.

Curatolo, P. W., & Robertson, D. (1983). The health consequences of caffeine. *Annals of Internal Medicine, 98,* 641–653.

D

D'Amicis, A., & Viani, R. (1993). The consumption of coffee. In S. Garattini (Ed.), *Caffeine, coffee, and health* (pp. 1–16). New York: Raven Press.

G

Gilbert, R. M. (1976). Caffeine as a drug of abuse. In R. J. Gibbins, Y. Israel, H. Kalant, R. E. Popham, W. Schmidt, & R. G. Smart (Eds.), *Research advances in alcohol and drug problems* (Vol. 3) (pp. 49–176). New York: John Wiley & Sons.

Gilbert, R. M. (1984). Caffeine consumption. *Progress in Clinical Biological Research, 158,* 185–213.

Goldstein, A. S., Kaizer, S., & Whitby, O. (1969). Psychotropic effects of caffeine in man. IV. Quantitative and qualitative differences associated with habituation to coffee. *Clinical and Pharmacological Therapeutics, 10,* 489–497.

Graham, D. M. (1978). Caffeine: Its identity, dietary sources, intake and biological effects. *Nutrition Reviews, 36,* 97–102.

Greden, J. F. (1974). Anxiety or caffeinism: A diagnostic dilemma. *American Journal of Psychiatry, 131,* 1089–1092.

Greden, J. F., & Walters, A. (1992). Caffeine. In J. H. Lowinson, P. Ruiz, & R. B. Millman (Eds.), *Substance abuse: A comprehensive textbook* (2nd edition) (pp. 357–370). Baltimore: Williams & Wilkins.

Griffiths, R. R., & Woodson, P. P. (1988). Caffeine physical dependence: A review of human and animal laboratory studies. *Psychopharmacology, 94,* 437–451.

Grobbee, D., Rimm, E., Giovannucci, E., Colditz, G., Stampfer, M., & Willett, W. (1990). Coffee, caffeine, and cardiovascular disease in men. *The New England Journal of Medicine, 323,* 1026–1032.

H

Hughes, J. R., Oliveto, A. H., Helzer, J. E., Higgins, S. T., & Bickel, W. K. (1992). Should caffeine abuse, dependence or withdrawal be added to DSM-IV or ICD-10? *American Journal of Psychiatry, 149,* 33–40.

I

Infante-Rivard, C., Fernandez, A., Gauthier, R., David, M., & Rivard, G. E. (1993). Fetal loss associated with caffeine intake before and during pregnancy. *Journal of the American Medical Association, 270,* 2940–2943.

J

James, J. E. (1991). *Caffeine and health.* New York: Academic Press.

Julien, R. M. (1992). A *primer of drug action* (6th edition). New York: W.H. Freeman & Co.

K

Kenny, M., & Darragh, A. (1985). Central effects of caffeine in man. In S. D. Iversen (Ed.), *Psychopharmacology: Recent advances and future prospects* (pp. 278–288).

Konner, M. (1988). Caffeine high. *New York Times Magazine,* January 17, pp. 47–48.

Koslowski, L. T., Henningfield, R. M., Keenan, R. M., Lei, H., Leigh, G. Jelinek, L. C., Pope, M. A., & Haertzen, C. A. (1993). Patterns of alcohol, cigarette, and caffeine and other drug use in two drug abusing populations. *Journal of Substance Abuse Treatment, 10,* 171–179.

L

Leonard, T. K., Watson, R. R., & Mohs, M. E. (1987). The effects of caffeine in various body systems: A review. *Journal of the American Dietetic Association, 87,* 1048–1053.

Levenson, H. S., & Bick, E. C. (1977). Psychopharmacology of caffeine. In M. E. Jarvic (Ed.), *Psychopharmacology in the practice of medicine* (pp. 451–463). New York: Appleton-Century-Crofts.

Lowe, G. (1988). State-dependent retrieval effects with social drugs. *British Journal of Addiction, 83,* 99–103.

M

Marks, V., & Kelly, J. F. (1973). Absorption of caffeine from tea, coffee, and Coca Cola. *The Lancet, 3,* 827.

Mills, J. L., Holmes, L. B., Aarons, J. H., Simpson, J. L., Brown, A. A., Jovanovic-Peterson, L. G., Conley, M. R., Granbard, B. I., Knopp, R. H., & Metzger, B. E. (1993). Moderate caffeine use and the risk of spontaneous abortion on intrauterine growth retardation. *Journal of the American Medical Association, 269,* 593–597.

R

Rall, T. W. (1990). Drugs used in the treatment of asthma. The methylxanthines, cromolyn sodium, and other agents. In A. G. Gilman, T. W. Rall, A. S. Niles, & P. Taylor (Eds.), *Goodman and Gilman's The pharmacological basis of therapeutics* (8th edition) (pp. 618–637). New York: Pergamon Press.

S

Sawyer, D. A., Julia, H. L., & Turin, A. C. (1982). Caffeine and human behavior: Arousal, anxiety, and performance effects. *Journal of Behavioral Medicine, 5,* 415–439.

Schivelbusch, W. (1992). *Taste of paradise.* New York: Pantheon Books.

Snyder, S. H., & Sklar, P. (1984). Behavioral and molecular actions of caffeine: Focus on adenosine. *Journal of Psychiatric Research, 18,* 91–106.

Syed, I. B. (1976). The effects of caffeine. *Journal of the American Pharmaceutical Association, 16,* 568–572.

Chapter 9

A

Abel, E. L. (1985). *Psychoactive drugs and sex.* New York: Plenum Press.

Adams, W. L., Yuan, Z., Barboriak, J. J., & Rimm, A. A. (1993). Alcohol-related hospitalizations of elderly people. *Journal of the American Medical Association, 270,* 1222–1225.

Adesso, V. J. (1985). Cognitive factors in alcohol and drug use. In M. Galizio & S. A. Maisto (Eds.), *Determinants of substance abuse* (pp. 179–208). New York: Plenum Press.

American Psychiatric Association (1981). DSM-III *Case Book.* Washington, DC: Author.

B

Babor, T. F., Kranzler, H. R., & Lauerman, R. J. (1987). Social drinking as a health and psychosocial risk factor. Anstie's limit revisited. In M. Galanter (Ed.), *Recent developments in alcoholism* (Vol. 5) (pp. 373–402). New York: Plenum Press.

Becker, C. E., Roe, R. L., & Scott, R. A. (1975). *Alcohol as a drug.* New York: Medcom Press.

Berild, D., & Hasselbalch, H. (1981). Survival after a blood alcohol of 1127 mg/dl. *The Lancet, 2* (8242), 363.

Brown, B. A., Christiansen, B. A., & Goldman, M. S. (1987). The Alcohol Expectancy Questionnaire: An instrument for the assessment of adolescent and adult alcohol expectancies. *Journal of Studies on Alcohol, 48,* 483–491.

C

Carroll, L. C., & Miller, D. (1986). *Health: The science of human adaptation* (4th edition). Dubuque, IA: Wm. C. Brown.

Cavanagh, J., & Clairmonte, F. F. (1985). *Alcoholic beverages: Dimensions of corporate power.* London: Croon Helm.

Charness, M. E. (1993). Brain lesions in alcoholics. *Alcoholism: Clinical and Experimental Research, 17,* 2–11.

Cohen, S., Tyrrell, D. A. J., Russell, M. A. H., Jarvis, M. J., & Smith, A. P. (1993). Smoking, alcohol consumption, and susceptibility to the common cold. *American Journal of Public Health, 83,* 1277–1283.

Collins, J. J., Jr. (Ed.) (1981). *Alcohol use and criminal behavior: An empirical, theoretical, and methodological overview.* New York: Guilford Press.

Collins, J. J., Jr., Guess, L. L., Williams, J. R., & Hamilton, C. J. (1980). *A research agenda to address the relationship between alcohol consumption and assaultive criminal behavior.* Final report submitted to the U.S. National Institute of Justice (Grant No. 78-NI-AX-0112).

D

Donovan, J. M. (1986). An etiologic model of alcoholism. *The American Journal of Psychiatry, 143,* 1–11.

E

Erenhart, C. B. (1991). Clinical correlations between ethanol intake and fetal alcohol syndrome. In M. Galanter (Ed.), *Recent developments in alcoholism* (Vol. 9) (pp. 127–150). New York: Plenum Press.

F

Franck, P. H. (1983). 'If you drink, don't drive' motto now applies to hangovers as well. *Journal of the American Medical Association, 250,* 1657–1658.

Frezza, M., di Padova, C., Pozzato, G., Terpin, M., Baraona, E., & Lieber, C. S. (1990). High blood alcohol levels in women: The role of decreased gastric alcohol dehydrogenase activity and first pass metabolism. *The New England Journal of Medicine, 322,* 95–99.

Frunkel, E. N., Kanner, J., German, J. B., Parks, E., & Kinsella, J. E. (1993). Inhibition of oxidation of human low-density lipoprotein by phenolic substances in red wine. *The Lancet, 341,* 454–457.

G

Galizio, M., & Maisto, S. A. (Eds.) (1985). *Determinants of substance abuse.* New York: Plenum Press.

H

Harvard, J. D. J. (1977). Alcohol and road accidents. In G. Edwards & M. Grant (Eds.), *Alcoholism: New knowledge and responses* (pp. 251–263). London: Croon Helm.

Heath, D. B. (1986). Happy hour in Sakiland. *The Wall Street Journal*, August 18, p. 21.

Higuchi, S., Parrish, K. M., Dufour, M. C., Towle, L., & Harford, T. C. (1992). The relationship between three types of the flushing response and DSM-III alcohol abuse in Japanese. *Journal of Studies on Alcohol, 53*, 553–560.

J

Jacobs, M. R., & Fehr, K. O'B. (1987). *Drugs and drug abuse: A reference text* (2nd edition). Toronto, Canada: Addiction Research Foundation.

Jacobson, J. L., Jacobson, S. W., Sokol, R. J., Martier, S. S., Ager, J. W., & Kaplan-Estrin, G. (1993). Teratogenic effects of alcohol on infant development. *Alcoholism: Clinical and Experimental Research, 17*, 174–183.

Julien, R. M. (1992). *A primer of drug action* (6th edition). New York: W. H. Freeman & Co.

K

Keller, M. (1979). A historical overview of alcohol and alcoholism. *Cancer Research, 39*, 2822–2829.

Kendler, K. S., Heath, A. C., Neale, M. C., Kessler, R. C., & Eaves, L. J. (1992). A population-based twin study of alcoholism in women. *Journal of the American Medical Association, 268*, 1877–1882.

Kitano, H. H. L. (1989). Alcohol and the Asian American. In T. D. Watts & R. Wright, Jr. (Eds.), *Alcoholism in minority populations* (pp. 143–158). Springfield, IL: Charles C. Thomas.

Knupfer, G. (1987). Drinking for health: The daily light drinker fiction. *British Journal of Addiction, 82*, 547–555.

L

Lang, A. R., Searles, J., Lauerman, R., & Adesso, V. (1980). Expectancy, alcohol, and sex guilt as determinants of interest in and reaction to sexual stimuli. *Journal of Abnormal Psychology, 60*, 285–293.

Levine, J. M., Kramer, G. G., & Levine, E. N. (1975). Effects of alcohol on human performance: An integration of research findings based on an abilities classification. *Journal of Applied Psychology, 89*, 644–653.

M

MacAndrew, C., & Edgerton, R. B. (1969). *Drunken comportment*. Chicago: Adline.

McKim, W. A. (1986). *Drugs and behavior*. Englewood Cliffs, NJ: Prentice Hall.

Mello, N. K. (1987). Alcohol abuse and alcoholism: 1978–1987. In H. Y. Meltzer (Ed.), *Psychopharmacology: The third generation of progress* (pp. 1515–1520). New York: Raven Press.

Mendelson, J. H., & Mello, N. K. (1985). *Alcohol: Use and abuse in America*. Boston: Little, Brown & Co.

Midanik, L. T., & Room, R. R. (1992). The epidemiology of alcohol consumption. *Alcohol Health Research World, 16*, 183–190.

N

Nace, E. P., & Isbell, P. G. (1991). Alcohol. In R. J. Francis & S. I. Miller (Eds.), *Clinical textbook of addictive disorders* (pp. 43–68). New York: The Guilford Press.

P

Parsons, O. A. (1986). Alcoholics' neuropsychological impairment: Current findings and conclusions. *Annals of Behavioral Medicine, 8*, 13–19.

Parsons, O. A., & Leber, W. R. (1982). Alcohol, cognitive dysfunction, and brain damage. In National Institute on Alcohol Abuse and Alcoholism, *Alcohol and health* (Monograph 2) (pp. 213–256). Rockville, MD: NIAAA.

Perez-Reyes, M., Hicks, R. E., Bumberry, J., Jeffcoat, A. R., & Cook, C. E. (1988). Interaction between marijuana and ethanol: Effect on psychomotor performance. *Alcoholism: Clinical and Experimental Research, 12*, 268–276.

R

Rall, T. W. (1990). Hypnotics and sedatives; ethanol. In A. G. Gilman, T. W. Rall, A. S. Nies, & P. Taylor (Eds.), *Goodman and Gilman's The pharmacological basis of therapeutics* (8th edition) (pp. 345–382). New York: Macmillan Publishing Co.

Renaud, S., & deLorgerd, M. (1992). Wine, alcohol, platelets, and the French paradox for coronary heart disease. *The Lancet, 339*, 1523–1526.

Riman, S., & E. B., Giovannucci, E. L., Willett, W. C., Colditz, G. A., Ascherio, A., Rosner, B., & Stampfer, M. J. (1991). Prospective study of alcohol consumption and risk of coronary disease in men. *The Lancet, 338*, 464–468.

Ritchie, J. M. (1985). The aliphatic alcohols. In A. G. Gilman, L. S. Goodman, T. W. Rall, & F. Murod (Eds.), *Goodman and Gilman's The pharmacological basis of therapeutics* (7th edition) (pp. 372–386). New York: Macmillan Publishing Co.

Roebuck, J. B., & Kessler, R. G. (1972). *The etiology of alcoholism*. Springfield, IL: Charles Thomas.

Roine, R., Gentry, R. T., Hernández-Muñoz, R., Baraona, E., & Leiber, C. S. (1990). Aspirin increases blood alcohol concentration in humans after ingestion of ethanol. *Journal of the American Medical Association, 264*, 2406–2408.

Rose, A. H. (1977). History and scientific basis of alcoholic beverage production. In A. H. Rose (Ed.),

Alcoholic beverages (pp. 1–41). New York: Academic Press.

S

Schuckit, M. A. (1987). Biology of risk of alcoholism. In H. Y. Meltzer (Ed.), *Psychopharmacology: The third generation of progress* (pp. 1527–1533). New York: Raven Press.

Sobell, M. B., & Sobell, L. C. (1981). *Alcohol abuse curriculum guide for psychology faculty* (Prepublication manuscript). Rockville, MD: U.S. Department of Health and Human Services.

Spitzer, R. L., Skodol, A. E., Gibbon, M., & Williams, J. B. W. (1981). *DSM–III casebook*. Washington, DC: American Psychiatric Association.

Suter, P. M., Schutz, Y., & Jequier, E. (1992). The effect of ethanol on fat storage in healthy subjects. *New England Journal of Medicine, 326,* 983–987.

T

Teichmann, B. (1993). A drinker goes free and kills. *USA Today,* August 30, p. 11A.

U

U.S. Department of Health and Human Services (USDHHS) (1987). *Alcohol and health.* Rockville, MD: Author.

U.S. Department of Health and Human Services (USDHHS) (1990). *Alcohol and health.* Rockville, MD: Author.

U.S. Department of Health and Human Services (USDHHS) (1993). *Preliminary estimates from the 1992 National Household Survey on Drug Abuse: Selected excerpts.* Rockville, MD: National Clearinghouse for Alcohol and Drug Information.

U.S. Department of Health and Human Services (USDHHS) (1993a). *Alcohol and health: Eighth special report to the U.S. Congress* (Prepublication copy).

W

Weil, A., & Rosen, W. (1983). *Chocolate to morphine.* Boston: Houghton Mifflin Company.

Williams, G. D., Stinson, F. S., Clem, D., & Noble, J. (1992). *Surveillance Report #23, Apparent per capita alcohol consumption: National, state, and regional trends, 1977–1990.* Rockville, MD: National Institute on Alcohol Abuse and Alcoholism.

Wilsnack, S. C., Klassen, A. D., & Wilsnack, R. W. (1984). Drinking and reproductive dysfunction among women in a 1981 national survey. *Alcoholism: Clinical and Experimental Research, 8,* 451–458.

Wolfe, S. M., & Victor, M. (1971). The physiological basis of the alcohol withdrawal syndrome. In N. K. Mello and J. H. Mendelson (Eds.), *Recent advances in studies of alcoholism* (pp. 188–199). Washington, DC: U.S. Government Printing Office.

Chapter 10

A

Abel, E. L. (1985). *Psychoactive drugs and sex.* New York: Plenum Press.

Ator, N. A. (1987). Self-administration of barbiturates and benzodiazepines: A review. *Pharmacology, Biochemistry and Behavior, 27,* 391–398.

American Psychiatric Association (APA). (1980). *Diagnostic and statistical manual of mental disorders* (3rd edition). Washington, DC: APA.

B

Barnes, G. E. (1979). Solvent abuse: A review. *International Journal of the Addictions, 14,* 1–26.

Brecher, E. M. (1972). *Licit and illicit drugs.* Boston: Little, Brown & Co.

Breese, G. R., Frye, G. D., Vogel, R. A., Mann Koepke, K., & Mueller, R. A. (1983). Comparisons of behavioral and biochemical effects of ethanol and chlordiazepoxide. In L. Pohorecky & J. Brick (Eds.), *Stress and alcohol use* (pp. 261–278). Amsterdam: Elsevier.

Bruckner, J. V., & Peterson, R. G. (1977). Review of the aliphatic and aromatic hydrocarbons. In C. W. Sharp & M. L. Brehm (Eds.), *Review of inhalants: Euphoria to dysfunction,* Research Monograph 15 (pp. 124–163). National Institute on Drug Abuse, Washington, DC.

C

Cappell, H. D., Sellers, E. M., & Busto, U. (1986). Benzodiazepines as drugs of abuse and dependence. In H. D. Cappell, F. B. Glaser, Y. Israel, H. Kalant, W. Schmidt, E. M. Sellers, & R. C. Smart (Eds.), *Research advances in alcohol and drug problems* (Vol. 9) (pp. 53–126). New York: Plenum Press.

Ciraulo, D. A., Barnhill, J. G., Greenblatt, D. J., Shader, R. I., Ciraulo, A. M., Tarmey, M. F., Molloy, M. A., & Foti, M. E. (1988). Abuse liability and clinical pharmacokinetics of alprazolam in alcoholic men. *Journal of Clinical Psychiatry, 49,* 333–337.

Cohen, S. (1977). Inhalant abuse: An overview of the problem. In C. W. Sharp & M. L. Brehm (Eds.), *Review of inhalants: Euphoria to dysfunction.* National Institute on Drug Abuse. Research Monograph 15 (pp. 2–13), Rockville, MD.

Costa, E., Guidotti, A., & Mao, C. C. (1975). Evidence for involvement of GABA in the action of benzodiazepines. Studies on rat cerebellum. In E. Costa & P. Greengard (Eds.), *Mechanism of action of benzodiazepines* (pp. 113–130). New York: Raven Press.

D

Dohrn, C. S., Lichtor, J. L., Finn, R. S., Uitvlugt, A., Coalson, D. W., Rupani, G., de Wit, H., & Zacny, J. P. (1992). *Behavioral Pharmacology, 3,* 19–30.

Dorow, R., Horowski, R., Paschelke, G., Amin, M., & Braestrup, C. (1983). Severe anxiety induced by FG 7142, a beta-carboline ligand for benzodiazepine receptors. *The Lancet, 2,* 98–99.

Dundee, J. W., & McIlroy, P. D. (1982). A history of the barbiturates. *Anesthesiology, 37,* 726–734.

Dykstra, L. (1992). Drug action. In J. Grabowski & G. R. VandenBos (Eds.), *Psychopharmacology: Basic mechanisms and applied interventions* (pp. 59–96). Washington, DC: American Psychological Association.

F

File, S. E., Pellow, S., & Braestrup, C. Effects of the beta-carboline, FG 7142 in the social interaction test of anxiety and the holeboard: Correlations between behavior and plasma concentrations. *Pharmacology, Biochemistry, and Behavior, 22,* 941–944.

G

Garriott, J. C. (1992). Death among inhalant abusers. In C. W. Sharp, F. Beauvais, & R. Spence (Eds.), *Inhalant abuse: A volatile research agenda.* National Institute on Drug Abuse, Research Monograph 129 (181–191), Rockville, MD.

Goode, E. (1993). *Drugs in American society* (4th edition). New York: McGraw Hill.

Gordon, B. (1979). *I'm dancing as fast as I can.* New York: Bantam Books, Inc.

Greenblatt, D. J., Shader, R. I., Abernethy, D. R., Ochs, H. R., Divoll, M., & Sellers, E. M. (1982). Benzodiazepines and the challenge of pharmacokinetic taxonomy. In E. Usdin, P. Skolnick, J. F. Tallman, D. Greenblatt, and S. M. Paul (Eds.), *Pharmacology of benzodiazepines* (pp. 257–270). London: Macmillan Press.

Griffiths, R. R., Bigelow, G. E., Liebson, I., & Kaliszak, J. E. (1980). Drug preference in humans: Double-blind choice comparison of pentobarbital, diazepam, and placebo. *Journal of Pharmacology and Experimental Therapeutics, 215,* 649–661.

Griffiths, R. R., Lukas, S. E., Bradford, L. D., Brady, J. V., & Snell, J. D. (1981). Self-injection of barbiturates and benzodiazepines in baboons. *Psychopharmacology, 74,* 101–109.

Griffiths, R. R., McLeod, E. R., Bigelow, G. E., Liebson, I. A., & Roache, J. D. (1984). Relative abuse liability of diazepam and oxazepam: Behavior and subjective dose effects. *Psychopharmacology, 84,* 147–154.

Griffiths, R. R., McLeod, E. R., Bigelow, G. E., Liebson, I. A., Roache, J. D., & Nowowieski, P. (1984). Comparison of diazepam and oxazepam: Preference liking and extent of abuse. *Journal of Pharmacology and Experimental Therapeutics, 229,* 501–508.

H

Harvey, S. C. (1980). Hypnotics and sedatives. In A. G. Gilman, L. S. Goodman, & A. Gilman (Eds.), *Goodman and Gilman's The pharmacological basis of therapeutics* (6th edition). (pp. 339–379). London: Macmillan.

Harvey, S. C. (1985). Hypnotics and sedatives. In A. G. Gilman, L. S. Goodman, & A. Gilman (Eds.), *Goodman and Gilman's The pharmacological basis of therapeutics* (7th edition). (pp. 339–371). London: Macmillan.

Hollister, L. E. (1983). *Clinical pharmacology of psychotherapeutic drugs* (2nd edition). New York: Churchill Livingston.

Hommer, D. W., Skolnick, P., & Paul, S. M. (1987). The benzodiazepine/GABA receptor complex and anxiety. In H. Y. Meltzer (Ed.), *Psychopharmacology: The third generation of progress* (pp. 513–526). New York: Raven Press.

Hutchens, A., & Miederhoff, P. (1989). Nitrous oxide: No laughing matter. *The Addiction Letter,* March, 5.

J

Johns, A. (1991). Volatile solvent abuse and 963 deaths. *British Journal of Addiction, 95,* 1053–1056.

L

Lader, M. (1983). Benzodiazepine withdrawal states. In M. R. Trimble (Ed.), *Benzodiazepines divided: A multidisciplinary review* (pp. 17–32). New York: John Wiley & Sons.

Lister, R. G., & Nutt, D. J. (1987). Is RO 15–4513 a specific alcohol antagonist? *Trends in Neuroscience, 10,* 223–225.

M

Mendelson, W. B. (1980). *The use and misuse of sleeping pills: A clinical guide.* New York: Plenum Press.

Moehler, H., & Okada, T. (1977). Benzodiazepine receptor: Demonstration in the central nervous system. *Science, 198,* 849–851.

O

Oetting, E. R., & Webb, J. (1992). Psychosocial characteristics and their links with inhalants: A research agenda. In C. W. Sharp, F. Beauvais, & R. Spence (Eds.), *Inhalant abuse: A volatile research agenda.* National Institute on Drug Abuse, Research Monograph 129 (pp. 117–171), Rockville, MD.

O'Hanlon, J. F., & de Gier, J. J. (1986). *Drugs and driving.* London: Taylor & Francis.

P

Pryor, G. (1990). Persisting neurotoxic consequences of solvent abuse: A developing animal model for toluene-induced neurotoxicity. In J. W. Spencer &

J. J. Boren (Eds.), *Residual effects of abused drugs on behavior* (pp. 156–166). Rockville, MD: National Institute on Drug Abuse Research, Monograph 101.

R

Roache, J. D., Cherek, D. R., Spiga, R., Bennett, R. H., Cowan, K. A., & Yingling, J. (1990). Benzodiazepine-induced impairment of matching-to-sample performance in humans. *Pharmacology, Biochemistry and Behavior, 36,* 945–952.

Rosenberg, N. L., & Sharp, C. W. (1992). Solvent toxicity: A neurological focus. In C. W. Sharp, F. Beauvais, & R. Spence (Eds.), *Inhalant abuse: A volatile research agenda.* National Institute on Drug Abuse, Research Monograph 129 (pp. 117–171), Rockville, MD.

S

Salzman, C. (1992). Behavioral side effects of benzodiazepines. In J. M. Kane & J. A. Lieberman (Eds.), *Adverse effects of psychotropic drugs* (pp. 139–152). New York: Guilford Press.

Sharp, C. W. (1992). Introduction to inhalant abuse. In C. W. Sharp, F. Beauvais, & R. Spence (Eds.), *Inhalant abuse: A volatile research agenda.* National Institute on Drug Abuse, Research Monograph 129 (pp. 1–12), Rockville, MD.

Shepard, R. A. (1986). Neurotransmitters, anxiety and benzodiazepines: A behavioral review. *Neuroscience and Biobehavioral Reviews, 10,* 449–461.

Smith, D. E., & Wesson, D. R. (1983). Benzodiazepine dependency syndromes. *The Journal of Psychoactive Drugs, 15,* 85–96.

Smith, T. C., Cooperman, L. H., & Wollman, H. (1980). The therapeutic gases. In A. G. Gilman, L. S. Goodman, & A. Gilman (Eds.), *Goodman and Gilman's The pharmacological basis of therapeutics* (6th edition), (pp. 321–338). London: Macmillan.

Spitzer, R. L., Gibbon, M., Skodol, A. E., Williams, J. B. W., & First, M. B. (1989). *DSM-III-R Case Book.* Washington, DC: American Psychiatric Press, Inc.

Squires, R. F., & Braestrup, C. (1977). Benzodiazepine receptors in rat brain. *Nature, 266,* 732–734.

Sternbach, L. H. (1983). The discovery of CNS active 1,4-benzodiazepines. In E. Costa (Ed.), *The benzodiazepines: From molecular biology to clinical practice* (pp. 1–6). New York: Raven Press.

Suzdak, P. D., Glowa, J. R., Crawley, J. N., Schwartz, R. D., Skolnick, P., & Paul, S. M. (1986). A selective imidazobenzodiazepine antagonist of ethanol in the rat. *Science, 234,* 1243–1247.

Ticku, M. K., Burch, T. P., & Davis, W. C. (1983). The interactions of ethanol with the benzodiazepine-GABA receptor-ionophore complex. *Pharmacology, Biochemistry, and Behavior, 18,* 15–18.

Tunnicliff, G., Eison, A., & Taylor, D. (1991). *Buspirone: Mechanisms and clinical aspects.* Orlando: Academic Press.

Chapter 11

A

American Psychiatric Association (APA). (1994). *Diagnostic and statistical manual of mental disorders* (4th edition). Washington, DC: Author.

B

Baldessarini, R. J. (1985). *Chemotherapy in psychiatry: Principles and practice* (revised edition). Cambridge, MA: Harvard University Press.

Boulenger, J. P., & Lader, M. (1982). Pharmacokinetics and drug metabolism: Basic principles. In P. J. Tyrer (Ed.), *Drugs in psychiatric practice* (pp. 11–30). London: Butterworths.

C

Caldwell, A. E. (1970). *Origins of psychopharmacology—From CPZ to LSD.* Springfield, IL: Charles Thomas.

Caldwell, A. E. (1978). History of psychopharmacology. In W. G. Clark & J. del Guidice (Eds.), *Principles of Psychopharmacology* (2nd edition) (pp. 9–30). New York: Academic Press.

Cooperrider, C. (1988). Antidepressants. In G. W. Lawson & C. A. Cooperrider (Eds.), *Clinical psychopharmacology* (pp. 91–108). Rockville, MD: Aspen Publishers.

Coryell, W., & Winokur, G. (1982). Course and outcome. In E. S. Paykel (Ed.), *Handbook of affective disorders.* New York: Guilford Press.

D

Deniker, P. (1983). Discovery of the clinical use of neuroleptics. In M. J. Parnham & J. Bruinvels (Eds.), *Discoveries in pharmacology* (Vol. 1): *Psycho- and neuropharmacology* (pp. 163–180). New York: Elsevier.

F

Fieve, R. R. (1976). Therapeutic uses of lithium and rubidium. In L. L. Simpson (Ed.), *Drug treatment of mental disorders* (pp. 193–208).

Flynn, K. (1985). The toll of deinstitutionalization. In P. W. Brickner, L. K. Scharer, B. Conanan, A. Elvy, & M. Savarese (Eds.), *Health care of homeless people.* New York: Springer.

G

Galenberg, A. J. (1991). Psychoses. In A. J. Galenberg, E. L. Bussuk, & S. C. Schoonover (Eds.), *The practitioner's guide to psychoactive drugs* (3rd edition) (pp. 125–178). New York: Plenum Medical Book Company.

Galenberg, A. J., & Schoonover, S. C. (1991). Depression (Eds.), *The practitioner's guide to psychoactive drugs* (3rd edition) (pp. 23–89). New York: Plenum Medical Book Company.

Gitlin, M. J. (1990). *The psychotherapist's guide to psychopharmacology*. New York: The Free Press.

Gutheil, T. G. (1980). In search of true freedom: Drug refusal, involuntary medication, and 'Rotting with your rights on.' *American Journal of Psychiatry*, 137, 327–328.

H

Hollister, L. E. (1983). *Clinical pharmacology of psychotherapeutic drugs* (2nd edition). New York: Churchill Livingstone.

K

Kalus, O., Asnis, G. M., & van Praag, H. M. (1989). The role of serotonin in depression. *Psychiatric Annals*, 19, 348–353.

Kerns, L. L., & Davis, G. P. (1986). Psychotropic drugs in pregnancy. In I. J. Chasnoff (Ed.), *Drug use in pregnancy: Mother and child* (pp. 81–93). Lancaster, PA: MTP Press.

L

Lader, M. (1976). Clinical psychopharmacology. In K. Granville-Grossman (Ed.), *Recent advances in clinical psychiatry* (Vol. 2). Edinburgh: Churchill Livingstone.

Lewine, R. R. J. (1988). Gender and schizophrenia. In M. T. Tsuang & J. C. Simpson (Eds.), *Handbook of schizophrenia: Volume 3, Nosology, epidemiology, and genetics of schizophrenia*. Amsterdam: Elsevier.

Lickey, M. E., & Gordon, B. (1983). *Drugs for mental illness*. New York: W. H. Freeman & Co.

M

Mackay, A. V. P. (1982). Antischizophrenic drugs. In P. J. Tyrer (Ed.), *Drugs in psychiatric practice*. London: Butterworths.

Magliozzi, J. R., & Schaffer, C. B. (1988). Psychosis. In J. P. Tupin, R. I. Shader, & D. S. Harnett (Eds.), *Handbook of clinical psychopharmacology* (2nd edition) (pp. 1–48). Northvale, NJ: Jason Aronson.

McNeal, E. T., & Cimbolic, P. (1986). Antidepressants and biochemical theories of depression. *Psychological Bulletin*, 99, 361–374.

O

OSMJ. (1986). PADS: A look at prescription drug abuse. *Ohio State Medical Journal*, 82, 33–38.

P

Poling, A. (1986). A *primer of human behavioral pharmacology*. New York: Plenum Press.

Potter, W. Z., Bertilsson, L., & Sojoqvist, F. (1981). Clinical pharmacokinetics of psychotropic drugs: Fundamental and practical aspects. In H. M. van Praag (Ed.), *Handbook of biological psychiatry* (Part 6) (pp. 71–134). New York: Marcel Dekker.

S

Sack, R. L., & DeFraites, E. (1977). Lithium and the treatment of mania. In J. D. Barchas, P. A. Berger, R. D. Ciaranello, & G. R. Elliott (Eds.), *Psychopharmacology: From theory to practice*. New York: Oxford University Press.

Snyder, S. H., & Largent, B. L. (1989). Receptor mechanisms in antipsychotic drug action: Focus on sigma receptors. *Journal of Neuropsychiatry*, 1, 7–15.

Spiegel, R., & Aebi, H. (1983). *Psychopharmacology*. New York: John Wiley & Sons.

Spitzer, R. L., Gibbon, M., Skodol, A. E., Williams, J. B. W., & First, M. B. (1989). DSM-III-R *case book*. Washington, DC: American Psychiatric Press, Inc.

Tyrer, P. J. (1982). Evaluation of psychotropic drugs. In P. J. Tyrer (Ed.), *Drugs in psychiatric practice* (pp. 31–44). London: Butterworths.

Tyrer, P. J. (Ed.), (1982). *Drugs in psychiatric practice*. London: Butterworths.

Tyrer, P. J., & Marsden, C. A. (1982). Classification of psychotropic drugs. In P. J. Tyrer (Ed.), *Drugs in psychiatric practice* (pp. 3–10). London: Butterworths.

Tyrer, S., & Shaw, D. M. (1982). Lithium carbonate. In P. J. Tyrer (Ed.), *Drugs in psychiatric practice*. London: Butterworths.

W

Weiss, K. J., & Greenfield, D. P. (1986). Prescription drug abuse. *Psychiatric Clinics of North America*, 9, 475–490.

Wells, K. B., Kamberg, C., Brook, R., Camp, P., & Rogers, W. (1985). Health status, sociodemographic factors, and the use of prescribed psychotropic drugs. *Medical Care*, 23, 1295–1306.

Chapter 12

A

Abel, E. L. (1985). *Psychoactive drugs and sex*. New York: Plenum Press.

B

Brecher, E. M. (1972). *Licit and illicit drugs*. Boston: Little, Brown & Co.

Burroughs, W. S. (1953). *Junky*. Middlesex, England: Penguin Books.

D

Dasgupta, S., Friedman, S. R., Jose, B., DesJarlais, D. C., Kleinman, P. H., Goldsmith, D. S., Neaigus, A., & Rosenblum, A. (1993). Risk factor for HIV-1 infection among street recruited intravenous drug users in New York City. In *National Institute on Drug Abuse Research Monograph 132: Problems of Drug Dependence*, 1992, p. 282, Rockville, MD.

Davis, J. (1984). *Endorphins: New waves in brain chemistry*. Garden City, NY: Doubleday and Company.

Dykstra, L. (1992). Drug Action. In J. Grabowski & G. R. VandenBos (Eds.), *Psychopharmacology*, pp. 59–96. Washington, DC: American Psychological Association.

E

The Economist (1991). An old opiate for the young. 320, p. 33. 12–13.

F

Farrell, P. A., & Gustafson, A. B. (1986). Exercise stress and endogenous opiates. In N. P. Plotnikoff, R. E. Faith, A. J. Murgo, & R. A. Good (Eds.), *Enkephalins and endorphins: Stress and the immune system* (pp. 47–58). New York: Plenum Press.

G

Gay, G. R., & Way, E. L. (1972). Pharmacology of the opiate narcotics. In D. E. Smith & G. R. Way (Eds.), *It's so good, don't even try it once* (pp. 32–44). Englewood Cliffs, NJ: Prentice Hall.

Goode, E. (1993). *Drugs in American society* (4th edition). New York: McGraw Hill.

H

Han, J. S., & Terenius, L. (1982). Neurochemical basis of acupuncture analgesia. *Annual Review of Pharmacology and Toxicology*, 22, 193–220.

Hawks, R. L., and Chiang, C. N. (1986). *Urine testing for drugs of abuse*. Research Monograph 73, National Institute on Drug Abuse, Washington, DC.

Hendrie, C. A. (1985). Opiate dependence and withdrawal: A new synthesis. *Pharmacology, Biochemistry, and Behavior*, 23, 863–870.

Henningfield, J. E., Lukas, S. E., & Bigelow, G. E. (1986). Human studies of drugs as reinforcers. In S. R. Goldberg & I. P. Stolerman (Eds.), *Behavioral analysis of drug dependence* (pp. 69–122). New York: Academic Press.

Ho, A. K. S., & Allen, J. P. (1981). Alcohol and the opiate receptor: Interactions with the endogenous opiates. *Advances in Alcohol & Substance Abuse*, 1, 53–75.

Hunt, G. H., & Odoroff, M. E. (1962). Follow-up study of narcotic drug addicts after hospitalization. *Public Health Reports*, 77, 41–54.

I

Inciardi, J. A. (1992). *The war on drugs* II. Mountain View, CA: Mayfield Press.

J

Jaffe, J. H., & Martin, W. R. (1985). Opioid analgesics and antagonists. In A. G. Gilman, L. S. Goodman, & A. Gilman (Eds.), *Goodman and Gilman's The pharmacological basis of therapeutics* (7th edition) (pp. 491–531). New York: Macmillan Publishing Company.

Johnston, L. D., O'Malley, P. M., & Bachman, J. G. (1991). *Drug use among American high school seniors, college students, and young adults, 1975–1990, Vol. one: High school seniors*. Rockville, MD: National Institute on Drug Abuse.

K

Kirsch, M. M. (1986). *Designer drugs*. Minneapolis: CompCare Publications.

Kramer, J. C. (1972). A brief history of heroin addiction in America. In D. E. Smith & G. R. Gay (Eds.), *It's so good, don't even try it once* (pp. 12–31). Englewood Cliffs, NJ: Prentice Hall.

L

Latimer, D., & Goldberg, J. (1981). *Flowers in the blood: The story of opium*. New York: Franklin Watts.

Luce, J. (1972). End of the road: A case study. In D. E. Smith & G. R. Gay (Eds.), *It's so good, don't even try it once* (pp. 143–147). Englewood Cliffs, NJ: Prentice Hall.

M

Mayer, D. J. (1987). The behavioral effects of opiates. In L. L. Iverson, S. D. Iverson, & S. H. Snyder (Eds.), *Handbook of psychopharmacology* (Vol. 19) (pp. 467–530). New York: Plenum Press.

Meyer, R. E., & Mirin, S. M. (1979). *The heroin stimulus: Implications for a theory of addiction*. New York: Plenum Press.

P

Pert, C., & Snyder, S. H. (1973). Opiate receptor: Demonstration in nervous system tissue. *Science*, 179, 1011–1014.

R

Rathus, S. A., Nevid, J. S., & Fichner-Rathus, L. (1993). *Human sexuality in a world of diversity*. Boston: Allyn and Bacon.

Robins, L. N., Helzer, J. E., & Davis, D. H. (1975). Narcotic use in Southeast Asia and afterward. *Archives of General Psychiatry, 32,* 955–961.

S

Scott, J. M. (1969). *The white poppy: A history of opium.* New York: Funk & Wagnalls.

Smith, D. E., & Gay, G. R. (1972). *It's so good, don't even try it once.* Englewood Cliffs, NJ: Prentice Hall.

Snyder, S. H. (1989). *Brainstorming: The science and politics of opiate research.* Cambridge, MA: Harvard University Press.

Steinberg, H., & Sykes, E. A. (1985). Introduction to symposium on endorphins and behavioural processes. Review of literature on endorphins and exercise. *Pharmacology, Biochemistry, and Behavior, 23,* 857–862.

T

Time Magazine (1993). Choose your poison. July 26, pp. 56–57.

W

Wei, E., Loh, H. H., & Way, E. L. (1973). Quantitative aspects of precipitated abstinence in morphine dependent rats. *Journal of Pharmacology and Experimental Therapeutics, 184,* 393–408.

Chapter 13

A

Abel, E. L. (1971). Marihuana and memory: Acquisition or retrieval? *Science, 173,* 1038–1040.

Abel, E. L. (1980). *Marijuana: The first twelve thousand years.* New York: Plenum Press.

Adesso, V. J. (1985). Cognitive factors in alcohol and drug use. In M. Galizio & S. A. Maisto (Eds.), *Determinants of substance abuse: Biological, psychological, and environmental factors* (pp. 179–208). New York: Plenum Press.

Adler, I., & Kandel, D. (1981). Cross-cultural perspectives on developmental stages in adolescent drug use. *Journal of Studies on Alcohol, 42,* 701–715.

Agurell, S., Halldin, M., Lindgren, J.-R., Ohlsson, A., Widman, M., Gillespie, H., & Hollister, L. (1986). Pharmacokinetics and metabolism of tetrahydrocannabinol and other cannabinoids with emphasis on man. *Pharmacological Reviews, 38,* 21–43.

Aldrich, M. R. (1977). Tantric cannabis use in India. *Journal of Psychedelic Drugs, 9,* 227–233.

B

Becker, H. S. (1953). Becoming a marihuana user. *American Journal of Sociology, 59,* 235–242.

Becker, H. S. (1963). *Outsiders: Studies in the sociology of deviance.* New York: Free Press.

Bloomquist, E. R. (1971). *Marijuana: The second trip* (rev. edition). Beverly Hills, CA: Glencoe Press.

Brecher, E. M., & the Editors of *Consumer Reports.* (1972). *Licit and illicit drugs.* Boston: Little, Brown & Co.

Brick, J. (1990). *Marijuana.* New Brunswick, NJ: Rutgers University Center of Alcohol Studies.

C

Carter, W. E. (1980). *Cannabis in Costa Rica.* Philadelphia: Institute for the Study of Human Issues.

Carter, W. E., & Doughty, P. L. (1976). Social and cultural aspects of cannabis use in Costa Rica. *Annals of the New York Academy of Sciences, 282,* 2–16.

Cherek, D. R., Roache, J. D., Egli, M., Davis, C., Spiga, R., & Cowan, K. (1993). Acute effects of marijuana smoking on aggressive, escape, and point-maintained responding of male drug users. *Psychopharmacology, 111,* 163–168.

Cohen, S., & Andrysiak, T. (1982). *The therapeutic potential of marijuana's components.* Rockville, MD: American Council on Marijuana and Other Psychoactive Drugs.

Comitas, L. (1976). Cannabis and work in Jamaica: A refutation of the amotivational syndrome. *Annals of New York Academy of Sciences, 282,* 24–32.

D

Day, N. L., & Richardson, G. A. (1991). Prenatal marijuana use: Epidemiology, methodological issues, and infant outcome. *Chemical Dependency and Pregnancy, 18,* 77–91.

DeLong, F. L., & Levy, B. I. (1974). A model of attention describing the cognitive effects of marijuana. In L. L. Miller (Ed.), *Marijuana: Effects on human behavior* (pp. 103–120). New York: Academic Press.

Devane, W. A., Dysarz, F. A., Johnson, R., Melvin, L. S., & Howlett, A. C. (1988). Determination and characterization of a cannabinoid receptor in the rat brain. *Molecular Pharmacology, 34,* 605–613.

Devane, W. A., Hanus, L., Breuer, A., Pertwee, R. G., Stevenson, L. A. Griffin, G., Gibson, D., Mandelbaum, A., Etinger, A., & Mechoulam, R. (1992). Isolation and structure of a brain constituent that binds to the cannabinoid receptor. *Science, 258,* 1946–1949.

Domino, E. F., Donelson, A. C., & Tuttle, T. (1978). Effects of 9-tetrahydrocannabinol on regional brain acetylcholine. In D. J. Jenden (Ed.), *Cholinergic mechanisms and psychopharmacology* (pp. 673–678). New York: Plenum Press.

E

Ehrenkranz, J. R. L., & Hembree, W. C. (1986). Effects of marijuana on male reproductive function. *Psychiatric Annals, 16,* 243–248.

F

Foltin, R. W., Fischman, M. W., Brady, J. V., Kelly, T. H., Bernstein, D. J., & Nellis, M. J. (1989). Motivational effects of smoked marijuana: Behavioral contingencies and high-probability recreational activities. *Pharmacology, Biochemistry, and Behavior,* 34, 871–877.

Foltin, R. W., Fischman, M. W., Brady, J. V., Bernstein, D. J., Capriotti, R. M., Nellis, M. J., & Kelly, T. H. (1990). Motivational effects of smoked marijuana: Behavioral contingencies and low-probability activities. *Journal of the Experimental Analysis of Behavior,* 53, 5–19.

Fried, P. A. (1986). Marijuana and human pregnancy. In I. J. Chasnoff (Ed.), *Drug use in pregnancy: Mother and child* (pp. 64–74). Lancaster: MTP Press.

G

Gaoni, Y., & Mechoulam, R. (1964). Isolation, structure, and partial synthesis of an active constituent of hashish. *Journal of the American Chemical Society,* 86, 1646–1647.

Gautier, T. (1844/1966). *Le club des hachichins.* In D. Solomon (Ed.), *The marijuana papers* (pp. 121–135). New York: Bobbs-Merrill.

H

Harris, L. S., Dewey, W. L., & Razdan, R. K. (1977). Cannabis: Its chemistry, pharmacology, and toxicology. In W. R. Martin (Ed.), *Drug addiction II: Amphetamine, psychotogen, and marihuana dependence* (pp. 371–429). New York: Springer-Verlag.

Hepler, R. S., & Frank, I. M. (1971). Marijuana smoking and intraocular pressure. *Journal of the American Medical Association,* 217, 1392.

Hepler, R. S., & Petrus, R. J. (1976). Experiences with administration of marijuana to glaucoma patients. In S. Cohen & R. C. Stillman (Eds.), *The therapeutic aspects of marijuana* (pp. 63–75). New York: Plenum Press.

Hollister, L. E., Richards, R. K., & Gillespie, H. K. (1968). Comparison of tetrahydrocannabinol and synhexyl in man. *Clinical Pharmacology and Therapeutics,* 9, 783–791.

I

Institute of Medicine (1982). *Marijuana and health.* Washington, DC: National Academy Press.

J

Johnson, B. D. (1973). *Marihuana users and drug subcultures.* New York: John Wiley & Sons.

Johnston, L. D., O'Malley, P. M., & Bachman, J. G. (1994). *National survey results on drug use from the Monitoring for the Future study,* 1975–1993. Rockville, MD: National Institute on Drug Abuse.

Jones, R. T. (1980). Human effects: An overview. In R. C. Peterson (Ed.), *Marijuana research findings: 1980* (pp. 54–80). Rockville, MD: National Institute on Drug Abuse.

K

Kandel, D. (1975). Stages in adolescent involvement in drug use. *Science,* 190, 912–914.

Kandel, D., & Yamaguchi, K. (1993). From beer to crack: Developmental patterns of drug involvement. *American Journal of Public Health,* 83, 851–855.

Kelly, T. H., Foltin, R. W., & Fischman, M. W. (1993). Effects of smoked marijuana on heart rate, drug ratings and task performance by humans. *Behavioural Pharmacology,* 4, 167–178.

Klonoff, H. (1974). Effects of marijuana on driving in a restricted area and on city streets. In L. L. Miller (Ed.), *Marijuana: Effects on human behavior* (pp. 359–397). New York: Academic Press.

L

LeDain Commission (1972). *A report of the Commission of Inquiry into the non-medical use of drugs.* Ottawa: Information Canada.

Ludlow, F. H. (1857/1979). *The hasheesh eater, being passages from the life of a pythagorean.* San Francisco: City Lights Books.

M

Martin, B. R., Cabral, G., Childers, S. R., Deadwyler, S., Mechoulam, R., & Reggio, P. (1993). International Cannabis Research Society meeting summary, Keystone, CO (June 19–20, 1992). *Drug and Alcohol Dependence,* 31, 219–227.

Mayor LaGuardia's Committee on Marihuana. (1944). *The marihuana problem in the city of New York.* Lancaster, PA: Jacques Cattell Press. (Reprinted by Scarecrow Reprint Corporation, Metuchen, NJ, 1983.)

McGlothlin, W. H., & West, L. J. (1968). The marihuana problem: An overview. *American Journal of Psychiatry,* 125, 370–378.

McKenna, T. (1992). *Food of the gods: The search for the original tree of knowledge.* New York: Bantam Books.

Mechoulam, R. (1973). Cannabinoid chemistry. In R. Mechoulam (Ed.), *Marijuana: Chemistry, pharmacology, metabolism, and clinical effects* (pp. 2–99). New York: Academic Press.

N

Nahas, G. G. (1973). *Marihuana—Deceptive weed.* New York: Raven Press.

National Institute on Drug Abuse (NIDA). (1982). *Marijuana and health* (Ninth Annual Report to the U.S. Congress from the Secretary of Health and Human Services). Rockville, MD: NIDA.

National Institute on Drug Abuse (NIDA). (1984). *Drug abuse and drug abuse research*. Rockville, MD: NIDA.

National Institute on Drug Abuse (NIDA). (1991). *National household survey on drug abuse*. Rockville, MD: NIDA.

P

Page, J. B. (1983). The amotivational syndrome hypothesis and the Costa Rica study: Relationship between methods and results. *Journal of Psychoactive Drugs, 15,* 261–267.

Paton, W. D. M., & Pertwee, R. G. (1973). The actions of cannabis in man. In R. Mechoulam (Ed.), *Marijuana: Chemistry, pharmacology, metabolism, and clinical effects* (pp. 288–333). New York: Academic Press.

S

Smith, D. E. (1968). Acute and chronic toxicity of marijuana. *Journal of Psychoactive Drugs, 2,* 37–47.

Spector, I. (1985). AMP: A new form of marijuana. *Journal of Clinical Psychiatry, 46,* 498–499.

U

Ungerleider, J. T., & Andrysiak, T. (1985). Therapeutic issues of marijuana and THC (tetrahydrocannabinol). *International Journal of the Addictions, 20,* 691–699.

W

Welte, J. W., & Barnes, G. M. (1985). Alcohol: The gateway to other drug use among secondary-school students. *Journal of Youth and Adolescence, 14,* 487–498.

Windle, M., Barnes, G. M., & Welte, J. (1989). Causal models of adolescent substance use: An examination of gender differences using distribution-free estimators. *Journal of Personality and Social Psychology, 56,* 132–142.

Z

Zinberg, N. E. (1984). *Drug, set, and setting*. New Haven: Yale University Press.

Chapter 14

A

Abraham, H. D. (1983). Visual phenomenology of the LSD flashback. *Archives of General Psychiatry, 40,* 884–889.

Anderson, E. F. (1980). *Peyote, the divine cactus*. Tucson, AZ: University of Arizona Press.

Appel, J. B., & Rosencrans, J. A. (1984). Behavioral pharmacology of hallucinogens in animals: Conditioning studies. In B. L. Jacobs (Ed.), *Hallucinogens: Neurochemical, behavioral, and clinical perspectives* (pp. 77–94). New York: Raven Press.

B

Barnes, D. M. (1988). New data intensify the agony over ecstasy. *Science, 239,* 864–866.

Boja, J. W., & Schecter, M. D. (1987). Behavioral effects of N-ethyl-3-4-methylenedioxyamphetamine (MDE; "eve"). *Pharmacology, Biochemistry and Behavior, 28,* 153–156.

Bowers, M. B. (1977). Psychoses precipitated by psychotomimetic drugs: A follow-up study. *Archives of General Psychiatry, 34,* 832–835.

Brecher, E. M. (1972). *Licit and illicit drugs*. Boston: Little, Brown & Co.

C

Carroll, M. E. (1990). PCP and hallucinogens. *Advances in Alcohol and Substance Abuse, 9,* 167–190.

Cohen, M. M., & Marmillo, M. J. (1967). Chromosome damage in human leukocytes induced by lysergic acid diethylamide. *Science, 155,* 1417–1419.

Commins, D. L., Vosmer, G., Virus, R. M., Woolverton, W. L., Schuster, D. R., & Seiden, L. S. (1987). Biochemical and histological evidence that methylenedioxymethylamphetamine (MDMA) is toxic to neurons in the rat brain. *The Journal of Pharmacology and Experimental Therapeutics, 241,* 338–345.

D

Davis, M. (1987). Mescaline: Excitatory effects on acoustic startle are blocked by serotonin-2 antagonists. *Psychopharmacology, 93,* 286–291.

Davis, W. (1988). *Passage of darkness: The ethnobiology of the Haitian Zombie*. Chapel Hill, NC: University of North Carolina Press.

Davis, W. M., Hatoum, H. T., & Waters, I. W. (1987). Toxicity of MDA (3,4-methylenedioxyamphetamine) considered for relevance to hazards of MDMA (ecstasy) abuse. *Alcohol and Drug Research, 7,* 123–134.

De Souza, E. B., Battaglia, G., & Insel, T. R. (1990). Neurotoxic effects of MDMA on brain serotonin neurons: Evidence from neurochemical and radioligand binding studies. *Annals of the New York Academy of Sciences, 600,* 682–698.

F

Feldman, H. W., Agar, M. H., & Beschner, G. M. (1979). *Angel dust*. Lexington, MA: Lexington Books.

G

Glennon, R. A., Titeler, M., & McKenny, J. D. (1984). Evidence for 5-HT-2 involvement in the mechanism of action of hallucinogenic agents. *Life Science, 35,* 2505–2511.

Grinspoon, L., & Bakalar, J. B. (1979). *Psychedelic drugs reconsidered*. New York: Basic Books.

Grinspoon, L., & Bakalar, J. B. (1983). *Psychedelic reflections*. New York: Human Sciences Press.

Grob, C. S., Bravo, G. L., Walsh, R. N., & Liester, M. B. (1992). The MDMA-neurotoxicity controversy: Implications for clinical research with novel psychoactive drugs. *Journal of Nervous and Mental Disease*, 180, 355–356.

H

Hawks, R. L., & Chiang, C. N. (1986). *Urine testing for drugs of abuse* (NIDA Research Monograph 73). Rockville, MD.

Hofmann, A. (1980). LSD: *My problem child*. New York: McGraw-Hill Book Co.

Huxley, A. (1954). *The doors of perception*. New York: Harper.

J

Jacobs, B. L. (1987). How hallucinogenic drugs work. *American Scientist*, 75, 386–392.

Johnson, K. M., & Jones, S. M. (1990). Neuropharmacology of phencyclidine: Basic mechanisms and therapeutic potential. *Annual Review of Pharmacology and Toxicology*, 30, 707–750.

Johnson, M., Letter, A. A., Merchant, K., Hanson, G. R., & Gibb, J. W. (1988). *The Journal of Pharmacology and Experimental Therapeutics*, 244, 977–982.

Johnston, L. D., O'Malley, P., & Bachman, J. G. (1991). *Drug Use Among American High School Seniors, College Students, and Young Adults, 1975–1990, Vol. I, High School Seniors*. National Institute on Drug Abuse, Rockville, MD.

K

Kaminer, Y., & Hrecznyj, B. (1991). Lysergic acid diethylamide-induced chronic visual disturbances in an adolescent. *Journal of Nervous and Mental Disease*, 179, 173–174.

King, W., & Ellison, G. (1989). Long-lasting alterations in behavior and brain neurochemistry following continuous low-level LSD administration. *Pharmacology, Biochemistry and Behavior*, 33, 69–73.

Kirsch, M. M. (1986). *Designer drugs*. Minneapolis, MN: CompCare Publications.

Kosten, T. R., & Price, L. H. (1992). Phenomenology and sequelae of 3,4-methylenedioxymethamphetamine use: Commentary. *Journal of Nervous and Mental Disease*, 180, 353–354.

L

Lewin, L. (1964). *Phantastica—narcotic and stimulating drugs: Their use and abuse*. London: Routledge and Kegan Paul.

Liester, M. B., Grob, C. S., Bravo, G. L., & Walsh, R. N. (1992). Phenomenology and sequelae of 3,4-methylenedioxymethamphetamine use: Commentary. *Journal of Nervous and Mental Disease*, 180, 345–352.

Linder, R. L., Lerner, S. E., & Burns, R. S. (1981). PCP: *The devil's dust*. Belmont, CA: Wadsworth.

Long, S. Y. (1972). Does LSD induce chromosomal damage and malformations? A review of the literature. *Teratology*, 6, 75–90.

M

Mathias, R. (1993). NIDA research takes a new look at LSD and other hallucinogens. NIDA *Notes*, 8, 6–9.

McCann, U. D., Ridenour, A., Shaham, Y., & Ricaurte, G. A. (1993). Evidence for serotonin neurotoxicity in recreational MDMA users: A controlled study. *Abstracts of the Society for Neuroscience Annual Meeting*, Vol. 19, p. 1169.

McCann, U. D., & Ricaurte, G. A. (1991). Lasting neuropsychiatric sequelae of (+-) methylenedioxymethamphetamine ("ecstasy") in recreational users. *Journal of Clinical Psychopharmacology*, 11, 302–305.

McCarron, M. M. (1986). Phencyclidine intoxication. *PharmChem Newsletter*, 15-3, 1–7.

N

Nichols, D. E., & Glennon, R. A. (1984). Medicinal chemistry and structure-activity relationships of hallucinogens. In B. L. Jacobs (Ed.), *Hallucinogens: Neurochemical, behavioral, and clinical perspectives* (pp. 95–142). New York: Raven Press.

O

Oberlender, R., & Nichols, D. E. (1988). Drug discrimination studies with MDMA and amphetamine. *Psychopharmacology*, 95, 71–76.

P

Peroutka, S. J. (1987). Incidence of recreational use of 3,4-methylenedioxymethamphetamine (MDMA, "ecstasy") on an undergraduate campus. *New England Journal of Medicine*, 317, 1542.

Pierce, P. A., & Peroutka, S. J. (1990). Antagonist properties of d-LSD at 5-hydroxytryptamine-2 receptors. *Neuropsychopharmacology*, 3, 503–508.

R

Randall, T. (1992). Ecstasy-fueled 'rave' parties become dances of death for English youths. *Journal of the American Medical Association*, 268, 1505–1506.

Ricaurte, G., Bryan, G., Strauss, L., Seiden, L., & Schuster, C. (1985). Hallucinogenic amphetamine selectively destroys brain serotonin nerve terminals. *Science*, 229, 986–988.

S

Schlieffer, H. (1973). *Sacred narcotic plants of the New World Indians*. New York: Hafner Press.

Schultes, R. E. (1976). *Hallucinogenic plants*. New York: Golden Press.

Siegel, R. K. (1992). *Fire in the brain: Clinical tales of hallucination*. New York: Dutton.

Siegel, R. K. (1984). The natural history of hallucinogens. In B. L. Jacobs (Ed.), *Hallucinogens: Neurochemical, behavioral, and clinical perspectives* (pp. 1–19). New York: Raven Press.

Smith, D. E., & Seymour, R. B. (1985). Dream become nightmare: Adverse reactions to LSD. *Journal of Psychoactive Drugs*, 17, 297–303.

Stevens, J. (1987). *Storming heaven: LSD and the American dream*. New York: Atlantic Monthly Press.

Stewart, O. C. (1987). *Peyote religion: A history*. Norman, OK: University of Oklahoma Press.

Stock, S. H. (1986a). Synthetic drugs: A history of ups and downs—Part 1. *PharmChem Newsletter*, 15-4, 1–6.

Stock, S. H. (1986b). Synthetic drugs: A history of ups and downs—Part 2. *PharmChem Newsletter*, 15-5, 1–6.

T

Thompson, H. S. (1971). *Fear and loathing in Las Vegas*. New York: Random House.

Time (1993). Cyberpunk. Vol. 141, No. 6, pp. 58–65.

Titeler, M., Lyon, R. A., & Glennon, R. A. (1988). Radioligand binding evidence implicates the brain 5-HT-2 receptor as a site of action for LSD and phenylisopropylamine hallucinogens. *Psychopharmacology*, 94, 213–216.

W

Wasson, R. G. (1979). Fly agaric and man. In D. H. Efron, B. Holmstedt, & N. S. Kline (Eds.), *Ethnopharmacologic search for psychoactive drugs* (pp. 505–514). New York: Raven Press.

Wolfe, T. (1969). *The electric Kool-Aid acid test*. New York: Bantam Books.

Y

Young, T., Lawson, G. W., & Gacono, C. B. (1987). Clinical aspects of phencyclidine (PCP). *The International Journal of the Addictions*, 22, 1–15.

Chapter 15

B

Buckley, W. E., Yesalis, C. E., Friedl, K. E., Anderson, W. A., Streit, A. L., & Wright, J. E. (1988). Estimated prevalence of anabolic steroid use among male high school seniors. *Journal of the American Medical Association*, 260, 3441–3445.

C

Colby, H. D., & Longhurst, P. A. (1988). Fate of anabolic steroids in the body. In J. A. Thomas (Ed.), *Drugs, athletes and physical performance* (pp. 11–30). New York: Plenum Press.

F

Friedl, K. E. (1990). Reappraisal of the health risks associated with the use of high doses of oral and injectable and androgenic steroids. In G. C. Lin & L. Erinoff (Eds.), *Anabolic Steroid Use*, National Institute on Drug Abuse Research Monograph 102, Rockville, MD.

G

Goldman, B., & Klatz, R. (1992). *Death in the locker room: Drugs and sports*. Chicago: Elite Sports Medicine Publications.

Grogan, F. J. (1987). The pharmacist's prescription. New York: Rawson Associates.

H

Hallowell, C. (1987). Ordinary medicines can have extraordinary side effects. *Redbook*, 169, 132–134, 156–157.

Hecht, A. (1985). *Addictive behavior: Drug and alcohol abuse*. Englewood, CO: Morton Publishing Co.

K

Katchadourian, H. A. (1989). *Fundamentals of human sexuality* (5th edition). New York: Holt, Rinehart and Winston.

L

Lamb, D. R. (1983). Anabolic steroids. In M. H. Williams (Ed.), *Ergogenic aids in sport* (pp. 164–182). Champaign, IL: Human Kinetics Publishers.

M

Marshall, E. (1988). The drug of champions. *Science*, 242, 183–184.

Moses, E. (1988). An athlete's rx for the drug problem. *Newsweek*, October 10, p. 57.

P

Pope, H. G., Jr., & Katz, D. L. (1988). Affective and psychotic symptoms associated with anabolic steroid use. *The American Journal of Psychiatry*, 145, 487–490.

R

Rathus, S. A., Nevid, J. S., & Fichner-Rathus, L. (1993). *Human sexuality in a world of diversity*. Boston: Allyn and Bacon.

Rogol, A. D., Martha, P. M., & Blizzard, R. M. (1990). Anabolic-androgenic steroids profoundly affect growth at puberty in boys. In G. C. Lin & L. Erinoff (Eds.), *Anabolic Steroid Use*, National Institute on Drug Abuse Research Monograph 102, Rockville, MD.

S

Steering Committee of the Physicians Health Study Research Group (1988). Preliminary report: Findings from the aspirin component of the ongoing Physicians Health Study. *New England Journal of Medicine*, 318, 262–264.

W

Wade, N. (1972). Anabolic steroids: Doctors denounce them, but athletes aren't listening. *Science*, 176, 1399–1403.

Y

Yesalis, C. E., Vicary, J. R., Buckley, W. E., Streit, A. L., Katz, D. L., & Wright, J. E. (1990). Indications of psychological dependence among anabolic-androgenic steroid abusers. In G. C. Lin & L. Erinoff (Eds.), *Anabolic Steroid Use*, National Institute on Drug Abuse Research Monograph 102, Rockville, MD.

Chapter 16

A

Alasuutari, P. (1992). *A cultural theory of alcoholism*. Albany: State University of New York Press.

Alcoholics Anonymous (1972). *If you are a professional* A.A. *wants to work with you*. New York: Alcoholics Anonymous World Services, Inc.

Alcoholics Anonymous (1983). *Questions and answers on sponsorship*. New York: Alcoholics Anonymous World Services, Inc.

Allison, M., & Hubbard, R. L. (1985). Drug abuse treatment process: A review of the literature. *The International Journal of the Addictions*, 20, 1321–1345.

American Health Consultants (1990). Little-known group provides non-spiritual alternative to AA. *Addiction Program Management*, 4, 57–61.

Annis, H. M. (1986). A relapse prevention model for treatment of alcoholics. In W. R. Miller & N. Heather (Eds.), *Treating addictive behaviors* (pp. 407–433). New York: Plenum Press.

Annis, H. M. (1987). Effective treatment for drug and alcohol problems: What do we know? Invited address presented at the Annual Meeting of the Institute of Medicine, National Academy of Sciences, Washington, DC, October 21.

Armor, D. J., Polich, J. M., & Stambul, H. B. (1976). *Alcoholism and treatment*. Report prepared for the National Institute on Alcohol Abuse and Alcoholism (R-1739-NIAAA). Santa Monica, CA: Rand Corporation.

B

Ball, J. C., Meyers, C. P., & Friedman, S. R. (1988). Reducing the risk of AIDS through methadone maintenance treatment. *Journal of Health and Social Behavior*, 29, 214–226.

Beidler, R. J. (1991). Treating drug addicts and alcoholics together: A clinical trial. *Journal of Addictive Diseases*, 10, 81–96.

C

Carroll, J. F. X., Malloy, T. E., & Kenrick, F. M. (1977). Drug abuse by alcoholics and problem drinkers: A literature review and evaluation. *American Journal of Drug and Alcohol Abuse*, 4, 317–341.

Carroll, K., Ziedonis, D., O'Malley, S., McKance-Katz, E., Gordon, L., & Rounsaville, B. (1993). Pharmacologic interventions for alcohol- and cocaine-abusing individuals. *The American Journal of Addictions*, 1, 77–79.

Crosby, R. D., Halikas, J. A., & Carlson, G. (1991). Pharmacologic interventions for cocaine abusers: Present practices and future directions. *Journal of Addictive Diseases*, 10, 13–30.

D

DeLeon, G. (1984). *The therapeutic community: Study of effectiveness* (NIDA Treatment Research Monograph 84). Rockville, MD: National Institute on Drug Abuse.

Diesenhaus, H. (1982). Current trends in treatment programming for problem drinkers and alcoholics. In USDHHS, *Alcohol and health* (Monograph) (pp. 219–290). Washington, DC: U.S. Government Printing Office.

Donovan, D. M., & Chaney, E. F. (1985). Alcoholic relapse prevention and intervention. In G. A. Marlatt & J. R. Gordon (Eds.), *Relapse prevention* (pp. 351–416). New York: Guilford Press.

E

Emrick, C. D. (1975). A review of the psychologically oriented treatment of alcoholism, II. The relative effectiveness of different treatment approaches and the effectiveness of treatment vs. no treatment. *Journal of Studies on Alcohol*, 36, 88–108.

Emrick, C. D. (1989). Alcoholics Anonymous: Membership characteristics and effectiveness as treatment. In M. Galanter (Ed.), *Recent developments in alcoholism* (Vol. 7) (pp. 37–53). New York: Plenum Press.

Emrick, C. D., Lassen, C. L., & Edwards, M. T. (1977). Nonprofessional peers as therapeutic agents. In A. S. Gurman & A. M. Razin (Eds.), *Effective psychotherapy: A handbook of research* (pp. 120–161). New York: Pergamon Press.

G

Gottheil, E. (1990). Emerging clinical issues in the treatment of alcohol and/or other drugs of abuse. In M. Galanter (Ed.), *Recent developments in alcoholism* (Vol. 8) (pp. 241–244). New York: Plenum Press.

H

Higgins, S. T., Delaney, D. D., Budney, A. J., Bickel, W. K., Hughes, J. R., Foerg, F., & Fenwick, J. W. (1991). A behavioral approach to achieving initial cocaine abstinence. *American Journal of Psychology, 148,* 1218–1224.

Holder, H. D., & Blose, J. D. (1991). Typical patterns and cost of alcoholism treatment across a variety of populations and providers. *Alcoholism: Clinical and Experimental Research, 15,* 190–195.

Hubbard, R. L., Marsden, M. E., Rachal, J. V., Harwood, H. J., Cavanaugh, E. R., & Ginzburg, H. M. (1989). *Drug abuse treatment: A national study of effectiveness.* Chapel Hill: University of North Carolina Press.

Hunt, G. M., & Azrin, N. H. (1973). A community reinforcement to alcoholism. *Behavior Research & Therapy, 11,* 91–104.

Hunt, W. A., Barnett, L. W., & Branch, L. G. (1971). Relapse rates in addiction programs. *Journal of Clinical Psychology, 27,* 455–456.

I

Institute of Medicine (1990a). *Broadening the base of treatment for alcohol problems.* Washington, DC: National Academy Press.

Institute of Medicine (1990b). *Treating drug problems* (Vol. 1). Washington, DC: National Academy Press.

L

Leach, B., & Norris, J. L. (1977). Factors in the development of Alcoholics Anonymous (AA). In B. Kissin & H. Begleiter (Eds.), *The biology of alcoholism* (Vol. 5) (pp. 441–544). New York: Plenum Press.

Lettieri, D. J., Sayers, M., & Pearson, H. W. (Eds.) (1980). *Theories on drug abuse.* Rockville, MD: National Institute on Drug Abuse.

Litman, G. K. (1986). Alcoholism survival: The prevention of relapse. In W. R. Miller & N. Heather (Eds.), *Treating addictive behaviors* (pp. 391–405). New York: Plenum Press.

Ludwig, A. M., & Wikler, A. (1974). 'Craving' and relapse to drink. *Quarterly Journal of Studies on Alcohol, 35,* 108–130.

M

Maisto, S. A., & Nirenberg, T. D. (1986). The relationship between assessment and alcohol treatment. Paper presented as part of the symposium, The Matching Hypothesis in Alcohol Treatment: Current Status, Future Directions, at the 94th Annual Convention of the American Psychological Association, Washington, DC, August.

Marlatt, G. A., & Gordon, J. R. (Eds.) (1985). *Relapse prevention.* New York: Guilford Press.

McKay, J. R., Murphy, R. T., & Longabaugh, R. (1991). The effectiveness of alcoholism treatment: Evidence from outcome studies. In S. M. Mirin, J. T. Gossett, & M. C. Grob (Eds.), *Psychiatric treatment: Advances in outcome research* (pp. 143–158). Washington, DC: American Psychiatric Press, Inc.

McLellan, A. T., Luborsky, L., Woody, G. E., O'Brien, C. P., & Druley, K. A. (1983). Increased effectiveness of substance abuse treatment: A prospective study of patient-treatment matching. *Journal of Nervous and Mental Disease, 171,* 597–605.

Mello, N. K., Mendelson, J. H., Bree, M. P., & Lukas, S. E. (1989). Buprenorphine suppresses cocaine self-administration by rhesus monkeys. *Science, 245,* 859–862.

Miller, W. R. (1992). The effectiveness of treatment for substance abuse: Reasons for optimism. *Journal of Substance Abuse Treatment, 9,* 93–102.

Miller, W. R., & Hester, R. K. (1980). Treating the problem drinker: Modern approaches. In W. R. Miller (Ed.), *The addictive behaviors: Treatment of alcoholism, drug abuse, smoking, and obesity* (pp. 11–141). New York: Plenum Press.

Miller, W. R., & Hester, R. K. (1986). Inpatient alcoholism treatment: Who benefits? *American Psychologist, 41,* 794–805.

Miller, W. R., & Hester, R. K. (1989). Treating alcohol problems: Toward an informed eclecticism. In R. K. Hester & W. R. Miller (Eds.), *Handbook of alcoholism treatment approaches* (pp. 3–14). New York: Pergamon Press.

O

O'Malley, S. S., Jaffe, A. J., Chang, G., Schottenfeld, R. S., Meyer, R. E., & Rounsaville, B. (1992). Naltrexone and coping skills therapy for alcohol dependence. *Archives of General Psychiatry, 49,* 881–887.

Orford, J. (1985). *Excessive appetites: A psychological view of addictions.* Chichester, England: John Wiley & Sons.

P

Peachey, J. E., & Annis, J. (1985). New strategies for using the alcohol-sensitizing drugs. In C. A. Naranjo & E. M. Sellers (Eds.), *Research advances in new psychopharmacological treatments for alcoholism* (pp. 199–216). Amsterdam: Elsevier Science Publishers B. V.

Prochaska, J. O., DiClemente, C. C., & Norcross, J. C. (1992). In search of how people change. Applications to addictive behaviors. *American Psychologist, 47,* 1102–1114.

R

Rawson, R. A. (1990–1991). Chemical dependency treatment: The integration of the alcoholism and drug addiction/use treatment systems. *The International Journal of the Addictions, 25,* 1515–1536.

Regier, D. A., Narrow, W. E., Rae, D. S., Manderscherd, R. W., Locke, B. Z., & Goodwin, R. K. (1993). The defacto U.S. mental and addictive disorders service system. *Archives of General Psychiatry, 50,* 85–94.

Rollnick, S., & Heather, N. (1982). The application of Bandura's self-efficacy theory to abstinence-oriented alcoholism treatment. *Addictive Behaviors, 7,* 243–250.

Rosenberg, H. (1993). Prediction of controlled drinking by alcoholics and problem drinkers. *Psychological Bulletin, 113,* 129–139.

S

Secular Organizations for Sobriety (1990). *Guidebook for group leaders.* Buffalo, NY: CODESH, Inc.

Sobell, M. B., & Sobell, L. C. (1993). *Problem drinkers. Guided self-change treatment.* New York: Guilford Press.

Sobell, L. C., Sobell, M. B., Toneatto, T., & Leo, G. I. (1993). What triggers the resolution of alcohol problems without treatment? *Alcoholism: Clinical and Experimental Research, 17,* 217–224.

Sokolow, L., Welte, J., Hynes, G., & Lyons, J. (1981). Multiple substance use by alcoholics. *British Journal of Addiction, 76,* 147–158.

Solomon, R. (1980). The opponent-process theory of acquired motivation: The costs of pleasure and the benefits of pain. *American Psychologist, 35,* 691–712.

Stimmel, B. (1991). Buprenorphine and cocaine addiction: The need for caution. *Journal of Addictive Diseases, 10,* 1–4.

T

The Alcoholism Report (1993). Drug czar calls for treatment of drug addicted criminals. *The Alcoholism Report, 21,* 6–7.

Tiffany, S. T. (1990). A cognitive model of drug urges and drug use behavior: Role of automatic and nonautomatic processes. *Psychological Review, 97,* 147–168.

Tiffany, S. T. (1992). A critique of contemporary urge and craving research: Methodological, psychometric, and theoretical issues. *Advances in Behavior Research and Therapy, 14,* 123–139.

Trimpey, J. (1990). How to empower the substance abuser. *The Humanist,* January–February issue.

Trimpey, J. (1992). *Rational recovery from alcoholism* (4th edition). New York: Delacorte Press.

Tuchfeld, B. (1981). Spontaneous remission in alcoholics: Empirical observation and theoretical implications. *Journal of Studies on Alcohol, 42,* 626–641.

U

U.S. Department of Health and Human Services (1984). *Drug abuse and drug abuse research.* Washington, DC: U.S. Government Printing Office.

U.S. Department of Health and Human Services (1993). *Alcohol and health: Eighth special report to the U.S. Congress* (Prepublication copy).

V

Volpicelli, J. R., Alterman, A. I., Hayashida, M., & O'Brien, C. P. (1992). Naltrexone in the treatment of alcohol dependence. *Archives of General Psychiatry, 49,* 876–880.

W

Walsh, D. C., Hingson, R. W., Merrigan, D. M. Levenson, S. M., Cupples, A., Heeren, T., Coffman, G. A., Becker, C. A., Barker, T. A., Hamilton, S. K., McGuire, T. G., & Kelly, C. A. (1991). A randomized trial of treatment options for alcohol abusing workers. *New England Journal of Medicine, 325,* 775–782.

Washton, A. M. (1990). Structured outpatient treatment of alcohol vs. drug dependence. In M. Galanter (Ed.), *Recent developments in alcoholism* (Vol. 8) (pp. 285–304). New York: Plenum Press.

Wise, R. A. (1988). The neurobiology of craving: Implications for the understanding and treatment of addiction. *Journal of Abnormal Psychology, 97,* 118–132.

Women for Sobriety (April, 1985). *Sobering thoughts.* Quakertown, PA: Author.

Chapter 17

B

Baer, J. S., Kivlahan, D. R., Fromme, K., & Marlatt, G. A. (in press). Secondary prevention of alcohol abuse with college student populations: A skills-training approach. In G. Howard (Ed.), *Issues in alcohol use and misuse by young adults.* Notre Dame University Press.

Bangert-Drowns, R. L. (1988). The effects of school-based substance abuse education: A meta-analysis. *Journal of Drug Education, 18,* 243–264.

Berkowitz, A. D., & Perkins, H. W. (1986). Problem drinking among college students: A review of recent research. *Journal of American College Health, 35,* 21–28.

Blane, H. T. (1976). Education and the prevention of alcoholism. In B. Kissin & H. Begleiter (Eds.), *The biology of alcoholism* (Vol. 4): *Social aspects of alcoholism* (pp. 519–578). New York: Plenum Press.

Blane, H. T. (1988). Research on mass communications and alcohol. *Contemporary Drug Problems, 15,* 7–20.

Botvin, G. J., & Botvin, E. M. (1992). School-based and community-based prevention approaches. In J. H. Lowinson, P. Ruiz, & R. B. Millman (Eds.), *Substance abuse: A comprehensive textbook* (2nd edition) (pp. 910–927). Baltimore: Williams & Wilkins.

Bruun, L., Edwards, G., Lumio, M., Makela, K., Pan, L., Popham, R. E., Room, R., Schmidt, W., Skog, O., Sulkunen, P., & Oesterberg, E. (1975). *Alcohol control policies in public health perspective.* Helsinki: Finnish Foundation for Alcohol Studies.

C

Cellucci, T. (1984). The prevention of alcohol problems: Conceptual and methodological issues. In P. M. Miller & T. D. Nirenberg (Eds.), *Prevention of alcohol abuse* (pp. 15–53). New York: Plenum Press.

Chen, T. T. L., & Winder, A. E. (1986). When is the critical moment to provide smoking education at schools? *Journal of Drug Education, 16,* 121–134.

D

DuPont, R. L. (1980). The future of primary prevention: Parent power. *Journal of Drug Education, 10,* 1–5.

E

Engs, R. C. (1977). Drinking behaviors among college students. *Journal of Studies on Alcohol, 38,* 2144–2156.

F

Flay, B. R. (1985). What we know about the social influences to smoking prevention: Review and recommendations. In C. Bell & R. Battjes (Eds.), *Prevention research: Deterring drug abuse among children and adolescents* (pp. 67–112). Rockville, MD: National Institute on Drug Abuse.

G

Geller, E. S., Russ, N. W., & Delphos, W. A. (1987). Does server intervention training make a difference? *Alcohol Health and Research World, 11,* 64–69.

H

Hewitt, L. E. (1982). Current status of alcohol education programs for youth. In *Special population issues* (Alcohol and Health Monograph 4) (pp. 227–260). Rockville, MD: NIAAA.

Hewitt, L. E., & Blane, H. T. (1984). Prevention through mass media communication. In P. M. Miller & T. D. Nirenberg (Eds.), *Prevention of alcohol abuse* (pp. 281–323). New York: Plenum Press.

J

Jahoda, G., & Cramond, J. (1972). *Children and alcohol.* London: HMSO.

K

Kimmel, C. K. (1976). A prevention program with punch: The national PTA's Alcohol Education Project. *Journal of School Health, 46,* 208–210.

Kinder, B. N., Pape, N. E., & Walfish, S. (1980). Drug and alcohol education programs: A review of outcome studies. *International Journal of the Addictions, 15,* 1035–1054.

Kivlahan, D. R., Coppel, D. B., Fromme, K., Williams, E., & Marlatt, G. A. (in press). Secondary prevention of alcohol-related problems in young adults at risk. In K. D. Craig & S. M. Weiss (Eds.), *Prevention and early interventions: Biobehavioral perspectives.* New York: Springer.

Kivlahan, D. R., Marlatt, G. A., Fromme, K., Coppel, D. B., & Williams, E. (1990). Secondary prevention with college drinkers: Evaluation of an alcohol skills training program. *Journal of Consulting and Clinical Psychology, 58,* 805–810.

Kraft, D. P. (1984). A comprehensive prevention program for college students. In P. M. Miller & T. D. Nirenberg (Eds.), *Prevention of alcohol abuse* (pp. 327–369). New York: Plenum Press.

L

Lewis, J. A. (1991). Alcohol abuse prevention in industrial settings. In B. Forster & J. C. Salloway (Eds.), *Preventions and treatments of alcohol and drug abuse* (pp. 137–152). Lewiston, NY: Edwin Mellen Press.

M

Marlatt, G. A., Larimer, M. E., Baer, J. S., & Quigley, L. A. (1993). Harm reduction for alcohol problems: Moving beyond the controlled drinking controversy. *Behavior Therapy, 24,* 461–504.

Mazis, M. B., Morris, L. A., & Swasy, J. L. (1991). An evaluation of the alcohol warning label: Initial survey results. *Journal of Public Policy and Marketing, 10,* 229–241.

Mosher, J. F., & Colman, V. J. (1986). Prevention research: The model Dram Shop Act of 1985. *Alcohol Health and Research World, 10,* 4–11.

N

Nathan, P. E. (1984). Alcoholism prevention in the workplace: Three examples. In P. M. Miller & T. D. Nirenberg (Eds.), *Prevention of alcohol abuse* (pp. 387–405). New York: Plenum Press.

Nathan, P. E., & Niaura, R. S. (1987). Prevention of alcohol problems. In W. M. Cox (Ed.), *Treatment and prevention of alcohol problems: A resource manual* (pp. 333–354). New York: Academic Press.

Nirenberg, T. D., & Miller, P. M. (1984). History and overview of the prevention of alcohol abuse. In P. M. Miller & T. D. Nirenberg (Eds.), *Prevention of alcohol abuse* (pp. 3–14). New York: Plenum Press.

P

Pellow, R. A., & Jengeleski, J. L. (1991). A survey of current research studies on drug education programs in America. *Journal of Drug Education, 21,* 203–210.

R

Rice, D. P. (1991). Estimates of economic costs of alcohol and drug abuse and mental illness: 1985–1988. *Public Health Reports*, 106, 280–292.

Richmond, L. B. (1977). Decisions and drinking: A prevention approach. *Alcohol Health and Research World*, Winter, 22–26.

Rush, B., & Gliksman, L. (1986). The distribution of consumption approach to the prevention of alcohol-related damage: An overview of relevant research and current issues. *Advances in Alcohol and Substance Abuse*, 5, 9–32.

S

Saltz, R., & Elandt, D. (1986). College student drinking studies, 1976–1985. *Contemporary Drug Problems*, 13, 117–159.

Scammon, D. L., Mayer, R. N., & Smith, K. R. (1991). Alcohol warnings: How do you know when you have had one too many? *Journal of Public Policy and Marketing*, 10, 214–228.

Schaps, E., DiBartolo, R., Moskowitz, J., Palley, C. S., & Churgin, S. (1981). A review of 127 drug abuse prevention program evaluations. *Journal of Drug Issues*, 9, 17–43.

Schmidt, W., & Popham, R. E. (1978). The single distribution theory of alcohol consumption. *Journal of Studies on Alcohol*, 39, 400–419.

Skirrow, J., & Sawka, E. (1987). Alcohol and drug abuse prevention strategies: An overview. *Contemporary Drug Problems*, 14, 147–241.

Skog, O. J. (1985). The collectivity of drinking cultures: A theory of the distribution of alcohol consumption. *British Journal of Addiction*, 80, 83–99.

Stuart, R. B. (1974). Teaching facts about drugs: Pushing or preventing. *Journal of Educational Psychology*, 66, 189–201.

W

Whitehead, P. C. (1975). Prevention of alcoholism: Divergences and convergences of two approaches. *Addictive Diseases*, 7, 431–443.

Wilkinson, R. (1970). *The prevention of drinking problems: Alcohol control and cultural influences*. New York: Oxford University Press.

Photographic Credits

Photo 1-1	Mike Marucci/Reuters Bettmann Newsphotos
Photo 1-2	Rue/Monkmeyer Press Photos
Photo 1-3	Comstock
Photo 1-4	*The New York Times*
Photo 2-1	Topham/The Image Works
Photo 2-2	From Alexander Lambert, "Underlying Causes of the Narcotic Habit," *Modern Medicine*, 2, January 1920.
Photo 2-3	The Bettmann Archive
Photo 2-4	Courtesy, Olympus America, Inc.
Photo 4-1	Comstock
Photo 4-2	Courtesy, American Cancer Society
Photo 4-3	John Maher/Stock Boston
Photo 5-1	Roswell Angier/Stock Boston
Photo 5-2	Courtesy, Sports Tower
Photo 5-3	Gilles Peress/Magnum
Photo 6-1	Courtesy, Drug Enforcement Agency
Photo 6-2	Courtesy, National Library of Medicine
Photo 6-3	Eugene Richards, Magnum
Photo 6-4	Eugene Richards, Magnum
Photo 6-5	AP/Wide World Photos
Photo 6-6	AP/Wide World Photos
Photo 7-1	Peter Menzel/Stock Boston
Photo 7-2	Courtesy, American Cancer Society
Photo 7-3	Culver Pictures
Photo 8-1	Mark Richards
Photo 8-2	G. Gardner/The Image Works
Photo 9-1	The Image Works
Photo 9-2	Ray Ellis/Photo Researchers
Photo 9-3	SEF/Art Resource
Photo 9-4	Courtesy, Intoximeters, Inc.
Photo 9-5	Stock Boston
Photo 9-6 A & B	Courtesy, Armed Forces Institute of Pathology
Photo 9-7	Ted Wood/Picture Group
Photo 10-1	The Bettmann Archive
Photo 10-2	Alberto Garcia/Picture Group
Photo 10-3	AP/Wide World Photo
Photo 11-1	Mary Evans Picture Library/Photo Researchers
Photo 11-3	Joel Gordon
Photo 12-1	Mikki Ansin/Gamma-Liaison
Photo 12-2	The Bettmann Archive

Acknowledgments of Permission

Table 1-5
"Diagnostic Criteria for Psychoactive Substance Abuse and Dependence, DSM-IV." American Psychiatric Association: *Diagnostic and Statistical Manual of Mental Disorders*, Fourth Edition. Washington, DC, American Psychiatric Association, 1994.

Table 2-1
"Schedules of Controlled Substances" by K. Blum. *From Handbook of Abusable Drugs*, pp. 667–670. Copyright © 1984. Reprinted by permission of The Gardner Press, Inc.

Table 2-2
"Examples of Scheduled Drugs." From *The Substance Abuse Problems* by Sidney Cohen. Copyright © 1981. Reprinted by permission of The Haworth Press, Inc., 10 Alice Street, New York, NY, 13904

Table 4-4
"Common Drugs of Abuse." From *The Pharmacology of Alcohol and Drugs of Abuse/Addiction*. Copyright © 1991 by Springer Verlag, Inc. Reprinted by permission.

Figure 4-5
"Dose-Effect Curve for Two Drugs" by Ross And Gilman. From *The Pharmacologic Basis of Therapeutics*, 7e. Copyright © 1985. Reprinted by permission of McGraw-Hill, Inc.

Figure 4-6
"Effective Doses for Sedation and Death" by Gilman. From *The Pharmacological Basis of Therapeutics*, 8e. Copyright © 1990. Reprinted by permission of McGraw-Hill, Inc.

Table 7-4
"Acetylcholine Effects" by Robert Julien. From: A *Primer of Drug Action* 6e by Robert Julien. Copyright © 1992 by W.H. Freeman and Company. Reprinted with permission.

Table 7-5
"Acute Pharmacological Effects of Nicotine" by Robert Julien. From: A *Primer of Drug Action* 6e by Robert Julien. Copyright © 1992 by W.H. Freeman and Company. Reprinted with permission.

Subject and Author Index